SPECIAL EDITION

USING

Adobe®

Creative Suite 2

Michael Smick
Pariah S. Burke
Francisco Meza
Steve Moniz
Carla Rose
Susan Smith

800 East 96th Street
Indianapolis, Indiana 46240

SPECIAL EDITION USING ADOBE® CREATIVE SUITE 2

International Standard Book Number: 0-7897-3367-6

Library of Congress Catalog Card Number: 2004114645

Printed in the United States of America

First Printing: September 2005

08   07   06   05   4   3   2   1

Trademarks

Warning and Disclaimer

Bulk Sales

Que Publishing offers excellent discounts on this book when ordered in quan-tity for bulk purchases or special sales. For more information, please contact

U.S. Corporate and Government Sales
1-800-382-3419
corpsales@pearsontechgroup.com

For sales outside of the U.S., please contact

International Sales
international@pearsoned.com

Acquisitions Editor
Linda Bump Harrison

Development Editor
Alice Martina Smith

Managing Editor
Charlotte Clapp

Project Editor
Andrew Beaster

Copy Editors
Nancy Albright
Kitty Jarrett

Indexer
John Sleeva

Proofreader
Elizabeth Scott

Technical Editor
Kate Binder

Publishing Coordinator
Vanessa Evans

Book Designer
Anne Jones

Page Layout
Kelly Maish
Michelle Mitchell
Julie Parks

Graphics
Tammy Graham

Contents at a Glance

CONTENTS

ABOUT THE AUTHORS

Michael Smick is a project manager and multimedia developer at Walsworth Publishing Company's Desktop Technology department. He produces animated video tutorials for Adobe Photoshop and InDesign and creates video presentations using Adobe Premiere and After Effects. He also writes technical manuals and travels to various design workshops teaching students how to use Adobe software to create their yearbooks.

Mike is also a freelance web developer and does graphics and publication training and consulting for small businesses and organizations. He is an Adobe Certified Expert in InDesign. He produced the InDesign CS training series for AtomicLearning.com and teaches Adobe software at community classes for the University of Missouri Kansas City. He also writes articles on graphics and other publishing topics and the occasional rant at his personal website Smick.net.

> *I would first like to thank the writing team who worked so hard to produce this book. Your tireless efforts during the difficult schedule have been nothing short of amazing. Also a huge thanks goes to the team at Que Publishing especially Linda Harrison, Alice Martina Smith, Matt Purcell, and Andy Beaster. Your hard work and attention to detail is unmatched. Thank you to my wife Juri Smick for her patience and understanding during the writing of this book and for sharing a scoop of ice cream with me on so many evenings. Thank you to my parents John and Ruth Smick who have been so understanding and always checked in to see if I was still alive. Also a special thank you to my friends Don Birkenmeyer and Susan Smith for your helpfulness and your infinite technical knowledge and support.*

Pariah S. Burke is the former Technical Lead for Illustrator, InDesign, InCopy, PageMaker, and Acrobat, and MVP for Photoshop, prepress, typography, and QuarkXPress of Adobe's technical support team. He is the author of *Adobe Illustrator CS2 @ Work: Projects You Can Use on the Job* (Sams Publishing, 2005), and the editor-in-chief of the websites *Quark VS InDesign.com* (www.QuarkVSInDesign.com) and *Designorati* (www.Designorati.com).

Throughout his 20 years as a creative professional, Pariah's greatest passion is, and has always been, using and teaching the tools and techniques of the graphic communication arts. Pariah travels the world teaching, speaking, and consulting on Illustrator, InDesign, Photoshop, QuarkXPress, InCopy, Creative Suite, and numerous other tools and processes in modern design and production workflows.

> *I am honored to be a contributor to this amazing book, in such distinguished company. I would like to specifically thank Linda Bump Harrison, Alice Martina Smith, Andy Beaster, Kate Binder, and Nancy E. Albright at Que Publishing for all their hard work behind the pages.*

Francisco Meza started his career in Graphic Arts at a very young age working a stat camera at an uncle's studio during school holidays. After surviving the shift from traditional to digital graphic production, Francisco has acquired a vast experience designing and producing for a varied assortment of media, from process offset to flexo, screening, embroidery, and the Web.

Currently Francisco runs his own graphics studio in Toronto, Canada. In his free time, he writes tutorials on Photoshop and writes stories for a publication in Seoul, Korea.

A big thanks to Mike Smick for the opportunity to participate in this project; to Linda Harrison and the Editors at Sams Publishing for keeping us on track; to Adobe for creating the amazing software I use in my day-to-day work; and to Mari and all the other friends and family who have cheered me and helped me keep my hair during this project. Thanks all!

Steve Moniz is the Prepress Director for Nameplates for Industry, Inc. in New Bedford, Massachusetts. Formerly the owner of SCM Training and Consulting in Boston, Massachusetts, Steve regularly consulted on web design and web design applications, including Macromedia Dreamweaver, Fireworks, and Flash and Adobe GoLive. As a computer software trainer for 10 years, Steve taught courses in everything from Macintosh basics to advanced Photoshop, QuarkXPress, HTML programming, and web design. On the cutting edge of desktop publishing and electronic pre-press technology since its inception in the early 1980s, Steve's background includes traditional offset printing, screen printing, publishing, digital prepress production, computer programming, and type-setting. Steve often lectures on digital prepress and Internet topics and provides customized training for corporate clients on both Macintosh and Windows platforms. He has also served as technical editor for a variety of computer graphics titles.

Thank you to Jenny and Nancy for keeping me focused and for their unfailing support and encouragement.

Carla Rose has written more than two dozen computer books including *Sams Teach Yourself Adobe Photoshop 7 in 24 Hours*, *Sams Teach Yourself Photoshop Elements 3 in 24 Hours*, and *Digital Memories: Scrapbooking with Your Computer*. She has written for publications ranging from *The Atlantic Fisherman* to *Adobe* magazine to *The New Yorker*.

Susan Smith has written various corporate manuals about using PageMaker, InDesign, QuarkXPress, and Photoshop. She regularly speaks at workshops and conventions across the country, teaching these programs to high school students and teachers. She has also edited a number of sports books. Susan currently works as a project manager, technical writer, and trainer.

I owe my sincerest thanks to a great number of people: First and foremost to Mike Smick for bringing me on board this project. Turns out you were right—I knew a lot more about InDesign than I thought I did.

To my colleagues, as well as the teachers and students I meet every day who constantly impress me with their ability to make these programs do what they want them to do: You inspire me and make me not feel crazy for loving software. To Linda Harrison and everyone at Que for their support and attention. To Alice Martina Smith, Kate Binder, and Nancy Albright for making sure the thoughts in my head got onto the page in a coherent, logical, and grammatically correct manner. You brought clarity to a sometimes jumbled mess. To my friends and family for their patience and love during this project and every day. You mean more to me than I can ever express. And especially to my friend Mike Callero, who has supported every word I've ever put on paper, whether he's read them all or not.

WE WANT TO HEAR FROM YOU!

As the reader of this book, *you* are our most important critic and commentator. We value your opinion and want to know what we're doing right, what we could do better, what areas you'd like to see us publish in, and any other words of wisdom you're willing to pass our way.

You can email or write me directly to let me know what you did or didn't like about this book—as well as what we can do to make our books stronger.

Please note that I cannot help you with technical problems related to the topic of this book, and that due to the high volume of mail I receive, I might not be able to reply to every message.

When you write, please be sure to include this book's title and author as well as your name and phone number or email address. I will carefully review your comments and share them with the authors and editors who worked on the book.

Email: graphics@quepublishing.com

Mail: Mark Taber
Associate Publisher
Que Publishing
800 East 96th Street
Indianapolis, IN 46240 USA

READER SERVICES

For more information about this book or another Que title, visit our website at www.quepublishing.com. Type the ISBN (excluding hyphens) or the title of a book in the Search field to find the page you're looking for.

INTRODUCTION

WHO SHOULD READ THIS BOOK?

If you happen to be in a bookstore right now deciding whether to purchase this book, studies show we have about 30 seconds to convince you. Not much time for persuasion, so we'll just give the facts. If you are already an expert in one or more Adobe programs, this book helps bring you to a full circle of understanding and using software to create your vision.

On the other hand, a lot of us aren't experts. We know a little bit of this and a little of that. This book helps fill in the gaps—so you not only understand the concepts in the Creative Suite 2, you get the work done. Our goal is to get you quickly and intimately involved in the Creative Suite 2 and help you pass that class you might be taking or tackle the new responsibilities that you've just been handed at your job. We understand that you not only need to know the Hows, but also the Whys of graphics, design, and printing. We also know to keep those Whys brief and easy.

The authors make some assumptions about your skill level. We assume you know how to use a mouse or other pointing device and that you have browsed the web, sent email, and used general office software. If you haven't grasped these general computing tasks, this book isn't for you. This book also isn't for you if you are a seasoned pro in all the Creative Suite programs. We have set our sights on giving you a manual for getting a foothold, not a lengthy academic study on specific areas. If you need a huge resource on color or Bézier geometry, this book is not for you.

Good luck—and make your decision soon because that lady has been waiting a while to look at the shelf you're leaning on.

WHY CHOOSE THE SPECIAL EDITION?

There are a lot of books on Adobe software. Some are better than others. We believe that most people are looking to learn as much as they can, without having it interfere with the rest of their lives. The Special Edition is designed to be friendly to your schedule and strong with information on things you'll likely encounter and question.

This volume is thorough but not exhaustive. A good book should not be intimidating in either its vocabulary or its size and weight. Most importantly, we've taken care to address how the Adobe Creative Suite 2 integrates *its* different programs so that *you* can integrate your workflow. There are so many things to learn in the Creative Suite, but the most common question people have is how they can bring their file from one program to another the right way. Understanding how the programs relate—and being able to use those relationships effectively—makes designing more fun and makes working with a team a heck of a lot easier. When you are certain that you know how to make graphic or page files compatible with your other programs, you have really gained confidence and you are able to reuse and repurpose your work.

WHY CHOOSE THE ADOBE CREATIVE SUITE?

If you haven't decided whether to buy just one Adobe program or the whole suite, we encourage you, if you have the means, to get the entire Creative Suite 2. If you are a budding creative professional, having the Creative Suite 2 makes sharing files with others very easy. You also will find that the Creative Suite 2 will pay for itself fairly quickly, not only with freelance projects you might take on but with the time you save by having all these tools at your disposal. It will open up opportunities for you to expand your toolset and give you more to offer to clients, customers, or your employer. With the Adobe Creative Suite 2 as a whole, you get more than the sum of its parts, and it's certainly cheaper than buying programs one at a time.

HOW THIS BOOK IS ORGANIZED

We thought long and hard about how to arrange this book so the information is logically presented. We wanted to give you the right information up front but still make it easy to jump around to the programs you use most. We begin with a chapter on the basics of the Creative Suite to orient you with the whole package. Because Adobe Photoshop is the most popular program in the Suite, we combined Photoshop and its companion ImageReady in Part I.

Part II explores Adobe Illustrator and all the vector fun therein. Part III is devoted to Adobe InDesign and how to create beautiful and memorable documents. Learn how to make interactive websites with Adobe GoLive in Part IV that are fun for everybody. Understand how to build and share lightweight press quality PDF documents in Part V with Adobe Acrobat 7.0.

Finally to wrap up this Special Edition, visit the book's website for bonus chapters that cover advanced Acrobat techniques, Adobe Designer, and Adobe Distiller.

COMMON CONCEPTS

In this book, we address both the Macintosh and the Windows platforms. Because the modifier keys on the keyboard differ between Windows and Macintosh, we use the following system of key identification:

- **⌘ and Ctrl**: The Mac Command key and the Windows Ctrl key are modifier keys that do nothing on their own and are always used in conjunction with another key and/or another modifier key.

- **Option and Alt**: The Option key on Mac and the Alt key on Windows are also modifier keys that are used in conjunction with other keys.

- **Control-click, right-click**: Although Mac OS has always supported multibutton mice and right-clicking (the machines just *ship* with single-button mice), we'll still use the traditional Control-click instruction, indicating the user holds down the Mac's Control key and clicks the mouse button (the left button on multibutton mice). Windows users click the right mouse button.

You may see a couple of modifier keys used with another key. For example, when we discuss the default keyboard shortcut used for copying to a new layer in Photoshop, you will see this convention used: ⌘-Shift-J (Mac users) or Ctrl+Shift+J (Windows users).

> Visit www.samspublishing.com and search on this book's ISBN (0789733676). From this page you can download bonus chapters to enhance your Creative Suite 2 experience.

CREATIVE SUITE 2 BASICS

IN THIS CHAPTER

1

In another dimension perhaps there are ways to magically manifest new creations through simple mind control. Unfortunately, in the Paleolithic world we live in we're still stuck using hammers, chisels, and even software for our design work. The good news is that hammers are getting harder, chisels sharper, and Adobe is lifting us out of the Stone Age with not one but a collection of programs, bringing the day closer when we can create merely by thinking about it. Until that day, at least we can make some pretty snazzy stuff on the computer.

Creative Suite 2 is a collection of world-class creative software that makes it easier to work, play, and use your imagination to create (see Figure 1.1). Not a bad idea, is it? Adobe has gone a step further. Not only do the programs work well together, they are largely based on a core technology—the Portable Document Format (PDF). PDF is most easily identified with Adobe Acrobat.

Figure 1.1
The Adobe Creative Suite 2.

CREATIVE SUITE VERSUS COMPONENT PROGRAMS

Purchasing the Adobe Creative Suite rather than the individual programs has a number of advantages. In addition to saving money, you work with a single serial number. In fact, the Adobe Creative Suite 2 is technically a single product. The most important differences between purchasing the Adobe Creative Suite 2 and the individual component programs are Version Cue and Adobe Bridge. These two applications can become the core of your file management routine.

Looking back over time, you see where Adobe has consistently added to its offerings. It has coincided with the needs of designers and improvements in digital technology and has often been the driving force of the industry (see Figure 1.2).

Figure 1.2
A timeline of Adobe software milestones from its humble beginnings to the release of CS2.

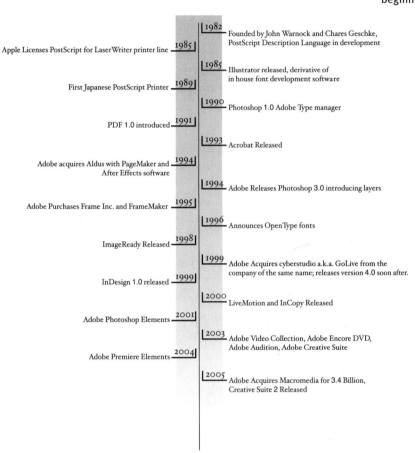

Adobe Timeline

1982 — Founded by John Warnock and Chares Geschke, PostScript Description Language in development

Apple Licenses PostScript for LaserWriter printer line — 1985

1985 — Illustrator released, derivative of in house font development software

First Japanese PostScript Printer — 1989

1990 — Photoshop 1.0 Adobe Type manager

PDF 1.0 introduced — 1991

1993 — Acrobat Released

Adobe acquires Aldus with PageMaker and After Effects software — 1994

1994 — Adobe Releases Photoshop 3.0 introducing layers

Adobe Purchases Frame Inc. and FrameMaker — 1995

1996 — Announces OpenType fonts

ImageReady Released — 1998

1999 — Adobe Acquires cyberstudio a.k.a. GoLive from the company of the same name; releases version 4.0 soon after.

InDesign 1.0 released — 1999

2000 — LiveMotion and InCopy Released

Adobe Photoshop Elements — 2001

2003 — Adobe Video Collection, Adobe Encore DVD, Adobe Audition, Adobe Creative Suite

Adobe Premiere Elements — 2004

2005 — Adobe Acquires Macromedia for 3.4 Billion, Creative Suite 2 Released

NEW GLOBAL FEATURES

Features new throughout the entire Creative Suite 2 include the introduction of Adobe Bridge, which is your control center and launch pad to your design work. Bridge is a standalone program that enables you to see multisize previews of your application files; simply double-clicking a file opens the file in the appropriate CS2 application (see Figure 1.3). View camera-recorded metadata in your image files and add your own notations to files. View PDF previews and even flip through pages right inside Adobe Bridge:

Figure 1.3
Adobe Bridge enables you to preview images before you select one to open.

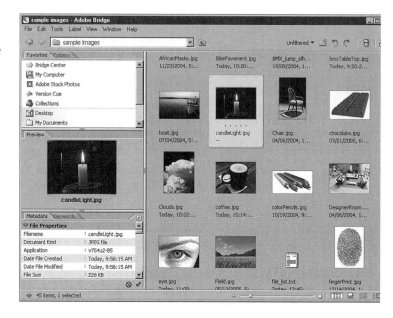

- A single integrated help system opens from inside each application (see Figure 1.4). Only Adobe Acrobat has separate online help. Help Center includes links to Adobe Support channels, links to external resources, and built-in and online tutorials to learn how to use the Creative Suite 2.

Figure 1.4
The Adobe Help Center contains help for all the Creative Suite 2 applications except Adobe Acrobat 7.0.

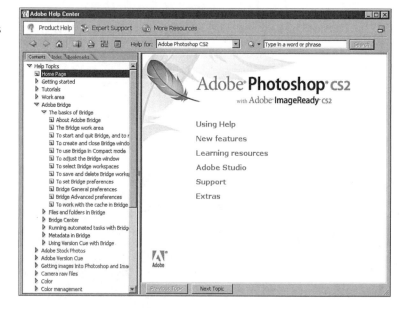

- Although it was introduced in the first Creative Suite, Version Cue is still considered a new feature for many. It's concept is unique. Version Cue helps you get into a project mentality: You can save, load, and share everything related to a project in an overall project directory. This keeps everything together, while Version Cue manages different file versions and prevents lost changes between users.

- CS2 enables you to synchronize your color settings for all CS2 applications in one place. This gives you accurate color display in your programs and consistent color output in your files (see Figure 1.5). From Adobe Bridge you can choose Edit, Creative Suite Color Settings and apply color settings appropriate for your work. After clicking Apply, all applications are synchronized.

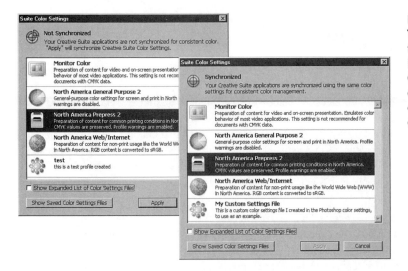

Figure 1.5
You can modify color settings from individual applications, but through the Adobe Bridge Color Settings, you can synchronize them to the same color profile settings to ensure consistent color display.

- Find and purchase stock images from Adobe Stock Photos (see Figure 1.6). The browsing interface to several top commercial stock libraries is extremely convenient when you need that photo yesterday.

Figure 1.6
The Adobe Stock Photos feature is accessed through Adobe Bridge.

You'll find that every application has loads of features—so many you may not even realize all of them until you work with them a few weeks or months. If you are new to Adobe software, it's certainly a good time to dig in and start playing. Try out Photoshop's Vanishing Point tool for cloning images with perspective, or use Illustrator's Live Trace to turn an image into a vector graphic. Create Object Styles in InDesign for consistent display of images, shapes, and tables. The new 3D support inside Acrobat is going to make waves, and improved CSS support in GoLive gives you much needed control over website layout and styling.

WHAT IS VERSION CUE?

Version Cue helps you manage your files efficiently. When you work on larger projects, sometimes you might be working on just a small portion of a large design. If the project is still in its infancy you might have to provide three or four mockups before you get the okay on one of them. The worst feeling is when you open a file and realize that 3 or 4 or *10* hours of work is lost because you overwrote your last few changes unintentionally. Version Cue helps prevent this. It enables *version control*, so you can track the most recent versions of documents while maintaining access to previous versions. It does this by enabling you to save multiple versions of a document, with notes describing the changes in each one, and by enforcing a check-in/check-out system that ensures that only one person can work on a document at a time.

Despite its benefits, many people avoided using Version Cue in the release of the first Creative Suite because they felt it wasn't worth their time to learn it, or they thought it may have been more of a barrier or hindrance between them and their files. Whatever your reasons for using or not using it, you can bet that many creative teams will make it an integral part of their workflow.

Where to Start?

In Version Cue, you create projects that you have access to from programs in the Creative Suite 2. Projects help you keep all the components in one place. Projects can contain Adobe files and non-Adobe files. What's important is your ability to find the right file you are looking for when you need it.

Look for the small Version Cue leaf icon in the system tray in Windows or in the menu bar in Mac (see Figure 1.7).

Version Cue icon in Mac

Figure 1.7
In Mac and Windows you can find the Version Cue icon near your system clock.

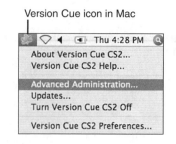
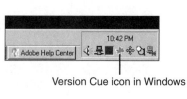

Version Cue icon in Windows

Click the Version Cue leaf icon (in Windows, right-click the icon) and choose Advanced Administration from the menu. Your default web browser opens the Web interface. This is similar to how you might set up a personal web server. The default username and password are both `system`. Log in and you can set up projects and administer them.

When the Version Cue CS2 Administration screen opens, click the Home tab and notice that Version Cue lists quite a bit of system information under the About This Workspace heading. You also see a Getting Started menu for the common tasks you will perform. These tasks mirror the other tabs in the Administration screen.

To create a project in Version Cue, follow these steps:

1. From the Getting Started menu on the Home tab, click Create a Project. The Projects tab opens (see Figure 1.8). Choose Blank Project. Give the project you are creating a Project Name. (I'll use `redgiraffe` as my project's codename.)

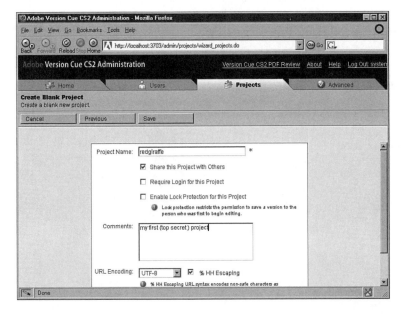

Figure 1.8
The Version Cue Projects setup table.

Note the options here for your new project. You can share this project, require a login for the project, and enable lock protection (which allows only you to save over files that you create). You can type any project note or comment in the Comments box, and you can set URL encoding to Unicode UTF-8, ISO-8859-1 (a standard western character set), or Shift_JIS (standard Japanese). UTF-8 is a good option to choose because it contains all international character fonts.

2. Click Save and your project is created. Now your project can be connected via your Adobe programs and through your network if you enable specific options.

3. Click the Advanced tab and then choose Preferences. You can change your workspace name and set other options like network server options.

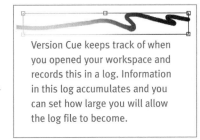

Version Cue keeps track of when you opened your workspace and records this in a log. Information in this log accumulates and you can set how large you will allow the log file to become.

4. Click on the Users tab and you can create new users who have access to the workspace. This is important when you have multiple projects with various security settings applied.

Whew! That was a lot of stuff, and we haven't even made anything yet. It's true, setting up and planning before you begin can sometimes seem tedious. You probably won't do it for many of your smaller projects. But when the big projects come down the pipe, consider setting up a Version Cue project to help you stay organized and to make backups.

Deleting Old Versions of Projects

When projects are in full swing you will probably be accumulating a lot of file versions. When you know you won't need some previous versions of files any longer you can delete them from the project via the Advanced Administration tab.

Click on the Advanced tab. Choose a project name in the pop-up menu and set a date by which to filter and delete old versions of files (see Figure 1.9). For example, to delete project files older than August 19, 2005, set that date in the date fields. Deleting older versions of files saves disk space when you're certain you won't be reverting to old designs. If you're not sure what to get rid of but you need to clear some hard drive space, back up this part of the project directory to a CD or DVD and then remove the old versions. The Version Cue projects and data can be found in the Version Cue folder in My Documents on Windows or in the Users/Documents folder on the Mac.

Figure 1.9
Removing old versions of project files using the Version Cue Advanced tab.

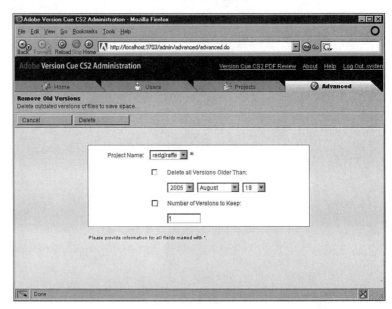

We'll save some of the other gory details about Version Cue when we're actually working within a project.

WHAT IS ADOBE BRIDGE?

Bridge is really the gem of CS2 as it helps pull together all the Suite programs in ways they weren't connected before. Bridge's core feature is its file browsing capability. It replaces Photoshop's old File Browser and is also a standalone program for the suite. From Bridge you can look at any image and PDF file previews and rename, sort, open, run actions, rotate, delete, and much more. It's like your own personal casting director for your files.

Bridge can be launched on its own by finding the Bridge application in your Start menu or Applications directory installed with the suite. It is helpful to make a shortcut to Bridge on the desktop or dock where you can easily get to it because it may become the program you use most frequently after you see its benefits.

Bridge opens with a number of panels showing (see Figure 1.10). Choose Window, Workspace, File Navigator from the menu bar to set up the workspace so that the panels on the left contain your favorites and the Folders panel shows your computer file system.

Figure 1.10
The Adobe Bridge Center as it looks originally.

In the Favorites panel, click Bridge Center. What looks like a web page appears containing some content such as your recent files and folders. If you are connected to the internet, you also see other features, such as an RSS news reader geared toward Adobe and design news (see Figure 1.11). Take a look at the Tips and Tricks panel where you can click through helpful hints on various programs. There are some excellent lesser-known tips in here when you have time to research them. At the bottom of the page (you may have to scroll) are links to create new Version Cue projects, synchronize your color management, and open the Adobe Help Center.

Save open files link

Figure 1.11
The Bridge Center Favorites panel.

Using Saved File Groups

The Saved File Groups panel is an interesting feature in Bridge. Let's say you are working on an intense project in both Photoshop and Illustrator. When lunch comes around you are ready for a break. You might have 15 files open. Instead of trying to remember which ones to close and which ones to save, switch to the Bridge and click the Save Open Files Into a File Group link. The files that are opened are saved and closed. Your applications are still open, but you can close them if you want.

If we had the luxury of doing only one project at a time, life would be good. But reality is that we have to plan and make progress on several projects every day. Using the saved file groups, you can in—just a few seconds—close one project and open another. All the background business is taken care of for you.

Come back to the Bridge Center and double-click on the group you want to open inside the Saved File Groups panel (see Figure 1.12). Whatever application was using those files opens for editing. Make sure that, if you've already saved and reopened a group, you don't have to save it and create a new group. Using the folder arrow button, you can save the contents back into the group. Otherwise you'd make unnecessary duplicates of your saved groups.

Browsing the Bridge

Adobe Bridge has a beautiful method to browse files. If you are used to looking for files in your computer, you've had to change your view to thumbnails or view files as a list. Instead of futzing with menus, Bridge gives you a slider to pick the size of the thumbnails you want to see onscreen (see Figure 1.13).

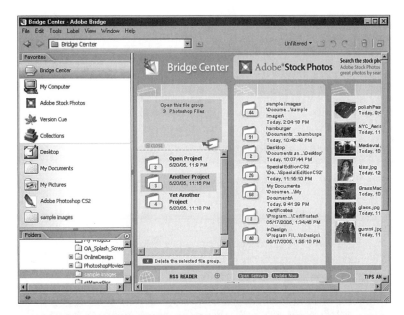

Figure 1.12
When you've saved multiple groups, click the one you want to use in the Bridge Center to open it again.

1

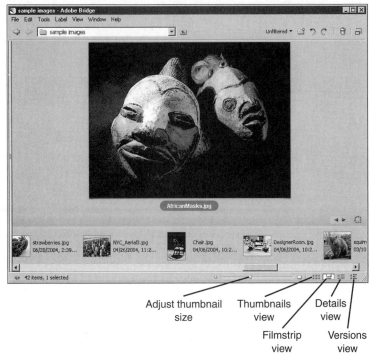

Figure 1.13
When you single-click a preview image and move the slider, your selected file remains in view.

Adjust thumbnail size

Thumbnails view

Details view

Filmstrip view

Versions view

In Bridge, choose Window, Workspace, LightBox. Your panels disappear, and you have only the main view of your files. Click the drop-down menu at the top of Bridge to navigate your file system. When you open a folder of images, you should see thumbnail previews display in the viewer area. At the very bottom of Bridge is a horizontal slider that enables you to change the size of the thumbnails. Next to the slider are buttons for other views: Thumbnails view, Filmstrip view, Details view, and Versions view. All views can also be accessed from the View menu at the top of Bridge. The slider works in all views, giving you maximum flexibility.

Viewing and Modifying Metadata

Choose Window, Workspace, Metadata Focus to display the Metadata panel on the right side of the Bridge window (see Figure 1.14). What is *metadata*? The generic definition states that metadata is data about data. Sounds like the stuff you want to show off at parties doesn't it? The purpose of meta-

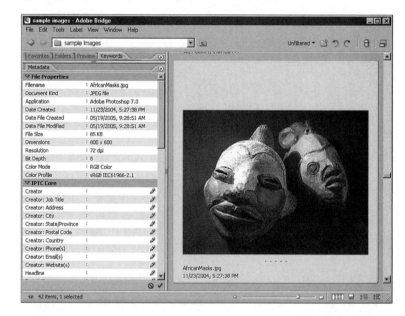

If you consistently refer to a particular directory, right-click in Windows (Control-click on the Mac) that folder when browsing Bridge and add it to the Favorites panel. Then you don't have to keep digging for it in the folder.

data is to help you label and identify files using other means besides the file's name and date created. When you work with hundreds of files within dozens of projects it helps to have a handle on things. Metadata in your files provides a way to identify more specifically what is important about that picture. The metadata you may have already been exposed to is EXIF data.

Figure 1.14
The Adobe Bridge Metadata panel.

When your digital camera stores an image it creates metadata about the way the camera was set when the image was generated. EXIF stands for Exchangeable Image File Format. It's a standard for storing information in image files, especially JPEG. Most cameras populate this metadata when an image is exposed. If you are a student of photography, this data is extremely helpful. You can see the camera settings that gave you the photograph. This means if you want to replicate something (or avoid something) you did in your next shot, just take a look at the metadata, and your answers are right there.

Nearly every file has metadata associated with it. At the very least the file will record the date and time it was created. As you navigate through your file directories in Bridge, you can click on any file to highlight it and view the Metadata panel (choose View, Metadata Panel). For JPEG image files taken with a digital camera, scroll down to the Camera Data (Exif) category to find information on lens aperture, flash, shutter, and even the lens focal length and much more. Metadata found in InDesign documents is also helpful and descriptive. Bridge metadata tells you the fonts and swatches used in your InDesign documents and shows you a thumbnail preview.

You can even add to a file's metadata information about yourself as the creator or photographer if you like. Using Bridge, navigate through your computer to find some JPEG images. Click the folder drop-down list at the top of the Bridge window to start your search. When you find some JPEG files you see their thumbnails pull up in the main view screen in Bridge. Single-click on an image and look at the Metadata panel on the left. Scroll down to see the IPTC Core entry in the panel. When you see a listing for Creator, click in the empty area and you can edit or create new metadata. Type your name as the Creator (see Figure 1.15).

Figure 1.15
Adding metadata to an image.

Now you might be thinking this would take forever to mark all these photographs with a new creator name. Using this example, it could take a while. So let's make it easier. Browse to a folder with multiple JPEG files. Holding down the Shift key, click to select multiple files. Then choose File, File Info. An information dialog appears containing all the metadata options that the Metadata panel had, just in separate views. On the left side of this dialog, click on IPTC Contact. Here you find the Creator tag you used a moment ago. Because you selected multiple files you see a small check box next to Creator. If you check the box and type your name, this information is applied to the metadata for all the selected files.

In the upper-right corner of this dialog there is a small menu arrow. Click to reveal the flyout menu. If you spent a lot of time adding new metadata to this group of pictures you might want to save a metadata template. A template holds all the information so you can apply it to other pictures. It's much easier than typing it in every time.

Labeling and Filtering Images

With all this talk about metadata, you'd think that metadata was the only way to label your images. Not true. Select an image in your viewing area and open the Label menu (see Figure 1.16). You have the option to label by using a star system or by color. For your first time labeling, choose the single star (*) to label the selected image file. Notice the keyboard shortcuts for applying these labels.

Figure 1.16
Apply labels to one or multiple images. You can label files by giving them a color or by using a star system.

Let's say you had some pictures from a photo shoot and you were given the task to find the perfect shot for a magazine ad. From an hour-long photo shoot, you may end up with 300 shots to narrow down. As you browse the photos, use the keyboard shortcut to label with a star the pictures you think are the ones to keep. You might use all five stars to label selected images or just one or two stars. At the top of the Bridge window, find the Filtering drop-down menu. Choose to filter by a certain number of stars. Or, if you labeled some images with a color, that color could be used to filter. This is a good way to narrow your search without having to move files around.

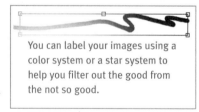

You can label your images using a color system or a star system to help you filter out the good from the not so good.

Processing Images in Batches

You'll read about batch processing later in the discussions about Photoshop, Illustrator, and InDesign. Essentially *batch processing* takes the monotony out of working with graphics. In Bridge you have access to these Batch features to work with many files at once. Unique to Bridge, in what was formerly the file browser, is a Batch Renaming feature. Photographs that come from your digital camera have generic names like DSC000145 and P1049543. Not very descriptive if you ask me, so you might want to rename the pics according to the subject matter or photographer. Renaming files individually can be a pain though. Here's how to batch rename hundreds of pictures at the same time:

1. Hold down the Shift key and click to select multiple image files in the main Bridge window. Because this is your first time working in batches, selecting only two files might be safer in case you don't like the results.

2. Choose Tools, Batch Rename. In the Batch Rename dialog (see Figure 1.17) select the radio button that defines how you want to treat your renamed files: Choose Rename in Same Folder, Move to Other Folder, or Copy to Other Folder. If you choose to move or copy the renamed files to another folder, a Browse button appears that you can click to designate the other folder.

   In the New Filenames area, options for renaming the file are available. Suppose that you want to rename the selected files with names such as **TestName MMDDYY_1**, **TestName MMDDYY_2**, and so on (where **MMDDYY** is today's date).

3. Select Text from the first pop-up menu in the New Filenames area; a text box to type in appears. Type the words **TestName** or something else if you like. To the right of that text box, click the + sign to add another part to the name.

4. In the new pop-up menu that appears after you click +, choose Date. The date defaults to Today, but you can specify another date by selecting it from the second drop-down list. From the third drop-down list in the Date row, pick the date format of MMDDYY. Click the + sign again to add another item to the new filenames you are creating.

5. From the new pop-up menu that appears, choose Text again. This time type only an underscore (_). Click the + sign one more time and choose Sequence Number. Keep the sequence number at 1, or type in any number for the start number in the sequence. In the last pop-up list, choose Four Digits (which means that your number sequence will have that many digits in the number). Later you can add images to this same sequence.

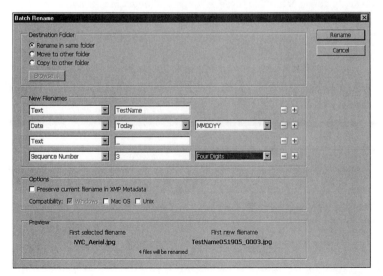

Figure 1.17
The Batch Rename dialog box.

If you followed the directions given in these steps, your files would be named similar to this:

TestName071205_0002.JPG

1

There are infinite ways you can rename image files with the Batch Rename command. Experiment with all the options to see how it suits you. Remember that if you are renaming batches of files, you probably need to use part of the existing unique name of the photo, or apply a number sequence to make the batch rename work properly. You can't have two files of the same name in the same folder.

Working with Color Settings

Setting up your color management in Bridge is a quick way to synchronize color across all the applications in the Creative Suite 2 at one time. In Bridge, choose Edit, Creative Suite Color Settings. The Suite Color Settings dialog gives a small list of possible color management options. Consider what is the best fit for your work. Everyone had different needs. If you are doing primarily onscreen work for the Web, choose North America Web/Internet. If you don't see the settings that apply to you, enable the Show Expanded List of Color Settings check box. Now you have three times as many options.

Color management is an area with mixed opinions in the industry. Your best bet is to talk to your printing service provider early in the project. It is not uncommon for printers to discard all color management data before rasterizing your pages and images for print, so don't be afraid to ask your vendor's technical support group for information so that you can be sure of their processes.

The color settings you specify in the Suite Color Settings dialog attach that color profile or instruction to the images you create. Talk to your printer to find out what settings to use. If you find that you need more specific options, open the Photoshop or Illustrator Color Settings dialog (choose Edit, Color Settings to display the dialog, as shown in Figure 1.18). You can create or load more detailed color settings and then save them. This custom profile then appears in the Suite Color Settings dialog where you can apply and synchronize these settings to the rest of the programs in the suite.

Figure 1.18
A custom color settings file created in Photoshop and saved.

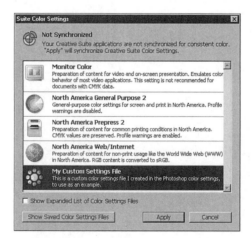

USING ADOBE STOCK PHOTOS

At first glance, you might think that Adobe is trying to corner the market on stock photography. Actually, it is much smarter than that. It knows that the best sites out there for stock photos are just aching to be pulled together into one enormous yet accessible library. The Adobe Stock Photos area of Bridge acts as an interface and shopping cart for several popular commercial stock photography sites. With Adobe Stock Photos, you browse all of them from one place.

Adobe Stock Photos is accessed from within Adobe Bridge. Find the link to open Adobe Stock Photos inside the Favorites pane within Bridge. Adobe Stock Photos opens in the main viewing window of bridge to its splash page.

Designers often don't have the time, equipment, or skill to capture that perfect image to be included in their work. Often it's not even geographically possible to snap your own pictures to place into your design. With the cost and skill required to get that perfect image, you'll wonder sometimes how you ever got by without using Adobe Stock Photos. I'm exaggerating a little here because a lot of the fun in designing is snapping the pictures yourself. You find after so many projects though that you wish you could just buy a picture that someone has already taken.

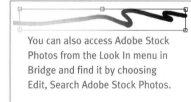

You can also access Adobe Stock Photos from the Look In menu in Bridge and find it by choosing Edit, Search Adobe Stock Photos.

With Adobe Stock Photos, you certainly can. There are well over 200,000 photos to pick from accessed through Adobe Stock Photos. You need only to type in a search.

Finding the Perfect Photo

Locate the search field at the top of the Adobe Stock Photos window. Type in a search keyword for a photo you might like to find. I think you'll be surprised how much ground has been covered with a camera after a few searches. I was impressed my first go-around with keywords. I didn't think I'd find more than 10 photos of licorice. Need some kind of baseball photo? You have about 500 to pick from there. Your search results display the photos in thumbnails in the main window. As the search finds more pictures, more thumbnails will accumulate. Hmmm, 26 pictures of tofu. Interesting!

Just like file browsing with Bridge, you can use the slider below the results window to change the size of the thumbnails to display a larger view of the stock photo. Having more visual information in a larger view helps you make a decision to use that picture. When you find a picture you like, what should you do with it? Are you charged right away? Absolutely not. In fact you can use low-resolution versions of the images known as *comps*. When you find a picture you like, double-click the thumbnail or film strip preview to open a comp version in Photoshop with which you can work.

You can also browse photos by category from the main Adobe Stock Photos page. Click on the Browse Link under Get Started in the main window. Navigate among hundreds of categories of images. Or use your knowledge of these categories to come up with more effective keyword searches.

Select an image from the search results and click the Download Comp button above the image thumbnails to download the low-res copy to your hard drive (see Figure 1.19). When you work on projects, you can use comps as placeholders for actual graphics. Just don't use them in your final design unless you purchase them.

Download a low-resolution comp

Figure 1.19
Download comps to your hard drive with the Download Comp button, or double-click a thumbnail to open the comp image in Photoshop.

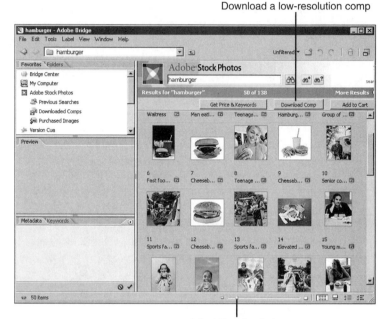

Adjust thumbnail size

Purchasing Photos

If you have found that perfect photo for use in your final design, you can purchase it through Adobe Stock Photos by creating an account. This account handles the photos purchased from all the different stock photo vendors used in the program. Highlight the photo you want and click the Add to Cart button. When you are ready to check out, click the Shopping Cart button near the top right of the Adobe Stock Photos window. Your shopping cart page appears with size options available for your selected photo (see Figure 1.20). Make sure to pick the right size for your output, whether screen or print because they come with vastly different price tags. Expect to pay between $40 and $300 for stock images. When you're designing for a large project, the price of the perfect picture may be a drop in the bucket.

Click the Check Out button to proceed. You are asked to sign in or to set up a new account. If you opt to create a new account, you are taken to a page where you create a login ID and provide your personal and credit card information. After the transaction goes through, your image is downloaded and available under the Purchased Images category in the Favorites pane in Bridge.

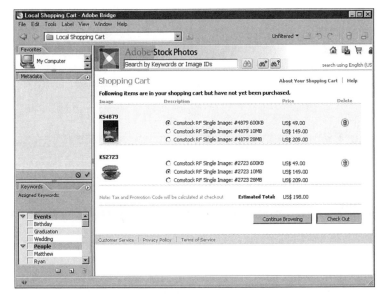

Figure 1.20
Choose the appropriate size for your image and click the Check Out button to create an account, or use your existing account to purchase one or multiple images.

Cleaning Up

After a lot of searches and comp downloads you may start to see your hard drive space declining. A lot of image data is cached in your hard drive to enable Adobe Stock Photos to operate smoothly. It's good to give it a cleansing every few weeks, or even more frequently depending on how much you use it. You can clean out these cache and comp folders right from inside Bridge:

1. In the Favorites pane, click on Previous Searches. Folders appear with the same search or category name you used when you browsed Adobe Stock Photos.

2. Hold down the Ctrl or ⌘ key and click to select multiple folders. Then right-click or Control-click the folders and choose Send to Recycle Bin from the context menu to move the folders to the trash/recycle bin. The thumbnails are removed from the AdobeStockPhotos folder located in your Documents or My Documents folder.

3. Click on the Downloaded Comps link in the Favorites pane and repeat steps 1 and 2 to remove unused comps from your hard drive.

You can perform these cleanups manually by finding the AdobeStockPhotos folder in your Documents folder (on the Mac) or in the My Documents folder (in Windows). Open the folders for Previous Searches and Downloaded Comps and throw away the contents. If you accidentally throw away the Previous Searches folder, don't worry. It will be re-created when you next search in Adobe Stock Photos.

THE HELP CENTER

1

Although we try to answer every question you have in this book, there's a great information option within the program: the Adobe Help Center. This resource contains complete information on all the features of all the applications in the Creative Suite, including step-by-step instructions for many tasks (see Figure 1.21).

Figure 1.21
The Help Center is your first line of defense for assistance with any part of the Creative Suite.

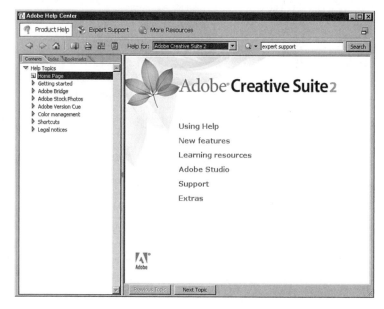

To access the Help Center from InDesign for example, select Help, InDesign Help. The Help Center browser opens.

The left pane of the browser window contains selections for the help contents, many hidden in pop-up arrows. Scroll through the pane and click a specific subject for help. The right pane contains the actual Help information.

Tabs at the top of the left pane take you to the alphabetical Index and Bookmarks, respectively.

The Bookmarks tab is empty when you first open the Help Center. If you find yourself returning to certain information over and over, or if there is a subject of particular interest to you, click the Add Bookmark button in the second line of buttons at the top of the screen (see Figure 1.22). These bookmarks are accessible in all programs, so if you add a bookmark about layer comps in Photoshop, for example, and want to access that information while you're working with a layered Photoshop document you've placed in InDesign, you can use the bookmark to jump quickly to the PSD layer comp information.

Rearrange bookmarks using the arrow buttons at the bottom-left of the pane. Rename a bookmark by selecting it and clicking the Rename button, or delete a bookmark by selecting it and clicking the Delete button.

Add Bookmark button

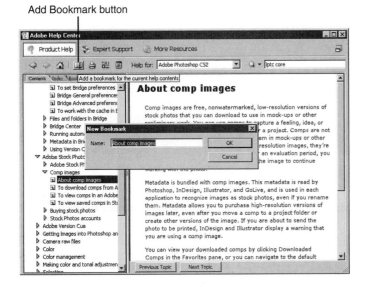

Figure 1.22
Create bookmarks to help you quickly return to commonly accessed Help topics.

To help navigate the Help Center, buttons above the left pane enable you to move forward or back through pages you visited or to return to the Help Center home page. Also at the top of the browser window is a button to print the contents of the right Help pane.

Select the program for which you'd like to view Help from the Help for pop-up menu. Search for the topic of your choice by entering your terms in the search box and clicking the Search button.

Expert Support is another option available in the Help Center. Expert Support is a subscription-based support option through which, using an Internet connection, you can submit support questions to experts at Adobe. There are several support subscription options depending on the level of support desired and the money you want to spend.

Finally, the More Resources button gives you links to Adobe's website that will prove helpful as you work with the software.

PHOTOSHOP AND IMAGEREADY

IN THIS PART

WORKING WITH PHOTOSHOP

IN THIS CHAPTER

If this is your first experience with Photoshop and ImageReady, I would like to bid you welcome. I am more than honored to be your first tour guide of this wonderful program. I would expect that you've heard a few things about Photoshop prior to buying the Adobe Creative Suite 2. Photoshop is always called Adobe's flagship program. Go into any bookstore and it's easy to see how popular the program is. In the computer book section you will likely find more Photoshop books than any other computer book.

There are three things that I hope you get out of your experience with Photoshop. Number one, the realization that you can't master this program without having a playful spirit. The only way you can absorb all of Photoshop is by having fun with it.

The second thing is that you realize that you are limited only by your imagination with this program. You can't say that about a lot of software, but it's definitely true here. If you can dream it and you can experiment, it can be done.

The third and most important thing to know is that even the masters of Photoshop will admit that they still have tons to learn. We are all at different levels of experience with programs. I can't count how many times in training sessions I've seen someone sit down to Photoshop for the first time and find some new control or command that does something so totally fresh and unknown that even the instructor is surprised. Enjoy your time with this software and remember this rule after you discover something new: You must share with others what you learn.

BEST PRACTICES

If Photoshop were the answer to all your graphic problems, you wouldn't need a creative suite. Photoshop is best suited for making raster graphics for high-quality print output. Digital photo editing and manipulation is what this program is for at its core. Use the Brush tools to create original art, or mix original art with existing photos. Take many pictures and assemble them into a collage. Perform color corrections and photo repairs. Use ImageReady to take your finished Photoshop creations and prepare them for the web using ImageReady's advanced compression options and slicing tools.

Photoshop seems to do everything, doesn't it?

Photoshop certainly does a lot. But that doesn't mean it outperforms other applications in the suite. You want to use the best tool for the job. For example, Photoshop can make PDF files, but they save as pretty large files even with simple graphics. If you need to make light PDF files for sharing on websites, use InDesign or Illustrator. Although Photoshop has some vector drawing tools for making logos and other objects, you should be using Illustrator for that sort of work because its design tools for vector art are superior. If you are creating websites, you should use Photoshop in combination with GoLive. It's surprising but there are a number of websites out there that are simply Photoshop graphics and text sliced and embedded into a page. Use Photoshop for your interface design, but your text should not be rendered out of Photoshop. Websites should be made up of HTML text, not Photoshop graphic text.

ImageReady is meant to work with Photoshop as a next step in creating web graphics. Though the differences between the programs seem small, more options for saving and optimizing web graphics and animations are available in ImageReady than in Photoshop.

FILE FORMATS

Table 2.1 lists the file formats that can be used, saved, exported, or imported by Photoshop.

Table 2.1 Photoshop File Formats

Format	Description/Comments
PSD, PDD	Photoshop document format
BMP (RLE DIB)	Bitmap format (Windows)
GIF	CompuServe Graphical Interchange Format; a web image format supporting transparency; 256 max colors
EPS	Photoshop EPS Encapsulated PostScript format
DCS 1.0 2.0	Desktop Color Separations format; a version of EPS; supports CMYK; DCS 2.0 supports spot channels
JPEG	Joint Photographic Experts Group; most common graphic format for the web and even for print despite its lossy compression; supports RGB, CMYK
PSB	Large Photoshop document format (Photoshop Big); allows files over 2GB
PCX	Older PC image format; opens in Microsoft Paint
PDF	Photoshop Portable Document Format
Raw	Photoshop raw format; different than camera raw format; cross-platform binary format supports RGB and CMYK, alpha, and more; cannot contain layers
PICT	Mac OS graphic format for the screen; supports RGB, index, grayscale, or bitmap modes
PXR	Pixar format; designed for high-end graphics commonly used in 3D work; su ports RGB grayscale and single alpha channel
PNG	Portable Networking Graphics format; a quality, patent-free alternative to GIF; well-supported web format; supports RGB, grayscale, bitmap modes, transparency; lossless compression options
PBM, PGM, PPM, PNM, PFM	Portable Bitmap formats; family of bitmap screen graphic formats
SCT	Scitex Continuous Tone high-end color format; sometimes used for magazine ads
Targa	Designed for systems using TrueVision boards; commonly used for video-editing systems
TIFF	Tagged Image File Format; raster format; supports CMYK, RGB, Lab, indexed color, grayscale, some transparency and Photoshop layers; bit depths of 8, 16, and 32
AI	Paths drawn in Photoshop can be exported as empty paths (no stroke or fill information) for use in Illustrator
WBMP	Images for mobile devices; 1-bit images contain only black or white pixels
CIN	Kodak Cineon Film System format; RGB 16-bit; channel image support
HDR, RGBE, XYZE	High Dynamic Range image formats; support higher range of luminance levels; used in high-end photography for more realistic lighting and exposure
SWF	Shockwave Flash format; still images and animations can be exported from ImageReady

2

Photoshop CS2 ships with optional plug-ins for a variety of file formats that are not needed by the vast majority of Photoshop users (see Figure 2.1). Should you need to work with one or more of these formats, drag the plug-in into the File Formats subfolder of Photoshop's Plug-ins folder. The next time you start Photoshop, the file format will be available.

Figure 2.1
Look for these plug-ins in the Optional Plug-ins folder, inside the Goodies folder, on the Photoshop CD.

Photoshop Format (.psd)

Photoshop's native file format supports all the program's capabilities. Files in this format can be placed in the latest versions of InDesign and GoLive as smart objects and can be opened in Adobe Illustrator. This is the default file format. Most workflows (but not all) benefit from maintaining a file in Photoshop format until it's time to create a final TIFF, EPS, JPEG, or other file. It's also usually a good idea to maintain the original image, with editable type and layers, for future use.

When saving in Photoshop format, you can see that the Save As dialog indicates which features are used in the image (see Figure 2.2). If a check box is grayed out, that feature is unavailable. If you disable a check box, the file is saved as a copy. If you disable a feature (layers, for example) and save the image as a copy, when the image is reopened, that feature is gone—no more layers.

Figure 2.2
The Save As dialog in Windows. Options such as Spot Colors, Annotations, Layers, and Alpha Channels are available only if they are actually used in your document.

UNDERSTANDING THE PHOTOSHOP CS2 INTERFACE

Open Photoshop and you will find more tools staring back at you than you'll want to count (see Figure 2.3). Fortunately you don't need to know how they all work, at least at first. Aside from the Tools palette and other floating palettes in the interface, it's pretty much like any other program. You have a menu bar and some icons along the top. All of the other palettes, which include the vertical Toolbox on the left and the smaller rectangular stacked palettes on the right, can be moved around in any arrangement that suits you. If you do not need a palette while you are working, just close it out by clicking the close button (the X) at the top of the palette.

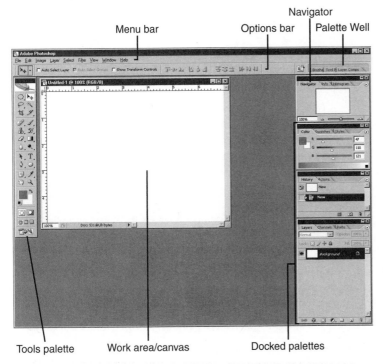

Menu bar   Options bar   Navigator / Palette Well

Tools palette   Work area/canvas   Docked palettes

Figure 2.3
The Photoshop interface.

When learning a new program, it's best to jump in with both feet, so let's create a new Photoshop document. Choose File, New to open the New dialog, which has a lot of options. From the Preset pop-up menu, choose Default Photoshop Size. The options underneath will change for the size. Spend a little time looking at all these options here. Understanding the purpose of your final graphic helps you make the right choices. A graphic for a printed poster has different sizes and dimensions than a button row you might design for a website. If you are not quite sure what size to specify, err on the larger size because it's very easy to crop your canvas later.

The Canvas

When you create a new document, the area where you make or work on your image is called the *canvas* (see Figure 2.4).

Figure 2.4
A new document in Photoshop has a canvas of a specified size on which you work. A canvas size has nothing to do with the size of the window in which it is displayed. You may be viewing your canvas at any zoom level inside the window. Resizing the window of the canvas does not change the canvas size.

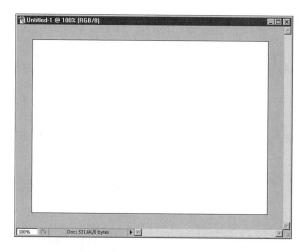

Options Bar

Choose Window, Options to show or hide the Options bar. Generally it's preferred to show the Options bar at all times rather than hide it because it gives you quick access to tool options and the Palette Well. The Options bar is contextual, so its options depend on the tool you have selected in the Toolbox. If you select the Paintbrush tool, the Options bar shows options for Brush size, opacity, and flow. Selecting the Type tool gives you type options such as font family, size, and justification. Think of the Options bar as an extension of the Toolbox.

The Palette Well in the Options bar is a smaller storage area for some of your palettes. You can dock a palette into the palette well by clicking the palette tab and dragging it into the well. Palettes that are docked in the Palette Well have all of their features hidden until you click their tab to reveal them. This works well for palettes you need access to, but not very often. The palettes that are docked in the Well by default are the Brushes, Tool Presets, and Layer Comps palette (see Figure 2.5).

Palettes

Palettes are everywhere. Sometimes you're working in Photoshop and it seems you are spending more time moving palettes around than actually creating something. When the view of your workspace gets too palette-cluttered, close a few out. If you need to open a palette again, remember that all the palettes are found under the Window menu. Think of palettes as your little windows and you won't forget that fact. Also take a look at how some palettes are in groups of tabs. This arrangement helps keep things clean, but you can still move palettes out from their group and use them individually. You can also regroup them in new ways that benefit your working style. Palettes help you further control the options for your tools, color, and other document arrangements. Look more closely at palettes and you see they have their own little interface. A lot of palettes look the same, but their extra buttons or controls are different.

Take a look at the Layers palette, which has more to it than you first think (see Figure 2.6). Your stack of layers show up in the middle of the palette. Around the outside is the palette's title bar, which includes close and minimize buttons. Not every palette has a palette menu. Most have them to contain extra options for the palette and even have duplicated options of those found under the

Photoshop menu. You may hear this palette menu referred to as a *flyout menu* or the arrow you click to display the palette menu referred to as a *caret*.

Brush tool selected

Options bar for the Brush tool

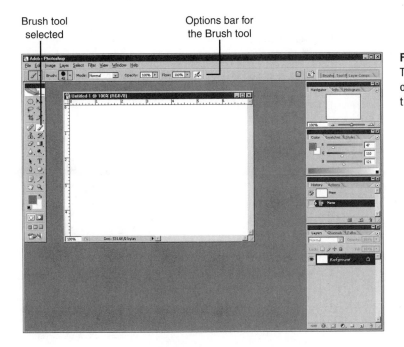

Figure 2.5
The Options bar showing options for the Brush tool and the Palette Well.

Palette title bar

Palette tab

Click here to open palette menu

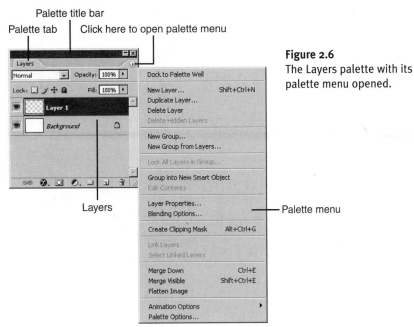

Layers

Palette menu

Figure 2.6
The Layers palette with its palette menu opened.

Each palette has the tab near the top that identifies it. The Layers palette has a tab called Layers. By clicking on these tabs and holding and dragging, you can move palettes out of their group and separate them. You can drag palettes into their own groups. When you drag a palette by its tab into another palette, the outside of the second palette is highlighted, enabling you to know that the palette you're dragging will dock with the highlighted palette. You can also dock palettes underneath each other by dragging into the bottom of a palette until you see a highlighted bar.

At the right end of the Options bar is a little rectangle called the Palette Well where you can also dock a few palettes to make them accessible but mostly hidden. The Palette Well is unique to Photoshop and ImageReady (see Figure 2.7).

Palette Well

Figure 2.7
Drag palettes inside the Palette Well and they stay hidden until you click the palette's tab. Here the Brushes palette is accessed from the Palette Well.

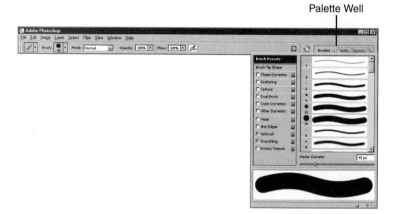

Workspace Hints

If you are getting overrun with palettes while you are working, you can press the Tab key to hide all the palettes at the same time. Press Tab again to bring them all back. If you need just the Tools palette, press Shift+Tab, and all palettes will disappear except for the Tools palette. What if you would like to keep your special arrangement of palettes? After you arrange your palettes, choose Window, Workspace, Save Workspace to make Photoshop remember the arrangement of the workspace; you give the workspace a name so that you can load it again later (see Figure 2.8). In the Save Workspace dialog that opens, enable the Keyboard Shortcuts check box to save your keyboard shortcuts and menus along with the workspace so that they are all easily accessible.

Figure 2.8
Save your workspace with a custom name and you can easily access your desired arrangement of palettes.

You can save your workspace and instantly set up your workspace the way you like at any time. Revert back to a saved workspace by choosing Window, Workspace and selecting the workspace you named.

Highlighted Menu Modes

Adobe has been the first I've seen to do this totally awesome menu trick with a program. Choose Window, Workspace, What's New in CS2. Then notice the color that is applied to some of your menus. As you drill down through menus you will see that Photoshop highlights the menu options corresponding to the new features of CS2. You have a lot of other choices for this menu-highlighting feature as well. Photoshop can highlight menu options corresponding to certain types of image editing you might be doing (see Figure 2.9). For example, you can choose to highlight menus related to Image Analysis, Painting and Retouching, Web Design, Typography and more. Kudos to Adobe for this neat little feature.

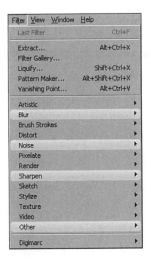

Figure 2.9
Choose from several menu-highlighting options, or customize your own. Here, the options in the Filter menu are highlighted based on Image Analysis related functions.

PHOTOSHOP HELP CENTER

As mentioned in Chapter 1, "Creative Suite 2 Basics," CS2 has an integrated Help Center with several programs included. From Photoshop or ImageReady, you can access the Help Center by choosing Help, Photoshop Help or Help, ImageReady Help. Help for some people is considered an afterthought, but when you work with the software, the Help Center can be a more convenient resource than a manual because of its text-searching capabilities. Adobe has also been known to put more information in its help system than in its user guides. When you have a question about something in the software or have a graphics-related question, type a keyword in the search field. Remember to make sure that Adobe Photoshop CS2 is selected in the Help For pop-up menu and then press Enter. Your keyword searches should get results.

A nice feature of the Help Center for Photoshop CS2 are the built-in tutorials. The left pane is full of help links; in this list, find the Tutorials category. If you can't see the category, click the Home button to take you back to the main menu and splash page. Click the small arrow to turn down the Tutorials category. You will find some great tutorials on making selections, color correction, and much more (see Figure 2.10).

Figure 2.10
Tutorials in the Help Center cover common tasks in Photoshop CS2.

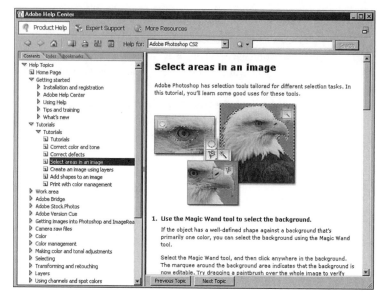

GRIDS AND GUIDES

Create a new document by choosing File, New. Open an existing image file by choosing File, Open. When the canvas appears and you are ready to work, you might like the benefit of having a grid or guidelines to help align elements in your composition. Show your document's grid by choosing View, Show, Grid. A grid will appear over your image, but it will not print or export with your image (see Figure 2.11). The grid is only for display, measurement, and alignment purposes.

If you need a custom grid or guide setup for working with your images, you can modify the grid spacing preferences and the grid and guide display colors. Choose Edit, Preferences, Guides Grid & Slices (Windows users) or InDesign, Preferences, Guides Grid & Slices (on the Mac). In this Preferences pane, choose the grid or guide color from the pop-up menus or pick a custom color from the swatch square. Guides can have solid or dashed lines. Grids can have solid, dashed, or dotted lines. Change the spacing between the grid lines so that it suits your workflow. You can work with several types of units for spacing your grid, such as inches, picas, millimeters, and points, to name a few. If your grid is showing on the canvas, you see your change to the grid updated on the canvas live so that you can preview your new grid.

> You cannot move guidelines if the Hand or Slice tool is active; first select the Move tool and then drag the guidelines.

If the grid is too much for you, but you still want some alignment tools, you can create just a few guidelines to help your design efforts. First, display the rulers by choosing View, Rulers. After the rulers are shown, you can create guides by clicking a spot on a rule, holding down the mouse button, and dragging from the ruler and into your image. The ruler guide will be created. If you need to move your guide somewhere else, choose the Move tool from the Tools palette (alternatively, press and hold the ⌘ key on the Mac or Ctrl in Windows). Hover the mouse pointer over the guide until the mouse pointer changes to a double-headed arrow; then slide the guide to another location (see Figure 2.12).

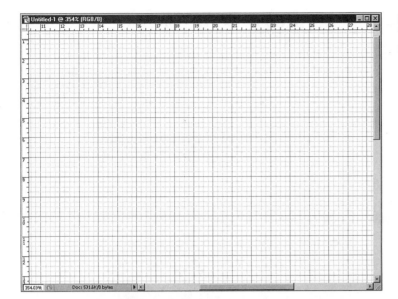

Figure 2.11
The document grid showing in the canvas.

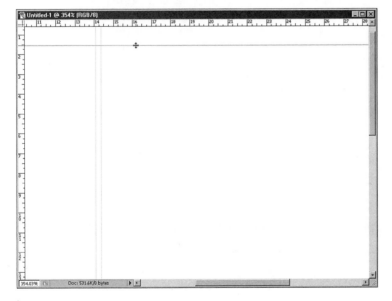

Figure 2.12
Create a guide by dragging from the ruler onto the canvas.

If your guidelines are not showing up or seem to be locked in place, choose View, Show, Guides. Your guides should now appear. If the View, Lock Guides menu option is checked, select that option again to unlock the guides.

Guides and the grid won't do you much good in aligning objects in your image area if you don't have snapping turned on. Choose View, Snap To and select whether you want the items you move around the canvas to have a magnetic snapping effect against the grid or guides.

CREATING A NEW PHOTOSHOP DOCUMENT

You've already created your first blank Photoshop document, but let's zero in on the options, so you know what you are getting. Let's just say this before anything else: If you create a document of the wrong size, you can always fix it when you open the canvas. However, after you have worked on the graphic for a while, it's rarely a good idea to size a graphic up, rather than size it down.

Choose File, New to open the New dialog, where there are a number of presets. You can create additional presets by setting up a custom size and then clicking the Save Preset button on the right size of the dialog. You can also delete presets you don't need any longer. The presets available in Photoshop represent a spectrum of sizes and needs, from business cards to high-definition video frames. There are also a variety of paper sizes, such as letter, legal, tabloid, A4, and B5 (see Figure 2.13). All the available presets cover most of the work you might do. Still, many people create their own custom-size documents to be certain they are on target with their final output.

Figure 2.13
Use the presets available in the New dialog or create your own custom presets by selecting options and saving them as a preset.

The following sections describe each of the fields in the New dialog box; understanding what each field controls can help you create documents that are appropriate for your intended use.

Width and Height

You can set the dimensions for the new document by typing in a width and height (see Figure 2.14). Be sure you are using the correct units for your document. When people say they need a 4 by 6 image, it's doubtful they mean 4 by 6 pixels. No matter what units you use, or what kind of document you have to make, it's always best to size things a little larger to leave room for cropping later.

When creating a document, your understanding of the units pixels, inches, cm, mm, points, picas, and columns helps tremendously. Let's quickly go over the units:

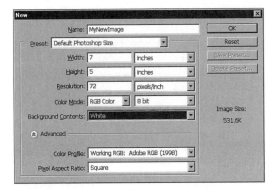

Figure 2.14
Choose appropriate options for size, resolution, and color mode in the New dialog.

- A *pixel* is the smallest graphic unit that makes up a digital onscreen image. A pixel can have only one color designation. It's the smallest unit your screen can render. Web graphics are displayed at 72 pixels per inch (ppi).

- *Inches* are used not only for page sizes, but also for image dimensions. There are 72 points per inch.

- *Centimeters* and *millimeters* are widely used internationally. For example, in Japan, a common paper size is B5. B5 measures 176mm by 250mm. Also in Japan, L-size photographs are the most common size printed and measure 12.5cm by 9cm.

- Used in layout design, a *pica* is a unit that has historically been identified as the ideal space between two columns of body text, or between images and body text columns. 12 points = 1 pica; 6 picas = 1 inch.

- A *column* is a custom unit of width, which can be set in the Photoshop Preferences window.

Resolution Guidelines

Print jobs vary, but here are a few guidelines to help you choose the right resolution for your image:

- Web graphics are displayed at 72ppi.

- Newspaper printed images should be from 100–150dpi.

- Newspaper line art (comics) are from 300–600dpi.

- Magazine and art book raster images (photos) are printed from 225–300 dpi.

- Line art graphics for commercial print are from 600–1200dpi.

- Photo quality prints are from 240–600dpi.

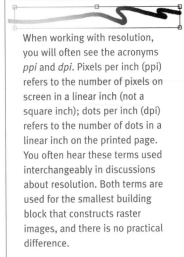

When working with resolution, you will often see the acronyms *ppi* and *dpi*. Pixels per inch (ppi) refers to the number of pixels on screen in a linear inch (not a square inch); dots per inch (dpi) refers to the number of dots in a linear inch on the printed page. You often hear these terms used interchangeably in discussions about resolution. Both terms are used for the smallest building block that constructs raster images, and there is no practical difference.

Color Mode

You can choose your color mode before you create your document or convert your document from one color mode to another after the canvas has opened. In many cases, you benefit from starting in one color mode and converting to another just before output. See Chapter 5, "Working with Images and Color in Photoshop," for more information on color modes.

Color Bit Depth

The default bit depth is 8 bits per channel. A *channel* stores information about the color elements in the image. You can create an image of up to 32 bits per channel. A 32 or 16 bits-per-channel image provides finer distinctions in color (but has a much larger file size) than an 8 bits-per-channel version of the same image. If you work with 32 or 16-bit images, you also don't have access to as many tools and filters as you do with an 8-bit image. Bitmap mode images use a 1-bit depth.

Background Contents

You can choose from three settings for your canvas background: White, Background Color, or Transparent. The White option is obvious enough. The Background Color option applies the most recently set background color in the Toolbox as your solid color background. Choosing the Transparent option does not create a background layer as the other choices do. Instead it creates a single transparent layer in your document. A transparent background is represented by a gray-and-white checkerboard pattern on the canvas. Note that even when choosing a transparent background, your image output format may not support it and might instead flatten it to a white background.

Color Profile

You can choose a color profile for your new document. Different profile types are shown depending on the color mode you select. Bitmap and Lab color images do not support color management settings. Also, not all image formats store color profile information. When supported, color profiles help with color consistency across multiple programs. Color profiles can help devices compensate for differences in their color display and capturing of an image.

Pixel Aspect Ratio

A computer's pixel aspect ratio, also known as its *height proportion to width*, is square. When creating graphics for output to the many video formats, use the appropriate aspect ratio for that chosen format. Otherwise, your graphic rendered may appear stretched in the final video. An example is if you are working in normal Digital Video NTSC (standard for North America and Japan), you would choose D1 DV NTSC 0.9. This is a slightly thinner pixel dimension. D1 DV NTSC Widescreen pixel size is 1.2, which is a bit wider than a normal pixel. Using the correct size for your video work ensures that what you create in Photoshop is consistent with the rest of your video footage size.

USING THE PHOTOSHOP TOOLBOX

3

The toolbox has gone through many incarnations since Photoshop was first introduced. More tools have been added and some modified and combined. Photoshop also shares most of the same tools as ImageReady, with a few differences that you'll see later. This chapter is a reference on each of the tools. Skim over it for just the tools you are trying to learn or read it straight through. Many tools have a keyboard shortcut assigned to them to access them immediately without having to locate them on the toolbox. When you hover your mouse over tools in the toolbox, a ToolTip gives you the name of the tool and the keyboard shortcut bound to it (see Figure 3.1). Some tools actually have groups of tools hidden underneath them. You can tell whether there are hidden tools if an arrow is fixed in the lower-right corner of the tool's button.

Figure 3.1
A ToolTip appears when the mouse pointer hovers over a tool in the toolbox.

USING THE OPTIONS BAR

When you have chosen a tool from the Toolbox, look in the Options bar for ways to apply settings to the tool. As you select a particular tool, the Options bar shows the settings for that tool in that context. So the Options bar always has different options available depending on the tool selected. Not all tools have options you can change, but most of them have some options you can change in the Options bar.

Understanding Paint Options

There are painting options available when one of the paint tools is selected. Paint tools include the Brush, the Pencil, the Gradient, and the Paint Bucket tools. Options you can change for these tools are the *mode* (which is the blending overlay effect as the tool paints), the opacity, and the flow, to name a few. Opacity settings for painting with these tools enable you to paint with a transparent ink, with one that is completely opaque, and with every percentage between.

Understanding Type Options

After you select one of the type tools, many options are available in the Options bar. Choose a font family from the font family menu. In Photoshop CS2, a preview of your font families shows up in the menu. If different font styles like Bold and Italic or Oblique are built into the font, those are available under the font style menu in the Options bar. Change the point size of the font from the Font Size menu. You can select one of the sizes in the menu or type your own value in the box. The highlighted text in the type layer is updated; if no type was selected, the next characters typed use these settings. When you use the Character and Paragraph palettes, these options and more are available, but the convenience of the Options bar is what makes it so valuable.

Many other options are available, depending on the tool selected. Although this book cannot cover all these options in detail, you will explore some of them as the tools are covered in the following pages.

USING THE SELECTION TOOLS

The Selection tools are used to designate areas that you will be cutting out, cropping, painting within, or applying filters to. The area not selected is usually unaffected when you manipulate the image in any of these ways. When a selection is made around an area of the image, you will see what is often referred to as *marching ants* or the *selection marquee* running around the edge (see Figure 3.2).

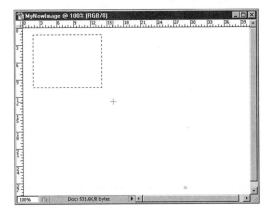

Figure 3.2
A rectangular marquee drawn in the canvas.

The following is a summary of the Selection tools:

- **Rectangular Marquee (M):** This tool creates a rectangle-shaped selection area. Holding the Shift key while drawing constrains your rectangle to a square shape.

- **Elliptical Marquee (M):** This tool makes an oval or ellipse-shaped selection. Hold the Shift key to constrain your selection to a circle.

- **Single Column Marquee (M):** This tool selects a one-pixel–wide line that runs the height of the canvas.

- **Single Row Marquee (M):** This tool selects a one-pixel–tall line that runs the width of the canvas.

- **Move (V):** This tool moves the content of the layer you are working with.

- **Lasso (L):** Use this tool to draw a freeform selection.

- **Polygonal Lasso (L):** After you select this tool, click, release, and drag the image to mark the corners (and draw the edges) of a polygonal selection.

- **Magnetic Lasso (L):** With an image on screen, this tool follows the contours of part of an image as it creates a selection marquee. It's one useful way to cut out a subject from its background.

- **Magic Wand (W):** This tool selects parts of the image by color similarity. Adjust the Tolerance setting in the Options bar to select more or fewer of the surrounding similar colors.

Like the marquee tools, many other tools share the same keyboard shortcut. To alternate between the different tools when this situation exists, hold down the Shift key when pressing the shortcut key on the keyboard. Pressing this key combination several times drills down through the tools nested together; the selected tool's icon shows up in the toolbox.

USING THE CROP AND SLICE TOOLS

The Crop and Slice tools are used to separate and eventually extract or use part of the image that is most important. Cropping takes out everything outside your cropping area. Slicing an image into multiple areas makes smaller image tiles from the main image.

- **Crop (C):** Click and drag with this tool to create an adjustable crop area of your image. Press Enter to crop the canvas to your rectangular area. Press Esc to cancel the crop. After you crop your image, part of the image is gone; make sure that if you save over the original image, you won't need the content you have cropped out.

- **Slice (K):** Used for creating web images, the slice tool creates rectangular slices from which you can export individual graphics. Build web button interfaces in one canvas and save to sliced areas for your web page.

- **Slice Select (K):** Select your image slices and adjust the size of the slices by moving the handles. Hold down the Shift key to select multiple slices at once.

USING THE RETOUCHING TOOLS

One of the most important benefits of Photoshop is your ability to retouch images to improve or perfect them. Frankly, the trickery and deception is quite fun. These tools help you patch and heal tears, scratches, and even red eyes from erratic camera flashbulbs:

- **Spot Healing Brush (J):** Click on a blemish in a photograph and this tool samples pixels in the area around the blemish to blend it out. This is similar to the Healing Brush tool, but with the Spot Healing Brush you do not need to select a source area.

- **Healing Brush (J):** Select this tool and hold the Alt key (in Windows) or the Option key (on the Mac) as you click to select a source area; then click on a blemish in a photo, such as a wrinkle on someone's face. The Healing Brush blends out the blemish by sampling pixels from the selected source area.

- **Patch (J):** Draw a marquee with the Patch tool or other marquee tools. Then click in the selected area with the Patch tool and drag the selection around the canvas. Wherever you drag will be visible through the selected area, enabling you to patch and blend that area with another part of the image.

- **Red Eye (J):** New in CS2, the Red Eye tool enables you to remove red eye with one click. Red eye is common in photos taken with a flash. This unfortunate red reflection from your eye can be scary, and removing it used to take a few steps in previous versions of Photoshop. Now, simply click in the middle of the subject's red eye with the Red Eye tool for a quick removal; click anywhere in the image to search the image for redness to remove. Because this tool couldn't possibly have knowledge of the original color of your subject's eyes, the color change is really a desaturation of the red color and a slight darkening. The effect looks natural, but that doesn't prevent you from altering the eye further using the Burn tool or some other paint tools. In the Options bar, set the percentage of Pupil Size and Darken Amount.

- **Clone Stamp (S):** Clone areas of an image into another part of an image with this tool. Press and hold the Alt key (in Windows) or the Option key (on a Mac) and click a source area. Then paint within another area of the image and watch the tool blend the source area into the destination area (see Figure 3.3). Works best with a soft-edged brush.

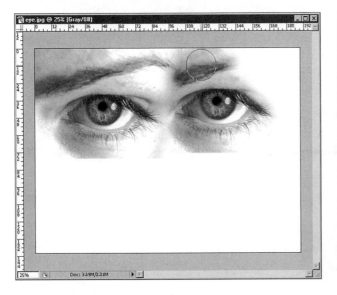

Figure 3.3
Cloning part of an image with the Clone Stamp tool.

- **Pattern Stamp (S):** Paints a pattern into your image where you paint with this tool. Choose a different pattern to clone in the Options bar using the pattern picker. Adjust the brush size and hardness, opacity, and flow, and the pattern is painted using those options. Enabling the Impressionist check box distorts the pattern as it is painted.

- **Eraser (E):** This tool erases the content on the layer you are working (see Figure 3.4) and reveals the background color underneath when erasing in the Background layer.

Figure 3.4
The Eraser tools.

- **Background Eraser (E):** This tool erases to transparency even on the Background layer of your image.

- **Magic Eraser (E):** This tool detects and erases areas in a similar color range. Adjust the Tolerance setting in the Options bar to select more or fewer of the adjacent areas.

- **Blur (R):** This tool enables you to brush areas (see Figure 3.5) and blur only those areas. It averages the pixel color and contrast of surrounding pixels to create a "softer" transition between the pixels and, consequently, the blur effect.

Figure 3.5
The Blur, Sharpen, and Smudge tools.

- **Sharpen (R):** This tool sharpens edges by creating more contrast between the pixels you brush over. This increased contrast creates the effect of a sharper edge.

- **Smudge (R):** Click on the image, hold the mouse button, and drag to smudge pixels. Like paint or pastels, this tool creates a realistic smearing of the pixels.

- **Dodge (O):** This tool mimics a photographic technique that underexposes or lightens parts of the image you brush over.

- **Burn (O):** This tool mimics the photographic technique that overexposes or darkens the parts of the image you brush over.

- **Sponge (O):** This tool saturates or desaturates areas of the image you brush over. Adjust the Flow percentage in the Options bar to weaken or strengthen the sponge effect.

USING THE PAINTING TOOLS

The Painting tools in the toolbox are used to paint pixels in the canvas. You can paint in an empty canvas and onto existing image layers. Using the Options bar, choose a brush size and adjust the hardness of the brush edge.

- **Brush (B):** Paint into your picture using this tool (see Figure 3.6). Adjust the Flow and Opacity settings in the Options bar to weaken or strengthen the effect of the brush. Select different brush styles from the Brushes palette. Hold down the Shift key and click in parts of your image to create straight, connected strokes.

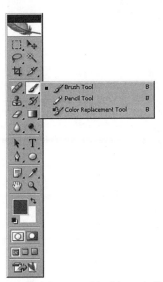

Figure 3.6
The Brush, Pencil, and Color Replacement tools.

- **Pencil (B):** Draw pencil strokes in your image with this tool. Similar to the Brush tool, the Pencil tool maintains a hard edge and has no flow adjustments. Hold down the Shift key and click in parts of your image to create straight, connected strokes.

- **Color Replacement (B):** Select a foreground color and replace colors by painting in the canvas with this new-to-CS2 tool. Colors similar to where the crosshairs are positioned are replaced with the foreground color. Adjust the Tolerance levels and Limits in the Options bar.

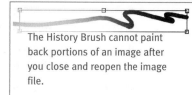

The History Brush cannot paint back portions of an image after you close and reopen the image file.

- **History Brush (Y):** This tool paints back the portions of your image to the selected history state in the history palette (see Figure 3.7).

Figure 3.7
The History Brush tools.

- **Art History Brush (Y):** Use this tool to paint your image back to any selected history state using one of ten paint styles that you can select from the Options bar. Adjust the brush size and shape, tolerance, and mode for different artistic effects.

- **Gradient (G):** Select this tool (shown in Figure 3.8) and click and drag in your image to create a gradient ramp across the canvas or selection area. In the Options bar, select from five gradient types and choose from several premade gradient libraries, or create your own custom gradient color ramp.

- **Paint Bucket (G):** Use this tool to click and fill areas of your image with the foreground color. Adjust the Tolerance level in the Options bar to fill more or fewer adjacent pixels of similar color with the Paint Bucket tool. In the Options bar, if the Contiguous check box is disabled, even non-adjacent pixels of similar color are filled.

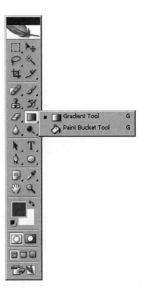

Figure 3.8
The Gradient and Paint Bucket tools.

USING THE DRAWING AND TYPE TOOLS

The Drawing and Type tools create and alter vector objects. Drawing tools work on vector paths, which are vector-based outlines you can turn into selections. Using the Options bar, choose whether to draw paths or shape layers. Type is created in type layers that can be transformed and warped and even set along paths.

- **Path Selection (A):** Use this tool to move entire paths around the canvas as a single object. The path or shape layer retains its shape.

- **Direct Selection (A):** Use this tool to select and move individual points and Bézier handles of a path or shape layer.

- **Pen (P):** Create paths with the Pen tool (shown in Figure 3.9). Single-click to create individual points to form the path. Click, hold, and drag to create a Bézier curve when drawing a path.

- **Freeform Pen (P):** With this tool, click, hold, and draw a path. Points of the path are created automatically.

- **Add Anchor Point (P):** Use this tool to click part of a path to add a point to the path. Adding an anchor point to your path or shape layer allows for more detail in the path or shape.

- **Delete Anchor Point (P):** Use this tool to click a point of a path to remove that point from the path.

- **Convert Anchor Point (P):** Single-click a point of a path to convert it to a corner point. Or click and drag to convert it to a curve point. Or Option-click (Mac users) or Alt-click (Windows users) and drag to convert it to a combination point.

Figure 3.9
The Path tools.

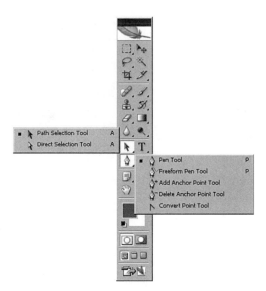

■ **Horizontal Type (T):** The Horizontal Type tool (shown in Figure 3.10) is the default Type tool. Click and drag to make a text box. Type your text with the keyboard to create text in the foreground color. Use the Options bar to set the font, size, and other text properties. Open the Character and or Paragraph palettes for more typography options.

Figure 3.10
The Type tools.

■ **Vertical Type (T):** This tool is similar to the Horizontal Type tool except that the type stacks vertically, and the text direction goes from right to left for Asian languages.

- **Horizontal Type Mask (T):** This tool is similar to the Horizontal Type tool, but a selection area is created rather than actual type. Although you can paint within the type selection area, adjusting the type options is not allowed after type is created.

- **Vertical Type Mask (T):** This tool is similar to the Vertical Type tool, but a selection area is created rather than actual type. Although you can paint within the type selection area, adjusting the type options is not allowed after type is created.

USING THE SHAPE TOOLS

Shape tools work in three ways (see Figure 3.11): In the Options bar you can choose to create a shape layer, a path, or a Fill Pixels shape.

A *shape layer* is a fill layer linked to a vector mask. This means you can double-click the fill layer in the Layers palette and change the fill color of the shape. A shape layer can also be resized infinitely because of its vector properties.

Selecting Paths in the Options bar before drawing your shape creates a *path* from the shape you draw. This creates a colorless vector shape that can be resized later without losing quality. You have all options available from the Paths palette when creating a Paths shape.

A Fill Pixels shape uses the foreground color and creates a *bitmap shape* on the current layer. This is a raster shape and if used in an image layer, is flattened over the image contents.

Figure 3.11
The Shape tools.

The following is a summary of the Shape tools:

- **Rectangle (U):** Creates a rectangle shape using one of the three options from the Options bar. Hold down the Shift key to constrain it to a square when drawing the shape.

- **Rounded Rectangle (U):** Creates a rectangle with rounded corners. In the Options bar adjust the corner radius options to suit your needs. Hold down the Shift key to constrain the shape to a square.

- **Ellipse (U):** Creates an ellipse or oval shape. Hold down the Shift key when drawing to create a perfect circle.

- **Polygon (U):** Creates a polygon shape. Choose the number of sides in the Options bar to draw the polygon of your choice.

- **Line (U):** Click, hold, and drag to create a straight line. Hold down the Shift key to constrain your line to a perfect horizontal, vertical, or 45-degree angle. Adjust the weight of the line in the Options bar.

- **Custom Shape (U):** Choose the Custom Shape tool; in the Options bar, click the Shape pop-up menu and choose from one of the shape icons. Click the fly-out menu to load a new shape library into the options. To create your own custom shape, draw a vector path in your image. Select the path from the Paths palette, and then choose Edit, Define Custom Shape. Name your shape; it will appear in the Shapes library for later use.

USING THE ANNOTATION, MEASURING, AND NAVIGATION TOOLS

The following list details the Annotation, Measuring, and Navigation tools:

- **Notes (N):** Click and drag with this tool to create a virtual sticky note for the image (see Figure 3.12). When you're finished typing the text of the annotation, click the close button on the note. Drag the note around by clicking and dragging the note's icon. Open the note by double-clicking it. Change the note's color in the Options bar. Notes are nonprinting elements.

Figure 3.12
The Notes and Audio Annotation tools.

- **Audio Annotation (N):** Select this tool and click in the canvas to create an audio recording. Speak into the computer's microphone to record your comments about the design and when finished, click Stop to finish recording. Drag the speaker icon to position your annotation anywhere in the canvas.

- **Eyedropper (I):** Use the Eyedropper tool (see Figure 3.13) to click and add a color from an image into the foreground color swatch in the toolbox. Open the Color and Info palettes to see the CMYK or RGB color values live as you click and drag across the canvas.

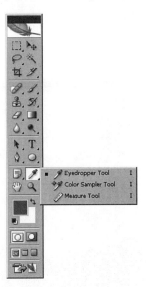

Figure 3.13
The Eyedropper, Color Sampler, and Measure tools.

- **Color Sampler (I):** Click in the image with the Color Sampler tool and get up to four separate color values. A crosshairs icon is placed on the image wherever the Color Sampler is used. Click and drag the crosshairs icon to reposition them elsewhere in the canvas. Open the Info palette to see the four sampled color values.

- **Measure (H):** Click, hold, and drag this tool across the canvas to create a measurement line. Hold down the Shift key to draw a straight horizontal, vertical, or 45-degree–angle line. Open the Info palette for line distances.

- **Hand (H):** Use the Hand tool to move your view of the canvas when you have zoomed in on the canvas. This is helpful when you are working on tiny areas across most of your entire image. To access the Hand tool quickly, press and hold the space bar; the Hand tool remains accessible until you let go of the space bar.

- **Zoom (Z):** Use the Zoom tool to zoom in and out of the canvas. Hold down the Alt key (in Windows) or the Option key (on the Mac) to zoom out. For zooming using only the keyboard, press Ctrl++ to zoom in in Windows (⌘-+ on the Mac) or Ctrl+- to zoom out in Windows (⌘— on the Mac). Use the Navigator palette for more controls for zooming your image.

SELECTING FOREGROUND AND BACKGROUND COLORS

Click the foreground and background color swatches in the toolbox to choose a color for working in your images (see Figure 3.14). Use the foreground color when you're painting with Brush tools or creating type on your page. Use the background color when you're deleting or erasing portions of the Background layer. The background color will be revealed underneath the portions you erase. Swap the foreground with the background color by clicking the Switch arrow just above and to the right of the color watches, or by pressing X on the keyboard. To set your colors to default black and white, click the Default Foreground and Background colors button just below and to the left of the color swatches or press the D key on the keyboard.

Figure 3.14
Click the foreground or background color swatch to display the Color Picker, from which you select colors. Click in the color ramp and your color appears in either color swatch on the toolbox.

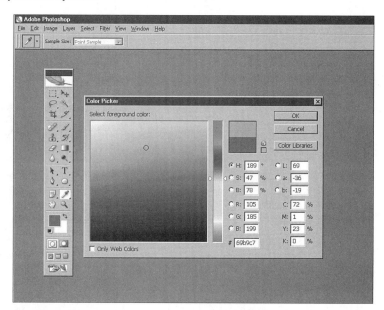

CHANGING VIEW MODES

Change the way Photoshop views the canvas area by selecting one of the three view modes (press the keyboard shortcut F):

- The default view mode is **Standard Screen Mode**. Photoshop appears in a window, and any open images appear in windows, too. This is the most common mode in which people use the program.

- **Full Screen Mode with Menu Bar** maximizes Photoshop, and also maximizes the image you have opened in your monitor. The Menu Bar is still available at the top of your screen, but the Photoshop title bar is hidden.

- **Full Screen Mode** also maximizes Photoshop and the active canvas. The only items visible are the palettes and the Options bar. This is a useful mode when you want to display your work to someone without any clutter. Press the Tab key on the keyboard and hide all palettes and the Options bar to get them out of the way of your masterpiece.

Click the Edit in ImageReady button at the bottom of the toolbox (see Figure 3.15) to close the file in Photoshop and reopen it in ImageReady. Closing and reopening the file in this way prevents loss of changes and creates two open versions of the same file.

Figure 3.15
The Edit in ImageReady button.

3

UNDERSTANDING PHOTOSHOP MENUS AND PALETTES

IN THIS CHAPTER

Like any other program, Photoshop CS2 has many of its functions located under various menus. Here we reference the submenu options so you get familiar with what can be done in this program. Not all menu options will be covered in detail here, however, as you will encounter more of the menu functions in depth in other chapters.

THE FILE MENU

Under the File menu are the majority of options for saving, exporting, and printing:

- **Open:** Open files from your local hard drive or server directory. You can choose in the Open dialog if you want to use Adobe's or your operating system's dialog. The Adobe dialog provides a means to save to a Version Cue project. Other than this advantage, there are no major differences between the OS and Adobe dialogs.

- **Browse:** Open Bridge so you can browse for files. If Bridge is already open, it comes to the front. Double-click on an image file in Bridge to open it in Photoshop.

- **Open Recent:** Show a list of most recent files accessed by Photoshop CS2. If the file still exists in the same place on the hard drive, you can open it via this list (see Figure 4.1).

Figure 4.1
The Open Recent submenu.
Change the number of recent files that will appear in this list in your Photoshop Preferences window under File Handling.

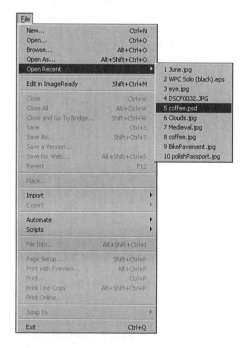

- **Close and Go To Bridge:** Closes the file you are working in, in case you opened the wrong file. Bridge opens and you can choose a new file.

- **Save** or **Save As:** If this is the first time you are saving, you are prompted to name your file, as in any other program. Afterward, use File, Save to overwrite your existing file.

- **Save a Version:** This option highlights only if you have chose File, Save As and actually saved to a Version Cue project. Otherwise this option stays grayed out. See Chapter 1, "Creative Suite 2 Basics," for information on setting up Version Cue projects.

- **Save for Web:** Though you can save files in web graphic formats through File, Save As, it is always best to use File, Save for Web. This dialog enables you to shrink your image files to more acceptable sizes for the web. You can also view your files in different format and quality previews (see Figure 4.2).

Figure 4.2
The Save for Web dialog provides many controls to bring your file size down for appropriate web delivery. Experiment with your own settings or try the various presets for JPEG, PNG, and GIF.

4

- **Revert:** Revert to the last saved state of the image. If you haven't saved it yet, it reverts to the image as it was when you first opened it.

- **Place:** Place an image or PDF file in your existing canvas. When the image comes into the canvas, you can adjust its size before accepting the placement.

- **Export, Paths to Illustrator:** If you have a vector image created with Photoshop paths, saving it to Illustrator gives you more control over the objects' paths. Be aware that any paths exported to Illustrator are empty paths and have no fill or stroke applied to them. Selections you make in Photoshop can be converted to paths. These paths are quite useful if you are tracing portions of a raster image into vector art.

- **Automate, Batch:** Choose a folder and apply an action to all the images within that folder (see Figure 4.3).

- **Automate, PDF Presentation:** Choose multiple image files to create a PDF file for a presentation. Each image file will be a page of the PDF file and Acrobat will play the PDF in a full screen slideshow mode.

Figure 4.3
Batch convert several images at once by using the Actions you specify.

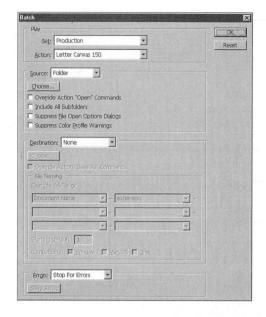

- **Automate, Create Droplet:** Save an action to run from your desktop. *Droplets* are shortcuts/aliases which you can drop files onto from your desktop or a folder (see Figure 4.4). When you drag and drop files onto a droplet, Photoshop launches and runs the corresponding action on those files. You can even drop entire folders onto the droplet and all images inside are run through the action.

Figure 4.4
A droplet icon. When you create droplets, the icon appears in your folder or desktop. Drag images onto the icon to run associated actions.

- **Automate, Contact Sheet:** Create a contact sheet of thumbnails from a selected directory of images. A separate Photoshop document is made from which you can print.

- **Automate, Crop and Straighten Photos:** Automatically straighten and crop multiple images that are scanned into one document into separate images. This makes working with scans much easier. Photoshop detects image edges and separates them from the solid color scanning background.

- **Automate, Web Photo Gallery:** Create a photo gallery from a directory of images instantly without all the busy work of resizing and making thumbnails. Photoshop creates all the necessary images and HTML pages.

- **Automate, Photomerge:** Create one panorama from several photos by using Photomerge. Browse to a directory of images but include the images in that connect, and Photomerge attempts to create a seamless overlap for you.

- **Automate, Merge to HDR:** Take several exposures of one image to create one high dynamic range image. Having more luminosity data from several shots can blend together to make a richer image.

- **Scripts:** Use existing scripts to automate certain functions of Photoshop. Choose from existing scripts or create your own if you are so inclined. Check Adobe Studio for scripts made by people around the world to enhance Photoshop's capabilities.

- **File Info:** Get file properties, including all metadata from a window inside Photoshop (see Figure 4.5).

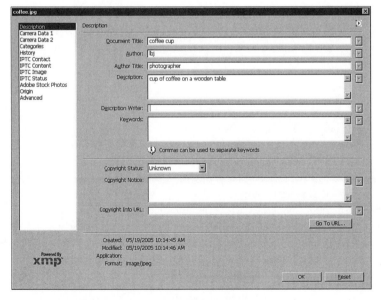

Figure 4.5
Edit your images metadata through the File Info dialog. This is the same dialog accessed through Adobe Bridge.

- **Print with Preview:** Get a preview of your image before printing (see Figure 4.6). Resize and position the image for the paper so you get the best printout possible. Set color options and rendering for specific printing needs.

Figure 4.6
When you print with preview you have the opportunity to position your image correctly on your page.

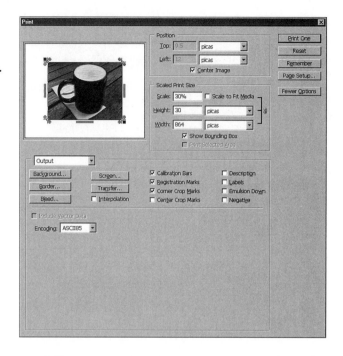

4

■ **Print Online:** Connect with Bridge and then Adobe's online print service and get your prints sent to you by mail. For use with JPEG files only.

THE EDIT MENU

In the Edit menu, you can cut, copy, paste, transform, undo, redo, warp, rotate your images, and much more. When working in type layers, you also have the ability to copy, paste, check spelling, and find and replace.

- ■ **Undo, Redo, Step Forward, Step Backward:** Undo and redo changes, and roll back through the History using these options.

- ■ **Fade:** After applying effects such as filters, changes in contrast, or even painting in the canvas, use this command to adjust the intensity of the color or filter or effect applied; you can also change the blend mode of the effect. The Fade command gives you an Opacity slider, which enables you to alter the previous effect, paint stroke, or fill, making it more or less intense. Try the Fade command with filters such as Gaussian Blur or Extract. Change contrast with Curves and then try the Fade command. The results are often quite useful.

- ■ **Cut** and **Copy:** Cut and copy portions of a layer within a selection.

- ■ **Copy Merged:** If multiple layers are visible in the document window, you can create a selection and copy it as a merged layer. The contents are merged and pasted.

- ■ **Paste:** Paste content that you have cut or copied to the Clipboard. You can paste from other Photoshop layers and documents as well as graphic and text content from other applications.

- **Paste Into:** Paste copied content into a selection area only, and within the active layer.

- **Check Spelling:** The spell check feature in Photoshop looks at all type layers in your document to find misspelled words. Be sure to check spelling before you rasterize any of your type layers.

- **Fill** and **Stroke:** Create a selection with a Marquee, Lasso, or any other method and fill the contents, or apply a stroke to the border of the selection.

- **Transform** and **Free Transform:** Resize and reshape selected areas, including layer content and path vector data. Hold down the Ctrl key (Windows users) or the ⌘ key (Mac users) and alter perspective by dragging the corners of the image selection or layer (see Figure 4.7). Hover outside the bounding box to rotate the contents of the selection or layer.

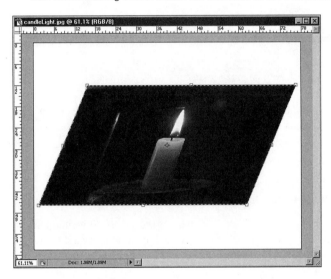

Figure 4.7
The content of a layer skewed by the Transform controls.

- **Transform, Skew, Distort,** and **Perspective:** Alter the shape of the selection area or layer by skewing or shearing the contents, distorting, or simulating perspective. Click and drag one of the eight handles to manipulate the selection or layer.

- **Transform, Warp:** Warp part of your image in the layer to give it a flexible quality. Simulate wrapping your image around a coffee mug or sagging it like a rubber band (see Figure 4.8). The best part is, Warp enables you to put things back in their original shape as long as you haven't closed the document and your warp changes still exist in the History palette.

- **Define Brush Preset** and **Define Pattern:** Make a selection in your image and Define Brush can create a new paintbrush type. Your new custom brush paints in a totally new way on your canvas. Make a brush out of your own eye or face and paint with it. Define a pattern from a selection area. Then use Edit, Fill to fill an area with your pattern for a background effect, or paint the pattern anywhere in the canvas with the Pattern Stamp tool.

Figure 4.8
Warping the content of a layer. Click and drag the netted mesh in the middle or pull the handles on the outside to warp the object.

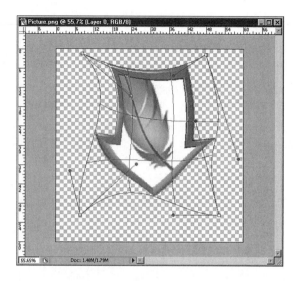

- **Purge:** If you are running out of memory due to intensive image editing, purge your history or Clipboard content to free some up. Remember, after the history is purged, you lose access to any of those history states you had during your image editing session as well as the ability to Undo or step backward through the history you just purged.

- **Color Settings:** Create your own custom color settings, and save them to a color settings file (.csf). Then apply custom settings to the entire Creative Suite using Bridge.

- **Assign Profile** and **Convert to Profile:** Add or change color profiles of the image you are working on. A digital may already have a profile attached from its digital camera or scanner output setting. Change and modify using these settings for consistent color in your projects.

- **Keyboard Shortcuts:** Modify the keyboard shortcuts for the features you use most. Many work with the default keyboard settings, but you have free reign to make complex tasks more streamlined by adjusting these to your specific needs.

- **Menus:** Modify the menus in Photoshop and create a custom menu setting for those tasks you want easy access to. Show or hide the existing menus and highlight menus in up to seven different colors to make them stand out. This option is new to Photoshop CS2.

- **Preferences:** Change preferences for file handling, grid and guidelines, and measurement settings (see Figure 4.9). Set general preferences for Photoshop's behaviors.

> The Preferences command (as well as other Photoshop menu commands) differ only slightly on Macintosh and Windows versions of Photoshop. On a Mac, the Preferences command is found under the Photoshop menu rather than the Edit menu.

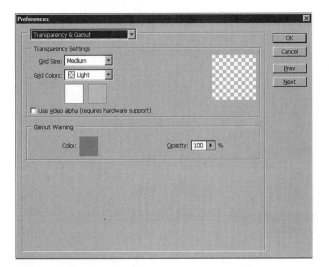

Figure 4.9
Transparency & Gamut preferences are just a few of the many preferences you have control over. The top pop-up menu in Preferences changes the category of preferences.

THE IMAGE MENU

Using the Image menu, you have control over the mode of the document you are working on and adjustments to image information such as contrast, hue, and brightness. You can change the canvas size and rotation so your image is oriented properly. The following are descriptions of most of the Image menu options:

- **Mode:** You must make sure your image mode is set properly for the way you intend to use it. CMYK and Grayscale is used for output on a commercial press. RGB and Grayscale would be used on the web and printing to your home printer. Indexed color is used by web graphics embedding a limited color palette to save space. Bitmap graphics are black or white only and used in certain line art graphics and to conserve space. Lab color provides a wider gamut of colors to work with and is a printable format. Multichannel mode is used for specialized printing for image formats such as Scitex CT.

- **Adjustments:** You can make infinite adjustment to images, affecting the color or lighting values.

- **Adjustments, Levels, Auto Levels:** Level adjustment works with shadows, highlights, and overall brightness of midtones. Using the Levels controls you can identify and set the darkest and lightest portions of an image in its printout. Auto Levels attempts to find a mix between contrast and detail.

- **Adjustments, Curves, Color Balance, and Brightness/Contrast:** Curves are the most powerful image-correction tools. An interface enables you to adjust the qualities of an image by working with the channels of color separately or all at once. Move the curve and the image changes (see Figure 4.10).

The Color Balance command gives similar adjustments but with a more rudimentary control. Move the sliders and adjust the colors by adding or taking away some of the hue. The Brightness/Contrast command provides a similar slider adjustment for those values.

Figure 4.10
Adjust the curvature in the Curves dialog and watch your image change. Move the curve for all channels or each individual channel to affect the image.

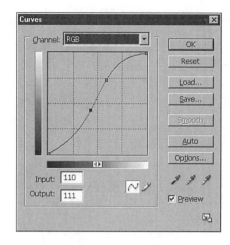

- **Adjustments, Hue/Saturation:** *Hue* is color, *saturation* is the amount of color. Adjust these values to add a color cast to an image layer or selection. Using the sliders, you can also remove color casts or change the brightness, intensity, and hue of an image.

- **Adjustments, Desaturate:** Take all the color from your image without having to convert it to grayscale mode. If you have a selection made in your image, only the area within the selection will be desaturated.

- **Adjustments, Shadow/Highlight:** Lighten the subject properly even in backlit photographs using this newer adjustment feature. Photoshop can see the subject against the background and adjusts them separately for you.

- **Adjustments, Invert:** Convert colors to their opposites along the color wheel. Black becomes white, greens become orange and so forth.

- **Adjustments, Variations:** See your image in several different variations on the screen at once. Preview your image with more cyan or magenta, darker or lighter, and much more.

- **Duplicate:** Create a copy of your image in a new canvas. With two versions of the image, you can apply different filters effects (or anything else) independently and view the results. Later, save the duplicate file as a separate document.

- **Image Size:** Resize your image or change the resolution. Resize in pixels, inches, percent, and more. When preparing for print, be aware that if you leave the Resample Image check box enabled, your pixels are interpolated, adding pixels but not necessarily enhancing quality. Constrain proportions ensures your picture won't become stretched out unevenly.

- **Canvas Size:** Change the size of the canvas around your image. Make more room to expand the size of your design, or crop out more of the canvas to suit your need.

- **Crop:** After making a selection, the Crop command removes the area outside your selection marquee. Works almost the same as the Crop tool in the toolbox.

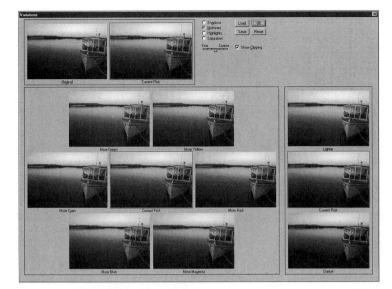

Figure 4.11
Looking at the variations of your image, you see where you might want to adjust color. This dialog is particularly good for looking at skin color and overall lighting in the scene to make sure the color of the subject and background looks the way it should.

THE LAYER MENU

The Layer menu gives you many options that create or effect the layers in your document: For example, you can apply layer styles to a layer, which can affect the color, shadow, and embossing. You can merge layers together and turn type layers into graphics. The Layer menu contains many commands that can also be accessed from controls on the Layers palette and its palette menu. There are so many layer commands they all could not be covered here. Chapter 6, "Working with Layers in Photoshop," focuses entirely on the subject of layers.

- **New:** Create a new empty layer above the layer you are working.

- **Duplicate:** Create an exact copy of the layer you are currently working in. Choose a name for the duplicate, or Photoshop assigns the duplicated layer the name of the original layer with the word COPY behind it.

- **Layer Style:** A library of layer effects are available under this menu. Selecting one effect from the menu gives you the Layer Style dialog, which gives you access to all styles (see Figure 4.12). Check the boxes to apply styles and make adjustments for all effects.

- **New Adjustment Layer:** Apply certain effects to the layer without changing the layer itself. An adjustment layer changes the layers below it without affecting pixel values. For example, you can create a levels adjustment layer to alter brightness and contrast of the layer below without affecting the actual lower layer's pixel values.

- **Group Layers:** Hold down the Shift key to select multiple layers. Then group them together to keep your Layers palette organized and easier to move around.

Figure 4.12
The layer styles give you options to affect the layer in many ways. This dialog is used most often for adding drop shadows or embossing effects to text and buttons.

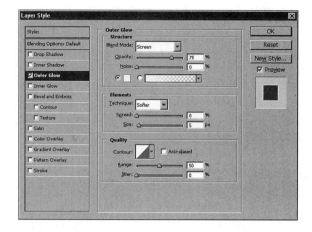

- **Merge Layers, Merge Visible, Flatten Image:** When you are ready to compress your image, use the different flatten options to combine layers. Sometimes you will use this to finalize an effect or make adjusting part of an image a little easier.

THE SELECT MENU

Much of the Select menu enables you to create or modify selections that you work with. For example, when you make a selection, you can shrink or expand it without redrawing the selection. You can also select multiple layers at one time or select only pixels within a specific color range.

- **All:** Create a selection marquee around the entire active layer.

- **Inverse:** Starting with a selection around portions of the image, this command inverts it by selecting everything else instead.

- **All Layers:** Select all layers in the Layers palette when you need to move or change everything at once.

- **Similar Layers:** Photoshop sees similar content in multiple layers and tries to select just those that are similar in case you need to apply a change to all of them or delete them collectively. For example, if you have a document with four shape layers and two raster image layers, selecting one shape layer and choosing Select, Similar Layers, Photoshop selects all the shape layers for you and leaves the raster layers unselected.

- **Color Range:** Sample a color in your document and then you can use this function to select that color throughout that layer so you can modify it or cut out portions with that color (see Figure 4.13). This works well with subjects in front of blue screens for cutting them out.

- **Feather:** After you make a selection, you can change the sharpness of the edge where the selection border is. Choose a number of pixels to create a feather or fuzzy edge; if you copy or cut out the content within the selection, the feathered edge is revealed.

Figure 4.13
Use the Color Range command to get more control over your selection than the Magic Wand tool. Adjust the Fuzziness slider and move the eyedropper around the preview area.

- **Modify, Smooth, Expand, Contract:** After you make a selection, sometimes you need to shrink it, expand it, or smooth it out to get the right portions of the image selected. Use Smooth, Expand, or Contract to make slight modifications to your selections.

- **Load/SaveSelection:** Save your temporary selection for use later within the same document. The saved selection is saved as an Alpha channel in the Channels palette. You can load it as a selection.

THE FILTER MENU

Filters are one of the most unique parts—and provide some of the most fun—of Photoshop. Filters can change an image into something completely different by running through a series of mathematical processes that may make the image look liquid, plastic, hand drawn, and much more. When you apply a filter, it affects the layer you have selected or only the area within a selection you have made. More information about filters can be found in Chapter 9, "Creative Imaging in Photoshop."

- **Last Filter:** This command works only if you used a filter in your current editing session. You can reapply the most recent filter used with the exact same options to any different layers and even in another document you may have open. In fact, the word *Last* is replaced with the name of the filter you used.

- **Extract:** Using the Extract window, you can draw a highlight around the edge of a subject and then fill the outline with the fill tool, and Photoshop will extract the subject from everything else (see Figure 4.14). It's one of the best ways to get a complex cutout created. If you need to clean up the extraction, you can use the History Brush to restore deleted portions of the image.

- **Liquify:** Liquify pixels for interesting effects. Use the Bloat and Pucker tools inside Liquify to expand and shrink your image in interesting and often frightening ways (see Figure 4.15).

- **Vanishing Point:** Identify the perspective in your image to help you clone difficult portions of the image. Works well when cloning straight lines that vanish in the distance, such as railroad tracks. This command is new in CS2.

Figure 4.14
The Extract window provides one way to remove the subject from its background. After you outline and fill your subject area, everything else is removed from the layer.

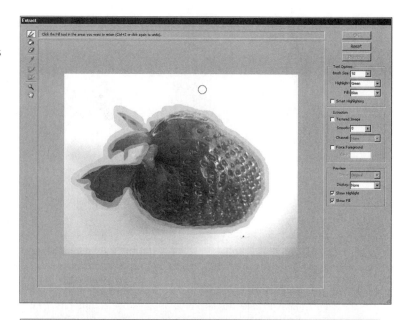

Figure 4.15
The controls in the Liquify window are immense. Not only can you severely alter an image, but also you can save your liquefied state to a mesh and change other images with the same mesh.

- **Artistic:** Make your image layer appear to have been created with some kind of artistic media, such as pastels, brushes, or water color.

- **Blur:** Blur images in many ways. The different blur filters in this category take out the contrast and smooth the gradation between pixels to create the blur illusion.

- **Render:** Create content in empty layers. You can create pixels in the form of clouds or fibers, which are rendered inside your layer or selection. The Lighting Effects filters enable you to simulate different types of lights beaming on your image and can completely change the mood of your image.

- **Texture:** Give your image a bumpy appearance as if it were painted on burlap or mosaic tiles. You can adjust the size of these textures to make them more or less prevalent.

There are way too many other filters and categories to mention here, so refer to Chapter 9 and experiment with the different filters and adjustments to them.

THE VIEW MENU

The View menu enables you to look at your document in different ways. You can see how your image will appear on a different monitor or a simulated press. You can view the colors that are out of range of your color space. You can zoom in and out or view the printed size onscreen.

- **Proof Setup:** Preview your image in different modes. Setup simulates a Mac or Windows monitor display or a printing press's color space.

- **Proof Colors:** Simulate your document colors in the window depending on the options.

- **Actual Pixels:** Zoom your image to 100% to see the actual pixel image.

- **Print Size:** Zoom your image to the size onscreen at which it prints, using the resolution settings for the image.

- **Show, Layer Edges, Grid,** and **Guides:** Layer edges, the document grid, and guides all help with visual alignment. Show or hide these nonprinting elements to help you get precise positioning. The grid looks like graphing paper lines overlaid on the image. Guides are the custom vertical and horizontal lines you created by dragging from the rulers into the image. If guides are hidden, you see the guide as it's positioned, but it becomes invisible when you let go of the mouse button.

- **Rulers:** When you show rulers they appear at the left and top of your document. Click, hold, and drag from the rulers into the document to create a guide. If you want to remove a guide, make sure it is unlocked and drag it back into the ruler area. Set the ruler measurements to inches, points, picas, and so forth in Photoshop's preferences.

- **Snap** and **Snap To:** When Snap is selected, the elements you move across the canvas have a magnetic snapping effect when brought into the same zone as the objects in which snap is activated. Under Snap To, you can give the grid, guides, layers, slices, and document bounds. Snap to Layers causes objects on separate layers to have a magnetic property to them, which is helpful for alignment purposes.

- **Lock Guides** and **Clear Guides:** When guides are locked, you are not allowed to move them after they have been initially dragged onto the screen. To move the guides again, select this option again. Clear Guides take out any guides you created. After guides are cleared they are deleted completely and have to be re-created if desired.

4

■ **Lock Slices** and **Clear Slices:** Slices that you draw in Photoshop can be locked. This prevents accidental movement or sizing. If you have this option checked in the beginning, you are unable to create any new slices.

THE WINDOW MENU

You find all your palettes in the Window menu. If a palette is not open in Photoshop, open the Window menu to select the palette. You can also load and save workspace arrangements.

All the palettes and even the Options bar are accessed from the Window menu. This is true for every Adobe program. If there is a palette to be found, it is accessed from the Window menu. When a palette is already visible onscreen, a check box appears next to the palette's name in the Window menu.

At the bottom of the Window menu is the list of all open documents. When you select an open document, it comes to the front for you to edit:

■ **Arrange, Tile Horizontally** and **Tile Vertically:** You can arrange all open images on the screen at once. Select Tile Horizontally or Tile Vertically and the images will be arranged onscreen fitting them as large as possible for you to view at once.

■ **Arrange, Match Zoom/Location:** With multiple images open at the same time, you can select one image window (suppose that it displays in the window at 315% of its actual size and reveals only the lower-left corner); the Match Zoom and Match Location commands find the other images and display them at 315%, revealing only the lower-left corners of those images as well.

■ **Workspace, Save, Delete,** and **Default Workspace:** If you find you have an arrangement of open palettes that suits your workflow, you can save this workspace to make it accessible at a later time. You can save several workspaces for different types of tasks you might perform. Select Window, Workspace, Save and name your workspace. After your workspace is saved you find it under Window, Workspace, *Your workspace name*. If you do not want to keep a workspace any longer, choose Window, Workspace, Delete, and the workspace is deleted. If you don't have a saved workspace, but you want to clean up the palettes in Photoshop quickly, choose Workspace, Default Workspace. The default workspace puts the toolbox on the left side and commonly used palettes neatly arranged on the right side.

■ **Workspace, Keyboard Shortcuts & Menus:** Customize your keyboard shortcuts to frequently used commands and create your own custom menu arrangements for work in Photoshop. Assign which menus are shown or hidden and which are colored. Keyboard shortcuts make it easier to handle tedious tasks. Create your own keyboard shortcuts for application menus, palette menus, and tools. Save your keyboard shortcut settings with a custom name.

■ **Workspace, Menus (various):** From the Workspace submenu you can choose from several menu arrangements. These menu arrangements fit with different types of workflows. Some of the pre-configured menus are Automation, Basic, Image Analysis, and Web Design. When choosing one of these menu options, your Photoshop menus display certain workflow-related menus in identifiable colors.

THE HELP MENU

Photoshop is no slouch when it comes to having plenty of available resources. The Help menu contains links to the Adobe Help Center, tutorials, plug-in information, and much more. There are also options for connecting with Adobe online for registration and updates.

- **Photoshop Help:** Photoshop Help launches the Creative Suite 2 Help Center. Find your answers quickly using the keyword search. Or access other Adobe CS2 applications from the pop-up menu in the Help Center.

- **Export Transparent Image:** Use this wizard after you make a selection in an image to create a background transparency.

- **Resize Image:** The Resize Image wizard helps you quickly change the size and resolution for your chosen print or online output.

- **Registration:** If you haven't registered your Creative Suite online, do it as soon as possible. This is helpful if you misplace your serial number or want to access some support options. Registration comes with a free gift from Adobe.

- **Activate, Transfer Activation:** If you are still using a 30-day trial version of CS2 and you have a valid serial number, you can activate it through this menu. When the program is already activated, this option is grayed out. If you change computers or need to alternate computers while you use CS2, use the Transfer Activation command so that your other computer can be activated to use the software.

- **Updates:** Check for software updates and set your update preferences for manual and automatic downloading and update install.

- **Photoshop Online:** Go to the main Photoshop page on the Adobe.com website. From there, you can find links to new stuff, movies, stories, and links to more and more links. Don't get lost out there, it's a big website.

- **How To's:** The How To options are shortcuts to popular Photoshop Help topics from within the Adobe Help Center. It's a great way to learn some of the complicated tasks that Photoshop CS2 can handle. You can even create your own instructional pages and add them to the list.

KEYBOARD SHORTCUTS

Photoshop is already set up with keyboard shortcuts to access menus, tools, and palette options. Not all of the options in Photoshop are attached to keyboard shortcuts and you can create your own shortcuts for options you use most. At first, find what existing keyboard shortcuts are set up. The easiest way is to browse the menus (see Figure 4.16).

The File menu is a good example of keyboard-accessible menus. Directly to the right of some of the menu options are the assigned keyboard shortcuts. With the menus closed and an image opened in Photoshop, press that key combination and the menu command is activated. This helps you control Photoshop faster with the keyboard and may reduce strain from constantly using the mouse. Spend some time remembering and practicing the keyboard shortcuts.

Figure 4.16
In all menus there are at least a few of the menu options with associated keyboard shortcuts. All of these can be customized to make your work easier.

Keyboard Shortcuts for the Toolbox

When you hover for a moment over a tool in the toolbox, a ToolTip appears identifying the name for that tool (see Figure 4.17). Next to the name you see a letter, which is the keyboard shortcut to activate that tool. The tools are explained and the default keyboard shortcuts are identified in Chapter 3, "Using the Photoshop Toolbox." The shortcuts make accessing tools much more convenient and keep you from pulling away from your design to find the tool you need.

Figure 4.17
Hover over each of the tools in the toolbox and see what keyboard shortcut might be associated. Some tools nested together have the same shortcuts, and can be accessed clicking Shift+ the shortcut key.

You might want to change some or all of the keyboard shortcuts to fit your own style of work. Choose Window, Workspace, Keyboard Shortcuts & Menus to open the dialog where you can start customizing (see Figure 4.18). Be sure and click the Keyboard Shortcuts tab so you can gain access to these options.

Click the pop-up menu next to Shortcuts For and change it to Application Menus. Each of the top-level menus are shown in gray with a pop-up arrow. Click the arrow to expand that menu. When you find an option you want to change, click on it. The keyboard shortcut field highlights for you to change. Click your desired combination to replace. If you have made a mistake, click the Undo button. Or at any time, you can click the Cancel button in the main dialog to exit without saving changes. One of the nicest features is the Summarize button.

Click Summarize and you are prompted to save an HTML file of your existing or modified keyboard shortcuts. This gives you a reference you can print. If you have made changes you want to save, click the Save button at the top of the dialog box (the button with an image of a floppy disk). Your keyboard shortcuts are saved as a .kys file and are accessible under the Set pop-up menu in this dialog.

Don't be discouraged about changing shortcuts, however. If you repeat certain functions the same way in your workflow, you benefit by changing that menu shortcut to something more easily reached by your fingers.

Though you have ultimate flexibility with altering keyboard shortcuts, there are reasons why you might want to leave them as they are. If you frequently read Photoshop tutorials in various resources, you might have trouble following along if keyboard shortcuts are used because yours are different from the default. If you work in an environment with shared computers, fortunately you can create and save different keyboard shortcuts for each person, or change back to the default shortcuts by choosing Window, Workspace, Reset Keyboard Shortcuts.

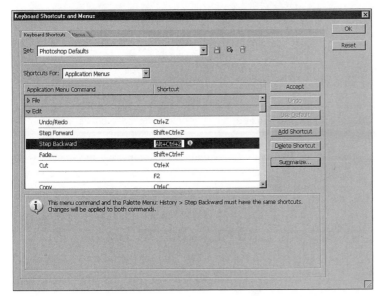

Figure 4.18
Editing keyboard shortcuts.

4

FILE MANAGEMENT

Photoshop offers a way to save your images to your Version Cue project. It's important to understand how to save your file versions properly and access them later. To allow Photoshop to access Version Cue, you must save to a Version Cue project. With a Photoshop document open, choose File, Save As. In the Save dialog box, change from the OS dialog to the Adobe dialog: Click the Use Adobe Dialog button at the bottom-left in this window (see Figure 4.19). The Adobe dialog appears and remains until you change it back. Both dialogs enable you to save normally. In the Adobe dialog, however, a panel appears showing your main document directories as well as Version Cue. Click the Version Cue button, and any local or network-accessible projects appear in the other pane. Double-click your desired project to open it or click the Project Tools button to create a new project.

Figure 4.19
You must be using the Adobe dialog to save your file to a Version Cue project.

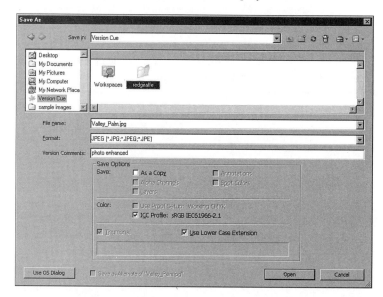

When you enter the project, save your image with a name as you normally would. When your image is saved, you can continue to work and save versions periodically when you make changes to your document.

To save a version, choose File, Save Version (this option is available only for images you saved to Version Cue projects already). You are prompted to add a version comment to this version (see Figure 4.20). You can comment on anything, but it might be good to comment on what changes you made. Your comments show up when you access the versions from Adobe Bridge. When you finish entering comments, click Save.

From Photoshop, you do not see multiple versions of a file you are saving. The versioned file appears as any other individual file. To open a version of a file, choose File, Open and navigate through Version Cue to your versioned file (see Figure 4.21). Right-click (in Windows) or Control-click (on the Mac) the file and choose Versions from the context menu. From the Versions dialog, you can choose to View Version to open a version or choose to promote a previous version to the current version if you like an older one better.

Figure 4.20
Saving a version of a file gives you a dialog to make a comment about the version.

Figure 4.21
Different versions of the file can be accessed from the Adobe dialog or accessed from Bridge. Remember, the more versions you save, the larger the file size becomes.

4

PHOTOSHOP PALETTES

Palettes provide ways to manipulate tools and objects in your documents. Here we take a look at the functions of various palettes in Photoshop CS2. You may not work with all the palettes when you first start using Photoshop, but given time you are exposed to everything.

The Actions Palette

In the Actions palette, you can record and play back actions, which, like macros, perform automated tasks in the program (see Figure 4.22). Actions are commands completed in Photoshop that have been recorded to be played back repeatedly on many images to save you time and energy. The default actions that are loaded in Photoshop CS2 modify only Photoshop menus; however, you can click the palette menu to choose Sample Actions. Experiment with these sample actions in your images and layers. There are libraries of actions you can load into the palette. Some of the different types of actions that ship with Photoshop are Image Effects, Text Effects, Production Actions, and Texture Actions. For more information on using actions, refer to Chapter 10, "Creating a Power Workflow in Photoshop."

Figure 4.22
The Actions palette.

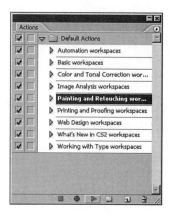

The Animation Palette

Photoshop CS2 includes an Animation palette, formerly available only in ImageReady (see Figure 4.23). Using layers of your document, you can take frame snapshots and simulate movement across the frames. Animate a text layer sliding across the image using the Tweens Animation button, for example. Send your document over to ImageReady where you can export your animation into a Flash movie (.swf).

Figure 4.23
The Animation palette.

THE BRUSHES PALETTE

Modify brush settings to paint any way you want on the canvas (see Figure 4.24). Change your smooth paintbrush into a spatter or particle effect by manipulating the brush's shape, scattering, and using color dynamics. Load different brush libraries or create your own brushes from images and see a preview of them in the palette.

The Channels Palette

The Channels palette enables you to view the color information that makes up your image (see Figure 4.25). An image can have between 1 and 56 channels. Add a spot channel to your image or create an alpha channel for a transparency effect. Refer to Chapter 5, "Working with Images and Color in Photoshop," for information about channels.

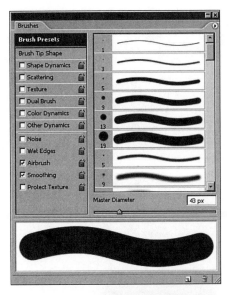

Figure 4.24
The Brushes palette.

Figure 4.25
The Channels palette.

4

The Character Palette

Control typography with the Character palette (see Figure 4.26). Change fonts, spacing, leading, kerning between letters, and size. Use the palette menu for more options including special options for OpenType fonts.

The Color Palette

Select your colors with the Color palette (see Figure 4.27). Click in the color band to choose a color, and adjust the sliders to choose a color more precisely.

The Histogram Palette

The histogram graphically displays the distribution of pixels in the image according to their tonality or brightness (see Figure 4.28). Use the histogram to evaluate your image. See how your image editing impacts the tonal distribution of the image. Show the palette in a compact or expanded view with or without statistics.

OpenType fonts were developed jointly by Adobe and Microsoft. The advantages of these fonts are that they are cross platform between Mac and Windows and they support the Unicode specifications (which means they can contain all sorts of international characters). Finally, each font can contain over 60,000 characters, known as *glyphs*, including multiple languages and ligatures. For more information about OpenType fonts go to www.adobe.com/type/opentype.

Figure 4.26
The Character palette.

Figure 4.27
The Color palette.

Figure 4.28
The Histogram palette.

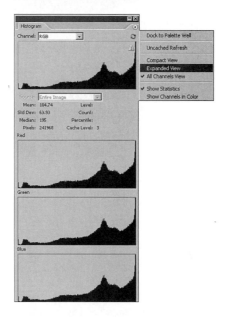

The History Palette

The History palette gives you a listing of your last steps performed in the program (see Figure 4.29). You can click in one of the previous steps to backtrack quickly. Be aware that if you go back in history and perform a new step, you can lose the steps that were ahead of it because you have altered the course of history. (See the movie "Back to the Future" for more information on altering the course of history.) To avoid this problem, choose History Options from the palette menu and enable the Allow Non-Linear History check box.

Figure 4.29
The History palette.

The Info Palette

The Info palette is a monitor of your image's color percentages, width and height measurements, and other sample information (see Figure 4.30). By viewing your Info palette, you can see what color pixel you are hovering over and how large a marquee you are drawing at that very moment.

Figure 4.30
The Info palette.

The Layer Comps Palette

The Layer Comps palette enables you to take layer snapshots of your compositions so you can quickly look at several image representations of layer stacking order and visibility (see Figure 4.31). This is useful for quickly toggling through different layer arrangements.

Figure 4.31
The Layer Comps palette.

The Layers Palette

Layers are one of Photoshop's most important features. Think of each layer as its own invisible glass canvas. Paint on one layer without affecting the others. Photoshop CS2 has updated layer features, like grouping, and improved how you select multiple layers at once. Adjust the opacity of the layer or the blend modes, create layer masks, layer styles, and adjust layers in one palette (see Figure 4.32).

Figure 4.32
The Layers palette.

The Navigator Palette

The Navigator palette gives you a smaller view of your entire image (see Figure 4.33). The red rectangle is called the *proxy view area*. Move the rectangle to adjust your view of an image you are zoomed into. Use the slider to control the zoom view quickly, and use the buttons to jump to specific zoom percentages.

Figure 4.33
The Navigator palette.

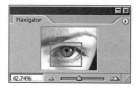

The Options Bar

The Options bar, as explained in Chapter 2, "Working with Photoshop," gives you options for the currently selected tool (see Figure 4.34). Click a tool in the toolbox and various options show and can be changed from the Options bar.

Figure 4.34
The Options bar showing the options for the Crop tool.

The Paragraph Palette

Control typography at the paragraph level with the Paragraph palette (see Figure 4.35). Change your paragraph justification, indent settings, and turn hyphenation on and off.

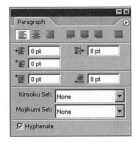

Figure 4.35
The Paragraph palette.

The Paths Palette

The Paths palette contains information on paths and shapes that you have drawn (see Figure 4.36). If you attached text to a path, the text is identified in the Paths palette. Convert your paths to selections, or selections to paths. Apply a fill or stroke color to the paths and create clipping paths to create transparent areas in the image for supported graphic formats.

Figure 4.36
The Paths palette.

4

The Styles Palette

The Styles palette contains premade or custom layer styles that you apply to text and graphic layers (see Figure 4.37). Quickly set a consistent emboss, shadow, and pattern or color overlay to layers for creative type and image effects. Create your own style and save it to the a styles library. Load 13 or more style libraries to make type effects, buttons, and much more.

Figure 4.37
The Styles palette showing the default styles. From the palette menu select Small List to view the list of styles with names and icons.

The Swatches Palette

Store and access colors you use most often in the Swatches palette (see Figure 4.38). Create your own colors and drag them to the swatches or use one of the premade swatch libraries. Access Pantone process and spot colors, and share solid color swatch libraries between applications.

Figure 4.38
View your Swatches palette as a small list by choosing Small List from the palette menu. This shows you the swatch's name and color icon at the same time.

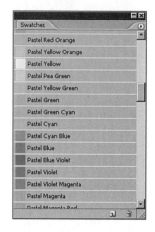

The Tool Presets Palette

When you use a tool for a specific purpose in a specific way, you can save it as a preset. Maybe you set up your Brush tool to paint white snowflakes; save your brush setting as a tool preset and have access to it any time. Save and load your tool presets from the Tool Presets palette menu (see Figure 4.39).

Figure 4.39
Customize tool presets if you are continuously using tools in the same way.

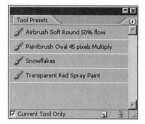

The Tools Palette

As mentioned in Chapter 2, you can open the toolbox with the Window, Tools command (see Figure 4.40).

Figure 4.40
When you see small arrows below the icons in the Toolbox, tools are nested underneath. Click and hold to see what those hidden tools are.

4

WORKING WITH IMAGES AND COLOR IN PHOTOSHOP

Because Photoshop is an image-editing program, you need to know how to get an image to the canvas and work with it. Of course, you can open an existing image or choose File, New to create a new document.

Remember that when you create a new document, you have a choice of the different color modes. If you don't choose the right mode when you create the document, you can change it later by choosing Image, Mode.

If you are already working in an image, you can place or import other image files into it. You choose File, Place to bring an image into an existing canvas. You have the ability to place nearly as many file types as you can open in Photoshop. After you place an image in a document, it becomes part of the new document as a new layer.

What is the advantage of placing an image into another image rather than just copying and pasting the contents? The difference is that when you place an image into another canvas, the placed image appears in a new layer as a Smart Object. This allows it to be placed at the document's resolution but still allows you to resize the contents in the future without any loss to the original resolution. This may not seem like a big deal, but when you work in multilayer documents and things are changing in your design, it's a very nice feature. It's especially beneficial if you place a vector EPS or PDF file. It means you'll always be working in the best quality possible. Earlier versions of Photoshop set placed images to the document's resolution immediately; transforming that layer was limited by that resolution.

One more thing to know about placing images is color mode limitations. If an image's color mode is Indexed Color, Bitmap, or Multichannel, you are unable to place other images, regardless of their mode. You will learn more about color modes in the next section.

All the programs in Adobe CS2 use color. One key to using color *correctly* is understanding how it works and how to control it digitally. Throughout this chapter you'll find references to Photoshop and Illustrator, with occasional mentions of ImageReady, InDesign, and GoLive. As you read, remember that GoLive and ImageReady are web oriented. They work with RGB color and subsets of RGB in Indexed Color mode. InDesign is primarily a print tool, and it works with CMYK and spot colors.

LOOKING AT ARTWORK, IMAGERY, AND COLOR

An image in Photoshop *is* color. Whether the image is in bright, vivid colors, various shades of gray, or even just black and white, it doesn't exist without color. At its heart, Photoshop is about assigning the correct color to each pixel.

Choosing Colors from the Color Picker

The toolbox contains buttons to set foreground and background colors. You can click the Set Foreground Color or Set Background Color button to open the Color Picker. The Color Picker shows you the spectrum of colors to choose from. The first time you use Photoshop CS2, the default state of the Color Picker displays the slider and field using the HSB color model, designated by the radio button. You can move the vertical color slider to choose a hue. Then in the large color field, you can click to change the saturation and brightness level of that hue. When you click a color, the values change in the HSB, RGB, Lab, and CMYK fields, and so does the RGB hexadecimal value (next to the # sign).

You can click the radio button for the components HSB, RGB, and Lab. When you select the radio button for a component, the color slider displays that component, and the color field displays the range for the remaining two components. For example, if you click the Brightness radio button, the color slider displays the range of brightness levels from white to black in the current color, and the color field displays the range of hue and saturation values at the current brightness level. If you want to enter a color value, you can highlight the values in the text boxes and type in the new value.

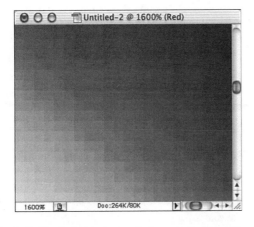

Be aware that the term *bitmap* can have two different meanings. First, it can be used as a synonym for *raster* (as in "That is not vector artwork; it's a bitmap image"). In this usage, *bitmap* refers to an image consisting of pixels arranged in rows and columns. Second, when you're talking about color, *bitmap* refers to black-and-white images. In Bitmap color mode (also called 1-bit color), each pixel is either black or white. There are no shades of gray or other colors. Think of the displays on older mobile phones or handheld devices.

Understanding How Photoshop Records Color

Photoshop works primarily with raster artwork, although it does have some sophisticated vector capabilities. A raster image, also known as a *bitmap image*, consists of a rectangular pattern of pixels, with a single color assigned to each of the tiny squares. The differences in color among the pixels determine the appearance of the image.

In simple terms, raster image file formats record image data pixel-by-pixel, keeping track of each pixel's location in the image and that particular pixel's color values. Theoretically, you could digitally re-create the *Mona Lisa* by assigning specific colors, one at a time, to each pixel. Remember that each pixel is a single color. The color can be changed, but a pixel can have only one color at any time (see Figure 5.1).

Figure 5.1
Even in a white-to-black gradient, each pixel has only one color.

In vector art, the individual objects have strokes applied to paths and fills within the paths. The color of the stroke and the color of the fill (or colors, for gradient and pattern fills) are recorded.

What Is a Color Model?

The actual recording of a pixel color or a vector object's assigned color depends on a couple factors. The file format you select determines, of course, how the actual data is recorded. (Photoshop handles that process transparently as the file is saved.) The document's *color mode* is assigned by the user and depends on the image's final destination and its content. This is the "color space" within which the document's colors are recorded. The most common color modes are RGB (for digital imaging and the Web) and CMYK (for commercial printing). This is in contrast to the term *color model,* which refers to the system within which you define specific colors. For example, in an RGB document, all colors are recorded in the RGB color mode, regardless of whether you defined the colors by using the Grayscale, HSB, Lab, or RGB color model. The color mode (along with the color model) determines what *component colors* are used to create the specific colors in the image.

The RGB color mode, for example, records the entire range of color as proportions of the component colors red, green, and blue. CMYK, on the other hand, records each color as percentages of cyan, magenta, yellow, and black (the CMYK component colors). A grayscale image is composed of grays, measured as percentages of black. Each of the major color modes and color models is discussed individually in this chapter.

UNDERSTANDING THE TWO TYPES OF COLOR

Colors in Photoshop can be considered additive or subtractive. *Additive colors* produce white when all colors are combined (added) at full strength. *Subtractive colors* produce white by removing (subtracting) all component colors. Conversely, a lack of color in an additive model produces black, whereas combining all colors in a subtractive model produces black.

Consider spotlights in a theater. The more spotlights you train on a specific area of the stage, the more brightly lit that area is; this is additive color. You can aim spotlights of many colors at the same spot, but when you've added enough different lights, regardless of their color, the audience sees only white light.

Now consider preparing paint for a blank canvas. Without any paint, the canvas is white. Because paints are subtractive colors, when you start mixing various paints together, they get darker. (The result is more likely to be muddy brown than black, but the concept is the same.)

Working with Additive Colors

Additive color is produced from a light source that's typically filtered to present color. For example, a household light bulb (which emits "white" light) behind a blue lampshade gives you blue. Behind a yellow lampshade, the same bulb gives you yellow. A stage spotlight can be filtered with a gel (a translucent piece of colored gelatin or acetate) to produce colored light. Multiple gels can be combined to create a wide range of colors.

Televisions and computer monitors produce additive color. The light is viewed directly or nearly directly, preferably without interference from other light sources. The light is filtered into red, green, and blue components that, in combination, produce all the colors that can be created with that device. Many large front- and rear-projection TVs actually use three synchronized lights, one of each of these colors, to produce images onscreen. Televisions, computer cathode ray tube (CRT) monitors, liquid crystal display (LCD) screens for computers, and other devices all use red, green, and blue light in combination to produce the colors of the spectrum.

When working in the Adobe CS2, you should remember these key concepts about additive colors (the colors you see on your monitor):

- The component colors (red, green, and blue), combined at full intensity, produce white.

- The complete lack of the component colors produces black.

- The light is seen directly, reaching the eye either from a colored source or from a source through a colored filter.

- In theory, by varying the amount of each component color (red, green, and blue), you can reproduce virtually all colors of the visible spectrum. (In reality, not all colors can be reproduced because of limitations of the devices.)

- Because the component colors are red, green, and blue, additive color is referred to as *RGB* in Photoshop and other graphics programs.

Working with Subtractive Colors

Subtractive colors are, generally speaking, seen with reflected light. A white or colored light source reflects off a colored surface to the eye. The color that's visible to the eye is the part of the spectrum that is *not* absorbed by the colored surface. For example, if you shine a white light on a wall painted yellow, you see yellow because all other colors are absorbed by the paint, and yellow is reflected back to the eye. The wall itself is not a light source; rather, light bounces off the wall to the eye.

As with the wall's yellow paint, subtractive colors are applied to a surface. The visible color of the paint or ink is the part of the spectrum that is reflected rather than absorbed. Subtractive color is used to design for print, where ink is applied to paper (or another substrate) to reproduce the artwork.

For Photoshop, Illustrator, and InDesign, subtractive color is reproduced by using cyan, magenta, yellow, and black inks. This color mode is called *CMYK*. Theoretically, the entire range of color can be produced with varying amounts of CMY inks, but it's necessary to add black to reach the darkest colors. (CMYK inks can be supplemented with other inks, called *spot colors*, to produce colors not available with just cyan, magenta, yellow, and black.)

Remember these key concepts about subtractive colors:

- The component colors (cyan, magenta, and yellow) can theoretically be combined to produce the full visible spectrum. However, in reality, printing inks are limited in the range of color they can reproduce.

- The lack of component colors results in white (or whatever is the color of the substrate—usually paper—to which the ink is applied).

- Combined at full intensity, CMY theoretically produces black. However, once again, there are limitations with real-world inks. Because mixing cyan, magenta, and yellow inks produces a dark brown rather than black, printers must add black ink (K) for CMYK printing.

5

- With subtractive colors, light is reflected rather than seen directly. The color perceived by the eye is the portion of the visible spectrum that the colored surface doesn't absorb. For example, when you're looking at a red wall, all parts of the spectrum *except* red are absorbed, and red is reflected to the eye.

- Printing on a press with CMYK inks is often referred to as *four-color process printing*, and the four inks are called the *process colors*.

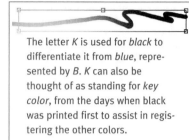

The letter *K* is used for *black* to differentiate it from *blue*, represented by *B. K* can also be thought of as standing for *key color*, from the days when black was printed first to assist in registering the other colors.

The Printing Gamut

In the Color Picker, to the right of the color slider, a small warning icon appears when the color chosen is out of gamut (see Figure 5.2). The *gamut* is the range of color that can be reproduced in printing. Because printed colors are subtractive, their color properties are based on what they reflect. This is a more narrow band of color than what a monitor can display. When you see that warning, the color you choose is out of the print range and will be altered when converting to CMYK color mode or when using that color in a CMYK image. When you click the gamut warning icon, the closest color within range inside the gamut is automatically selected in place of your color.

One of the biggest differences between RGB and CMYK color modes is the number of channels. Each component color is recorded in a separate color channel. Because RGB has three component colors, it has three color channels (plus a composite channel). CMYK has four component colors—so it has one more color channel than RGB—plus a composite channel.

In printing, CMYK inks can be supplemented with additional inks, often called *spot colors*. Spot colors are usually predetermined, premixed inks of a specific color. They are typically applied to a specific area (spot) on an image. It is not unusual to use one or more spot colors in place of CMY inks to create two- or three-color images. Spot colors can add color that the CMYK inks cannot produce. Neon, metallic, and even white are examples of colors that can be printed only with spot inks.

Figure 5.2
The warning symbol (the exclamation point in a triangle) tells you that the chosen color is out of gamut. Click the symbol, and Photoshop picks the closest color within the gamut, often a noticeably darker color.

WORKING WITH RGB, CMYK, AND SPOT COLORS

The vast majority of work in Photoshop—and all work in Illustrator—is done in RGB or CMYK color mode. Virtually all output is done in RGB, CMYK, or Grayscale mode, although Photoshop actually supports eight color modes. Illustrator can accept grayscale artwork in either RGB or CMYK documents, but each document can contain artwork of only its own color mode.

For more on the additional color modes, see "Understanding Photoshop's Other Color Modes and Models," later in this chapter.

Understanding the Relationship Between RGB and CMY

Theoretically (but not in practice), all RGB colors could be replicated by using cyan, magenta, and yellow. Likewise (and also theoretically), all CMY colors could be reproduced by using red, green, and blue. (Black [K], remember, is added to CMY to compensate for impurities in the inks. It is not one of the theoretical component colors.) The relationship among the six component colors is shown in Figure 5.3. The relationship is also shown in Table 5.1.

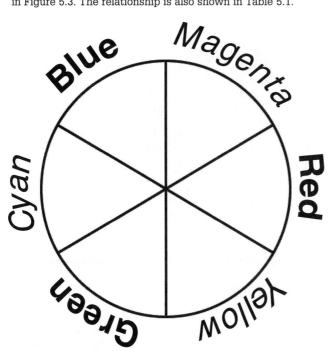

Figure 5.3
Notice that RGB and CMY alternate.

5

Table 5.1   RGB and CMY Relationships

Combine	And	To Create
Red	Green	Yellow
Red	Blue	Magenta
Green	Blue	Cyan
Cyan	Magenta	Blue
Cyan	Yellow	Green
Magenta	Yellow	Red

These relationships may not be the same as those you learned in elementary school, or even art school, but they are the relationships among component colors in Photoshop and Illustrator (and other digital imaging and illustration programs).

When displayed in a *color wheel* (a circular arrangement of colors), the relationships among the component colors is clear. A color wheel, such as the one in Figure 5.3, shows the way that the component colors interact with each other. Red is at zero degrees, the three o'clock position on the circle (see Figure 5.4).

Figure 5.4
The 0° point is typically on the right side of a color wheel.

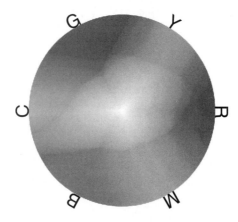

In a color wheel, each of the RGB colors is opposite a CMY color. These opposites represent the *inverse relationships* among colors. The inverse color relationships are summarized in Table 5.2.

Table 5.2   Inverse Relationships

Color	Inverse
Red	Cyan
Green	Magenta
Blue	Yellow
Cyan	Red
Magenta	Green
Yellow	Blue

Choosing a Color Mode

An image's color mode should be dependent on the image's final destination. The two major color modes, RGB and CMYK, are intended for different applications. CMYK is for use with commercial four-color printing presses and smaller printers specifically designed for the CMYK color mode. These devices include color laser printers, proofers (printers that simulate a printing press's output), and some high-end inkjet printers used for fine-art prints.

The RGB color mode is intended for use on the Internet, on monitors and kiosks, with film recorders, for broadcast and digital video, and with most desktop inkjet printers. Virtually all Photoshop and Illustrator work not destined for a commercial printing press should be done in RGB mode.

In the following discussions, Photoshop's 8-bit color mode is assumed. Photoshop also permits you to work in 16-bit and 32-bit color. You'll find more information on that subject in the section "A Note on Color Bit Depth," later in this chapter.

The inverse relationships among the component colors simplify color correction. For example, if an RGB image has a magenta cast to it, adding green is the same as subtracting magenta.

Working with RGB Color Notation

RGB colors are designated as proportions of the three component colors: red, green, and blue. Each value can range from 0 to 255. These 256 possible values for each component color are a product of 8-bit color depth. The standard notation is (red value)/(green value)/(blue value). For example, 35/120/57 means that the red value is 35, green is 120, and blue is 57.

When using the terms *print*, *printing*, and *printer*, keep in mind that there are differences between the inkjet printers likely to be found in studios, offices, and homes and the commercial offset printing presses, color laser printers, high-end inkjet proofers, and fine-art printers. When designing for home/office inkjets, remember to use RGB rather than CMYK. Although these printers actually use cyan, magenta, yellow, and black ink, these desktop printers' software requires RGB image data.

When all three component colors are 0, black results, and when all three are 255, you get pure white. When the component color values are equal and between 0 and 255, you get shades of gray.

The specific color for each pixel is broken down into the three component colors. Each component color value is recorded in the appropriate color channel. In practice, each color channel is a grayscale copy of the image, with only the component color values recorded in the channel.

Because each color channel can have 256 possible values, the total number of different colors that can be reproduced in 8-bit RGB is 16,777,216. That's 256×256×256. Consider, if you will, the sequence of colors 0/0/0, 0/0/1, 0/0/2, 0/0/3 through 135/87/42, 135/87/43, 135/87/44, 135/87/45 all the way to 255/255/252, 255/255/253, 255/255/254, and 255/255/255. The difference between 135/87/42 and 135/87/43 is too subtle for the human eye to see, even with the two color swatches side-by-side. In fact, variations of as much as 5 in a single color component are difficult to detect in most circumstances. A variance of 5 in *two* color components can, on the other hand, be very noticeable.

5

Working with CMYK Color Notation

Like RGB colors, CMYK colors are recorded as proportions of the component colors. Unlike RGB, CMYK has four components. Therefore, the notation is a bit longer. If you have a green color recorded in RGB as 35/120/57, a comparable shade of green could be recorded as 85/29/100/17 in CMYK. (Depending on the color settings in use, there could be considerable variation in the specific values. Also note that several different combinations of CMYK colors could produce similar shades of green.)

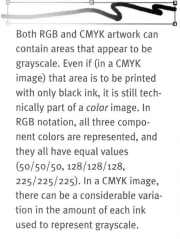

Both RGB and CMYK artwork can contain areas that appear to be grayscale. Even if (in a CMYK image) that area is to be printed with only black ink, it is still technically part of a *color* image. In RGB notation, all three component colors are represented, and they all have equal values (50/50/50, 128/128/128, 225/225/225). In a CMYK image, there can be a considerable variation in the amount of each ink used to represent grayscale.

Besides the additional component, CMYK notation differs from RGB notation in a very significant way: RGB values range from 0 to 255, but CMYK components are measured in percentages. Each of the four values can range from 0% to 100%. In practical terms, the percentage represents the ink density for that particular color. Values less than 100% can be thought of as "thinning the ink."

Although in theory a particular spot on a page could have 100% each of cyan, magenta, yellow, and black ink, in practice, that is not done. Depending on the paper used, maximum ink density is typically between 250% and 300%.

Like RGB color mode, CMYK records the component color value for each pixel in a separate color channel. CMYK images have one channel for each of the component colors, plus a composite channel used for editing the image.

Identifying Spot Colors

Photoshop and Illustrator enable you to specify a particular color by using *spot colors*. These predesignated colors, chosen from a library of color, represent premixed inks for use in commercial printing. Spot colors are used in addition to, or in place of, CMYK inks. The color is identified by name in the image, and the press operator mixes the exact color, using a specific formula or a premixed ink.

Photoshop supports a variety of spot color collections. Most common in North America are the Pantone collections. These and other spot color collections can be accessed through Photoshop's Swatches palette menu (see Figure 5.5).

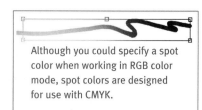

Although you could specify a spot color when working in RGB color mode, spot colors are designed for use with CMYK.

One of the most common uses of spot colors is to ensure an exact color match. For example, the specific red of the Adobe logo can be specified in a print image as PANTONE 485. This particular shade of red can also be reproduced by using CMYK 0/100/100/0.

Spot colors can also be used to supplement an image's tonal or color range. And they can provide a cost-effective printing method: using black ink and one spot color rather than all four process (CMYK) colors. Keep in mind that although most spot colors can be reproduced by using process colors, the premixed inks require only a single pass through the press, instead of three or four.

Figure 5.5
Photoshop's Swatches palette menu contains a wide variety of spot color libraries, often referred to as *books*.

Some colors cannot be reproduced on a printing press by using the CMYK inks, so other spot colors are added. Metallic and neon colors, for example, can be added to an image only through the use of spot colors. These inks cannot be duplicated with process inks.

Spot color names are assigned by the companies that produce the inks. The notation varies from company to company (and within brands, to some extent). Pantone inks for use with uncoated paper have a three- or four-digit number, followed by the letter *U*. Pantone inks for use with coated paper have the letter *C* following the number. A specific color has the same number, whether the ink is for use with coated or uncoated paper. Most other manufacturers also use numeric designations for their inks.

Here are descriptions of some of the spot color collections installed with Photoshop CS2:

- **ANPA Colors:** These 300 colors are designed for use on newsprint. The name ANPA comes from the American Newspaper Publishers Association, now known as the Newspaper Association of America.

- **DIC Color Guide:** This is a collection of 1,280 CMYK spot colors that can be matched against the *DIC Color Guide* from Dainippon Ink & Chemicals. These spot colors are most commonly used in Japan.

- **FOCOLTONE Colors:** Focoltone colors are designed to be used with the parent company's charts, showing overprint and absorbency characteristics with different stocks. Focoltone International, Ltd., of the United Kingdom, provides these 830 CMYK colors.

- **HKS E:** HKS-Farben is a German firm with four different collections of colors for use with inks from BASF or Hostmann-Steinberg. The E series (from the German *Endlospapiere*) is composed of the 88 colors designed for use with continuous forms papers.

5

- **HKS K:** The K (*Kunstdruckpapiere*) series is for use with glossy art papers. This set also has 88 colors.

- **HKS N:** These 86 colors are for uncoated paper (*Naturpapiere* in German).

- **HKS Z:** The *Z* stands for *die Zeitung* (German for *newspaper*), and this collection of 50 spot colors is for newsprint.

- **TOYO Colors:** These colors are as common in Japan as the Pantone colors are in the United States. There are 550 predesignated colors in this set.

- **TRUMATCH Colors:** Trumatch is a system for designating CMYK colors. The first component of each color's name represents one of 50 hues. The next pair of digits represents the saturation (*a* through *h*) and the amount of gray (1 through 7).

UNDERSTANDING PHOTOSHOP'S OTHER COLOR MODES AND MODELS

Photoshop enables you to work in six color modes in addition to RGB and CMYK: Grayscale, Bitmap, L*a*b (or just *Lab*), Indexed Color, Duotone, and Multichannel. Each of the color modes has specific characteristics and can be used for specific purposes. In the following sections, each of the color modes—and a pair of color models—are explained.

Grayscale Color Mode

Often referred to (incorrectly) as *black and white*, Grayscale color mode offers 256 shades of gray, including black and white. Grayscale mode uses one color channel. Although Grayscale is an 8-bit color mode (with 256 shades of gray), Photoshop measures each pixel's color as a percentage of black. Grayscale can be used in commercial printing, on the Web, or for output to other devices, such as inkjet printers and film recorders. Photoshop also permits you to work with 16-bit grayscale images (see "A Note on Color Bit Depth," later in this chapter), which can contain up to 65,536 shades of gray.

When you convert color images to grayscale, all color information is lost. The image retains only the brightness value of each pixel, expressed in varying shades of gray. Converting a grayscale image to RGB or CMYK mode does not add color to the image; rather, it adds color *channels*, allowing you to add color.

If you place a CMYK Photoshop document into an RGB Photoshop document, the new smart object that is created has some unique properties. From the Layers palette, you can click the placed smart object and then from the palette menu, choose Edit Contents. You then have access to the CMYK image you placed, with all of its layers intact. You can edit the image and click Save. The Smart Object layer then updates in the main document. This means that the smart object created from the placed Photoshop file is really a Photoshop document housed within a Photoshop document. This arrangement can help limit the scattering of all your different project files.

Bitmap Color Mode

Bitmap color mode is true black and white. Perhaps the phrase "black *or* white" would be clearer. Each pixel in such an image is either black *or* white; there are no shades of gray and no colors.

As you can see in Figure 5.6, each pixel is either white or black. The Navigator palette indicates the area of the image that is shown in the document window. In addition, note that the Channels palette shows only a single channel (and the image is somewhat identifiable in the palette thumbnail).

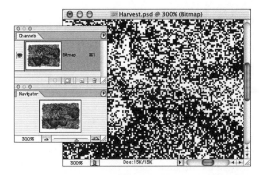

Figure 5.6
The image is shown at 300% zoom so that individual pixels are recognizable.

Bitmap color mode can be used effectively with certain line art and for special effects. Bitmap color mode greatly reduces file size but generally is not appropriate for most images. It is the color mode of the WBMP file format, designed for graphics viewed on some wireless devices and cell phones.

A file must be in Grayscale mode or Duotone mode before you can convert it to Bitmap mode. When converting from Grayscale mode to Bitmap mode, you have several options for how the gray pixels are converted to black or white (see Figure 5.7).

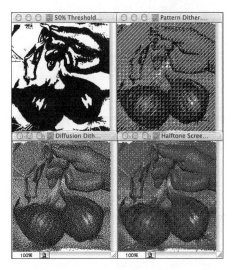

Figure 5.7
The results of four different bitmap conversions are shown.

5

Photoshop uses different criteria for the four types of bitmap conversion:

- **50% Threshold:** Pixels with gray values higher than 128 (50% gray) are converted to white. Pixels with gray values lower than middle gray are converted to black (refer to Figure 5.7, upper left).

- **Pattern Dither:** Geometric patterns of black and white dots are created to represent the image's general appearance (refer to Figure 5.7, upper right).

- **Diffusion Dither:** This technique bases the conversion on the color of the pixel in the upper-left corner of the image. Unless that pixel is pure white or pure black, the transformation to either white or black produces some margin of error. That error is transferred among the surrounding pixels and thus "diffused" throughout the image (refer to Figure 5.7, lower left).

- **Halftone Screen:** By specifying a halftone screen, you create a bitmap image that simulates reproduction with halftone dots. You can specify the line screen frequency (up to 999 lines per inch, or *lpi*) and the dot shape. (Typically, newspapers are printed at 85 lpi and magazines at 133 lpi or 150 lpi.) The example in Figure 5.7 at the lower right uses 133 lpi and a diamond-shaped dot to convert a grayscale original at 72 dpi.

> After an image is converted from Grayscale to Bitmap mode, converting back to Grayscale mode does not restore the image to its earlier appearance. Each pixel is still black or white, until editing the image changes the color values.

A closer look at the results of the four bitmap conversions shows the different distributions of black and white pixels (see Figure 5.8).

Figure 5.8
Here, each of the bitmap images shown in Figure 5.7 is zoomed to 300% at the center of the image.

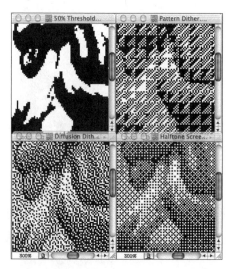

In Photoshop, you can also specify custom screens when converting to Bitmap mode, but you must create a pattern first. If the pattern is smaller than the image, it is tiled. The Custom Pattern option simulates shades of gray by making the halftone pattern thicker and thinner.

L*a*b Color Mode

The L*a*b color mode, often called simply *Lab*, uses three channels. Unlike the RGB and CMYK modes, the channels in Lab mode do not contain component color information. Rather, one channel contains only the Lightness value for each pixel (L), and the additional channels (a and b) split the color spectrum into two pieces (see Figure 5.9).

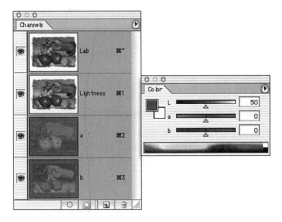

Figure 5.9
The top channel is the composite channel. Next is the Lightness channel (L), followed by the two color channels (a and b).

The L channel controls the brightness of a pixel, with a range of 0 to 100. The a channel contains the color value of the pixel along a red–green axis. The value normally ranges from –120 (green) to +120 (red). The b channel contains color information running along a blue–yellow axis. This value, also normally –120 (blue) to +120 (yellow), is combined with the L and a channels to produce the pixel's color.

The Lab color gamut is wider than RGB or CMYK, containing a range of colors not otherwise reproducible. When Photoshop converts between RGB and CMYK, it uses Lab as an intermediate color model.

Lab images can be printed to many PostScript devices (Levels 2 and 3 only) and can be used to edit photo CD images. In addition, converting from RGB mode or CMYK mode to Lab mode enables you to work directly with the luminance values in the image.

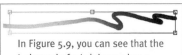

In Figure 5.9, you can see that the L channel of a Lab image has a good grayscale likeness of the image as a whole. If converting from RGB mode or CMYK mode to Grayscale mode leaves your image looking flat, try converting to Lab mode and then deleting the a and b channels.

Don't submit Lab images or place them into a page-layout document without approval from your service bureau or printer. If they can't work with the Lab color mode, you'll likely incur additional expenses.

Indexed Color Mode

Indexed Color mode is a subset of RGB. Rather than 8 bits of information for each of the *color channels*, files in Indexed Color mode contain only a total of 8 bits of color information for each *pixel*. For that reason, each image can contain a maximum of 256 different colors. They can be any RGB colors, even 256 different shades of blue or red or yellow, but there can be only 256 different colors.

Indexed Color mode is used with GIF and PNG-8 file formats, and it can be specified for some other formats. The advantage of 8-bit color is smaller file sizes, but that is often outweighed by the sometimes drastic degradation in image quality. Many photographic images cannot be accurately reproduced with such a limited color palette.

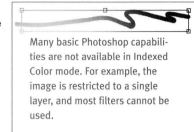

Many basic Photoshop capabilities are not available in Indexed Color mode. For example, the image is restricted to a single layer, and most filters cannot be used.

An image in Indexed Color mode has a single color channel, called *Index*, in the Channels palette. Photoshop records the colors used in an Indexed Color mode image in a color lookup table (CLUT). The CLUT is recorded with the file and might be unique to that file or to a standardized color table. If you attempt to add a color to the image that isn't among the 256 available colors, that color is converted to the nearest color.

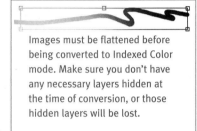

Images must be flattened before being converted to Indexed Color mode. Make sure you don't have any necessary layers hidden at the time of conversion, or those hidden layers will be lost.

Only RGB and Grayscale mode images can be converted to Indexed Color mode. Grayscale conversions happen automatically because there are a maximum of 256 shades of gray in an 8-bit grayscale image. When you're converting an RGB image, however, the Indexed Color dialog appears (see Figure 5.10).

Figure 5.10
The Indexed Color dialog offers some control over an image's reduction to 256 colors.

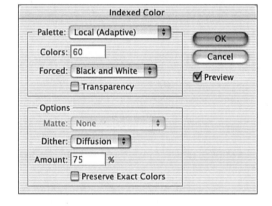

The Palette pop-up menu in the Indexed Color dialog offers several conversion options:

- **Exact:** If the RGB image contains 256 or fewer colors before conversion, the Exact option lets you create a color table using those colors. The image's appearance is maintained.

- **System (Mac OS):** The image's colors are converted to the Macintosh system's 8-bit palette.

- **System (Windows):** The 8-bit palette that is standard for Windows is used to produce the color table.

- **Web:** The web-safe palette of 216 colors that are common to both the Macintosh and Windows system palettes is used.

- **Uniform:** The color table is created by taking samples from the RGB spectrum. Six evenly spaced values for red, green, and blue are taken: 6×6×6 = 216. If the total number of colors is limited to fewer than 216 in the dialog, the next smallest perfect cube (125, 64, 27, or 8) is used.

- **Perceptual:** The color table is created, giving priority to those colors for which the human eye has greatest sensitivity. (The Local option emphasizes colors within the image, and the Master option relies on the RGB gamut.)

- **Selective:** Large areas of consistent color are taken into account when creating the palette with this option. Otherwise, the palette follows the guidelines for Perceptual. Generally, the Selective option does the best job of preserving an image's appearance.

- **Adaptive:** An adaptive palette of color is created by using the colors that appear most frequently in the image. If the color of a specific area of the image is most important, you can make a selection of that area before converting and choose Adaptive.

- **Custom:** This option enables you to edit the color table directly. It opens with the adaptive palette. You also have the option to load a previously saved palette of color.

- **Previous:** The most recently used custom palette is used to create the color table. This option enables you to convert numerous images using the same palette.

The difference between Local and Master for the Perceptual, Selective, and Adaptive options is most apparent when the color table is reduced from 256 to a smaller number of colors. The Local option emphasizes colors that exist in the image, whereas Master looks at the RGB gamut. Dithering can be critical when using the Master options.

You can enter a specific value in the Colors field to shrink the file size even more by choosing to retain fewer than 256 colors.

The Forced pop-up menu enables you to specify colors that must be maintained in or added to the image's color table. Forcing black and white adds those two colors to the table, regardless of whether they're used in the image. The Primaries option adds black, white, red, green, blue, cyan, magenta, and yellow. Web adds the 216 Web-safe colors. (See the following section, "Web-Safe RGB Color Model," for more information on the web-safe palette.) If you select Forced: Custom, you can specify colors that must be added to the image's color table.

Enabling the Transparency check box maintains any areas of transparency that exist in the image. When this option is not selected, any existing transparent pixels are filled with the specified matte color or, if no matte color is selected, with white.

Selecting a matte color uses anti-aliasing to help edges along a transparency blend with the designated color. If, for example, the image will be placed on a web page with a specific background color, using that color as the matte color helps the edges blend into the background. Choosing None in the Matte pop-up menu results in a hard-edged transparency or, if Transparency isn't selected, a white fill for transparent pixels.

You can also select the type and amount of dithering to apply. *Dithering* simulates colors missing from the color table. Pixels of colors that *are* in the color table are interspersed to simulate the missing color. Diffusion, Pattern, and Noise dithering are all available (as is the choice None). Here's how these options differ:

5

- **None:** Instead of attempting to simulate a color, this option substitutes the nearest color in the color table.

- **Diffusion:** An error-diffusion method of dithering is applied, which results in a less structured appearance than does Pattern dithering.

- **Pattern:** A pattern of dots similar to a halftone pattern is used to simulate colors that are not in the color table.

- **Noise:** Adding noise along edges helps break up potentially visible seams in sliced images. (Slices are used with web graphics to control optimization and downloading.)

The Preserve Exact Colors option, which is available with Diffusion dithering and mandatory for Noise dithering, ensures that colors already existing in the color table are not dithered. This option is helpful for preserving fine lines and type. Preserve Exact Colors is not available for Pattern dithering.

You can edit an image's color table directly by selecting Image, Mode, Color Table. The dialog that appears, shown in Figure 5.11, enables you to make changes to the individual colors saved with the file.

Figure 5.11
This color table shows the maximum 256 unique colors allowed for any image in Indexed Color mode.

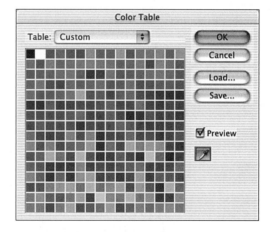

You have several options when editing a color table:

- Select the Preview check box to see the effect of your changes on the image.

- Select a standardized color table from the Table pop-up menu, if desired. Leave Table set to Custom to use the color table created during the color mode conversion.

- Click any color in the color table to select it and open the Color Picker. In the Color Picker, you can designate a new color to replace the selected color throughout the image.

- Drag the cursor through the table to select multiple colors. You can then use the Color Picker to assign a range of colors to replace those selected. When the Color Picker opens, you select the first color. After you click OK, the Color Picker reopens so that you can choose the ending color. A gradient is then generated, with each step replacing one of the selected colors.

- ⌘-click (on the Mac) or Ctrl+click (in Windows) to delete a color from the table.

- Option-click (on the Mac) or Alt+click (in Windows) a color to designate that color for transparency. You can also click the Eyedropper tool in the dialog and use it to designate the transparent color.

- Save and load custom color tables. Color tables should be saved with the file extension .act. Tables can be loaded from ACT files or from GIF files.

Web-Safe RGB Color Model

The Web-Safe color model is the subset of an 8-bit RGB gamut (Indexed Color) that is common to both the Macintosh and Windows system palettes. The two operating systems have built-in color palettes for use with 8-bit color (256 maximum colors, not 8 bits per channel). Color values are recorded in a single color channel.

Both the Macintosh and Windows system palettes contain 256 colors (the maximum allowed under 8-bit color), but only 216 of the colors are common to both palettes. These are the web-safe colors.

HTML, the basic language used with the World Wide Web, records color as a base-16 (hexadecimal) value. Rather than 10 possible values for each digit (the numerals 0 through 9), hexadecimal notation permits 16 different values for each digit. In addition to the 10 numerals, the letters *A* through *F* are used.

Web-Safe RGB is a subset of the RGB color mode, but it should actually be considered a variation of the Indexed Color mode. The Web-Safe colors are locked to specific color values that are considered to be reliable display colors for web browsers. Most modern browsers can display a much wider spectrum of color, so being "web–safe" isn't as much of a concern with developers as is the challenge of keeping graphic file size as small as possible. Also, because 40 of the Web-Safe colors differ between Windows and Mac, Photoshop limits the color field to 216 colors. To view these colors, you open the Color Picker and enable the Only Web Colors check box. Then you click one of the R, G, or B radio buttons. These 216 colors are available in the color field and color slider.

Duotone Color Mode

Duotone color mode in Photoshop actually refers to four different types of color images. *Monotones* use a single colored ink, much like printing a grayscale image with an ink other than black. *Duotones* use two inks, typically black and a color. *Tritones* use three inks, and *quadtones* use four inks.

What sets these color modes apart is that the inks are used throughout the image, rather than placed in specific areas. Each of the inks is, by default, distributed according to the single color channel.

Duotones can be created only from grayscale images. To convert RGB, CYMK, or another color mode to Duotone color mode, you first choose Image, Mode, Grayscale. The Duotone Options dialog, shown in Figure 5.12, enables you to select Monotone, Duotone, Tritone, or Quadtone from the Type pop-up menu.

Clicking a color swatch to the left of a color name opens the Color Picker in Custom Color mode. You can select a Pantone or other custom color.

5

Hexadecimal Colors

For use with Hypertext Markup Language (HTML), the basic language of the Web, hexadecimal color notation is based on 16 possible values for each digit. (The more familiar decimal system, called base-10, allows for only 10 possible values for each digit: the values 0 through 9.) To work with this system and not have to invent another six numbers to replace what we call 10 through 15, letters are substituted.

Hexadecimal uses 0 through 9 to represent themselves and adds the letters A through F as single-digit replacements for 10 through 15. In this system, therefore, the number 11 is represented by B, and 17 is recorded as 11. Likewise, 0F is 15, and F1, in base-10, is 241.

Why this base-16 system? Each of the 256 possible values for red, green, and blue (0 to 255) needs to be represented by only two digits in HTML. Using base-10, the purest white would have to be recorded as 255255255 (R-255, G-255, B-255). In base-16, it is FFFFFF—a six-digit number rather than nine digits. (Higher values represent lighter colors; lower values are darker.) Base-16 can represent any of the 16.7 million (16×16×16×16×16×16 = 16,777,216) possible RGB colors in a total of six digits.

Although learning the translation from decimal to hexadecimal may have some value to web designers and HTML coders, the majority of Illustrator users can rely on the Color Picker and Color palette to make adjustments. You simply choose a color and let the program determine the color's hexadecimal designation. If you need to be able to read or write hexadecimal, refer to the translation table shown in the following figure.

Using letters to represent the numbers from 10 through 15, hexadecimal notation is a base-16 system.

Decimal															
0	1	2	3	4	5	6	7	8	9	10	11	12	13	14	15
Hexadecimal															
00	01	02	03	04	05	06	07	08	09	0A	0B	0C	0D	0E	0F
Decimal															
16	17	18	19	20	21	22	23	24	25	26	27	28	29	30	31
Hexadecimal															
10	11	12	13	14	15	16	17	18	19	1A	1B	1C	1D	1E	1F
Decimal															
32	33	34	35	36	37	38	39	40	41	42	43	44	45	46	47
Hexadecimal															
20	21	22	23	24	25	26	27	28	29	2A	2B	2C	2D	2E	2F
• • •															
Decimal															
95	96	97	98	99	100	101	102	103	104	105	106	107	108	109	110
Hexadecimal															
5F	60	61	62	63	64	65	66	67	68	69	6A	6B	6C	6D	6E
• • •															
Decimal															
240	241	242	243	244	245	246	247	248	249	250	251	252	253	254	255
Hexadecimal															
F0	F1	F2	F3	F4	F5	F6	F7	F8	F9	FA	FB	FC	FD	FE	FF

Clicking the thumbnail in the left column, which by default has a diagonal line, opens the Duotone Curve dialog for that ink. Adjusting the curve gives you control over the distribution of the ink in the image. By default, each ink is printed at the gray value of each pixel. For example, a 50% gray midtone pixel is printed at 50% tint of the ink, whereas a darker pixel in a shadow area is printed with a higher tint. The straight-line curve uses the pixel's brightness value as the tint percentage for each ink.

The curve can be modified to change the distribution of an ink. To try this, you can reopen the Duotone Options dialog by choosing Image, Mode, Duotone. In Figure 5.13, the curve has been changed to eliminate the yellow ink from the image's highlights and shadows, and to print yellow at a darker tint in the midtones. Note that both the curve thumbnail and the image preview are automatically updated.

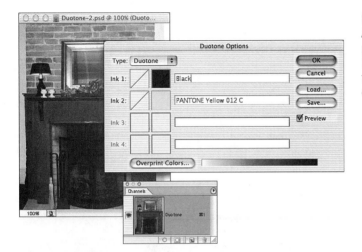

Figure 5.12
As you can see in the Channels palette, this image has already been converted to Duotone, and the dialog is reopened, enabling a change of color, if necessary.

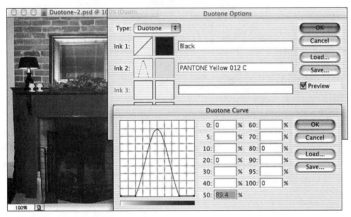

Figure 5.13
In this example, the yellow ink will be printed only in the image's midtones.

The Info palette shows you the "before" and "after" values when you're modifying a duotone curve. You can move the cursor around the image to get the ink percentages at any point (see Figure 5.14).

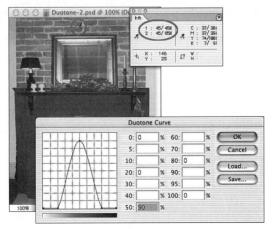

Figure 5.14
The cursor changes to the eyedropper when moved in the image window. The Info palette tells you each ink's tint percentage before (left) and after (right) the new curve is applied.

Note that custom curves can be saved and loaded in the Duotone Curves dialog. The Duotone Options dialog also has Load and Save buttons. Photoshop ships with a variety of predesigned duo-

tones, tritones, and quadtones. You'll find them all in the Duotones folder, inside the Presets folder, within the Photoshop folder. The presets include a variety of duotones, tritones, and quadtones in shades of gray, with Pantone custom colors and with process (CMYK) inks.

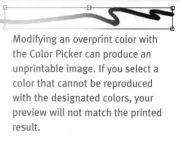

Modifying an overprint color with the Color Picker can produce an unprintable image. If you select a color that cannot be reproduced with the designated colors, your preview will not match the printed result.

The Overprint Colors button in the Duotone Options dialog shows you how the inks will interact (see Figure 5.15). Clicking a color swatch in the Overprint Colors dialog opens the Color Picker, allowing you to modify the overprint color.

Figure 5.15
With a duotone, only 1+2 is available. With a tritone, 1+2, 1+3, 2+3, and 1+2+3 are available.

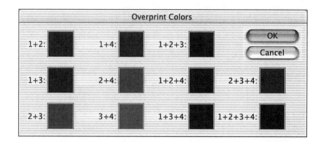

Images in Duotone color mode can be saved and printed in the Photoshop (PSD), EPS, PDF, and RAW file formats. In PSD format, all of Photoshop's capabilities are available, including spot channels, layers, and filters. Photoshop CS2's large document format (PSB) can be used to save extremely large images in Duotone mode. (PSB must be activated in Photoshop's file-handling Preferences window.)

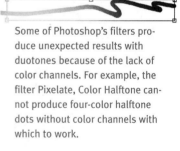

Some of Photoshop's filters produce unexpected results with duotones because of the lack of color channels. For example, the filter Pixelate, Color Halftone cannot produce four-color halftone dots without color channels with which to work.

Multichannel Color Mode

Multichannel color mode uses a separate color channel for each of an image's component colors, just as the RGB and CMYK color modes do. However, Multichannel mode does not include a composite channel, so each color channel can be considered a spot color.

Multichannel mode is designed for use with some specialized image printing (such as some Scitex CT format images) and can be used to edit individual color channels. In Photoshop, this color mode is typically used with images destined for commercial printing, including CMYK and duotone images.

Although most of Photoshop's capabilities are available for Multichannel mode images, they can be used on only one color channel at a time. Because there is no composite channel as there is in RGB or CMYK mode, the entire image cannot be manipulated at once.

Multichannel images can be created from CMYK, RGB, Lab, Duotone, and Grayscale files. Converting a CMYK image creates spot channels from each of the four color channels and deletes the composite channel. The four resulting channels are cyan, magenta, yellow, and black. There might be some color shift during the conversion. RGB images converted to Multichannel mode typically undergo a large color shift. During the conversion, the red, green, and blue channels are changed to cyan, magenta, and yellow.

Converting an image from Lab color mode to Multichannel mode creates three alpha channels rather than spot channels. Because a Grayscale mode image starts with only one color channel, converting to Multichannel mode results in an image with only one channel. The channel's name is switched from Gray in Grayscale mode to Black in Multichannel mode, but it's otherwise identical.

A duotone image can be converted to Multichannel mode, creating one color channel for each of the inks. This allows direct editing of the color placement, which is not possible in Duotone mode.

When working in Multichannel color mode, you can't apply a filter to the entire image at once because there's no composite channel. Remember that a filter can be repeated on each channel individually with the keyboard shortcut ⌘-F (on a Mac) or Ctrl+F (in Windows). You apply the filter to one channel and then switch to the next and use the keyboard shortcut to apply the same filter with the same settings. You repeat this for each channel.

HSB: The Non-Mode Color Model

Photoshop offers one additional way to define color, but it's not found under the Image, Mode menu. *HSB* stands for hue, saturation, brightness. Rather than a color mode, it is a *color model* used with the Color palette and the Color Picker. Images themselves are not recorded as HSB, but this color model can be used to define colors in the file in RGB, CMYK, Indexed Color, Lab, or Multichannel mode. (HSB is not available for images in Grayscale, Bitmap, or Duotone color mode.)

An image converted from Duotone mode to Multichannel mode cannot be converted back to Duotone mode. It can, however, be converted to Grayscale mode and then back to Duotone mode. Doing this, however, eliminates any changes made to the color channels in Multichannel mode.

HSB is designed to replicate the way the human eye and brain recognize color, breaking it down into color, purity, and brightness. Hue (color) is based on the color wheel and is measured in degrees. The six primary component colors (RGB and CMY) are found evenly spaced around the wheel (see Table 5.3 and Figure 5.16).

Table 5.3 Hue Values for Photoshop's Primary Colors

Color	Hue Value
Red	0°
Green	120°
Blue	240°
Cyan	180°
Magenta	300°
Yellow	60°

Figure 5.16
The hue values for the primary colors are typically measured from the three o'clock position on the color wheel.

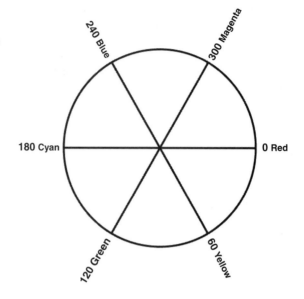

Saturation determines the purity of the color, from gray (0%) to pure or fully saturated (100%). Brightness (also sometimes called *lightness*) is the relative darkness (0%) or lightness (100%) of the color. When brightness is at 0%, the hue and saturation are insignificant—and black results. When brightness and saturation are both at 100%, the result is white, regardless of the hue.

Most Photoshop users employ HSB on a regular basis, perhaps without realizing it. By default, Photoshop's Color Picker is set to Hue (see Figure 5.17).

Figure 5.17
The H stands for hue. The Color Picker can also be set to use saturation (S), brightness (B), the RGB colors, or the Lab components as the basis for color selection. As you can tell from the lack of radio buttons, the CMYK colors cannot be used as a basis for color definition.

Comparing Color Modes

A number of Photoshop's capabilities cannot be used in certain color modes. Table 5.4 summarizes what features are and are not available for images in the various color modes.

Table 5.4 Photoshop Features for the Color Modes

Color Mode	Channels	Layers	Paint Tools	Filters	Composite Channel
RGB	3 (R, G, B)	Yes	All	All	Yes
CMYK	4 (C, M, Y, K)	Yes	All	Most	Yes
L*a*b	3 (L, a, b)	Yes	All	Most	No
Indexed Color	1 (Index)	No	Most	No	No
Grayscale	1 (Gray)	Yes	All	Most	No
Bitmap	1 (Bitmap)	No	Some	No	No
Duotone	1 to 4	Yes	All	Most	No
Multichannel	Varies	No	All	Most	No

A Note on Color Bit Depth

In addition to the various color modes, Photoshop permits you to work in 16-bit color for RGB, CMYK, Grayscale, Lab, and Multichannel modes. Rather than 256 possible values for each pixel in each color channel, 16-bit color theoretically has 65,536 possible values. With over 65,000 possible values for each of the three channels, the theoretical number of colors available is overwhelming.

Although most output devices can't handle the additional color information or don't have the capability of reproducing such fine variations among similar colors, 16-bit mode can be printed. Some film recorders, especially with grayscale images, can show improved tonal range.

In older versions of Photoshop, few editing options were available for an image in 16-bit color. There were no layers, you couldn't cut or paste, and most of the filters were grayed out. Photoshop CS introduced expanded support for 16-bit images, making it feasible to edit images using most of Photoshop's capabilities. Now Photoshop CS2 includes some support for 32-bit images.

Using Multiple Color Modes

Some images, including logos and other small art, are multipurpose. When you're preparing an image for both RGB (web or monitor) and print (CMYK), consider the following:

- If the colors must match exactly for every employment of the image, ensure that your RGB version doesn't contain any out-of-gamut colors. One way to do so is to work in CMYK and then convert a copy to RGB when you're finished.

- If a piece of art is headed for both print and the Web, and the colors must match, consider working in the web-safe RGB palette. Those 216 colors don't give you any out-of-gamut warnings.

- If color matching is not critical, take advantage of RGB's larger gamut by doing your work in that mode. At the end of the creation process, reduce a copy for your web needs and convert a copy to CMYK for print. Maintain the original in the full RGB spectrum for later use.

5

UNDERSTANDING CHANNELS

In Photoshop CS2, an image can have up to 56 total channels, up from 24 in older versions of Photoshop. (The total does not include the composite channel, RGB, CMYK, or Lab, which doesn't actually hold color data.) There are three types of channels:

- **Component color channels:** Component color channels contain the basic color information for an image. They are used with RGB, CMYK, and Lab color modes. The single channel in a Grayscale mode image can also be considered a component color channel. Component color channels store the color information for all artwork on layers in the image.

- **Spot channels:** Spot channels are used in CMYK images to hold special color information. A spot channel represents ink that will be printed independently of and in addition to the component inks (cyan, magenta, yellow, and black). Spot colors and their channels are independent of the layers in the image and are defined only in the spot channel.

- **Alpha channels:** Alpha channels do not hold color information. Rather, they are saved selections and are referred to as *masks*. Black, white, and shades of gray are used to store the selection information. A hard-edged selection made with the Rectangular Marquee tool would appear by default as a white rectangle on a black background. A heavily feathered selection made with the same tool would appear as an area of white blending through gray to black. Alpha channels can also be used to store transparency information for a variety of file formats.

Figure 5.18 shows a Channels palette containing an image's CMYK channel and includes a spot channel using a metallic Pantone color and an alpha channel to mask out portions of the image. You can use the palette menu or buttons at the bottom of the Channels palette to add these channels.

Figure 5.18
The Channels palette contains the image's CMYK channel, a spot channel, and an alpha channel.

Spot Color Channels

Spot color channels are primarily used with CMYK and Multichannel documents. They are designed to provide a channel for additional inks to be used in commercial printing. The location in the image where the ink should be applied is stored in the spot channel. A separate printing plate is generated, and an additional run through the press is required. This usually increases the cost of the print job. (Remember that Photoshop CS2 can now work with as many as 56 channels.)

If you need to ensure an exact match for a corporate logo, you might want to use a spot color. Another typical use is extending an image's color range beyond what can be produced by using CMYK inks. For example, you can add neon and metallic colors to an image with spot channels. Spot channels are also used to identify areas of an image over which a varnish will be applied.

A spot channel is added to the image—and to the Channels palette—by using the Channels palette menu command New Spot Channel. In the dialog, you click the color swatch to open the Color Picker.

Spot channels don't interact with layers, so adding a type layer in a spot color is out of the question. Instead, you create a type mask in the spot channel and fill the selection with black.

Color Channels: Grayscale at Heart

The key to working directly in the Channels palette is remembering that each channel is nothing more than a grayscale image. You can treat a channel as a single-layer grayscale image and use the same tools and commands that you would use on the layer of a grayscale image. Each pixel can be any of 256 different "gray" or brightness values. When considered with the other component color channels of the image, that value is actually the proportion of the channel's color.

To edit an individual channel, you click it in the Channels palette. By default, the image appears in grayscale, with only the values of the selected channel visible. Changes made are applied to only that active channel.

You can also make two or more channels active at the same time by Shift-clicking them. When multiple color channels are active, the image appears in color, using a blend of the selected colors (see Figure 5.19).

Remember that conversion to CMYK color mode often happens late in a workflow. You can add the spot color channels at any time; they're maintained when you do your final preprint color conversion. In addition, you can use a spot channel as an interim step in an RGB image. You create the spot channel and apply the color. Because the spot color is in a separate channel, it is protected while you continue editing and adjusting the rest of the image. Later, you can use the Channels palette menu command Merge Spot Channel to integrate that channel into the RGB channels.

5

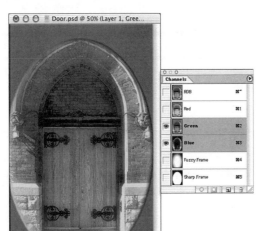

Figure 5.19
The Green and Blue channels are active in the Channels palette, so the window displays the image in a combination of greens and blues rather than in grayscale.

You can also work with one or more channels active and all channels visible. By clicking in the left column, next to the composite channel, or next to any channel of your choice, you can make the channel visible without being active. Likewise, you can hide the active channel by clicking the eyeball icon. At least one channel must be visible at all times.

Filtering and Adjusting Individual Channels

You can apply Photoshop's filters to channels individually. You might do this to control the impact of a filter, to produce a special effect, or to fix a problem that occurs in only one or two channels.

Digital camera images often have a lot of noise. When you examine the channels individually, you often find that the noise is primarily or exclusively in the Blue channel. Instead of applying a Gaussian Blur or Dust & Scratches filter to the entire image—which results in a general softening of detail—you can filter only the noisy channel, retaining detail in the other channels.

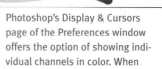

Photoshop's Display & Cursors page of the Preferences window offers the option of showing individual channels in color. When one channel is active, you see a monotone image rather than a grayscale image in that channel's color. Although this may be a handy reminder of what channel is active, it can be very difficult to see detail in the Yellow and Cyan channels when they're shown in color.

Using the Channel Mixer to Create Perfect Grayscale from Color

Using the Channel Mixer is an excellent way to create grayscale images from color pictures. To see for yourself, try this:

1. Open a copy of an RGB image.

2. If it has multiple layers, flatten it.

3. Click twice on the leftmost button at the bottom of the History palette. This makes a pair of copies of the image. Zoom out, if necessary, and position the windows so that you can view all three images onscreen at the same time. (Choose the Windows, Arrange, Tile menu command.)

4. Use the Image, Mode, Grayscale menu command to convert one image.

5. Click another copy of the image. Use the Image, Adjustments, Desaturate menu command followed by the Image, Mode, Grayscale command on this second copy of the image.

6. Switch to the third copy and use Image, Adjustments, Channel Mixer to open the Channel Mixer dialog.

7. Click the Monochrome check box.

8. Set the Red, Green, and Blue fields to 40 and change the Constant slider to –7.

9. Concentrate on an area of extreme highlight or extreme shadow. Slowly move the sliders back and forth, juggling the amounts of each channel you add or subtract. Watch how you can target certain tonal ranges, depending on the content of each channel.

10. As you work, compare this image with the other two. Look for a balance in your mix that makes the image "pop" and provides the best tonal range.

11. When the image looks perfect, click OK and then select Image, Mode, Grayscale.

You can even make selections and work on different areas on an image according to their needs. Generally speaking, for a normal key image, you want the total of the sliders to equal about 100. When doing the math, triple the value—positive or negative—of the Constant slider.

WORKING WITH GRADIENTS

A *gradient* is a blend of two or more colors, either in a straight line or as concentric rings of color. Gradient options are modified primarily in the Options bar. This, in conjunction with the Color and Swatches palettes, allows you to customize the colors and blending (see Figure 5.20).

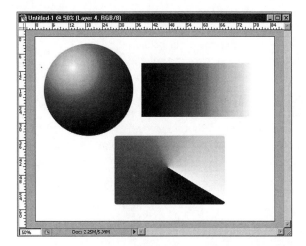

Figure 5.20
Three different gradients used in a canvas. You can fill the entire canvas or just select areas with gradients. You also have control over the colors within a gradient and how wide or narrow the gradient should be.

5

Nested with the Fill tool in the toolbox is the Gradient tool (see Figure 5.21). When the Gradient tool is selected, the Options bar displays one of the default gradients if a gradient hasn't been used before, or it displays the last gradient used. Some of the gradients loaded by default are affected by your chosen foreground and background colors. To choose a different gradient, you have several options. In the Options bar, you can click the pop-up menu to display the gradients currently loaded. You can click one of these gradient icons to use it in your image. To create your own gradient, you locate in the Options bar the preview of the gradient. Then you click in the middle of the preview to edit the gradient. The Gradient Editor dialog appears. The gradients loaded are shown in the presets area. You can click the Load button to load another library of gradients. (Photoshop ships with several different gradient libraries.) Or you can create your own gradients and save them to a gradient library file (.grd).

Figure 5.21
The Gradient tool depends on the Options bar to change the way gradients are made.

Creating a Custom Gradient

To create a custom gradient, you click in the Name field and type a name for your gradient. After naming your gradient, you click the New button. A duplicate of the previous gradient is created but with the new name. Make sure your Gradient Type is solid. Below you see the gradient ramp. The smaller squares that appear to be attached to the ramp by small wires are called *stops*. The handles attached to the top of the gradient ramp are called *opacity stops*. Below the ramp, they are called *color stops*. When you double-click the square of one of the color stops, the Color Picker appears, and you can choose a color for that color stop.

Instead of clicking the other color stop, you click in an empty area underneath the gradient ramp; a new color stop appears. You can double-click to choose a color (try a light gray) for your middle color stop. After you choose your color, you can change the color of your last color stop to another dark or light brown color. Your gradient might look like something in Figure 5.22.

When the Color Picker appears for you to choose one of the gradient colors, you can instead choose a color from your color libraries. But remember that the use of spot colors (Pantone, for example) can result in extra charges from your service provider.

Figure 5.22
If you mistakenly created a stop where you didn't want one, drag the stop up or down off the gradient bar until the stop disappears. This applies to both color and opacity stops.

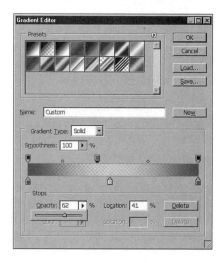

Working with Opacity Stops

You can create as many color or opacity stops as you want. These stops cause the desired shift of colors you'd expect from a gradient. To create or modify an opacity stop, you click in an area above the gradient ramp or click an existing opacity stop. In the Stops area at the bottom of the Gradient Editor dialog, the Opacity control becomes active. You change the percentage by moving the slider or typing in a value for the opacity.

Working with Midpoints

When selecting an opacity or color stop, small diamonds appear on either side of the stop. These diamonds are midpoints, and sliding them alters the transition of the gradient in either direction toward the next gradient color.

After you have mixed your gradient in the Gradient Editor, you can click OK, and your gradient is displayed in the Options bar, and it will be active the next time you use the Gradient tool.

Drawing Gradients

To use the Gradient tool, you click, hold, and drag a line across the canvas or a selection you have made in your document. The gradient is created inside the canvas or selection (see Figure 5.23). If you hold down the Shift key while dragging the line for the gradient, you constrain your straight line to a perfectly vertical, horizontal, or 45-degree angle.

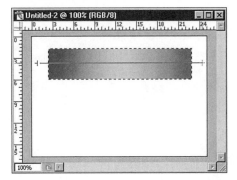

Figure 5.23
Even if you have designated a selection area, you can start and finish your gradient line outside it. This stretches the band of the gradient further and usually hides some of the outside colors and shades in the gradient. You can also drag your gradient outside the canvas border for a similar effect when filling the entire canvas with a gradient.

As you practice with the Gradient tool, you learn to anticipate where to start and finish your line so the gradient looks the way you want it to.

Using the Five Gradient Tools

The appearance of a gradient depends both on which tool is selected in the Options bar and on how you drag the tool through the selection or layer. Here are the basic capabilities of the five gradient tools (shown in Figure 5.24):

- **Linear Gradient tool:** When you drag a linear gradient, the colors are distributed perpendicularly to the line of drag (see Figure 5.25, top left). The distribution of color starts where the drag begins, and it ends where the button is released (or the stylus is lifted). Any selected areas outside the drag are filled with the first and last colors of the gradient (or transparency, if built in to the gradient). Everything before the drag is the first color; everything after is the last color. The Linear Gradient tool is typically dragged all the way across a selection.

Linear Gradient

Angle Gradient

Diamond Gradient

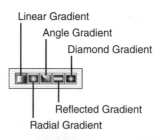

Figure 5.24
The five gradient variations all apply the selected gradient; they just apply it in different directions.

Reflected Gradient

Radial Gradient

Figure 5.25
From left to right, here are gradients made from the five gradient tools: Linear Gradient, Radial Gradient, Angle Gradient, Reflected Gradient, and Diamond Gradient. The arrow shows the start and direction of drag. The sample gradient that created these is also shown.

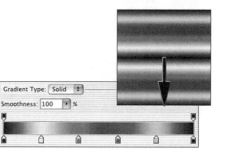

■ **Radial Gradient tool:** The colors in the gradient form concentric circles from the start to the end of the drag (see Figure 5.25, top center). Any areas beyond the drag are filled with the last color. Remember that transparency in the gradient and selections can limit the outer fill. The Radial Gradient tool is typically dragged from the center (or somewhat off center) of a selection to the edge.

■ **Angle Gradient tool:** The Angle Gradient tool "wraps" the gradient around the line of drag (see Figure 5.25, top right). Consider the line of drag to be the minute hand of a clock. The gradient is applied clockwise, centering on the point where you start the drag. Like the Radial Gradient tool, the Angle Gradient tool is typically dragged from the center to the edge of a selection.

■ **Reflected Gradient tool:** The Reflected Gradient tool produces the same gradient, extending outward from either side of the line of drag (see Figure 5.25, bottom center). Think of the start of the drag as the point from which the reflection begins and the length and direction of drag as the extent of the gradient. The Reflected Gradient tool is typically dragged from the center of a selection outward.

■ **Diamond Gradient tool:** The Diamond Gradient tool is somewhat of a cross between the Reflected Gradient and Angle Gradient tools (see Figure 5.25, bottom right). Multiple copies of the gradient are produced (as with the Reflected Gradient tool), but they rotate around the line of drag (as with the Angle Gradient tool). Regardless of the shape of the selection, the Diamond

Gradient tool always produces gradients along straight lines. Note that in the sample image, if the tool had been dragged to a side of the selection rather than a corner, the pattern would be a diamond rather than a square; picture the gradient rotated 90 degrees, with the square selection remaining oriented to the page.

GETTING PRINTING RESULTS

The best guarantee of a good final product is a quality source image. If your color was good coming in, it's more likely to look good for output. So if your subject has an odd green skin tone, your print will probably have the green skin, too. If you are printing on an inkjet printer, realize that despite an inkjet's CMYK color space, it actually prints from RGB images. A great many programs that don't even support CMYK images print just fine to inkjet printers.

Regarding commercial printing, the most important piece of advice I can give you is to simply talk with your commercial printer. Just as a racecar driver trusts his mechanic to prepare a multimillion-dollar vehicle, so should you trust your printer to run his or her machinery at maximum efficiency. Communication is the key. Instead of wondering what you can do past calibrating your monitor and choosing the correct color management settings, you might request a proof from your printer. Some test prints are prohibitively expensive, but depending on the facility, your printer may have a specialized color laser printer calibrated with the press for accurate proofing.

If you are not satisfied with the color proof, communication is still the key. You should express your concerns and find out what modifications should be made. Many jobs have non-critical color requirements. That means that if the skin tones look correct and nothing looks out of the ordinary, the slight color variance will likely go unnoticed. With logos and other specific company brand colors, you have critical color needs. Make sure you are using the right CMYK or spot colors. Never just eyeball your color in these situations. Sample the important color from existing art or get the CMYK or spot color numbers from the marketing department. When you match the numbers, you know that even if it doesn't look quite right onscreen, at least your prints will be correct.

You will find that different printers may print the same graphic just a little differently. These variations come from color mixing differences and machine calibration differences. Using a spot color such as one from the Pantone Matching System helps guarantee accurate color matching because print vendors mix Pantone colors to exact specifications.

Viewing and Correcting Colors

Because the range of color in CMYK is limited and because not all of Photoshop's filters are available in that color mode, design and creation are often done in RGB mode, and the artwork is later converted to CMYK for print. The difference in gamut, however, allows you to design in RGB with colors that can't be printed in CMYK. Photoshop warns you if you select an RGB color that cannot be reproduced with CMYK inks.

Photoshop enables you to *soft proof* your work. This means viewing your image onscreen while Photoshop attempts to simulate different outputs onscreen. By choosing View, Proof Colors, you can check how your project is expected to print.

The View, Proof Setup, Custom command enables you to select a color profile for the printer. You then use the View, Proof Colors command to toggle the preview on and off. The Custom option opens the Customize Proof Condition dialog, shown in Figure 5.26.

The Simulate Paper Color check box, when enabled, compensates for the medium defined in the profile (if any). The Simulate Black Ink option simulates onscreen the dynamic range of the selected profile.

Selecting the appropriate color profile is critical if the Proof Setup command is to give you an accurate representation of the image. Your printer may be able to supply you with a profile for the particular press and inks that will be used on your project.

Soft proofing is not usually considered an acceptable substitute for hard (printed) proofs. Soft proofing is feasible only when the monitor has been properly calibrated and an appropriate profile for the specific printer is available.

The Preserve Color Numbers option shows you what your artwork would look like if it were thrown on the press "as is." This setting simulates printing the color values without compensating for the profile space. Normally, you should leave this option unchecked.

Figure 5.26
Changes made in the Customize Proof Condition dialog do not change the selections in the Color Settings dialog.

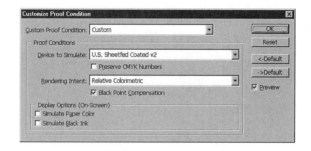

The Intent pop-up menu gives you the same four options that you can find in the Advanced section of the Color Settings dialog:

- **Perceptual:** This option preserves the relationships among colors. The range of colors can be changed, but the visual differences among them are maintained. Color values can also change. Perceptual is not suitable for images, such as logos, that must use specific colors.

- **Saturation:** The Saturation option is not acceptable for print in many circumstances. It attempts to make colors more vivid and is designed for use with presentation graphics.

Using the Custom option enables you to select a CMYK setup other than that selected in the Color Settings dialog. You can select Working CMYK to use that setting.

- **Relative Colorimetric:** This option, the default, strives to preserve all colors that fall inside the target gamut, maintaining their color accuracy. Colors that are outside the target gamut are mapped as closely as possible but might overlap with other colors. The extreme highlight of the image (white) is mapped to white in the destination space. If the artwork is within the CMYK gamut, you need to consider only the differences among output devices. These differences are usually minor.

- **Absolute Colorimetric:** Like the Relative Colorimetric option, this one tries to preserve colors that are within the target gamut. However, it does not take into account the image's white point.

WORKING WITH LAYERS IN PHOTOSHOP

IN THIS CHAPTER

Using layers—along with understanding how layers work with each other—is what makes Photoshop such a powerful tool for the digital imagist. Everything else you do in Photoshop is affected by what you do on specific layers.

This chapter looks at how to create and manage layers within a Photoshop document, as well as how to control the visibility of a layer's contents. This is done through opacity changes, layer masks, and clipping masks, which enable you to isolate specific areas to be hidden or revealed. This chapter also looks at how to use layer styles and layer comps to add special effects to layers and experiment with layer combinations.

WORKING WITH LAYERS

The clear, logical layout of the Layers palette, with the "stacking" of layers one on top of the other, helps you keep track of the images and elements you have on each layer. The top layers are the most visible. If the content of the top layer fills the canvas and is set to 100% opacity, the content of the layers underneath is hidden. Sometimes an image has only one layer. A JPEG image taken with a digital camera, for example, if opened in Photoshop contains only one layer, called *Background*. This single layer means the image is flattened. When you create a new document in Photoshop, you always create a document with one layer. If you choose Transparent from the Background Contents drop-down menu, your layer is called `Layer 1` and the layer is empty.

Photoshop layers work like stacks of clear plastic film on which elements of the complete composite reside. Figure 6.1 starts with a black background. Add to that your base image and then the shadow of your subject—each added on a piece of clear plastic film. Continue adding your subjects on stacked layers of plastic film.

Figure 6.1
Consider the arrangement of layers in the Layers palette as a stack of clear film; each layer is like one sheet of clear celluloid. Each can be moved, reordered, and painted without disturbing the others in the stack.

The top layer is in the foreground, and the subsequent layers are viewed as being beneath it, creating a complete, composite image. In this example, the word ZEN is the top layer and is visible in the foreground (see Figure 6.2).

Figure 6.2
A composite can have several layers that make up the final image, with the top layers visible in the foreground.

If the top image layer is moved beneath the next layer down, it appears to be behind the object in the next layer—as though you were shuffling stacks of clear film. To reorder layers, click a layer's name in the Layers palette and drag it beneath the next layer in the stack. See Figure 6.3.

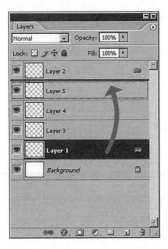

Figure 6.3
You'll often change the stacking order of the layers to bring contents of one layer to the front, back, or somewhere in the middle. Click a layer in the Layers palette and drag it to your chosen location in the stack.

6

UNDERSTANDING THE LAYERS PALETTE

The Photoshop Layers palette provides complete control over how layers are organized and displayed. In addition to reordering layers and turning on and off their visibility, the Layers palette enables you to lock various layer characteristics, apply blending modes, and set opacity.

Showing and Hiding Layers

To hide layers, simply click the eye icon of each layer you want to hide. Click the empty box in the left column to make it visible again. Making a layer visible does not select it or make it active. You must click near the layer name to make a layer active.

Linking Other Layers to the Active Layer

You often find the need to link multiple layers together. When layers are linked, you can use the Move tool to drag the contents of one layer; the content inside its linked layer moves with it. For example, if you work on a highly detailed logo, your logo design might require several layers. When you need to move the entire logo to another location in the document, linking the layers makes it easy to drag the logo and reposition it. If you leave the layers unlinked, you must drag several times and reposition each layer every time.

Linking layers is simple. Hold the ⌘ key (Mac users) or the Ctrl key (Windows users) and click to select multiple layers in the Layers palette. After you select the layers you want to link, they are highlighted. Click the Link Layers button at the bottom of the palette.

You can see the link icon (it looks like a small chain link) in Figure 6.4. Moving one linked layer up or down in the Layers palette does not affect the other layers in the stack, but moving the contents of the layer inside the canvas causes the linked layers' contents to move with it. To unlink layers, select a linked layer in the layers palette. (You can tell that the layer is linked to others by its chain link icon.) Click the Link Layers button at the bottom of the Layers palette to unlink that layer. If you have more than two layers linked and you want to unlink them all, select all the linked layers at once by holding the ⌘ key (Mac users) or the Ctrl key (Windows users) as you click to select the layers; then click the Link Layers button.

To link layers, Shift-click or ⌘-Control-click to select the layers, and then click the Link Layers button at the bottom of the Layers palette. You can link only to the active layer; however, links are maintained when you make another layer active.

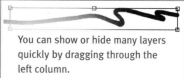

When a layer is named *Background* (in italics) in the Layers palette, it represents a solid layer. Background layers differ from regular layers in a number of ways: They don't support transparency, no layer can be moved below the Background layer, and by default they cannot be moved. You can convert a Background layer to a regular layer by renaming it in the Layers palette.

You can show or hide many layers quickly by dragging through the left column.

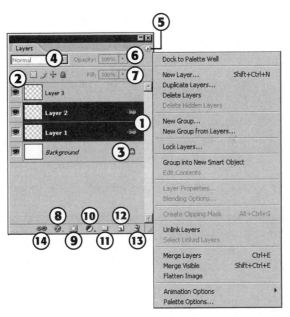

Figure 6.4
The Layers palette is one of Photoshop's most powerful components. Here are multiple layers selected at the same time. Using the Move tool, you can move the contents of linked layers at the same time.

1. Highlighted layer indicates that it is the "active" layer. What you choose to do in the canvas will happen directly to this layer.
2. Eye icon indicates that the layers visibility is turned on. Click to hide the eye icon and the layer will hide.
3. Lock icons allow you to lock individual layers of transparency, paint or editing, movement or lock all.
4. Blending modes that can be applied to the layer.
5. Layer palette menu selector.

6. Sets opacity of layer and layer styles, effects and masks
7. Sets the fill opacity of the layer, excluding layer styles, effects or masks.
8. Adds a layer style to the active layer.
9. Adds a layer mask to the active layer.
10. Creates a new layer group.
11. Creates a new adjustment or fill layer.
12. Creates a new layer. You can also drag a layer to this icon to duplicate it directly
13. Deletes the active layer. You can also drag a layer to this icon and delete the layer.
14. The Link Layers button is self-explanatory.

ALIGNING AND DISTRIBUTING LAYERS

You can align or evenly distribute the content of layers using the Alignment and Distribute buttons in the Options bar (see Figure 6.5). For example, you may be creating button graphics for a website interface and you need to align them and evenly distribute them so they are equally distant from one another. First choose the Move tool in the toolbox. This ensures that the Align and Distribute commands appear in the Options bar. Then ⌘-click (Mac users) or Ctrl-click (Windows users) to select multiple layers in the Layers palette and choose one of the Align or Distribute button commands.

Align command buttons

Bottom Edges
Top Edges | Left Edges

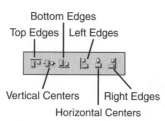

Vertical Centers | Right Edges
Horizontal Centers

Distribute command buttons

Bottom Edges
Top Edges | Horizontal Centers

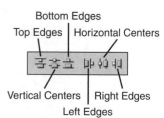

Vertical Centers | Right Edges
Left Edges

Figure 6.5
The Align and Distribute buttons in the Options bar. These commands are accessible only when the Move tool is selected in the toolbox.

Locking Layers

You can lock the active layer's transparency by clicking the square checkered box in the Lock area at the top of the Layers palette. To lock the editing of a layer, click the paintbrush in the Lock area. Click the four-headed arrow icon to lock the location of the layer's content or the transforming of the layer, and click the padlock icon to lock everything on a layer.

USING LAYER STYLES

You can quickly add three-dimensional effects and realism to raster and vector image layers by applying a layer style. Choose from a large variety of layer styles in the Preset Library or create one of your own. You can even modify existing or saved layer styles to create a look that's just right for your project, and you can save the customized style as a preset in your library. You can trade and email custom layer style preset libraries with colleagues and clients. Saved Photoshop files retain the applied style effect on any layer.

Layer style effects range from simple drop shadows and embossed edges to transparent glass and textured 3D patterns. The effects remain with the layer even while you're editing—whether it's a type layer, a vector shape, or a paint layer. Not all effects can be applied to Background layers, locked layers, or layer sets.

A layer style can have several effects, and each is fully editable after it has been applied. The layer styles remain fully editable because the layer effects don't degrade or destroy the image layer data. The layer with the layer style effects applied has the layer style icon (a scripted white *f* in a black circle) next to the layer name in the Layers palette (see Figure 6.6).

Layer Style Effects Overview

When you apply a layer style effect to a layer, the Layer Style dialog opens with the Blending Options section displayed at the top (see Figure 6.7). Click one of the Styles options in the list to the left to apply an effect and modify its settings. You can then create and customize your own layer style effects.

The following sections briefly explore the Styles categories listed on the left side of the Layer Styles dialog:

6

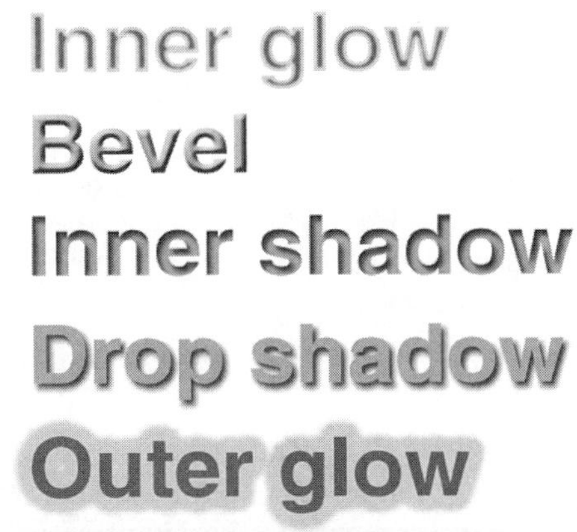

Inner glow

Bevel

Inner shadow

Drop shadow

Outer glow

Figure 6.6
A few layer styles applied to text layers can turn ordinary text into fancier ordinary text.

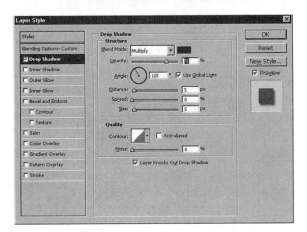

Figure 6.7
The Layers Style dialog lets you control the application of a dozen layer styles.

- **Drop Shadow:** The default Drop Shadow settings have Multiply as the blending mode, with black as the shadow color and Opacity set to 75%. Generally, these settings are good for most applications. For the angle of the lighting, the Use Global Light option has been selected by default, which means that all instances of effects lighting are linked together. The distance and size options are scalable to the image layer and effect you want to achieve.

- **Inner Shadow:** The Inner Shadow effect places a drop shadow along the inside edges of the image's fill area—such as cutout text—maintaining the layer's fill color and texture. It looks as though the content of the layer has been pressed inward, such as a button depressed or a stamp impression. Adjust the distance and shadow size to create the effect you want.

6

- **Outer Glow:** The Outer Glow effect can be used to add a glowing color beaming around it. Adjust the Spread and the Size sliders to change the appearance of the glow. You can choose to have a solid color glow or use an gradient to create a multicolored outer glow around the contents of the layer. Outer glow looks especially cool on text and shape layers.

- **Inner Glow:** The Inner Glow effect adds a glow around the inside edges of the image layer's fill area. The blending mode is set to Screen with Opacity at 75% for its default, the same default settings as is used with the Outer Glow effect.

- **Bevel and Emboss:** The Bevel and Emboss layer styles are quite useful because they turn flat text into type that bulges off the page. You are not limited to text though. You can emboss shapes for very cool results and even give images an interesting appearance.

- **Satin:** Create the reflective gradient effect that appears as though the content of the layer is made out of satin or other shiny cloth. This effect is quite unpredictable and produces interesting results on all kinds of images.

- **Color Overlay:** The Color Overlay layer style is a simple but useful feature that enables you to apply a different color to your object layer without changing the layer's fill color. Using the blending mode options gives you the same versatility to work with other layer style effects so that they show through or work together.

- **Gradient Overlay:** The Gradient Overlay layer style applies gradients from the Preset Manager Gradients Library to the image layer's fill area. Clicking the gradient thumbnail in the dialog opens the Gradient Editor, where you can fine-tune your gradients.

- **Pattern Overlay:** The Pattern Overlay style works with other layer style effects, especially if the object layer's fill is solid and needs some texture to bring it to life.

- **Stroke:** The Stroke layer style creates a smooth outline of the object's fill edges. Adjust the Position drop-down menu to place the stroke on the outside, middle, or inside of the border of the layer's contents. Change the Size slider to alter the stroke width. This layer style gives you a result similar to the result you can get in Illustrator or InDesign by changing the stroke of objects using the stroke palette. Use the stroke layer style for great results on type layers and shapes, but also to quickly apply a border color to image layers.

The best effects are usually combinations of layer styles that work together to create an interesting—and often 3D—image, shape, or text effect.

Choosing a Blending Mode

You use the Blending Mode pop-up menu to change the way the layer color, contrast, and opacity interacts with the layers beneath it. The effect of a layer's blending mode is dependent on the layer(s) underneath. To use this powerful feature of Photoshop, you must create or build an image with at least two layers and fill the layers with a photo or fill the layer with brush strokes using the Brush tool. The default blending mode is Normal (see Figure 6.8). Try going down the list and selecting the different blending modes to see what effect each has on your image. The blending modes are

- Normal, Dissolve

- Darken, Multiply, Color Burn, Linear Burn

- Lighten, Screen, Color Dodge, Linear Dodge

- Overlay, Soft Light, Hard Light, Vivid Light, Linear Light, Pin Light, Hard Mix

- Difference, Exclusion

- Hue, Saturation, Color, Luminosity

Like the Photoshop filters, the blending modes can be described in great technical detail, but no matter how much you read about these powerful features, you must try them out. The following are descriptions of a few of the blend modes:

- **Normal:** There is no interaction between the selection and the base color.

- **Dissolve:** Between filled and transparent areas, make a gritty random jagged edge transition. When the entire canvas is filled, the effect is not visible until you change the opacity or fill settings for the layer.

- **Darken:** Select the darker of the base and blend colors and use it as the resulting color.

- **Multiply:** Make the base color darker by adding the selection color to it. This color is always darker than the other colors.

- **Color Burn:** Make the base color darker to reflect the blend color.

- **Screen:** The opposite of multiply. Lighten the base color by adding the inverse of the selection color to it. This color is always lighter.

- **Color Dodge:** Make the base color brighter to reflect the blend color.

- **Overlay:** Depending on the colors involved, you can either multiply or screen. The blend color reflects either the lightness or darkness of the base color.

- **Soft Light:** Darken or lighten the colors, depending on the blend color. If the blend color is lighter than 50% gray, it lightens the artwork. If the blend color is darker than 50% gray, it darkens the artwork.

- **Hard Light:** Multiply or screen the color, depending on the blend color. If the blend color is lighter than 50% gray, it screens the artwork and adds highlights. If the blend color is darker than 50% gray, it multiplies the artwork and adds shadows.

- **Lighten:** Select the lighter of the base and blend colors and use it as the resulting color.

- **Difference:** Depending on whether the base color or the blend color is brighter, subtract one from the other.

- **Exclusion:** This mode is similar to Difference, but with less contrast.

- **Hue:** Create a color from the base and blend color.

- **Saturation:** Create a color from the base and blend color.

6

■ **Color:** Create a color from the base and blend color. This mode is especially useful with black and white.

■ **Luminosity:** Use like Color, but create the inverse of the blend and base color.

Figure 6.8
Select the blending mode from the pop-up menu in the Layers palette.

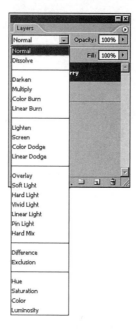

You can set a layer's blending mode in the Layer Styles dialog by choosing Layer, Layer Styles, Blending Options or by simply clicking the Blending Mode pop-up menu in the Layers palette and selecting a mode.

Working with the Layers Palette Menu

The Layers palette menu contains some commands and options similar to those available using the icons at the bottom of the Layers palette, but it also offers some additional options (see Figure 6.9). You can create new layers, duplicate layers, create layer sets from linked layers, merge layers together, and delete selected individual or grouped layers. You can also dock the palette to the Palette Well at the top of the screen or set palette options from this menu.

Understanding the Opacity and Fill Settings

There is a fundamental difference between a layer's Opacity and its Fill settings. The Opacity setting affects the entire layer, including any masks or layer styles applied to it. The Fill settings, on the other hand, apply only to the layer's content, without affecting anything that has been applied, masked, or stylized.

Figure 6.9
The Layers palette menu offers noteworthy options including Opacity and Fill settings, blending modes, and the ability to move layers up and down in the "stack."

Using the Layers Palette Buttons

Across the bottom of the Layers palette are several buttons. Although they duplicate commands available in the Layer menu and the Layers palette menu, the buttons at the bottom of the Layers palette are more easily accessible

Adding Layer Masks

Click the Add Layer Mask button at the bottom of the Layers palette to create a rasterized (pixel-based) layer mask that you can paint, edit, and fill with selections. Just as you can use a face mask to hide your facial features, use a layer mask to paint out and hide portions of the layer. Click the button a second time to create a linked vector mask that can be filled with custom shapes or vectors drawn with the Pen tool. If you have an active selection in the canvas, click the Add Layer Mask button to use your active selection as the basis of the mask. This is a preferred method to make a cutout of your layer because it isn't destructive to the actual layer.

When painting within layer masks, you are limited to shades of gray, ranging from black to white. Paint in the mask with black and you effectively paint out that portion of the image. Painting with a shade of gray gives it a transparent, but not completely invisible effect. Painting with solid white enables that portion of the layer to show through completely. To reveal the masked portions of the image, erase part of the mask. The image comes back. Layer masks make the Paint and Eraser tools work opposite from normal.

Working with Layer Groups

Layer groups were called *layer sets* in previous versions of Photoshop. Click the Create a New Group button at the bottom of the Layers palette. By organizing multiple layers into groups, you can maintain organization in your palette with related layers. Since some of your designs may have tens of layers, grouping them makes organizing easier. You can then move groups of layers within your document's layer hierarchy.

In addition to using layer groups to streamline the Layers palette, you can use them to isolate the effects of adjustment layers. Normally, an adjustment layer affects all layers below it in the Layers palette. Likewise, by default, an adjustment layer within a layer set affects all layers below it, regardless of whether they're in the group. Changing the layer group's blending mode from Pass Through to Normal prevents any adjustment layer in the set from having an effect on layers outside the set.

There are several ways to create layer groups. When you know what layers you want to add to the same group, hold down the Ctrl or ⌘ key and select the layers. Then open the Layers palette menu and choose New Group from Layers. A dialog appears enabling you to name the new group, choose a color for identifying the group, and set the blending mode and opacity (see Figure 6.10). Make your selections and click OK.

Figure 6.10
Create a new layer group and choose a color, blending mode, and opacity options for the group.

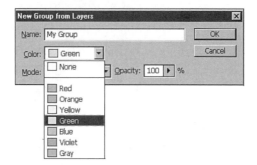

To create a nested layer group, create a new group and drag it into an existing group. Click the arrow next to the layer group name to show the contents of the group. A nested layer group is indented and so are the layers inside it (see Figure 6.11).

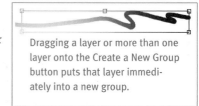

Dragging a layer or more than one layer onto the Create a New Group button puts that layer immediately into a new group.

Figure 6.11
Nested layer groups appear below the parent layer and are indented.

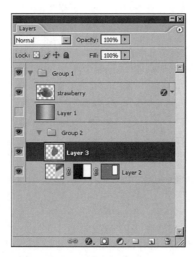

6

Selecting a Fill or Adjustment Layer

Fill layers can be filled with a solid color, gradient, or pattern. They are often used with a layer mask and a layer style. Click the Layers palette's New Fill or Adjustment Layer button and select the type of fill layer from the top of the pop-up menu. When you select Color, the Color Picker opens. Select Gradient and the Gradient Fill dialog opens. When you select Pattern, the Pattern Fill dialog appears. A pattern is tiled throughout the layer or an active selection.

Using an adjustment layer is the best way to color-correct the layers beneath it without permanently affecting the image layers. You can reverse or eliminate any modifications, corrections, or effects applied to the adjustment layer without any impact on the original image layers. Adjustment layers can be reopened at any time to change the settings, unlike changes made to the layers themselves with the Adjustments commands. Click and hold the New Fill or Adjustment Layer button and select the type of adjustment layer required from the pop-up menu.

You can perform several menu functions by simply Control-clicking (on the Mac) or right-clicking (in Windows) a different area of a layer in the Layers palette. The context menus that appear change depending on whether you click the visibility icon, layer thumbnail, or layer name. Available functions include Layer Label Colors, Show/Hide, Layer Properties, Blending Options, Duplicate or Delete Layer, Enable Layer Mask, Rasterize Layer, Copy Layer Style, Paste Layer Style, Paste Layer Style to Linked, and Clear Layer Style.

Adding and Deleting Layers

Among the most basic layer-related steps are creating and deleting layers. The familiar buttons to the right of the Layers palette handle these tasks. You can add a new layer by clicking the New Layer button or using the keyboard shortcut Shift-⌘-N (on the Mac) or Shift+Ctrl+N (in Windows). You can quickly duplicate an existing layer—and its content—by dragging the layer from its position in the Layers palette to the New Layer button.

You can delete the active layer by clicking the Trash icon. Alternatively, you can drag a layer (or a layer mask) to the Trash icon to eliminate it.

UNDERSTANDING LAYER BLENDING OPTIONS, OPACITY, AND TRANSPARENCY

6

Transparency means allowing light to pass through. When you think of transparency, think of windows or cellophane; your eye can see through an object to whatever is behind it. In Photoshop, you can set a transparency level of a layer by adjusting the Opacity slider in the Layers palette. By default, a layer's opacity is 100% (See Figure 6.12). You can change a layer's opacity so that objects in layers underneath become visible. Click the Opacity slider pop-up and move the slider or enter a percentage in the text field for the opacity (see Figure 6.13).

Figure 6.12
Setting the Opacity slider to 100% makes the selected layer fully opaque.

Figure 6.13
Setting the Opacity slider to 50% adjusts the opacity of the selected layer and its elements.

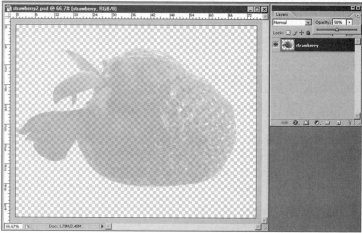

A lot of people know about blending modes because they are accessible from the pop-up menu on the palette, but the Blending Options make the layer's blending modes a lot more powerful. Blending Options are also great fun and extremely useful when you are trying to get that blending effect just right in your design.

Control-click (on the Mac) or right-click (in Windows) a layer and select Blending Options from the context menu to open the Layer Style dialog (see Figure 6.14). Although this dialog is the same as the one that opens when you select a layer style, choosing Blending Options from the left pane displays the Blending Options section at the top with the default settings.

These advanced blending options enable you to change the opacity and fill opacity for the blending modes (see Figure 6.15). You can also manipulate the two gradients at the bottom to control the blending for both the current layer and the layer underneath. Check the boxes for each of the channels to include or exclude those channels when the layer is blended. The Blend If drop-down menu enables you to blend specific channels. Changing the Blend If drop-down menu to Cyan in a CMYK image, for example, enables you to move the sliders in the gradient so that you can blend in more or fewer of the cyan pixels in the image.

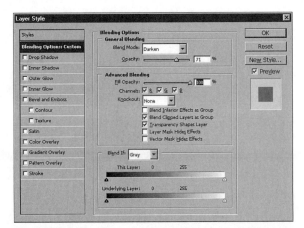

Figure 6.14
The Layer Style dialog doubles as the Blending Options dialog, with the default settings visible at the top.

Figure 6.15
Advanced blending options give you more control over blending modes.

Adjusting the Fill Opacity slider (or entering a percentage number in the numeric field) affects only the contents of the layer, not the layer styles applied to it. Notice how the stroke outline and drop shadow are still visible, but the layer content is totally transparent (see Figure 6.16).

Figure 6.16
Only the filled contents of a layer are affected by adjusting the Fill Opacity slider on the selected layer.

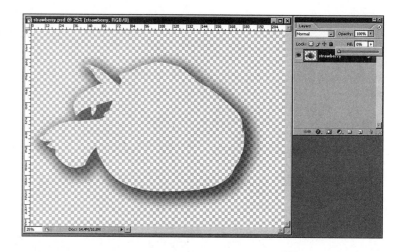

WORKING WITH PHOTOSHOP'S SPECIALTY LAYERS

In addition to layers that contain your artwork's pixels, Photoshop uses a number of other types of layers. Adjustment and fill layers change the appearance of regular layers below them without actually changing their pixels. Type layers contain any text you add to an image. As long as the type layer is not converted to a regular layer (using the Layer, Rasterize, Type command), the text remains editable and vector based for sharp output to PostScript devices. Shape layers, which simulate vector objects, are filled with a color, pattern, or gradient that is selectively exposed by using one or more vector paths.

Adjustment and Fill Layers

Using fill and adjustment layers over a regular layer enables you to create effects and color corrections nondestructively—no pixels are permanently changed. Fill layers can be added to create overall tonal shifting and colorization, patterns, and effects. Adjustment layers are used in place of the Image, Adjustment commands (which make permanent changes to the image). They affect all the layers beneath, not just the adjoining layer, so more layers can be affected globally by the placement of your adjustment layer. You can restrict the effect of an adjustment layer to the one layer immediately below it by Option-clicking (on the Mac) or Alt-clicking (in Windows) the line between the layer and the adjustment layer in the Layers palette. To create a fill layer, choose Layer, New Fill Layer and choose from the three types: Solid Color, Gradient, or Pattern. These fill layers are also available from the palette by clicking the black-and-white circle button on the Layers palette.

To create an adjustment layer, first start with an image. (*Hint:* Open a JPEG file of a photograph to see the difference adjustment layers can make.) Choose Layer, New Adjustment Layer and choose the Curves option. The Curves dialog appears for you to make some curves adjustments. After you make changes to the diagonal line in the Curves dialog, click OK. Your Curves adjustment layer is created. Notice that the small black-and-white circle icon appears on the left side of the adjustment layer. At any time, you can double-click this icon and open the Curves dialog to adjust the curves again. If you want to hide this adjustment, click the eye icon to turn off the visibility of the adjustment layer. Your original image layer is intact without change. The separate adjustment layer makes it easy to alter the look of your image without worrying about changing individual layers permanently.

The different types of adjustment layers are

- Levels
- Curves
- Color
- Balance
- Brightness/Contrast
- Hue/Saturation
- Selective Color
- Channel Mixer
- Gradient Map
- Photo Filter
- Invert
- Threshold
- Posterize

You can create multiple adjustment layers for an image layer to affect the layer in different ways. And you can create Adjustment Layers to affect multiple layers at the same time.

The nondestructive nature of adjustment and fill layers means you can experiment with an image until you're satisfied with the results, without actually changing the original image data or risking a burning contrast or oversaturation that can destroy an image. You can always remove or replace an adjustment layer later with no permanent effect to your image or a drastic increase in the image size. In addition, each adjustment can always be changed, so you can go back and tweak your layers again—you don't have to start over.

Two different context menus are used for the Type tool and type layers. When text is selected or the Type tool is being used to edit, the context menu contains font-related and editing options. To access commands that enable you to convert the layer to paths or a shape layer, as well as to access the commands for Check Spelling and Find/Replace, make sure that the type layer is active in the Layers palette *but no text is selected*. Then Control-click (on the Mac) or right-click (in Windows) directly on a character with the Type tool.

Type Layers

Type layers are created with the Type tool. Clicking in the canvas with the Type tool automatically creates a new layer that contains the vector-based type. The type's appearance is regulated through the Options bar and the Character and Paragraph palettes. You can rasterize type layers or convert them to shape layers that can be modified as paths. To rasterize the type layer, use the Layer, Rasterize, Type command or Control-click or right-click the layer and select Rasterize Layer from the context menu (see Figure 6.17).

6

Figure 6.17
A type layer shows a different
layer icon than a pixel or shape
layer.

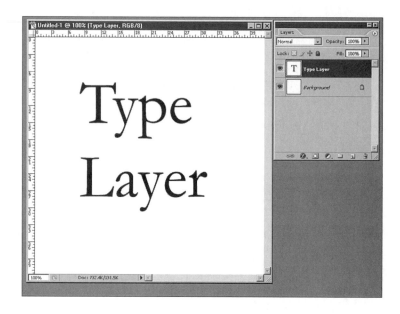

Figure 6.17
A type layer shows a different
layer icon than a pixel or shape
layer.

Shape Layers

Vector shape layers are layers that use vector masks on selective exposed parts of the layer. They can be filled with colors, patterns, or gradients. The exposed parts simulate vector objects and appear as artwork in your image. The individual path segments and anchor points of the vector mask can be edited with the Direct Selection and Path Selection tools and the various pen tools (see Figure 6.18). There are several ways to create shapes. Using one of the Shape tools nested in the toolbox, choose the Shape Layers button in the Options bar. Draw the shape in your canvas. The vector mask of the Shape layer is created using the current foreground color.

Figure 6.18
Two shape layers created in the
document. The different shape
tools visible in the toolbox and the
Custom Shape Picker reveal many
of the shapes available in the
library. In the Layers palette, the
Shape layers have been created as
vector masks.

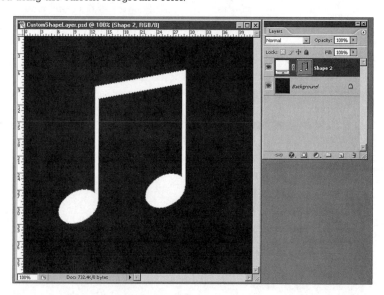

Using the Pen tool, you can create a Shape layer by changing the Pen's options in the Options bar. Click the Shape Layers button in the Options bar and create your vector shape layer (see Figure 6.19).

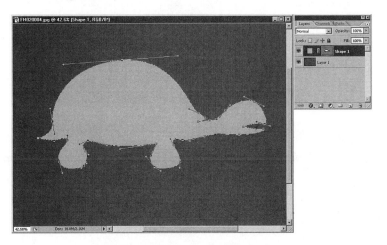

Figure 6.19
Use the Pen tool to create solid fill layers with a vector mask custom shape.

You can save custom shapes, whether created by converting a type layer or with the Pen tool, in the Custom Shapes Library. Use the Edit, Define Custom Shape command. You can later reuse these shapes with the Custom Shape tool by selecting them from the Custom Shape Picker.

TRANSFORMING LAYERS

When you *transform* a layer, you modify the position, scale, shape and even rotation of the layer. Transforming a layer is useful for changing the size or placement of a layer, as well as for adding perspective or distortion. You cannot apply the transformation process to the Background layer; you must convert that layer to a standard layer before you can transform it. To convert the background layer, double-click it in the Layers palette and rename it in the dialog that appears. Alternatively, duplicate the Background layer and transform the copy, leaving the original Background layer untouched. To transform layers, follow these steps:

1. Choose File, Open and select the file you want to modify.

2. Choose Window, Layers to open the Layers palette.

3. In the Layers palette, click the name of the layer you want to transform.

4. Choose Edit, Free Transform to begin the transformation process. A bounding box with handles at the sides and the corners surrounds the layer or the objects on the layer. To transform just a portion of a layer, select the area before choosing Free Transform so that the bounding box covers only the selected area (see Figure 6.20). Background areas left by the transformation will be transparent, enabling lower layers to show through.

Figure 6.20
Select a layer to transform.

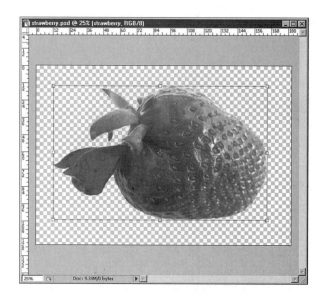

5. Apply any of the following transformations to the area in the bounding box:

- To move the bounding box, place the cursor inside it and drag.

- To scale the bounding box, click and drag a handle (use the Shift key to keep the original proportions).

- To rotate the bounding box, position the cursor outside it (until the cursor turns into a curved, two-headed arrow) and then drag.

- To distort freely, press and hold the ⌘ key or the Ctrl key and drag a handle. To skew, press and hold ⌘-Shift (on the Mac) or Ctrl+Shift (in Windows) and drag a side handle. Press Return or Enter to apply the effect.

You also can apply individual transformation options by choosing Edit, Transform and then choosing the transformation option you want from the submenu that appears. This approach limits the transformation to only the selected task, such as rotating or scaling. In addition, you can transform a layer with numeric precision by choosing Edit, Transform, Free Transform. In the Options bar, you can adjust the Position, Scale, Rotation, and Skew options. This approach is especially valuable when you have to repeat the same transformation across multiple unlinked layers.

USING LAYER COMPS

Layer comps are not actual layers at all. Rather, they are saved layer configurations that preserve the current layer order between all the layers in the Layers palette—as well as any existing settings for opacity, layer styles, and blending modes. Think of them as being similar to snapshots created from the History palette in that they preserve a specific image state that can be loaded and accessed at any time.

The Layer Comps feature is especially valuable for designers who create multilayered montage files with several layers of images, text, adjustments, and shapes. Design success often comes through experimentation because the designer shifts settings and layer order to modify the composite result. Layer comps give the designer the ability to preserve different design variations and access them with a single mouse click.

Layer comps are created and stored in a separate palette (the Layer Comps palette) that can be opened through the Window menu. To create a layer comp, start by creating a layer configuration as desired, combining layer order, styles, masks, and any other attributes. Click the Create New Layer Comp button at the bottom of the Layer Comp palette to open the Layer Comp Save dialog. Name the new Layer Comp, specify which characteristics should be preserved, and add comments about the current state if a description would be useful. Click OK and the Layer Comp is created, which now has the Layer Comps palette (see Figure 6.21). You can create and access multiple layer comps by clicking them in the Layer Comps palette. You can also click the forward and back arrows at the bottom of the palette to cycle through the list of layer comps.

Figure 6.21
Arrange your layer stack and set visibility options; then create a layer comp for quick viewing. The Layer Comp palette is especially useful for others to preview your design work.

As you can see, there is a lot of flexibility and control available when working in layers. Knowing which layer to work in and how your layers work is essential to understanding Photoshop. When you get used to working in layers, you will wonder how you could ever edit images without them.

6

7

USING SELECTIONS, PATHS, AND TRANSFORMS IN PHOTOSHOP

IN THIS CHAPTER

Selections are used to identify pixels that are to be the target of your editing. Selections are stored in masks, which can be used to create complex selections. Masks are also used to show and hide parts of a layer or an image. Photoshop has many tools and commands available for creating selections and masks.

Photoshop uses vector *paths* in a variety of ways, for a variety of purposes, including converting to selections. Paths are nonprinting, mathematical descriptions of lines and shapes, also called Bézier curves. They can be used to precisely define selections, create objects, and even be used to clip out portions of the image for page layout programs.

This chapter looks at how selections and paths work, as well as the tools and commands you use to make them and apply transformations to them.

TELLING PHOTOSHOP WHERE TO WORK

Whether it's deleting part of an image, adding color, or perhaps applying a filter, you need to let Photoshop know which pixels you want to change. Using a painting tool (or other tool that works with brushes), you select a brush and drag. The size, shape, and hardness of the brush, combined with the course along which the tool is dragged, control what happens.

When working with adjustments, filters, and many other menu commands, you must first identify the target area. You can, of course, apply a filter or other command to an entire layer. By not isolating a section of the layer, you have, in effect, identified where you want the filter to work: the entire layer. However, often you need to apply a filter to only a section of a layer. That's when you need to use selections and masks.

Defining Selections

Experienced Photoshop users understand that selections are critical to effective use of the program. Understanding the theory behind selections can be a key to mastering their application.

Consider a selection to be an area of an image that is activated, the part on which you're working. Pixels within the selection can be changed; those outside the selection are protected. Selections can be made with tools and commands, and you can also create selections from paths and masks.

Generally speaking, a pixel is either inside a selection or outside a selection. However, under a variety of circumstances, a pixel can be *partially selected*. Any filter or adjustment command applied to the selection is partially applied to any partially selected pixels—the filter or effect is applied with less intensity. Selections that are anti-aliased or feathered can have partially selected pixels along their edges. Selections made from masks can have up to 256 variations of a selected status among the pixels.

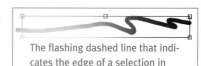

The flashing dashed line that indicates the edge of a selection in Photoshop is technically referred to as a *selection border*, *selection marquee*, or *selection edge*, but you are far more likely to hear the term *marching ants*.

As an example, consider two selections. One has no feathering or anti-aliasing: A pixel is either inside the selection or outside. The second selection has two pixels partially selected on either side of the line of selection. When the two selections are filled with black, there are two different results (see Figure 7.1).

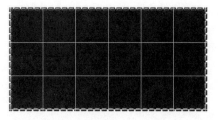

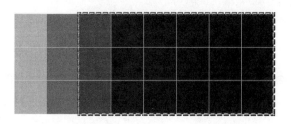

Figure 7.1
At the top, the black fill is consistent and stops at the edge of the selection. Below, the partially selected pixels get filled with black but are partially transparent.

When a selection is feathered, anti-aliased, or otherwise contains partially selected pixels, the selection marquee indicates which pixels are at least 50% selected. It is certainly possible to have selections that contain *only* pixels that are less than 50% selected. In such cases, the pixels are affected by whatever additional steps you take (fill, delete, filter, and so on), but the marching ants are not visible around those areas. Photoshop provides a warning when no selection border appears or when the feathering is so large that no selection is made at all (see Figure 7.2).

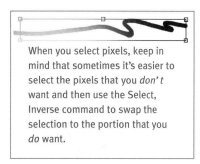

When you select pixels, keep in mind that sometimes it's easier to select the pixels that you *don't* want and then use the Select, Inverse command to swap the selection to the portion that you *do* want.

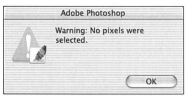

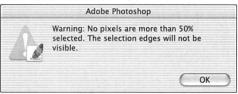

Figure 7.2
When pixels are less than 50% selected, the effect of a filter or an adjustment might be extremely subtle, but the command is executed nonetheless. If no selection is made, no pixels are changed.

Unmasking Masks

Just as a painter uses masking tape to protect parts of a surface and expose others, so, too, can you use *masks* in Photoshop. Masks are used to create and store selections. (Until a mask is loaded and used as a selection, it has no effect on the appearance of an image.)

7

Masks can be created from selections or created from scratch. In either case, masks are stored in *alpha channels*, which are grayscale representations of an image. The shades of gray determine levels of selection for individual pixels.

You can use painting tools, selection tools, and even adjustment commands and filters to alter masks. Virtually anything you can do with a grayscale image can be done with an alpha channel.

Photoshop also offers Quick Mask mode, which enables you to make a selection with all the flexibility of masks but without creating an additional channel.

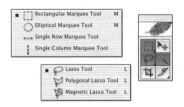

If one of the warnings shown in Figure 7.2 appears and you don't know why, take a look in the Options bar. Make sure your selection tool doesn't have some unwanted feathering.

WORKING WITH THE SELECTION TOOLS

Photoshop has a collection of tools used to make selections. As shown in Figure 7.3, there are eight primary selection tools: four Marquee selection tools, three Lasso tools, and the Magic Wand.

When creating a selection, remember that the Shift key can be used with selection tools to add to an existing selection. Likewise, the Option (on the Mac) or the Alt key (in Windows) can be used with a selection tool to subtract from an existing selection. When both modifier keys are used with a selection tool, anything outside the new selection border is deselected, and anything inside remains selected (see Figure 7.4).

Figure 7.3
Click and hold on an icon to show the tools on the fly-out palettes. Hold down the Shift key and use the keyboard shortcut shown in the fly-out to rotate among the related tools.

■ ⬚ Rectangular Marquee Tool	M	
○ Elliptical Marquee Tool	M	
⋯ Single Row Marquee Tool		
▯ Single Column Marquee Tool		

■ ⬭ Lasso Tool	L	
⬠ Polygonal Lasso Tool	L	
⬭ Magnetic Lasso Tool	L	

Figure 7.4
The Shift and Option (Mac users) or Alt (Windows users) keys are pressed down; therefore, when the mouse button is released, nothing outside the loop being dragged is selected. Within the loop, only what is already selected stays selected.

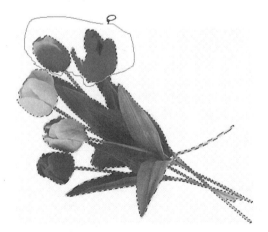

Using the Marquee Tools

Photoshop offers two major and two minor marquee selection tools. The Rectangular Marquee and Elliptical Marquee tools have several options and a great deal of flexibility. The Single Row Marquee and Single Column Marquee selection tools are one-trick ponies, with a specific job to do and few options.

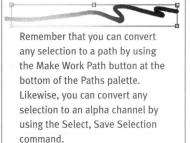

Remember that you can convert any selection to a path by using the Make Work Path button at the bottom of the Paths palette. Likewise, you can convert any selection to an alpha channel by using the Select, Save Selection command.

Using the Rectangular and Elliptical Marquee Selection Tools

The Rectangular Marquee tool is used to make rectangular and square selections. Its round counterpart, the Elliptical Marquee tool, creates oval and circular selections. To select squares and circles, respectively, hold down the Shift key while dragging. This constrains the selection to a 1:1 aspect ratio, forcing an identical width and height. You can also hold down the Option key (Mac users) or the Alt key (Windows users) to drag the selection from the center with either tool. The Options bar enables you to use the tools in several modes (see Figure 7.5).

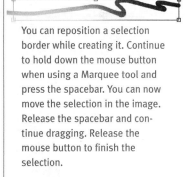

You can reposition a selection border while creating it. Continue to hold down the mouse button when using a Marquee tool and press the spacebar. You can now move the selection in the image. Release the spacebar and continue dragging. Release the mouse button to finish the selection.

In Normal mode, the tool can be dragged as you want, creating a selection of whatever proportions you desire. The Fixed Aspect Ratio option gives you the opportunity to establish a width-to-height ratio in the numeric fields to the right. A ratio of 1:1 creates a square (Rectangular Marquee) or a circle (Elliptical Marquee). You can specify any ratio, constraining the shape of the selection. When you use the Fixed Aspect Ratio option, no matter what size the marquee, the proportions remain the same. The button between the Width and Height fields swaps their values, offering a quick way to switch between landscape and portrait orientations.

The Fixed Size option not only restricts the selection to a set aspect ratio but also determines the selection's actual dimensions. Set the desired size in the Options bar and then click once with the selection tool. The selection is made to the lower right of the clicked point. The Options bar assumes the unit of measure specified in the Preferences dialog box. You can use another unit of measure by including the appropriate abbreviation in the fields of the Options bar. The button between Width and Height is also available in Fixed Size mode to swap the values in the two fields.

Figure 7.5
The pop-up menu is part of the Options bar when the Rectangular or Elliptical Marquee tool is active.

7

The Options bar also offers several other variables for the marquee selection tools. Normally, the tools are used to create a selection. If a selection already exists in the image, the tool can be set to add to, subtract from, or intersect with that selection (see Figure 7.6).

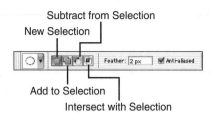

Subtract from Selection

New Selection

Add to Selection

Intersect with Selection

Figure 7.6
Feathering and the tool behavior options are the same for both the Rectangular Marquee tool and the Elliptical Marquee tool. With no active selection, the tools create a new selection with any of the four behaviors selected.

The Feather field enables you to specify how "soft" to make the edges of the selection. (Remember that feathering lessens the effect of whatever you do on the edges of a selection, whether it's adding a fill, deleting, or applying a filter or an adjustment.)

Feathering can be as high as 250 pixels and is always measured in pixels, regardless of the document's unit of measure. Keep in mind that feathering actually affects several times as many pixels as the number specified. To ensure that the effect appears seamless, a feather of 2 pixels actually affects a band that is approximately 10 pixels wide along the selection border.

In Figure 7.7, a square selection border is visible, measuring slightly more than 100 by 100 pixels. With feathering set to 50 pixels, the actual selection border when the mouse button

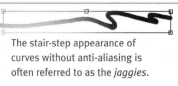

The Fixed Aspect Ratio option is invaluable in preparing images for Picture Package and other photograph printing. Dragging with a 5:7 or 4:6 aspect ratio ensures that the image can be properly cropped with the menu command Image, Crop.

is released is shown by the circular selection within. (Remember that the marching ants are drawn around pixels at least 50% selected.) When the heavily feathered selection is filled with white on a black background, the impact extends far beyond the selection border, as you can see.

Figure 7.7
The square selection border indicates where the Rectangular Marquee tool (set to Feather: 50 pixels) was dragged. The circular selection edges indicate pixels at least 50% selected. Filling with white affects pixels almost to the corners of the 300- by 300-pixel black square.

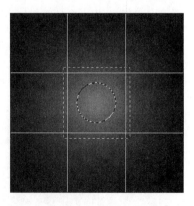

Anti-aliasing softens the edges of curves. It is not available for the Rectangular Marquee, the Single Row Marquee, and the Single Column Marquee selection tools because these tools make selections with straight edges. When an anti-aliased selection is filled with color or deleted, the appearance of the

The stair-step appearance of curves without anti-aliasing is often referred to as the *jaggies*.

7

edges is softened by using pixels that are intermediate in color between the selected area and the background. For example, filling an anti-aliased selection with black on a white background results in gray pixels to soften the curves (see Figure 7.8).

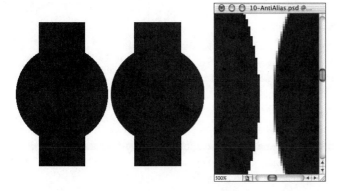

Figure 7.8
On the left, the selection was not anti-aliased. The selection on the right was. Both were filled with black. The inset shows a close-up comparison of the edges.

Notice, too, that the straight edges of the filled selections form perfect horizontal and vertical lines with and without anti-aliasing.

Selecting Single Rows and Columns

Photoshop offers two additional marquee selection tools: the Single Row Marquee and the Single Column Marquee. As their names indicate, they select a row or column of pixels exactly 1 pixel high or wide. The row or column extends from edge to edge of the image and is made at the point where you click the mouse.

These tools, set to Feather: 0, are excellent for creating grid lines 1 pixel thick. Click to place the first line and then fill with the foreground color. With the tool still selected and the selection still active, you can use the arrow keys (with or without the Shift key) to reposition the selection for the second line. Each line will be perfectly horizontal or vertical and exactly 1 pixel in width or height.

Although designed to work with 1-pixel selections, the Single Row and Single Column tools offer the option of feathering. Any feathering with these tools generates a warning that no pixels are more than 50% selected.

Making Irregularly Shaped Selections

The marquee selection tools are fine for making regularly shaped selections. However, they lack the kind of flexibility needed for many selection jobs. Photoshop's Lasso tools are designed to help you make irregular selections, with and without assistance.

The Lasso Tool

The Lasso tool itself is a freeform tool. Drag it in any shape or direction. When you release the mouse button, the selection is established. You need not move the mouse back to the point from which you started; the Lasso finishes a selection with a straight line from the point where you release the mouse button to the point where you started to drag.

7

Like the Marquee selection tools, the three Lasso tools offer buttons in the Options bar to make new selections or to have the tools add to, subtract from, or intersect with an existing selection. Anti-aliasing and feathering are also options for the Lasso tools.

The Polygonal Lasso Tool

The Polygonal Lasso tool is not a freeform tool. Rather than drag the tool, you click, move, click, move, click to establish a selection with straight sides. Although the edges of the selection are straight, they can be at any angle, not just horizontal and vertical. Using the anti-aliasing option can help prevent jaggies along angled edges.

To complete a selection with the Polygonal Lasso tool, position the tool over the start point and click. When the cursor is directly over the start point, a small circle appears to the lower right of the tool's icon. Alternatively, double-click or

Use the Option key (Mac users) or the Alt key (Windows users) to switch between the Lasso tool and the Polygonal Lasso tool on the fly. While dragging the Lasso, hold down the modifier key and click-move-click to place straight selection edges. When working with the Polygonal Lasso tool, hold down the key and drag to make freeform selections.

press the Return or Enter key to complete the selection with a straight segment from the cursor's location to the selection start point. Use ⌘-click (on the Mac) or Ctrl-click (in Windows) to do the same. Press the Esc key to leave the selection process before a selection is complete.

The Magnetic Lasso Tool

The third Lasso tool is a bit more complex. The Magnetic Lasso tool attempts to follow existing edges in an image to make a selection. Using contrast to identify edges, the Magnetic Lasso is best suited for use on images that have uncomplicated backgrounds (see Figure 7.9).

Figure 7.9
This image is a perfect candidate for the Magnetic Lasso tool because of the strong contrast between the foreground and background.

While working, the Magnetic Lasso tool places a series of temporary anchor points as it follows the path you trace. (Note that the tool does not create a path; the anchor points disappear when the selection is completed.) Double-clicking, clicking the start point, and pressing the Return or Enter key all close the selection.

As you move the mouse (or drag it), you can click the mouse button to place anchor points manually at spots where the edge you're tracing takes a sharp turn. If the tool places an anchor point in an incorrect location, press the Delete key (on the Mac) or the Backspace key (in Windows) to remove it. You can also back up along the edge to retrace a segment.

In addition to the options common to all three lasso tools, the Magnetic Lasso tool has four options of its own (see Figure 7.10).

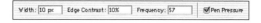

Figure 7.10
The first three of these four options are unique to the Magnetic Lasso tool.

Width determines the Magnetic Lasso's search area. It is always measured in pixels and can range from 1 to 256. It follows the line of pixels with the highest contrast within this radius. If the image has few edges, a high Width setting enables you to move quickly and requires less precision. If there are multiple areas of contrast closely placed in the image, a lower width is required, forcing you to keep the cursor precisely along the desired edge. When Photoshop's Preferences are set to Precise for Other Cursors, the width is displayed as a circle around the tool's crosshair. If you see the tool's icon as the cursor, you need not change the Preferences. Before you start working with the tool, press the Caps Lock key to show the width cursor.

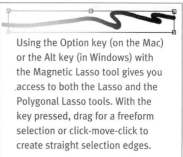

Using the Option key (on the Mac) or the Alt key (in Windows) with the Magnetic Lasso tool gives you access to both the Lasso and the Polygonal Lasso tools. With the key pressed, drag for a freeform selection or click-move-click to create straight selection edges.

Edge Contrast can be considered the sensitivity setting for the Magnetic Lasso tool. It ranges from 1% to 100%. Lower values reduce the amount of contrast required to define an edge. However, that can also lead to the selection border being placed along false edges—areas where a texture or shadow/highlight create contrast. Likewise, too high a setting might lead to the tool not finding any edge at all and a very confused selection border.

Frequency determines the automatic placement of anchor points as you drag. Ranging from 0% to 100%, the higher numbers produce more anchor points. Remember that you can manually add anchor points by clicking.

You can change the Width setting for the Magnetic Lasso on the fly. Think of it as a brush size. The left and right bracket keys increase and decrease the width by 1 pixel. Add the Shift key to jump to the maximum (256 pixels) and minimum (1 pixel) widths.

The Pen Pressure check box is used with pressure-sensitive tablets, such as those from Wacom. Increased pressure on the tablet constricts the tool's width, and lighter pressure results in a higher Width setting. The width varies from twice the value in the Options Bar (very light pressure) to 1 (very hard pressure).

Using the Magic Wand Tool

Designed to select similar colors throughout an image, the Magic Wand enables you to specify a *tolerance* (the range of sensitivity) and click on a sample. Pixels similar in color to that on which you clicked will be selected. Depending on choices in the Options bar, you can restrict the Magic Wand to the active layer or use all visible layers. (Although the check box is labeled Use All Layers, hidden layers are excluded.) The Magic Wand can also create a selection of all similar pixels throughout the image or only those similar pixels contiguous to the pixel you click.

When Contiguous is selected in the Options bar, clicking selects only pixels that adjoin pixels of the selected color. If pixels of another color are between the clicked pixel and similarly colored pixels, those pixels are not selected (see Figure 7.11).

Because the Magic Wand selects in a range that extends to both the high and low, you should click a pixel that's in the midtones of the color you want to select.

Figure 7.11
To the left, the Magic Wand was set to Contiguous-only—similarly colored pixels adjacent to the clicked pixel are selected. On the right, Contiguous was not selected—all similarly colored pixels throughout the image were selected.

You can Shift-click with the Magic Wand to add to a selection and Option-click (on the Mac) or Alt-click (in Windows) to subtract from a selection. The Options bar also enables you to set the tool to add to or subtract from a selection. The tolerance can be changed between clicks as well.

Removing a White Background

There are a number of ways to extract a subject from a plain white background. One of the simplest uses the Magic Wand:

1. Go to the Photoshop folder on your hard drive and then to the Samples folder, and open the image `Ducky.tif`.

2. In the Layers palette, double-click the layer Background and rename it **Layer 0**. (Background layers don't support transparency.)

3. Click the New Layer button at the bottom of the Layers palette.

4. Drag the new layer below Layer 0 in the Layers palette.

When you select a uniformly colored background for deletion or want to extract an image, it's usually a good idea to use the Select, Modify, Expand command with a setting of 1 or 2 pixels. This helps eliminate any fringe or halo from anti-aliasing.

5. Press D on the keyboard to restore your colors to black and white; then press Option-Delete (Mac users) or Alt+Backspace (Windows users) to fill the layer with the foreground color (black).

6. In the Layers palette, click Layer 0 (the Ducky layer) to make it active.

7. Select the Magic Wand in the Toolbox. The default settings in the Options Bar are fine. If necessary, restore the defaults by Control-clicking (on the Mac) or right-clicking (in Windows) the Magic Wand icon at the left end of the Options bar and selecting Reset Tool.

8. Click once anywhere in the white background of Layer 0. Note that because Contiguous is selected in the Options bar, the whites of the eyes are not selected.

9. Press the Delete key (on the Mac) or the Backspace key (in Windows) to remove the white background. Your results should be similar to those shown in Figure 7.12.

Figure 7.12
The default settings for the Magic Wand produce a fringe-free extraction from the uniform white background of this image.

Making Selections from Paths

Paths can be used to create extremely precise selections. Any path, including work paths and those created with Photoshop's shape tools, can be used to create selections. With the path selected in the Paths palette, either click the Load Path as a Selection button at the bottom of the palette or use the Paths palette menu command Make Selection (see Figure 7.13).

You can also ⌘-click (on the Mac) or Ctrl-click (in Windows) a path in the Paths palette to load it as a selection. Adding the Shift and Option key (Mac users) or Alt key (Windows users) adds the path to or subtracts the path from an active selection.

When you choose the Make Selection command, you're presented with the Make Selection dialog box. If a selection is already active in the image, you can add to, subtract from, intersect with, or replace the selection (see Figure 7.14). You also can specify feathering and choose or forgo anti-aliasing.

7

Figure 7.13
Simply clicking the button makes an active selection from the path; the menu command opens a dialog box.

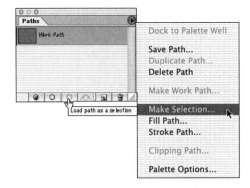

Figure 7.14
The Make Selection dialog box can also be opened by Option-clicking (Mac users) or Alt-clicking (Windows users) the Load Path as a Selection button at the bottom of the Paths palette.

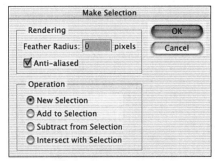

WORKING WITH SELECTION COMMANDS

Photoshop's Select menu includes commands in five basic categories (see Figure 7.15). The commands All, Deselect, Reselect, and Inverse can be thought of as the *macro commands*—they work on a large scale. In contrast, the modification commands (Feather, Modify, Grow, and Similar) can be considered the *micro commands*—they fine-tune or adjust an existing selection.

Transform Selection also modifies an existing selection, but it does so on the basis of selection shape rather than content. Selections can be saved as alpha channels (masks) and loaded later. This method is especially useful for protecting the work that went into a complex selection and for modifying a selection as a mask.

Figure 7.15
Although this image shows no commands grayed out for illustrative purposes, not all commands are available at the same time. For example, the command Reselect is grayed out when there is an active selection, so it can't be available at the same time as Deselect.

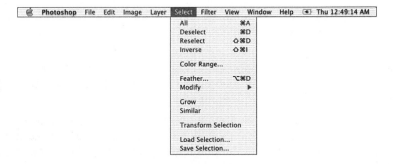

The Color Range command is also a macro selection command, but it's far more complex than simply selecting all or deselecting. It offers the capability of selecting based on one or more colors within an image.

Using the Basic Selection Commands

The four basic selection commands are rather simple in nature. Select, All makes a selection of the entire active layer. If the layer contains transparency, the transparent pixels are selected with the others. If you press Option-Delete (on the Mac) or Alt+Backspace (in Windows) next, the entire layer is filled with the foreground color.

Deselect does exactly what you would expect from the name. It is available only when there is an active selection in the image. After you use this command, no pixels in the image are selected.

Reselect is extremely useful for those occasions, among others, when an unintended click inadvertently deselects. Although you can use the Undo command immediately after deselecting to restore the selection, Reselect is available until another selection is made or the image is closed (or the history purged).

Select, Inverse reverses an active selection—pixels that were selected are now deselected, and pixels that were not selected are now selected. Inverse also recognizes anti-aliasing, feathering, and other partially selected pixels. If, for example, you load a mask containing pixels selected at 25%, Inverse switches them to 75% selected.

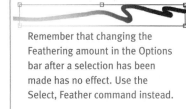

Remember that changing the Feathering amount in the Options bar after a selection has been made has no effect. Use the Select, Feather command instead.

Modifying Existing Selections with Commands

The Select menu offers a number of commands that enable you to modify an existing selection. Feathering softens the edges of a selection, which results in a reduced effect on those pixels. Whether deleting, filling, filtering, or adjusting, you can use feathering to produce a subtle transition between those pixels 100% affected by the command or tool and those pixels that are unaffected. Selecting this command opens a dialog box in which you enter the amount of feathering, which is always measured in pixels.

The Modify commands, accessed through the Modify submenu of the Select menu, are rather clumsy tools and are best applied using very small pixel values. Like Feather, they open dialog boxes into which you enter a value in pixels.

Border

The Border command creates a new selection and discards the original selection. The new selection is centered on the original selection border, with or without anti-aliasing and feathering, at the width specified in the Border dialog box. That width, however, extends both inward and outward from the original selection border, so the term *width* is somewhat misleading. The affected area is actually twice the Width value.

The selection created by Border is feathered. Only the two pixels immediately on either side of the original selection border are 100% selected, with the balance of the width tapering to 0% selected. If,

7

for example, you drag a square selection with the Rectangular Marquee tool, use Border with a Width value of 10, and then press (Option-Delete) [Alt+Backspace] to fill with the foreground color, you do not get a beautiful frame around the original selection. Instead, you see a line of color that fades inward and outward, with angled corners rather than square.

Smooth

The Smooth command is designed to eliminate jagged edges in selections. It uses the pixel value you enter into the Sample Radius field to see which pixels should be included in the active selection. It rounds the corners of a rectangular or angular selection.

The Smooth command can be used effectively with the Magic Wand tool and the Color Range command. If your initial selection has numerous unselected pixels scattered around within it, try Smooth set to 1 or 2 pixels.

Expand

You can move a selection border outward by as much as 100 pixels by using the Expand command. However, any rectangular corners in the original selection become angles (and the angles are rounded) when a selection is greatly expanded. The number of pixels you enter into the Expand By field can be considered a radius from the center rather than a linear measure from the selection border.

The Expand command can be very effective in eliminating a halo. When a background is selected for deletion, expanding by 1 or 2 pixels can eliminate any fringe pixels.

Instead of using Border to create a frame, consider using the menu command Edit, Stroke. If the pixels to be framed are on a separate layer, select Layer Style, Stroke for an even better alternative.

Contract

The Contract command brings in a selection border toward its center. If the active selection consists of a variety of discrete areas, each is contracted individually. Just as Expand can help eliminate a fringe when a *background* is selected, Contract helps eliminate a fringe when a *foreground* is selected.

Caution

If all or part of a selection extends to the edge of the canvas, neither Expand nor Contract is effective along that edge. A selection cannot be expanded beyond the edge of the canvas, and any part of a selection border on the edge is not affected by the Contract command.

Other Selection Commands

In addition to the commands under the Modify submenu, Photoshop's Select menu offers the Grow and Similar commands. Grow searches for and adds to the active selection any pixels of a similar color to those already selected. The command uses the Tolerance value set for the Magic Wand tool. Only adjacent pixels are considered for inclusion in the selection. The Grow command can be applied multiple times to achieve a desired selection.

The Similar command is identical to Grow with one exception: The pixels need not be contiguous. All similarly colored pixels in an image are included in the selection, regardless of their location in the image. Use Similar to select a color throughout an image.

Transforming Selections

An active selection can be scaled, rotated, skewed and distorted by using the Select, Transform Selection command. A bounding box is created around the active selection (see Figure 7.16).

Figure 7.16
The bounding box originates as a rectangle surrounding the selection. You can manipulate it in a variety of ways with the cursor and modifier keys.

You can drag within the bounding box to move the selection, drag an anchor point to scale, Option-drag (on the Mac) or Alt-drag (in Windows) to scale from the center, and Shift-drag to scale proportionally. Adding the ⌘ key (Mac users) or Ctrl key (Windows users) enables you to skew, distort, or add perspective to a transformation. The Options bar is also available for numeric transformations.

After manipulating the selection boundary, you can accept the changes by clicking the check mark icon in the Options bar, double-clicking within the selection, or using the Return or Enter key. The Esc key cancels a transformation.

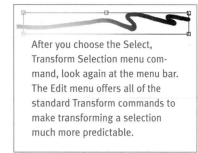

After you choose the Select, Transform Selection menu command, look again at the menu bar. The Edit menu offers all of the standard Transform commands to make transforming a selection much more predictable.

Warping Selections

With Photoshop's new Warp feature, you can warp the area of your selection. You can also warp a path. Make a selection with one of the lasso or marquee tools. To warp a selection, choose Select, Transform Selection. Then immediately choose Edit, Transform, Warp. Just as you can warp part of an image, you can drag the warp mesh or the control points to warp the selection (see Figure 7.17).

When you warp part of your image, you are given a grid that you can click within, drag, and reshape. Grab the control points and the handles to warp your image from the outside. You can warp a path, subpath (a portion of the path), or shape layer the same way. Reshape your pixels or paths considerably using the Warp feature.

7

Figure 7.17
In the same way you can warp a pixel image and a vector path using the Warp feature, you can transform and warp a selection.

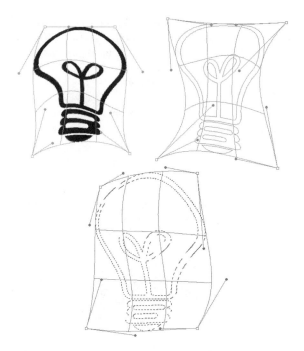

Saving and Loading Selections

Any selection that takes more than a couple of keystrokes and a drag to create is worth saving. Re-creating a selection might not produce the exact results. It could also be time consuming. Photoshop has the capability to store any selection as an alpha channel—a mask—that can be reloaded at will.

The menu commands Save Selection and Load Selection enable you to create an alpha channel from a selection and to load that channel as a selection.

Selection Tips

Accurate selections, with appropriate feathering or anti-aliasing, can make or break a project. Quick and efficient selection can make or break deadlines. Here are some tips that can improve your selection procedures:

- Open the Channels palette and look at each color channel individually. Your intended selection area may stand out in better contrast on one layer or another. Working with just that layer active improves the performance of the Magic Wand, Color Range, or Magnetic Lasso. After creating the selection, remember to make the composite channel active again in the Channels palette.

- The Filter, Extract command provides an automated way of creating a selection and deleting the inverse, all-in-one step. You can use the command to make a selection, too. Duplicate the target layer and hide all other layers. Use Extract on the duplicate layer. Click once in the now-transparent background with the Magic Wand. Delete that layer and restore the visibility of others. To finish selecting the subject, use the menu command Select, Inverse.

7

- If you do a lot of complex selecting that involves hair, fur, glass, clouds, fabric, and the like, you might be best served by a special-purpose plug-in or program. Mask Pro from Extensis and KnockOut from Corel are two such choices. They are far more capable of making selections of wispy hair, semitransparent objects, and other difficult subjects.

- When a subject has been removed from a background and your selection wasn't perfect, you might see a halo around the edges. The command Layer, Matting, Defringe can be used to clean up the selection. Photoshop searches along edges within the specified width to remove remnants of the background color.

- Showing the grid and/or guides and turning on snapping for the grid and the guides can give you an added level of precision when working with selection tools.

- A selection can be dragged from one open document to another. You can copy your document, use Levels or Curves to create extreme contrast, make a selection, and then drag that selection back to the original document. With a selection active, use any selection tool to drag from one window to the other.

- When you have a selected area you want to make a copy of, instead of going through steps to create a new layer, choose the Move tool. Click in the selection holding down the Option key (Mac users) or the Alt key (Windows users). Your selection areas are duplicated in a new layer.

UNDERSTANDING ALPHA CHANNELS AND MASKS

Alpha channels are channels in the image that store transparency information in the form of masks. You can use alpha channels to show and hide particular parts of the image without erasing the image itself.

Basic Alpha Channel Creation

The easiest way to create an alpha channel to store a selection in is to make the selection first. With any selection active in the image, use the menu command Select, Save Selection to open the Save Selection dialog box (see Figure 7.18).

The Document pop-up menu lists all files open in Photoshop that have *exactly* the same pixel dimensions; it also includes the option to create a new document. (Open files that are a different size than the document in which you made the selection do not appear in the list.) Selecting New creates a new document with the same dimensions and resolution as the original. The document consists of only the single alpha channel and is in Multichannel mode. Although the new image contains no color channels and holds only the saved selection, you can convert the document to any color mode (after first converting it to Grayscale). The name selected in the Save Selection dialog box is applied to the channel, not to the new document.

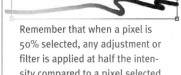

Remember that when a pixel is 50% selected, any adjustment or filter is applied at half the intensity compared to a pixel selected at 100%. This behavior also holds true for deleting, painting, and other steps performed on a selection.

7

The Channel pop-up menu lists all available alpha channels in the image selected in the Document field. You can create a new channel or add to, subtract from, or intersect with an existing alpha channel. When you're working with an existing channel, the Name field is grayed out.

Figure 7.18
The Destination area of the dialog box is where you choose both the document and the channel in which to save the selection. You can also select a name when creating a new channel.

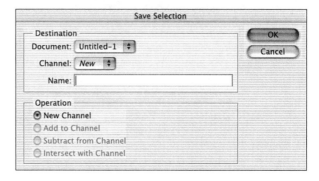

With a selection active in the image, you can also create a new alpha channel through the Channels palette (see Figure 7.19). Clicking the Save Selection as Channel button at the bottom of the palette creates a new alpha channel and bypasses the Save Selection dialog box. (The new channel is named Alpha 1 or the next available number.)

Figure 7.19
A new channel added with the Save Selection as Channel button can be renamed by double-clicking the name in the Channels palette.

The third technique for adding an alpha channel from an existing selection is through the Channels palette menu. Select the command New Channel (not New Spot Channel). You have an opportunity to name the channel and decide the channel's options (see Figure 7.20).

Figure 7.20
The Color Indicates and Color options determine the appearance of the mask when it is activated over one or more channels.

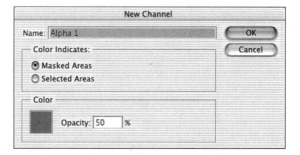

Quick Mask Mode

Photoshop offers a convenient way to edit selections through the use of masks—without ever having to look at the Channels palette. Quick Mask mode takes you directly to a red overlay that is active and ready to be edited as an alpha channel. Simply press Q on the keyboard or click the button in the Toolbox to enter Quick Mask mode (see Figure 7.21). After editing the mask, press Q again or click the opposite button to exit Quick Mask mode.

When you're in Quick Mask mode, a temporary channel is created in the Channels palette. Just as a work path disappears when it's no longer needed, so, too, is a quick mask deleted when you exit Quick Mask mode. After you exit Quick Mask mode, a selection is active in the image, and you can, of course, save that selection as a regular alpha channel.

In terms of the actual content of a newly created alpha channel, there is no difference among the Select, Save Selection menu command, the Channels palette Save Selection as Channel button, and the palette menu command New Channel. Each generates the same channel from the same selection.

In Quick Mask mode, the Channels palette menu also offers the Quick Mask Options command. You can change the overlay's opacity or color and even decide whether it shows or hides the masked areas. You can also open the dialog box by double-clicking the Quick Mask button in the Toolbox.

Figure 7.21
The button to the left of the cursor returns you to Standard mode.

Alpha Channels and File Formats

Alpha channels can be stored in several file formats. Photoshop's native format (PSD) supports multiple alpha channels, as does Photoshop's large image format (PSB). TIFF images in RGB or CMYK mode can support multiple alpha channels, as can PDF files created in Photoshop. The RAW file

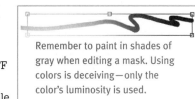

Remember to paint in shades of gray when editing a mask. Using colors is deceiving—only the color's luminosity is used.

7

format can support numerous channels, but it can present problems of its own. For example, when reopening a RAW file, you must know the exact dimensions of the image, the correct number of channels, and whether the color data was interleaved when saved.

A single alpha channel can be saved with BMP, PICT, and Pixar files. The PNG-24 file format can generate an alpha channel to store transparency in an image, but that information cannot be accessed directly or edited. Rather, it is updated if you change the transparency of the image.

PATHS: WORKING WITH VECTORS IN PHOTOSHOP

Photoshop is primarily a raster image-editing program, designed to work with the pixels that make up a digital image. However, it does offer some rather powerful vector capabilities. Vector type, clipping masks, vector masks for layers, and Photoshop's shape layers are examples of vectors in raster images.

Vector artwork is based on paths that are recorded in a file as mathematical descriptions. The advantage of vectors is that artwork can be scaled to any size without loss of quality. Raster images, in contrast, can be drastically degraded when scaled either up or down. What this means is the work paths you draw can be scaled as large or small as you like within the bitmap image. If you are making use of a lot of shapes, scaling them may be necessary from time to time.

The Many Faces of Paths

Vector paths in Photoshop can exist independent of a layer, or they can be tied to a layer to create artwork. Vector type layers, for example, must contain nothing but the vector type (keeping in mind that any path on which you place type is independent of the layer). Likewise, shape layers can have no other artwork unless the layer is rasterized. Paths not used directly to create vector shapes or type can be used to create selections or masks for layers and can be stroked or filled.

Photoshop can use vector paths in a variety of ways:

- **Type layers:** Although you can't edit the paths directly, type on a type layer consists of filled vector paths. (However, don't overlook the command Layer, Type, Create Work Path. It creates editable paths from the letters.) Photoshop CS2 can also use paths to bend and warp type baselines.

- **Shape layers:** Photoshop's shape layers are actually layers filled with color, a gradient, or a pattern and selectively exposed using vector masks. When a shape layer is selected in the Layers palette, the path is visible (and selectable) in the Paths palette. When the layer is not active, its path is not visible in the Paths palette.

- **Clipping paths:** The term *clipping path* describes those vector paths that determine areas of visibility for raster images placed into page layout documents. (*Clipping path* and *clipping mask* were also used in earlier versions of Photoshop as the names for paths used to show/hide areas of a layer. The term *vector mask* is now used.) When placing a raster image in a page layout program, you can use a clipping path to selectively hide the background (see Figure 7.22).

- **Vector mask:** Paths can be used to selectively show and hide areas on a layer, much as a clipping path is used for an image as a whole.

- **Selection definition:** A path can be used to precisely define a selection in Photoshop. The Paths palette offers a button that converts any selected path to a selection.

- **Stroke and fill:** Using the Paths palette menu, you can place color along an active path. Consider the Stroke and Fill commands to be ways to precisely control a painting tool. Remember that unlike true vector objects, if you stroke and/or fill a path and then move the path, the colored pixels remain behind. A path retains no connection to a stroke or fill in Photoshop.

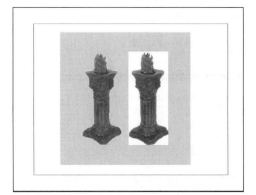

Figure 7.22
The left image was placed into a page layout document with a clipping path. To the right, the same image was placed without a clipping path.

Creating Paths in Photoshop

Paths can be created in a variety of ways. The Pen tools can be used to create paths from scratch, selections can form the basis of paths, shape layers are created with paths, and type can be converted to paths. Photoshop uses the Paths palette to manage paths.

A path is called a *work path* until saved. There can be only one work path at a time. With a work path selected in the Paths palette, you continue to add subpaths. If the existing work path is *not* active in the Paths palette when you begin to create a new path, it is replaced by the new path (which then assumes the name Work Path). The prior work path is lost. Renaming a work path saves it. You can change the name by double-clicking Work Path in the Paths palette and overtyping or by using the Paths palette menu command Save Path.

Remember that when a path is active in the Paths palette, creating another path with the Pen tool adds a subpath. Converting a selection into a path replaces an existing work path or, if the active path has been saved, starts a new work path.

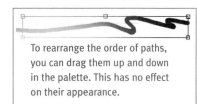

To rearrange the order of paths, you can drag them up and down in the palette. This has no effect on their appearance.

Using the Paths Palette

The appearance of a path's name in the Paths palette gives you a good indication of what type of path it is. The palette also offers several buttons for use with paths (see Figure 7.23).

The Paths palette menu offers commands to create a new path or new work path; to duplicate, delete, fill, and stroke a selected path; and to convert a path to a selection or a clipping path. When

7

a work path is selected in the palette, you can also use a menu command to save it, which opens a dialog box in which you can assign a name. However, you can achieve the same result by double-clicking Work Path in the Paths palette and typing a new name.

Figure 7.23
The Shape 1 Vector Mask path and the Layer 1 Vector Mask path would not normally be visible at the same time—only one layer can be active, and an inactive layer's vector mask is not shown in the palette.

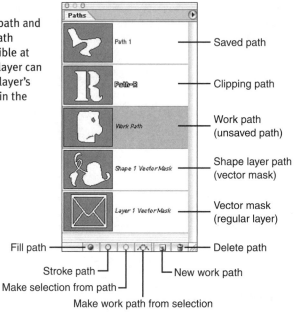

Saved path

Clipping path

Work path
(unsaved path)

Shape layer path
(vector mask)

Vector mask
(regular layer)

Fill path

Delete path

Stroke path

New work path

Make selection from path

Make work path from selection

Using the Pen Tool

The Pen tool enables you to place each anchor point individually as you work, deciding between corner and smooth points on the fly.

You should remember a few basic concepts when working with the Pen tool:

- To place a corner anchor point with the Pen tool, simply click.

- To create a smooth point, click and drag. The direction and distance dragged set the anchor point's direction line and determine the appearance of the curved path segment.

- To close a path, click (or click and drag) the first end point. The Pen tool cursor shows a small circle to the lower right when it's directly over the path's start point. Clicking elsewhere with the Pen tool then starts a new subpath.

- To end an open path, either switch tools or ⌘-click (Mac users) or Ctrl-click (Windows users) away from the open path.

- To add to an existing open path, select the path in the Paths palette, click once with the Pen tool on an end point, and then continue creating anchor points.

Creating a path with the Pen tool can be as simple as clicking in two different locations—a straight path segment is created between the points. More complex paths can be created by clicking and dragging. The key to creating paths with the Pen tool is understanding how dragging affects curved path segments. In Figure 7.24, four paths were created by clicking and dragging with the Pen tool. In each case, the Pen was clicked and dragged straight down to form the left anchor point.

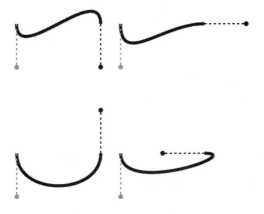

Figure 7.24
The dashed lines show the direction and distance of drag for each anchor point. Note that the left points for each of the path segments were created with identical drags.

The only difference among the four path segments shown in Figure 7.24 is the direction in which the Pen tool was dragged when creating the anchor point on the right side. (The distance is identical in each case.)

The multiple-segment paths shown in Figure 7.25 illustrate the difference between dragging in opposite directions at each end of a path segment and dragging in the same direction. In the line shown at the left of the figure, each anchor point was created by dragging the Pen tool in the same direction. The second path was created by dragging in alternating directions. However, as you can see in the pair of lines on the right side of the figure, the actual direction lines for the anchor points between path segments look identical.

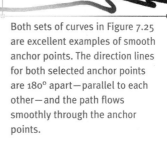

Both sets of curves in Figure 7.25 are excellent examples of smooth anchor points. The direction lines for both selected anchor points are 180° apart—parallel to each other—and the path flows smoothly through the anchor points.

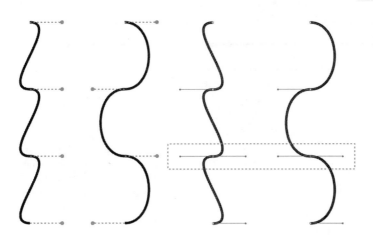

Figure 7.25
In the pair of images on the left, the dashed lines show the direction and distance of drag for each anchor point. The pair on the right show the direction lines for the anchor points.

7

Note on the right of Figure 7.25 that, although only the two anchor points within the dashed box are selected (their squares are filled), one direction line for each of the neighboring points is visible. Even though those neighboring points aren't selected, the direction line for the path segment bordering the selected anchor point is available. This enables you to use the Direct Selection tool to modify the path segments from either end.

Understanding Pen Tool Options

When the Pen tool is active, the left part of Photoshop's Options bar offers you the choice of creating a work path or a shape layer (see Figure 7.26). (The option to create an area filled with the foreground color isn't available with the Pen tool.) You can also easily switch to the Freeform Pen tool or any of the Shape tools.

> When paths are placed close together, disabling Auto Add/Delete can make it easier to start a new subpath. Enabling the option in other situations can save you time switching tools.

When set to create a work path and a path is active in the Paths palette, the right side of the Options bar offers several different behaviors for a new subpath. You can add to, subtract from, intersect with, or exclude overlapping areas. The icons in the Options bar show the differences.

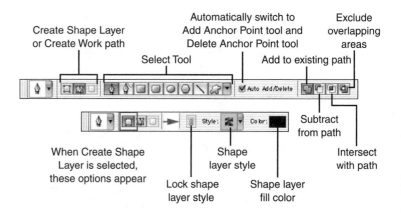

Create Shape Layer or Create Work path

Select Tool

Automatically switch to Add Anchor Point tool and Delete Anchor Point tool

Add to existing path

Exclude overlapping areas

Figure 7.26
The Options bar differs, depending on whether Create Shape Layer or Create Work Path is selected.

When Create Shape Layer is selected, these options appear

Lock shape layer style

Shape layer style

Shape layer fill color

Subtract from path

Intersect with path

Selecting the Auto Add/Delete check box in the Options Bar enables the Pen tool to change to the Add Anchor Point and Delete Anchor Point tools automatically. If this option is selected and the Pen tool is positioned over a path segment, it automatically prepares to add an anchor point when you click with the tool. When this option is activated and the tool is positioned over an existing anchor point, it can be used to delete the point.

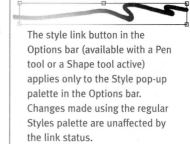

> The style link button in the Options bar (available with a Pen tool or a Shape tool active) applies only to the Style pop-up palette in the Options bar. Changes made using the regular Styles palette are unaffected by the link status.

When the Pen tool is set to create or edit shape layers, additional options enable you to apply a style and color directly in the Options bar. You notice a link icon to the left of the Style example in the Options bar. When a style is selected, using the Style Link button links the Style pop-up palette to the active layer. Changes made to the style through the pop-up palette in the Options bar are applied to the active layer. When the link is not selected, changes to the style made in the Options bar do not affect the active layer.

Clicking the down arrow to the right of the shape tools in the Options bar exposes some additional tool-related options. For the Pen tool, you have the Rubber Band check box. With Rubber Band activated, the Pen tool previews the path that will be created by tracking the cursor's movement with the mouse button up. Without Rubber Band, you won't see the path until you click and drag. Additional options for the Freeform Pen tool are discussed in the following section.

Using the Other Pen Tools

In addition to the Pen tool, Photoshop offers the Freeform Pen, Add Anchor Point, Delete Anchor Point, and Convert Point tools. The Freeform Pen tool can be used to drag a path, much like using the Pencil or Brush tool. You don't have to click to add anchor points, however; the points are added automatically as you drag. (You can also add an anchor point to the path manually by clicking.) How closely the path follows the cursor's movement is a function of the additional tool options (accessed through the arrow to the right of the shape tool icons in the Options bar). The default Curve Fit setting of 2 pixels is usually a good balance between path accuracy and complexity. Higher numbers (to a maximum of 10 pixels) reduce the number of anchor points, but accuracy can suffer (see Figure 7.27).

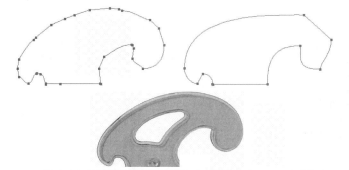

Figure 7.27
The image at the bottom was traced with the Freeform Pen tool twice. On the left, Curve Fit was set to 2 pixels. On the right, the setting was 10 pixels.

The Magnetic option for the Freeform Pen tool enables it to follow edges. It uses contrast to determine where an edge exists. The Magnetic option is best suited for use on images with plain backgrounds.

When working with the Magnetic option, the Freeform Pen places a series of anchor points as it follows the path you trace. As you drag, you can click the mouse button to place anchor points at spots where the edge you're tracing takes a sharp turn. If the tool places an anchor point in an incorrect location, press the Delete key (Mac users) or the Backspace key (Windows users) to remove it. You can also back up along the edge to retrace a segment. Clicking the start point closes the path. Double-click the tool and it attempts to follow the nearest edge back to the start point. Pressing the Return or Enter key finishes the path and leaves it as an open path.

7

With the Freeform Pen tool selected, click the arrow to the right of the shapes in the Options bar to set the Magnetic option's behavior. Width determines the radius within which the tool searches for an edge to follow. Contrast, measured in percent, governs how different the pixel color must be to constitute an edge. Frequency controls how often an anchor point is placed as you drag.

With an existing path selected in the image, the Add Anchor Point tool enables you to add both corner (click) and smooth (drag) anchor points to the path. Similarly, the Delete Anchor Point tool removes existing anchor points from a selected path when you click them. You can use the Convert Point tool to change a smooth anchor point to a corner point (by clicking it) or to convert a corner point to a smooth point (by clicking the point and dragging).

The Option key (Mac users) or Alt key (Windows users) converts the Pen tool to the Convert Point tool when the cursor is over an anchor point. You can use it to convert corner anchor points to smooth, and vice versa. Click and drag a corner point to create direction lines for a smooth point. Click once on a smooth point to change it to a corner point. You can also drag a direction point with the Convert Point tool to change the shape of only that side of the curve.

Editing Paths

Paths as a whole can be edited, or you can work with subpaths or even individual anchor points and path segments. To select an entire path, click it in the Paths palette. You can stroke, fill, delete, and use the Edit, Transform commands.

To isolate a subpath from the entire path, use the Path Selection tool, whose icon is a plain black arrow (see Figure 7.28). Click the subpath in the image window to select it.

When using the Freeform Pen tool with the Magnetic option, you can temporarily disable the capability by holding down the Option key (Mac users) or the Alt key (Windows users). With the key pressed, drag a freeform path without regard for following edges. Release the modifier key to resume using the Magnetic option.

When working with the Pen tool, you can enable or disable the Auto Add/Delete check box in the Options bar. This option, enabled by default, deletes or adds points automatically if you click existing points or segments in your path. If you disable this option, the Pen tool no longer edits existing points on the path; it only creates new points. This may be useful when drawing detailed images with the Pen tool where your points overlap. Most simple images can be drawn just fine with this option checked—in fact, it can be downright useful for creating pen drawings.

When you use the Path Selection tool to select a subpath, all the anchor points are selected. If you drag with the tool, you can reposition the subpath. You can also use the Paths palette menu commands to stroke or fill a selected subpath.

You can control the operation of the Path Selection tool in the Options bar using these techniques:

- When Show Bounding Box is selected, you can manipulate a path with the Path Selection tool much like using the bounding box with the Free Transform command. Drag a side or corner anchor to scale the path. Holding down the Shift key while dragging constrains the proportions, maintaining the original height-to-width ratio. You can use the Option key (Mac users) or the Alt key (Windows users)—with or without the Shift key—to scale from the center. Add the ⌘ key (Mac users) or the Ctrl key (Windows users) for skew and perspective transformations. The Edit,

Transform commands are available with paths; for numeric transformations, you can use the Options bar.

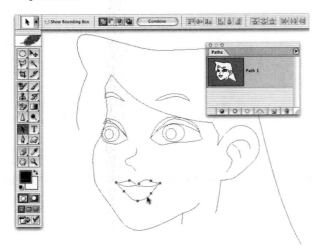

Figure 7.28
The path must be selected in the Paths palette to make it visible. You can then use the Path Selection tool to select a subpath, making its anchor points visible.

- Shift-clicking multiple subpaths with the Path Selection tool activates several buttons in the Options bar. You can combine the paths by adding, subtracting, intersecting, or excluding areas of overlap. Select the preferred operation and then click the Combine button.

- Multiple subpaths can also be aligned or distributed, according to their centers or any side. Shift-click the subpaths or drag across them with the Path Selection tool and then use the appropriate buttons in the Options bar.

To select an individual anchor point or path segment to edit the shape of a path, use the Direct Selection tool, identified by the white arrow icon (see Figure 7.29). The Direct Selection tool has no options in the Options bar. Selected anchor points are identified as filled squares; anchor points in the same subpath that are *not* selected appear as hollow squares. (Other subpaths are visible, but their anchor points are not.) If a selected anchor point has direction lines, those lines will be visible.

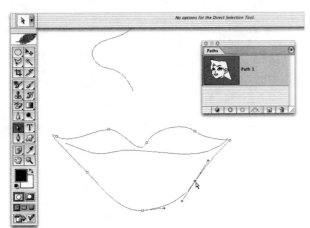

Figure 7.29
The direction lines for the selected anchor point are visible, as is one direction line from each of the neighboring points. The additional direction lines are visible so that you can edit the path segments connected to the selected anchor point.

7

The Direct Selection tool can be used to drag an anchor point or a path segment or to drag direction points, which alters the shape of a curve. Remember that dragging a direction point for a smooth anchor point affects the direction lines—and curves—on *both* sides of the anchor, but changing a direction line for a corner point alters only the curve on that side (see Figure 7.30).

The Direct Selection tool can also be used to drag path segments. When a straight path segment is dragged, the neighboring anchor points move as well, altering not only the segment dragged but also those on either side. When you drag a curved path segment, the adjoining anchor points remain in place and the neighboring path segments are undisturbed. Note that dragging a curved path segment automatically converts any adjoining smooth anchor point to a corner point. In Figure 7.31, dashed lines represent the original paths, and you can see how dragging path segments affects shapes.

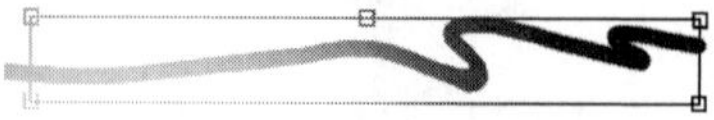

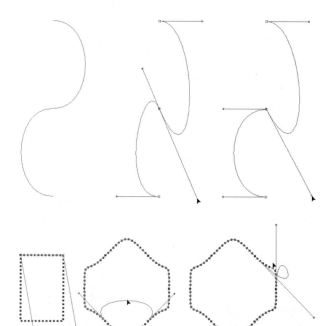

To alter a curve connected to a smooth anchor point without disturbing the adjoining curve, hold down the Option key (Mac users) or the Alt key (Windows users) and drag a direction point. The smooth anchor point is converted to a corner anchor point with direction lines.

Figure 7.30
On the left is the original curve. In the center, you can see how dragging either of a smooth anchor point's direction lines changes the path segments on each side. On the right, the same curve with a corner anchor point has independent path segments.

Figure 7.31
To the left, a straight path segment is being dragged. In the center, a curved path segment is being dragged straight up. On the right, you can see one example of what can go horribly wrong when dragging a curved path segment. To avoid the unexpected, click and drag in the middle of a path segment.

Stroking and Filling Paths and Subpaths

To add color to an image, you can stroke and fill paths and subpaths. Use the Path Selection or Direct Selection tool to make the target path active. Make sure you're on the correct layer in the Layers palette. Use the Paths palette buttons or the commands from the Paths palette menu (see Figure 7.32), which open dialog boxes.

The Stroke Path dialog box (or Stroke Subpath, depending on the active selection) offers all the tools that use brushes. You can even apply the Healing Brush, Clone Stamp, and Pattern Stamp tools along paths for incredible precision.

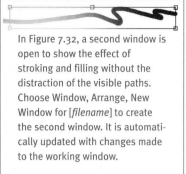

In Figure 7.32, a second window is open to show the effect of stroking and filling without the distraction of the visible paths. Choose Window, Arrange, New Window for [*filename*] to create the second window. It is automatically updated with changes made to the working window.

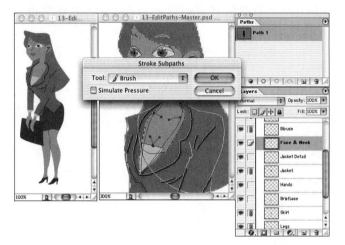

Figure 7.32
The buttons at the bottom of the Paths palette use the settings selected in the Stroke and Fill dialog boxes. Open the dialog boxes using the Paths palette menu, select the appropriate options, and afterward you can simply click the buttons to use the same settings.

Changeable Names

When your path consists of a single subpath, the commands are Fill Path and Stroke Path. When you have multiple subpaths and all are selected, the commands and dialog boxes also show Fill Path and Stroke Path. When there are multiple subpaths and only one is selected, the commands and dialog boxes are Fill Subpath and Stroke Subpath. When you have multiple subpaths and some but not all are selected, the commands and dialog boxes adapt themselves grammatically and read Fill Subpaths and Stroke Subpaths.

The Fill Path (or Fill Subpath) options include filling with the foreground or background color or with a pattern, history state, black, white, or 50% gray. You can select a blending mode, opacity, feather radius, and anti-aliasing for the fill. Remember that filling an *open path*—a path with two identifiable ends—fills an area that includes a straight line between the start and end anchor points.

Making Paths from Selections

The Paths palette offers two ways to create a path from a selection. At the bottom of the Paths palette, the Make Work Path from Selection button loads an active selection as a work path. Alternatively, the Paths palette menu offers the Make Work Path command, which opens a dialog box where you can specify a tolerance setting. Ranging from 0.5 to 10 pixels, the Make Work Path command tolerance setting determines the accuracy with which the path is created as well as the complexity of the final path.

If a selection is heavily feathered or created from a mask, the path follows the marching ants (selection border), which indicates pixels at least 50% selected. If no pixels are at least 50% selected and you attempt to create a work path, a work path appears in the Paths palette, but there will be no anchor points or path segments.

Compound paths can be created from selections, as shown in Figure 7.33. You can create the selection with selection tools, from a mask, or by using selection commands.

Compound paths can be used as vector masks for layers and as clipping paths for images to be placed in page layout programs (see Figure 7.34).

After you stroke or fill a path, the menu command Edit, Fade is available. You can use this command to change the opacity or blending mode of the stroke or fill. Remember that Fade is available only immediately after you apply the stroke or fill.

Caution

Remember that when you create a path from a selection, you create a work path. It replaces any existing work path in the Paths palette. And, unless saved, it is lost as soon as you start another work path (although you can add more subpaths). Save a work path by renaming it in the Paths palette.

Figure 7.33
When the Option key (Mac users) or Alt key (Windows users) is used along with a selection tool, areas within a selection can be deselected. The Options bar also offers this capability for selection tools.

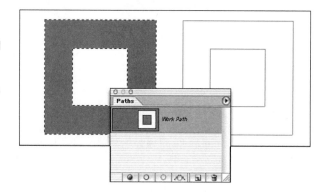

Converting Type to Paths

Editable paths can also be created from vector type. With a type layer selected in the Layers palette, use the menu command Layer, Type, Create Work Path. The original type layer is untouched, and a work path is created in the shape of the letters (see Figure 7.35). Although the original type layer remains editable as text, the work path is no longer type.

Caution

Creating paths from large amounts of small type can cause problems. The paths can be too complex to output properly.

Before filling or stroking a work path, make sure you are on the appropriate layer.

A Note About Illustrator Paths

You can copy and paste paths between Photoshop and Illustrator. However, when you copy from Illustrator, it's important that the Illustrator Preferences be set correctly. In Illustrator's File Handling & Clipboard preferences pane, select AICB (Adobe Illustrator Clipboard) in the Copy As area. If you're copying paths, click Preserve Paths.

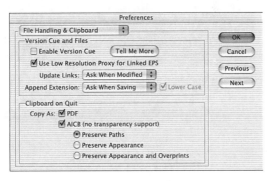

The PDF option can be used along with AICB, but when you're working with Photoshop, AICB must be selected.

When you copy one or more objects from Illustrator and switch to Photoshop, the Paste command opens a small dialog box. You have the option of pasting from the Clipboard as pixels, as just paths, or as a shape layer.

You can, in fact, use the Paste command twice—once to paste the path and again to paste the pixels. The two remain separate, and they don't become a vector object. However, you have both the substance (paths) and appearance (pixels) of the original object.

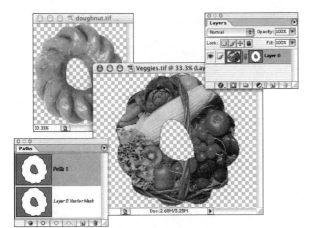

Figure 7.34
A compound path was created from a selection of the doughnut and used to mask an image of vegetables. Then the path was duplicated in the Paths palette and the copy converted to a clipping path. When placed in a page layout program, only the pixels between the paths are visible.

7

Figure 7.35
The two existing layers have reduced opacity to better show the work path. The Direct Selection tool can be used to move anchor points and direction points, customizing the letter shapes. The paths can then be filled or stroked.

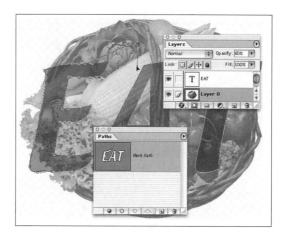

USING PHOTOSHOP'S SHAPE LAYERS

Photoshop simulates vector objects with shape layers. A *shape layer* is actually a layer in the image, completely filled with the selected color or pattern. The layer is selectively shown and hidden by a vector mask. The pixels on the layer inside the path are visible; those outside the path are hidden (see Figure 7.36).

Figure 7.36
A shape layer's vector mask is visible in the Paths palette when the layer is selected in the Layers palette.

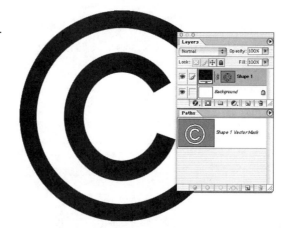

In the Options bar, you can assign a color for a shape layer. With the shape layer selected in the Layers palette, you can use the menu command Layer, Change Layer Content to assign a gradient or pattern to the layer or to convert the layer to an adjustment layer. You can also use the Layer, Layer Content Options command to adjust the fill of a shape layer.

Using the Shape Tools

The shape tools are, at their heart, scalable preset path tools. When you use a shape tool, you create one of three things: a shape layer, a work path, or colored pixels in a specific shape on an existing layer. The choice is made by selecting one of the three buttons to the left in the Options bar.

The shape that is created can be selected in the Toolbox or the Options bar (see Figure 7.37). The standard preset tools include Rectangle, Rounded Rectangle, Ellipse, Polygon, and Line. Custom shapes can also be selected from a palette, which can be loaded with Photoshop-supplied shapes, third-party shapes, or custom shapes you define.

Regardless of which shape is selected—or whether you're creating a shape layer, a work path, or a filled region—the basic operation of the Shape tools is the same: Click and drag. (When size options are selected, you need only click.) Use the Shift key to constrain the shape to its original height:width ratio; use the Option key (Mac users) or the Alt key (Windows users) to create the shape from the center. The two modifier keys can be used together.

Each of the individual Shape tools has characteristics that you can control through the Geometry palette of the Options bar (see Figure 7.38).

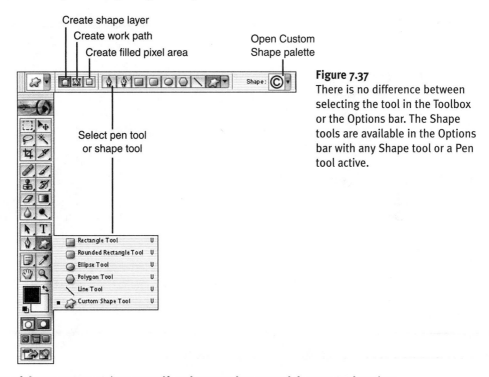

Figure 7.37
There is no difference between selecting the tool in the Toolbox or the Options bar. The Shape tools are available in the Options bar with any Shape tool or a Pen tool active.

Most of the geometry options are self-explanatory, but several deserve explanation:

- When the Rounded Rectangle tool is selected, you see the Radius field in the Options bar. The value entered here determines the curve of the corners.

- Snap to Pixels is primarily used when creating web graphics. By snapping the horizontal and vertical edges of the shape to pixels, this option ensures that web graphics are crisp. The option is used only with the Rectangle and Rounded Rectangle tools and is not available for the shapes that don't have horizontal and vertical edges.

- The Polygon tool offers the option to create stars. When it's checked, you have the opportunity to specify the indentation of the star's arms. Percent is the unit of measure.

7

Figure 7.38
To open the Geometry palette, click the down arrow to the right of the Custom Shape tool icon.

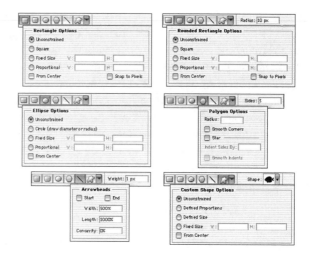

- The Line tool can have arrowheads at either or both ends. However, when you have arrowheads at both ends, they must be identical. (You can, of course, transform the line later.)

- The Defined Proportions and Defined Size options for the Custom Shape tool refer to the size and proportions at which the custom shape was originally created.

Editing Shape Vector Masks

The vector masks that selectively show and hide the fill of a shape layer can be edited like any other path in Photoshop. The path, of course, must be selected in the Paths palette. For the path to be visible in the palette, the shape layer must be selected in the Layers palette. The Path Selection tool selects all the anchor points in a path or subpath, enabling you to move the entire path or subpath as a unit.

The Direct Selection tool enables you to select one or more individual path segments or anchor points to manipulate. It is also used to drag the direction points of anchor points adjoining curved path segments.

Using, Creating, and Saving Custom Shapes

Custom shapes are selected from the Custom Shape palette (see Figure 7.39). This palette, opened through the Options bar, is available only when the Custom Shape tool has been selected in the Toolbox or the Options bar.

After you select a custom shape from the palette and set options in the Geometry palette, the custom shape can be added to the image like any other shape. Shape layers, work paths, and filled pixel regions can all be added with custom shape tools.

You can create custom shapes and add them to the Custom Shape palette. Create a path or select an existing path and then use the menu command Edit, Define Custom Shape. You have the opportunity to name the new custom shape (see Figure 7.40).

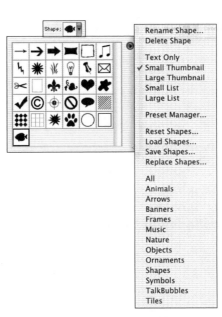

Figure 7.39
The Custom Shape palette's menu offers available sets of custom shapes at the bottom. The newly added shapes can be added to or replace those already in the palette.

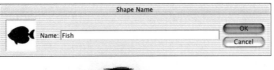

Figure 7.40
Naming the shape is the only option. It is saved at the size created, although as a vector, the original size is insignificant.

Remember that custom shapes are not saved when you add them to the palette. Rather, you must use the palette's menu command Save Shapes. Should you need to replace your Preferences file or reinstall Photoshop, any unsaved shapes you have defined will be lost. The shapes are, by default, added to Photoshop's Custom Shapes folder within the Presets folder, but you have the option of choosing another location. Shapes (and brushes, tool presets, styles, and other such elements) can also be saved in sets using the Preset Manager, found under the Edit menu.

CLIPPING PATHS AND VECTOR MASKS

Clipping paths and vector paths serve the same purpose—identifying what will be visible or invisible—but they do so at two different levels. Clipping paths are used with images destined for page layout programs, delineating areas of visibility for the image as a whole. Vector masks are used in a similar manner to show and hide areas of individual layers within an image.

7

Open, closed, and compound paths can all be used to create both clipping paths and vector masks. You must name a work path to save it before you can convert it to a clipping path. Double-clicking a work path in the Paths palette and renaming it saves it, and you can then use the Paths palette menu command Clipping Path.

You can create a vector mask for a layer in either of two ways. You can first create the path and then assign it as a vector mask, or you can create the vector mask and then define it with a path. With or without an active path, use the menu command Layer, Add Vector Mask. Alternatively, you can ⌘-Option-click (Mac users) or Ctrl+Alt-click (Windows users) the Add Layer Mask button at the bottom of the Layers palette.

Caution

The Clipping Path dialog box includes a Flatness field. Never enter a value for flatness unless your imagesetter is having trouble outputting curves. The field overrides the device's native setting for vector reproduction.

WORKING WITH TYPE
IN PHOTOSHOP

IN THIS CHAPTER

8

Although Photoshop cannot be mistaken for a page layout program, it does have some rather sophisticated type-handling features. You can add a single character, word, or line of type. You can add paragraphs of type that automatically adjust to changes in the enclosing rectangle. Introduced in Photoshop CS was type on a path, the capability to have a line of type follow a path created by the Pen tool or a shape tool. Both spell checking and find/replace for text are built in to Photoshop. You also have incredible control over the appearance of text, especially when using OpenType fonts. This chapter looks at the type and text capabilities built in to Photoshop CS2, the tools and palettes you use to take advantage of those capabilities, and issues involving fonts and font embedding.

UNDERSTANDING PHOTOSHOP'S TYPE CAPABILITY

As the subject of type and text in Photoshop is discussed, it's important to keep one basic concept in mind: Photoshop is an image-editing program. It is not designed to be a page layout program nor a word processor. Don't consider Photoshop's type-handling capabilities to be substandard, however; rather, think of them as a bonus. If you have large amounts of text to add to a document or need to work with very small type, consider Adobe InDesign or Illustrator.

Just a few versions ago, Photoshop's type capability was restricted to creating masks in the shape of letters. The biggest problem with type masks is that the type isn't "live." You can't edit the words or change the typographic attributes without re-creating the entire type element (see Figure 8.1).

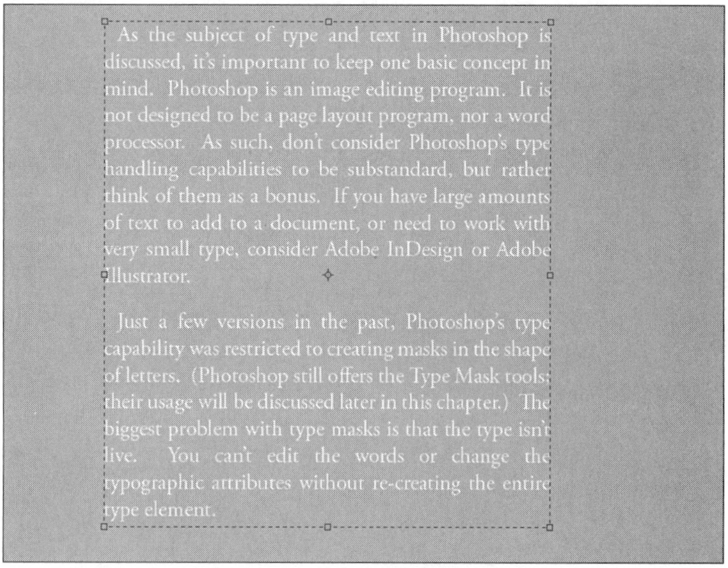

Figure 8.1
After a type mask is set, it becomes nothing more than filled pixels. Changing the font or even one misspelling might mean re-creating the entire image when type is added as a mask.

Photoshop 5 introduced type layers, and Photoshop 6 added vector type. Photoshop 7 refined the type engine and added both a spell checker and the find/replace capability. Photoshop CS went a bit further with type on a path and support for type layers in 16-bit color and layered PDF files. Now Photoshop CS2 adds the long-awaited WYSIWYG Font menu. Now when you are choosing fonts from the Font menu, you can see what the font looks like. Also added is more control in the Options bar and enhanced Japanese font options. Internationalization is an important need in software, and Adobe is focused on supporting other languages as best it can.

Working with Vector Type

You already know there are numerous advantages to vector artwork, and this is especially true for vector type. For example, when printed with a PostScript output device, the artwork's edges remain crisp and clean, without the so-called *jaggies*—the visible stair-step edges of pixels along a curve. Vector artwork can be scaled in an illustration program or by a PostScript printer and still retain those high-quality edges. Because it consists of mathematically defined paths, it can also be manipulated in ways impossible with raster art. Figure 8.2 shows the difference between scaling vector type and raster type.

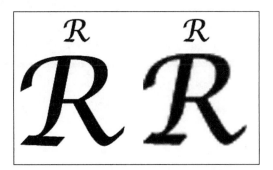

Figure 8.2
The original letters are shown for comparison. Notice the dramatic difference in quality when vector and rasterized type are scaled to 400%.

One primary advantage of raster art is its capability of reproducing fine transitions and gradations in color. Because vector type is usually a single color, that is not of particular value. However, Photoshop's vector type can be rasterized whenever necessary, in case you need that feature.

Saving Files with Type

The difference between vector and rasterized type is primarily important during the creation process and when preparing artwork for placement in a page layout program. In most other circumstances, the type is automatically rasterized. In Photoshop, the PostScript file formats, those that support vectors, are limited to these:

- Photoshop (.psd)

- The large image version of Photoshop's format (.psb)

- Encapsulated PostScript (.eps)

- Portable Document Format (.pdf)

- Desktop Color Separations (.dcs)

Caution

EPS and DCS support vector type when you're saving from Photoshop. However, reopening either of these image formats in Photoshop results in rasterization. PDFs saved without layers are also rasterized when reopened in Photoshop. After you save a file with vector text in one of these formats, don't reopen it in Photoshop. It's a good idea to keep the original in Photoshop's own PSD format.

When saving in a format that can maintain vector artwork or type, you need to ensure that the Include Vector Data option is selected. In Figure 8.3, you can see the check boxes for the various PostScript file format options. Note that both the EPS Options dialog box and the DCS 2.0 Format dialog warn about reopening files in Photoshop, but the PDF Options dialog does not.

8

Figure 8.3
EPS, PDF, and DCS file formats all offer (but don't require) saving vector data in a file. If there are no vector paths or type in the image, the option is grayed out.

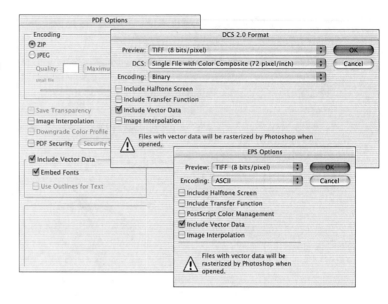

Working with Type on a Path

When you create a path, as you learned from the last chapter, you can manipulate the path any way you like. By hovering the type tool over your path, you can attach your type to the path (see Figure 8.4). While type is attached to the path, reshaping the path causes the type to follow the new shape. Type on a path was introduced with Photoshop CS not long ago, but it has been available in Illustrator and InDesign for quite some time.

Figure 8.4
To the left, type has been placed along a path created with the Pen tool. To the right, the type is inside a path created with a Shape tool. As you can tell from the Paths palette and the visible path, the type layer of the left object is active.

Working with type on a path requires knowledge of both path creation and editing and placing type in Photoshop. Here are the basic steps for creating type on a path in Photoshop:

1. Create or paste the path and then click it with the Type tool. To add type inside the path, simply click inside the path. The Type tool's cursor changes appearance to indicate that you're adding type on a path.

2. Type on a path can be adjusted with the Character palette. For example, baseline shift can be used to raise the type from a path that will be stroked or filled. (The Character palette is discussed later in this chapter.)

3. When you finish editing the type, press ⌘-Return (Mac users) or Ctrl+Enter (Windows users) to accept the type editing. Press it again to hide the path.

4. With the Type tool active, click in the type, hold down the ⌘ key (Mac users) or the Ctrl key (Windows users), and position the Type tool near the type to alter its position in relation to the path. Drag the beginning and ending points to move the type along the path. Drag the cursor across the path to flip the type upside down. When the cursor is not near the type or the type isn't being edited and the modifier key is pressed, you (as usual) have the Move tool available.

5. The Path Selection tool (the black arrow tool) can also be used to manipulate type on a path.

6. The original path is retained separately in the Paths palette. A duplicate of the path is visible in the Paths palette when the type layer is active in the Layers palette. (This behavior is comparable to that of shape layers and their paths.)

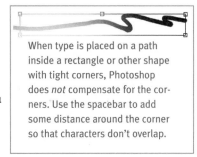

When type is placed on a path inside a rectangle or other shape with tight corners, Photoshop does *not* compensate for the corners. Use the spacebar to add some distance around the corner so that characters don't overlap.

7. Type path layers cannot be stroked or filled (because you cannot add pixels to a type layer). However, because the original path is retained, you can add a new layer and then stroke or fill *that* path (see Figure 8.5).

8. Shape layers can be used as type containers. Select a Shape tool, make sure it's set to create a shape layer in the Options bar, and drag. Switch to the Type tool, position the cursor inside the shape, and click. The shape layer's vector clipping path is copied and serves as a type container. Remember, too, that shape layers can be created with the Pen tool.

9. Using the Warp Type feature disassociates the type from the path but warps the type from its path-based shape.

10. If you need to add regular point or paragraph type near an existing path, either deselect the path in the Paths palette first or hold down the Shift key when clicking or dragging the Type tool.

Working with Type Layers

As long as type remains part of a type layer, it remains editable. You can return to the type layer at any time and make changes to the character and paragraph characteristics, or you can edit the text. After the layer is rasterized or merged or the image is flattened, the type can no longer be edited as type. (You can, of course, edit the pixels; but you cannot, for example, highlight a word with the Type tool and overtype to correct a spelling error.)

8

Figure 8.5
A custom shape was used to create the copyright-shaped work path. Type on a path was added (and the baseline decreased 35 points) and then the original path was stroked and filled.

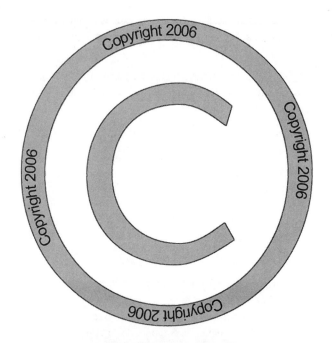

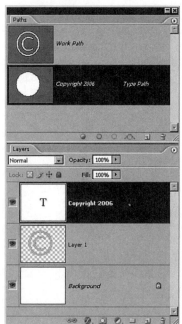

In many ways, type layers are comparable to other nonbackground layers. Layer styles can be applied, type layers can be moved in the Layers palette and become part of a layer set, and adjustment layers can be applied (see Figure 8.6).

Layer Style Applied

Adjustment Layers Applied

Figure 8.6
The Layers palette indicates what effects and adjustments have been applied to the type layers.

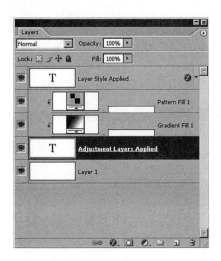

A type layer is always indicated by the letter *T* in place of a layer thumbnail in the Layers palette. As with other layers, you can click the layer's name and rename it. (By default, Photoshop names a type layer using the first characters of the layer's content.) You can change the blending mode and opacity of a type layer and create layer-based slices from type layers.

Unlike with other nonbackground layers, you cannot add pixels to a type layer. You cannot paint on a type layer, nor can you stroke or fill a selection. The adjustment tools (Blur, Sharpen, Dodge, Burn, Sponge, Smudge) cannot be used on type layers.

Warping Type

Among the features in Photoshop that are the most fun is Warp Text. You can apply preset distortions to type and customize their effects, and the type remains completely editable. You can apply layer styles to the warped text as well (see Figure 8.7).

The Warp Text dialog box can be opened with the button to the right of the color swatch in the Options bar (when a Type tool is active) or with the menu command Layer, Type, Warp Text. The dialog box enables you to select any of 15 shapes and then use three sliders to adjust the result (see Figure 8.8).

When warping text some of the different warp effects will look more balanced when your type is centered. Open the Paragraph palette or click the Center Text button in the Options bar.

Figure 8.7
Each of the five examples is on a
separate type layer.

Figure 8.8
To remove an existing warp effect,
select None from the top of the
Style pop-up menu.

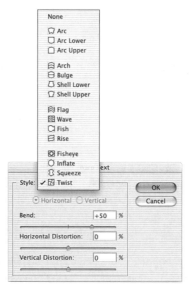

WORKING WITH THE TYPE TOOLS

Photoshop offers four related tools for adding type to an image. The Horizontal Type tool (usually
referred to as simply the *Type tool*), the Vertical Type tool, the Horizontal Type Mask tool, and the
Vertical Type Mask tool are shown in their flyout palette in Figure 8.9.

Figure 8.9
To open the flyout palette, click
and hold on whichever Type tool
icon is visible in the toolbox.

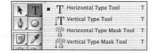

The Horizontal and Vertical Type Tools

The only difference between the Horizontal Type and Vertical Type tools is the orientation of the characters added to the image. Note in Figure 8.10 the difference between vertical type and horizontal type that has been rotated.

Both the Horizontal and Vertical Type tools create type layers when used. Unless you rasterized the type, as long as the file remains in a format that supports layers (Photoshop's native format, the Photoshop Large Document Format, or TIFF or PDF with layers), the type remains editable. You can change the font, size, or other attributes as well as change the content of the text. You can click with either tool anywhere in an image window to create a new type layer and add point type. You can also drag with either tool to create a type layer and add paragraph type.

To make changes to an entire type layer, don't select any type; merely select the type layer in the Layers palette. You can change any attributes in the Character or Paragraph palettes, and the change is applied throughout the type layer.

To edit existing type, click and drag with either tool to make a type selection. Changes are restricted to the selected type.

V
e
r
t
i
c
a
l

T
y
p
e

Horizontal Type Rotated 90°

Figure 8.10
Consider vertical and horizontal to be references to the relationship among letters.

The Type Mask Tools

Also available for horizontal and vertical type, the Type Mask tools do not create type layers. Rather, they create masks in the shape of the letters. (A nontype layer must be active in the Layers palette.) These masks become selections when you change tools, click the check mark in the Options bar, or press ⌘-Return (Mac users) or Ctrl+Enter (Windows users).

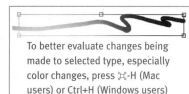

To better evaluate changes being made to selected type, especially color changes, press ⌘-H (Mac users) or Ctrl+H (Windows users) to hide the selection highlighting.

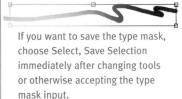

If you want to save the type mask, choose Select, Save Selection immediately after changing tools or otherwise accepting the type mask input.

Using the Type Mask tools is comparable to using Photoshop's Quick Mask mode. As in Quick Mask mode, the temporary mask that is created is not retained after the selection is made. You see the translucent red overlay while adding the type, but the mask is lost when the type is converted to a selection (see Figure 8.11).

Type masks are often used to create layer masks in the shape of letters. A Type Mask tool is usually not the tool of choice for creating large amounts of text, and it's especially inappropriate for small type sizes.

Figure 8.11
On the left, the mask is visible while the type is being set. On the right, the type is a selection and the mask is discarded. This happens automatically when you change tools or otherwise accept the type.

UNDERSTANDING THE TYPE PALETTES AND COMMANDS

In addition to the Type tools in the Toolbox and the Options bar, some 16 menu commands and two palettes are designed for use specifically with type. Some of the commands duplicate options found in the Options bar (such as anti-aliasing), which enables you to access the capabilities without having the Type tool active. (Check Spelling and Find and Replace Text are discussed separately, later in this chapter.)

In addition, virtually all other commands and palettes can be used with type in one way or another. Styles can be applied, colors can be changed, transformations are available—these are just some of the ways that Photoshop enables you to work with type.

Type Commands Under the Layer Menu

The Type submenu found under the Layer menu offers 13 commands, each of which is available only when a type layer is active in the Layers palette. Two of the commands can be used to convert the editable type into vector paths, either as work paths or as shape layers.

Create Work Path Command

The Create Work Path command converts the type layer from editable type to a work path. The work path consists of all the subpaths used to create the vector type. Photoshop does nothing with the work path, nor does it change your type layer in any way. You can, however, open the Paths palette and save the work

Caution
Be aware that paths created from type are very complex. When created from large amounts of text, they can be complex enough to cause output problems for image setters and printers. Unlike Illustrator, Photoshop has no Simplify command to reduce the complexity of paths.

path, you can use it to create a layer mask or clipping mask, you can stroke the paths (on a separate layer, not on the original type layer), or you can use the work path as a basis for a selection. Paths created from type can also be exported to Illustrator. In addition, you can edit the individual anchor points of the subpaths to customize the type (see Figure 8.12).

Figure 8.12
The type has been converted to a work path, and the Direct Selection tool is being used to edit the letterforms. The path can be converted to a selection and filled or stroked.

In Figure 8.13, you can see the number of anchor points for the converted type. Note the density of points in the type.

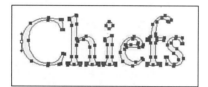

Figure 8.13
The type is set at a relatively large 18 points. The density of the anchor points is increased at lower font sizes because the number of points per character remains the same.

The font used can play a major role in the number of anchor points created when type is converted to work paths. Serif fonts and some script fonts often require a substantially higher number of anchor points to be reproduced as editable paths. Multiply the increased number of anchor points, as shown in Figure 8.14, by the number of letters in a several-word type layer, and you can calculate the increased complexity of the work path.

Convert to Shape Command

Like the command Create Work Path, the Convert to Shape command uses a vector type layer to create paths. However, rather than creating a work path, this command produces a shape layer (see Figure 8.15). The original type layer becomes a layer comparable to those produced by Photoshop Shape tools. A shape layer consists of a filled layer with a layer clipping mask. The clipping mask selectively reveals areas of the filled layer.

Figure 8.14
The fonts are Arial (27 anchor points), Times New Roman (38 anchor points), Brush Script (74 anchor points), and Lucida Calligraphy (34 anchor points).

Figure 8.15
The Layers palette shows the layer thumbnail as well as the layer clipping mask created from the type layer. The Paths palette shows the clipping path as a vector mask.

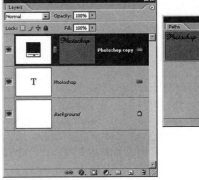

The new shape layer is filled with the same color that was originally applied to the type. If more than one color is applied to the type, the shape layer is filled with the color of the first character. When a style has been applied to the type layer, it is retained in the shape layer.

The paths created by the Convert to Shape command are identical to those created by the Create Work Path command. The caution presented earlier also applies to the shape layer path—paths with too many anchor points can create output problems.

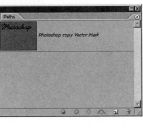

Both Convert to Shape and Create Work Path are available for type that has been warped. The paths that are created, whether work paths or layer clipping paths, follow the contours of the warped type. You can also use these commands with type on a path.

Anti-aliasing Type

Anti-aliasing is the process of adding transitional pixels along the edges of objects in Photoshop images to soften the appearance of curves. Selection tools offer the option of anti-aliasing, but Photoshop's type engine is more sophisticated, offering several levels of anti-aliasing. Because the appearance of type is usually critical, and because different fonts and type sizes have different requirements, Photoshop's type engine offers these anti-aliasing options:

- **Anti-Alias None:** Smooth the edges of type onscreen. This command removes all anti-aliasing, which can result in jagged-edged type (see Figure 8.16). However, None is often the appropriate choice for very small type and small type at low resolution.

Figure 8.16
Although the differences in the other four types of anti-aliasing are virtually impossible to spot in the examples in this figure, None (at the upper left) is certainly apparent.

- **Anti-Alias Sharp:** Select for the lowest amount of anti-aliasing. If the type appears rough or jagged along curves, select another option.

- **Anti-Alias Crisp:** High-contrast edges take precedence over smoothing when you use the Crisp option.

- **Anti-Alias Strong:** Add anti-aliasing outside the character in an attempt to maintain the individual character's width.

- **Anti-Alias Smooth:** Apply the greatest amount of anti-aliasing. If characters become blurry, consider Crisp or Sharp. If the characters seem to lose optical weight (the strokes appear too thin), opt for Strong.

Anti-aliasing makes curves and angled lines appear smoother by adding colored pixels along edges. Think of the transitional pixels as a minigradient, blending from the foreground color to the background color. When you look at black type on a white background, the added pixels are shades of gray (see Figure 8.17).

Keep in mind that anti-aliasing is not always a good idea. Very small type can become quite blurry onscreen when anti-aliased. Especially when you're preparing images for the Web, think carefully about anti-aliasing. Using larger type, particularly the more linear sans serif fonts, such as Arial, can do far more to improve legibility and appearance than anti-aliasing. In addition, if the image is to be saved as a GIF or PNG-8 file, remember that anti-aliasing introduces several new colors to the color table, potentially increasing file size.

Remember, too, that anti-aliasing is not used when you print vector type to a PostScript printer.

8

Figure 8.17
The number 2 has no anti-aliasing applied, but the letter s is set to Crisp. The inset is at 100%, and the image behind is at 800% zoom.

One other command deserves special attention. The menu command Layer, Rasterize, Type converts a vector type layer to pixels, and the type is rasterized at the image's resolution. This command is not available if the active layer in the Layers palette is not a type layer (identifiable by the *T* symbol in place of the layer thumbnail).

The Options Bar and the Type Tools

Photoshop's Options bar includes the capability to save tool presets. This is a great way to speed your work with the Type tool. If you regularly use certain fonts at certain sizes, they can be saved as presets in the Tool Presets Picker at the left end of the Options bar (see Figure 8.18).

Figure 8.18
Select the font, size, anti-aliasing, alignment, and color, and then use the palette's menu command New Tool Preset. You have the opportunity to name the new configuration.

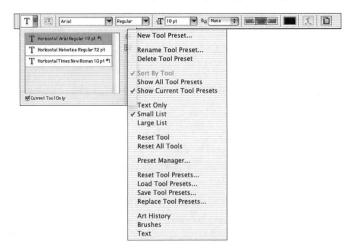

Each of the settings in the Options bar can be changed for a preset. The values in the Character and Paragraph palettes are recorded as well. Note that the Horizontal Type tool and the Vertical Type tool have separate presets. The Tool Presets palette is available for use with the Type tool only when the Type tool is selected, but not in the act of adding type to the image. (When you're actually adding type, the preset palette's button is grayed out.)

Immediately to the right of the Tool Presets Picker button is a button that enables you to switch existing type between horizontal and vertical. The button is available when a type layer is active in the Layers palette, regardless of whether the type itself is selected in the window. Swapping the type orientation applies to the entire type layer; you cannot change part of a sentence from horizontal to vertical.

With a Type tool active, you can use the Options bar to change the font, font style (when the font has multiple styles available), type size, anti-aliasing, alignment, and color. To the right, the Options bar offers four additional buttons. Just to the right of the color swatch is a button to open the Warp Text dialog box. The only difference between using this button and the menu command Layer, Type, Warp Text is convenience.

To the right of Warp Text is a button that toggles the visibility of the Character and Paragraph palettes. Again, this is comparable to using the appropriate commands in the

Because the Options bar is contextual, these fields and buttons are available only when the Type tool is active. However, when a type layer is active in the Layers palette, no matter what tool is selected, all these capabilities are available in the Character and Paragraph palettes or using the Layer, Type menu.

Window menu to show and hide the palettes. Next are the Cancel Current Edits and Commit Current Edits buttons, which are visible only while a Type tool is in action. Clicking the Cancel button returns the type layer to its previous state (or cancels a new type layer), and the Commit button accepts the type entry or edit. The keyboard shortcuts for these two buttons are Escape and ⌘-Return (Mac users) and Ctrl+Enter (Windows users).

The Character Palette

You can show and hide the Character palette (see Figure 8.19) through the Window menu or a button in the Options bar when a Type tool is active. The palette replicates many of the fields and options available in the Options bar for Type tools. Unlike the type-related fields in the Options bar, the Character palette is also available when a non-Type tool is active.

The Character palette can be used in several ways:

- It can be used without any active type layer to establish presets for the Type tools. This affects all type that is entered later until additional changes are made in the Character palette or the Options bar.

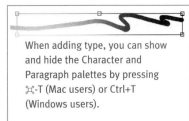

When adding type, you can show and hide the Character and Paragraph palettes by pressing ⌘-T (Mac users) or Ctrl+T (Windows users).

- With a type layer active in the Layers palette but no type selected in the image, changes can be made to the entire layer. These changes affect all type on the layer, but *only* type on that layer. The changes remain in effect in the Character palette and Options bar.

- When some type on a type layer is selected with a Type tool, changes can be made to that portion of the type without affecting the rest of the type layer. Such changes affect only the selected type and remain in effect.

Figure 8.19
Not all menu options are available at the same time or with all fonts.

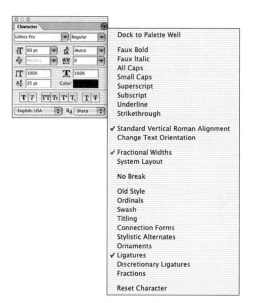

- If a Type tool is active and in use, the Character palette can be used to set the characteristics of type that has not yet been entered. All type entered from that point on has the new characteristics, but previously entered type is unaffected.

The Character palette has 12 fields and 8 style buttons (the 8 buttons are duplicated by commands in the palette's menu). You can navigate among the fields in the Character palette with the Tab key. Tab advances you to the next field, and Shift+Tab returns you to the previous one. Note that this method works even with the Font Family (name) and Font Style fields. In these fields, you can type the first letter of an entry in the pop-up list to jump to it.

In the Style field, you can jump only to styles available for that font. If you press I for italic and the current font doesn't offer italic, you hear an error tone.

Font Family

The Font Family pop-up menu includes a list of all fonts available to Photoshop on your system. Font families include Helvetica, Times New Roman, Arial, and so on. All properly installed TrueType, Type 1, and OpenType fonts should appear. This menu selects only the font family.

Font Style

The Font Style pop-up menu shows the font styles and weights built in to the font itself. The options can include Regular or Roman, Bold, Italic, Semibold, Condensed, Expanded, and combinations of these options, such as

You can preview how your type looks in a particular font. Select the type layer in the Layers palette (or select some type with the Type tool). Click once in the Font field of the Character palette or the Options bar. Use the up and down arrow keys on the keyboard to navigate through the fonts, which changes the appearance of the type in the image. Take a snapshot in the History palette first, because each change is registered there.

Semibold Italic. Some fonts, such as Stencil and Techno, are designed at a single weight and style, in which case the menu's arrow is grayed out.

Font Size

The Font Size field determines how large the font appears in the image. In addition to the preset values in the pop-up menu, you can type any size between 1/10 of a point and 1296 points. By default, Photoshop uses points as the unit of measure for font size. One point is equal to 1/72 inch. You can change the unit in Photoshop's Preferences window. In addi-

For really large projects, you can work around Photoshop's font size limitation. Enter the text at 1296 points and then choose Edit, Transform, Scale. Make the type larger than you need. You can now return to the Font Size field and enter any point size up to the scaled size.

tion, you can type any unit of measure directly into the field. For example, typing **28 px** makes the font size 28 pixels. The other available abbreviations are in (inches), cm (centimeters), pica (picas), and pt (points). Fractional values can be entered as decimals.

Styles and Weights

When we talk about *style* for variations in a font's appearance, we're often misusing the term. Styles include condensed, extended, italic, roman, small caps, strikethrough, and underline. The terms *bold*, *light*, *regular*, and *semibold* are actually referring to a font's *weight*. Think of weight as the thickness of the stroke used to create the character. Consider style to be what you do to the characters: pushing and pulling, tilting and leaning, adding lines through and under.

There's no real reason to differentiate between style and weight in Photoshop, but typographers know the difference.

Character and Line Spacing

In addition to controlling the appearance of type through fonts, you can determine positioning among characters and between lines of type using these options:

- **Leading:** Pronounced like the metal rather than the verb *to lead*, *leading* determines the distance between lines of type. Like size, leading is normally set in points, but you can enter values in any unit of measure. The pop-up menu defaults to Auto, which sets the leading at 120% of the font size (although this can be changed in the Justification dialog box, opened through the Paragraph palette's menu).The values in the pop-up menu mirror those of the Font Size field. Leading is based strictly on the specified point measurement, from the baseline of one line to the baseline of the line below. Twelve-point leading, regardless of the character's

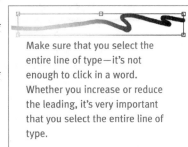

Make sure that you select the entire line of type—it's not enough to click in a word. Whether you increase or reduce the leading, it's very important that you select the entire line of type.

actual size, measures 12 points from the base of one line to the base of the next.

8

- **Kerning:** *Kerning* is the space between a pair of characters. It affects only those two adjoining characters. Each font is designed with specific kerning for various pairs of characters, applied with the default setting of Metrics, but you can fine-tune the appearance of type with judicious use of kerning. Kerning is especially valuable when letters of different font size adjoin (see Figure 8.20).

  To adjust kerning, select a Type tool and click between the letters that need adjustment (do not select the letters). Use the pop-up menu or enter a numeric value in the Kerning field. Pressing Return (Mac users) or Enter (Windows users) commits the change. If you change your mind while still in the numeric field, you can use ⌘-Z (Mac users) or Ctrl+Z (Windows users) to undo the change, or you can press Escape to cancel.

  Kerning is measured in 1/1000 em, a unit of measure based on the particular font's size. One em in a 24-point font is equal to 24 points.

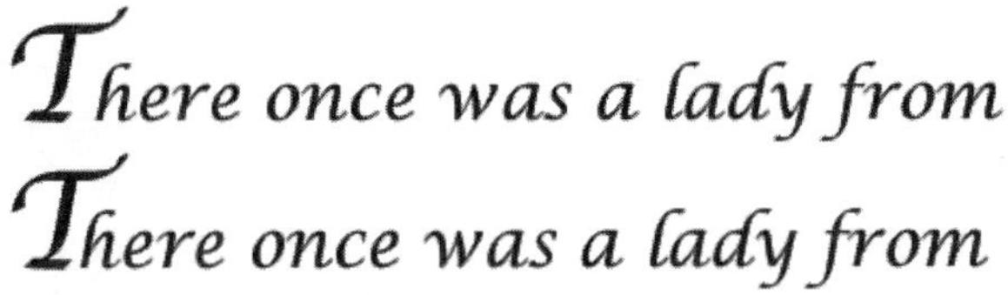

Figure 8.20
The top example shows the default kerning. By manually changing the Kerning value, you can improve the overall appearance, as was done in the bottom example.

There once was a lady from

There once was a lady from

- **Tracking:** Whereas kerning sets the distance between two letters, *tracking* adjusts the spacing among a group of selected letters. Tracking is measured like kerning. It can also be applied to an entire type layer by selecting the layer in the Layers palette and then making the change. When tracking is adjusted for a group of letters in a selection, selected letters shift to meet the adjustment. Tracking is often used to spread the letters out in a title or heading.

Reducing the tracking can be an excellent way of squeezing type into a space that's just a little too small. Whether you're working with paragraph or point type, tightening the tracking can be far preferable to scaling or resizing the type.

Changing Scale, Shifting, Coloring, and Styling

Photoshop's Character palette enables you to change the vertical and horizontal scaling of one or more characters as well as to move a character up or down in relation to the baseline. You can also assign a specific color to a character or block of type and add style characteristics not built in to the font, such as bold, italic, strikethrough, and even anti-aliasing. Here are the Character palette fields that govern these options:

- **Vertical Scale:** Because Photoshop's type is vector based, you can scale it without loss of quality. The Character palette enables you to adjust the height of selected characters from 0% (invisible) to 1000%. The font's default appearance is always 100%. You can apply vertical scaling to selected type or to an entire type layer. Keep in mind that this scaling is independent of the menu command Edit, Transform, Scale. The Character palette still shows 100% after a scale transformation.

- **Horizontal Scale:** Useful for simulating expanded or compressed font styles, horizontal scaling can be adjusted from 0%–1000%. When used proportionally with vertical scaling, the effect is comparable to changing the font size.

- **Baseline Shift:** The *baseline* is the imaginary line on which most letters in a font rest. (Some letters, of course, extend well below the baseline, such as *g, j, p, q,* and *y*; others extend slightly below the baseline, such as *e* and *o*.) Shifting a letter above the baseline creates a *superscript*; shifting a letter below the baseline produces a *subscript* (see Figure 8.21).

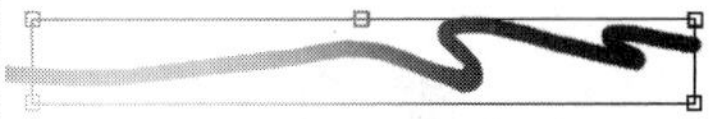

> True superscripts and subscripts are typically smaller than the other characters in the text. Shifting the baseline changes the position of the character(s) without changing the size.

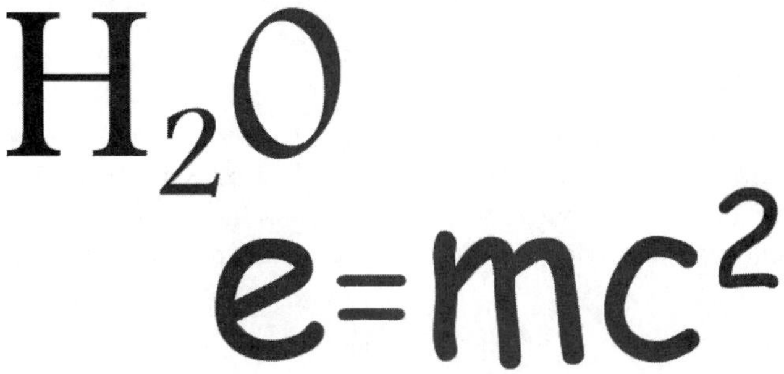

Baseline shift can be adjusted by using the Option-Shift keys (Mac users) or Alt+Shift keys (Windows users) with the up and down arrow keys. Adding the ⌘ or Ctrl key changes the increment from 2 points to 10 points.

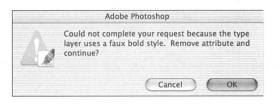

H_2O

$e=mc^2$

Figure 8.21
These "2" examples show a common use of subscript and perhaps an equally familiar superscript.

- **Text Color:** The swatch in the Character palette indicates the current type color. Click it to open the Color Picker. Remember that Photoshop allows multiple colors in a single type layer, so each letter can be a different color, if desired. Use a Type tool to select text to change, or select a type layer in the Layers palette to apply the change to the entire layer.

- **Style Buttons:** From the left, the buttons are Faux Bold, Faux Italic, All Caps, Small Caps, Superscript, Subscript, Underline, and Strikethrough.

When the selected font offers a bold weight or an italic style, it's definitely preferable to choose it in the Font Style pop-up menu than to apply the faux style. On the flip side, using Photoshop's Superscript and Subscript buttons is usually easier than working with Baseline Shift and then scaling the character. Remember, too, that Photoshop does not allow you to warp type to which faux bold has been applied (see Figure 8.22).

Adobe Photoshop

Could not complete your request because the type layer uses a faux bold style. Remove attribute and continue?

Cancel   OK

Figure 8.22
The other faux styles do not interfere with warping.

- **Language:** Select the dictionary to use for spell checking and hyphenation (paragraph type only). All available dictionaries are listed. Photoshop enables you to mix languages on a type layer. Select a word or words with a Type tool and then select a language in the pop-up menu.

- **Anti-Aliasing:** You have the option of applying one of four types of anti-aliasing to selected type or a type layer or having no anti-aliasing applied. (Anti-aliasing is discussed in the section "Anti-aliasing Type," earlier in this chapter.)

Remember that the difference between changing kerning and changing tracking is the selection. If the cursor is between two characters and there is no selection, the shortcuts adjust kerning. If one or more letters are selected, the tracking is changed. Otherwise, the keystrokes are identical.

Also keep in mind that adjusting leading might show no effect unless the entire line is selected. If part of a line has leading set to 24 and another part of the same line has a leading of 48, the entire line appears as 48-point leading. Leading is applied to an entire line, but baseline shift can be applied to individual characters.

The Character Palette Menu

The Character palette's menu contains a number of commands that simply duplicate the style buttons found in the palette itself. Faux Bold, Faux Italic, All Caps, Small Caps, Superscript, Subscript, Underline, and Strikethrough show a check mark to the left when the style is applied to the selected type or type layer. To select or deselect a style, choose the style from the menu or use the palette's button.

The palette's other menu commands deserve additional attention:

- **Dock to Palette Well:** Docking the Character palette to the palette well makes it easily accessible.

- **Standard Vertical Roman Alignment** and **Change Text Orientation:** The option Change Text Orientation rotates type. Horizontal type is rotated to vertical, and vertical is rotated to horizontal. However, when the option Standard Vertical Roman Alignment is applied to one or more characters, those characters are reoriented to the top of the image. In Figure 8.23, the word *Vertical* can be set with the Vertical Type tool or by changing the text orientation of horizontal type. The word *Rotated* uses the Standard Vertical Roman Alignment option. In the words *Mixed Rotation*, the *M* and *R* have standard alignment; the rest of the characters do not.

- **Fractional Widths:** Adjust spacing between letters on an individual basis, using fractions of a pixel. Although this method often improves legibility for large type (20 points and over), it can cause problems for smaller type sizes. It is especially inappropriate for small type destined for the Web. Fractional widths can be applied only to entire type layers.

- **System Layout:** Simplify the characteristics of the selected type layer to match as closely as possible the type of Windows Notepad or Apple's SimpleText and TextEdit. This option's settings include Kerning:0, Tracking:0, Vertical Scaling:100%, Horizontal Scaling:100%, Baseline Shift:0, and Anti-Aliasing:None, and it disables the Fractional Widths option. It does not change font, font size, leading, character style settings, color, or dictionary. System Layout is used primarily for screen mockups and user interface elements.

Figure 8.23
Standard Vertical Roman Alignment orients characters to the top of the page.

- **No Break:** Disable hyphenation in paragraph type. It can be applied on a word-by-word basis by selecting the type with a Type tool and then selecting the command from the menu. No Break can be applied to specific letter combinations to force the break to occur elsewhere in the word. It can also be applied to a group of words to force Photoshop to keep those words on the same line. It is not used with point type because all breaks are inserted manually with the Return or Enter key.

- **Old Style, Ordinals, Swash, and so on:** These options are available only for those fonts that have the specific capabilities built in, primarily OpenType fonts. (Fonts with the word *Pro* in the name are OpenType fonts.) *Ligatures* are two or three letters combined into one character to improve the look of certain letter combinations (see Figure 8.24). *Old Style* refers to number characters. These are lowercase numbers, used primarily with lowercase type. Many old-style numerals have ascenders and descenders, as shown in Figure 8.25.

  Many non-OpenType fonts have the *fi* and *fl* ligatures built in, and you can add them with Shift-Option-5 (Mac users) or Shift+Alt+5 (Windows users) and Shift-Option-6 (Mac users) or Shift+Alt+6 (Windows users). You find ligatures in such common fonts as Times and Geneva, but not in many others, including Arial, Helvetica, and any all-caps fonts.

- **Reset Character:** Return the Character palette (and any selected type or type layer) to the default settings. You can reset selected type or an entire type layer. Either use a Type tool to highlight type on a type layer or select the type layer in the Layers palette. The default settings are not user definable.

Figure 8.24
The top two lines compare the same letter combinations without and with ligatures. The lowest line shows old-style numerals with their natural baseline. (The font is Adobe Garamond Pro.)

fi ff fl ffi ffl
fi ff fl ffi ffl
0123456789
0123456789

The Paragraph Palette

When nested with the Character palette (as it is by default), the Paragraph palette can be shown and hidden by using the button in the Options bar or the ⌘-T (Mac users) or Ctrl+T (Windows users) shortcut while editing or inputting type. You can also show and hide the Paragraph palette through the Windows menu. This palette and its menu, shown in Figure 8.25, govern the appearance of a body of type. Photoshop considers a paragraph to be any amount of text followed by a return.

Figure 8.25
Some of the Paragraph palette menu commands are not available when point type is selected.

All options in the Paragraph palette can be set individually for each paragraph. The entire paragraph need not be selected; click with the Type tool in a paragraph to indicate that it's the target of the changes. You can highlight one or more characters from several paragraphs to select them all. If you don't click in the text, Photoshop assumes that changes made in the Paragraph palette should be applied to the entire type layer. If no type layer is active in the Layers palette, any changes made are used the next time type is added to the image.

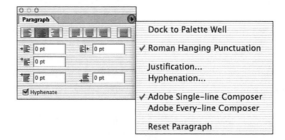

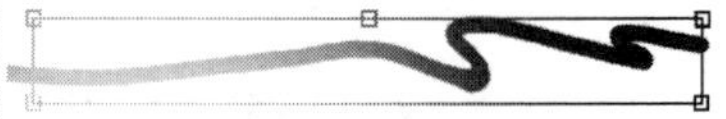

Point type that appears on a single line without a return at the end is considered a paragraph for Photoshop's alignment options.

Across the top of the palette are seven buttons that govern the alignment and justification of paragraphs. What they do to a paragraph of text is apparent from the button icons. The first three buttons are for alignment—arranging the text to have an even margin on the left, have each line centered, or have an even margin on the right. In each case, the text remains within the boundaries of its rectangle.

Photoshop's criteria for justifying text are set in the Justification dialog box opened through the Paragraph palette's menu. (Justification rules are discussed in the next section.) When applied to point type, the left align, center, and right align text buttons determine where the type appears in relation to the spot you clicked with the Type tool.

The four remaining buttons at the top of the Paragraph palette determine justification. *Justified* text has even margins on both the left and right. These four options govern the last line of a paragraph. When the final line is not full—that is, it does not naturally stretch from the left to the right margin— Photoshop offers several options. The final line can be aligned left, centered, aligned right, or justified. To justify the final line, space is added between words and, if necessary, letters. Should the final line be substantially shorter than the others, the amount of whitespace added can be unsightly and interfere with legibility (see Figure 8.26).

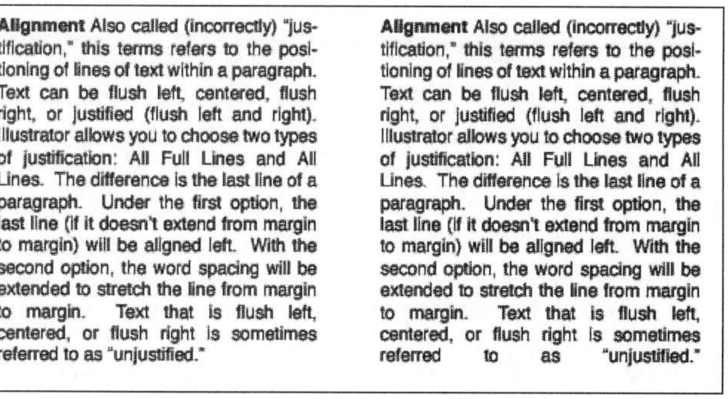

Alignment Also called (incorrectly) "justification," this terms refers to the positioning of lines of text within a paragraph. Text can be flush left, centered, flush right, or justified (flush left and right). Illustrator allows you to choose two types of justification: All Full Lines and All Lines. The difference is the last line of a paragraph. Under the first option, the last line (if it doesn't extend from margin to margin) will be aligned left. With the second option, the word spacing will be extended to stretch the line from margin to margin. Text that is flush left, centered, or flush right is sometimes referred to as "unjustified."

Alignment Also called (incorrectly) "justification," this terms refers to the positioning of lines of text within a paragraph. Text can be flush left, centered, flush right, or justified (flush left and right). Illustrator allows you to choose two types of justification: All Full Lines and All Lines. The difference is the last line of a paragraph. Under the first option, the last line (if it doesn't extend from margin to margin) will be aligned left. With the second option, the word spacing will be extended to stretch the line from margin to margin. Text that is flush left, centered, or flush right is sometimes referred to as "unjustified."

Figure 8.26
The same text is shown with Justify Last Left and with Justify Last All. Note the difference in the final line of each paragraph.

The second section of the Paragraph palette governs indenting. Entire paragraphs can be indented to the left, to the right, or both (the upper pair of buttons), and you can specify indenting separately for the first line of a paragraph (the lower button in the middle section of the palette). By default, the unit of measure for indenting is points. That can be changed in Photoshop's preferences under Units & Rulers. The Paragraph palette uses the unit of measure specified under Type. Figure 8.27 shows how indenting can be used effectively. (The first lines of the subparagraphs are indented with a negative number to shift them to the left.)

Also visible in Figure 8.28 is paragraph spacing. Using the lower set of buttons in the Paragraph palette, you can specify spacing before a paragraph (left), or space can be added after a paragraph (right). Like indenting, the unit of measure specified for type in the Preferences is used.

At the bottom of the Paragraph palette is a check box that turns hyphenation on and off in the paragraph. Like the other Paragraph palette options, hyphenation can be set on a paragraph-by-paragraph basis. Specific rules for hyphenation are set by using the Paragraph palette's menu command of the same name (discussed in the following section).

The Paragraph Palette Menu

Several commands appear in the Paragraph palette's menu. Like most palettes, the top command, Dock to Palette Well, enables you to add the palette to the palette well.

Roman Hanging Punctuation is an advanced typesetting option. With paragraph type, certain punctuation marks fall outside the margins to the left and right, creating a cleaner look to the margins (see Figure 8.28).

8

Figure 8.27
As you can see in this comparison, adding space before or after paragraphs and indenting can improve the appearance and legibility of text.

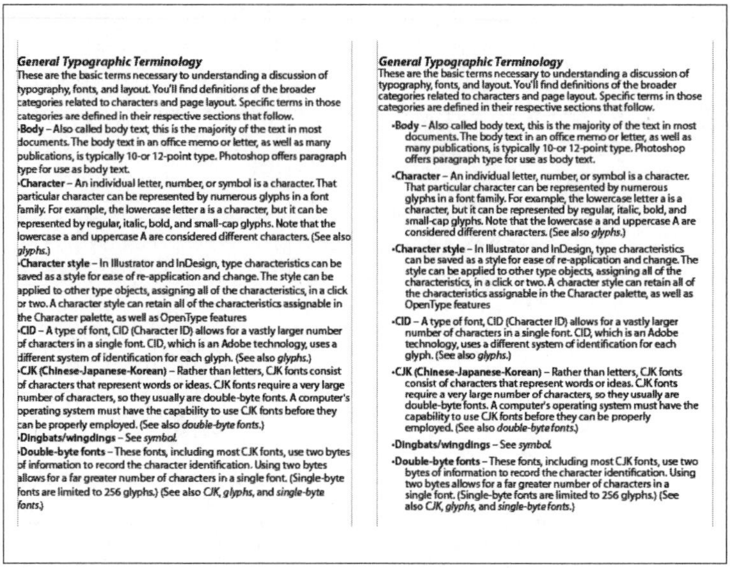
General Typographic Terminology
These are the basic terms necessary to understanding a discussion of typography, fonts, and layout. You'll find definitions of the broader categories related to characters and page layout. Specific terms in those categories are defined in their respective sections that follow.
•**Body** – Also called body text, this is the majority of the text in most documents. The body text in an office memo or letter, as well as many publications, is typically 10-or 12-point type. Photoshop offers paragraph type for use as body text.
•**Character** – An individual letter, number, or symbol is a character. That particular character can be represented by numerous glyphs in a font family. For example, the lowercase letter a is a character, but it can be represented by regular, italic, bold, and small-cap glyphs. Note that the lowercase a and uppercase A are considered different characters. (See also *glyphs*.)
•**Character style** – In Illustrator and InDesign, type characteristics can be saved as a style for ease of re-application and change. The style can be applied to other type objects, assigning all of the characteristics, in a click or two. A character style can retain all of the characteristics assignable in the Character palette, as well as OpenType features
•**CID** – A type of font, CID (Character ID) allows for a vastly larger number of characters in a single font. CID, which is an Adobe technology, uses a different system of identification for each glyph. (See also *glyphs*.)
•**CJK (Chinese-Japanese-Korean)** – Rather than letters, CJK fonts consist of characters that represent words or ideas. CJK fonts require a very large number of characters, so they usually are double-byte fonts. A computer's operating system must have the capability to use CJK fonts before they can be properly employed. (See also *double-byte fonts*.)
•**Dingbats/wingdings** – See *symbol*.
•**Double-byte fonts** – These fonts, including most CJK fonts, use two bytes of information to record the character identification. Using two bytes allows for a far greater number of characters in a single font. (Single-byte fonts are limited to 256 glyphs.) (See also *CJK*, *glyphs*, and *single-byte fonts*.)

Figure 8.28
Hanging punctuation enables the larger letterforms to align to the margins. This option gives the text more of a "block" look, producing the illusion of straighter margins.

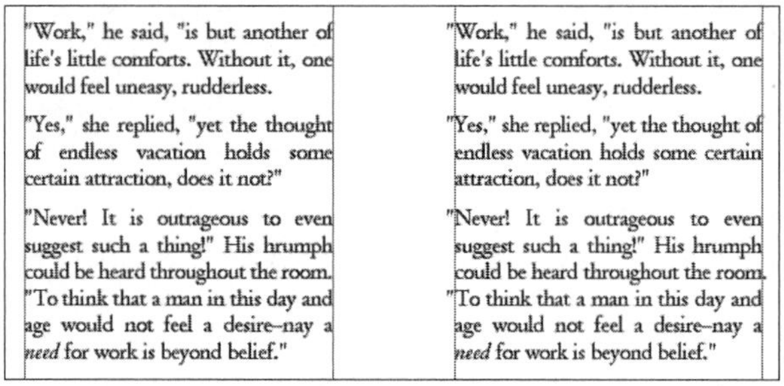
"Work," he said, "is but another of life's little comforts. Without it, one would feel uneasy, rudderless.

"Yes," she replied, "yet the thought of endless vacation holds some certain attraction, does it not?"

"Never! It is outrageous to even suggest such a thing!" His humph could be heard throughout the room. "To think that a man in this day and age would not feel a desire–nay a *need* for work is beyond belief."

The Justification dialog (shown in Figure 8.29) controls how Photoshop justifies paragraphs. Making changes here enables you to make tiny adjustments to how Photoshop spaces words and letters to create full justification.

Figure 8.29
Other than Auto Leading, these values are applied only when text is justified.

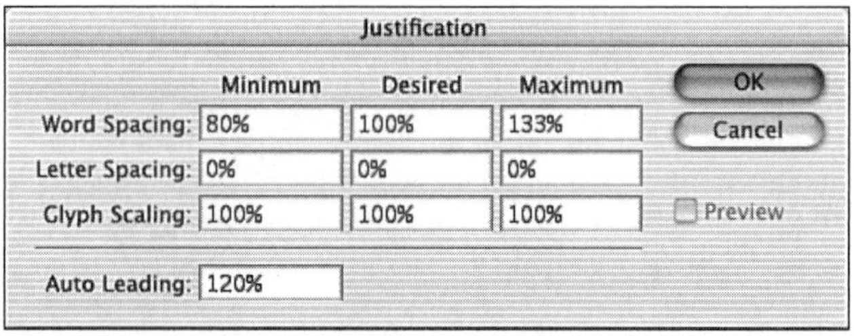

Word Spacing establishes minimum, maximum, and target amounts for space between words. A value of 100% represents the font's built-in spacing plus any changes you've made to tracking in the Character palette. Values can range from 0%–133%.

Letter Spacing determines how much change Photoshop can make to spaces between letters within words. Justifying relies on letter spacing only after word spacing has been applied and only if necessary. Although percents are shown in the dialog, the unit of measure is actually fractions of an em. Inputting 0% in all three fields turns off letter spacing.

Glyph Scaling, a method of last resort, actually changes the width of individual characters to create justification. Sacrificing the appearance of the letters for the appearance of the margins is rarely a good idea. A value of 100% represents the original width of each character.

At the bottom of the Justification dialog, you can specify what percentage of a font's size will be used for the Auto setting in the Character palette's Leading pop-up menu.

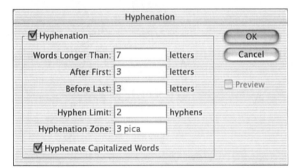

The default values for justification in Photoshop CS2 are appropriate for most purposes. Make changes to the settings when you need to tweak the type a little, perhaps to make a specific amount of text fit in a specific area or to adjust the overall appearance of the text.

The Hyphenation dialog, shown in Figure 8.30, is opened with the Hyphenation command on the Paragraph palette's menu. It controls what rules Photoshop applies when breaking words at the end of a line. Photoshop uses the assigned dictionary to determine where a word is hyphenated; these settings determine whether a word is hyphenated at all.

Figure 8.30
Remember that only paragraph type can be automatically hyphenated.

You use the Hyphen Limit field to control how many consecutive lines can end with hyphens and the Hyphenation Zone field to establish a distance from the right margin in which words will not be hyphenated. For example, if the preceding word enters the designated zone, the following word is moved in its entirety to the following line. Likewise, if a word to be broken does not have a dictionary-defined break within the zone, the word remains unhyphenated.

If you deselect the Hyphenate Capitalized Words check box at the bottom of the dialog box, words that begin with a capital letter cannot be hyphenated. This includes proper nouns as well as words that start sentences. (The possibility that a word is long enough to both start a sentence and require hyphenation in Photoshop indicates very narrow columns or a very long word.) This setting has no effect on type set in all caps or entered with the Caps Lock key locked down.

The difference between the Adobe Single-line Composer and the Adobe Every-line Composer commands is the approach to hyphenation. Single-line looks at one line, decides the appropriate hyphenation, and then moves to the next line. Every-line examines all the selected text before making decisions, which usually produces fewer word breaks and a generally more pleasing look to the text.

The Reset Paragraph command restores the Paragraph palette to its default settings.

USING SPELL CHECK AND FIND/REPLACE

8

Introduced in Photoshop 7, the Spell Check and Find/Replace features are indispensable tools when you're adding large amounts of type to a project.

The Spell Checker

The menu command Edit, Check Spelling opens Photoshop's Check Spelling dialog box (see Figure 8.31). Similar to spell checking systems found in many word-processing programs, this tool offers suggestions and enables you to input your own changes in the dialog box. In addition, you have the choice of ignoring that particular word, ignoring all instances of that word in the image, changing that instance to a suggested spelling or a word you type in the Change To field (thus changing all instances to the selected new spelling), or adding the word to the dictionary.

Caution

Think twice about using the Add button in Photoshop's spell checker because the dictionaries are not editable. After you add a word, it's there for good. Instead, rely on the Ignore and Ignore All buttons unless the word appears often—and you're absolutely certain the spelling is correct.

Figure 8.31
The spell checker is rather basic, but it certainly is functional.

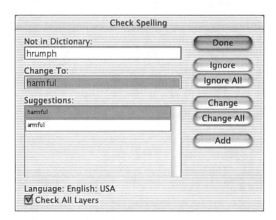

The spell checker uses the dictionary assigned to the selected text. If more than one dictionary is assigned, it automatically switches to the appropriate dictionary on the fly. The spell checker does not check grammar.

Find/Replace

The Find and Replace Text command, also located under Photoshop's Edit menu, functions much like the Find and Replace command in a basic word processor (see Figure 8.32). Unlike Microsoft Word, however, it doesn't allow you to search by format or style, nor can it search for special characters.

Enter the word or phrase that you want to find and then enter a replacement word or phrase. The Find Next button initiates the search. When an instance of the word or phrase is located, it is highlighted in the text. You have the option of changing that instance, changing all instances in the image, or changing and continuing the search for the next instance (Change/Find). You can also click Change All immediately after entering the target and replacement words.

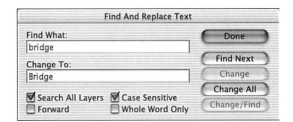

Figure 8.32
To find without replacing, simply enter the word or phrase and click Find Next. You can then click Done without making any changes.

You have the option of restricting the search to the active type layer or searching all type layers. You can make the search case sensitive, requiring a match in capitalization as well as spelling. When you select the Forward check box, Photoshop searches from the current Type tool insertion point to the end of the text. Selecting the Whole Word Only check box prevents Photoshop from finding matches within longer words. For example, when this option is deselected, a search for *ten* also returns such words as *often*, *intent*, *tension*, and *tents*.

WORKING WITH FONTS AND FONT EMBEDDING

Many types of fonts are currently available in various qualities. Photoshop, like most high-end computer programs, works best with high-quality fonts. Although you can get good results with inexpensive and free fonts, they are often troublesome. TrueType and Type 1 fonts are the most common high-quality fonts available, with more and more OpenType fonts reaching the marketplace. (Adobe has discontinued support for multiple master fonts.)

Fonts (also called *typefaces*) classified as TrueType, Type 1, multiple master, and OpenType typically perform flawlessly with Photoshop. (Any font, however, is subject to corruption over time and might need to be reinstalled.) Bitmap fonts should not be used with Photoshop.

> Although Photoshop can use multiple master fonts, it cannot take advantage of the special characteristics of these fonts. Unlike Illustrator, Photoshop has no provisions for customizing the appearance of multiple master fonts.

Fonts and Font Families

Technically, a certain typeface at a certain size in a certain style constitutes a font. More generally, we tend to use the term to refer to an entire family of fonts. For example, Times 12 pt is different from Times 24 pt and Times (Italic) or Times (Bold). Each was designed to serve a separate purpose. Colloquially, we refer to all the Times typefaces as a single font. Technically, Times is a font family, with numerous individual fonts.

> Many fonts come in both Macintosh and Windows versions. Make sure you install the appropriate font. OpenType fonts can use the same font file on either platform.

When does terminology make a difference? Primarily, the subject comes up in marketing. Such-and-such a laser printer may have 52 fonts installed, and a competitor might claim more than 250 fonts. One font package could include more than 1,000 fonts, and another might have 85 font families. As long as you are aware of the difference in terminology, you can make informed decisions.

CREATIVE IMAGING
IN PHOTOSHOP

IN THIS CHAPTER

There are infinite ways you can alter an image, whether for purposes of repair, creative enhancement, or color correction. Most of the effects in this chapter require that a layer be rasterized if it contains type or a vector shape. We'll look at different filters and how you can make use of them.

A detailed look at the ins and outs of every filter is beyond the scope of this chapter. Besides, more than half the fun of working with Photoshop and the filters in particular is trying things on your own.

Images can be fixed and enhanced—from such minor things as sharpening blurry images and removing dust and blemishes from scanned images, to extracting foreground objects from backgrounds and creating custom patterns from portions of images. If you encounter a filter that is unavailable for your particular image, it is likely due to the color mode of the image. RGB is the color mode where the most filters are available.

USING THE EXTRACT TOOL

The Extract tool was mentioned in Chapter 7, "Using Selections, Paths, and Transforms in Photoshop." Although Extract is part of the Filter menu, it falls under the category of selections. In the Extract interface, you can separate the subject from its background, and it will be extracted onto a transparent layer for you.

Simple Extraction

When you select Filter, Extract or press Option-⌘-X (Mac users) or Alt+Ctrl+X (Windows users), you get the Extract dialog (see Figure 9.1). The basic operation of the Extract feature is fairly simple: Use the Highlight tool to trace the edge of the object you want to isolate and then click the Fill tool within the outline you just drew to fill the object with a mask. This indicates the area(s) you want to retain (see Figure 9.2).

Next, either click Preview to preview the extraction or go ahead and click OK to begin the extraction process. You end up with the extracted object against a transparent background (see Figure 9.3).

Caution

The Extract filter discards all the background pixels. If you want to keep a copy of the original, duplicate the layer and apply the extraction to the copied layer.

Highlight Options

You can alter the size of the Highlight tool by adjusting the Brush Size slider in the Tool Options portion of the Extract dialog. You can also choose a different highlight color if the default of lime green disturbs you (or, more importantly, if a similar color is used in the image and you can't see the highlighting).

A good option for many extractions is the Smart Highlighting check box. With this checked, you don't need to precisely draw a highlight around the edge of the object; the tool automatically seeks out the edge of the object and "snaps" to that edge. However, the effectiveness of the Smart Highlighting feature (as with the Magnetic Lasso selection tool) is a function of how distinct the edge of the foreground image is from the background. You may need to do some repair to the highlight after the fact (more about this in a moment).

Fill Eyedropper Clean edges

Highlight Erase Cleanup Zoom Move

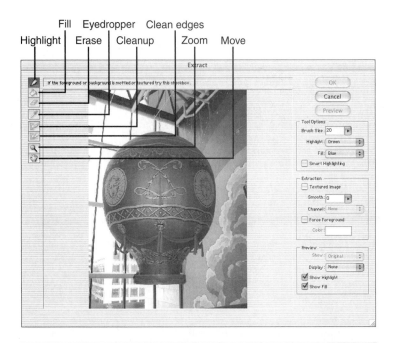

Figure 9.1
The Extract dialog has a set of tools, the controls and settings for those tools, and a large preview window.

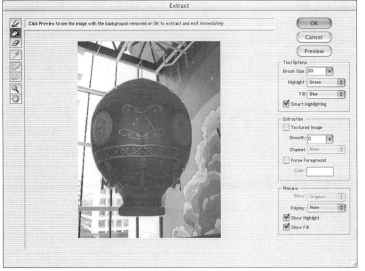

Figure 9.2
An outline is drawn around the object with the Highlight tool and then is filled with a mask using the Fill tool.

Enlarge the brush size to cover intricate areas of the object, such as fine hairs, or other parts of the image that are not easily separated from the background. If you are unable to draw a definable border that can be filled (for example, it's hard to draw a highlight around a wispy strand of hair or a blade of grass), highlight all of what you want to include and then check the Force Foreground check box. Select the Eyedropper tool and select the color in the highlighted area that you want the Extract filter to base the extraction on. Naturally, this process works best on objects that have large areas of a single color, such as a blade of grass.

Figure 9.3
The Extract filter strips away the background outside the masked area and leaves you with the extracted object against a transparent background.

If you make a mistake while drawing with the Highlight tool, unlike with the Magnetic Lasso tool (or any other lasso tool), you can stop, switch to the Erase tool, erase the errant line, reselect the Highlight tool, and soldier on.

If your highlight is completely out of whack, hold down the Option key (Mac users) or the Alt key (Windows users). The Cancel button changes to a Reset button. Click it, and whatever highlight or fill you've drawn is erased, and you can start over without having to exit the dialog.

Unless you are using a stylus on a drawing tablet (such as Wacom's), you may need to go back over your border and fix any erratic portions of it. After all, a mouse is not a precision drawing tool. Also, this process may not be terribly effective if you've consumed a lot of coffee!

Caution

If you do stop and start with the Highlight tool and Erase tool, make sure that there are no tiny gaps in the finished, highlighted border; otherwise, the Fill tool will not place a mask within that border, but rather over the entire image. Use the Zoom tool to enlarge the highlighting and inspect it for small gaps. Use the Erase and Highlight tools to fix the border as necessary.

Previewing and Editing Extractions

After you have drawn a highlight around an object and filled it with a mask, click the Preview button to see a preview of what the extracted object will look like. If the edges are not clean, you can select either the Cleanup tool or the Edge Touchup tool.

Clicking and dragging with the Cleanup tool lets you erase portions of the mask, if there is still some background peeking through, either along the edge of the object or in the middle of the object. This is also good for adding "punch-through" parts of an image, such as transparent windows if you are removing a car from a background, for example. You can hold down the Option key (Mac users) or the Alt key (Windows users) while clicking and dragging the Cleanup tool to restore the mask, in case you erased too much (see Figure 9.4).

The Edge Touchup tool lets you sharpen the edges of the object. Holding down the ⌘ key (Mac users) or the Ctrl key (Windows users) while clicking and dragging lets you move an edge in or out, if the extraction process "missed."

Figure 9.4
In Preview mode, the Cleanup tool lets you erase any portions of the background that got picked up by the mask.

If you like what you have created, click OK. Photoshop goes ahead and applies the Extract filter.

After you extract an object from an image, you can use any of Photoshop's other retouching tools and filters to make any further corrections or tweaks.

You can, of course, drag the extracted object to a new document to composite it on a new background (see Figure 9.5).

Figure 9.5
An extracted object can be composited over a new background without exhibiting any fringing around its edges.

USING THE FILTER GALLERY

The Filter Gallery (see Figure 9.6) is a separate interface used to quickly apply filters in Preview window. If you don't like the way a particular filter is working, click a category and try on another filter. Many filters use the Filter Gallery as their interface, so you are going to encounter it frequently. If you wish to turn off the gallery to free screen space for the preview, click the small double arrow button. The thumbnails of the filter gallery hide until you click the arrow again.

Figure 9.6
The Filter Gallery contains the preview on the left, categories of filters in the middle pane, and the filter controls on the right side.

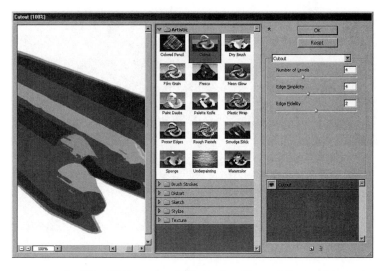

In a single image or layer, you can use the Filter Gallery cumulatively: One filter can be used on top of another filter, on top of another, and so on. You can also apply the same filter several times. Under the filter controls appears a list of filters that are applied. Beneath that, at the very bottom-right corner, are buttons to create new effect layers or delete effect layers. You click the New Effect Layer button, and the list above populates with a new filter. When you click that list item, you can then find a filter from the gallery drop-down list of filters. Each filter builds on the one underneath it. For a different effect, you can change the stacking order of the filters by clicking and dragging the filter up or down through the list. You click the trash icon to delete an effect layer you have selected. When you click OK, your single or multiple filters are applied to the image.

USING THE LIQUIFY FEATURE

Liquify is perhaps one of the most fun tools in Photoshop. By using the Bloat and Pucker tools inside the Liquify interface, you can expand and shrink parts of your image until it becomes downright scary (see Figure 9.7). Liquify really gives you an opportunity to push pixels around. You can smear them, twirl them, and expand or shrink them, and you can also save your liquefied area as a mesh for use on other images.

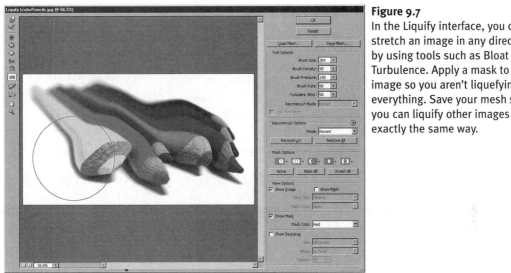

Figure 9.7
In the Liquify interface, you can stretch an image in any direction by using tools such as Bloat and Turbulence. Apply a mask to the image so you aren't liquefying everything. Save your mesh so you can liquify other images exactly the same way.

9

USING PATTERN MAKER

Pattern Maker takes the image layer you are working with and lets you designate from that area a portion that will be duplicated and tiled across the entire image layer. This is a fast way to make a pattern from a portion of any image you choose, and it takes very little effort.

WORKING WITH THE VANISHING POINT FEATURE

New in Photoshop CS2, Vanishing Point is perhaps one of the tools that will encourage users of previous versions of Photoshop to upgrade. You have already been introduced to the Clone Stamp tool, which you use to clone part of an image in order to fill in an area or cover up a blemish. Cloning gets difficult when you have to account for the change in visual perspective in the image. One aspect of perspective is that the eye perceives objects in a scene that are further away as appearing smaller. The Vanishing Point feature lets you identify the angle of perspective in an image so that the Clone Stamp tool will follow that perspective when cloning your image.

Choose Filter, Vanishing Point. The Vanishing Point window opens. Several steps are required to use this tool successfully. Most importantly, you need to be able to identify the angles of perspective in your image. If you have a picture of a hilly landscape with some rocks but nothing geometric to help you with perspective, don't bother using Vanishing Point. Use

To use the Vanishing Point tool, your image must be in RGB color mode. Other color modes currently do not support editing with this filter. If you are working in another color mode, try converting your image to RGB and then using the Vanishing Point tool. After applying the filter, change your mode back to where you need it. Be aware that converting color modes can affect the look of the image significantly.

Vanishing Point for images with homes and buildings or other objects with obvious straight lines. Fences, railroad tracks, and wooden planks come to mind.

In the Vanishing Point window, you choose the Create Plane tool and locate the area you wish to clone. Click in four places with the Grid tool to create the grid. You should be using the perspective of the image to create the grid, so follow the lines and angles with the Grid tool. Using the perspective from your grid, Photoshop interpolates the pixels as you clone. This means that as a portion of your subject gets smaller in the distance, the cloned area is smaller at that distance. In the example in Figure 9.8, we have created a plane for cloning the building into a much larger skyscraper.

Figure 9.8
A plane has been created for the skyscraper located in the center of this image and extended upward. Although you can draw anywhere outside the plane, use the plane to help you with perspective where you will clone by using the Clone Stamp tool.

To clone an area, select the Clone Stamp tool. Alt-click (Windows users) or Option-click (Mac users) in the area you want to clone. Let go of the Alt or Option key and find a location to start stamping the cloned area. Click, and you begin cloning.

When you are satisfied with your image, click OK. Your resulting image appears back in the canvas (see Figure 9.9).

For more detailed information on the Vanishing Point tool, search for Vanishing Point in the Adobe Help Center. You will find tutorials covering all aspects of uses of the Grid tool and other Vanishing Point options.

Don't expect your first attempt with the Vanishing Point feature to be successful. Also don't expect every one of your images to be a good candidate for using Vanishing Point.

Figure 9.9
A moderately successful use of the Vanishing Point tool.

UNDERSTANDING FILTER CATEGORIES

Many filters in Photoshop are organized into categories to help you find what you need faster. The following sections list the categories of filters.

The Artistic Filters

The Artistic filters simulate some artistic styles you may already be familiar with. As with applying any other filter, applying these re-renders the image or layer with the artistic look you choose:

- **Artistic, Film Grain:** Film Grain makes your image look like it is a frame from an old movie. Adding grain can be a way to quickly age your picture or make it look more gritty. You can control the look of the film grain with the sliders for Grain, Highlight Area, and Intensity. Grain enlarges the size of the simulated film grains. Highlight Area brightens the lighter portions of the grained image overall. Lowering the Intensity setting of the grain gives you more grain in the image area.

- **Artistic, Palette Knife:** Applying the Palette Knife filter takes away the photographic realism and makes the image appear scraped on with a palette knife. Make adjustments to the Stroke Size, Stroke Detail, and Softness, and your image also changes considerably. Altering the size can really change the detail level to an abstract geometric appearance (see Figure 9.10).

- **Artistic, Sponge:** Applying the Sponge filter waters down your detail and gives the image layer a water droplet effect. Move the sliders for Brush Size, Definition, and Smoothness. A higher Smoothness number overlays your sponged image with an almost camouflage pattern. If you have ever done any sponge painting on walls, you will see a similarity with this filter. The pattern is usually obvious in the areas of solid color and washes out the detail in the image underneath.

Figure 9.10
When the Palette Knife filter is applied to an image of a street sign, notice how the painted version still looks "digital."

9

The Blur Filters

The Blur filters attempt to simulate every type of blur you have ever experienced through your weary eyes, camera lens, photograph, video, or car window. Often you need to blur part or all of an image layer to produce a special effect or to force focus on another part of the image. Sometimes you want a subtle blur applied to an image to simulate a soft focus or a glow on the subject. Other times, your goal may be to make the image unrecognizable. Although we can't cover all the different blurs in this section, the most popular ones are listed here:

- **Blur, Gaussian Blur:** The Gaussian Blur filter is an all-purpose blur filter that gives you some degree of control over the blur effect, going from a slight softening to a glaucoma-vision effect (see Figure 9.11).

- **Blur, Motion Blur:** Applying the Motion Blur filter blurs the image as if the subject in the image or the camera taking the photo is traveling quickly through space.

- **Blur, Lens Blur:** The Lens Blur filter is a photography-centric filter that can be used to simulate all kinds of camera lens effects. This blur filter contains more options than any of the others. If you need the absolute tightest control over your blur, use the Lens Blur filter.

- **Blur, Radial Blur:** This filter realistically simulates a shaky or spinning camera lens in your image even more than the Lens Blur filter does.

The Brush Strokes Filters

Although many of the Brush Strokes filters could fall under the Artistic category, they don't fall in that category in Photoshop:

- **Brush Strokes, Angled Strokes:** Angled Strokes changes the image so that the lighter and darker strokes are painted in opposite directions (see Figure 9.12).

Figure 9.11
A Gaussian blur takes off all the hard edges. Move the Radius slider to the right to increase the blur intensity.

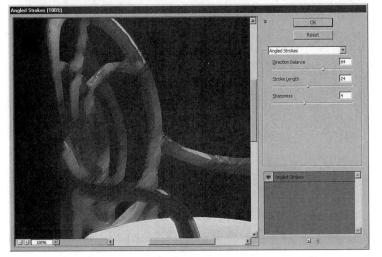

Figure 9.12
Angled Strokes is a filter that produces a painted look. Adjust the Direction Balance, Stroke Length, and Sharpness sliders to control the effect of the brush stroke.

- **Brush Strokes, Dark Strokes:** Dark Strokes renders dark areas as short, tight, dark strokes, and it renders lighter areas with long, white strokes.

The Distort Filters

The Distort filters alter an image geometrically, creating 3D or other reshaping effects. Some of the many Distort Filters are listed here:

- **Distort, Displace:** A displace is often referred to as a *displacement map* or *bump map*. By using the contrast of one image, you displace or shift the pixels of another (see Figure 9.13). The result looks like a three-dimensional imprint displacing your source image. For example, if you have an image of a coin, you can use it as a displacement for a picture of a flag. So your final image of the flag has the texture of the coin. The flag's colors are retained. In any image used to displace, the darkest and lightest colors produce the most displacement. In order to displace, the displacement image must be saved in Photoshop document format (.psd). You can change the horizontal and vertical scaling of the displacement image to enlarge or reduce the effect. You can also tile the displacement image across the canvas in case you want to create a repeating subtle watermark across the canvas.

Figure 9.13
Displacing the image of the city by using the image of the fingerprint.

- **Distort, Shear:** The Shear filter lets you bend your image horizontally in many ways by adjusting the vertical band. Easily apply some flexibility to your image by making new points along the band and bending it in opposing directions.

  Click the Wrap Around radio button or the Repeat Edge Pixels radio button to allow or prevent your image from overlapping on the opposite side of the image.

- **Distort, Wave:** The Wave filter gives you an interface of sliders to create a wavy mess of your picture (see Figure 9.14). Actually, *mess* isn't really a good word for it as the Wave effect is quite cool looking. Moving the sliders too far can render the image unrecognizable.

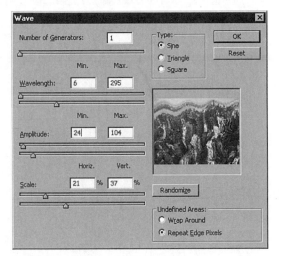

Figure 9.14
The Wave filter controls affect all images differently. Wave is based on calculations that are random. If you like the wave settings, but the wave is not quite right, click the Randomize button to see a different version of the same wave effect.

The Noise Filters

Noise is a random disturbance that reduces the clarity of a signal. The Noise filters in Photoshop create and remove noise. You can add noise like that from a broken television set, or remove the dust and scratches from an image that Photoshop may be detecting from a scanned or older photograph. The following are the Noise filters:

- **Noise, Despeckle:** If you have an image that has a dirty appearance from scanning or having some nasty stuff on the lens, it may benefit from a despeckle. Despeckle removes the tiny highlights that are most likely bits of dirt in your image. It does more than a decent job on images and may save you quite a bit of cleanup time. Be aware that despeckling sometimes inadvertently removes specular highlights that belong in the image.

- **Noise, Dust and Scratches:** This filter reduces noise by changing dissimilar pixels. It works best when the dust or particles are in high contrast to their background.

The Pixelate Filters

Imaging in computers involves pixels. The words you are reading right now were originally created as pixels. The Pixelate filters break up your selection or layer by using stiff geometric pixel effects. These are the Pixelate filters:

- **Pixelate, Crystallize:** The Crystallize filter breaks up the image into a crystal pattern. It limits image color depth to fewer colors. Adjust the size of the individual crystal cells to make the polygon shapes larger or smaller (see Figure 9.15).

Figure 9.15
Crystallize uses the colors of the image but limits the number of colors for the solid-color shapes. This effect is similar to stained glass, without the dark edges in between cells.

- **Pixelate, Mosaic:** The Mosaic filter produces an effect of enlarging pixels and taking out the detail in the selected area. Because of the wide use of this effect to obscure the identifying features of crime suspects on police television shows, many people are familiar with the mosaic pixelated look.

The Render Filters

The Render filters are a hodgepodge of different effects that add clouds, textures, backgrounds, and lighting effects:

- **Render, Clouds:** Whereas most filters require that an image already exist that can be manipulated, Clouds is one of the few filters that actually creates an image. The cloud color generated uses your background and foreground colors to create the pixel effect. Because the Clouds filter creates random shadows and highlights from whole cloth, many Photoshop tutorials for creating "natural" textures begin with creating a cloud layer.

- **Render, Lighting Effects:** The Lighting Effects filter gives you the most for your money. An interface is provided where you can create and move virtual lights on your image to alter its overall light quality. You can wash out your image in light, or you can darken the image to make it more mysterious or dramatic (see Figure 9.16). You can even choose the type of light and its intensity. You can also choose how the image "material" reacts to the light, with glossy or dull finish. If you like your lighting arrangement, you can save it to use in other images.

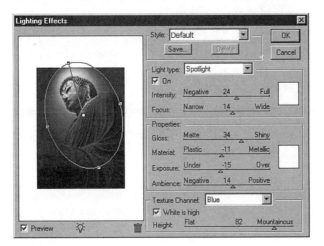

Figure 9.16
Practice with the Lighting Effects filter to get used to how you expand the light source by using the handles on each light. Each light type has different handles.

9

The Sharpen Filters

You know how it is. You take a bunch of digital pictures, and when you start downloading them, you find that the one you really want to use is blurry. Now, when it comes to images, there is blurry and then there is *blurry*. In the former case, we're talking about images that are a little soft or slightly out of focus. In the latter case, we're talking about images that are little more than indistinguishable blurs. Photoshop's Sharpen filters can fix the slight softness, but they're not going to resurrect a hideously out-of-focus image:

- **Sharpen, Sharpen Edges:** Blurriness or softness is caused, in part, by decreased contrast between the "edges" in an image. An *edge* in an image is where adjacent pixels demonstrate major color changes. Major color changes provide detail in an image, and when these edges are softened, a loss of detail results. Sharpen Edges improves on the detail in the selection by increasing the contrast between colors or shades.

- **Sharpen, Smart Sharpen:** The Smart Sharpen filter, which is new in Photoshop CS2, outperforms the other sharpening filters. The Smart Sharpen dialog gives you a lot of control over the sharpening, contrast, and the shadow and highlight areas (see Figure 9.17). You can click the Advanced radio button to access all this control over sharpening. Whenever possible, you should zoom in to the image in the dialog by using the zoom buttons so you can see the subtle changes of the effect in the preview. Smart Sharpen can use an algorithm to remove a Gaussian or Lens Motion blur from an image.

Figure 9.17
The Smart Sharpen dialog gives
you control never before available
for sharpening your images in
Photoshop.

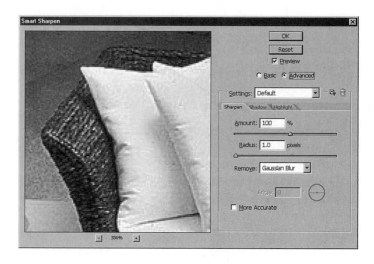

The Sketch Filters

The Sketch filters attempt to simulate a sketch by using different drawing media. Applying a Sketch filter to an image alters it considerably, forcing its color and contrast to fit within the range of the filter you choose. These are the Sketch filters:

- **Sketch, Chalk and Charcoal:** This filter converts an image into a chalk-and-charcoal sketch. The background is rendered in coarse chalk, and foreground objects are rendered in charcoal. You can vary the amount of charcoal used versus the amount of chalk used. Charcoal strokes are applied in the foreground color you have selected, whereas chalk strokes are applied in the background color you have defined. Black (or dark gray) and white are the traditional choices for this filter, but you can choose whatever combination of colors you'd like.

- **Sketch, Conté Crayon:** A Conté crayon is a type of crayon made of graphite and clay, usually available in black, brown, and red. The Conté Crayon filter draws images in this style, giving images a rough-textured illustration effect. The filter uses the selected foreground color for dark areas of the image and the background color for light areas.

- **Sketch, Halftone Pattern:** The Halftone Pattern filter simulates an exaggerated halftone dot pattern. You can adjust the size of the dots, the contrast, and the shape of the dot pattern. This filter is useful for simulating the look of old newspaper photos or Roy Lichtenstein paintings (see Figure 9.18).

The Stylize Filters

Stylize filters create an impressionistic effect on a layer or selection. These are the Stylize filters:

- **Stylize, Extrude:** Extrude applies to your image a 3D effect where blocks or pyramids radiate out from the surface of the image or selection.

Figure 9.18
The halftone pattern simulates an offset printed image viewed under a loop or magnifying glass.

■ **Glowing Edges:** This filter identifies the edges in the image and creates a glow as if beaming from a neon light.

■ **Stylize, Wind:** The Wind filter streaks the brighter areas of your image to make it look as though it is being affected by winds (see Figure 9.19). Depending on the subject in your image, it may look like dust is being blown off in a wind or as if your image's color is starting to bleed. You can choose the direction of the wind, whether left or right. You can also choose the method. For a more realistic effect, choose Wind for the method. Unfortunately, the Blast and Stagger methods tend to look computerized.

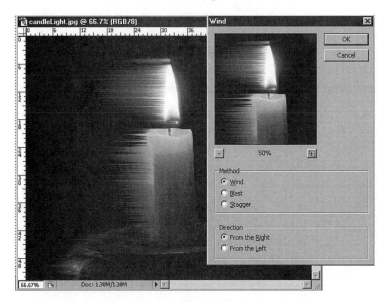

Figure 9.19
The Wind filter used on an image smears the brighter portions of the image more. If you find that the Wind filter isn't intense enough for your needs, reapply it under the Filter menu. The most recent filter used is always available for reapplication as the first filter item in the menu.

The Texture Filters

These are the Texture filters, which let you add surface effects to images:

- **Texture, Patchwork:** Patchwork breaks up your image into smaller squares. It has a textured appearance, with a more limited color distribution in the image. The pattern created looks a lot like it was sewn in with colored yarn.

- **Texture, Texturizer:** The Texturizer filter provides four types of textures with different options for each: Brick, Burlap, Canvas, and Sandstone. When you use one of these options, your image looks like it is painted onto the texture. The scaling and relief options affect the perceived depth of the texture.

The Video Filters

The Video filters help you correct an image for use in a frame of video:

- **Video, De-Interlace:** Video is interlaced frames, and you see only every other line of resolution. De-Interlace smoothes out your image by interpolating or duplicating the even or odd fields.

- **Video, NTSC:** The gamut of color used by television is more restricted, and this filter prevents some of the oversaturated colors from bleeding inside the scan lines of the television.

The Other Filters

The filters under the Other category have been around for some time, certainly long enough to call Photoshop their home. For whatever reason, they have never fallen into a more descriptive category than Other:

- **Other, High Pass:** The High Pass filter reveals the edge details of your image, using your specified radius (see Figure 9.20).

- **Other, Offset:** Offset takes your image within the view of the canvas and shifts it. One use for Offset is to prepare an image for a pattern by shifting it evenly and allowing the image to wrap around. This makes the outer edges capable of meeting smoothly on all sides.

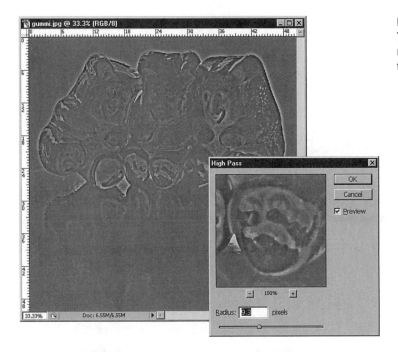

Figure 9.20
The High Pass filter grays out most of the image, revealing only the edge details.

WORKING WITH DIGIMARC

Embedding a digital watermark in an image embeds information about the creator of the image. Watermarks are invisible to the naked eye, but they can be detected by Photoshop and can be used to track purloined images. Digimarc lets you embed watermarks in images, which aids in protecting copyrighted images.

For more information on embedding Digimarc digital watermarks, refer to the Digimarc website, at www.digimarc.com.

CORRECTING IMAGES

A lot of your time working in Photoshop will be used correcting images so that they are displayed in all their splendor. Most cameras capture a decent image, but rarely do images come right off the camera in perfect contrast, brightness, and color. In traditional photography and development, even the most experienced developer might spend days or weeks developing a photo to get the desired result from the film negative. Photoshop makes these corrections much faster and provides immediate results.

Brightness/Contrast and Auto Contrast

The Brightness/Contrast command is the easiest correction concept to understand, and use of the tonal adjustments is also simple. However, Brightness/Contrast is also the least flexible and the least powerful of the image-correction tools. The Brightness/Contrast dialog, shown in Figure 9.21, consists of a pair of sliders and their related numeric fields, along with OK and Cancel buttons and a Preview check box. It can be used on the active layer or on an active selection. It always affects all selected color channels equally, but you can apply it to channels individually by selecting the target channel(s) in the Channels palette.

Figure 9.21
Each of the sliders ranges from −100 to +100.

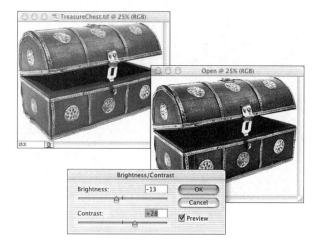

Dragging the Brightness slider to the right lightens the image (or selection), and dragging it to the left darkens the image (or selection). The Contrast slider, in effect, increases or decreases the difference between light and dark pixels. Dragging the slider to the left (reducing the contrast) makes the image more gray and consolidates the pixels' luminosity values in the midranges; dragging the Contrast slider to the right distributes the luminosity values (see Figure 9.22).

Figure 9.22
The top image represents the original. In the middle, Contrast has been changed to −50. At the bottom, Contrast has been changed to +50. Note that Brightness/Contrast was applied only to the subject, not to the white background.

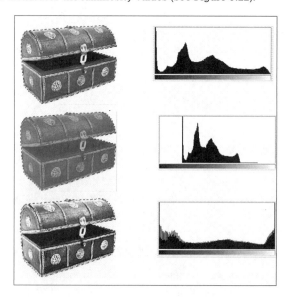

The Auto Contrast command adjusts image tonality by making light pixels brighter and shadows darker. It attempts to preserve the overall color relationship in the image while making the change.

Levels and Auto Levels

The Levels adjustment dialog, shown in Figure 9.23, works with shadows, highlights, and overall gamma (the brightness of an image's midtones) independently. It also gives you separate control over input and output values, includes special eyedropper tools for identifying the highlight and shadow areas of an image, and offers a neutral gray eyedropper for removing color casts.

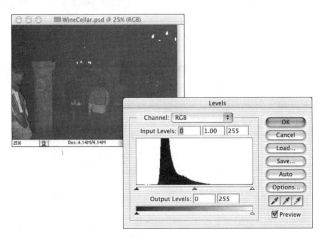

Figure 9.23
The image's tonal range is very compressed. Using Levels spreads the range out by moving values apart to reveal more of the image's details.

Input Levels

One of the most common uses of Levels is to expand an image's tonal range. Typically, the left and right sliders are dragged inward to the beginning of the image data in the Levels histogram. The middle slider is repositioned under what is likely to be the "center mass" of the histogram—the average value, or *mean*, rather than the median (see Figure 9.24).

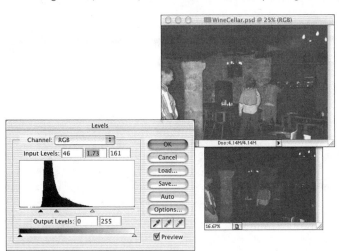

Figure 9.24
Note that the few stray pixels at the far left and right of the histogram are ignored, and the adjustment concentrates on the bulk of the pixel values in the image.

Levels works by adjusting the brightness of pixels. The left and right sliders, and their corresponding Input Levels fields, are used to define where black and white begin. For example, in Figure 9.25, the left slider is at 25, meaning that any pixels that have a brightness between 0 and 25 will be changed to 0 and become black. The right slider is at 225, so any pixels with a brightness higher than that become white (255).

As the left and right sliders are brought closer together, the number of possible brightness values in the image decreases. In Figure 9.26, the image goes from 256 possible tones (0–255) to 201 possible tones (25–225). Figure 9.25 shows what the histogram looks like *after* the adjustment in the previous figure is applied. The 201 values that were retained in the previous adjustment (25–225) are now spread over 256 total tonal values (0–255).

Figure 9.25
The middle slider, Gamma, reposi-
tions itself automatically and
remains set to 1.00 as the left and
right sliders are changed.

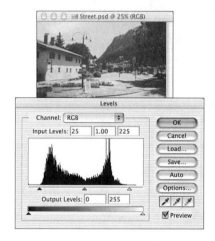

Figure 9.26
Notice the new empty columns in
the histogram. Levels didn't create
any new brightness values; rather,
it redistributed the values that
were retained in the previous
adjustment.

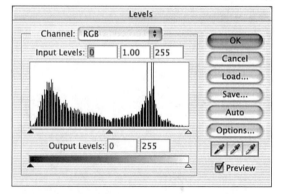

Output Levels

The lower slider in the Levels dialog controls the tonal range of an image from a different direction. It is used to compress the range (which reduces contrast) and to *clip* highlights and shadows. (Clipping occurs when multiple tonal values at either end of the tonal range are compressed into a single value.) These sliders can be used very effectively with the Gamma (middle) slider below the histogram. In Figure 9.27, the correction is being made to the foreground only. This method not only provides a more accurate histogram, it also maintains the brightness of the white background.

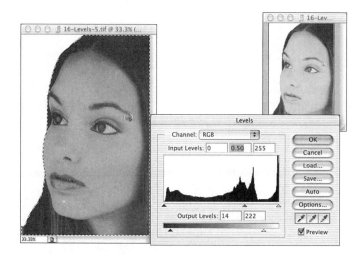

Figure 9.27
The original image, shown in the upper right, is skewed to brightness. Changing the Output slider on the right trims the highlights, and using the middle slider below the histogram adjusts the overall gamma.

Curves

The most powerful of Photoshop's image-correction tools is, without a doubt, Curves, although with that power comes complexity. The Curves dialog itself (see Figure 9.28), however, is not particularly complicated when you understand a few basic techniques and concepts.

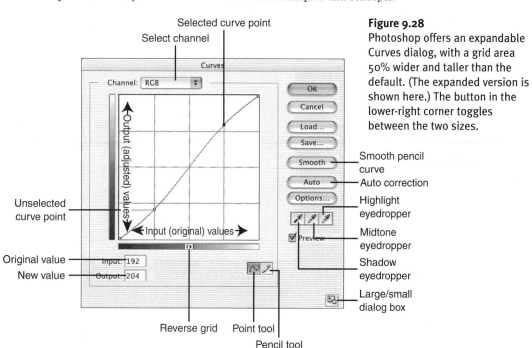

Figure 9.28
Photoshop offers an expandable Curves dialog, with a grid area 50% wider and taller than the default. (The expanded version is shown here.) The button in the lower-right corner toggles between the two sizes.

You can apply curves to a flattened image, an active layer, a channel, or a selection. Curves adjusts images much as Levels does, but it uses 256 separate values (RGB) or 100 values (other color modes) rather than just the three available in Levels. (When adjusting 16-bit images, you still see the 256 or 100 value scale.) The eyedropper tools in Curves work the same way they do in Levels.

Making Tonal Adjustments with Curves

Images that already look good can often benefit from some additional help to make them look even better. Typically, minor adjustments to the curve of the diagonal band are all that is needed to improve the image (see Figure 9.29). The grid is made up of vertical and horizontal lines that divide the image, and typically your adjustments originate from the lower-left quarter and the upper-right quarter of the grid. These are called *quarter tones* and *three-quarter tones*.

Figure 9.30 shows a pair of common Curves adjustments. The adjustment shown in the upper figure tones down the brightest highlights and lightens dark shadows. In the lower example, the contrast of the image is increased by moving the quarters away from each other.

To simplify the Curves dialog in your mind, picture it *without* the horizontal grid lines. The vertical grid lines help you identify input values; you can drag points straight up and down and watch the Output field.

Dragging an anchor point up or down on the curve can have an effect on the entire curve. To keep a section of the curve stable, place pairs of anchor points at either end of that section of the curve. You can use two closely spaced anchor points to prevent changes from flowing past a specific value.

Figure 9.29
By default, vertical grid lines appear at the 25%, 50%, and 75% levels.

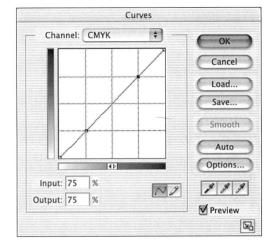

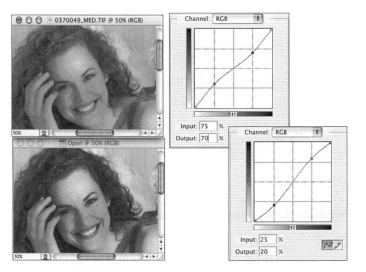

Figure 9.30
In each example, the adjustments are small—25% to 20% or 30%, 75% to 80% or 70%.

9

You can also make more complex adjustments, such as target specific groups of pixels in an image. Shift-clicking in the image with the Curves dialog open places color samplers on the image, and you can use them with the Info palette to track adjustments as you make them. As you can see from the smaller original in the upper-right corner in Figure 9.31, the highlights on the forehead are too light and the shadows lack detail. The Curves adjustment targets those specific areas.

Hold down the ⌘ key (Mac users) or the Ctrl key (Windows users) and click in an image to place a point on the curve at that value. For example, you can ⌘-click (Mac users) or Ctrl-click (Windows users) the color samplers to add points.

When you're working with RGB images, the Input and Output fields are calculated from 0 to 255 rather than 0 to 100. The 25% equivalent is 64, 50% is equal to 128, and 75% is comparable to 191.

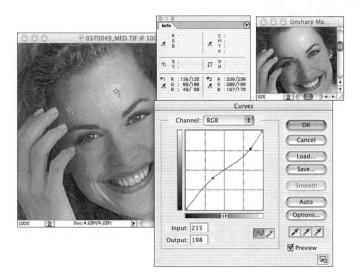

Figure 9.31
In the Info palette, the numbers to the left are the original color values, and those to the right are the values after the correction is applied.

Color Correction with Curves

The Channel menu at the top of the Curves dialog enables you to target a correction to a single component color in an image. You can remove color casts by adjusting the individual channels. Keep in mind the relationship among the RGB and CMYK component colors:

- When working in RGB, you can increase or decrease yellow in an image by adjusting both the Red and Green channels (R+G=Y).

- In an RGB image, you can adjust cyan by increasing or decreasing green and blue (G+B=C).

- Magenta in an RGB image is a function of red and blue (R+B=M).

- In a CMYK image, you can correct a blue cast by reducing both cyan and magenta (C+M=B).

- You adjust the amount of red in a CMYK image through the Magenta and Yellow channels (M+Y=R).

- Green in a CMYK image is a function of cyan and yellow (C+Y=G).

You can also use Curves with channels. In Figure 9.32, the RGB image has yellow accent lighting that is too prominent. To adjust the yellow lighting without destroying the color in the remainder of the image, you can isolate it by using Select, Color Range.

Figure 9.32
Curves can be applied to a selection. Color Range is an excellent tool for creating that selection

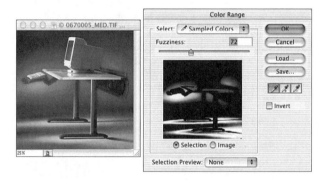

In Figure 9.33, you can see that the red and green channels are active in the Channels palette but that all channels are visible. This allows you to work on a pair of channels and continue to monitor the overall effect on the image. In this example, the Red and Green channels are active because, combined, they are responsible for the yellow content of an RGB image.

Auto Color

Photoshop's Auto Color command is much more powerful than Auto Contrast or Auto Levels. The key to its accuracy in color correction is based on its method of evaluating an image. Instead of looking at the histogram to determine shadows, highlights, and midtones, it examines the image itself. Using the values you specify in the Auto Color Correction Options dialog, it clips the highlights and shadows, identifies the image's midtone, and neutralizes the color by balancing the component color values. You can open the Auto Color Correction Options dialog by clicking the Options button in the Curves or Levels dialog.

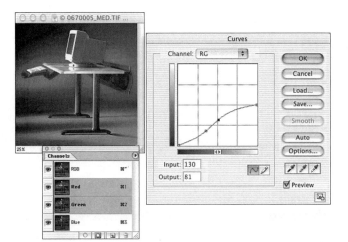

Figure 9.33
In the Channels palette, select the channels on which you'll be working before you open the Curves dialog box. The Channel pop-up menu shows RG, indicating that both the Red and Green channels are active.

9

Color Balance

The Color Balance command is available only when the composite channel is active in the Channels palette. The selection you make in the Tone Balance section of the dialog enables you to concentrate (but not restrict) the effect in shadows, midtones, or highlights. The Preserve Luminosity option protects the image's tonality. Typically, this command is used to compensate for color casts.

With Preserve Luminosity selected, moving all three sliders to the right equally has no effect on the image. Without the option, such a change would lighten the image by uniformly increasing the amounts of red, green, and blue throughout the image. Likewise, moving the three sliders equal distances to the left darkens the image when luminosity is not preserved.

Hue/Saturation

The Hue/Saturation command actually works with hue, saturation, and lightness. It can be used to correct or add a color cast, increase (or decrease) the saturation of an image, or generally lighten or darken an image. When used in combination, the three components of Hue/Saturation can produce dramatic effects and subtle adjustments. Hue/Saturation can be used with flattened images, active layers, and selections, and you can manipulate the composite channel (all colors at once) or individually selected colors.

If the skin tones in your image look good, make sure to exclude them from any selection before using Hue/Saturation. To exclude portions of the image inside your selection, you can choose Edit in Quick Mask Mode from the toolbox while the selection is active and paint in or erase portions of the mask as needed. You can choose Edit in Standard Mode to see how your selection has been altered.

Desaturate

The Image, Adjustments, Desaturate menu command removes the color from an image but does not convert the image to Grayscale mode. The original channels are retained. The brightness values of the pixels are retained, but the component colors RGB or CMY are equalized to create gray. Desaturate can be applied to a flattened image, an active layer, or a selection.

Selective use of Desaturate can be an excellent way to simulate a spot color in an RGB or a CMYK image. Simply make a selection of an area you want to keep in color, invert the selection, and desaturate. You can invert again and use the Hue/Saturation Colorize feature as well.

Shadow/Highlight

The Shadow/Highlight command is designed to give you control of the far ends of an image's tonal range (see Figure 9.34). If a flash overexposes the subject of a photo, you can adjust the highlights. If the subject is in shadow because the image was exposed for a bright background, you can adjust the shadows.

Figure 9.34
The Shadow/Highlight dialog also offers a Save As Defaults button and can be minimized to show only the Shadows and Highlight sliders.

Tonal Range determines how much of the image will be considered highlight or shadow. Reducing the value prevents alteration of the image's midtones. You use the Radius slider to identify the specific pixels that will be adjusted. A low value tends to select all very dark/light pixels individually. A higher Radius value includes the surrounding pixels. When Radius is too high, the entire image is adjusted.

The Color Correction slider helps remove color casts from newly lightened shadows. It affects only those pixels identified for adjustment by the Radius and Tonal Width sliders.

Midtone Contrast reduces an image's contrast (negative numbers) or increases the contrast (positive numbers). Clipping the shadows or highlights forces more colors to black or white. Higher clipping values can produce posterization in the shadows and highlights, causing a loss of detail.

Invert

Invert is used primarily to create grayscale images from scanned black-and-white negatives. It is not appropriate for use with scanned color negatives because of their orange mask. When Invert is used with a color image, each channel is calculated independently.

Using the 256 possible values for each pixel in each color channel, Invert simply flips the color across the midpoint. Pixels with high values in one channel get low values, and vice versa. For example, a pixel with an RGB value of 240/130/65 changes to 15/126/190. To calculate this, subtract the beginning value from 255, and you get the resulting value.

The Skinny on Skin

Is there a magic formula for correcting skin tones? How can you make sure the people in your images look right?

Producing accurate flesh tones is among the greatest challenges in Photoshop. One of the reasons for the difficulty is that we see and evaluate skin colors constantly: "You look a little pale." "Too much sun this weekend?" "You must be freezing!" In part because of how aware we are of the appearance of people around us, we are sensitive to the appearance of skin in images, too.

There is no single color mix for skin. There is no single relationship among component colors for skin. There is a tremendous range of skin tones in nature and, therefore, in images. Remember, too, that an individual's skin has a range of colors. The top and bottom of the forearm are typically different colors, as are the area beneath the chin and the chin itself. Parts of the body exposed to sun are typically darker, and how much darker often depends on the time of year.

In addition, the way an image is captured presents differences in skin tones. Because of reflections and lighting, foreheads, cheekbones, and noses might be lighter than the areas below the eyes, along the jaw, and on the neck.

That having been said, here is some *general* guidance on skin color:

- Even when working with RGB images, evaluate skin in terms of CMYK. Set the Info palette's second color reading to CMYK. Also, use color samplers set to CMYK in key areas, such as the forehead, the side of the nose, the cheeks, and the chin.

- The key component is magenta. Determine appropriate cyan and yellow proportions based on the magenta content.

- Too much yellow makes the skin look jaundiced. Too little yellow creates sunburn. In Caucasians, too much cyan produces grayish skin.

- Don't think in terms of specific percentage values for each of the component colors; rather, consider the relationship among the three values. The actual percentage of each CMY ink depends on the image's tonality.

- The skin of babies and northern Europeans can have a yellow content only slightly higher than the magenta. Southern Europeans may range to 25% more yellow than magenta. African-Americans might have only slightly more yellow than magenta. Africans may show equal values. Asians may have 30% to 50% again as much yellow as magenta. Native American skin might even show more magenta than yellow, but only slightly.

- Cyan values should be very low for pale skin and babies. The cyan component might be only 10% of the magenta. Darker Caucasian and Asian skin may have cyan equal to 30% of the magenta. Cyan for Africans and African–Americans can range from 50% to 75% of the magenta value. Tanned skin typically needs a higher cyan value than "winter-white" skin.

- With the exception of shadow areas, there should be little if any black ink in northern European and Asian skin tones. There may be trace amounts in darker Caucasian tones. African-Americans and Africans can range from 25% of the magenta value to as much as 75%.

9

10

CREATING A POWER WORKFLOW IN PHOTOSHOP

IN THIS CHAPTER

The most important thing to be aware of when you work with Photoshop is your output of the graphics you work with. Graphics you spend time on will get a lot of uses in many formats. Your awareness of which graphic formats and sizes you need is your most valuable tool. Images for print have a higher resolution than images for use on the Web. When you are designing for both print and Web, you need to be able to save and export the right image for the job. The steps you take to get there become your personal workflow. A *workflow* is a combination of the tools you use most often, your methods of solving problems, and your ability to increase your efficiency and lessen your turnaround time. Your efficiency comes through experience, but it also can come from automation tools in Photoshop. This chapter looks at several tools to help you crank out the work by putting Photoshop in charge of the repetitive tasks. The first time you let Photoshop convert 350 images while you grab a snack and relax you will feel like you stepped out of the last century.

UNDERSTANDING PHOTOSHOP SCRIPTING

Scripting and actions both help you automate tasks in the Adobe Creative Suite. *Scripts* are actual programs you write (or record) to perform tasks. Photoshop, Illustrator, and InDesign can use OLE-compatible scripting languages (such as Visual Basic) on Windows computers, AppleScript on Macintosh computers, and the less-powerful JavaScript on both. Scripts not only can perform tasks within a program, they can *call* or *invoke* other programs (accessing the second program and its features) and even work with hardware and the operating system.

Actions, in contrast to scripts, are a series of recorded steps within the program. They cannot talk to other programs. Logic can be built into actions using Conditional Mode Change. Conditional Mode Change is a Photoshop automation function that applies rules to change the image color mode based on certain conditions. For example, part of an action may require the image to be in CMYK mode and another part of an action may require RGB mode. Here, Conditional Mode Change is helpful. Refer to the Adobe Help Center for information on Condition Mode Change.

Scripting and the Adobe Creative Suite

Think of scripting as that studio assistant you can't afford to hire—the one who does all the little tasks, freeing you to be creative and dynamic. No, scripting won't make coffee (yet), but it *will* handle many of the small-but-important tasks that seem to eat up the workday.

Scripting can also be used for those jobs not within the scope of actions. Have you ever wanted to add the name of a file in, say, the lower-left corner of the image, along with your copyright information? And you wanted to do this to an entire folder of images—without losing a night's sleep? What if the images are not the same size or orientation? An action in Photoshop or Illustrator isn't capable of determining whether an image is portrait or landscape oriented. Scripts, on the other hand, can be written to handle such jobs. A script can get information, evaluate that information and perform calculations, and make decisions based on the information. Actions, on the other hand, are "dumb"—they can perform only the same steps and settings with which they were recorded.

Each of the scriptable members of the Adobe Creative Suite can be controlled with JavaScript, Visual Basic (Windows), or AppleScript (Mac). Again, the purpose of this chapter is not to teach programming or scripting languages. Instead, this chapter introduces you to the possibilities and then provides you with resources that enable you to capitalize on those opportunities to improve efficiency and free more time for creativity.

Virtually every aspect of Photoshop, Illustrator, and InDesign can be controlled through scripting. Visual Basic and AppleScript can call programs outside of the program within which you're running the script. Running a script in Photoshop could, for example, open Illustrator, find a specific piece of artwork, copy it, switch back to Photoshop, paste the artwork, save the file in a format appropriate for print, open InDesign, add the Photoshop file to a document, save the document, and print the proof. In a nutshell, if *you* can do it using the keyboard and mouse, it can probably be recorded in Visual Basic or AppleScript. And don't overlook the fact that a script can play an action within Photoshop or Illustrator.

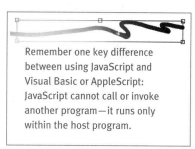

Remember one key difference between using JavaScript and Visual Basic or AppleScript: JavaScript cannot call or invoke another program—it runs only within the host program.

Understanding JavaScript, AppleScript, and Visual Basic: Which One?

JavaScript is cross-platform—meaning the same script performs identically on both Windows and Macintosh versions of your programs. However, a JavaScript must be run from within the program and cannot call another program. AppleScript and Visual Basic are more powerful, can be run from outside a specific program, and can run multiple programs. However, they are both platform specific—an AppleScript cannot be used in Windows, and Visual Basic cannot run on a Macintosh.

Keep in mind that both AppleScripts and Visual Basic scripts can execute a JavaScript, but JavaScripts can't call the others.

Scripting Resources Supplied with the Adobe Creative Suite

Each of the scriptable members of the Adobe Creative Suite (Photoshop, Illustrator, and InDesign) has some scripts included with the program, as well as additional resources and information either on CD or available through www.adobe.com.

Inside Photoshop CS2's Scripting Guide folder, you find the ScriptListener plug-in. When installed, ScriptListener records most of what you do in Photoshop as JavaScript code in a file at the root level of your hard drive. For Windows, it also creates VBScript code in a separate file. (AppleScripts call the JavaScript.) Install ScriptListener in Photoshop's Plug-Ins folder *only* when you actually use it to create scripts. Photoshop might run more slowly with the plug-in installed, and it generates a file on your hard drive that is otherwise not required.

Photoshop CS2 Scripts

Under the File, Scripts menu, you find a few JavaScripts that can be very handy: Export Layers to Files, Layer Comps to Files, Layer Comps to PDF, and Layer Comps to WPG. New in Photoshop CS2 is the excellent Image Processor and the Script Events Manager.

Inside the Photoshop folder on your hard drive, you find the Scripting Guide folder. In PDF format, you see reference guides for Photoshop scripting in general (91 pages), JavaScript (335 pages), AppleScript (251 pages), and Visual Basic (178 pages). That is definitely a lot of reading, and these

10

guides and sample scripts are the very best resource for learning scripting in Photoshop. In addition, the folder contains additional prerecorded scripts (27 JavaScript, 18 AppleScript, and 19 Visual Basic). You can use these scripts, or open them for study.

Remember, too, that resources are available to you at www.adobe.com in the Expert Centers for each product. You also find assistance and information in the various scripting forums within the product forums of www.adobe.com.

Loading a Sample JavaScript

The sample scripts mentioned earlier can be added to Photoshop as long as you know where to put them. You can load a script for use one time, or copy them to the Scripts directory to put them under the Scripts menu the next time you launch Photoshop. Choose File, Scripts, Browse. From here you can browse to the Sample Scripts folder in the Scripting Guide folder. Select the ExecuteMoltenLead.jsx script and click Load. A new layer of molten lead is created by the script. If you don't have a document open, the script creates a new document for you and emblazons it with lead. You can put any of these sample scripts permanently under the Script menu. Copy the JSX files to your Presets, Scripts folder in the Photoshop CS2 folder. Close and relaunch Photoshop, and look under the File, Scripts menu for your sample scripts to appear in the list. For more scripts go to http://share.studio.adobe.com.

Learning More About Scripting...

Here are some online resources you can use to learn more about scripting:

- www.javascript.com

- www.javascriptcity.com

- http://javascript.internet.com/tutorials/

- http://www.apple.com/macosx/features/applescript/

- www.applescriptsourcebook.com

- www.macscripting.com

- www.scriptweb.com

- http://msdn.microsoft.com/vbasic/

- www.developer.com/net/vb/

The Internet is just one source of information on scripting. Especially if you're new to high-level automation, check out these additional resources:

- *Special Edition Using JavaScript* by Paul McFedries (Que Publishing)

- *JavaScript Goodies* by Joe Burns and Andree Growney (Que Publishing)

- *Sams Teach Yourself JavaScript in 24 Hours* by Michael Moncur (Sams Publishing)

- *Sams Teach Yourself JavaScript in 21 Days* by Jonathan Watt, Andrew Watt, and Jinjer Simon (Sams Publishing)

- *Visual Basic .NET Primer Plus* by Jack Purdum (Sams Publishing)

UNDERSTANDING PHOTOSHOP'S ACTIONS

Automating tasks with actions not only saves time but ensures precision by applying the same steps every time.

Actions are simply prerecorded steps in Photoshop. You play an action to repeat those steps on one or more images. Photoshop ships with dozens of actions, and others are available at minimal cost or free on the Web. The true power of actions, however, is in recording your own to automate your tasks. You can also share your actions with others through the process of saving and loading actions.

Some actions are completely automated and can be run while you're away from the computer; other actions require you to enter specific values for certain procedures. Photoshop also enables you to specify whether to use the values originally recorded with an action or to pause the action for you to input new values.

You create, store, organize, and play back actions by using the Actions palette. You can create *droplets*, which are miniapplications that run actions when one or more files is dragged onto them. Droplets are available for both Photoshop and ImageReady. You can even run actions on multiple files sequentially as a *batch*. Batch processing of a folder of files can include subfolders.

Remember that painting tools can be applied along paths and that paths can be inserted into actions. You can insert a path and apply a painting tool (or other brush-related tool) along that path.

How Actions Work

An action consists of a series of steps in Photoshop. They are the same steps you use to accomplish the same thing manually. For example, if you want to prepare an image for a page layout program, you might need to change the resolution, sharpen it, change the color mode to CMYK, and then save the file in the correct format. In this case, here are the four steps you take:

1. Choose Image, Image Size.

2. Choose Filter, Sharpen, Unsharp Mask.

3. Choose Image, Mode, CMYK Color.

4. Choose File, Save As, TIFF with LZW compression.

When this process is recorded as an action, the same four steps are taken when the action runs.

An action can record the same settings as those applied when the action was recorded, or it can pause so that you can input different settings. Commands and paths can be inserted. The use of painting tools, which require dragging the cursor in the image, cannot be recorded, however.

The Actions Palette

You use the Actions palette to record, play, and manage actions. The palette contains three columns and a series of buttons across the bottom. Figure 10.1 shows the first action of the Default Actions set, installed in the Actions palette when you installed Photoshop.

Figure 10.1
Click the triangles next to action sets, actions, and the individual steps of the action to expand them, as shown here.

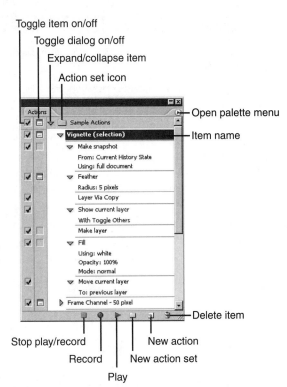

The On/Off Column

You use the first column in the Actions palette to toggle items on and off. You can toggle off actions and entire sets of actions. If they are toggled off, they are not playable until you check the box to turn them back on.

The Modal Control Column

The second column shows an icon of a dialog box, an empty box, or nothing next to each step, action, or set. These are the *modal* indicators. An icon or an empty box shows that the step (or one or more steps within an action or set) has user-definable parameters: a dialog box. The action can play with the options used when the step was recorded (empty), or it can stop at the step and wait for you to change the dialog box and click OK (icon).

Like the first column, the second column is color coded. A black icon indicates that every step that has a dialog box is set to open its dialog box and wait for input. A red icon shows that one or more steps will play with the prerecorded values. An empty box tells you that *all* steps will play with pre-recorded values. If there is no icon and no empty box, none of the steps within the Action (or set) are modal.

The Palette Body

Examine the third column of the Actions palette shown in Figure 10.1:

- The top line is the action set to which the action belongs. `Sample Actions.atn` is identifiable as a set by the folder icon. You can click the downward-pointing triangle to hide the contents of the set.

- The second line, indented slightly, is selected and therefore highlighted. It is the action named Vignette (selection). Selection is part of the name (assigned by the person who prepared the action) to indicate that a selection must be made before running the action. Clicking the triangle to the left of the name hides or shows the action's steps.

The Sample Actions can be loaded from the Actions palette menu by choosing Sample Actions. In previous versions of Photoshop these Sample Actions were known as the Default Actions.

- Below the action name are the steps of the action, indented slightly. They are the actual commands that are executed when you run the action. Some can be expanded and collapsed with triangles; some steps require a single line in the palette.

- The last item visible in the Actions palette is another action, named Frame Channel-50 pixel. Note that it is aligned with the action Vignette (selection), showing that it is also a member of the Default Actions set.

The Actions Palette Buttons

Use the six buttons across the bottom of the Actions palette to create, record, play, and delete actions. All these capabilities are duplicated by commands in the Actions palette menu:

- The Stop button (just like on a VCR) ceases the recording or playing of an action.

- The Record button begins recording a new action. You can also record steps somewhere in the middle of an action. If you click on an Actions command and press the Record button, your steps record after that command. Any commands that were below your inserted command(s) stay below them.

- The Play button, which should also look familiar, plays the selected action on the active document. The action executes according to the check marks in the first two columns next to each step.

- Create a set of actions by using the button with the folder icon. You can create new actions within the sets or drag actions from one set to another.

10

- When you click the New Action button, a dialog box opens in which you can name the new action and assign it to a function key for quick-and-easy play. Duplicate an action set, an action, or a step by dragging it to the button.

- Clicking the Trash icon enables you to delete actions, entire sets, and individual commands within an action. Alternatively, you can drag items onto the Trash button to delete them.

The Actions Palette Menu

The Actions palette's menu contains a variety of commands for creating, using, and managing actions. Much of the palette menu commands are already covered using the palette's interface controls. There are a few options to note.

Several of the palette's menu commands can be considered palette maintenance commands. You can use the menu to remove all action sets and actions (Clear All Actions), return the palette to its default content (Reset Actions), add action sets or actions to the palette (Load Actions), exchange the current content for a different set of actions (Replace Actions), and save a set of actions so that it can be reloaded at a later time (Save Actions).

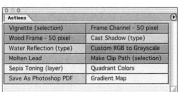

Recording actions and creating action sets in the palette doesn't preserve them. To ensure that you won't accidentally delete your custom actions by resetting the palette, use the Save Actions command.

You can save actions as text files and view or print them.

Select a set of actions or create a new set and copy one or more actions into it. Hold down the Option-⌘ keys (Mac users) or the Alt+Ctrl keys (Windows users) and select Save Actions from the Actions palette menu; a text file (.txt extension) is generated. (Remember that you can only use the Save Actions command with sets of actions, not individual actions.)

Button Mode

The Actions palette can also be displayed in Button Mode (see Figure 10.2). In this configuration, you play an action by clicking it. Note that the palette shows no buttons for recording actions; this mode is for playing actions only. In fact, when in Button Mode, the Actions palette's menu commands related to creating, recording, and even playing are grayed out.

Figure 10.2
Depending on the size and shape of the palette, Button Mode can display actions in one column or multiple columns.

Actions are sorted in the palette according to their order, not by assigned color. (An action's color can be assigned when recorded or through the palette's menu command Action Options.) Action sets are ignored in Button Mode.

WORKING WITH ACTIONS IN PHOTOSHOP

An action can be played on a selection, an image, or even a folder filled with images (using the Batch command). The action can run while you're away from the computer—even at home, fast asleep—or you can sit at the keyboard and make changes to how the action is applied to each image.

Running an Action

In a nutshell, you select the action in the Actions palette and click the Play button at the bottom of the palette. Some actions require that a selection be made first to identify a part of the image with which to work. Other actions may require that a type layer be available or that an image meet minimum or maximum size requirements. Color mode can also be a factor, especially when an action applies a filter or uses an Adjustment command.

Loading Actions

The Actions palette menu's bottom section shows a list of all action sets in the Photoshop Actions folder. By default, Photoshop installs several sets of actions. You can add your own sets to the list by placing them in the folder. You find the Photoshop Actions folder inside the Presets folder, within the Adobe Photoshop CS2 folder.

You can load sets of actions not located in the Photoshop Actions folder into the palette by using the palette's menu command Load Actions. In the dialog box, navigate to the actions, select them, and click Load. They appear at the bottom of the Actions palette, ready to be played.

The palette menu also offers the commands Clear All Actions (which empties the palette), Reset Actions (which restores the palette to its default content), Replace Actions (which clears the current content and adds the selected set), and Save Actions (which saves the selected actions set).

Before switching to Button Mode, you can rearrange actions by dragging them up and down in the Actions palette.

Caution

When you play an action by clicking it in Button Mode, it plays as last configured. Steps that are unchecked do not play, and modal controls are shown or not shown as last set. Button Mode gives no indication if one or more steps of an action will not play.

Because actions typically execute a number of steps, taking a snapshot in the History palette beforehand is a great idea. Should the action not produce the expected results, you've got a one-click Undo.

Remember that you risk losing your custom actions until you use the Save Actions command. If Photoshop needs to be reinstalled, or if you use the Clear Actions or Reset Actions command, any unsaved action sets will be lost.

10

Batching It

A folder full of files can have the same action applied to it with one command. Choosing the File, Automate, Batch command opens the Batch dialog shown in Figure 10.3.

You select a number of settings in the Batch dialog box. Most importantly you need to choose which folder of images to batch and which action to play for these images. You can choose to include subfolders of images to batch and also various save options. When batching, it's always a good idea to save a new copy of the images rather than overwriting the existing files, in case you made a mistake in your action or chose the wrong action all together.

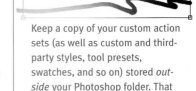

Keep a copy of your custom action sets (as well as custom and third-party styles, tool presets, swatches, and so on) stored *outside* your Photoshop folder. That helps prevent accidental loss, should you ever need to reinstall Photoshop. Also, it's a good idea to back up your custom elements to CD or an external disk, too.

Figure 10.3
Shown to the right of the Batch dialog is the message that appears when you check or uncheck the option Override Action Save As Commands.

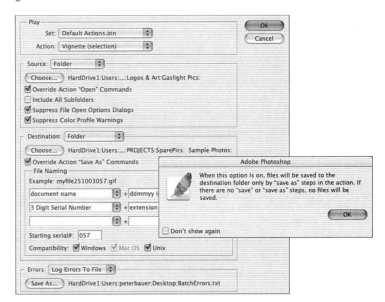

Using Batch to Change File Formats

The Batch command saves files in their original format, whether the Destination field is set to Save and Close or to Folder. To automate a change of file format, you must include three steps:

1. When recording the action, include a Save As command followed by a Close (Don't Save) command.

2. In the Actions palette, check to make sure that the modal column is not checked next to the Save As command or the Close command.

Aliases (Macintosh) or shortcuts (Windows) to other folders are considered subfolders by Batch. You can use them to process multiple folders with a single Batch command.

3. In the Batch dialog, choose Folder in the Destination pop-up menu and then select the Override Action Save As Commands check box.

The end result will be copies of the original images in the file format specified in the action. The original files will be unchanged.

Using Actions as Droplets in Photoshop

Recall that a droplet is a little shortcut icon that can play an action. Instead of clicking the droplet icon, you drag and drop files or folders onto the icon. A droplet must always have an action associated with it. Droplets do not work on their own. You convert actions to droplets by using Photoshop's File, Automate, Create Droplet menu command. The Create Droplet dialog is shown in Figure 10.4.

Use the Save Droplet In section of the dialog box to name the droplet and choose a location. Select the action from which the droplet is created in the Play section. If the action needs to open another file to execute a step—for example, to copy from one image and paste into another—do not override Open commands. You also have the option of including any subfolders when a droplet is played on a folder. If you'll run the droplet while away from your computer, make sure you suppress color warnings; otherwise, you might return to find a warning showing onscreen and no files processed.

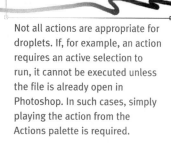

Depending on the file format selected for the Save As command, you might need to flatten the file and delete alpha or spot channels. Record these steps in the action before the Save As command.

Not all actions are appropriate for droplets. If, for example, an action requires an active selection to run, it cannot be executed unless the file is already open in Photoshop. In such cases, simply playing the action from the Actions palette is required.

10

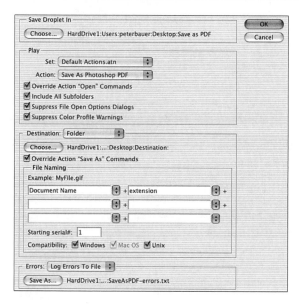

Figure 10.4
The Destination section of the dialog box looks familiar to anyone who uses the Batch command or the File Browser's Batch Rename command.

What Photoshop does with the files processed by the droplet is determined in the Destination section of the dialog box. You can elect to leave the files open (None), save the changes and close each file (Save and Close), or save the files to a new location (Folder). When Folder is selected, you have access to the options shown in Figure 10.4.

CREATING CUSTOM ACTIONS IN PHOTOSHOP

If a droplet is created with the option to include subfolders, it plays its action on all files in the folder and the subfolders. You can also include aliases or shortcuts to other folders.

The true power of actions comes through when you record them yourself. Because your custom actions are tailored to your needs and your work, they are best suited to improving your productivity.

Recording a New Action

An action must belong to a set. Actions are not allowed to float free in the Actions palette. You can assign an action to an existing set by clicking the set in the Actions palette. Alternatively, you can create a new set by using the Create New Set button at the bottom of the Actions palette or the New Set command from the palette's menu. Both open the New Set dialog (see Figure 10.5), in which you can give the set a name.

Figure 10.5
The only option available for action sets is the name, which can also be changed by double-clicking it in the Actions palette.

Clicking the New Action button (or using the New Action command from the palette menu) opens the New Action dialog shown in Figure 10.6.

In addition to giving the new action a name, you can assign it to a function key, with or without modifier keys. Pressing the assigned key combination executes the action, even if the palette is hidden. Any color assigned to the action is used only in Button Mode.

After you click the Record button, virtually every move you make in Photoshop becomes part of the action. You can pause the recording at any time by clicking the Stop button or using the Stop Recording command from the palette menu. To continue, click the Record button. The Record button gives a visual indicator when an action is actually being created.

Figure 10.6
You can change your mind and assign the action to a different set right in the New Action dialog.

The New Action and New Set commands are not grayed out while recording an action. You can, in fact, create new sets and actions while recording an action. You can even work in the Actions palette, deleting actions and sets, while recording. These activities are not recorded as steps in the current action.

The actual steps that can be recorded in an action fall into several categories: recordable commands and tools, non-recordable commands and tools, inserted paths, and stops. In addition, you can decide whether a command will use the settings with which it was recorded or pause while you enter new settings (modal commands).

> Remember that Photoshop executes commands while you're recording. For that reason, it's best to work on a copy of your file when recording an action.

After you go through all the steps you want in the action, click the Stop button at the bottom of the palette or use the Stop Recording menu command. It is usually a good idea, especially with more complicated actions, to make another copy of the original file and test the action.

What Can and Can't Be Recorded

Generally speaking, any tool that relies on cursor movement cannot be recorded in an action, including the Move tool and the Painting, Toning, Healing, and Eraser tools. The Zoom and Hand tools cannot be recorded, nor can the Pen tools. You can, however, record options for many tools, including brushes.

Photoshop's other tools are recordable, as are these palettes: Actions, Channels, Color, History, Layers, Paths, Styles, and Swatches.

> You can record some movements of the Move tool as long as you are nudging with the arrow keys rather than using the mouse pointer. For larger movement increments, hold the Shift key when pressing the arrow keys.

Recording Menu Commands

Most menu commands can be recorded in an action. There are, however, two ways to do so. If, while recording, you select a menu command, enter values in any dialog box, and click OK, the action is recorded with *those* values. You can record the action without assigning any value (and without changing the current image while recording). From the Actions palette's menu, choose Insert Menu Item. With the Insert Menu Item dialog open (see Figure 10.7), move the cursor to select the desired command. After selecting the command, click OK to close the dialog box.

Figure 10.7
This dialog box remains open while you mouse to the command that you want to record in the action.

When the action is played back, nonmodal commands are executed immediately. If the command is modal, it doesn't execute until you approve the values in the dialog by clicking OK. Remember that you cannot disable the modal control for an inserted command—when you play the action, the dialog *will* open and wait for you to click OK, whether you're sitting at your computer or not.

Inserting Paths

Although the Pen tool cannot be recorded, the Shape tools can, and you can save a custom shape to be added in an action. You can also insert paths into an action. The path must already be available in the Paths palette while the action is recorded. Select the path in the Paths palette and then choose Insert Path from the Actions palette menu. When the action is played back, the path is added as a work path. If you need to retain the path in the image, make sure to also record a Save Path command from the Paths palette menu.

In Figure 10.8, you can see how the action records a rather simple path.

Figure 10.8
Coordinates of the anchor points are recorded in the action when recording a path. Although only the first six anchor points (corner or smooth) get listed in the Actions palette when a path is recorded, all points of the path are still recorded. Coordinates for anchor points and direction points for smooth anchor points are specified from the upper-left corner of the image.

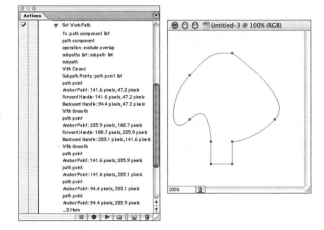

Inserting a Pause for Playback

When an action is played back, you can force it to stop and display a message. Use the Actions palette menu command Insert Stop at any point in the recording process. You type a message to be displayed in the Message window of the Record Stop dialog (see Figure 10.9).

The Allow Continue option determines which buttons are available in the message box when the action is played. When Allow Continue is selected, the box contains two buttons: Stop and Continue (see Figure 10.10). When the option is not selected, only one button is available.

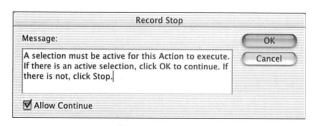

Figure 10.9
The message can be up to 255 characters (and spaces) long.

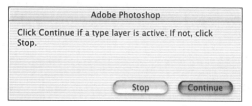

Figure 10.10
The best stops are recorded with explicit instructions.

Editing an Existing Action

You can perform seven basic types of editing on an existing action:

1. **Delete a step.** Select the step in the Actions palette and either drag it to the Trash icon or click the icon.

2. **Rerecord a step.** Double-click the step, perform the task as you want it, and then click Stop.

3. **Add a step.** Click the step in the action immediately above where you want the new step(s) and then click the Record button. When you finish adding to the action, click the Stop button.

4. **Rearrange the order of steps.** Drag a step from one spot in the action to another.

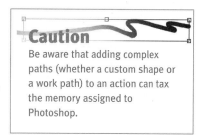

Caution

Be aware that adding complex paths (whether a custom shape or a work path) to an action can tax the memory assigned to Photoshop.

5. **Duplicate a step.** Option-drag (Mac users) or Alt-drag (Windows users) a step from one location to another in the action, drag a step to the New Action button, or use the Actions palette menu's Duplicate command.

6. **Turn a step off (or on).** Click in the left column of the Actions palette next to the step. When the check mark is visible, the step runs when the action is played. If there is no check mark, that step is skipped when the action is played.

7. **Change the modal setting.** The second column of the Actions palette determines whether the dialog box for a modal command or tool shows when the action is played. If the icon is visible next to a step, the action stops at that step, shows the dialog box, and waits for you to change options and click OK. If there is an empty box in the column, the action plays using the values recorded in the step. If the icon is grayed out, the step was added with the Insert Menu Command command, and the dialog always shows. If there is neither an icon nor an empty box in that column, the step is nonmodal.

Sources of Actions

In addition to the Default Actions set loaded in the Actions palette, seven other action sets are immediately available. You can load any of them by selecting the set from the bottom of the Actions palette menu. The new actions are added to the bottom of the palette.

Actions are also available, commercially and free, from a wide variety of sources on the Internet. ActionFX (www.actionfx.com) is an excellent source of useful, practical, and fun actions. You also find a wide variety of actions and more at the Adobe Studio site (www.studio.adobe.com).

You can also save action sets and exchange them with other Photoshop users. Make sure that you attach the .atn extension to the filename when saving. To save actions, follow these steps:

1. Select the action set in the Actions palette. Remember that only action sets, not individual actions or steps, can be saved. To save a single action, create a new set, Option-drag (Mac users) or Alt-drag (Windows users) the action into the set to copy it and then save the new set.

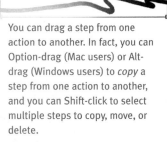

You can drag a step from one action to another. In fact, you can Option-drag (Mac users) or Alt-drag (Windows users) to *copy* a step from one action to another, and you can Shift-click to select multiple steps to copy, move, or delete.

2. With the set selected, choose Save Actions from the Actions palette menu. If the command is grayed out, it's likely that an action or a step, rather than an action set, is selected in the palette.

3. In the Save dialog box, specify a name and location for the saved action set. Include the .atn file extension in the filename.

USING OTHER PHOTOSHOP AUTOMATE COMMANDS

The commands found in the File, Automate submenu don't do anything that you can't do manually in Photoshop. They simply do it faster and more efficiently (although sometimes not as flexibly as you might like).

PDF Presentation

Photoshop CS introduced a feature that enables you to create a multipage PDF file or an onscreen presentation that can be played back in Adobe Reader. You select a series of images in the PDF Presentation dialog (see Figure 10.11), choose to create a presentation or a multipage PDF, and decide whether you want to open Acrobat (or Reader) and see the finished product right away. If you're creating a presentation, you specify how long you want each slide to appear (or uncheck the Advance Every box for manual slide switching), specify whether you want the slideshow to play once or repeat, and select a transition for moving from slide to slide.

Caution

If a PDF presentation will (or may) be viewed in Acrobat Reader 5 or earlier, do *not* include 16-bit images. Although they can be shown in Adobe Reader 6 and later versions, 16-bit images generate an error message in the earlier versions.

When a presentation is opened in Reader or Acrobat, the program automatically goes into full-screen mode, hides the program interface, and surrounds each slide with a plain black background. Slides can be advanced manually with the Return key (Mac users) or the Enter key (Windows users), and a slideshow can be halted with the Esc key.

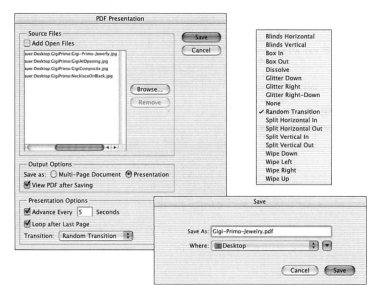

Figure 10.11
After clicking Save, you select a name and location for the presentation or Multipage PDF document. The slide transitions available in PDF Presentation are shown in the upper right.

Conditional Mode Change

This command is designed to be recorded in an action to prevent error messages while using the Batch command. When an action changes a color mode or contains a step that can be run only in certain color modes, Conditional Mode Change should be included. If, for example, you record an action that relies on a specific channel and apply it to a folder of images that are not of the same color mode, an error message appears when the color channel isn't found (see Figure 10.12).

By using the Conditional Mode Change command, you indicate that all images processed by the action are changed to the appropriate color mode. You select the color mode to which you want to convert the images, and you designate which color modes to convert *from* (see Figure 10.13).

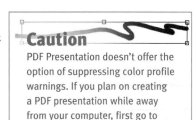

Caution

PDF Presentation doesn't offer the option of suppressing color profile warnings. If you plan on creating a PDF presentation while away from your computer, first go to Color Settings and uncheck the profile mismatch warning options. Remember, too, that PDF Presentation does not suppress File Open option dialog boxes for Raw images.

Contact Sheet II

You can create pages of thumbnail images with captions by using Contact Sheet II. Use the dialog box shown in Figure 10.14 to select the source folder of images, describe the page on which the thumbnails will be placed, specify the layout, and add captions from the filenames, if desired.

Figure 10.12
The action requires the presence of a channel named Blue, but the image is CMYK. An error message stops the Batch process.

Figure 10.13
If this command had been recorded in the action before the step shown in Figure 10.12, the image would have been converted to RGB mode and the Batch command would not have aborted.

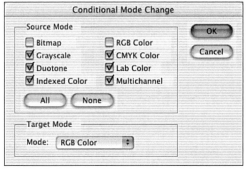

Figure 10.14
Remember that the document size should be the printable area of your page, not the paper size.

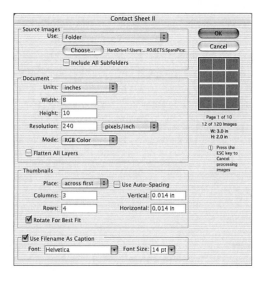

Fit Image

The Fit Image command is comparable to using the Image, Image Size command to resample an image. Use the Fit Image command to make images fit a specific pixel dimension quickly and easily, especially for websites. The advantage to using the Fit Image command rather than choosing Image, Image Size and recording an action is that you can set a maximum dimension for the image and fit images—whether they are in landscape or portrait proportions—to a certain size.

> **Caution**
>
> Converting from Bitmap to a color mode requires that Conditional Mode Change first convert the image to Grayscale and then to RGB. The conversion to Grayscale is modal and requires that you be at the computer to click OK, even if the modal icon is not visible next to the step in the Actions palette.

Multi-Page PDF to PSD

Photoshop's Open command can handle only one PDF page at a time. The Multi-Page PDF to PSD command automatically creates a series of PSD files from a multipage PDF document. In the Convert Multi-Page PDF to PSD dialog shown in Figure 10.15, you select the original document, determine which pages to translate, select the resolution and color mode for the resulting Photoshop files, and select a destination folder.

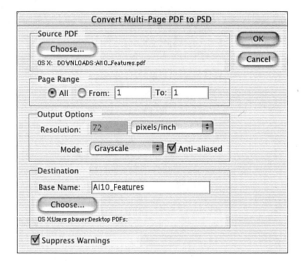

Figure 10.15
Use the Base Name field to create the filename for the resulting Photoshop files. A four-digit sequential number is added to the base name for each PSD file.

Picture Package

Use this command to place multiple images on a single sheet for printing. You can add multiple copies of a single image or copies of various images from a folder. The dialog box shown in Figure 10.16 gives you the choice of three paper sizes: 8 by 10, 10 by 16, and 11 by 17 inches. The resulting document can be of any resolution, and the color mode can be RGB, CMYK, Grayscale, or LAB. The document can also be flattened if desired.

Figure 10.16
In the Use pop-up menu, choose
Frontmost Document, File, or
Folder for the source image or
images.

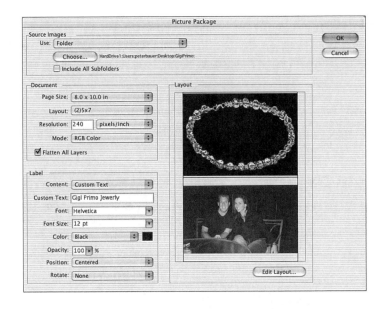

Web Photo Gallery

The Web Photo Gallery command can create an entire website, ready for posting to your host server.
Keep in mind, however, that this is a very basic capability, and you won't be creating any award-win-
ning e-commerce sites with Web Photo Gallery.

Aimed at assisting photographers and digital artists in posting examples of their work on the Web,
Web Photo Gallery takes folders filled with images and creates web pages in which they are displayed. A simple dialog box gives you a number of variations, but limited control, over the final product (see Figure 10.17).

Figure 10.17
One dialog box is all Photoshop
requires to build a website to display your artwork.

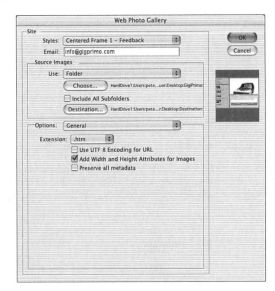

Photomerge

Photomerge is an automated panorama creator. You select two or more images in the Photomerge dialog box, tell Photomerge whether you want it to attempt to arrange the images automatically, and click OK.

After the images are identified and you click OK, the images are opened into the Photomerge workspace. The Photomerge dialog shown in Figure 10.18 includes a lightbox at the top for images not currently being used, a large central work area for arranging and compositing, and several options and tools.

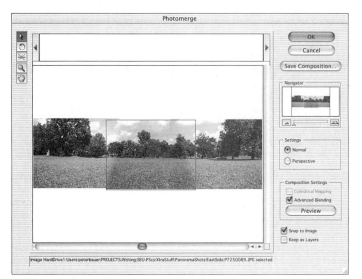

Figure 10.18
The Navigator section can be used in conjunction with or instead of the Zoom and Hand tools. Cylindrical mapping is available only with Perspective selected; Advanced Blending can be used with or without Perspective. Choosing Snap to Image lets Photomerge try to mate overlapping areas of images, and Keep as Layers prevents the flattening of the image after you click OK.

Image Processor

When working with images for print and web, you are required to change image sizes for a lot of images. The Image Processor makes it even easier than using actions for resizing a lot of images at once. Previously you would have to record an action and then use batching to run the action on folders of images. Open the Image Processor dialog by choosing File, Scripts, Image Processor (see Figure 10.19).

The Image Processor contains options for creating up to three different formats: JPEG, PSD, and TIFF. You can create one or all of these formats by checking the check boxes. You also control some of the file format options.

Whether saving your processed images to the same folder or a different folder, separate folders for the processed images are always created. The folders are named JPEG, PSD, or TIFF. When processing a folder of images, you can check the box to Open first image to apply settings. Like an action, the steps you perform on the first image, for example, contrast changes, are applied the same way to all images in the folder. Unlike actions, after the settings are applied and used once, they are lost. Actions keep the recorded commands for use at a later time. You can save the Image Processor options by clicking the Save button. This enables you to load them again later.

Figure 10.19
When image processing, you can choose from JPEG, PSD, or TIFF as the file format to process to. A folder is created that contains the processed images. The folders are creatively named JPEG, PSD, or TIFF. Along with processing the images, in this example we simultaneously play an action for the output images. After everything happens, the files are saved.

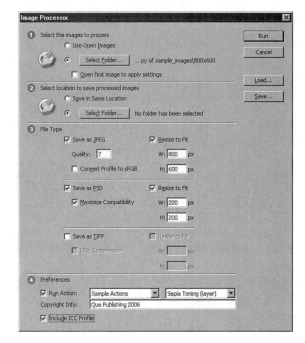

Another nice feature of processing images is your ability to resize the processed images differently. Your JPEG output can be resized small for the Web, and your TIFF output files are kept larger. No matter the pixel dimensions, your processed images stay in proportion.

At the bottom of the Image Processor dialog under the number 4 are the Preferences. Here you can run an action from the Actions palette while you process the images. All this control in an easy interface makes Photoshop CS2 a powerhouse for working with hundreds or thousands of images. Just don't tell your supervisor how easy it is. Insert Copyright Info to apply text to your metadata. Check the box to Include ICC Profile to match all your images' color profiles. Again, sit back and relax or walk away while the work is done for you. Who knew a power workflow required so little energy?

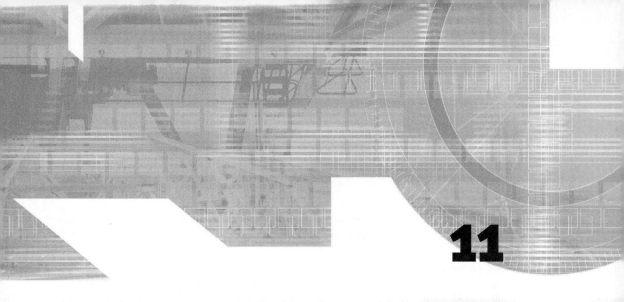

11

WORKING WITH IMAGEREADY

IN THIS CHAPTER

In this chapter, you learn about Adobe ImageReady. Although you can easily jump back and forth from ImageReady to Photoshop with a single click, you can also use ImageReady as a standalone program without ever opening Photoshop. Its sole purpose is to prepare your photos and art for use on the Web. It includes most of the same functions as Photoshop. You can set type for headlines, crop, adjust color and saturation just as you would in Photoshop. But because its purpose is specifically web graphics, it also handles tricks like animation, rollovers, and image slices that Photoshop doesn't do.

Why are web graphics different? When a picture is printed, you look at it on a piece of paper, or possibly a T-shirt or as the frosting on a cake. But when you see it on a video monitor, it doesn't necessarily have to just sit there. It can move. The earliest way to do this on the web was with GIF (Graphics Interchange Format) animation. You explore this and other motion techniques like slices and rollover buttons in the next chapter, but first you need to learn more about putting a simple image on a web page.

WEAVING PHOTOS INTO THE WEB

When the Internet was first opened to the general public, it was a text-only medium. One computer could send a message to others using a system not unlike the ones used by the telegraph company or news wire service. Signals went from the computer to a box called a modem, and then as tones over a telephone line to another computer. The signals again passed through a modem and were translated back into letters and numbers on the receiver's computer screen. The system was originally developed as a means of secure communication for science facilities, the armed forces, and university researchers. Eventually, it was opened to the general public.

Words are good, but some things require pictures. ASCII graphics, like the example in Figure 11.1, were the first attempt at graphics on the Internet. Obviously, they weren't very successful.

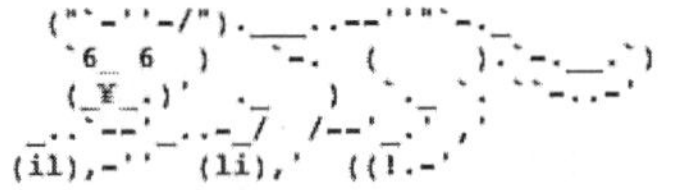

Modem stands for modulate/demodulate. The modem translates ASCII text into audible signals that are sent back and forth on a normal telephone line.

Figure 11.1
ASCII graphics were cute, but not very successful as art.

```
("`-''-/").___..--''"`-._
 `6_ 6  )   `-.  (     ).`-.__.`)
 (_Y_.)'  ._   )  `._ `. ``-..-'
   _..`--'_..-_/  /--'_.' ,'
  (il),-''  (li),'  ((!.-'
```

CompuServe developed the first usable graphics format, called GIF, which let users display either line art or photos with a limited palette by downloading them to the screen, one picture at a time. The GIF format was originally the exclusive property of CompuServe, which was also one of the earliest web service providers. GIF pictures were first shared among CompuServe users who downloaded them from text files. Before long the web was opened to businesses and individuals who signed up for their own web addresses, called *domains*, and used a service provider to host these websites.

The most popular language used to publish documents on the web is still HTML (Hypertext Markup Language). HTML isn't really a computer *programming* language, so relax. It is, as its name suggests, a *markup* language. A series of relatively simple *tags* enables you to specify how text appears in the browser and arranges for images and links to other sites. HTML isn't difficult to learn, but you really don't need to. (If you decide to get into it, look for *Sams Teach Yourself HTML and XHTML in 24 Hours*. It's an excellent reference.)

There are programs, including web page design programs, desktop publishing programs, web browsers, and word processors you might already own, that can translate your pages into HTML with just a couple of mouse clicks. All you do is lay out the page the way you'd like it to look with your Photoshop pictures pasted in. Most of the programs described convert your images to web formats automatically. If the one you're using doesn't offer that service, you have to do the conversion first. Because web pages can be viewed on all kinds of computers, the graphics have to be in a format that's common to as many as possible and compatible with the HTML requirements. A web browser will not, for example, display a PSD or TIFF file. Instead, it requires that graphics files be compressed or *optimized* so that they are as small as possible. This limits your web graphic options to the GIFs previously mentioned or to JPEG (Joint Photographic Experts Group) or PNG (Portable Network Graphics) formats. ImageReady saves in all three of these formats.

WORKING WITH THE IMAGEREADY DESKTOP

Before we start to use ImageReady, let's take a minute to look at the program. Much of it is already familiar from Photoshop. The Photoshop Save for Web dialog is very similar to the ImageReady interface. It has a toolbox at the left, a tool options bar across the top of the screen, and a collection of palettes on the right. Below the tool's Options bar you can see the Window tabs at the top of the window in ImageReady and starting in the upper-left corner of the Save for Web dialog. They determine the content of the preview area. You can show the original image alone, a single image that is updated to show you current optimization settings, or you can compare images. When you select 2-Up, a pair of images is visible in the preview area. By default, the original image and an optimized image are shown, although you can change the original to any optimization settings. When you choose 4-Up, you can see the original and three different optimization possibilities for comparison or see four different sets of optimization options.

In both the 2-Up and 4-Up views, you activate a pane by clicking it. That version's settings is shown and can then be changed. Figure 11.2 shows the 4-Up view.

The Tools

To the left of the preview area, you have four tools available (see Figure 11.3). In 2-Up and 4-Up views, the tools can be used only in the active pane. They function similarly to the comparable tools in Photoshop:

- **Hand tool:** When the entire image doesn't fit in the window, click and drag with the Hand tool to reposition it. You can temporarily activate the Hand tool by holding down the spacebar.

- **Slice Select tool:** When the image has multiple slices, you can use the Slice Select tool to choose a slice to optimize. Different slices can have different optimization settings.

- **Zoom tool:** Click or drag to zoom in, and Option-click (on the Mac) or Alt-click to zoom out. You can also change the magnification by using the pop-up menu in the lower left of the dialog or by using the contextual menu.

11

Figure 11.2
The ImageReady 4-Up is the most useful view.

Figure 11.3
These are the tools in Photoshop's Save for Web dialog box.

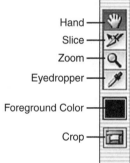

Hand
Slice
Zoom
Eyedropper
Foreground Color
Crop

■ **Eyedropper tool:** The Eyedropper is used to select a color. You can select colors only in the active pane. If the optimization settings selected are GIF or PNG-8, the color you click is selected in the color table. For 24-bit images (JPEG and PNG-24), the color is shown only in the swatch below the Eyedropper tool on the left.

The *color swatch*, which shows the color most recently selected with the Eyedropper, is below the tools. (When you open the Save for Web dialog, the last selected color is still visible, even if it's not present in the current image.)

The button below the color swatch toggles slice visibility on and off. Clicking the Slice Select tool automatically shows slices, too.

Figure 11.4 shows the ImageReady toolbox. As you can see, many of the icons are familiar from Photoshop. The tools work

Although the Save for Web dialog offers preset zoom magnifications from 12.5% to 1600%, you can use the Zoom tool to zoom out as far as 1%. Remember, however, that you should always make your final evaluation of web graphics at 100% zoom—that's how they'll be seen in a web browser.

exactly the same in ImageReady, so it doesn't really matter which application you access them from. You can toggle back and forth between Photoshop and ImageReady by clicking the icon at the bottom of the toolbox.

The tools that are unique to ImageReady enable you to create and view image maps, rollovers, and slices. The button with the browser icon opens your browser, displaying the image you're working on, so you can check to see that the actions you insert work as expected. The button with the browser icon opens your browser, displaying the image you're working on, so you can check to see that the actions you're inserting work as expected.

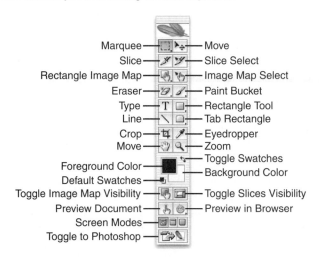

Figure 11.4
Click the button at the bottom of the toolbox or press ⌘-Shift-M (on the Mac) or Ctrl+Shift+M (in Windows) to switch between ImageReady and Photoshop.

To use any of these tools, select the one you want and apply options as needed from the tool's Options bar.

GETTING HELP

Help is always at hand in any of Adobe's programs. If you go to the Help menu in ImageReady, you see the menu in Figure 11.5. The submenu items walk you step by step through common actions.

Figure 11.5
If you want to optimize an image, the Help system takes you through the steps, carefully explaining each one.

There's even a topic that explains how you can export your ImageReady or Photoshop files into Macromedia Flash SWF format, retaining layers as part of the animation.

EXPORTING FILES TO IMAGEREADY

ImageReady includes many of the basic color correction, painting, and selection tools that you've already learned in Photoshop, plus a powerful set of web tools for optimizing and previewing images and creating GIF animations and rollovers. But before you can work on a picture in ImageReady, you have to get it there. There are a couple of ways to do this. If you've been working in Photoshop, click on the small icons at the bottom of the toolbox. Initially, this action opens ImageReady with the current Photoshop image loaded; when both ImageReady and Photoshop are launched, click this button to toggle back and forth between the two applications. You can use the keyboard command Shift-⌘-M (on the Mac) or Shift+Ctrl+M (in Windows), to toggle between the two programs. Of course, you can always open the picture to be worked on from within the application.

What ImageReady *can't* do is print. Because it's intended for web creation, it works only in RGB mode, and only in 8-bit color (what a monitor displays). Now that we're seeing web pages on TV sets and even on cell phones, it's more important that images on the page fit with the display standards.

PREPARING IMAGES FOR THE WEB

If Photoshop and ImageReady have the same tools—and both can save images in GIF, JPEG, and PNG formats—how do you know when to use which one? If you're just dealing with one picture, you can use either. If you want to optimize several pictures so that they display well while using as little memory as possible, use ImageReady to do the optimization. You can edit, apply filters and type, and color correct in either program. Obviously, if you're going to be designing animations or using rollovers and slices, or any other kind of motion graphics, you have to do them in ImageReady.

The first thing you need to learn about preparing web graphics is the type of file format to use. File formats for web use are optimized in one of several ways to make the file as small as possible without losing detail in the image or having colors turn blotchy instead of making the smooth continuous transitions that we expect to see in a photograph. As you learned earlier, there are two standard choices: GIF and JPEG. The third format, PNG, has been out for several years and promised to be the best choice of all three, but it never really caught on.

File Optimization and Compression

File compression means to save the file by making it as small as possible. For saving and archiving documents, you're probably already familiar with such compression programs as Allume StuffIt and PKZiP. Compression works on text by surveying the document for frequently used combinations of letters and substituting a single character for a group. Let's look at a quick example: "These three trees are beeches." Looking for recurring patterns, you see "th" and substitute *. The pattern "ee" becomes !, and "es" becomes @. So, you get *@e *r! tr!s are b!ch@. By simply substituting a single character for each common group of two or three letters, you go from 25 letters to 18. That's better than a 28% drop, and well worth doing when storage space or transmission time is an issue. Obviously a file that's 50% compressed sends from one computer to another twice as fast. Similarly, compressing JPEG graphics works by looking at adjacent pixels on the screen and finding averages in each group. This works great the first time you do it. But, as in the text example, you lose half of your data. When the program that's uncompressing the file puts the averaged pixels on the screen, you lose some color data. The transitions from one group of averaged pixels to the next isn't as smooth, and you also lose some contrast because blacks and whites are averaged into grays. If you again save as a JPEG, you lose more data and more contrast, and soon the image starts to look like a bad photocopy. You could turn a spotted Dalmatian dog or a leopard into a gray or beige animal with enough saves. (That's why it's called the *lossy compression* method—it loses data each time it's applied.)

Optimization is the process of minimizing file size while protecting image quality. It's sort of a two-way street. As the file gets smaller, which is good, it gets harder to see, which is bad. Smaller files download from the web server to the visitor's computer faster, so they display onscreen quicker. The more quickly the image displays, the less disruption for the site's visitor. The balance between file size and image quality is not an exact science—there is no specific formula for optimization.

Files optimized for web display are stripped of nonessential data. Image previews and custom icons, for example, are not saved with the file. Such data is not visible over the web and serves to increase file size, thus slowing download time.

> Remember that Photoshop and ImageReady are designed to create *graphics*, not to produce web pages. Although it is certainly possible to produce rudimentary web pages using only Photoshop and ImageReady, they are *not* web development tools. Use Adobe GoLive instead.

Lossy versus Lossless Compression

JPEG files use the lossy compression scheme. Image data is discarded to reduce file size and is re-created to display the image. The more data that is thrown away, the smaller the file size. However, the more information that must be re-created, the more likely the image quality will be degraded. When a JPEG image is opened onscreen (or printed), the pixels that were deleted during compression must be restored. Because the exact color of the missing pixels is not recorded, the JPEG process estimates their color, based on surrounding pixels. The more pixels that must be re-created, the fewer original pixels that are available from which to estimate.

GIF and PNG (both 8-bit and 24-bit) use *lossless compression*. The data is compressed without discarding any, so the image can be rebuilt as it was. GIFs rely on a limited color table, with no more than 256 different colors. It's ideal for line art and pictures with large areas of flat color. It's not capable of showing subtle differences or continuous tones, so it's not very good for photography. GIF and PNG-8 file size can be further minimized by reducing the actual number of colors recorded in the file. If you have a piece of line art that uses only black, red, and green, for instance, you can limit the GIF color table to three colors and lose nothing. PNG-24 has no such color table option.

The Role of the Web Browser

A web page typically consists of both text and images, laid out with HTML tags so that the page can be displayed on the viewer's computer. You use a web browser to translate that HTML and re-create the page on your screen. The HTML file contains the page's text and tells the browser where to find the images on the web server. Some of the more popular web browsers are Microsoft Internet Explorer, Apple Safari, Netscape Navigator, and Opera. They, and most of the lesser-used browsers, can interpret HTML and similar languages natively and can use plug-ins for additional capabilities

11

(such as Scalable Vector Graphics and Java). Without the web browser, the page can't be downloaded and displayed. (However, numerous programs, including some word processors, can display a web page if you download it and save it to your hard drive.)

Remember, too, that cellular telephones and personal digital assistants (PDAs) can access the Internet. PDAs typically use wireless connections and have limited color capability. Although older cell phones are limited to 1-bit color—they can display only black and white (or black and gray or green)—the newer color cell phone displays are very common. If your intended viewers will access your website with cell phones or PDAs, plan accordingly. Use fewer colors, make sure your text and background have good contrast, and "think small" (consider the size of a PDA screen). If possible, check your page with a cell phone as soon as you post it, so you can see what might need to be changed.

Color Modes on the Web

Most modern web browsers (and HTML) support bitmap (black and white), grayscale, indexed color, and RGB modes. CMYK is a print mode and can't be displayed on a monitor; therefore, it can't be used for web work. Indexed color and grayscale images contain a maximum of 256 different colors or shades of gray. RGB images can have millions of subtly different colors in a single image. Because less color information per pixel is required in indexed color mode, an image of the same pixel dimensions is typically smaller and displays more quickly in a web browser because it downloads faster.

Indexed color mode is appropriate for web graphics that have few colors or large areas of solid color or transparency and for any image smaller than 256 pixels. RGB mode is better suited to capture and present the fine gradations of color typically found in photographs.

SAVING FOR THE WEB

Whether you're working in Photoshop or ImageReady, choosing File, Save for Web opens a dialog similar to the one shown in Figure 11.6. I selected JPEG Medium from the Preset pop-up menu in the upper-right corner. Medium is a good compromise between file size and image detail. After a short calculation, and because I clicked the 4-Up tab at the top of the window, you see my original image, plus the image with three different JPEG settings. The file size and download time are displayed for each image.

You can see that the upper-right image, which has been compressed the most, is the softest. (In photography terms, "soft" means soft focus or fuzzy, with diminished contrast.) For some uses, it's probably good enough. I prefer the middle quality version in the lower-left window. It's noticeably sharper and looks fine. There's not a great deal of visible difference between it and the largest JPEG shown (the one in the upper-left corner) but the difference in size is remarkable. By the way, the upload times shown have very little to do with reality. You'll find that most pictures upload very quickly, especially on a cable modem or any other high-speed system. Even dial-up modems using the regular phone lines are much faster than they were even a couple of years ago. Technology keeps improving, but file size is still worthy of consideration. If you create an absolutely beautiful image and it weighs in at something like 40MB, it takes something like forever to download. It will be far too high and wide to display all at once on a typical computer screen, and there's really no point in using a resolution setting greater than 96 dpi because that's what a good quality home/office monitor can display. HDTV isn't really here for computer users yet. Although print images need as much resolution as your printer can manage, screen images are limited by the hardware.

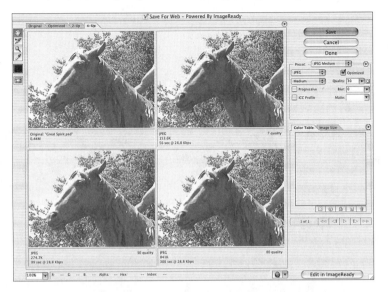

Figure 11.6
Photoshop's Save for Web function is powered by ImageReady.

Looking at the same picture in ImageReady, in Figure 11.7, you can see that the interface is similar but not identical. The biggest difference is that settings are displayed on palettes on the right side of the screen, rather than as a cluster of options on the dialog itself.

Figure 11.7
Saving in ImageReady gives you many more options than Photoshop's Save for Web dialog.

11

When you save an image, you can compare it as a JPEG at any quality level you choose from low to extremely high, and you can also compare JPEG, GIF, and PNG formats to the original. Doing so with a photo clearly shows the disadvantages of GIF for this kind of image. Figure 11.8 shows an example of this.

Figure 11.8
Quality settings from left to right, above: Original, GIF; below: JPEG, PNG.

You can see that both the GIF and the PNG versions of the image reflect the limitations of indexed color, and the JPEG version looks most like the original file.

JPEG (Joint Photographic Experts Group)

Depending on your needs, JPEG could be the best file format for your web graphics. It is great for photographs and other continuous-tone (full-color) images, primarily because it can display 16 million colors. Of course, some web browser programs and display screens, such as those on a cell phone, can't handle that color depth. Instead, they display a reasonable approximation of your artwork. JPEG maintains pretty good color information but does, however, employ a lossy compression scheme, which means that you can adjust and reduce the file size—at the expense of the image quality. Image data is discarded to reduce file size and is re-created to display the image. The more data that is thrown away, the smaller the file size. However, the more information that must be re-created, the more likely the image quality will be degraded. When a JPEG image is opened onscreen (or printed), the pixels that were deleted during compression must be restored. Because the exact color of the missing pixels is not known, the JPEG algorithm estimates their color, based on taking an average of the surrounding pixels and inserting new pixels in those colors. You can see the difference in file quality arising from choosing a low, medium, or high file size.

WORKING WITH QUALITY SETTINGS

If you choose to save your image as a JPEG, the second section in the Optimize palette enables you to select an image quality—specifically, balancing the file size against the quality of the photo on the screen. In ImageReady, you can view an image in 4-Up view and then change the format and quality settings for each of the four images by activating one of the image windows and then using the Optimize palette to apply different settings.

JPEG Format

When the file format is set to JPEG in the Save for Web dialog or the main ImageReady window, the Settings area changes to the configuration shown in Figure 11.6 (Photoshop Save for Web) or 11.7 (ImageReady). To change the settings, use the pop-up menus in the Optimize palette, as shown in Figure 11.9.

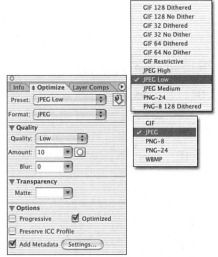

Figure 11.9
The Preset pop-up is at the top right and the Format pop-up is just below it.

You can select a preconfigured set of JPEG compression options from the pop-up menu at the top of the Settings area, or you can create custom settings. The various pop-up menus are shown in Figure 11.10. With JPEG selected as the file format, you have the following options:

- **Quality pop-up menu:** The pop-up menu directly below the Format pop-up menu offers Low, Medium, High, and Maximum options. The pop-up menu and the Quality slider are linked—a change to one updates the other. When you select from the pop-up menu, the Quality slider is adjusted to these values: Low: 10, Medium: 30, High: 60, and Maximum: 80.

- **Quality slider:** You can select precise levels of compression by using the Quality slider or by entering a value into the Quality field. The Quality slider setting is tied to the Amount pop-up menu: Quality settings of 0–29 are Low, 30–59 are Medium, 60–79 are High, and 80–100 are Maximum. The Amount setting is automatically updated as you change the Quality field or its slider.

- **Blur:** Applying a slight blur to an image can substantially reduce file size when it's compressed as a JPEG. The tradeoff is, of course, a degradation of image sharpness.

- **Transparency matte:** The color you choose in the Matte pop-up menu determines how the JPEG file handles transparency. Because the JPEG format doesn't support transparency, any pixel in the original that has reduced opacity must be filled with color. The matte color is used for any pixel that is 100% transparent, and it's blended with the existing color in any pixel with partial transparency.

- **Progressive:** When the Progressive check box is selected, the JPEG image appears in the web browser window in stages. Each stage clarifies the image until the final image is displayed. This display option can result in a slight delay in download, but the viewer gets feedback as the image loads, giving the impression of faster loading.

- **Preserve ICC Profile:** You can include an ICC color profile with the image. Some web browsers can adjust the image's appearance according to an embedded profile, but at the expense of increased file size—and therefore a slightly slower download speed. Browsers that do not support ICC profiles display the image as uncorrected.

> ICC profiles are mathematical descriptions of how a scanner, printer, or monitor sees colors. For the most accurate reproduction, the International Color Consortium (ICC) developed specific profiles for different scanners, printers, and monitors, even down to the level of what kind of paper you're printing on. Because you have no control over the kind of monitor that will be used to view your web images, ICC profiles are less important for web work, but critical for printing.

- **Optimized:** Optimizing a JPEG file can result in a slightly smaller file size. However, some older web browsers cannot display optimized JPEGs.

- **Add Metadata:** In ImageReady, the Optimize palette offers the option of preserving any metadata in the image, including EXIF data, typically generated by a digital camera, can include information about how and when the image was created and its print resolution.

Figure 11.10
Use the mouse to drag the Quality Amount slider or enter an amount in the window above it.

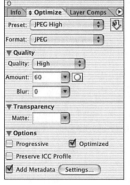

GIF Format

GIF is ideal for work with limited color art, such as line drawings and posterized photos. It's not so great for continuous tone photographs or full-color painting, because the GIF format works by evaluating the color of each pixel in your image and assigning it to one of only 256 colors.

When you save a picture as a GIF, you have a completely different set of options from those available when you save the file as a JPEG. Figure 11.11 shows the GIF palette options.

Saving as a GIF gives you choices for the color table algorithm used, the size of the color table, dithering method or No Dither, and whether to interlace the GIF and save its metadata. *Dithering* is a means of making color appear to blend more evenly. *Interlacing* draws the image on the screen, skipping alternate lines, so that you see the picture sooner. The second, and sometimes third, passes fill in the gaps to complete the picture.

Caution

Each time you save the file as a JPEG, you lose some data to compression. This can create *artifacts*—blocky areas or color bands in your picture. Never save a file as a JPEG a second time. If you make a conversion to JPEG and then decide to make changes, go back to the original Photoshop file. Don't make changes and resave the previously saved JPEG.

Figure 11.11
The GIF settings are not the same as the JPEG or PNG-24 options, but they are similar to the PNG-8 option set.

The Color Table palette shows the individual colors of an 8-bit image. You can edit, delete, and shift the color swatches. The Color Table palette is used only with GIF and PNG-8 images. It is empty when working with JPEG and PNG-24 files and shows only the uneditable black-and-white swatches for WBMP files.

Color Table Algorithms

When you reduce the number of colors in an 8-bit image, Photoshop makes decisions in accordance with your choice of color-reduction algorithm. You have several options:

- **Perceptual:** Different colors are viewed differently by the human eye. Some colors appear more prominent than others. Perceptual color reduction favors the colors that you see with greater sensitivity.

- **Selective:** Like the Perceptual algorithm, the Selective option favors the colors for which the human eye is more sensitive. However, it also considers the image itself. Areas of broad color are prioritized, and web colors are retained over similar non-web colors. The image's overall appearance is best maintained by using Selective, which is the default setting.

> Remember that the color table represents either the colors in the selected pane of the images in the Save for Web dialog or those of the selected slice in that pane. Each slice can be optimized separately.

- **Adaptive:** The Adaptive color-reduction procedure evaluates the image and gives preference to the range of color that appears most in the image. For example, color reduction of a picture of a banana preserves most of the yellows at the expense of other colors in the image.

- **Restrictive (Web):** The colors in the image are converted to web-safe colors, those 216 colors common to both the Windows and Macintosh system palettes.

- **Custom:** When an image's color table is created by using the Custom option, the colors are locked in. Further editing of the image won't change the color table. If, for example, you create a custom color table that does not include RGB 255/0/0 (hexadecimal value FF0000) and then attempt to paint with that shade of red, the nearest color already present in the color table is substituted.

- **Black & White:** The color table is reduced to only black and white and consists of only those two colors. The color table is locked after the conversion.

- **Grayscale:** The color table is reduced to grayscale and is then locked.

- **Mac OS:** Only the 256 colors of the Macintosh system palette are used.

- **Windows:** Only the 256 colors of the Windows system palette are used.

Number of Colors Used

You have the option of choosing a specific number of colors for the GIF or letting ImageReady or Photoshop do so for you, by selecting Auto, rather than a number between 2 and 256. Why does it matter? Again, the reason is to save a smaller file with no more information than is necessary to re-create the picture. The posterized cat in Figure 11.11 required only 20 colors. There's no reason to keep 236 unused colors in the table for this picture. Set the number of colors to use in the Color Table pane.

Dithering

Dithering is, in its most basic form, mixing two colors to simulate a third color. When viewed at 100% in a web browser, the dithering results in a smoother transition between colors than an undithered image. In Figure 11.12, I'm comparing a reduced and dithered GIF to the original.

If your image should have distinct edges, as is the case for many interface items, set the Dither Method pop-up menu to No Transparency Dither to prevent softening of the edges.

> You can use dithering to further reduce the number of colors in the color table. When you optimize an image, reduce the number of colors to the point where the image is starting to degrade; then select Diffusion from the Dither Method pop-up menu and adjust the slider to regain image quality.

The Image Size Palette

Docked with the Color Table palette in the Photoshop Save for Web dialog, the Image Size palette enables you to change the size of the image directly in the dialog box (see Figure 11.13).

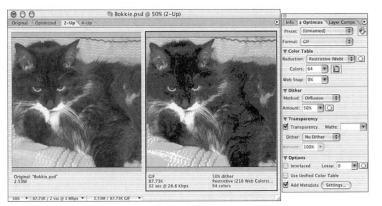

Figure 11.12
If your image should have distinct edges, as is the case for many interface items, set the Dither Method pop-up menu to No Transparency Dither to prevent softening of the edges.

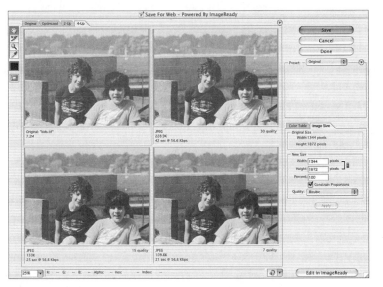

Figure 11.13
The Image Size palette has options comparable to those found in the Image Size dialog (opened with the command Image, Image Size), with the exception of resolution (which isn't required for web graphics).

You can specify an exact pixel dimension or a percentage. Selecting the Constrain Proportions check box automatically maintains an image's width/height ratio (as does sizing by percent). One of the Bicubic options in the Quality pop-up menu should be used with photographic or other continuous-tone images. Use Bicubic Sharper when reducing image size, and use Bicubic Smoother when enlarging an image. The Nearest Neighbor method is often more appropriate for inter-face elements and other web graphics that have large areas of solid color or distinct edges.

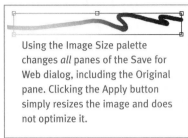

Using the Image Size palette changes *all* panes of the Save for Web dialog, including the Original pane. Clicking the Apply button simply resizes the image and does not optimize it.

PNG-24 Format

Unlike the JPEG file format, PNG-24 supports transparency. However, you can also choose to use a matte color in place of transparency. As you can see in Figure 11.14, when the Transparency check box is selected in the Optimize palette, the Matte pop-up menu is grayed out. To select a matte color, uncheck the Transparency option.

Figure 11.14
Matte choices are None, Eyedropper Color, Foreground, Background, and Other, which opens the Color Picker. ImageReady offers a palette of web-safe colors rather than the Eyedropper color.

In addition to a choice between transparency and matte, PNG-24 offers an interlacing option, which is comparable to the JPEG progressive option and to GIF interlacing: The image begins to appear in the web browser more quickly.

WBMP Format

The WBMP file format is intended for the creation of tiny black-and-white image files that transfer speedily to wireless Internet devices, including web-surfing cellular phones. Because the images are 1-bit color, file size is minimized. As you can see in Figure 11.15, the color table contains only white and black. Essentially, everything that's less than 50% black becomes white. Everything that's greater than 50% dark turns black. To change the ratio of black and white, go back to the original picture and experiment with the contrast.

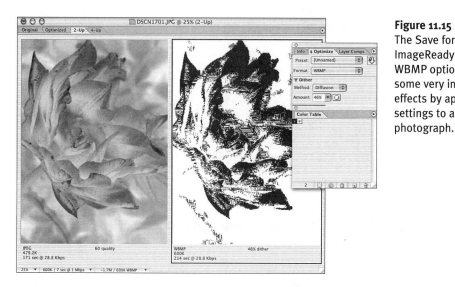

Figure 11.15
The Save for Web dialog and ImageReady offer the same WBMP options. You can create some very interesting etching effects by applying these settings to an appropriate photograph.

UNDERSTANDING RESOLUTION AND PIXEL SIZE

Web browsers ignore any resolution information recorded in an image. (The exception is Scalable Vector Graphics, which requires a plug-in for the web browser and cannot be created in Photoshop or ImageReady.) There's a reason for this: Your monitor isn't capable of showing 300 dots per inch, or 1200, or whatever resolution you may have set for an image. Images are displayed onscreen strictly according to their pixel dimensions, not their print dimensions. Consider resolution to be an instruction to the printer about how to reproduce the image on paper, not an instruction to the browser about how to reproduce the image onscreen.

USING THE REPOPULATE VIEWS MENU

The Repopulate Views menu command is available only in 4-Up view (click the fly-out menu at the top of the Optimize pane to find it). It generates a pair of new optimization settings based on the selected pane. The new options use the same file format but different options for comparison. If you select the Original pane and change it to show an optimization configuration, the Repopulate Views command restores it to its original status and replaces the other three panes with their original content.

WORKING WITH TRANSPARENCY IN GIF AND PNG-8 IMAGES

When a GIF or PNG-8 image is on a transparent background, you can maintain the transparency by selecting the Transparency check box in the Save for Web dialog or the ImageReady Optimize palette. When this option is not selected, the transparent areas of the image are filled with the matte color. If the Matte pop-up menu is set to None, white is used. The Transparency check box must be active when you map colors to transparency using the color table.

Transparency Dither

The Transparency Dither option softens the transition from colors to transparency. It works similarly to the standard Dither option (discussed in the section "Dithering," earlier in this chapter), but instead of blending colors, it blends from color to transparent.

As with regular dithering, you're offered the choice of Diffusion, Pattern, and Noise methods for Transparency Dither. In addition, when using the Diffusion method, you can choose the amount of diffusion dithering to apply by using the slider to the right in the Settings area.

Transparency Matte

If you deselect the Transparency option, the matte color is used to fill transparent areas of the image. The matte color can be used to blend the image with a solid-color web page background. The options are None (no matte), Eyedropper Color (the color most recently selected with the Save for Web dialog's Eyedropper tool), White, Black, and Other (which opens the Color Picker). ImageReady doesn't offer the Eyedropper Color option, but it does display a palette of the 216 web-safe colors from which you can select.

If your image has a transparent background and uses feathering or anti-aliasing, selecting your web page's background color in the Matte pop-up menu can prevent or reduce any halo around your image.

Interlacing

Interlaced GIF and PNG-8 images appear in the web browser as they download. Although it *seems* that the image is loading faster, interlacing doesn't actually speed up the process. Rather, the viewer gets feedback while the page loads. Interlacing is recommended for images over a few kilobytes in size.

SAVING THE PICTURE

It's the final step, but arguably the most important one of all. If you're using the Save for Web dialog in Photoshop, clicking the Save button opens a second dialog box titled Save Optimized As. Directly below the title is a field in which you enter the title of the picture. Below that is a pop-up menu with the following choices: HTML and Images, Images Only, HTML Only. If you're a wizard at hand-coding web pages, you may decide to choose either HTML Only—which gives you the script (in your preferred browser format) for inserting the file into a page—or Image Only, which saves just the picture in a folder called Images. Choosing HTML and Images obviously gives you both the hypertext and the image.

When you open the image you've saved, it opens in the browser rather than in Photoshop or ImageReady. If you then choose View Source from the browser's View menu (typically accessed with the shortcut key combination Shift-⌘ on the Mac or Ctrl+V in Windows), you see a batch of HTML text something like this:

```
<!DOCTYPE html PUBLIC "-//W3C//DTD XHTML 1.0 Transitional//EN"
"http://www.w3.org/TR/xhtml1/DTD/xhtml1-transitional.dtd">
<html xmlns="http://www.w3.org/1999/xhtml">
<head>
<title>Bokkie</title>
<meta http-equiv="Content-Type" content="text/html; charset=iso-8859-1" />
</head>
<body bgcolor="#FFFFFF">
<!-- ImageReady Slices (Bokkie.psd) -->
<img id="Bokkie" src="images/Bokkie.gif" width="710" height="600" alt="" />
<!-- End ImageReady Slices -->
</body>
</html>
```

To place this image into a previously coded web page, copy and paste the code where you want the picture to appear. If you are working in a program that generates pages, such as Adobe GoLive, place the picture on the page, and the program generates the code.

If you have other plans for your picture, such as posting it on a forum or sending it in email, don't bother with the HTML file. All you need is the picture.

A shortcut for saving your work is to let ImageReady make arbitrary decisions for optimizing the photo and choose File, Save Optimized. The dialog that appears looks like the one in Figure 11.16.

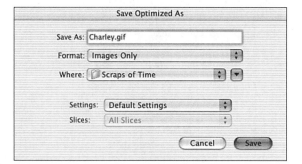

Figure 11.16
When you're in a hurry, let the computer do the work.

11

EMAILING YOUR PICTURES

You have all these great pictures and you want to share them, right? There are several ways to go about this. You can send them as email attachments, just like stuffing a handful of prints into a letter. You can post them on a forum, if you belong to one. You can set up your web gallery on your own website, or you can join a service such as Webshots (http://www.webshots.com) that gives you online storage and enables you to share your pictures with others as well as make digital prints and photo gifts.

To post a picture in a forum or on a service such as Webshots, follow its instructions. In any case, make sure that the picture is a reasonable size. You wouldn't want someone to tie up your mailbox by sending you a huge file, so don't do it to them.

To add a photo to an email, use the Add Attachment button or command in your regular email program and locate the picture you want to send. You can't send mail directly from Photoshop. The photo needn't be any special format, as long as you know your recipient has software that can open it. JPEG is always safe, because it opens in any web browser.

MASTERING IMAGEREADY

1. *Can I mix the kinds of images I use on a web page? Suppose I wanted a GIF background, a couple of JPEGs, and the head title done as a PNG 24. Will the combination automatically crash the browser when someone tries to open the page?*

    It shouldn't. There's no reason not to mix image types, provided that there is a reason for saving the files that way in the first place. If you have an image with only black and white, why save all those colors that aren't included? Make it a 2-bit GIF and enjoy the savings in file size. Photos need to be saved as JPEGs so they look better onscreen. But sure, so ahead and mix the image formats you use on your web pages.

2. *What's the deal about 216-color GIFs? Are there different kinds of GIFs for Macs and Windows computers?*

    It used to be that the Mac and the PC had an 8-bit color mode, which meant that they could display 256 colors. But, just to be difficult, the people who designed the two systems used slightly different colors. Only 216 of the 256 colors were close enough to be considered the same color on either screen. So, to be completely compatible, to make sure that what you saw was exactly what everyone else saw, we used 216 colors as the limit for a GIF. Now, monitor displays have improved and most computer graphics users agree that "close enough is good enough" and use the entire 256-color table.

3. *Are there any advantages to lossy compression, and if not, why isn't there a better way?*

    Lossy compression simply means that you lose some data when you save the picture. Groups of pixels are merged into a single value, and only that value is saved. The first time you save a photo as a JPEG, you suffer some loss, but so slight as to be unnoticeable. The second time you save the same file, more data is lost. Think about the numbers. Suppose, in the first save, you had groups of 9 pixels (3 by 3) that were averaged down to 1 pixel color for all 9. In the second save, pixels were again divided into groups of 9 and averaged. But this time, each of the 9 is already the average of 3 pixels, so you now have 27 by 27 pixels or 729 total, averaged into groups of 9 and reduced to 1. At this point, you have visible loss of data. Further saves make it worse. Lossy compression isn't a problem if you save as a JPEG only once—in fact, it's a very efficient system. The problem builds as you repeat the save. Why isn't there a better way? Many users think PNG is better. I'm not convinced, but with the entire Internet and everything that goes on it in a constant state of flux, we shouldn't have long to wait for the ideal solution.

BUILDING WEB GRAPHICS
IN IMAGEREADY

IN THIS CHAPTER

Back in the early days of the Internet, there was only text on the screen. In 1993, we first saw a graphical interface called Mosaic. It was based on HyperText Markup Language (HTML), which was a series of tags applied to the contents of the web page. In the case of text, the tags described the font, size, and color to be used, and where to start the text string. For graphics, the HTML tag included the name of the picture, its location in a folder, and its placement on the web page. The main point about HTML was—and still is—that it's a universal language. What you see on your screen as you design a page is pretty much identical to what a viewer on a different computer system and perhaps halfway around the world sees. Today, there are at least a half a dozen different browsers in use, and they all interpret HTML the same way.

HTML is good for more than just display specifications. You can also use it to create moving graphics, animations, and rollover buttons that change state when they see a mouse. (But so did my Aunt Hilda….) It's the ability to maintain transparencies, and therefore to build a graphic in layers, that makes these tricks possible.

You can also create some very interesting images that change when you click and hold the mouse button. They're done by dividing the picture into slices. You explore this a bit further along in the chapter, because you need to understand how to work with transparent images and GIF layers first.

TRANSPARENCY ON THE WEB

Every graphic you create for screen display in Photoshop and ImageReady is rectangular, and generally is landscape rather than portrait view. If you want the image to appear to be another shape, perhaps circular, or an irregular object with no background showing, you must make parts of the rectangle *transparent*. The pixels will still be there; they'll just be invisible. If you want the image to fade to the background or appear with a translucent shadow, you need *partially transparent* pixels. When each pixel is either completely opaque or completely transparent, the transparency is said to be *hard edged*. Images that have partially opaque pixels are said to have *variable transparency* or to fade.

> Remember that, with the exception of SVG, all graphics are displayed in a web browser window at 100% zoom—pixel for pixel—onscreen. Always preview your graphics at 100%.

The key to transparency in web graphics is understanding the capabilities—and limitations—of the web-compatible file formats:

- **GIF:** Create images with hard-edged transparency and save them as GIF. The file format does not support variable transparency.

- **JPEG:** JPEG does *not* support transparency.

- **PNG-8:** Photoshop handles hard-edged transparency automatically in PNG-8—create the image on a transparent background and save it as PNG-8. Variable transparency is simulated in PNG-8 with dithering.

- **PNG-24:** Both hard-edged and variable transparency are supported natively by PNG-24.

In Figure 12.1, an image using both hard-edged and variable transparency is shown in the three web-related image transparency formats.

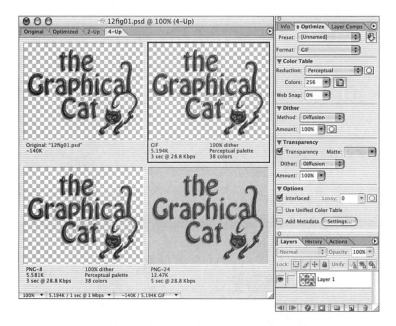

Figure 12.1
Clockwise, starting from the upper left, the images are Original, GIF, PNG-24, and PNG-8.

OPTIMIZING A COLOR TABLE

The more you work with GIF conversion, the more you realize that the most critical step is in mapping the original colors to a minimal yet representative table set. To most people, it sounds inconceivable that 32 colors can replace the thousands of colors in an image. Although you *can* do it, you must be careful about which colors you keep and which you throw away. Follow these steps to optimize a color table:

1. In Photoshop, choose File, Open. The Open dialog appears. Select the file you want to convert to the GIF format and click Open. Choose File, Save for Web.

2. Choose GIF from the Format pop-up menu. From the Colors pop-up menu, select the lowest number of colors without changing the file. Click the Optimized tab to review the results.

3. Click the Color Table tab. Choose the Eyedropper tool in the Save for Web dialog and click a prominent color in the image. The corresponding color in the Color Table is highlighted.

4. Lock the selected color by clicking the Lock button (marked with a padlock icon) at the bottom of the Color Table palette (see Figure 12.2). Locking a color prevents it from being removed or dithered. Repeat this step for any critical colors in the image. You see a small white square in the lower-right corner of the color chip, denoting that it's locked.

5. With the image showing on the Optimized tab, choose Sort by Luminance from the Color Table palette menu. In the color table, select a color close to a locked color and click the trash icon in the Color Table section (see Figure 12.3). The screen redraws to delete the selected color from the image. Continue deleting colors until you get a core set that represents the image well. Note that you can delete multiple colors by pressing the Shift key as you select adjacent color chips.

Figure 12.2
Select a color from the image and
lock it in the color table.

Figure 12.3
Click the trash icon to delete a
color.

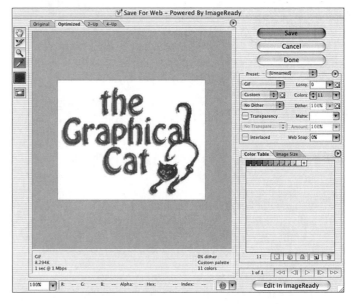

6. With the important colors locked down, decide whether you need to change other colors. To change color swatches, double-click the color in the color table; the Color Picker dialog opens (see Figure 12.4). Change the current color, paying close attention to the web-safe icon in the picker (the three-sided box icon), which shows you the nearest web-safe color.

7. If you're working with the same kind of image, or you want a series of images to use the same color set, save the color table you just fine-tuned. Choose Save Color Table from the Color Table palette menu. In the Save As dialog that appears, type a name for the color table and click OK.

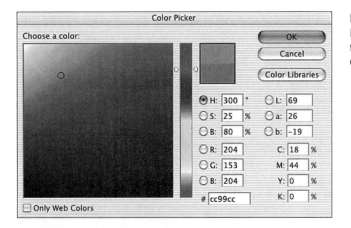

Figure 12.4
Double-click a color in the color table to change its value in the Color Picker.

PREPARING BACKGROUNDS

I admit that I have mixed feelings about backgrounds on web pages. These can really add personality to a website, but they also can make reading the text of your site difficult and frustrating. To quote web designer David Siegel, "Gift-wrap makes poor stationery."

If you use backgrounds with discretion, however, they can add to a site's presence and look. Because HTML includes the capability to tile any image as a background, your background file can be quite small. You just have to make sure that it doesn't have obvious edges or pictures that end abruptly, unless that's what you want. In Figure 12.5, I've created a tile for a web page background, and I'm saving it as a GIF using the Save for Web dialog in Photoshop.

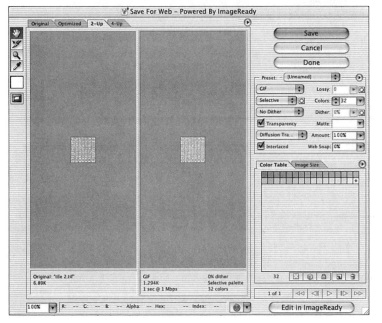

Figure 12.5
This tile combines several filters applied to a plain white background.

12

To convert the single tile into a background is easy: Open a page in your favorite web page layout program and import the image. Depending on the program, you might import it as an image and click a check box in the dialog box to make it a background. Some other web page layout programs such as InDesign and GoLive have a specific dialog for placing backgrounds. Netscape Composer's is called Page Colors and Background and is shown in Figure 12.6.

Figure 12.6
You can also preview text colors in the sample swatch.

Now, all you have to do is to be sure that when you upload your page to the web, the background image goes into the same folder as the page itself. Figure 12.7 shows the tiled background with some type and a picture (with transparency) placed over it.

Saving HTML with Images

If you are not using a web page construction program, but instead you are hand-coding your own web page hypertext, you probably already know that you need a few lines of text to describe the graphic being inserted. Without this HTML coding, nothing happens. For a static image, the coding is simply the source of the image file, its size, and its placement on the page. If the image has rollovers, is an animation, includes a special background color or background image, or will be used as a tiled background on a web page, you must save both the image and the associated HTML. With this saving option, HTML code is generated and an HTML file is saved along with a folder named, by default, Images.

To incorporate the artwork into an existing web page, you typically must copy and paste the HTML into the appropriate section of the web page's HTML document. The Images folder must be saved (and uploaded) with the HTML and other web page graphics.

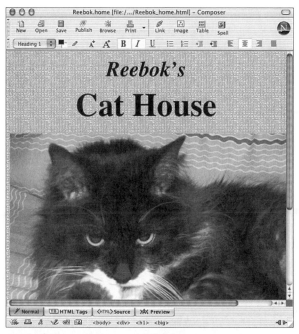

Figure 12.7
The background looks even, and the tiling hardly shows at all.

Adding an Accent Stripe

Here's a trick for placing a stripe down one side of your page. Make a single tile that's a little wider than the width of the screen by as few pixels high as needed. Place your color and/or texture on it and then save it as a GIF or JPEG. The file will probably look something like Figure 12.8.

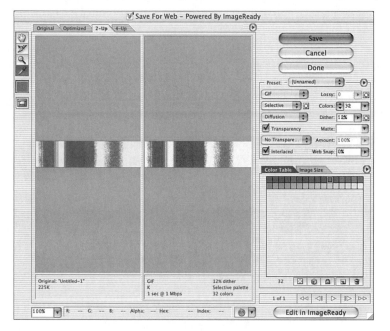

Figure 12.8
Note that this image has been cut off in the window. The background color continues across the entire screen.

12

When you place this file as a background, it is tiled vertically but not horizontally because it's already as wide as the screen. It's a good idea to check this in a high-resolution monitor setting to be sure you haven't left room for the stripe to tile again. You end up with a nice stripe, as wide as you care to make it, in the color and texture of your choice. It makes a good accent for a plain page, or you could design a wide stripe to set off a column of buttons. There's no limit except your own imagination.

Web graphics can also be *sliced*—divided into subsections—and with ImageReady you can create special effects associated with the image. The image can change appearance depending on the mouse's location or behavior, and you can even create animations that play in the web browser window.

dow. You can hide one image behind another and have the second one appear gradually as you click on, or drag the mouse over, slices of the top image, hiding the top slices or toggling them behind the other image. To make a slice, use the Slice tool and drag the box over part of the picture. This action actually makes two slices: the one you defined and the rest of the image. Make as many slices as you need. Slices are automatically numbered as they are created.

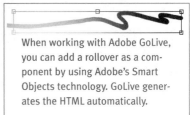

When working with Adobe GoLive, you can add a rollover as a component by using Adobe's Smart Objects technology. GoLive generates the HTML automatically.

Building Animations

GIF animations are commonplace on web pages, and you'll probably see dogs wagging their tails endlessly, cats catching mice, leaves falling, balls bouncing…. It's enough to make you dizzy. Photoshop and ImageReady can create the graphic elements and add motion to any of these goodies. If they aren't too big and flashy, GIF animations can be very effective.

Animation is done, as it was 50 years ago, in layers. The difference is that for a GIF animation, each layer must be a complete frame with the entire picture in it. In the old days, you could put the body on one layer and the arms, which moved, on a different layer. Now, because the animation is accomplished by scrolling through the layers, everything needs to be kept together or you see an armless torso, followed by waving arms.

Figure 12.9 is an animation model, a Japanese Happy Cat. This one, in black, represents good health. You make him wave at you in a very simple three-step animation. I'm working on this animation in ImageReady, but you could also do it in Photoshop CS2, as of this revision.

Figure 12.9
This cat will soon wave his paw.

The first step is to open a new image file in Photoshop and then to copy the cat into it on a separate layer.

Next, duplicate the layer twice, so there are three layers in all. The bottom layer is the *resting* state for the animation, so you don't need to do anything to it. It will be the first frame in the animation. The second layer is the *transition* state, and the third layer is the *final* state. You can insert as many transition layers as you need. More steps give you smoother animation, and a much larger file. Unfortunately, it might not play well on some computers, or if the Internet is running slowly, as it sometimes does.

Now, move to the top layer and make the changes necessary to take the picture to the final state. In Figure 12.10, you can see the cat's paw moved to a fully extended wave position. To do so, cut it loose with the Lasso, rotate it, and fill in the gaps in black and pink with a small brush.

Figure 12.10
The waving cat.

Next, move to the middle layer. Because this is a small animation and the cat's paw has to move only a short distance, one middle step is enough. If the paw had farther to travel, you could put in more transitional steps, but the animation looks fine with just one step here. Cut the paw loose and rotate it halfway between where it is on the first and third layers. Again, use a small brush to fill in any gaps. Now your animation should look like Figure 12.11. The "art" part of the job is nearly complete.

Figure 12.11
Midpoint of the wave.

12

Finally, copy the middle layer and add it to the top of the stack; then copy the background layer and add it to the top so the cat's paw ends up where it started. You now have five layers.

In ImageReady, open the Animation palette. Open the pop-up menu and choose Make Frames from Layers. You see the frames in the Animation window and clicking the forward arrow runs through them so you can preview the animation.

From the pop-up menu at the bottom of the Animation palette, choose Forever or Other if you want the animation to go continuously. Otherwise, it runs its steps once and stops. If you choose Other, you can specify a number of repeats—usually 10 is plenty. If it seems to run too fast, you can add a delay between each frame in the animation by setting the Frame Delay value. Figure 12.12 shows the final settings for the animation. You don't need very many colors for this particular example, so you can make it a 16-color GIF with no noticeable change.

Figure 12.12
Here are the five frames in order.

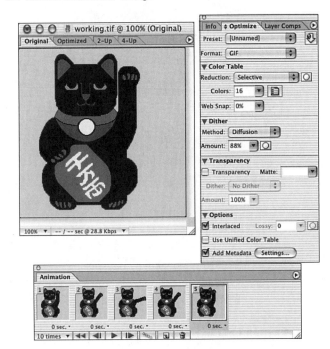

Choose Save Optimized from the File menu to save your work as an animated GIF. Choose HTML and Images to let ImageReady write the code and optimize the individual frames. Then add it to the source code for the web page and place the frames in the image folder. Check it out in your regular browser, and then—if possible—in other browsers to make sure it works for all.

Creating Slices

Slices are not the easiest concept to grasp, but they can save you a lot of file space, after you determine what they are about. Recall that slices divide an image into smaller files. Each slice is an independent file, containing its own optimization settings, color palettes, URLs, rollover effects, and animation effects. Slices can give you increased image quality when you are working with documents that contain more than one kind of image or text and images. They can make pages seem to load faster because each slice becomes visible as soon as it's loaded, giving the viewer something to look at while the rest of the image loads. Slices also allow you to create image maps that do useful things when you click part of an image. They can take you to new pages, show an enlarged view of the slice, or anything else you care to program them to do.

Slices are assembled in an HTML table in the document's HTML file. By default, the document starts with one slice that comprises the entire document. You can then create more slices in the document. Both Photoshop and ImageReady automatically make additional slices to complete the full table in the HTML file.

Slices are created by dragging the Slice tool, which looks like a drawing of an X-Acto knife. Select it from the ImageReady toolbox or the Photoshop toolbox, or press the K key to activate it. Drag a selection box across the area you are slicing. If you make a slice across the middle of an image, by default, you have defined three slices: the slice itself and one above and one below where you have sliced. Slices that you create are called *user-slices*. Slices that Photoshop generates are called *auto-slices*. If you place a slice across the middle of a picture, Photoshop places auto-slices above and below it. Slices can be vertical as well as horizontal. Subslices are created when you overlap two or more user-slices. Figure 12.13 shows a sliced image.

Figure 12.13
The numbers in the upper-left corner of the sections are their slice numbers (slices 3 and 5 are hidden under slices 4 and 6).

12

Slice Options

Slices options (see Figure 12.14) are necessary only when you're working with a sliced image. They determine how the slice-related information is recorded in the HTML file. To open this pane, you can select Slices from the Photoshop Save for Web dialog box's Preset pane pop-up menu. Click the Next button to reach the Slices pane. In ImageReady, you can select Slices directly from the File, Output Settings submenu.

Figure 12.14
These options do not pertain to
unsliced images.

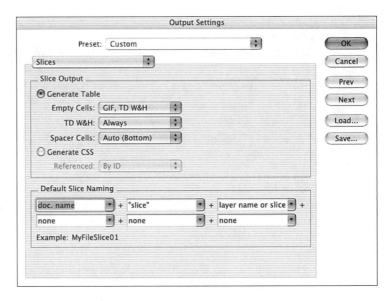

The Save for Web dialog and ImageReady offer these options for slice-related HTML:

- **Generate Table:** When you save a sliced image in Photoshop or ImageReady, you create a separate image from each slice—the slices are saved as individual files. The web browser requires HTML to tell it how to arrange those slices back into a cohesive whole, the original image. The browser uses the HTML to reassemble the jigsaw puzzle. You can generate an HTML table within which the slices are placed by using these options:

  - **Empty Cells:** Empty cells, used to ensure correct table spacing, can be recorded as single-pixel GIF images, with their width and height (W&H) recorded with the <IMG> (image) tag or the <TD> (table data) tag. The NoWrap option creates a nonstandard attribute and records W&H in the table data tag.

  - **TD W&H:** You can choose to include the width and height for all table data, never include the width and height, or let Save for Web determine when it is necessary. The Auto option is recommended.

  - **Spacer Cells:** A row or column of empty cells can be generated to ensure that a table displays properly in the web browser window. Spacer cells are particularly important when slice boundaries don't align. Save for Web can generate the extra cells automatically, always, or never, and you can also choose to have the spacer cells only at the bottom of the table. Auto generation is recommended.

    > For in-depth information on creating and editing code for web pages, see *Special Edition Using HTML and XHTML* by Molly Holzschlag (Que, ISBN 0-7897-2731-5).

- **Generate CSS:** With this function, you can create Cascading Style Sheets (CSS). The slices can be identified by a unique ID, in the <DIV> tag as an inline style, or by class.

- **Default Slice Naming:** Save for Web offers six fields for choosing names for slices. You choose the name options from pop-up menus for each field. A generic sample name is generated based on your choices and is displayed below the six fields. The available options are shown in Figure 12.15.

Figure 12.15
The slice names must be unique, so you must include at least one variable that changes from slice to slice.

The Output Settings dialog has five panes (see Figure 12.16). In addition, you can select from any available saved setting configurations from the pop-up menu at the top of the dialog.

HTML Options

The HTML pane of the Output Settings dialog governs how HTML is written (see Figure 12.16). The Save for Web dialog offers these HTML options:

- **Output XHTML:** Generate XHTML 1.0 Transitional–compliant code when selected.

- **Tags Case:** Create the HTML tags in all uppercase, uppercase and lowercase, or all lowercase. Web browsers can read tags in any style—this option is primarily for your convenience. If you edit or review the HTML, you might prefer to have the tags stand out by putting them in uppercase.

- **Attribute Case:** Record attributes in all uppercase, uppercase and lowercase, or all lowercase. Again, it makes no difference to the web browser.

- **Indent:** Format the HTML to indent using tabs or a specified number of spaces. If you edit the HTML in a word-processing program, either is appropriate. However, some text editors don't recognize tabs, so specifying a number of spaces better preserves the indenting.

12

Figure 12.16
These options determine the formatting of the HTML file generated by the Save for Web command.

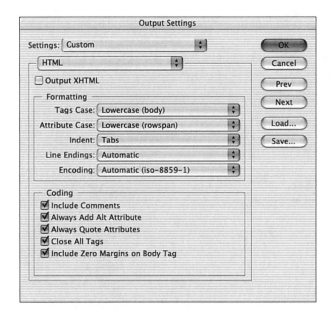

- **Line Endings:** Macintosh uses carriage returns at the end of lines, Unix uses line feeds, and Windows uses both. If you know what platform will be hosting your website, choose that platform from the pop-up menu. Generally speaking, however, there is no need for concern.

- **Encoding:** Select a customized text-encoding option. Options include ISO-8859-1, Mac OS Roman, and Unicode.

- **Include Comments:** Add explanatory comments to the HTML. Comments do not appear in the web page but rather are used by web design programs and can be used by ImageReady when updating HTML.

- **Always Quote Attributes:** Strict compliance with HTML standards requires that tag attributes be enclosed in quotation marks. The earliest web browsers also require the quotes. However, you should leave this option unchecked to allow the Save for Web dialog to include quotes only when necessary.

- **Always Add Alt Attribute:** Images are identified in HTML by the <IMG> tag. When a browser can't display the image, it looks for the ALT attribute and displays any text entered there, along with a symbol indicating that the image wasn't found. Without the ALT attribute, nothing is displayed. Save for Web includes the ALT attribute and quotation marks; you open the HTML file in a web design program, word processor, or text editor to add a message within the quotes. If you don't add any message, just the symbol is displayed. ALT attributes maintain links, even if the image is missing. Be aware that ALT attributes are required for compliance with U.S. government accessibility standards.

- **Close All Tags:** If the HTML will be incorporated into an XHTML page, select this check box. It ensures that all tags in the HTML have closing tags to match.

- **Include Zero Margins on Body Tag:** Margins are used by the web browser much as they are used in a word-processing document to offset the document. When you include the margins, you can later simply change the zeros to your desired margin by editing the HTML document.

EDITING OUTPUT SETTINGS

If you're familiar with Photoshop and ImageReady's set of nested Preferences dialogs, the Output Settings dialogs will be just as easy to work through. Choose File, Save for Web and then choose Edit Output Settings from the Settings pop-up menu to change how Save for Web handles slices, HTML, the filename, and any background image associated with the file. In ImageReady, use the File, Output Settings command to access the Output Settings dialog.

Unless an image has been sliced, normally you save only the image itself from Photoshop's Save for Web dialog. Generating an HTML web page for a single image is possible, but unless the image will be posted as a standalone web page, there's no need to create the HTML in Save for Web. In ImageReady, you need to save HTML with any artwork that has been sliced, has rollovers, or is an animation. Figure 12.17 shows what the source code for such a sliced photo might look like.

Figure 12.17
The source HTML is shown in a Safari window. You can open the HTML document in a word processor or text editor to change the margin information and add ALT messages.

File-Saving Options

The Saving Files pane of the Output Settings dialog box, shown in Figure 12.18, enables you to specify how slices are named (when generated) and several additional options.

Figure 12.18
Here's the first slice with its dialog box.

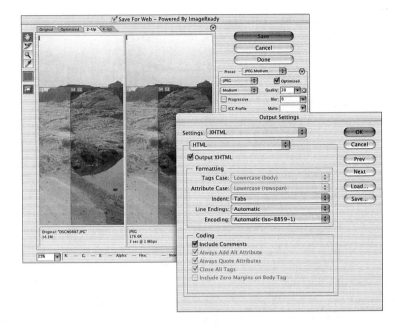

When an image is sliced, each slice is saved as a separate image. The Save for Web dialog automatically generates a separate file for each slice, using filenames that follow the guidelines you choose in the File Naming section of the Output Settings dialog.

Each slice name can contain up to nine elements, the last of which must always be the file format extension. You select the components from a list in each field (see Figure 12.19). You can also enter text into any of the fields, but remember that file extensions *must* be included at the end.

Figure 12.19
Here's the second slice.

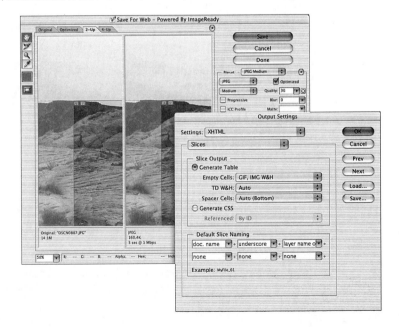

If you know what type of web server is hosting the site in which the image will be used, you can disable the unnecessary Filename Compatibility options. However, keep in mind that equipment gets upgraded, servers get replaced, and hosting services get changed. Keeping maximum compatibility helps prevent unexpected problems related to server changes.

Image Maps

An image map links specific areas on the web page to the index of URLs it generates. When you're working with images that contain image maps, ImageReady offers several ways to encode link information. Client-side image maps use the visitor's web browser to interpret the links. When you opt to use server-side links, the link information is generated as a separate MAP file, instead of being embedded in the HTML. The browser must query the server before navigating a server-side image map link. Client-side links are generally much faster for the browser to open. However, server-side links can be updated separately from the web page's HTML file.

When you generate client-side links, the Placement buttons at the bottom of the Image Maps pane are available. They determine where in the HTML the image map declaration is placed. The information can appear at the beginning or end of the BODY section of the HTML (Top and Bottom options, respectively), or it can be placed directly above the appropriate <IMG SCR> tag (the Body option). The difference is insignificant for the web browser, but you might have a preference if you edit HTML.

The Optimized Files section of the Image Maps dialog offers three options:

- **Put Images in Folder:** Select a name for the folder that holds the images created as slices or backgrounds. The default name, Images, is standard for most web purposes. The folder is created at the location where you choose to save the file. If a folder with that name already exists, the images are added to it.

- **Copy Background Image When Saving:** When you specify a background image to be tiled behind the image you're saving, the file can be copied to the folder you create. If this option is not selected, you must remember to include the background image separately when adding the image to a web page or website.

- **Include Copyright:** Automatically add the copyright information and file title in File Info to each image. If no information is available in File Info, nothing is added. To add the information, use the File, File Info menu command. Enter the data in the Copyright Notice and Title fields. The copyright information is added to the file but is not visible in the image.

CREATING SWF FLASH FILES

If you work with Shockwave, you'll be delighted to learn that it's quite simple to prepare your work in ImageReady and then save it as a Shockwave-compatible file, ready to drop into your Shockwave application.

12

Saving Files in SWF Format (ImageReady)

Technically speaking, you don't save your ImageReady file in Shockwave format, you export it; but this makes no real difference. In a multilayered Photoshop file, each layer of the file is exported as one SWF object, or each layer can be exported as separate SWF files using the Layers As Files command. When the entire file is exported to one SWF file, animation frames are exported as SWF animation frames. URLs in slices and image maps are preserved when exported. Rollovers are ignored. The exported images do not change when you roll over them.

Layers in a Photoshop document, layered GIF, or PNG-24 file can be preserved when exported from ImageReady and then imported into Macromedia Flash. Use the Layers As Files command to export the individual layers as separate SWF files. When the SWF files are imported in a SWF document, they each appear on separate layers. You can also export individual animation frames as separate SWF files using the Animation As Files command. Again, each SWF file appears on a separate layer when imported into Macromedia Flash.

Use the File, Export menu in ImageReady to open the simple dialog shown in Figure 12.20. Choose the appropriate options and click OK to save the file as an SWF document, which you can then open in Shockwave.

Figure 12.20
This figure shows the original image and the Export to SWF dialog.

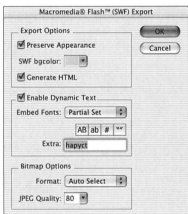

If you prefer, each layer can be exported as separate SWF files using the Layers As Files command. When the entire file is exported to one SWF file, animation frames are exported as SWF animation frames. URLs in slices and image maps are preserved when exported. Rollovers are ignored. The exported images do not change when you roll over them.

Layers in a Photoshop file can be preserved when exported from ImageReady and then imported into Macromedia Flash. Use the Layers As Files command to export the individual layers as separate SWF files. When the SWF files are imported in a SWF document, they each appear on separate layers. You can also export individual animation frames as separate SWF files using the Animation As Files command. Again, each SWF file appears on a separate layer when imported into Macromedia Flash.

PREPARING IMAGES FOR GOLIVE

If you work with GoLive, or certain other page creation programs, you already know how helpful it might be to export an image directly into a particular application rather than saving it and reopening it. For that reason Adobe has added Export Layers as Files to the File, Export submenu, as shown in Figure 12.21.

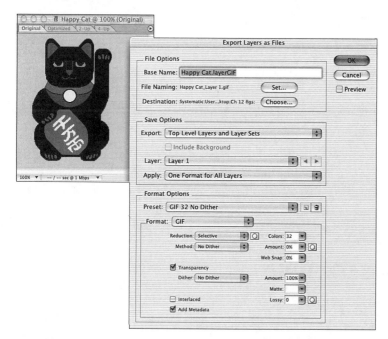

Figure 12.21
This figure shows the original image and the Export Layers as Files dialog.

WORKING WITH TEXT FOR THE WEB

Text appears in a web page one of two ways: as text, embedded in the page's HTML, or as part of an image. Generally speaking, large amounts of type are typically incorporated into the page as HTML; images that contain type often include buttons and banners.

Type displayed in a web browser window is displayed as pixels, whether HTML or in an image. Because the type is displayed at 100% onscreen, small type is often blurry or jagged. You can use Photoshop's anti-aliasing to smooth the curves of type you incorporate into an image. Fonts with strong, even strokes reproduce more cleanly with pixels than do cursive or ornamental fonts.

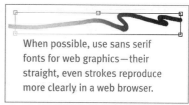

When possible, use sans serif fonts for web graphics—their straight, even strokes reproduce more clearly in a web browser.

HTML web standards include a handful of different type sizes and fonts, some for headings, some for text, and some for emphasis. Uh-huh. "Bor-ing," to quote the kids. However, you're not necessarily limited to what HTML has to offer. If you want a more elaborate title for your page, create it in Photoshop (you can also use ImageReady for this task), using filled letters, filters, drop shadows, glows, or whatever other special effects you like. Crop it tightly and save it as either a GIF or JPEG. Figure 12.22 shows a title I created for my page. Compressed, the file is only 6.3KB.

Figure 12.22
I used Photoshop's filters to create the 3D effect.

You have the option of converting your file to JPEG or PNG or to GIF. One good thing about text is that it usually, but not always, is applied to a white background. If this is the case with your website, there is no need to go through the trouble of exporting a transparent GIF89a file. Just make sure that your background is white and save it as a plain GIF file.

GIF or JPEG?

Professional web page designers apply one rule of thumb to choosing formats: With line art or anything with a limited palette (fewer than 216 colors), choose GIF or PNG-8; with photos or full-color art, choose JPEG or PNG-24.

MASTERING IMAGEREADY

Creating Transparent JPEGs

Suppose that you want to cut out the foreground of an image and see the web page's background, but you want to keep the image as 24-bit color. I suggest that you rethink your intent. Why do you need 24-bit color? You can, of course, save it as a PNG-24 if you feel that you really need every possible color available on a computer screen. Although it produces larger file sizes than JPEG, it natively supports transparency. Remember that some older web browsers can't display PNG files. That is rarely a problem, however.

Alternatively, you can get the benefits of the JPEG format's smaller file size and wider compatibility by simulating transparency. Here's how:

1. Make a copy of the image.

2. Merge all layers. If the image is flattened, convert the Background layer to a regular layer by renaming it.

3. Make a selection of the area that you want to be transparent and delete it. (The area should actually become transparent in the image.)

4. Open Save for Web.

5. Select JPEG as the file format and choose your Quality setting.

6. In the Matte pop-up menu, choose Other.

7. Select the web page's background color. For best results, the web page (and the matte color) should use a web-safe color.

8. Save the image.

This technique is *not* recommended for use with web pages whose background is a pattern or tiled image. It's difficult to ensure that the pattern will be properly aligned. To get the best possible color match, do not save an ICC profile with the JPEG.

Creating Letters by Pixel

Why does type look so bad on the web? Type doesn't *have* to look bad on your web pages. Keep in mind one simple concept as you design and create, and you'll get excellent quality. In a nutshell, you need only remember that everything on the web is reproduced with square pixels.

Because web pages are generally viewed on a computer monitor, everything is created from pixels, and every pixel is square. Trying to use square, evenly spaced pixels to show the subtle variations and curves of a script font or an italicized type, for example, can be difficult. And the smaller the type, the fewer the number of pixels that can be used for each character. Here are some suggestions:

- Use the largest type size possible. The more pixels you have for each character, the better they reproduce.

- Sans serif fonts are typically easier to show onscreen. They have uniform stroke sizes throughout the letter and lack the fine details at the end of strokes that often get too fuzzy to see properly.

- Sharp anti-aliasing is designed for use with type. It's especially effective for smaller font sizes.

If you use a video monitor, you can elect to change the shape of the pixels by applying the corrections available on the Image, Pixel Aspect Ratio menu. The Help screen in Photoshop explains them very well.

12

Understanding Pre-optimization

What do I need to do to get an image ready for Save for Web? What color mode? What resolution? What else?

Actually, you don't have to do anything—Save for Web automatically converts CMYK to RGB and 16-bit to 8-bit. Layers are flattened, type is rasterized, and blending modes are applied. Save for Web handles all the conversions necessary for the selected file format.

Remember, too, that there's no resolution on the web. All raster images are displayed according to their pixel dimensions. You don't even need to use Image Size to adjust those dimensions. Instead, leave your original as is, and use the Image Size tab in Save for Web to resize the image. You can use the same resampling algorithms as in Image Size, so there's no worry about additional image degradation.

ImageReady, on the other hand, requires 8-bit RGB images. Use the Image, Mode command if necessary before jumping to ImageReady.

ILLUSTRATOR

IN THIS PART

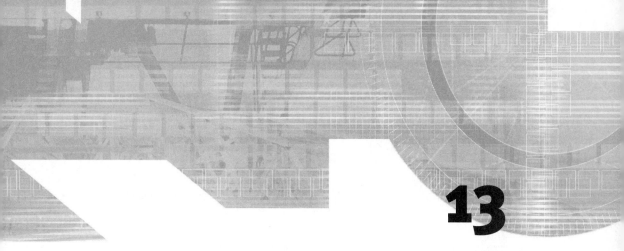

13

UNDERSTANDING THE ILLUSTRATOR ENVIRONMENT

IN THIS CHAPTER

Adobe Illustrator is one of the venerable programs in the Adobe stable. This vector drawing program has been around since 1987 and has undergone some amazing changes over the years. With the last few versions, Adobe has continued to perfect Illustrator, and the CS2 version contains many new features and improvements that make it a natural next step in the progression.

BEST PRACTICES

Recommending when to use and when not to use Illustrator involves a brief discussion about a couple of other programs in the Creative Suite: Photoshop and InDesign. Especially for new users, many of the tools and capabilities appear the same. They are, but there are both subtle and not-so-subtle differences between the programs that make differentiation necessary.

To explain this fully, let's talk about graphics first. There are two types of graphic formats: vector and bitmap. *Vector graphics* are created with curves and lines based on mathematical formulas. After you create a vector graphic, you can enlarge it, reduce it, or change it as much as necessary without having to worry about the graphic losing resolution.

Bitmap graphics, also called *raster graphics*, are resolution-dependent. The graphic itself is made up of individual pixels that hold color information about the graphic. When you work with bitmap images, you alter pixels, as opposed to manipulating lines and curves as you do with vector graphics. The most common use of bitmap graphics is in the form of digital photographs.

Although both Photoshop and Illustrator can work with either type of graphic, Illustrator is primarily a vector-graphic program. You can import bitmap images into Illustrator and work with them, but you have to be careful because what you see in Illustrator may not accurately reflect the graphic when it is output. In the same vein, Photoshop's true strength lies in the ability to manipulate bitmap graphics and images. You can work with vector graphics in Photoshop, but your tools and options are much greater in Illustrator.

As far as how Illustrator stacks up against InDesign, there are many similarities in the programs. However, it's all a matter of utility—you need to look at what the programs were originally intended for. InDesign is a page layout program. It was created to help you design large documents with more than one page, particularly text-heavy documents. Although you can create vector objects in InDesign, you have more options for working with them in Illustrator.

Illustrator, for its part, does what the name says it does: creates illustrations. It does have some page layout and text features, and it might be suitable for creating simple, one-page documents. But for the most control over document functions, look to InDesign.

The great thing about all these similarities, and even the differences, is that with the entire Creative Suite, you have access to all these tools and more. In addition, because the three programs work so well together, you end up with a tightly integrated workflow that can help you create better documents than you thought possible.

NEW FEATURES AND TOOLS

For those of you who have used Illustrator before, there are several new features and tools that make working with Illustrator in CS2 a process that is both easier and more exciting.

Live Trace

Live Trace may very well end up being your favorite new feature (see Figure 13.1). It's certainly the one that has garnered the most attention and praise from the technology press. Import a bitmap graphic—including photos—into your Illustrator document, and then use Live Trace to convert it to a vector graphic. After the conversion has taken place, you can edit the object as if you created it yourself in Illustrator. Live Trace also works on scanned graphics. That means those great ideas you have that end up drawn on cocktail napkins no longer need to be traced—or even worse, redrawn—on the computer. Just scan the drawing, import it into Illustrator, and convert it with Live Trace. In three steps you're ready to start working with your drawing.

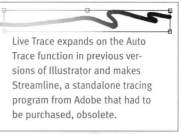

Live Trace expands on the Auto Trace function in previous versions of Illustrator and makes Streamline, a standalone tracing program from Adobe that had to be purchased, obsolete.

Figure 13.1
The Live Trace feature has received a lot of attention because it makes creating vector graphics out of bitmap objects a fast and easy process.

Live Paint

The Live Paint feature makes applying color easier and more intuitive. In previous versions of Illustrator, you had to plan your graphics in advance to be able to apply color and shading exactly the way you wanted. Live Paint picks up on the different parts of a drawing that are created by intersecting paths and enables you to apply color to each one separately (see Figure 13.2). It also has a feature, Gap Options, which enables you to specify how fills should be applied to objects whose paths don't completely meet or overlap. This is especially important with scanned drawings.

13

Figure 13.2
Fill in any area created by an intersecting path using the Live Paint Bucket tool, which automatically detects the shapes created by the paths.

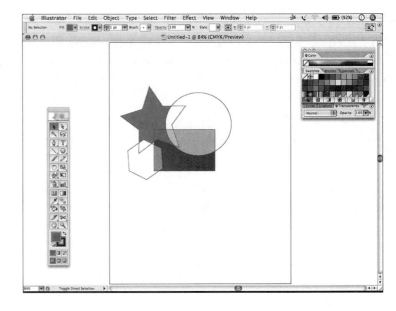

Control Palette

Finally—an end to the need for constantly opening and closing palettes depending on the tool you're using at any given time. A context-sensitive Control palette appears at the top of the screen based on the tool you select and the action you're performing (see Figure 13.3). Like the Options bar in Photoshop, the Illustrator Control palette enables you to access quickly options such as font, size, style, and alignment when you are working with type, and options such as fill, stroke, brush, opacity, and style with most other tools.

Figure 13.3
The contextual Control palette, which appears and changes based on the tool you have selected, is one of the features that makes using Illustrator a simpler experience.

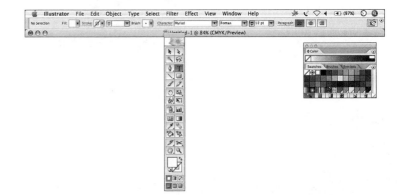

Support for Photoshop Layer Comps

Hide or show layer comps in any Photoshop document you place, embed, or open in Illustrator because it gives you more control and options for how images with layer comps are displayed.

Colorize Grayscale Images

Add a spot or process color to any placed, embedded, or open grayscale images, a process that was not automated in previous versions of Illustrator. With Illustrator CS2, you simply select the object and then fill the object with a color from the Color palette. Because you do not have to create an opacity mask for the object, you can apply color with more assurance that your image will separate properly when printed.

Expanded Stroke and Type Options

Create strokes that are aligned to the inside or outside, or are centered to the object's anchor points; previous versions of Illustrator gave you only one choice for how the stroke was positioned. Quickly apply underline or strikethrough to text.

New Filter Gallery

Many of Photoshop's filters have been duplicated in Illustrator's Filter Gallery, which enables you to apply effects to your vector graphics (see Figure 13.4).

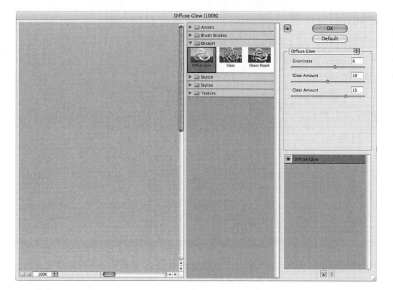

Figure 13.4
The Filter Gallery enables you to alter filters that are applied in Photoshop after you open your document in Illustrator.

Custom Workspaces

Specify and save how the workspace should be arranged, including palette locations. This is useful if more than one person is using the same computer, or if you work on a variety of projects, each of which requires you to have different palettes open for an easier workflow.

Wacom Tablet Support

If you use a Wacom drawing tablet, Illustrator has support for the tablet's new features, including the new pressure tip and eraser, tilt two side switches, barrel rotation, and the large felt-marker-shaped nib.

Adobe Bridge

The Bridge enables you to preview objects and documents you create in any of the Adobe applications, including Illustrator (see Figure 13.5). Right-click (Windows users) or Control-click (Mac users) on any document and select Open With to choose the Creative Suite 2 program you want to use to open the file. Remember that you can open Photoshop files in Illustrator and vice versa, but with InDesign you must choose File, Place to open a native Illustrator or Photoshop document and place it in your InDesign file.

Figure 13.5
Adobe Bridge makes file management and working between applications a much easier proposition.

Color Management

Like the rest of the programs in the Creative Suite 2, color can be synchronized across the applications if you choose Edit, Creative Suite Color Settings in Adobe Bridge. For more information on color managing your Creative Suite files, refer to the Color Management section of Chapter 1, "Creative Suite 2 Basics."

PDF Support

Use PDF presets you created in Illustrator or other applications to specify how a document or piece of artwork should be exported. Illustrator also enables you to export in the PDF/X format. Finally, to create multiple-page PDFs, you can tile your Illustrator documents, called *artboards*, into the appropriate number of pages and then export.

Tiling Control

A new overlap feature enables you to output a large document to a standard printer, printing 8.5- by 11-inch sheets and then pasting them together using the overlap to create a seamless document.

Support for Nearly Every Graphic Format

As you'll see later in this chapter, Illustrator supports the creation of, importing of, and exporting of almost all graphic formats. This includes a new ability to export documents to the SWF (Macromedia Flash) format, as well as SVG formats, including those that can be used for display on mobile devices, such as cell phones.

ILLUSTRATOR HELP

Obviously, our goal with this book is to provide you with a complete overview of the programs in the Creative Suite and how to use them to get the best results possible. But we know that you're always going to have questions. That's why the Adobe Help Center is such a great addition to the Suite. It's a resource that gives you definitions, step-by-step instructions and examples of different effects.

To get to the Help Center, select Help, Illustrator Help, or press F1 on your keyboard. The browser opens with the Help Center ready to assist you.

ILLUSTRATOR PREFERENCES

Before you start working in any application, give some thought to setting up your preferences. Each Adobe application gives you numerous preference options that control the way the application performs specific actions or reacts in specific situations. Access the Illustrator Preferences window by selecting Edit, Preferences in Windows environments, and Illustrator, Preferences on your Mac.

The Preferences window contains several panes. You can select a specific pane from the Preferences submenu, or use the pop-up menu at the top of the Preferences window to choose the set of preferences you want to see. Use the Next and Previous buttons to move from set to set. In the following sections, you explore the different options in the Preferences window. In many cases you may choose to stay with Illustrator's default preferences, but it's good to become familiar with these because there might be certain options that are very meaningful to you and the way you work.

General Preferences

Figure 13.6 shows the General pane of the Illustrator Preferences window. The following options are available:

- **Keyboard Increment** refers to the amount a selected object moves when one of the arrow keys on the keyboard is pressed.

- **Constrain Angle** enables you to change the angle of the x and y axes. They are horizontal and vertical by default; enter another degree in these text fields to rotate the axes. A positive number moves the rotation angle counterclockwise, and a negative number moves it clockwise.

13

Figure 13.6
Illustrator's General Preferences.

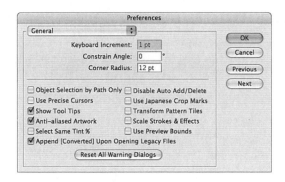

- **Corner Radius** refers to the corner appearance when rounded rectangles are drawn.

The following check box options enable you to turn the features on or off:

- **Object Selection by Path Only:** When this option is checked, you can select an object only by clicking on the path or an anchor point. When it is not selected, you can click the fill of an object and select it.

- **Use Precise Cursors:** This turns on an option that gives you a very precise pointer when you are working with the tools in the Toolbox. The precise cursors help your accuracy when you're dealing with detailed artwork.

- **Show Tool Tips:** Uncheck this option if you do not want to display the name of a tool when you hover your mouse over it.

- **Anti-Aliased Artwork:** Turn on anti-aliasing, which displays your vector artwork much smoother than is usually possible on a monitor, giving you a more precise view of how it will be printed.

- **Select Same Tint %:** The Select, Same menu commands in Illustrator enable you to select all objects that have the same fill and/or stroke color. When this box is checked, these commands will select only those objects that have the same tint percentage of the given colors.

- **Append [Converted] Upon Opening Legacy Files:** If you are opening files from previous versions of Illustrator, text in those files is not editable until you update it. When you update text, Illustrator will automatically add the word [Converted] to the end of your filename. Deselect this option if you do not want to add [Converted] to your filename.

- **Disable Auto Add/Delete:** When you are working with a path using the Pen tool, by default the tool automatically changes to the Add Anchor Point tool or Delete Anchor point tool, depending on where you position it on the path. Check this box to turn that feature off.

- **Use Japanese Crop Marks:** This turns on the double crop marks common in Japanese printing environments.

- **Transform Pattern Tiles:** If you are transforming an object with a patterned fill, checking this box also automatically applies the transformation to the fill. When this option is disabled, the default will be to leave patterns unchanged when the object is transformed.

- **Scale Strokes and Effects:** When this option is selected, an object's stroke and any effect applied to it, such as a drop shadow, will be scaled when the object is scaled. Uncheck it to scale the object only, leaving the stroke and effect the same.

- **Use Preview Bounds:** This selection determines how the dimensions of any object are displayed in the Info palette. When this box is checked, the stroke width and any other parts of the element are included in the measurement; when this option is not enabled, only the vector path is measured.

Click the Reset All Warning Dialogs button to reset any warning dialogs you might have turned off or changed in the application.

Type Preferences

Figure 13.7 shows the Type pane of the Illustrator Preferences window.

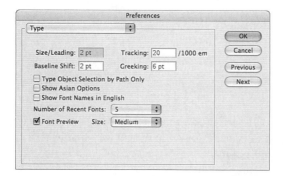

Figure 13.7
Illustrator's Type Preferences.

Keyboard shortcuts exist to help you automatically enlarge or reduce type and type characteristics incrementally. The numbers in the Size/Leading, Tracking, and Baseline Shift fields are the default increments when you use these keyboard shortcuts.

The Greeking field refers to the size type has to be to avoid being *greeked*, or displayed as a gray bar, when you are looking at your artboard. The point size is relative to the zoom level of the artboard. For example, with the default setting, type below 6 points is greeked at 100%. With that same setting, type below 12 points is greeked at 50% zoom.

The following options are available:

- **Type Object Selection by Path Only:** When this is checked, you must click on a type path to select the type. When it is deselected, you can click anywhere in the type bounding box to select the type.

- **Show Asian Options:** Determine whether different letter forms are visible in the Glyphs palette for Asian fonts. The term *glyph* refers to a single character in a font family. The Glyphs palette displays all available characters or letterforms in a font.

- **Show Font Names in English:** When this is selected, all font names display in English. When unchecked, the font names display in the native language.

13

- **Number of Recent Fonts:** This pop-up menu specifies the number of fonts you want to see in the Type, Recent Fonts menu.

When the Font Preview option is checked, fonts will be displayed with previews in the Type menu and all other places where fonts are selected. You can also choose a general size at which the font should display.

Units & Display Performance Preferences

Figure 13.8 shows the Units & Display Performance pane of the Illustrator Preferences window.

Figure 13.8
Units & Display Performance
Preferences.

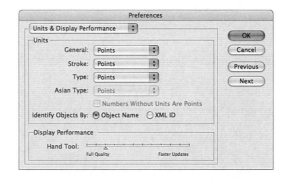

The Units pop-up menus enable you to select the units of measurement in which general items (page objects, tabs and rulers), strokes, type, and Asian type (if you selected Show Asian Options in the Type Preferences pane) are displayed.

The following options are available:

- **Numbers Without Units Are Points:** When this check box is checked, Illustrator assumes that any number you enter in a palette without specifying a unit of measurement is a point. Otherwise, the default unit of measurement will be used.

- **Identify Objects By:** This setting determines how object names are displayed in the Variables palette. Object Name is the standard setting; XML ID refers to the XML name that Illustrator assigns to every object you create.

- **Display Performance:** This setting determines the quality of display when you move the artboard with the Hand tool. The closer you are to Full Quality, the better the display will look, but the slower you will move. The closer you are to Faster Updates, the faster you will move, but your display will not look as good.

Guides & Grid Preferences

The Guides & Grid pane of the Preferences window enables you to set the style and color of grids and guides on your artboard (see Figure 13.9). Enter a number to indicate how often a gridline should appear when grids are turned on and how many subdivisions are between each gridline. For example, if you were working in picas (a unit of measurement common in printing) and wanted a gridline every inch, you would put a gridline every 6p0 (6 picas equal 1 inch), with six subdivisions to represent the individual picas. The check box enables you to place grids behind page objects.

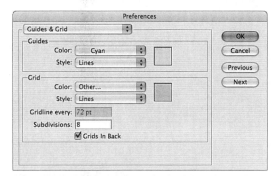

Figure 13.9
Guides & Grid Preferences.

Smart Guides & Slices Preferences

Figure 13.10 shows the Smart Guides & Slices pane of the Illustrator Preferences window. The following options are available:

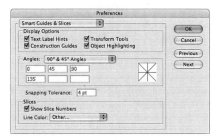

Figure 13.10
Smart Guides & Slices Preferences.

- **Text Label Hints:** Display labels similar to ToolTips indicating where the cursor will snap as you move the mouse. For example, if you move an object with Smart Guides turned on, the text label hints tell you what you are aligning to.

- **Construction Guides:** Display guidelines when you use Smart Guides.

- **Transform Tools:** Display information when you transform items by scaling, rotating, and shearing them.

- **Object Highlighting:** Highlight the object below the pointer while you drag around it.

The Angles area enables you to set how Smart Guides appear to help you position other objects near existing objects. Choose from the predefined angles in the pop-up menu or enter your own angles, which automatically changes the default to Custom. The preview square shows how the Smart Guide angles display. The Snapping Tolerance option refers to the number of points within which an object automatically snaps to a Smart Guide.

The Slices options define the boundaries of elements on a web page based on object type. In these preferences, you can set to show the slice number on the page and what color the boundary line for the slice should be.

13

Hyphenation Preferences

Choose your default language for hyphenation on the Hyphenation pane of the Preferences window (see Figure 13.11). If there are words you do not want to hyphenate automatically, like company names or proper names, enter them in the New Entry field and click Add to include them in the Exceptions list. You can also delete from the Exceptions list here.

Figure 13.11
Hyphenation Preferences.

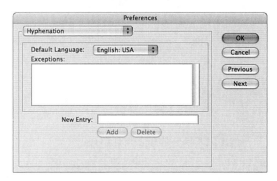

Plug-ins & Scratch Disks Preferences

If you are using Illustrator plug-ins, you can choose their default location on the Plug-ins & Scratch Disks pane of the Preferences window (see Figure 13.12). Use this pane if you want all plug-ins to be stored in a certain location.

Figure 13.12
Plug-ins & Scratch Disk Preferences.

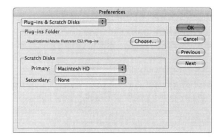

Certain Adobe programs ask you to specify a *scratch disk* to help handle the memory requirements of the program. When you are working with certain types of effects, Illustrator needs to store a lot of temporary information about the effects. If you have a partitioned drive or other hard drives you can use for the temporary storage of this information, choose your primary and secondary scratch disks here if necessary.

File Handling & Clipboard Preferences

Figure 13.13 shows the File Handling & Clipboard pane of the Illustrator Preferences window. The following options are available:

- **Enable Version Cue:** Turn Version Cue on for the application.

- **Use Low Resolution Proxy for Linked EPS:** Help cut down on file memory requirements by displaying only a low-res version of any placed EPS.

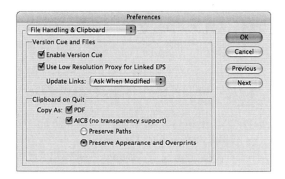

Figure 13.13
File Handling & Clipboard
Preferences.

- **Update Links:** When a link has changed, you can choose to have it updated in your file automatically or manually, or have Illustrator ask whether you want to update when it has modified.

- **Copy As:** For those applications that support the pasting of PDFs or AICBs, use this option to specify how to paste. A PDF preserves any transparency. If you choose the AICB option, the Preserve Paths radio button discards transparency in the copied item. The Preserve Appearance and Overprints radio button flattens transparency, maintains the appearance of the artwork, and preserves overprints. You can select PDF, AICB, or both.

Appearance of Black Preferences

The Appearance of Black pane in the Preferences window (see Figure 13.14) enables you to set how Rich Black and Pure Black (K = 100) appear onscreen and when they are printed/exported to RGB and Grayscale devices. Pure black tends to appear onscreen as a dark gray; rich black displays as more of a true black. If you select the Output All Blacks Accurately option, files that are printed on RGB or grayscale devices print blacks as they are defined. If all blacks are not created in the same way, you could have a difference between black elements on your page. If you select the Output All Blacks as Rich Black option, files that are printed on RGB or grayscale devices print the black as 100K, so it appears as dark as possible.

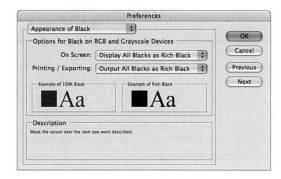

Figure 13.14
Appearance of Black
Preferences.

13

SETTING UP THE WORKSPACE

Before you start a document, it's helpful to set up the workspace the way you prefer it to make your efforts more efficient. Because there are numerous palettes in Illustrator, several of which you might be using at any given time, it's easy for the workspace to become cluttered and possibly even take your focus away from your work.

As with any Adobe program, you can press the Tab key at any time to hide all palettes and see your workspace. If you'd like to hide all palettes except for the Toolbox, select Window, Workspace, Minimal or press Shift-Tab. This command also keeps the Control palette open, but it docks it at the bottom of the screen.

You can also set custom workspaces if more than one person will be using the computer or if you have different workspace preferences for different projects. To create a custom workspace, first arrange your workspace the way you want, with all palettes open and in the space you want. Select Window, Workspace, Save Workspace. A dialog enables you to name your workspace; click OK to save it. From that point on, this named *workspace* (a collection of your preferred working environment) is available at Window, Workspace, *Workspace Name*. You can also select Window, Workspace, Manage Workspaces to add or delete workspaces.

SETTING UP A DOCUMENT

After your preferences are set, you're ready to start working with documents. To create a file, select File, New. Name your document in the New dialog that opens and choose your artboard size from the Size pop-up menu (see Figure 13.15). If you want to set up a custom document size, enter the measurements in the Width and Height fields. Choose your paper orientation.

Select whether you want the color mode of the document to be CMYK or RGB. RGB is generally used for documents that are displayed only onscreen; CMYK is usually chosen for documents that print in full color.

Figure 13.15
Set these options for new files you create.

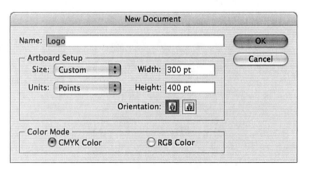

Choose File, Document Setup to see the Document Setup dialog, which gives you more options for how your document is set up. Choose the panel you want to display at the top of the dialog.

The Artboard Panel

The Artboard panel of the Document Setup dialog provides the same page size options as does the new Document dialog (see Figure 13.16). To speed up document display, select the Show Images in Outline check box. This option displays any linked files as an outlined box with an X through it. It displays artwork as paths only, without any paint attributes.

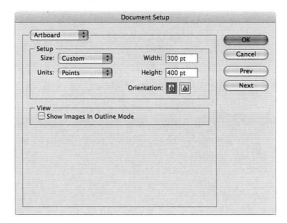

Figure 13.16
Artboard options in the Document Setup dialog.

The Type Panel

Figure 13.17 shows the Type panel of the Document Setup dialog. Enable the Highlight Substituted Fonts and Highlight Substituted Glyphs options to show you the type that is affected when you open a document that uses a font you do not have installed.

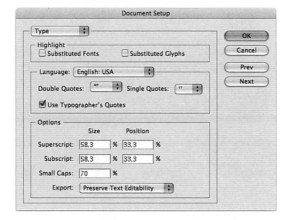

Figure 13.17
Type options in the Document Setup dialog.

From the Language pop-up menu, select the one you will be working in. Choose how double and single quotes are displayed. If the Use Typographer's Quotes option is checked, "curly" quotes, as opposed to straight quotes, are automatically used.

13

In the Options area, you can customize the size and/or position of superscript type, subscript type, and small caps. You can also choose how text should be handled when your Illustrator files are exported—whether you want to preserve editability or appearance.

The Transparency Panel

It's important to know when you are using transparency in your document, so Illustrator has a transparency grid that you can display on your artboard (View, Show Transparency Grid). The Transparency panel of the Document Setup dialog determines how the grid is displayed (see Figure 13.18).

Figure 13.18
Transparency options in the Document Setup dialog.

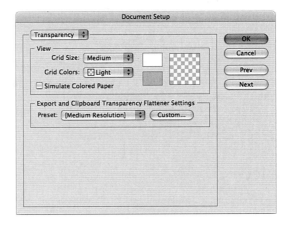

You can also choose the transparency preset here, which determines how transparency is handled when you export your document. Choose low, medium, or high resolution. To create custom settings, click the Custom button. The following options are available in the Custom Transparency Flattener Options dialog:

- **Raster/Vector Balance:** This setting determines to what point artwork is rasterized. Rasterization converts vector graphics, or those created with curves and lines, to dots. The higher the setting, the less the graphics will be rasterized. This means your page objects will be smoother, but they will take longer to load and print.

- **Line Art and Text Resolution:** This setting determines the resolution for those objects that are rasterized when you flatten. If you are outputting to low-resolution devices, this number can equal the output resolution. If you are outputting to a high-resolution device, you should check with your printer or the device manual for resolution suggestions.

- **Gradient and Mesh Resolution:** Use this setting to determine the resolution for gradients and drop shadows or feathers when flattened. Adobe recommends keeping this setting between 150 and 300. Higher resolutions cause slower printing and exporting and larger file sizes, without any equivalent return in quality.

- **Convert All Text to Outlines:** On spreads with transparency, this option converts all type to outlines and discards glyph information for that font. It helps ensure that text retains its proper width during flattening, but small type sizes may appear thicker when these documents are viewed onscreen or printed on low-resolution output devices.

- **Convert All Strokes to Outlines:** This setting converts all strokes to filled paths on spreads with transparency to ensure that the stroke width stays consistent when flattened. As in the Convert All Text to Outlines option, thin lines may appear thicker onscreen or when printed on low-resolution output devices.

- **Clip Complex Regions:** This setting reduces stitching that can result where vector and raster objects meet. Stitching shows up as blocky areas where colors don't exactly match. If you check this box, know that it also creates complex paths that might make your document harder to print.

Note that you also have other places where you can set up transparency flattening within Illustrator, including in the PDF saving options, which are covered in Chapter 20, "Working with Placed Graphics and Filters in Illustrator."

USING GRIDS AND GUIDES

You may have set the way grids and guides display in your Preferences window; now let's look at displaying those grids and guides.

Grids

When you create objects on your page, grids can be helpful because they show exact placement of objects in relation to one another. The settings that determine the increments of the gridlines and colors are set in the Preferences window, on the Guides & Grid pane.

To display the grid, choose View, Show Grid.

If you want the objects you create on the page to snap to the grid automatically, choose View, Snap to Grid.

Guides

There are two kinds of guidelines in Illustrator. The first are ruler guides, which are vertical and horizontal lines. These are dragged out of the rulers at the top and side of your artboard (if you don't see the rulers, choose View, Show Rulers).

You can also create guides from vector objects. Create the object you want to use as a guide and select View, Guides, Make Guides (see Figure 13.19). To turn the object back into a vector object, choose View, Guides, Release Guides.

To hide any guides you temporarily place on the page, select View, Guides, Hide Guides. Bring the guides back by choosing View, Guides, Show Guides. To delete all guides, choose View, Guides, Clear Guides.

Lock guides on your page so they cannot be moved or deleted by selecting View, Guides, Lock Guides. Unlock them by reselecting that same menu command.

13

Figure 13.19
In this example, the two diagonal lines have been transformed into guides to help align a specific polygon shape.

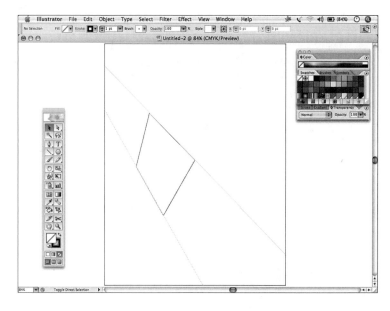

As long as guides are unlocked, you can move them freely on the page or delete them by selecting the guide and pressing Delete or Backspace.

Smart Guides

Smart Guides are temporary guides that appear when you move objects around on the page (see Figure 13.20). Remember that you can set your preferences for how Smart Guides appear by choosing Edit, Preferences, Smart Guides & Slices in Windows or by choosing the Apple menu, Preferences, Smart Guides & Slices on the Mac.

Figure 13.20
Smart Guides give you information about your selection and how it aligns with other guides.

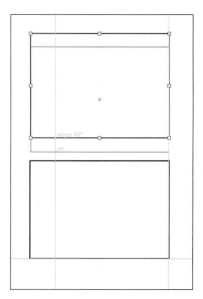

Turn Smart Guides on and off by choosing View, Smart Guides. As you move objects around on the page, you'll see the Smart Guides, which can be used to help you line up objects.

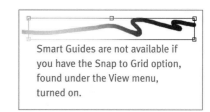

Smart Guides are not available if you have the Snap to Grid option, found under the View menu, turned on.

UNDERSTANDING FILE FORMATS

Illustrator enables you to import, export, and save files of nearly every graphic type. This section lists those formats and gives more explanation when necessary. Again, the Adobe Help Center is a great source of information for specific file formats and some of the options it offers.

Importing

Import files into Illustrator by selecting File, Place. If you have the Link option selected in the Place dialog, it creates a linked file—one that is not stored inside the document but is merely referenced in it. This creates smaller files. If you do not select Link, the file is embedded in the document, creating a larger document.

Following are the file types that can be imported into Illustrator. Different file types give you different import options in the case of PDFs and Photoshop files (PSDs). See Chapter 21, "Importing, Exporting, and Saving in Illustrator," for more specific information on Import options:

- Adobe PDF
- AutoCAD Drawing or AutoCAD Interchange file
- Bitmap (BMP)
- Computer Graphics Metafile
- CorelDRAW, versions 5–10
- Encapsulated PostScript (EPS)
- Enhanced Metafile
- FreeHand versions 4–9
- GIF89a
- JPEG
- JPEG 2000
- Macintosh PICT
- Microsoft RTF
- Microsoft Word
- PCX
- Photo CD

13

- Photoshop

- Pixar

- PNG

- SVG and SVG Compressed

- Targa

- Text

- TIFF

- Windows Metafile

Exporting Illustrator Files

You can export Illustrator files to various file formats. Following is a list of those formats. See Chapter 21 for more specific information about each format and the options it has:

- AutoCAD Drawing and AutoCAD Interchange File

- BMP (Bitmap)

- Enhanced Metafile

- GIF

- JPEG (Joint Photographic Experts Group)

- Macintosh PICT

- Macromedia Flash

- Photoshop

- PNG (Portable Network Graphic)

- Targa

- Text Format

- TIFF (Tagged-Image File Format)

Saving As

The options available when you save your Illustrator file are

- Adobe Illustrator

- Adobe PDF

- Illustrator EPS

- Illustrator Template

- SVG and SVG Compressed

More information about the various options can be found in Chapter 21.

Saving for Microsoft Office

The Save for Microsoft Office option, found under the File menu, saves the file as a PNG, as is. If you want to set options in the PNG, export the file instead of choosing this option.

In general, the differences between saving documents and exporting them is in the amount of control you have over the output after it's done. Saving a file preserves layer and path options so you can edit them after the object is placed or pasted in another application. When you export files, certain export options can flatten your files or make them uneditable.

Saving for the Web

Selecting the File, Save for Web command opens a dialog that gives you the following file format options:

- GIF

- JPEG

- PNG-8

- PNG-24

- SVG

- SWF

- WBMP

See Chapter 21 for a complete explanation of these file formats.

13

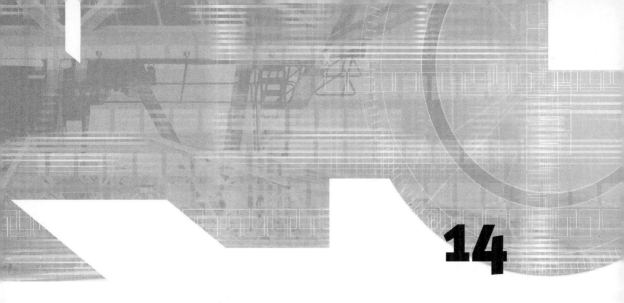

WORKING WITH ILLUSTRATOR TOOLS

This chapter serves as an overview of Illustrator's tools, contained in the toolbox (see Figure 14.1). As you read the following chapters, you will learn specific ways to use these tools in the creation and manipulation of page elements.

Figure 14.1
Use the toolbox to access all of Illustrator's tools.

Illustrator's tools are grouped in the toolbox based on their function. Like the other Adobe applications, if a tool has a small black arrow in the lower-right corner of its space, one or more other tools live underneath it.

When you click the arrow to expose the other tools in that space, drag to the tearoff tab at the very end of that row of tools. This separates the main tool and all hidden tools from the toolbox and puts them in their own palette, making them quickly available.

Tools often work in conjunction with palettes. In those cases, this chapter briefly looks at the related palette and some of its functions, but be aware that more detailed descriptions of how these items work together is given in later chapters when you investigate Illustrator's functions in depth.

Also remember one of Illustrator's most recent additions: the Control palette. By default, the Control palette sits at the top of the workspace, although it can be moved elsewhere (see Figure 14.2). Depending on which tool is selected, various options for the tool and the object(s) created with it are available in the Control palette. In some cases, the options in the Control palette can help you maintain an uncluttered workspace because you won't have to have as many "specialty" palettes open at the same time.

The following sections group the tools based on their function, not by how they appear in the toolbox.

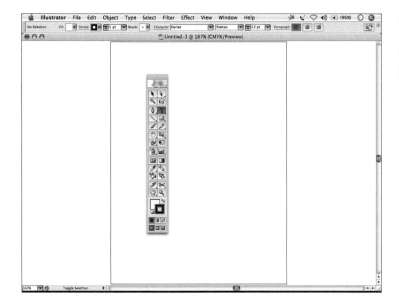

Figure 14.2
The Control palette gives you options for working with various objects you create on your page, including text.

UNDERSTANDING THE SELECTION TOOLS

Illustrator's selection tools are used to select or move shapes and anchor points, select objects within groups, or select parts of objects based on attributes (see Figure 14.3):

- **Selection tool:** Click to select entire objects. Drag around objects to select multiple items.

- **Direct Selection tool:** Click to select specific anchor points or paths on objects.

- **Group Selection tool:** Click to select specific items within groups of items. Click again on the same item to select the entire group, and again to select other groups of items that are grouped with the first one. Continue clicking until everything you want to select has been selected.

- **Magic Wand tool:** Click to select objects with similar attributes, such as the same color fill. Hold down the Shift key to select multiple objects. To set specifics of how the Magic Wand tool makes selections, either double-click on the tool itself or use the Magic Wand palette (choose Window, Magic Wand).

- **Lasso tool:** Drag around objects to select them. If you drag around a part of an object, it is selected, but only those anchor points you dragged around are active.

14

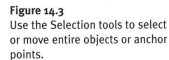

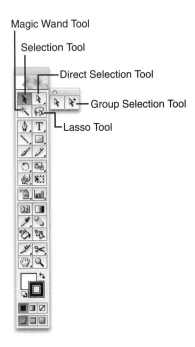

Figure 14.3
Use the Selection tools to select or move entire objects or anchor points.

UNDERSTANDING THE DRAWING TOOLS

Illustrator's drawing tools are used to draw paths and closed shapes, as well as to alter the paths that are created (see Figure 14.4). The Pen tool draws either straight line paths or Bézier curves, and the Add, Delete, and Convert Anchor Point tools help you work with the paths you create:

Figure 14.4
Illustrator's drawing tools are its greatest strength.

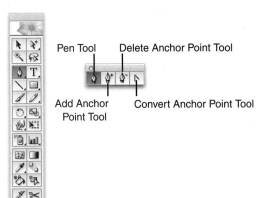

14

- **Pen tool:** Click to create paths or closed paths; an anchor point is created every time you click. Clicking multiple times creates straight curves between anchor points. Clicking and then dragging creates a Bézier curve. To close a path created with the Pen tool, click again on the first point of the frame.

- **Add Anchor Point tool:** Click on any path to add an anchor point.

- **Delete Anchor Point tool:** Click an existing anchor point along a path to delete it. Deleting a point in the middle of two others joins the two points on either side of the deleted point.

- **Convert Anchor Point tool:** Click on curves created with the Pen tool to create a straight line point. Click on a straight line point to create a curve. You can also click and drag a single direction point to modify one side of the curve without affecting the other side.

- **Line Segment tool:** Click and drag to draw individual straight lines. Double-click on the tool to set the line length, angle, and whether you want to fill the line with the current color (see Figure 14.5).

With any of the following drawing tools selected, click on the artboard to open a dialog that enables you to set many of the specifications for the object you are drawing, including size. For any of the tools that create lines or closed shapes, use the Stroke palette, Swatches palette, and/or Color palette to set specific page object options like path stroke and fill color.

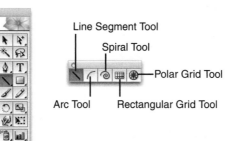

Figure 14.5
Create lines and paths of any shape.

Line Segment Tool

Spiral Tool

Polar Grid Tool

Arc Tool

Rectangular Grid Tool

- **Arc tool:** Click and drag to draw individual curved lines. Double-click on the tool to set options like the length, slope, and whether it should fill with the current color.

- **Spiral tool:** Click and drag right to create counterclockwise spirals; click and drag left to create clockwise spirals.

14

■ **Rectangular Grid tool:** Click and drag to draw rectangular grids. Double-click on the tool to set the grid size and specifications for the horizontal and vertical dividers.

■ **Polar Grid tool:** Click and drag to draw circular grids. Double-click on the tool to set the grid size and division specifications.

■ **Rectangle tool:** Click and drag to draw rectangles. Hold down the Shift key as you draw to create perfect squares (see Figure 14.6). Click on the artboard to set the width and height of your rectangle.

Figure 14.6
Illustrator gives you tons of options for creating closed shapes on your page.

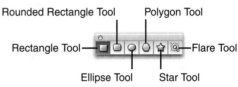

Rounded Rectangle Tool   Polygon Tool

Rectangle Tool —| Flare Tool

Ellipse Tool   Star Tool

■ **Rounded Rectangle tool:** Click and drag to draw rectangles with rounded corners. Hold down the Shift key while drawing to draw rounded corner squares. Click on the artboard to set the width, height, and corner radius of the rectangle.

■ **Ellipse tool:** Click and drag to draw oval shapes. Hold down the Shift key to draw a perfect circle. Click on the artboard to set the width and height of the ellipse.

■ **Polygon tool:** Click and drag to draw multisided shapes. Hold down the Shift key to draw shapes with equal sides. With this tool, clicking the artboard enables you to specify the radius of the polygon as well as the number of sides.

■ **Star tool:** Click and drag to draw star shapes. Clicking the artboard also enables you to change the number of points and set the radius from the inner and outer points of the star.

■ **Flare tool:** Click and drag to create a solar flare effect. Click the artboard or double-click the tool to set various options like size and halo and to make adjustments to the resulting rays and rings.

■ **Pencil tool:** Click and drag to create a continuous path or closed shape (see Figure 14.7). Double-click on the tool to set the tolerance of the path created and other pencil options.

14

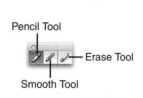

Pencil Tool

Erase Tool

Smooth Tool

Figure 14.7
The Pencil and its related tools enable you to control your freehand paths.

- **Smooth tool:** When you drag the Smooth tool over anchor points on a path, it makes the angles or corners smooth. This might delete anchor points from the path. Double-click the tool to control the tolerance of the Smooth tool.

- **Erase tool:** Click and drag over anchor points to erase them. If you drag over more than one point, you might break the path. This tool works only on paths created with the Pencil tool.

In relation to the Pencil tool, the word *tolerance* refers to the tool's sensitivity to your mouse or stylus movement. The lower the tolerance settings, the more anchor points are created on your path, and the more complex the path.

UNDERSTANDING THE TYPE TOOLS

Illustrator's Type tools enable you to create text in a variety of ways. Choose the proper tool to create either standard, straight-line text, text inside a closed path, or type on a path (see Figure 14.8):

- **Type tool:** Click to start typing, or click and drag to draw a type container of a specific size. When the Type tool is selected, your cursor becomes an I-beam, which enables you to select text by dragging over it.

- **Area Type tool:** Click with this tool inside a closed path to change the shape to a type container.

- **Type on a Path tool:** Click on a path and start typing to create text that adheres to the path.

- **Vertical Type tool:** Click to start typing vertically, or click and drag to draw a type container that contains vertical type. When the Vertical Type tool is selected, your cursor becomes a vertical I-beam, which enables you to select vertical text by dragging over it.

14

Figure 14.8
The various Type tools give you a great deal of control over how type is displayed and created.

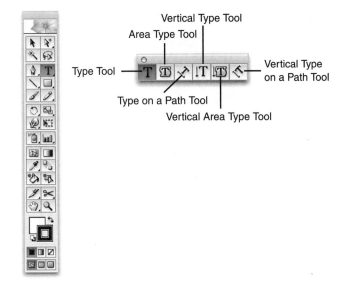

■ **Vertical Area Type tool:** Click with this tool inside a closed path to change the shape to a vertical type container.

■ **Vertical Type on a Path tool:** Click on a path and start typing to create vertical text that adheres to the path.

UNDERSTANDING THE PAINTING TOOLS

The Painting tools create not only brush strokes but can also be used to add color and shading effects to the shapes you create (see Figure 14.9):

■ **Paintbrush tool:** Click and drag to create freehand lines. Double-click the tool to set tolerance and Paintbrush options. Use the Brushes palette to set the width and shape of your brushstroke.

■ **Mesh tool:** The Mesh tool works with previously drawn objects to create multicolored effects. When you click with the Mesh tool, it creates mesh lines across an object that enable you to set color transitions to create a more dimensional look, for example. Use the Color palette and/or the Swatches palette to apply colors to the various parts of the mesh patches or mesh points.

■ **Gradient tool:** Click and drag across a page object to apply a gradient, setting the start and endpoints and the direction of the gradient, based on how you drag. The Gradient tool works in conjunction with the Gradient palette, Swatches palette, and/or Colors palette to create multicolored gradients and determine details about the gradient, such as type, angle, and location.

■ **Eyedropper tool:** Use this tool to sample object attributes and apply them to other objects (see Figure 14.10). Double-click on the tool to select the attributes the Eyedropper picks up and the attributes it applies.

Paintbrush Tool

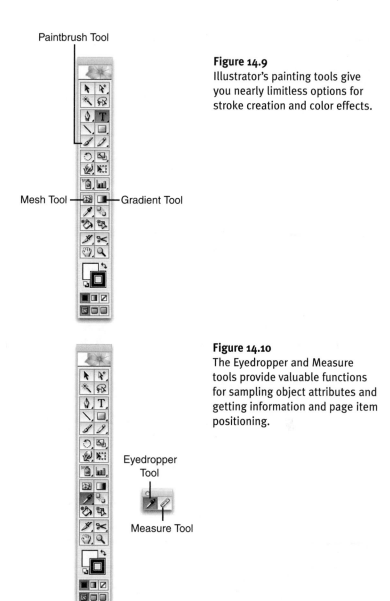

Figure 14.9
Illustrator's painting tools give you nearly limitless options for stroke creation and color effects.

Mesh Tool —————— Gradient Tool

Figure 14.10
The Eyedropper and Measure tools provide valuable functions for sampling object attributes and getting information and page item positioning.

Eyedropper
Tool

Measure Tool

- **Measure tool:** Click and drag to measure the distance between two points or the angle of a line. The measurement information is displayed in the Info palette. Double-click on the Measure tool to bring up the Guides & Grids Preferences dialog.

- **Live Paint Bucket tool:** Click to paint faces and edges of Live Paint objects with the current set of color attributes (see Figure 14.11). Double-click the tool to show Live Paint Bucket Options, including what is painted and the highlight color. There is also a button on this dialog that gives you tips for working with the Live Paint feature.

14

Figure 14.11
These two tools specifically deal with Illustrator's new Live Paint feature.

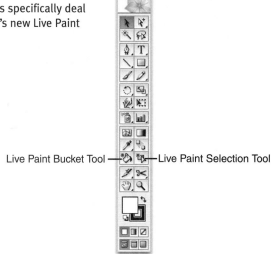

Live Paint Bucket Tool ———— ————Live Paint Selection Tool

- **Live Paint Selection tool:** Click to select faces and edges of Live Paint objects. Double-click the tool to show Live Paint Selection Options, including what is selected and the highlight color.

UNDERSTANDING THE RESHAPING TOOLS

The Reshaping tools alter the appearance of page elements while still maintaining the element's basic characteristics (see Figure 14.12):

Figure 14.12
Reshaping tools can change any page object or its arrangement.

Rotate Tool

Reflect Tool

- **Rotate tool:** Click, hold, and drag to rotate a selected object. This is a manual rotation, but use the Control palette or the Transform palette to see your angle of rotation. After you click with the Rotate tool, you see crosshairs. This indicates the point from which the item will be transformed. The crosshairs can be freely moved by clicking and dragging them. Double-click on the tool to enter a specific rotation angle.

- **Reflect tool:** Click, hold, and drag to flip a selected object over the crosshairs. You can flip by dragging horizontally or vertically. Double-click on the tool to select how to reflect the item, or enter a specific reflection angle.

- **Scale tool:** Select an object, and then click and drag on any anchor point or the side of the object to resize (see Figure 14.13). The item is resized from the crosshairs, which can be moved at any time by dragging. Hold down the Shift key to resize proportionally. Double-click the tool to enter a specific scale percentage, either proportional or nonproportional.

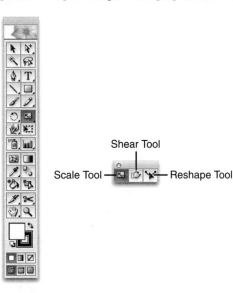

Figure 14.13
The Scale, Shear, and Reshape tools size, skew, and change the shape of objects, respectively.

Shear Tool

Scale Tool ——— Reshape Tool

- **Shear tool:** Select an object and then click and drag with the Shear tool to skew the object around the crosshairs. Move the crosshairs to skew from another point. Double-click the tool to specify the direction and angle of shear.

- **Reshape tool:** Click and drag on an anchor point of a selected object to reshape the object from that anchor point only.

- **Warp tool:** This tool bends and shapes the selected object (see Figure 14.14). Think of it as though the object you are reshaping is made out of Silly Putty, and the Warp tool is your finger or hand reshaping the object. Double-click to open the Warp Tool Options dialog, which enables you to set the brush dimensions and warp options.

14

Figure 14.14
These reshape tools create special detailed effects for elements.

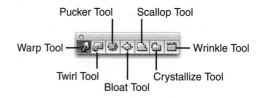

- **Twirl tool:** Click and drag on a selected object to create a swirled effect. Double-click to open the Twirl Tool Options dialog, which enables you to see the brush dimensions and twirl options.

- **Pucker tool:** Click and drag on an object to deflate it. Double-click to open the Pucker Tool Options dialog, which enables you to set the brush dimensions and pucker options.

- **Bloat tool:** Click and drag on an object to puff it up. Double-click to open the Bloat Tool Options dialog, which enables you to set the brush dimensions and bloat options.

- **Scallop tool:** Click and drag to add points to the outside of an object and add curves to the path. Double-click to open the Scallop Tool Options dialog, which enables you to set the brush dimensions and scallop options.

- **Crystallize tool:** Click and drag to add points to the outside of an object and add spikes to the path. Double-click to open the Crystallize Tool Options dialog, which enables you to set the brush dimensions and crystallize options.

- **Wrinkle tool:** Click and drag along the path of an object to add random wrinkles to it. Double-click to open the Wrinkle Tool Options dialog, which enables you to set the brush dimensions and wrinkle options.

- **Free Transform tool:** This tool can be used to rotate, scale, and shear an object (see Figure 14.15). With the item selected, when you position the tool at the corner of the frame you see a double-ended curved arrow. Click, hold, and drag to rotate. Scale by clicking and holding an anchor point. Hold down the Option or Alt key to scale from the center of the object. To shear an element, click, hold, and drag a side anchor point while you hold down the Ctrl+Alt keys (Windows users) or ⌘+Option keys (Mac users).

Figure 14.15
The Free Transform tool can be used to rotate, scale, or shear an object, and the Blend tool creates a continuous gradient between multiple selected shapes.

—Free Transform Tool

—Blend Tool

- **Blend tool:** Use with a series of selected objects. Click on the first object and then click on the last object you want to blend. This creates a gradient of the objects' colors, as well as of the objects themselves. Double-click to open the Blend Options dialog, which enables you to set either automatic or manual spacing of objects and the orientation that is aligned to the page or path.

UNDERSTANDING THE SYMBOLISM TOOLS

The tools shown in Figure 14.16 work with symbols in the Symbols palette. To add a new symbol, create the symbol on your page and then select New Symbol from the palette menu.

Double-click on any of the Symbolism tools to open the Symbolism Tool Options dialog. Diameter, Method, Intensity, and Symbol Set Density are set in this dialog. Click on the small buttons representing the Symbolism tools in the middle of the palette to set options or see shortcut keys for the specific tool:

- **Symbol Sprayer tool:** Click and drag to place symbols on the page in a series of what are called *symbol instances*.

- **Symbol Shifter tool:** Click and drag to move symbol instances on the artboard.

- **Symbol Scruncher tool:** Click and drag to move symbol instances closer together.

- **Symbol Sizer tool:** Click and drag to resize symbol instances.

- **Symbol Spinner tool:** Click and drag to rotate symbol instances.

- **Symbol Stainer tool:** Click and drag to color symbol instances.

14

Figure 14.16
Use these tools to work with symbol instances, both placing them on the page and changing their display.

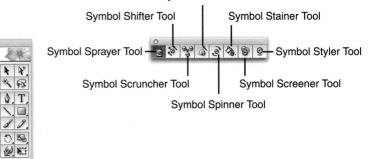

Symbol Sizer Tool

Symbol Shifter Tool

Symbol Stainer Tool

Symbol Sprayer Tool

Symbol Styler Tool

Symbol Scruncher Tool

Symbol Screener Tool

Symbol Spinner Tool

- **Symbol Screener tool:** Click and drag to add opacity to symbol instances. The opacity is based on settings in the Transparency palette.

- **Symbol Styler tool:** Click and drag to add styles to symbol instances.

> The term *symbol instances* refers to the series of symbols, or elements, that are placed on the page with the Symbol Sprayer tool. Symbols are often used when creating web animation because the items that are placed on the page can be animated so they appear one at a time in a specific pattern. Examples of Illustrator's predefined symbols can be found in the Symbols palette by choosing Window, Symbols.

UNDERSTANDING THE GRAPH TOOLS

All the tools shown in Figure 14.17 create various types of graphs to communicate information. When you click and drag with a graph tool, a spreadsheet-type window opens where you can enter the information with which the graph should be created. You can also import graph data from another program. Each type of graph has a specific way that information has to be entered for it. See the Adobe Help Center and Chapter 22, "Speeding Up Illustrator and Data Functionality," of this book for step-by-step instructions on creating each type of graph.

To place a graph on your page, you can click and drag with a Graph tool to create a specific graph area or click on the artboard to enter specific measurements for your graph.

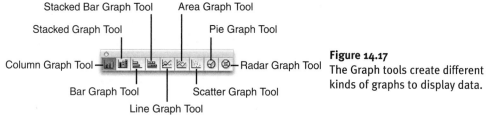

Stacked Bar Graph Tool   Area Graph Tool

Stacked Graph Tool   Pie Graph Tool

Column Graph Tool ─   ─ Radar Graph Tool

Bar Graph Tool   Scatter Graph Tool

Line Graph Tool

Figure 14.17
The Graph tools create different kinds of graphs to display data.

Double-click on any of the graph tools to set the options for graph creation:

- **Column Graph tool:** Use to create vertical column graphs.

- **Stacked Graph tool:** Use to create vertical column graphs with more than one measurement in each column to communicate relationships of data.

- **Bar Graph tool:** Use to create horizontal column graphs.

- **Stacked Bar Graph tool:** Use to create horizontal column graphs with more than one measurement in each row to communicate relationships of data.

- **Line Graph tool:** Use to create graphs that use trend lines in different colors to compare data.

- **Area Graph tool:** Use to create line graphs that fill with color, indicating totals that are created by the trend line.

- **Scatter Graph tool:** Use to create graphs that compare data as sets of points on an x-y axis.

- **Pie Graph tool:** Use to create graphs that contain wedges representing data's percentage of a whole.

- **Radar Graph tool:** Use to create graphs that compare data at points in time or different categories, demonstrated by slices and markings in a circle.

14

UNDERSTANDING THE SLICING AND CUTTING TOOLS

The Slicing tools are used in web page creation, to select and specify certain parts of the page to help with load times (see Figure 14.18). The Cutting tools—the Scissors tool and Knife tool—are used to break paths:

Figure 14.18
Slicing tools work on web documents; cutting tools cut objects or paths.

Slice Tool   Slice Select Tool

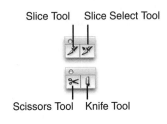

Scissors Tool   Knife Tool

- **Slice tool:** Click and drag to cut your artwork into separate elements for web display.

- **Slice Select tool:** Click to select a specific slice you created.

- **Scissors tool:** Click to cut a path at a specific point.

- **Knife tool:** Click and drag to slice through objects or paths.

UNDERSTANDING THE MOVING AND ZOOMING TOOLS

The Moving and Zooming tools are stalwarts of every Adobe toolbox, and help you gain more control over what is displayed onscreen at a given time (see Figure 14.19):

- **Hand tool:** Click and drag to scroll around the currently open artboard.

- **Page tool:** When you click with the Page tool, it creates an outline of the page as it would print. Drag the page outline to position the artboard for printing.

- **Zoom tool:** Click to zoom into that area, or click and drag to draw a marquee around a specific area you'd like to zoom to. Click as you hold down the Ctrl key (Windows users) or Option key (Mac users) to zoom out of an area.

14

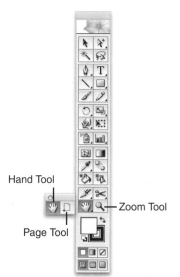

Figure 14.19
The Moving and Zooming tools give you control over your artboard view and printing setup.

Hand Tool

Zoom Tool

Page Tool

UNDERSTANDING OTHER CONTROLS

There are several important controls below the tools in the toolbox (see Figure 14.20). The first is the Fill and Stroke control. The outline box controls the stroke of the selected object. Click it to bring it to the front. The solid box controls the fill of the selected object. Click it to bring it to the front. Click the curved arrow to switch the application of fill and stroke. Click the fill and stroke proxy to return to the default settings.

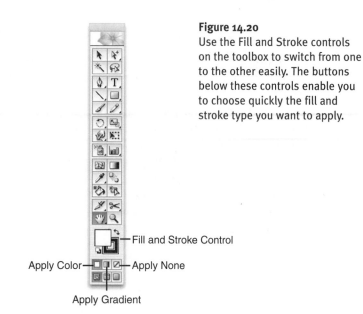

Figure 14.20
Use the Fill and Stroke controls on the toolbox to switch from one to the other easily. The buttons below these controls enable you to choose quickly the fill and stroke type you want to apply.

Fill and Stroke Control

Apply Color — Apply None

Apply Gradient

14

Below these controls, the Apply Color button applies the last-selected color to the fill or stroke, the Apply Gradient button applies the last-selected gradient to the fill or stroke, and Apply None switches the color choice to none.

Finally, Illustrator offers several view controls for the artboard (see Figure 14.21). The first button is a Normal view. The second button shows a Full-screen view with only the menu bar showing. The third button shows Full-screen mode without the menu bar.

Figure 14.21
View options on the toolbox enable you to see your document three different ways.

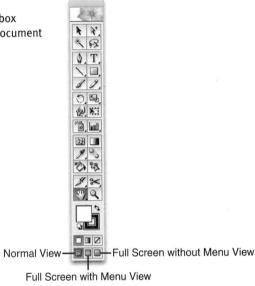

Normal View—┐ ┌—Full Screen without Menu View

Full Screen with Menu View

WORKING WITH KEYBOARD SHORTCUTS

Illustrator has hundreds of keyboard shortcuts to help make menu commands and tool selection as easy as clicking a button or two. Keyboard shortcuts are a great time-saver, but they can take a while to learn.

Don't sweat it, though. The best advice for learning keyboard shortcuts is simply to pay attention. When you're selecting a command from a menu, look to the right of the command name to see the keyboard shortcut. Do the same with the tools in the toolbox; when you hover your mouse over a tool, you see a ToolTip that shows the tool name and its keyboard shortcut.

You also have a certain amount of control over keyboard shortcuts. Choose Edit, Keyboard Shortcuts from the menu bar. Select either Tools or Menu Commands from the pop-up menu to see the keyboard shortcuts for each item (see Figure 14.22). For a learning experience, click the Export Text button to save a text file that lists all Illustrator shortcuts. You can print it out and use it as a study guide if you like.

14

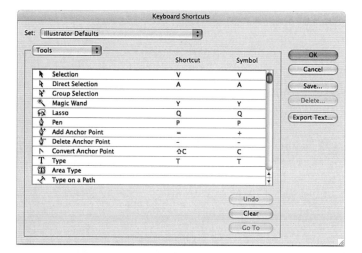

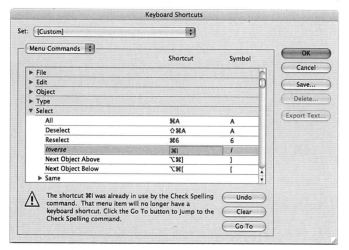

Figure 14.22
Scroll through the Keyboard Shortcuts dialog to see all keyboard shortcuts for tools and menu commands. Click on any keyboard shortcut to highlight the current shortcut and change it to make using Illustrator more convenient.

To change a keyboard shortcut, click on the shortcut you want to change under the Symbol column. Press the keyboard shortcut you'd like to apply. If the shortcut is already assigned to another command, you see an alert, but you are enabled to override the current shortcut.

When you finish setting up keyboard shortcuts, click Save. You are prompted to give your shortcut set a name. This saves your set with any changes you made. If another person will be using your computer, or if you have certain sets of keyboard shortcuts that you customize for certain projects, change back to the default by choosing Edit, Keyboard Shortcuts and selecting the Illustrator Defaults from the drop-down at the top of the dialog.

14

15

UNDERSTANDING ILLUSTRATOR PALETTES AND MENUS

IN THIS CHAPTER

As you may have surmised by this point in the book, much of Illustrator's functionality is contained within its elegant and malleable palettes; the rest is in ever more intuitive menus and nested menus. Though not quite as many as the palette-prolific InDesign with 38 palettes, Illustrator's 32 far outweighs Photoshop's paltry 19.

Although many other applications place the bulk of their commands and features on long and nested menus or inside dialog boxes, Adobe puts as many as possible on palettes. When open, dialog boxes prohibit access to the objects within the document; to apply the same commands to multiple objects, select each one individually, navigate back through the menus to open the dialog box, set its options, and apply them.

Palettes, on the other hand, do not prevent access to the objects within the document. Therefore commands are typically faster to apply to a single object or sequentially to multiple objects.

Still, as the number of palettes grows, their utility diminishes by creating screen clutter, reducing the amount of document working space available, and sowing confusion as to which palette contains a given command. Although Adobe and other software publishers continue to struggle with solving the matter of confusion as they work to improve and extend the commands available in their programs, relief for the first two drawbacks of palettes is already built in.

In Photoshop, palette clutter can be reduced by inserting palettes into the Palette Well on the Options bar. In InDesign and its sister program InCopy, palettes may be docked to, and collapsed into, the side of the screen, monopolizing only a small fraction of the horizontal screen space until palettes need to be accessed. Regrettably, Illustrator has neither of these extra palette-handling features. It does, however, share the Common Adobe User Interface capabilities of grouping multiple palettes together in a tabbed interface, stacking palettes atop one another, and rolling up palettes into their tabs.

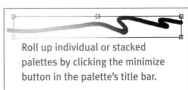

Roll up individual or stacked palettes by clicking the minimize button in the palette's title bar.

None of these methods make up for the fact that the number of palettes grows with each release of the program, but the innovations that *are* in the programs prove that Adobe is still working on answers.

WORKING WITH ILLUSTRATOR PALETTES

Among all the palettes discussed in the following chapters, a few stand out as necessitating in-depth discussion and extra detail.

Layers Palette

In Figure 15.1 there are but four layers as traditionally defined by other creative tools—and as noted in the bottom-left corner of the palette. The other entries are sub-layers, paths, objects, and groups on the layer. Every path, object, mesh, point text, area text, placed image—*everything*—has an entry on the Layers palette in a sub-layer, which makes selecting, hiding, or locking objects a breeze no matter how nested they may be.

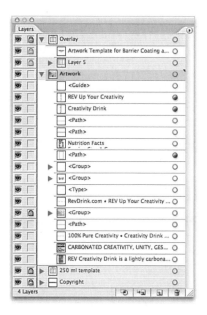

Figure 15.1
Inside layers, each object is represented by sub-layers.

15

Bearing the Photoshop-esque eye is the visibility column. To hide a layer or sub-layer, click the eye; to make it visible again, click the empty area where the eye should be.

Next in is the lock column. Absent a padlock icon, the layer or sub-layer is selectable and editable. A black-and-white lock, such as the one beside the Overlay layer in Figure 15.1, indicates that the layer and all its sub-layers are locked; you cannot select or edit these items. The faded lock beside the sub-layers of Overlay denote that the top-level layer is locked, overriding the individual lock state of sub-layers. If Overlay was not locked, each of the paths and objects it contains could be individually locked or unlocked.

Alt-click (in Windows) or Option-click (on the Mac) the visibility eyeball to hide all but the clicked-on layer; Ctrl-click (in Windows) or ⌘-click (on the Mac) to outline the targeted layer.

Between the lock column and the icon preview of the layer or sub-layer is the expand triangle. When a layer or sub-layer contains additional objects and sub-layers, the triangle will appear (generally pointed right). Clicking it once swivels the triangle, expanding the layer to reveal its sub-layers or closing it up to show just the top-level layer as is the case with the Overlay layer in Figure 15.2.

As you create new objects, Illustrator automatically names sub-layers according to the type of object. New layers that you manually create are named sequentially—Layer 1, Layer 2, and so on. Sub-layers—objects—however, are named initially according to what they are. For example, drawing a new path creates a <Path> entry; when converting a path to a mesh object, the layer is renamed to <Mesh>. The exception is type objects, which are named after the first few words of text you type. All these layers may be renamed.

Alt-click (in Windows) or Option-click (on the Mac) the lock column to lock all but the clicked-on layer; click while holding Alt+Shift (in Windows) or Option+Shift (on the Mac) to unlock or lock all layers.

15

Figure 15.2
With the Artwork layer fully expanded, sub-layers and sub-layers within sub-layers—all the objects in the layer—are evident.

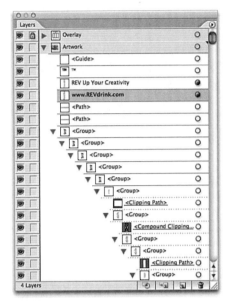

Double-clicking the title of a layer brings up the Layer Options dialog (see Figure 15.3). In the Layer Options dialog, you may rename the layer; change the color used to indicate the edges and bounding boxes of objects on the layer; and set whether the layer is shown, locked, printable, and previewed (as opposed to outlined). The Dim Images to X% option is most often used with the Template option checked to fade or "ghost" placed images for manual tracing, in which case you would trace on another layer just above the template. These options apply only to top-level layers; if you double-click a sub-layer your options are limited to renaming it and checking Show or Lock.

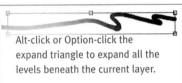

Alt-click or Option-click the expand triangle to expand all the levels beneath the current layer.

Figure 15.3
The Layer Options dialog (for top-level layers).

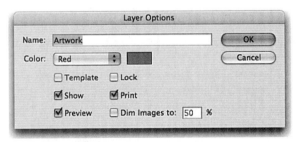

To the right of the layer name in the Layers palette is the target indicator, which tells you which object(s) are selected by the presence of a double-ring (see Figure 15.4) and, with a filled circle, which objects have Appearance attributes that may be copied to other objects. In a complex document, clicking on the target indicator is often the fastest way to select the correct object or objects—press Shift or Ctrl (in Windows) or Shift or ⌘ (on the Mac) as you click to select multiple targets concurrently). Clicking on the target of a layer or sub-layer automatically selects all visible and unlocked sub-layers and objects it may contain; Shift-clicking deselects.

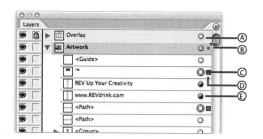

Figure 15.4
The target indicators in the Layers palette.

A: Unselected layer with empty target
B: Some sublayers selected
C: Target ring showing object selected
D: Selection and layer color indicator
E: Object has appearance attributes

The Layers palette uses symbols to identify what has been selected. The final column serves a few functions. When an object is selected, a large rectangle the color of the layer (from the Layer Options dialog, remember?) appears in this column. If a sub-layer is selected, but not the entire layer, a similar but smaller square appears beside the top-level layer. Dragging the colored square to drop atop a different layer actually moves the selected art objects to the new layer. Clicking or Shift-clicking the colored square has the same effect as clicking the target indicator.

Layers and sub-layers may be reordered easily by dragging them and dropping them higher or lower in their existing layer nest, or by dragging them into or out of layers, sub-layers, and groups (you cannot make an object equal to a top-level layer; it must be contained within one). Reordering sub-layers here is especially useful because changing the stacking or *z-order* of sub-layers is the same as sending an object forward or backward on the artboard—often with much less effort.

At the bottom of the Layers palette are four buttons:

- **Make/Release Clipping Mask:** If the selected object(s) contain a clipping mask (indicated by a <Clipping Path> sub-layer), it is removed, expanding both the mask path and clipped object(s) back to their individual status. Conversely, two separate objects selected are converted to a clipped object and mask path, the latter forming from whichever object is higher in the z-order.

- **Create New Sub-Layer:** Makes a new sub-layer beneath the currently selected layer or sub-layer.

- **Create New Layer:** Makes a new top-level layer above the currently selected top-level layer.

- **Delete Selection:** Deletes all the selected objects, sublayers, or layers.

As you arrange palettes to create a comfortable workspace (see the "Understanding Workspaces" section later in this chapter), consider giving the Layers palette plenty of vertical room. Each time you create a new document you will have only a single layer, Layer 1, with the remainder of the palette looking like wasted space. Very quickly, however, your average drawing will fill in that space in the form of other layers and their sub-layers. And, having a long list already visible onscreen is easier to work with than scrolling through a long list.

Paragraph Styles and Character Styles Palettes

Discussed in greater depth in Chapter 19, "Working with Type in Illustrator," the sibling Paragraph Styles and Character Styles palettes (see Figure 15.5) list text *styles,* reusable recordings of type properties, such as font family, type size, color, and paragraph alignment.

Figure 15.5
The Paragraph Styles palette (left) and Character Styles palette (right), with a few styles listed, are very similar in both appearance and function.

At the bottom of the Paragraph Styles and Character Styles palettes are two buttons each:

- **Create New Style:** Create a new style, with or without text selected.

- **Delete Style:** Delete the currently selected style(s).

Transform Palette

When you want to *transform* an object—change its width, height, rotation, skew, or location on the artboard—reach for the Transform palette (see Figure 15.6).

Figure 15.6
The Transform palette.

The grid on the left is the reference point locator (familiar to users of InDesign or PageMaker as the *proxy*). Corresponding to the control corners on an object's bounding box, the *reference point locator* determines to which quadrant, side, or center of the object transformations will be relative. For example, selecting the top-left reference point and rotating an object 90° causes it to swivel around its top-left corner and out to the side; the same rotation with the center reference point selected simply twirls the object in place (see Figure 15.7).

The X and Y measurement boxes are the coordinates or location of the selected reference point relative to the document's rulers. Illustrator's horizontal ruler begins its 0-point at the left edge of the artboard, and its vertical ruler starts at the *bottom* of the artboard, which is somewhat counterintuitive. Be wary of this distinction because setting an object's Y coordinate to 8 inches on an 8.5- by 11-inch page places the chosen reference point half an inch from the bottom edge not the typically expected top edge.

To change the coordinates or the content of any measurement box, highlight the existing content with the mouse and type a new value, with or without a unit notation (for example, "in").

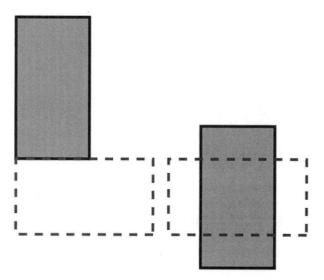

Figure 15.7
The left object was rotated 90° relative to its top-left reference point; the right object was rotated the same 90° but with its center point selected in the reference point locator (dotted lines indicate the original locations of both objects).

W is the width of the selected object(s), and H is the height. By default, both dimensions operate independently—changing one has no affect on the other. Clicking the Constrain Width and Height Proportions chain, however, links them such that a change in one proportionately changes the other to match. When Constrain Width and Height Proportions is active, a bold line connects the two measurement boxes.

Below the coordinates and dimensions boxes are Rotate and Shear. Both accept any typed degree from 0–360, either positive (clockwise) or negative (counterclockwise), and yet both also have pop-up menus from which common degree settings may be chosen without using the keyboard. Rotate swivels the selected object(s) around the axis selected in the reference point locator, and Shear skews the object(s) relative to the same axis. With Shear, positive degrees shear to the right, negative degrees to the left (see Figure 15.8).

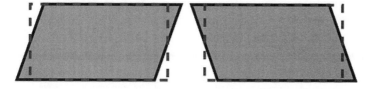

Figure 15.8
The object on the left was sheared 20° and the object on the right was sheared –20° (dotted lines indicate the original locations of both objects).

Neither Rotate nor Shear remembers its settings. After an object is rotated and/or sheared, both measurement boxes in the Transform palette reset to 0°, making it impossible to determine via that palette the angle used. Rotating or shearing again will compound the transformation already in effect.

To find out the angle of a rotated or sheared object after the fact, click and hold on the Eyedropper tool in the toolbox to reveal the Measure tool. With the Measure tool, click and drag from one end of the object, path, or surface to the other. Upon releasing the mouse button, the angle from start to endpoint is displayed in the Info palette (see Figure 15.9).

15

Figure 15.9
The Info palette displays the angle of a line drawn with the Measure tool.

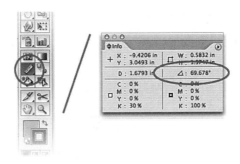

Like virtually all of Illustrator's measurement boxes, the coordinates and measurement boxes on the Transform palette accept any unit of measure Illustrator understands—not just the one chosen during creation of the new document. If your document is set to inches, but you know you want an object 200 pixels wide, merely type **200 px** in the W box; Illustrator automatically handles the unit conversion to inches. Illustrator understands inches (in or "), millimeters (mm), centimeters (cm), pixels (px), picas (p), and points (pt).

Appearance Palette

As the name implies, the Appearance palette is devoted to cataloging and managing the appearance properties of an object, group, or layer. That includes everything from simply a fill and stroke (both color and weight), to dozens of fills, path offsets, drop shadows, brushed strokes, transparency, warps, and just about anything that affects how your objects *look* (see Figure 15.10).

Figure 15.10
The Appearance palette showing the attributes comprising the neon check mark.

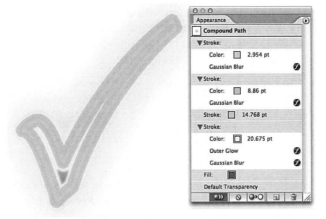

It might help to think of the properties on the Appearance palette as layers of visual attributes. Each property builds upon the one below it, and each property can have certain types of subproperties. For example, an object may contain a stroke and a fill, with an Outer Glow effect applied to the fill (as a subproperty) but not to the stroke. At the same time, the stroke may be set to 50% opacity while the fill remains completely opaque.

At the top of the Appearance palette is an entry noting the kind of object(s) selected. It may say Layer, Group, Path, Type, Characters, Mesh, or any other kind of object Illustrator is capable of creating. Any attributes below the object identifier are assigned to this object.

When an object is contained within another—such as a path that is part of a group—the Appearance palette lists the container at the top, with the currently selected object beneath it. Because appearance attributes may be applied to a Layer, other attributes to a group within that layer, and still others to the path within the group within the layer, selecting the path causes the Appearance palette to display all three levels hierarchically in the top: Layer, Group, and Path.

Figure 15.11 shows a common nesting of container and content appearance: Type and Characters. In this usage, *Type* refers to the Area Type object, to which has been assigned a fill, an empty stroke, and a Drop Shadow effect (not filter) as denoted by the stylized *f* icon. Area Type is a *container* for characters. Although many appearance properties like effects cannot be applied to individual characters in an Area Type object, they *can* be applied to the object as a whole, manifesting as effects on all the characters. It is not possible to apply an effect to only certain characters in Area Type.

Figure 15.11
Appearance attributes of the Area Type object, with the Characters entry representing that it contains other objects capable of having their own attributes.

Double-clicking the Characters entry accesses the properties of the characters themselves (see Figure 15.12). At the top is a reminder that Characters, the active object, is contained within Type. Icons to the container entry's right indicate that it contains paint (a fill color in this instance) and effects (the Drop Shadow), which are applied atop and in combination with the attributes of individual characters. Container appearance attributes override content appearance attributes. In Figure 15.11, for example, the Type container carries a fill, which overprints the Character fill shown in Figure 15.12.

Figure 15.12
When editing the Characters entry and its attributes, the Type entry at the top acts as a reminder that the Type container can have additional attributes.

Though effects cannot be applied to individual characters in Area Type, different strokes, fills, and/or transparency settings can. Theoretically, every character in a paragraph could be assigned a different fill color and blending mode. Note that the Appearance palette does not record type styling options like font family, point size, and paragraph attributes; these are the domain of the Character and Paragraph palettes and of character and paragraph styles. They are not attributes of visual appearance.

The best way to understand the function of the Appearance palette is to use it:

1. Using the Type tool, click and drag out a rectangle for Area Type.

2. Enter some text—for example, *Mary had a little lamb. It was salty.*

3. Highlight all of the text and select one of the red color swatches in the Swatches palette, which should fill the text with red.

4. With the Selection tool (the black arrow), click on the Area Type object. The Appearance palette should indicate that a Type object is selected, that it has Default Transparency, and that there are characters present.

5. From the Effect menu select Stylize, Drop Shadow. Leave all settings at their defaults and click OK. The type should now display a soft drop shadow, and a Drop Shadow attribute will appear on the Appearance palette.

6. Double-click the Characters entry to access the content of the Type object. The Appearance palette should display Type and then Characters with the attributes of an empty stroke, red fill, and Default Transparency.

7. After the phrase *It was salty* add *but the taste lingered.*

8. Highlight the new phrase and change its color to one of the green swatches. Its Appearance attributes will change to reflect the new fill color, but the soft drop shadow will also fall from this newly typed text because it is inherited from the parent or container object, the Type.

9. To change the Drop Shadow options, double-click the Type container entry and then double-click Drop Shadow.

Deselecting the Area Type object leaves the Type container's attributes in the Appearance palette. This is a *major* gotcha. Many Illustrator users—even experienced ones—occasionally find themselves scratching their heads over the fact that attribute changes are not being reflected in the object. They realize too late that the entity listed at the top of the Appearance palette is No Selection—they are not working with the attributes of the desired object (see Figure 15.13); they're working with nothing. This behavior enables the rapid creation of multiple styled objects through setting attributes on the Appearance palette and *then* creating the objects, which automatically inherit the attributes. Of course, that works only if the New Art Maintains Appearance button is active at the bottom of the Appearance palette.

Before making changes to appearance attributes, check the upper lines to ensure that the desired object is indeed selected.

15

Figure 15.13
Though the top line informs
that nothing is selected, the
appearance attributes persist,
often leading to confusion and
unrealized attribute changes.

At the bottom of the Appearance palette are five buttons:

- **New Art Maintains Appearance/New Art Has Basic Appearance:** Toggle button. When deselected, whatever attributes are listed above for the current object are automatically inherited by
new objects upon creation. When depressed, this button becomes New Art Has Basic
Appearance, meaning new objects will conform to the basic appearance (a single, simple fill
and stroke).

- **Clear Appearance:** Strips away all attributes of the selected object(s), rendering it with an
empty fill and empty stroke and removing any other effects.

- **Reduce To Basic Appearance:** Returns the selected object(s) to a single stroke and fill and
Default Transparency and removes any effects.

- **Duplicate Selected Item:** Creates a duplicate instance of the selected attribute, including any
subproperties, above the currently selected attribute.

- **Delete Selected Item:** Deletes the selected attribute (clears but does not delete Fill and Stroke).

Graphic Styles Palette

In short, graphic styles are encapsulated and reusable definitions of appearance attributes. If it's an
attribute on the Appearance palette—fills, strokes, effects, blending modes, and so on—it can be
saved in a graphic style and applied to any other Illustrator object. The Graphic Styles palette (see
Figure 15.14) and the Appearance palette go hand in glove. In fact, the best way to learn how to use
the Appearance palette is by selecting an object and applying different graphic styles.

Figure 15.14
The Graphic Styles palette in
default thumbnail view.

Graphic styles are stored in the Graphic Styles palette and may be imported to other Illustrator documents, saved as a Graphic Styles library, and even shared among other Illustrator users.

15

With each new Illustrator document the Graphic Styles palette populates with a set of default styles—separate sets for RGB and CMYK documents. Installed with Illustrator are eight other graphic style libraries, including Artistic Effects, Buttons and Rollovers, Image Effects, Neon Effects, Scribble Effects, Textures, and Type Effects (see Figure 15.15). Open any or all of the libraries into their own floating palettes from the Window, Graphic Styles menu or from the Graphic Styles palette menu.

On the Adobe Studio website (http://studio.adobe.com) are hundreds of graphic styles created by other Illustrator users and available for (usually free) download.

To use a graphic style, select a layer, group, or object and click the desired graphic style. The appearance attributes stored in the style instantly apply to the selected item and are reflected in the Appearance palette. To change to a different graphic style, repeat the process—there's no need to undo between because each graphic style automatically replaces any existing appearance attributes.

Figure 15.15
All these graphic styles are already installed on your computer in eight separate libraries.

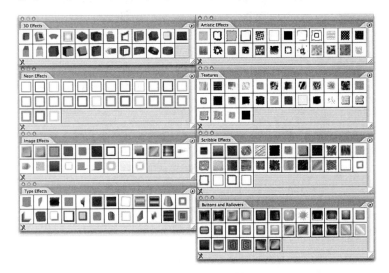

Creating new graphic styles is almost as easy:

1. Create an appropriate object.

2. Style it via the Appearance palette until the desired effect is achieved.

3. On the Graphic Styles palette click the New Graphic Style button (or drag the object into the palette).

4. Double-click the new style and rename it to something more meaningful than the default title.

When a graphic style is applied to one or more items, the item(s) are linked to the style. Altering the style causes those alternations to reflect instantly in all objects to which the style has been assigned (see Figure 15.16). If this behavior is undesired, select the object and click the Break Link to Style button on the Graphic Styles palette. The object will retain all the appearance attributes of the style, but will no longer update with it.

Figure 15.16
All these objects are assigned to the same graphic style. Redefining the style immediately causes all of them to update to match, saving significant time that would otherwise be spent making the repetitive appearance changes to each object individually.

Unlike symbols and paragraph and character styles, there is no Redefine Graphic Style menu item. To change a graphic style stored in the palette, changes must be made on an object:

1. To redefine a graphic style, select an object to which the style has been applied.

2. Disconnect the object from the stored style with the Break Link to Style button.

3. Make appearance attribute changes directly to the selected object.

4. Select the object with the Selection tool and, while holding the Alt key in Windows or the Option key on the Mac, drag it to the Graphic Styles palette and drop it onto the icon of the style to be updated. Both the style thumbnail and any objects to which the style has been assigned instantly reflect the new changes. As an added bonus, the source object will now have the updated style reassigned to it.

Experiment with different predesigned graphic styles and then begin building your own. Like any reusable element, graphic styles are a huge time-saver when used judiciously.

At the bottom of the Graphic Styles palette are three buttons:

- **Break Link to Graphic Style:** Dissociates a styled object from the graphic style entry, making changes in either independent of the other.

- **New Graphic Style:** Creates a new graphic style based on the attributes active in the Appearance palette—with or without objects selected.

- **Delete Graphic Style:** Deletes the currently highlighted style(s).

Other Notable Palettes

Throughout the rest of the Illustrator chapters many of the remaining palettes are discussed in great depth. The palettes detailed in this chapter bear special note because they are used in virtually every task Illustrator will be called on to perform. Here are a few other, less obvious, palettes that deserve attention:

- **Document Info:** A wealth of information about the document—its objects, colors, fonts, and styles used—is presented in this convenient and resizable palette, making it a valuable working aid as well as a useful troubleshooting tool. It can even generate a report of all the information it tracks via the Save option on the palette menu.

- **Navigator:** While zoomed in on details, this window on a document is often the fastest way to move around. Drag the view area rectangle to change the working view. Use the slider at the bottom right or type a percentage in the box on the bottom left to zoom.

- **Info:** Relevant to the selected object or tool, the Info palette can display the active color in up to two color modes simultaneously, as well as the width, height, and angle of an object and the X and Y coordinates of the mouse pointer.

- **Control:** Docked beneath the menu bar by default, the Control palette is a context-sensitive toolbar of the most commonly used features and functions relative to the task at hand. When working with text, for example, the Control palette displays font family, font style, size, paragraph alignment, and other commonly used tools. With nearly all objects, the Control palette mirrors most of the features of the Transform palette.

- **Magic Wand:** The Magic Wand tool makes it easy to select objects by fill color, opacity, stroke weight, and other options. On the Magic Wand palette the options for the tool are set and always accessible.

USING PALETTE MENUS

In the top-right corner of many palettes is the palette's menu. Though easy to overlook, it shouldn't be forgotten. Many useful commands are hidden there; some—such as the ability to convert type to All Caps, Small Caps, Superscript, and Subscript via the Character Palette's menu—are not accessible by any other means in Illustrator. In addition to hidden commands, the palette menu often contains the toggle to enable or disable access to key features of the palette. The Gradient palette, for instance, shows up by default as only the preview ramp (see Figure 15.17); by choosing Show Options from the Gradient palette's menu, however, you may access features that exercise much more control over the appearance of a gradient.

Most of Illustrator's palettes have a palette menu.

Figure 15.17
The default Gradient palette (left) and the expanded Gradient palette (right) after selecting Show Options from the palette menu.

UNDERSTANDING WORKSPACES

Illustrator CS2 is an incredibly robust application with toolsets for dozens of different creative workflows. Although a minority of users will never do more than a single type of project in this amazing program, most users find themselves performing many different types of tasks. The same person who draws street maps in Illustrator may also trace scanned images and build Flash animations. A web designer may use Illustrator to sketch, slice, and export a website template, build variable data SVG content for delivery on mobile devices, and end the day working on a photo-realistic drawing of a fruit still life. The uses for the program are virtually limitless, and so are its arrangement of job-specific palettes.

Rarely does any one project require all of Illustrator's many palettes onscreen simultaneously. Instead of dealing with either a cluttered screen or hidden palettes, create multiple workspaces specific to different types of projects:

1. Choose a single type of project you perform in Illustrator and decide which palettes are needed for such projects.

2. Open the needed palettes, closing all others.

3. Arrange and size the palettes into a productive work area.

4. From the Window menu choose Workspace, Save Workspace.

5. In the resulting dialog, type the kind of project for which the arrangement has been optimized— for example, `Web Design` or `Animation`. Click OK.

6. Repeat the previous five steps for another kind of project, with a different palette arrangement.

7. From the top of the Window, Workspace menu choose the first project. The entire work area will reconfigure to *your* project-specific organization. Switching between different computer users' workspaces is just as easy.

UNDERSTANDING MENU COMMANDS

It isn't possible to go through every menu command, when to use it, and what it does under all circumstances. Most menu items come into play throughout the chapters of this book. However on each menu there is at least one new or oft-overlooked item to which drawing special attention is warranted.

File Menu

Universal commands, such as Open, Save, and Print are found on the File menu, as are these important commands:

- **New From Template:** Included with Illustrator CS2 are dozens of predesigned templates for everything from websites to business cards. With this menu option, these templates may be opened as new documents for adapting to a particular project or to examine as examples.

- **Save for Microsoft Office:** With no options and no preamble, the current Illustrator document is exported as an Office-optimized PNG file ready for import into PowerPoint, Word, or Excel.

- **Scripts:** With support for added features and complicated processes written in JavaScript (Windows and Mac), AppleScript (Mac), or VBScript (Windows), Illustrator is more extensible than ever. Look for many free scripts on the Creative Suite Resources and Extras CDs and around the Web.

- **Document Setup:** If, after creation, a document size, units of measure, or other options must change, this is where to make those changes.

Edit Menu

In addition to Copy and Paste and the new Check Spelling options, the Edit menu contains these significant options:

- **Undo <action>:** Undo the last action. Undo enables you to step backward through time—as one action is undone, the Undo entry in the Edit menu is updated to refer to the action before.

- **Tracing, Print,** and **Adobe PDF Presets:** Create or edit preset options that appear in various places throughout Illustrator such as Live Trace, the Print dialog, and when saving as PDF.

- **Keyboard Shortcuts:** Just about everything in Illustrator CS2 can be bound to a keyboard shortcut of the user's choosing—even existing keyboard shortcuts can be changed!

Object Menu

Containing transformation and most of the other functions for working with objects, the Object menu also includes these useful commands:

- **Rasterize:** Especially when working with very large or very complex documents, converting objects from vector to pixel-based raster images can save plenty of time Illustrator would otherwise consume with screen redraws and effects rendering.

- **Transform, Transform Each:** Changing the dimensions or rotation of multiple selected objects via the Transform or Control palettes treats all the objects as a single unit, transforming them in relation to one another. When several objects must be transformed similarly but individually, use Transform Each. No matter how many objects are selected, the transformation is applied to each independent of the others.

Type Menu

With options for controlling and changing Type on a Path and Area Type, the Type menu augments the Character and Paragraph palettes, especially with features such as these:

- **Font:** Unlike the Font Family menu on the Character palette, this new menu shows all installed fonts in their respective typefaces, enabling visual selection of a font without guesswork.

- **Find Font:** A search and replace for type faces, Find Font locates and replaces one font with another in each or all instances of text.

- **Create Outlines:** Convert point or area text from live, editable type to nontext compound paths for path modification, export, or a variety of other purposes.

Select Menu

Grouping together commands to select or deselect objects, the Select menu features these handy commands:

- **Same:** Use the Select, Same submenu to select automatically all objects with attributes in common with the currently selected object. For example, select all objects that share a common fill or stroke color.

- **Save Selection:** Select the same objects again and again by doing it once and saving the selection. Recall the selection at any time from the bottom of this menu.

Filter Menu

In addition to the numerous nondynamic filters on the Filters menu are these useful commands:

- **Apply Last Filter:** Reapply the last used filter without having to navigate back through the submenus and dialogs.

- **Colors, Convert To Grayscale:** Convert all colors in the selected object (except raster images) to shades of gray.

Effect Menu

Differing from the commands on the Filter menu in that these are live and ever-editable effects, the Effect menu also features these commands:

- **Apply Last Effect:** Just like the Filter, Apply Last Filter command, this command reapplies the same effect, with the same settings, to another object much faster than reissuing the original command.

- **Document Raster Effects Settings:** Photoshop Effects and others create a raster result, the quality of which is specified with this option.

View Menu

Among options to show or hide various indicators and onscreen devices, the View menu includes these commands:

- **Outline/Preview:** In Preview mode, artwork appears with fills, strokes, and effects; but precision drawing is more accurate in Outline mode, which shows only the paths of objects.

- **Pixel Preview:** When creating graphics for use in a digital environment such as the Web, turn on Pixel Preview to display the resolution-independent vector paths in resolution-dependent pixels exactly how they would export to a raster image format such as JPG, GIF, or PNG.

- **New View:** Establish and save the view state of the current document, including zoom level, location, and show/hide options, and return to those identical settings at any time during a subsequent editing session.

Window Menu

Primarily dealing with the display of palettes, the Window menu also features these commands:

- **New Window:** Open another window, with its own independent zoom level, view mode, and show/hide options, onto the same document. Great for keeping an eye in Preview mode while working in Outline mode or for seeing the whole document while zoomed in to touch up detail.

- **Brush, Graphic Style, Swatch, and Symbol Libraries:** Gain fast access to dozens of preinstalled or user-created libraries.

Help Menu

In addition to providing access to Illustrator's help topics in the Adobe Help Center, the Help menu also includes these useful options:

- **Welcome Screen:** If the Welcome Screen has been disabled by unchecking the Show This Dialog at Startup check box, you can restore it here so that it automatically launches again when you start Illustrator.

- **About Illustrator** (On the Illustrator menu on Macintosh): This option shows the Illustrator About or splash screen displaying the exact product version and registered user information. Have the About Illustrator splash screen onscreen when contacting Adobe Technical Support.

FINAL THOUGHTS

All components of the Creative Suite share the elegant and simple Common Adobe User Interface, including similar—and in some cases identical—tools, palettes, and menu items. Illustrator, the predecessor and, in its twelfth version with CS2, the most mature of them all, has its own unique place in Creative Suite. Owing to its rainbow of professional illustration, graphic design, technical, and Web uses, it has palettes and features unlike anything found in InDesign, Photoshop, and GoLive.

Illustrator's creative freedom, precision, and element reuse is, for lack of a better term, unprecedented. What once required dozens of duplicate objects can now be created in a single, editable instance with the Appearance palette—and totally redesigned and restored on a whim. Nested a dozen levels deep, even the smallest path in the most complex document can be isolated and edited accurately without fear of accidentally changing surrounding or even containing objects and paths. And, with graphic styles, hours of intricate designs and careful construction can be replicated infinitely with a single mouse click.

When a new project rises or boredom begins to seep in, the entire workspace can be reconfigured—with the ability to return always assured. Customizable and multiple palette arrangements, windows, and views make any comfort level, any work habit, within reach of a menu.

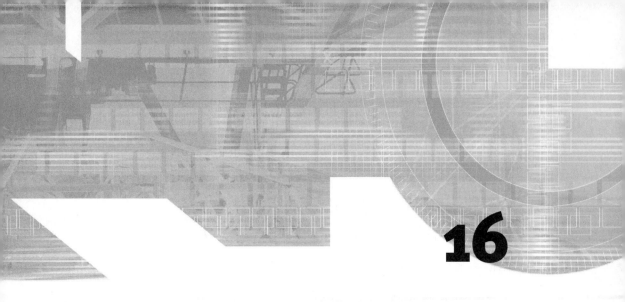

UNDERSTANDING AND DRAWING PATHS IN ILLUSTRATOR

IN THIS CHAPTER

Illustrator creates *vector*, or mathematically plotted, artwork comprised of points and Bézier curves that connect those points. A *path* is a sequence of at least two *points* joined by *path segments*, which may be straight or curved. Although Illustrator imports, exports, and works with pixel-based raster images, its main function—and the area in which it leads all others—is in drawing vector paths and shapes.

WORKING WITH VECTOR ART

There are two types of computer graphics: raster images and vector drawings.

Raster Images

Raster images, the primary domain of Photoshop, are dependent on a grid of square pixels (in broadcast media, the pixels are non-square, but the principle is the same). Each raster image is defined by its resolution, or the number of pixels occurring within every inch of the grid. Thus raster images are *resolution dependent*, meaning they look best when displayed on a monitor or other device that fits the same number of pixels within an inch.

Because a pixel is the smallest unit of measure in a raster image, it cannot be divided. All image data must partition evenly into the pixel grid. Each pixel must also be solid—either filled with a single color, empty to create transparency, or semitransparent so that, when laid atop another object, the pixel appears to be filled with a single solid color. One pixel equals one color; it cannot be half one color and half another. The fewer pixels per inch (*ppi*), the less detail and color variations possible.

Scaling a raster image up to a larger size increases the ppi, forcing the existing filled image pixels to expand across more pixels. For example, a 100- by 100-pixel image blown up 200% horizontally and vertically spreads the image data from each individual pixel across the adjacent 3—1 pixel becomes 2 horizontally, 2 vertically, and 2 diagonally (see Figure 16.1). At the same time, new pixels mix the colors from adjacent pixels above, below, and to both sides because *every* pixel is expanding to fill four slots. This is why blown up images appear fuzzy.

Figure 16.1
Original image magnified 8×
(top). The same image blown up
400% of the original size and
magnified 4× (center). The same
image reduced to 50% of the
original size and magnified 8×
(bottom). Note the pixel grid visible in the original and the quality
loss resulting from enlargement
and reduction in the lower two.

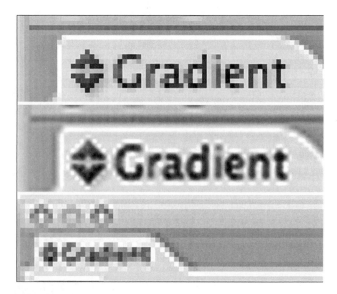

Shrinking or scaling down images is even more destructive (though it typically looks better) because, to fit *X* number of pixels into *Y* number of slots is impossible. The pixels that don't fit must be thrown away. Scaling the same 100- by 100-pixel image down to a 50- by 50-pixel image, for example, throws away exactly half of the original pixel data.

Vector Drawings

Because they are resolution dependent, raster images are limited in their utility. Sizing or viewing a raster image to or at any percentage other than 100% results in quality loss. By contrast, *vector drawings* are *resolution independent*—they are not based on a pixel grid, and quality cannot be lost by resizing. A vector does not *have* a size.

Vector is geometry. The anchor and end points of a path are plotted by their coordinates in space relative to the axes—x for horizontal positioning, y for vertical location, and z for depth positioning. Recall that path segments are mathematically defined curves or straight lines that connect points. Neither points nor lines have size or resolution, merely location.

Fonts are vectors. Each character or glyph in a font is a vector path, which is what enables type to display and print sharply at any resolution.

Zooming in on a raster image quickly shows its grid of solid pixels. Angled edges that appear smooth at 100% become jagged or stair-stepped (see Figure 16.2). Vectors may be zoomed in to the one-billionth percentage without any sign of jaggedness in smooth angled edges. Moreover, even zoomed, more paths may be added without any difference between the new and old paths.

Figure 16.2
A raster image of a 72-ppi angled shape (left), magnified 6×. Compare with the same shape still in vector (right) magnified by the same amount.

An original 1- by 1-inch vector drawing may be scaled up to 100 by 100 *feet* while remaining perfectly sharp—this is an example; it may actually be scaled ad infinitum in either direction without quality loss. The versatility of vector artwork to be put to use in almost any situation, at any imaginable size, is its greatest strength. Indeed, that is why many professional designers and illustrators choose to create in Illustrator rather than immediately reaching for Photoshop.

Points and Paths

Paths are the actual drawings to which fills, strokes, and effects may be applied. Other than imported or *placed* raster images, everything created in Illustrator is built from paths.

Points are the basic building blocks of paths. Between points are path segments, lines that are either straight or curved. *End points* define the beginning or end of a path, with a single path segment running into, or out from, the end point. *Anchor points* have path segments on two sides, and occur everywhere the path changes direction or curvature. Paths must include a minimum of two points to begin and end them.

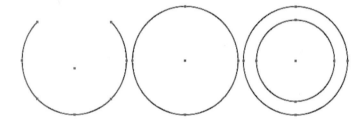

On the artboard, points and path segments are drawn as small boxes and lines in the color assigned to the layer on which the path resides.

Paths may be either open or closed (see Figure 16.3). Open paths have beginnings and ends, with two end points defining such. Whereas closed paths have no discernible beginning and end. In closed paths, points connect to other points infinitely via path segments, and end points—where the path drawing actually began and finished—are indistinguishable from anchor points.

Figure 16.3
Open (left), closed (center), and compound (right) paths.

Compound paths are objects comprised of two or more paths. For example, the letter *O* drawn in vector has two paths—the outside path (shape) and the hole. Though they form a single object, the paths themselves never meet; they are two disconnected loops. Together they form one object, compounding each other—the inner path creates a hole in the fill of the outer path.

Vectors Across the Creative Suite

Borrowed from Illustrator by both Photoshop and InDesign are the Pen tool for precision drawing, several of the Shape and Line tools to create common geometric path shapes, and the Direct Selection tool for modifying paths (see Figure 16.4). Although the Pen tool is, but for a few keyboard shortcuts, identical across the Creative Suite applications, the Shape and Line tools tend to vary. Only Illustrator, for example, has a vector-based Flare tool or the Spiral tool. Still, Photoshop and InDesign have common shape tools such as Rectangle, Ellipse, and Rounded Rectangle. They both also have the Line tool, which creates perfectly straight path segments between two points.

Illustrator is the vector drawing powerhouse of the Creative Suite, with the tools and commands to create almost anything imaginable. The reason InDesign and Photoshop include the most basic of Illustrator's drawing and shape tools is not to usurp the role of Illustrator in the creative workflow; when only a simple object like a rectangle is required, it's more efficient to remain in InDesign or Photoshop and draw it directly than to open Illustrator. Each of the Creative Suite applications has its own distinct role, but the roles often overlap for convenience.

Figure 16.4
The Tools palettes from Illustrator (left), Photoshop (center), and InDesign (right) showing the common vector tools.

16

Because the functionality of the common vector tools is identical or nearly identical between the applications, and because the underlying technology is superposable, paths created in any one application can be manipulated in the others. An ellipse drawn in InDesign, for example, may be copied from the InDesign document and pasted into Illustrator to take advantage of Illustrator's more advanced, purpose-built vector features. After the Illustrator work is completed, that path may be dragged from Illustrator and dropped back into the InDesign document or even into Photoshop for an effects stopover before returning to InDesign.

For more on drawing and working with paths in Photoshop, see Chapter 7, "Using Selections, Paths, and Transforms in Photoshop"; for information about using paths in InDesign, see Chapter 30, "Creating and Modifying Paths in InDesign."

USING THE SHAPE TOOLS

Illustrator comes presupplied with basic shapes such as rectangle, ellipse, polygon, and even flare, making it easy to draw both simple and complicated forms using familiar shapes at the heart of many shapes. With the exception of the Flare tool, which creates multiple paths with each use, shapes are single, closed paths.

By default, the Rectangle tool is active (in the Tools palette just beneath the *T* of the Type tool). Clicking and holding on the Rectangle tool reveals the other Shape tools behind it (see Figure 16.5).

Rectangle Tool

A *rectangle*, by definition, is four right-angle corners (anchor points) with two pairs of parallel and equal length sides (path segments). A square, of course, is a rectangle with all four of its sides equal in length.

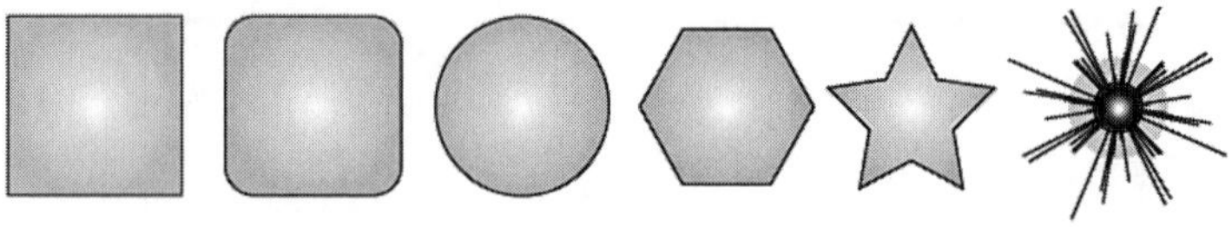

Figure 16.5
Illustrator's six default shapes, from left to right: Rectangle, Rounded Rectangle, Ellipse, Polygon, Star, and Flare.

Draw rectangles (including squares) with the Rectangle tool by clicking on the artboard and dragging until the rectangle has the desired dimensions. To create a square, hold the Shift key while dragging, which constrains all sides to equal lengths.

When the desired dimensions of the rectangle are known in advance, click once on the artboard and release rather than clicking and dragging. The Rectangle dialog appears, displaying Width and Height input boxes. Fill in the desired dimensions and click OK; that rectangle appears on the artboard.

Hold the Alt/Option key while dragging with the Rectangle tool to draw from the center outward.

Rounded Rectangle Tool

A *rounded rectangle* is merely a rectangle with rounded corners. However, because paths may change their angle or curvature only at an anchor point, rounded rectangles contain eight anchor points instead of four. One appears at the top of each straight line leading into the rounded corner, and one appears at the end of the corner curve leading into the next straight path segment.

Rounded rectangles may be drawn in the same manner as rectangles, by clicking and dragging free-hand, or by clicking and releasing. In addition to Width and Height measurements, the Rounded Rectangle dialog also contains a box for the corner radius, where you determine how rounded the four corners will be.

Hold the Alt/Option key while dragging with the Rounded Rectangle tool to draw from the center outward.

Ellipse Tool

An *ellipse* is a shape without corners or angles, like a circle or oval. It too contains four anchor points, each one defining the curvature of a quarter of the shape. In circles, the four anchor points are *equidistant*—the same distance apart—at the four points of the compass.

Draw ovals by clicking and dragging with the Ellipse tool. Draw circles by holding Shift while dragging. Clicking once and releasing brings up the Ellipse dialog with Width and Height measurement boxes.

Hold the Alt/Option key while dragging with the Ellipse tool to draw from the center outward.

Polygon Tool

Technically, rectangles are polygons because the definition of a *polygon* is any closed figure formed by more than two segments. The Polygon tool creates shapes constructed of 3–1000 path segments of equal length. Anchor points are created only at the points of the polygon.

Although Illustrator's Polygon tool *can* make a square, its primary use is for making triangles or objects with more than four sides.

Clicking and dragging with the Polygon tool draws, from the center outward, an equilateral hexagon where all six sides are the same length. The rotation of the polygon also changes dependent upon the dragging direction, so holding the Shift key while drawing maintains the correct orientation of the polygon.

To create a polygon of a specified size, click once on the artboard with the Polygon tool and specify the *radius*, or the distance from the center to one point on the path; the resulting polygon is twice the radius in both height and width. Changing the number of sides is accomplished the same way. In the Polygon tool dialog, set the number of sides to between 3 (to create a triangle) and 1000 (a *chiliagon*).

Increase or decrease the number of polygon sides by pressing the up or down arrow on the keyboard while drawing with the Polygon tool.

Star Tool

Though, by default, the Star tool makes five-pointed stars, it, like the Polygon tool, is much more versatile than would first appear. Whereas the Polygon tool deals in *sides*, the Star tool is used for creating points or peaks and valleys, with anchor points created at both the peak and the valley—even when, in the case of shapes like the three-sided star in Figure 16.6, that contains no visible valleys (see Figure 16.6).

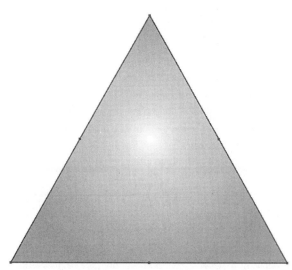

Figure 16.6
Using the Star tool to create a triangle (one radius exactly half the length of the other) creates anchor points at the vertices of the triangle as well as at the midpoints of its sides.

Clicking and dragging with the Star tool draws a star from the center outward, rotated along with the direction of drag. Hold Shift to keep the star's original orientation while dragging.

With the Star tool selected, click and release on the artboard to activate the Star dialog. Radius 1 is the distance from the center point to the outside (peaks) of the star, and Radius 2 is the distance from the center to the inner diameter (the valleys). The number of points may be anywhere from 3 to 1000.

To straighten the star's sides—for example, to create a star such as may be seen in the American flag—hold the Alt key (in Windows) or the Option key on the Mac while dragging. Holding the Ctrl key (in Windows) or the ⌘ key on the Mac while drawing a star keeps the inner radius constant at 0 inches, resulting in a flare.

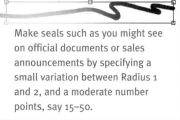

Make seals such as you might see on official documents or sales announcements by specifying a small variation between Radius 1 and 2, and a moderate number points, say 15–50.

Increase or decrease the number of star sides by pressing the up or down arrows on the keyboard while drawing with the Star tool.

Flare Tool

Though grouped with the shape tools, the Flare tool is typically used more as an effect than as a shape. A *flare* is a reflection of light, such as might flash across the lens of a camera when taking a photo in sunlight. It is comprised of a bright center, halo, rays, and rings (see Figure 16.7).

Figure 16.7
Diagram of a Flare: (A) Halo, (B) Rays, (C) Bright Center Point, (D) Rings, and (E) End Point.

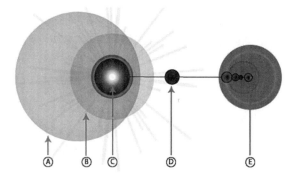

Clicking and dragging with the Flare tool creates a flare with the default or last-used settings, drawing from the center (brightest) point outward. Clicking and dragging again within the area of the first flare draws the rings and end handle to define the angle of the rings from the center point.

By default, clicking and then dragging with the Flare tool increases the size of the entire flare—bright center, halo, and rays. Hold the Ctrl key (Windows users) or the ⌘ key (Mac users) to fix the center point so that further dragging resizes the halo and rays. Hold Shift to constrain the angle of the rays. Press the up or down arrow to increase or decrease the quantity of rays while drawing.

When drawing the end point and rings, up and down arrows increase or decrease the number of rings, holding the tilde (~) key randomizes their placement, and the Ctrl key (Windows users) or the ⌘ key (Mac users) fixes the position and angle of rings while still resizing the end point halo.

Unlike the other shape tools, the flare remains editable via its tool after creation. Clicking on the center point or end point of an existing flare with the Flare tool enables repositioning and editing of that flare. With a flare selected, double-click on the Flare tool to bring up the Flare Tool Options. Grouped into settings germane to the center, halo, rays, and rings are various settings for precise control over the flare's appearance. Rays and rings may even be disabled entirely.

USING LINE TOOLS

Adjacent to the shape tools are the Line tools, which create open paths that are either simpler or more complicated than the basic closed shapes discussed in the previous section (see Figure 16.8). They appear on the Tools palette to the left of the shape tools; the Line tool shows by default, with the rest behind it. Click and hold on the Line tool to access the other path tools.

Figure 16.8
Illustrator's five default line constructs, from left to right: Line, Arc, Spiral, Rectangular Grid, and Polar Grid.

Line Segment Tool

When a straight line is desired, the Line tool is often the fastest way to create it. Merely click to set the start point and drag until the desired end point is reached. Hold the Shift key while dragging to constrain the line to angles that are increments of 45°:0°, 45°, 90°, 135°, 180°, 225°, 270°, 315°, and 360°. Hold the Alt key (Windows users) or Option key (Mac users) to draw from the center outward, as with the Rectangle, Ellipse, and other tools.

Click and release to produce the Line Segment Tool Options, which enable precise length and angle definition. Filling the line has no effect unless the line is incorporated into a larger path, at which point the fill color floods the space between line segments.

Arc Tool

Similar to the Line Segment tool, the Arc tool creates curved segments rather than straight segments. Click to initiate the arc and then drag to the desired end point. Hold Shift while dragging to constrain the angle of the end point relative to the start point to 45°, 135°, 225°, or 315°. Hold the Alt key (Windows users) or the Option key (Mac users) while dragging to draw the arc from the center outward.

Click and release with the Arc tool to access the Arc Segment Tool Options, where the length of the arc across the x axis (horizontally) and y axis (vertically) may be specified, as well as the Type (open or closed), along which axis the arc is based, the slope of the arc (positive values are convex, negative concave), and whether to fill the arc with the active fill swatch.

Spiral Tool

Spirals are collections of arcs, with four in each complete wind. The winds *decay*, or decrease in size, with each revolution. A spiral may have between 2 and 1000 arc segments (see Figure 16.9 for several different spirals).

Figure 16.9
Different spirals created with the
Spiral tool.

16

Create spirals by clicking and dragging with the Spiral tool. Click to set the center point and then drag to draw outward from the center and determine the overall size and the space between winds. The rotation of the cursor determines the rotation of the spiral, from center point to end point. Hold Shift while drawing to constrain the angle of rotation to an increment of 45°.

While drawing, hold the up or down arrow to increase or decrease the number of winds in the spiral. To increase or decrease the number of winds relative to the size of the spiral, hold the Alt key (Windows users) or the Option key (Mac users) while dragging, which also increases or decreases the spiral's *decay rate*, or the amount of space between winds.

Click and release with the Spiral tool to set Spiral options like the radius, decay percentage, number of segments, and the style.

Rectangular Grid Tool

Create rectangular grids to hold tabular data, to use as the basis for meshes and warps, and to aid in perspective drawing by using the Rectangular Grid tool.

With the Rectangle Grid tool selected, click and drag until the grid is the desired size. Increase or decrease the number of horizontal lines by pressing the up or down arrow while dragging; use the left and right arrows to control the number of vertical lines while dragging. Adjust the skew of horizontal dividers in 10% increments by pressing V to increase or F to decrease. Use C and X to increase or decrease the skew of vertical dividers while dragging.

Click and release to access the Rectangular Grid Tool Options, which enables advanced control over the construction of the grid. Width and Height are the dimensions of the entire grid—dividers distribute evenly across this area—and the reference point locator determines from which corner the grid is drawn. Specify the number of horizontal and vertical dividers and their skew. Checking Use Outside Rectangle as Frame creates a rectangle path instead of using strokes for the top, right, bottom, and left borders. Fill Grid fills the grid with the currently selected fill color.

To deconstruct the grid into a rectangle—the fill and/or frame—and horizontal and vertical rules, select Object, Ungroup.

Polar Grid Tool

Line constructs such as concentric circles and lines radiating around a circle—used to create tick marks on a clock, for example—are easy to create with the Polar Grid tool (see Figure 16.10).

Click and drag with the Polar Grid tool to create the default polar grid, drawing from the upper-left corner. Hold the Alt key (Windows users) or the Option key (Mac users) while dragging to draw from the center outward. The grid will be sloped or oval-shaped very much like drawing with the Ellipse tool. Hold Shift while drawing to constrain the polar grid to a circle.

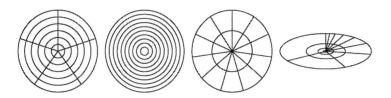

Figure 16.10
Different constructs created with the Polar Grid tool.

Increase or decrease the number of radial dividers (the lines emanating from the center point) by pressing the left or right arrow while dragging; use the up or down arrow to control the number of concentric (circle) dividers while dragging. Adjust the skew of radial dividers in 10% increments by pressing V to increase or F to decrease. Press C or X to increase or decrease the skew of concentric dividers while dragging.

Click and release with the Polar Grid tool to access the Polar Grid Tool Options dialog. Set the overall width and height, the number and skew of concentric and radial dividers, whether to create a compound path from the ellipses of the concentric dividers, and whether to fill the polar grid with the currently selected fill color.

USING THE DRAWING TOOLS

Though the Shape and Line tools often give many drawing objects a head start, most vector artwork is the product of heavy Pencil and Pen tool use. If the Pencil tool is freedom, the Pen is precision. Both tools can create open or closed vector paths, and each has functions for modifying existing paths.

Pencil Tool

As its name implies, drawing with the Pencil tool is as familiar as drawing with a pencil. With this tool selected, simply click and drag; wherever the cursor travels, so does the path. Illustrator automatically creates an anchor point every time the path changes direction. This makes drawing easy, but it also tends to make overly complicated paths, with too many direction changes. See the "Modifying Paths" section for the tools and techniques of cleaning up and massaging paths.

Let's try a quick drawing with the Pencil tool:

1. Select the Pencil tool from the Tools palette.

2. Click and drag to draw a path in the shape of an apple (see Figure 16.11).

3. Close the path by dragging back to the start point.

The Pencil tool can not only draw paths but modify existing ones as well. Try this exercise to take a bite out of the apple:

1. Select the apple path by clicking on it with the Selection tool.

2. With the Pencil tool, click directly on an anchor point in the apple path and drag a roughly round shape inside the apple.

Figure 16.11
A rough apple sketch drawn with
the Pencil tool.

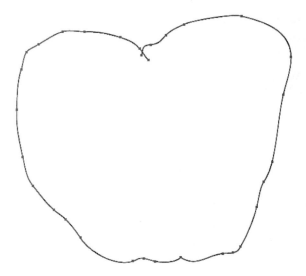

3. End the path on another existing anchor point on the apple path. The bite should be subtracted from the apple path (see Figure 16.12); if not, you probably missed the anchor point either at the beginning of the bite path or its end. Undo and try again.

Figure 16.12
The apple with a bite out of it
courtesy of the Pencil tool.

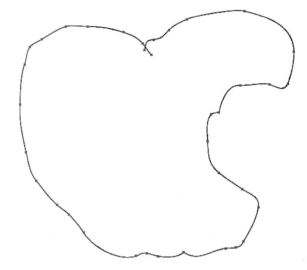

Choosing Undo from the Edit menu or with the keyboard shortcut Ctrl+Z (Windows users) or ⌘-Z (Mac users) will undo the entire Pencil drawing; with the Pen tool it will undo only the last anchor point created.

With an electronic stylus and tablet, Pencil tool drawing is far easier than with a mouse or trackball. Mastering the Pencil tool with such an input device is easy because it becomes just like drawing with a real pencil on paper—you even have the optional luxury of varying stroke weight according to the angle of the stylus or the pressure exerted on the tablet.

Pen Tool

With the Pencil tool, the focus is on the shape; draw the path segments, and Illustrator automatically creates the anchor points to define them. This behavior facilitates freedom and rapid sketching of an idea. The Pen, the precision drawing tool, is the Pencil's opposite: Draw the anchor points and Illustrator automatically connects them with path segments.

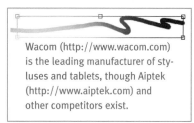

Wacom (http://www.wacom.com) is the leading manufacturer of styluses and tablets, though Aiptek (http://www.aiptek.com) and other competitors exist.

Each click with the Pen tool creates an anchor point (or end point). Each click subsequent to the first connects the points with path segments. Try this exercise:

1. Ctrl-click (Windows users or ⌘-click (Mac users) to deselect the previous path and prepare to draw a new one.

2. Click and release once on the artboard with the Pen tool. It should result in an end point.

3. A few inches away, roughly parallel with the first end point, click again, which connects the two points with a straight path segment.

4. Directly below the second anchor point, at a distance of a few inches, click a third time.

5. Now click a fourth time to create an anchor point beneath the first end point and parallel to the third.

6. Click once more on the first point to close the path. As you hover over it, a small circle appears beside the Pen cursor. This circle indicates that you are closing a path. You should now have a rectangle.

In the rectangle drawing there are four *corner points*, anchor points defining and attached to independently angled (often straight) path segments. More often than corner points, drawings require *smooth points* with curvature. It's important to note that, though the path segments *display* the curvature, anchor points *control* the curvature and direction of path segments leading into and out from them.

Smooth points are created by clicking to create the anchor point (or end point) and dragging to introduce curvature. They are easily identified by the presence of *direction lines* or *curve handles* emanating from them (see Figure 16.13).

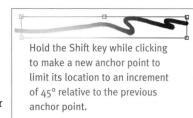

Hold the Shift key while clicking to make a new anchor point to limit its location to an increment of 45° relative to the previous anchor point.

Figure 16.13
After clicking and dragging, direction lines appear.

16

Try this exercise:

1. Ctrl-click (Windows users) or ⌘-click (Mac users) to deselect the previous path and prepare to draw a new one.

2. With the Pen tool, click and hold on the artboard.

3. Drag the mouse upward a bit, away from the end point to introduce curvature. Direction lines should appear beneath the cursor, which becomes a black arrow.

4. Drag the direction line upward and to the right an inch or two at approximately a 45° angle.

5. A few inches to the right, click and release to create the second end point. You should now have a curved path segment (see Figure 16.14).

Figure 16.14
A simple arc path segment.

Each anchor point has its own curvature settings, making *both* ends of a path segment malleable. Try creating an S-curve:

1. Ctrl-click (Windows users) or ⌘-click (Mac users) to deselect the previous path and prepare to draw a new one.

2. With the Pen tool, click and hold on the artboard.

3. Drag the mouse upward and to the left, an inch or two at approximately a 45° angle.

4. A few inches to the right, create the second end point by clicking, but don't release.

5. Drag the second end point up and to the left, trying to mirror the angle and distance as in step 3. Notice how the path segment changes from a simple arc to a smoothly sloping S-shape (see Figure 16.15).

Figure 16.15
A simple S-curve made from two points.

Smooth points have *inheritance*, that is, the curvature assigned to one point automatically applies to the next (but not the one following). So, clicking and dragging to create a curved path segment on one smooth point automatically carries over to the next anchor point, following the path segment through and converting this second point automatically to a smooth point. This is what occurred in the exercises you've done so far. To illustrate the point, try this:

1. Ctrl-click (Windows users) or ⌘-click (Mac users) to deselect the previous path and prepare to draw a new one.

2. With the Pen tool, click and release on the artboard, creating a corner point.

3. A small distance away, click and hold to create another point and introduce curvature.

4. Click and release to create a third point, which inherits the curvature from the second.

Curvature inheritance is a convenient way of making complex paths—making the two to four arcs of an ellipse, for example, requires little more than half the effort. When inheritance is not desired, however, there is an easy way to eliminate it. After creating one curve, but before clicking to establish the next anchor point, click once on the last smooth point. This action converts the anchor point from a smooth to a corner point, creating independent curvature and angling to the path segments on either side of that point. Now the next anchor point may be defined exclusive of the previous; click and release to create a corner point and straight path segment, or click and drag to create a smooth point with independent curvature.

Let's try creating independent points:

1. Ctrl-click (Windows users) or ⌘-click (Mac users) to deselect the previous path and prepare to draw a new one.

2. With the Pen tool, click and release on the artboard, creating a corner point.

3. A small distance away, click and hold to create a smooth point. The path segment should be curved.

4. Move the cursor back over this second point, which shows a small, inverted V beneath the Pen tool cursor, denoting that it is acting as the Convert Anchor Point tool (see the section titled "Adjusting and Converting Anchor Points," later in this chapter).

5. Click on the second point; one of the direction handles disappears.

6. Click and drag to create a third point—an independent smooth point—a few inches away. Inheritance has been canceled, and this new point is completely independent of the prior points and path segments.

The more points in a curve, the more complicated it becomes when working with changes and when printing. Many beginners draw complex paths as a series of corner points or very shallow smooth points, clicking and creating a new anchor point at each minor course or curvature change. Exploit the curvature of smooth points to reduce the overall number of points, the complexity of the path, and the likelihood of unsightly bumps that can be caused by anchor points at awkward places in a curve (see Figure 16.16).

16

Figure 16.16
In the main curve an extraneous anchor point is causing an unwanted bump (left). By eliminating this point and adjusting the direction handles of the smooth points on either side of it, the curve renders smoothly (right).

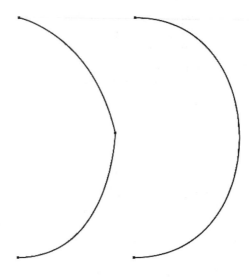

MODIFYING PATHS

After paths are created, they must often be modified. It simply isn't possible to draw perfect paths every time.

Selecting Anchor Points and Path Segments

On the Tools palette, the Direct Selection tool (the white arrow) is used for most postdrawing anchor point manipulation. Using the Direct Selection tool, any anchor point may be selected individually or in combination with others. A selected anchor point is solid; unselected points are hollow.

Select anchor points with the Direct Selection tool by clicking directly on the anchor point, or by clicking away from the path and dragging a selection rectangle to encompass the desired point or points (see Figure 16.17). Hold the Shift key while clicking or dragging with the Direct Selection tool to select multiple, nonsequential points.

Figure 16.17
Using the Direct Selection tool to select a point in a path by dragging a selection rectangle.

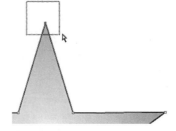

Path segments may be selected just like points. Click on or as close as possible to the path segment, or drag a selection area to encompass part of the path segment.

Below the Direct Selection tool is the Lasso tool. In Photoshop, the Lasso tool creates a *marquee* or selection area to select an area of a pixel-based image. In Illustrator, which deals in points and paths rather than pixels, the Lasso tool selects points or path segments. Click and drag the Lasso tool in any shape needed to select the points or path segments desired, and then close the loop by returning to the start of the Lasso selection area. All the points and path segments that fall within the area of the lasso are selected and ready for manipulation.

To select all the points and segments in a path, do one of the following:

- Drag a selection rectangle around the entire path with the Direct Selection tool.

- Drag a selection marquee around the entire path with the Lasso tool.

- Click on the path with the black Selection arrow.

- If the path is closed and filled, click the fill with the Direct Selection tool.

Adding and Deleting Anchor Points

Working with paths often requires adding anchor points to create more bends or curves, or removing extraneous points that may be hindering or unnecessarily complicating paths. Doing either is quite easy.

Use any of the following methods to delete an anchor point without breaking the path or converting a closed path to an open path:

- Click on it with the Delete Anchor Point tool accessible by clicking and holding on the Pen tool in the Tools palette. The Delete Anchor Point tool looks like the Pen with a minus sign in the upper right.

- With the Pen tool selected, move the cursor over a point in the currently selected path. The cursor automatically changes to the Delete Anchor Point tool. Click to remove the point.

Add additional points to existing paths by any of the following methods:

- Click on the path, in the desired location for a new point, with the Add Anchor Point tool accessible by clicking and holding the Pen tool in the Tools palette. The Add Anchor Point tool looks like the Pen with a plus sign beside it.

- With the Pen tool selected, move the cursor over a path segment and away from an anchor point. The cursor automatically changes to the Add Anchor Point tool. Click to add a point at the current location.

- Choose Object, Path, Add Anchor Points to add a new anchor point between every existing pair of points, effectively doubling the number of anchor points (see Figure 16.18).

Figure 16.18
The original square (left) contains four points at its corners. After using the Add Anchor Points command (right), points have been added midway between each of the four, resulting in eight anchor points.

To prevent temporarily the Pen tool from becoming either the Add or Delete Anchor Point tools, hold the Shift key while clicking to create the first end point. Release Shift after that to enable unrestricted drawing.

Adjusting and Converting Anchor Points

After being selected, points may be moved by dragging with the Direct Selection tool or by using the arrow keys on the keyboard. Each press of an arrow key moves the anchor point(s) 1 pixel (which is equivalent to 1 point, 1/12th pica, 0.0139 inches, 8mm, and 0.0353 cm); hold Shift when pressing the arrow keys to move points in 10 pixel increments. As points move, their connected path segments transform to accommodate. When multiple points are selected, the path segments between them move undistorted with them.

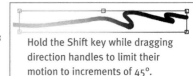

The distance in which arrow keys move or nudge objects is set in Illustrator's Preferences window on the General panel. In the Keyboard Increment field set the unit to move for each press. That field displays measurements in the units defined as General on the Units & Display Performance panel—you can select from Points, Picas, Inches, Millimeters, Centimeters, or Pixels—and accepts measurements in any of those formats.

The Direct Selection tool also grants access to the direction handles of selected points, enabling their curvature to be manipulated. Direction handles control the angle at which segments attach to points. With curved segments, the length of the direction handle directly corresponds to the depth of the curve; a short handle equals a shallow curve, a long handle a deep curve. To adjust the depth of curves, drag direction handles toward or away from their parent anchor points. To change the angle of path segments, rotate direction handles around their points.

Rotating one of the direction handles on a smooth point mirrors the changes through to the path segments on *both* sides of the smooth point, causing the segments to the left and right (or top and bottom) of a point to react equally to changes in one direction handle. To prevent changes in the angle of one direction handle from causing equal and opposite reactions in the other, they must be decoupled with the Convert Anchor Point tool.

Hold the Shift key while dragging direction handles to limit their motion to increments of 45°.

The last tool behind the Pen tool (click and hold on the Pen tool in the Tools palette), the Convert Anchor Point tool looks like an inverted V. With this tool selected, click and drag a direction handle to move it independently of its opposing handle, and thus only affect the path segment on the same side of the anchor point as the handle. This action converts the smooth point to a corner point, where the path segments move free and independent of one another. A point with autonomous path segments—either two curves or a curve and a straight path segment—is often referred to as a *combination point*.

To convert an entire point from a smooth point to a corner point, click directly on it with the Convert Anchor Point tool. The path segments on either side of a smooth point instantly straighten, but the straight segments attached to a corner point do not immediately curve when the point is converted to a smooth point. Instead, click with the Convert Anchor Point tool to convert and drag to expose the direction handles.

If an anchor point was previously already converted to a combination point, either with the Convert Anchor Point tool or while drawing with the Pen tool, clicking on it with the Convert Anchor Point tool straightens only one side but not the other. Click it with the Convert Anchor Point tool a second time to convert the entire point from a combination point to a corner point.

Smoothing and Simplifying Paths

Existing paths—particularly those drawn with the Pencil tool—often need to be simplified. When that can be accomplished by deleting just a few points, doing it manually is the more controlled method. However, if the path contains many more points than it needs, it is typically easier to employ Illustrator's automated tools.

Clicking and holding on the Pencil tool in the Tools palette reveals the Smooth tool. Drag the Smooth tool along a path or path segment to reduce its number of anchor points and smooth it out. Several passes may be required.

Double-click the Smooth tool in the Tools palette to access the Smooth Tool Preferences where Tolerances may be adjusted. Fidelity is the distance between automatically created (or undeleted) anchor points, from 0.5–2.0 pixels. The higher the Fidelity, the more anchor points are removed with each pass of the Smooth tool, and the smoother the resulting path. Smoothness is the amount of change applied to the path with each pass of the Smooth tool; the higher the percentage, the more the path may reshape or smooth.

The Simplify command on the Object, Path submenu changes the entire path at once, regardless of whether only certain points or segments are selected. The goal of Simplify is to reduce the number of anchor points in a path. Curve Precision gives Illustrator its criteria about which is more important, keeping a curve or reducing the number of points attached to it. The lower the percentage, the fewer resulting points and separate path segments, but the less like the original path segments may appear. *Angle threshold* is the maximum angle of a corner point before it is removed or converted. Setting an angle threshold of 90°, for example, leaves all corner points of 90° or less unchanged. Checking Straight Lines converts all path segments to straight lines and all points to corner points, removing any curvature (which is why the Curve Precision slider dims with this option checked). Show Original works in conjunction with the Preview option. When both are checked, the results of the Simplify command are superimposed over an outline of the original path (see Figure 16.19).

Joining Paths

Lining up points and path segments to draw symmetrical closed paths can be a challenge for even the most seasoned Illustrator user. Often the easiest way is to draw only one half and then combine them.

The Object, Path, Join command connects the end points of two paths, bridging any gap with a path segment. Object, Path, Average moves the end points to overlap midway between their original locations.

Figure 16.19
Simplifying the path with the
Object, Path, Simplify command
(shown with Show Original
checked).

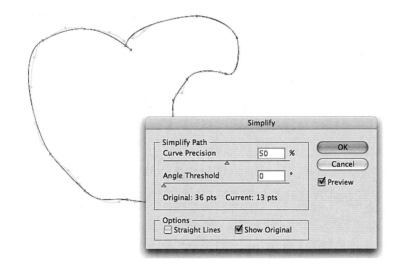

Try this, using Figure 16.20 as a guide:

1. Using either the Pencil or Pen, draw a path open on the right.

2. Select the path with the Selection tool.

3. Click and hold the Rotation tool to reveal the Reflect tool hidden behind it.

4. Double-click the Reflect tool and choose the Vertical axis and then the Copy button. This creates a second copy of your path.

5. With the Selection tool, Shift-drag the new copy until its left edges line up with right edges of the first path.

6. Zoom in on one pair of end points and then reposition the second path to get as close as possible to the first.

7. Drag a selection rectangle with the Direct Selection tool that encompasses the single end point from each.

8. Choose Object, Path, Average.

9. Select Both axis and click OK. The two end points move to a new location at an average distance between both starting points.

10. Choose Object, Path, Join, and the two paths become one, removing the extraneous, overlapped point.

11. Repeat steps 6–9 to combine the other pair of end points and close the path.

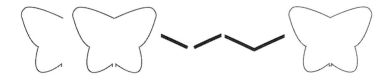

Figure 16.20
Drawing a single side of an object and then reflecting and joining the paths is a fast and accurate way of achieving symmetry in a drawing. Left to right: Step 1, Step 5, Step 9, and Step 11.

Dividing Paths

Just as creating one object is often easier by drawing only half of it, sometimes it's more convenient to draw a single object when two or more are desired. There are several ways to divide or break paths. The Pathfinder commands and effects, which are discussed in the next section, is one group. The others are the Erase, Scissors, and Knife tools, and the Divide Objects Below and Split Into Grid commands (see Figure 16.21).

Figure 16.21
Before (top) and after (bottom) using each of the path division tools and commands. From left to right: Results of using Erase, Scissors, Knife, Divide Objects Below, and Split Into Grid.

The Erase tool (behind the Pencil and Smooth tools) erases path segments or parts of them. Drag it across a short path segment in the selected path and that segment disappears, converting the anchor points on either end to end points. In longer path segments, the Erase tool does not remove the entire segment. Instead, it punches a hole in the path, creating two new endpoints on either side of the hole. The further the Erase tool is dragged along the path, the wider the gap it creates. If the direction of drag includes an anchor point, that anchor point is erased along with the path segment.

With the Scissors tool (above the Zoom tool on the Tools palette), click on an anchor point or path segment where the path should be split. New end points are added, one atop the other, to define the new ends of the open or severed paths. To break a closed path into two separate open paths, use the Scissors tool on both sides, such as in the star in Figure 16.21.

Located behind the Scissors tool, the Knife tool cuts objects and closed paths to divide them into multiple closed paths. With the Knife tool, click on the artboard beside the object and then drag across the entire object or path, ending on the artboard on the other side of the object. The result is two separate closed paths. To maintain a straight edge on the knife, hold the Alt key (Windows users) or the Option key (Mac users).

Choose Object, Path, Divide Objects Below if you want to use the selected object to cut its shape through all objects below it. A star, for example, placed atop a square and circle of·the same size cuts both the square and circle into multiple objects—one each in the shape of the star, with multiple other objects created from the areas that fall outside the star.

Choose Object, Path, Split Into Grid to divide a selected object into rectangular rows and/or columns, as specified in the Split Into Grid dialog. The number of rows and columns—as well as the dimensions of each cell—and the *gutter*—the space between them—may be specified.

The Pathfinder Palette

Many of the more powerful shape combination and division commands are stored in the Pathfinder palette (from the Window menu choose Pathfinder), and are only one or two clicks. On the Pathfinder palette are two groups of buttons—Shape Modes and Pathfinders.

Shape modes create live interactions between two or more objects as a *compound shape* (see Figure 16.22):

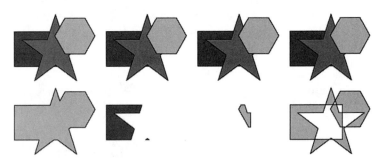

Figure 16.22
Before (top) and after (bottom) using each of the shape modes. From left to right: Results of using Add to Shape Area, Subtract from Shape Area, Intersect Shape Areas, and Exclude Overlapping Shape Areas.

- **Add to Shape Area:** Combine the shapes of all selected objects. The resulting compound shape has the fill and stroke settings of the topmost object.

- **Subtract from Shape Area:** Cut out the shape of all other selected objects from the bottom object.

- **Intersect Shape Areas:** Clip or mask all selected objects to only the area of overlap. The resulting compound shape has the fill and stroke settings of the top object.

- **Exclude Overlapping Shape Areas:** Clip or mask all selected objects to omit all areas of overlap, leaving only the areas that do not overlap. The resulting compound shape has the fill and stroke settings of the top object.

Clicking the Expand button commits the shape mode, permanently altering the object's path(s).

Pathfinders make permanent changes to objects and their paths without the need to click the Expand button (see Figure 16.23). For nonpermanent pathfinder effects—as well as other permanent pathfinder filters—see Chapter 20, "Working with Placed Graphics and Filters in Illustrator."

Figure 16.23
Before (top) and after (bottom) using each of the Pathfinder Effects. From left to right: Divide, Trim, Merge, Crop, Outline, and Minus Back.

- **Divide:** Divide all shapes by each other, resulting in new paths from each visible section of the originals, broken into new shapes at any overlap point.

- **Trim:** Remove all overlapping areas from each shape. Also remove strokes assigned to any of the objects.

- **Merge:** Combine the paths of any overlapping objects of the same fill color (and without strokes). Objects not of the same color are trimmed to remove overlap.

- **Crop:** Remove all portions of the selected shapes that fall outside the area of the top object. Also remove strokes assigned to any of the objects.

- **Outline:** Divide the selected objects into their non-overlapping path segments. Fills are removed while strokes are preserved.

- **Minus Back:** Knock all shapes overlapping the top object out of the area of the top object.

The shapes resulting from Pathfinders are not compound shapes. Rather they are individual paths grouped together. To access paths separately, choose Ungroup from the Object menu.

FINAL THOUGHTS

Raster art is like a painting: The brush may swipe across the canvas with caprice or purpose. Aesthetics are created by layering paint, one pixel atop another, with the ability to paint over the same canvas again and again with lucid direction or absent a single preconceived color or shape. However controlled the action, raster is always liquid paint with fuzzy edges; however magnificent the art, it is always limited by the immutable size of its canvas.

Vector artwork, with its anchor points and path segments, requires slightly more attention to detail, a little more forethought, like sculpting in clay. Paths may be layered, divided, and combined to form new shapes and rich artwork, though their mere existence never scathes other paths unless directed to do so. Each bump and curve of the sculpture must be crafted by hand, a more tactile and immersive experience than painting on flat canvas with a brush. Roll the clay between your fingers, smooth this bump, lengthen that side. Affix the nose to the bust and smooth it into the face, then tear it off without injury to the face and shape it some more.

With path-based drawing, no alteration is ever truly permanent or unforgiving. Vector artwork and its paths are at the heart of all Illustrator work. On a whim they may be divided, sliced, and broken, and just as easily reconstructed, merged, or joined with variety as infinite as the uses made possible by resolution independence.

WORKING WITH COLOR
IN ILLUSTRATOR

Color is as important to communication as structure and organization. Illustrator has the full range of color tools, commands, and features that any other creative pro application includes—and more.

IDENTIFYING AND CHOOSING COLOR

Various tools, palettes, menu commands, and features manage and display color in Illustrator.

Tools Palette Color Swatches

At the bottom of the Tools palette are *swatches* indicating fill and stroke colors active in the currently selected object or appearance attribute. If no object is selected, the displayed stroke color and fill color, gradient, or pattern applies to newly created objects. The exception is new type, which always starts out with a 100% pure black fill and no stroke.

Surrounding the swatches are various features related to them (see Figure 17.1).

17

Figure 17.1
On the Tools palette, fill and stroke swatches and additional features provide quick access to commonly used features.

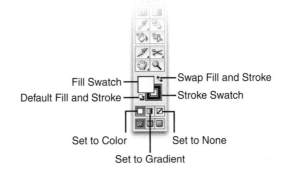

Fill Swatch ——
Default Fill and Stroke ——
—— Swap Fill and Stroke
—— Stroke Swatch

Set to Color — Set to None
Set to Gradient

The buttons and features in this area are

- **Fill Swatch:** Display the active fill color, gradient, or pattern. A white swatch with a red slash through it signifies no fill. Click to bring to the front (if behind the stroke swatch).

- **Stroke Swatch:** Display the active stroke color or pattern. A white swatch with a red slash through it signifies no stroke. Click to bring to the front (if behind the fill swatch).

- **Swap Fill and Stroke:** Exchange the colors, gradients, or patterns in the fill for that in the stroke and vice versa.

- **Default Fill and Stroke:** Return the fill and stroke to their default states—white and black, respectively.

- **Set to Color:** Set the foremost swatch, either fill or stroke, to the solid color active in the Colors palette.

- **Set to Gradient:** Set the fill swatch to the gradient active in the Gradients palette.

- **Set to None:** Set the foremost swatch, either fill or stroke, to none, vacating any color, gradient, or pattern present.

Here are some keyboard shortcuts to make working with the fill and stroke features easier: Press X to exchange the active swatch, either fill or stroke, for the inactive swatch. Press D to set both swatches back to their defaults. Press / to set the active swatch to none.

Color Palette

Mix or adjust fill or stroke colors on the Color palette in one of three ways: by typing values into the measurement fields, by clicking on and dragging the sliders below each color, or by clicking inside the color ramp at the bottom of the palette. Swatches may also be chosen from the Swatches palette and adjusted via the measurement fields or color sliders. Click the fill or stroke swatches to choose which to edit.

Depending on the document color mode and the currently selected object or swatch, the Color palette may show between one and four sliders and measurement fields in any of five color models (See Figure 17.2):

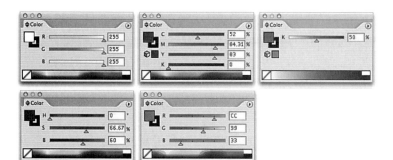

Figure 17.2
The Color palette, in each of its five color models: (top row) RGB, CMYK, Grayscale; (bottom row) HSB, Web Safe RGB.

- **RGB:** Red, green, and blue, the largest of Illustrator's color models, used for onscreen or on-web graphics. Enter mixes in the form of 0–255, no color (black) to full color (white).

- **CMYK:** Cyan, magenta, yellow, and black, the color model of process printing ink used in for-press projects. Enter mixes in percentages, from 0–100%, no color (white) to full color.

- **Grayscale:** A misnomer, the grayscale mode of the Color palette is actually a *tint* mode. One color—black or another pure ink or spot color—is accessible at a time, and the measurement field and slider affect the tint of that ink, from 0%–100%.

- **HSB:** Hue, saturation, and brightness: Equivalent to RGB, but instead of mixing percentages of red, green, and blue, the color is mixed in a more intuitive fashion by adjusting levels of hue (color), saturation (amount of color), and brightness (tone). Enter measurements in percentages, from 0%–100%.

- **Web Safe RGB:** The same as RGB, but optimized for the web-safe 216-color palette and with measurement fields that display HTML hexadecimal color codes rather than the 0–255 RGB values.

Choose any of the above color modes from the Color palette menu.

Sliders on the Color palette dynamically inform about how changes in the sliders affect the selected swatch. In HSB mode, for example, the B slider lightens on the right side, indicating that moving the slider to the right achieves the colors shown. Simultaneously, the remaining sliders update to reflect potential adjustments relevant to the state of all other sliders.

Below the swatches on the Color palette may appear two warnings and accompanying swatches (see Figure 17.3). Out of Web Color Warning indicates that the active color does not fall within the 216 Web Safe colors; Out of Gamut Color Warning reveals that the color will not print reliably in the limited CMYK color space. Both warnings present accompanying swatches displaying the closest, in-gamut, match to the active color. Clicking on a warning swatch makes that swatch the active color, discarding the previously active swatch.

Figure 17.3
The active color is Out of Web Color and Out of Gamut.

Out of Web Color Warning

Out of Gamut Color Warning

Color Picker

The Color Picker, which may be accessed by double-clicking the active swatch in either the Tools or Color palettes, provides additional methods for color choice (see Figure 17.4).

Figure 17.4
The Color Picker.

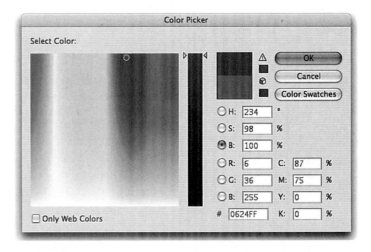

In the same Color Picker dialog are all the Color palette's models, HSB, RGB, CMYK, and hexadecimal. Enter values in any group to create a new color. To define a new color, click somewhere inside the spectrum (which changes modes depending upon the active measurement field), or click inside the color slider or drag the slider arrows.

Above the HSB measurement fields are two swatches, the current color (top), and the color selected prior to accessing the Color Picker (bottom). Any warnings appear beside the swatches.

Clicking the Color Swatches button limits the display to colors saved in the Swatches palette; clicking Color Models returns to the default Color Picker view.

Swatches Palette

Colors, gradients, and patterns that will or may be used again are stored in the Swatches palette, enabling single-click application to objects (see Figure 17.5). Clicking on a swatch in the palette automatically applies it to the selected object's fill or stroke, whichever is foremost at the bottom of the Tools palette and Color palette. If no objects are selected, choosing a swatch loads it for application to new objects as they are created.

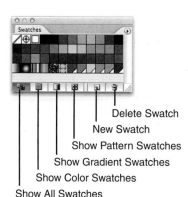

Figure 17.5
The Swatches palette (swatches shown are the defaults in a new RGB document).

Delete Swatch
New Swatch
Show Pattern Swatches
Show Gradient Swatches
Show Color Swatches
Show All Swatches

Any type of fill may be made into a swatch—solid colors (of various types), gradients, and patterns. Mix the desired RGB, CMYK, HSB, or grayscale color on the Color palette or create the gradient or pattern desired, and click the New Swatch button at the bottom of the Swatches palette to add it to the library.

The Swatches palette may contain any or all of the following types of swatches:

- **Process Color:** Process typically refers to colors printed by some combination of cyan, magenta, yellow, and/or black inks. In Illustrator's case, however, all new solid color swatches created in CYMK, RGB, or HSB mode are saved as process swatches.

- **Global Process Color:** Marked by a white triangle in its corner, global process colors are pure colors that update automatically throughout the entire document if edited.

- **Spot Color:** Marked by a white triangle with a black spot inside it, a spot color is a premixed ink color.

- **Color Tint:** A tint or percentage of a global process or spot color.

- **Gradient:** A smooth transition between two or more colors, either linear or radial.

- **Pattern:** Paths, type, or other vector artwork to be used as a fill or stroke.

- **None:** No color. Appears on the Swatches, Color, and Tools palettes as a white square with a red slash through it.

- **Registration Black:** A special swatch that prints on all plates of a color separation. It appears black onscreen, but it is *not* black. Appears on the Swatches, Color, and Tools palettes as a white square with black target or registration symbol.

Swatches are document-specific, meaning swatches added to or removed from the Swatches palette save within, and remain with, the document. When a new document is created, it contains only the default swatches—either the default RGB or CMYK swatches, depending upon the color space of the document.

Load one or more additional, preinstalled or user-created color libraries by choosing Window, Swatch Libraries. Any swatch libraries opened in addition to the default Swatches palette appear in their own free-floating palette. Swatches from these other libraries are automatically appended to the normal Swatches palette upon use in the document.

Use spot colors (special premixed inks used universally throughout the creative, prepress, and press industries for reliability) and add them to the Swatches palette by loading the appropriate swatch library (choose Window, Swatch Libraries), as shown in Figure 17.6.

Figure 17.6
The Pantone process coated library, one of many additional swatch libraries installed with Illustrator (shown in List View).

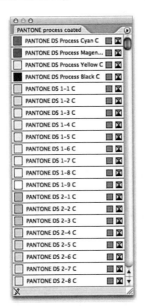

There are six buttons along the bottom of the Swatches palette:

- **Show All Swatches:** Display all defined swatches, including colors, gradients, and patterns.

- **Show Color Swatches:** Filter the list to display only color swatches, hiding gradients and patterns.

- **Show Gradient Swatches:** Filter the list to display only gradient swatches, hiding colors and patterns.

- **Show Pattern Swatches:** Filter the list to display only pattern swatches, hiding colors and gradients.

- **New Swatch:** Add the currently active fill or stroke (whichever is foremost on the bottom of the Tools palette) as a swatch.

- **Delete Swatch:** Delete the currently selected swatch(es).

Color Filters

Choosing Illustrator's Filters, Colors menu displays several useful filters and commands for working with the colors in a selected object or objects:

- **Adjust Colors:** Adjust all fill and/or stroke colors in the selected object(s).

- **Blend Front to Back:** When three or more objects are selected, this filter fills the objects between the top and bottom objects with colors mixed from the fills of the top and bottom objects' fills.

- **Blend Horizontally:** When three or more horizontally aligned objects are selected, this filter fills the objects between the left and right objects with colors mixed from the fills of the left and right objects' fills (see Figure 17.7).

Figure 17.7
Before using the Blend Horizontally filter (top), and after (bottom). The middle star is filled with an even mix of the fills on either side.

17

- **Blend Vertically:** When three or more vertically aligned objects are selected, this filter fills the objects between the top and bottom objects with colors mixed from the fills of the top and bottom objects' fills.

- **Convert to CMYK:** Convert colors present in the selected object(s) to CMYK, changing any out-of-gamut colors to fit within the CMYK gamut or range of colors.

- **Convert to Grayscale:** Convert colors present in the selected object(s) to Grayscale.

- **Convert to RGB:** Convert colors present in the selected object(s) to RGB.

- **Invert Colors:** Change colors present in the selected object(s) to their opposites on the color wheel. For example, blue becomes yellow and red becomes cyan.

- **Overprint Black:** Print black ink on top of cyan, magenta, and yellow ink to reduce the noticeable effects of *misregistration*, or colors not lining up perfectly on a printing press. By default, black knocks out or prevents printing of other colors beneath it.

- **Saturate:** Adjust the saturation of colors present in the selected object(s).

Eyedropper

In Photoshop, the Eyedropper tool picks up color from a pixel or range of pixels. In Illustrator, the Eyedropper tool can also select a color from a pixel- or path-based object, but it does far more. It copies most appearance attributes, including fill color, transparency, and overprint; stroke color, transparency, overprint, weight, cap, join, miter limit, and dash pattern; and, with type, the character and paragraph styles.

To use the Eyedropper, first select the object(s) that is the destination for another's style. Then click on the source object with the Eyedropper. Instantly its appearance attributes apply to the destination object(s). Any appearance attributes in the destination object(s) are replaced with those of the source.

Hold the Shift key while clicking to select only the color directly beneath the Eyedropper cursor and not all the appearance attributes of the source object or an entire gradient.

Hold Shift+Alt (Windows users) or Shift-Option (Mac users) to *add* the source object's appearance attributes to the destination object's instead of *replacing* them.

To customize what the Eyedropper picks up and applies, as well as the size of the sample area when sampling colors from placed raster images, double-click the Eyedropper tool in the Tools palette. In the Eyedropper Options dialog deselect the undesired options and set the Raster Sample size to either Point Sample (selecting color from the pixel directly beneath the Eyedropper cursor when clicked) or an average of the colors in a 3- by 3-pixel or 5- by 5-pixel area.

USING COLOR

Now that you understand the basic tools for choosing, mixing, and saving colors, let's look at the different ways to use color in Illustrator drawings.

Fills and Strokes

Open or closed paths, shapes, type, and just about everything except placed images can be colored with fills and/or strokes.

Both fill and stroke colors may be chosen or created in a number of ways:

- Predefined colors may be selected from the Swatches palette.

- Colors may be chosen from additional swatch libraries.

- New colors may be mixed on the Colors palette.

- Pattern fills and strokes may be loaded from additional libraries or created.

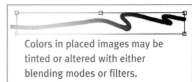

Colors in placed images may be tinted or altered with either blending modes or filters.

- Multiple colors may be blended together via the Gradient palette or with a gradient mesh.

- A graphic style containing fill and/or stroke colors may be applied to objects.

17

- Colors may be picked up from other objects or even images with the Eyedropper tool.

- Objects or their fills or strokes may be rendered semi-transparent or assigned a blending mode so that they mix with other fills, strokes, or objects to create color from the mixture of the two.

Multiple fills and strokes, each with their own transparency settings and effects, may be added to an object via the menu on the Appearance palette (see the section on the Appearance palette in Chapter 15, "Understanding Illustrator Palettes and Menus"). Select Add New Fill or Add New Stroke and then set its options. Intricate designs may be achieved by layering either fills or strokes or both, and applying blending modes and transparency to them (see Figure 17.8).

Use the Transform and Offset Path effects on multiple fills or strokes to create unlimited effects without necessitating multiple copies of an object or text (see Chapter 20, "Working with Placed Graphics and Filters In Illustrator").

Figure 17.8
Multiple fills and/or strokes assigned as appearance attributes replace cumbersome layering of objects.

17

Strokes

Strokes are colored or patterned lines that follow the outside of a path. They may be either solid, dashed, or dotted, and can be rendered transparent or assigned a blending mode, either as part of such an effect on the entire object or independently of the rest of the object's fill and other appearance attributes.

The color of a stroke is defined on the Color palette, but all other attributes are handled by the Stroke palette (choose Window, Stroke to display it). By default, the Stroke palette displays only the weight or thickness of the stroke. Choose Show Options from the Stroke palette menu to access the rest of the palette (see Figure 17.9).

Change the weight either with the pop-up menu of common weights or by manually typing a value in points. Choose the style of end cap—how far and in what shape the stroke extends beyond the path—and the Miter Limit—the angle of a stroked corner—and the style of corners. Align Stroke decides how strokes align to the path, whether straddling it (the default, where a 4-point stroke results in 2 points outside the path and 2 points inside overlapping the fill), stroke inside the path (all 4 points overlapping the fill), or aligned to the outside of the path (all 4 points of the stroke appear outside the fill).

Figure 17.9
The Stroke palette (with options shown).

To create a dashed or dotted line, check Dashed Line at the bottom of the Stroke palette. There are six measurement fields—three dashes and three gaps—to help define very complicated dash patterns (see Figure 17.10). Only the first is required. Filling in the length of the first dash (in points) automatically creates gaps of the same size. For example: A 2-point dash creates a 2-point corresponding gap. If an even on-off-on dash is desired, no gap needs be entered. To widen or shorten the gap, enter a value. Create more complicated patterns—for example: 4 pt dash-2-pt gap-3 pt dash-2 pt gap-2 pt dash—by filling in the appropriate boxes. To create dotted lines, use a small dash size equal to the stroke weight—for example, 1 or 2 points.

Figure 17.10
Different dash patterns and their settings.

InDesign enables you to specify a separate gap color for dashed or dotted lines. Illustrator does not include that feature because it has a much more powerful mechanism for creating a gap color and other advanced effects: the Appearance palette. Choose Add New Stroke from the Appearance palette menu, adding a second stroke to the original artwork. Set the options of the stroke appropriately and then drag its entry below the first, dashed stroke entry in the Appearance palette. The result is a dashed stroke with a separate gap color. Add additional strokes for more complicated patterns or effects.

Patterns

Patterns are vector artwork used to fill other vector artwork. They may be wallpaper-like repetitions, single objects (that are tiled or repeated automatically by Illustrator), solid-filled or unfilled type, or any path-based creation in Illustrator.

Creating a pattern is simple: Draw and style the object(s) to be used as a fill, select the object(s), and then choose Edit, Create Pattern. Give the pattern a name and click OK. The new pattern appears on the Swatches palette, ready to apply as a fill or even stroke (see Figure 17.11).

Figure 17.11
An object filled with the Grid on Grid pattern (in the default RGB Swatches palette).

Gradients

Gradients are two or more colors blended smoothly together, which is why a few other applications call them *blends*. They are created on the Gradient palette (choose Window, Gradient to display it).

On the Gradient palette menu choose Show Options to access all the palette's features (see Figure 17.12). The type choices are Linear—colors blend linearly into one another—or Radial—colors blend outward in a circle. When Linear is the chosen type, Angle becomes active, enabling the gradient to be tilted to any positive or negative angle. Location becomes accessible when one of the gradient stops beneath the gradient preview is selected.

Figure 17.12
The Gradient palette (options shown).

Gradient stops store the colors in a gradient, injecting them into the fluent transition at the site of the stops' points. Click and drag gradient stops to change their locations and adjust the number of color shades appearing between them. Pushing two stops up against each other, for instance, creates a shallow transition between their colors—almost a hard edge. Alternative to manually dragging the gradient stops, select them and use the location measurement field to define their position relative to the entire gradient.

To change the color of a gradient stop, click once on it; the arrow at the top of the gradient stop fills, denoting selection. The stop's color also loads into the Color palette. Edit the color using the Color palette, by Alt-clicking (Windows users) or Option-clicking (Mac users) a swatch in the Swatches palette, or by dragging a color swatch from the Swatches palette and dropping it directly onto the stop.

Add more colors or shades to the gradient by clicking beneath the preview but away from a gradient stop, which creates a new gradient stop (see Figure 17.13). Pressing Alt (Windows users) or Option (Mac users) while dragging a gradient stop duplicates it. Dragging one gradient stop onto another while holding Alt or Option swaps them—for example, in a duotone (two-color) gradient, swapping the gradient stops flips the direction of colors. Swatches may also be dragged from the Color or Swatches palette and dropped directly onto the gradient preview or the gradient stop area below it. A gradient may have as many colors as can be managed.

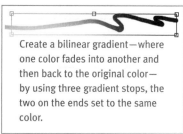

Create a bilinear gradient—where one color fades into another and then back to the original color—by using three gradient stops, the two on the ends set to the same color.

Figure 17.13
Complex gradients may be created
by adding gradient stops.

Click and drag in a gradient-filled object with the Gradient tool from the Tools palette to define the
start point and endpoint for gradients and the angle of transition. Any colorable areas not touched by
dragging the gradient tool fill with the solid color on the corresponding end of the gradient.

Gradient Meshes

Gradients may be only linear or radial; they cannot flow around shapes, transition in an arc or diamond form, or even give asymmetric priority to one color in the gradient. When an object requires
smooth, nonbanded transition between colors, turn to gradient meshes (see Figure 17.14).

Figure 17.14
A photo-realistic painting (in-
progress) created with a gradient
mesh.

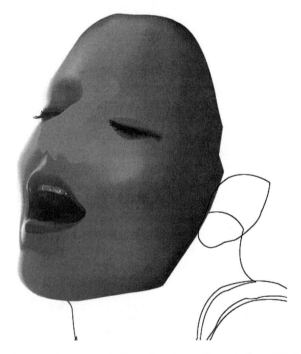

A mesh is a grid of points and path segments, called *mesh points* and *mesh lines*. Mesh points are
fillable, and colors flow smoothly across the grid from one point to mix with the colors assigned to
the mesh points (up to eight) surrounding it. Mesh lines define the direction of color flow. Between
mesh points and lines are *mesh patches*, in which the color transitions are actually visible.

To convert a path to a gradient mesh, select the object and choose Object, Create Gradient Mesh. In
the Create Gradient Mesh dialog specify a number of rows and columns into which initially to divide
the object. The Appearance pop-up menu starts off the gradient mesh by applying a white highlight,

either radiating from the center outward or from the edges inward. Highlight percentage controls the intensity of the highlight. Alternatively, select a path and click on it with the Mesh tool to initiate a gradient mesh.

A mesh follows the shape of the path. If opposing sides of a path are not identical, Illustrator extrapolates each stage of shape morphing between them, creating mesh lines and points that follow the extrapolation (see Figure 17.15). The default points and lines can be edited, however.

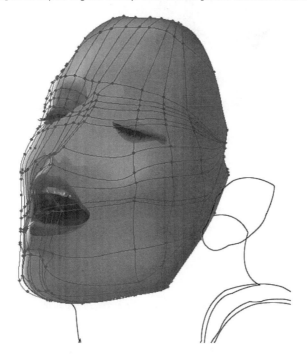

Figure 17.15
Mesh lines and mesh points follow the shape of the object.

Mesh points behave like anchor points: They have direction handles that may be modified with the Direct Selection tool, the Mesh tool, or the Bézier tools behind the Pen. The direction handles of mesh points control the angle and curvature of mesh lines.

With the Direct Selection tool or Mesh tool, click to highlight a mesh point and fill it by either choosing a swatch from the Swatches palette or mixing a color on the Colors palette. Swatches may also be dropped onto mesh points or mesh patches without selecting them in advance. Anchor points on the outside of the mesh path are also fillable.

Like anchor points, mesh points may be selected, moved, and modified by clicking or dragging across them with the Direct Selection tool, by using the Lasso tool, and with the Mesh tool (see Figure 17.16).

Further divide the mesh by clicking on a mesh line with the Mesh tool, which creates a new row or column perpendicular to the one clicked on. Clicking inside a mesh patch adds both a new column and a new row at that point. To remove rows and columns, Alt-click (Windows users) or Option-click (Mac users) the mesh point with the Mesh tool. Clicking on a mesh line while holding Alt or Option removes only that row or column without also deleting the other.

Figure 17.16
Mesh points may be selected and manipulated like anchor points.

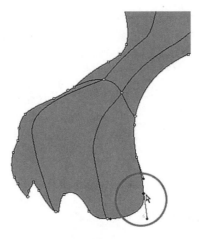

To move a mesh point along the mesh line—thus, reshaping only the column *or* row, not both—hold the Shift key while dragging the mesh point with the Mesh tool. Twirl all four mesh lines emanating from a mesh point by holding Shift while dragging one of the direction handles.

Gradient meshes are the secret to all levels of realism in Illustrator drawings—from cartoons to photorealistic portraits. They can be controlled and colored with precision, affording the artist absolute control over the coloring of an object, with much less effort and discombobulation than using separate objects and normal gradients for every color area.

Transparency

Transparency is the process of making an object less than perfectly opaque so it may interact with other objects. In Illustrator transparency takes many forms. Entire objects may be rendered partially transparent—from 0% opaque (invisible) to 100% (fully opaque)—as may each of their fills and strokes independently (see Figure 17.17). Effects like drop shadows and glows are also forms of transparency (see Chapter 20), as are blending modes (see the section on blending modes later in this chapter).

Figure 17.17
Objects with transparency blend with the objects behind them.

Simple opacity changes are accomplished by selecting the object or appearance attribute for transparency, and, on the Transparency palette (choose Window, Transparency to display it), entering an opacity percentage or clicking the arrow and moving the Opacity slider (see Figure 17.18). Any object in Illustrator—shape, path, placed graphic, type—can be rendered transparent.

Figure 17.18
The Transparency palette (options shown).

In the middle of the Transparency palette are options for opacity masks (see the section on opacity masks in Chapter 20).

On the bottom of the Transparency palette are three check boxes:

- **Isolate Blending:** Prevent the blending mode of the group or layer from affecting objects below the group or layer.

- **Knockout Group:** Prevent objects in a group from blending with each other when checked. A square in the check box indicates that some objects in the group have knockout assigned and some do not.

- **Opacity & Mask Define Knockout Shape:** Use opacity and an opacity mask to define the area in which other inks will be knocked out or not printed.

Blending Modes

Also on the Transparency palette is the blending modes pop-up menu. Blending modes control how the colors of one object affect the colors of other objects beneath. To blend the colors of one object with another, you apply a blending mode to only the upper object.

There are sixteen blending modes:

- **Normal:** No blending mode; the colors of stacked objects have no interaction (other than that created by the Opacity setting or other device).

- **Darken:** Display the darker of the blended objects' over-lapping colors, discarding the lighter.

- **Multiply:** Multiply stacked colors by each other, resulting in darker tones.

> With the Multiply blending mode, blending black always produces black, and multiplying by white has no effect on other colors.

- **Color Burn:** Darken lower object colors by burning with the blended object colors. Blending with white has no effect on other colors.

- **Lighten:** Display the brighter of the blended objects' overlapping colors, discarding the darker.

- **Screen:** Multiply stacked colors by the inverse of each other, resulting in lighter tones.

- **Color Dodge:** Lighten lower object colors by dodging with the blended object colors. Blending with black has no effect on other colors.

> With the Screen blending mode, blending black produces no effect, and screening by white creates white.

- **Overlay:** Mix the luminosity and blended object color into lower object colors.

- **Soft Light:** Depending on the luminosity of the blended object colors, Soft Light either dodges lower objects (if the blended colors are less than 50% gray) or burns (if the blended colors are more than 50% gray).

- **Hard Light:** Depending on the luminosity of the blended object colors, Hard Light either screens lower objects (if the blended colors are less than 50% gray) or multiplies (if the blended colors are more than 50% gray). Blending with white or black produces only white or black.

- **Difference:** Subtract the brighter of the blended objects' overlapping colors, discarding the darker. Blending with white inverts the colors. Blending with black has no effect on other colors. Convert spot colors to process.

- **Exclusion:** Similar to the Difference blending mode, but with lower contrast. Blending with white inverts the colors. Blending with black has no effect on other colors. Convert spot colors to process.

- **Hue:** Apply only the hue of the blended object colors to the luminosity and saturation of the lower object colors. Blending with white, black, or any percentage of black desaturates all colors, resulting in grayscale. Convert spot colors to process colors.

- **Saturation:** Apply only the saturation of the blended object colors to the luminosity and hue of the lower object colors. Blending with white, black, or any percentage of black desaturates all colors, resulting in grayscale. Convert spot colors to process.

> **Caution**
>
> In CMYK process printing, 100% black ink *knocks out* all colors beneath, resulting in no blending. When employing a blending mode, use a rich black that includes black as well as a small bit (even 1%) of each of cyan, magenta, and yellow instead of pure black.

- **Color:** Apply the hue and saturation of the blended object colors to the luminosity of the lower object colors. Blending with white, black, or any percentage of black desaturates all colors, resulting in grayscale. Convert spot colors to process.

- **Luminosity:** Apply only the luminosity of the blended object colors to the hue and saturation of the lower object colors. Blending with white or black produces white or black. Convert spot colors to process.

Color Management During Printing

All the applications in Creative Suite 2 share a common color management engine and interface, and all handle the process in their respective print dialogs the same. In Illustrator's (choose Print from the File menu and then click on Color Management) are three pop-up menus: Color Handling, Printer Profile, and Rendering Intent (see Figure 17.19):

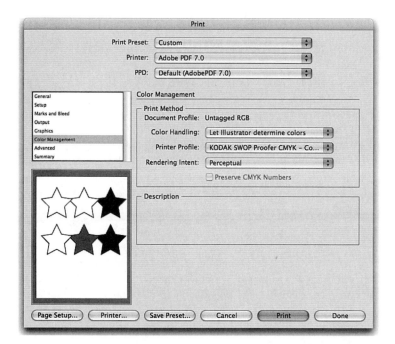

Figure 17.19
The Color Management tab of Illustrator's Print dialog.

- **Color Handling:** Select whether Illustrator or the printer handles the color management processes. Let Illustrator Determine Colors is the recommended option.

- **Printer Profile:** This pop-up menu lists all ICC printer profiles installed on the computer. Select the profile matching the printer or output device. How the print device handles color is communicated to Illustrator by the printer ICC profile, and the Rendering Intent makes decisions based upon this profile.

- **Rendering Intent:** Select the method employed when calculating how to convert out-of-gamut colors or colors that present in the document that cannot be reproduced with absolute fidelity by the print output device. Each rendering intent has a specific methodology for making these calculations:

  - **Perceptual:** Attempts to preserve the relationships between, and tonal range of, hues. Works best for artwork with subtle color changes like photographs and gradient meshes.

  - **Saturation:** Best for business graphics and artwork with large areas of one color, this rendering intent keeps the saturation level or vividness in out-of-gamut colors constant even if hues shift.

  - **Relative Colorimetric:** Converts out-of-gamut colors to the closest match color in the printer profile using the white point of both the source (the monitor's or document's assigned profile) and destination (printer) profiles as the common point of origin. Colors that fall within the gamut are scaled and altered to retain their relative distance from converted colors.

- **Absolute Colorimetric:** Clips out-of-gamut colors to the first available in-gamut color in the hue range. In-gamut colors are not changed to preserve relationships, and white points are not matched and calculated.

FINAL THOUGHTS

A picture, the worn cliché postulates, is worth a thousand words. Words are meaningless without context, without language, structure, or grammar. So, too, are pictures meaningless without form, composition, or color—even if that color is in tones of gray or just black and white.

Color is about communication—speaking of aesthetics, organization, importance, or emotion. Choose warm colors such as orange to attract attention, subdued hues like green to distract it. Fill an object with red to evoke passion, with blue to promote serenity. Use gradients and gradient meshes for subtlety and realism or to create faux dimensionality or motion. Tell a story with your Illustrator drawings.

Each field of design—for print, the Web, or broadcast, and all the smaller fields within them—has its own language of color. For print, that language is limited by the abridged dictionary of CMYK ink, but the other two are more intricate, fuller languages the breadth of human vision, in the larger gamut of light-spectrum-derived RGB. Learn to speak each language fluently, adjusting for the dialects spoken by various color-rendering devices such as computer monitors, scanners, printers, and imagesetters through their ICC profiles.

Compose your illustrations—tell a story—as would a writer. Describe beauty in the meter and rhyme of a poet, schematics and diagrams in the crisp pragmatism of technical writing, advertisements with the languid flourish of a copywriter, and illustrations with the variegated and robust adjectives of fiction.

Simple, concise sentences are usually the most effectively communicated—don't draw in an overly complicated tongue. Neither should your illustrations be laconic. Using only short, simple sentence structures robs your prose of the richness of language variance, ultimately sacrificing interest. Verbalize the language of your art in CMYK or RGB, using not only the basic nouns and verbs of fill and stroke, but also the fertility of the language's adjectives and adverbs—gradients and transparency.

In this chapter you learned the alphabet—the basic building blocks for the languages and dialects of color possible within Illustrator CS2. What will you now write?

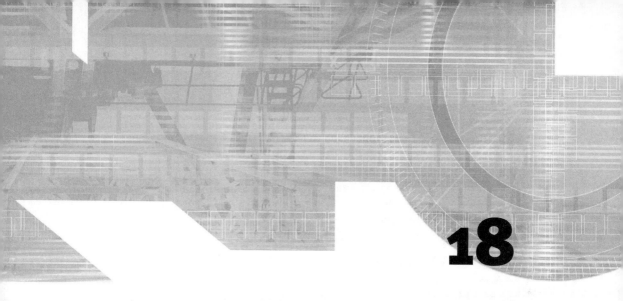

WORKING WITH OBJECTS IN ILLUSTRATOR

IN THIS CHAPTER

Drawing is the foundation for objects, and color is the beginning of illustration. The ways to work with and style objects doesn't end there, however.

ARRANGING AND GROUPING OBJECTS

When every area of artwork is a separate, stacked, and modifiable object, isolating just one or organizing multiple objects can become cumbersome. Fortunately, Illustrator includes several features to ease the task of working with—and around—objects.

Grouping and Ungrouping

Often working with multiple objects is easier when they behave as a single unit. This is where grouping comes in.

Grouped objects are still individual paths, shapes, placed images, text, or even other groups. They are simply treated as a unified object (see Figure 18.1). Groups may be transformed—moved, scaled, rotated, skewed, and so on—as a single unit; effects and appearance attributes may be applied to grouped objects without affecting the attributes of the component elements; and groups may be used as symbols.

Figure 18.1
When individual objects (left) are grouped (right), they remain individual objects, though they behave, and are only selectable, as a unit.

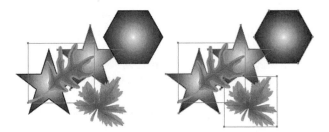

Group individual objects by selecting them and then by choosing Object, Group or by pressing the keyboard shortcut Ctrl+G (Windows users) or ⌘-G (Mac users). Ungroup, or release the group to autonomous objects, with the Object, Ungroup command or by pressing the keyboard shortcut Shift+Ctrl+G (Windows users) or Shift-⌘-G (Mac users).

When grouping, all objects selected become part of a group sub-layer on the top object's layer regardless of their origin layers. In the Layers palette the group object is listed as a <Group> sublayer, with each of its components below it (see Figure 18.2). As with any sub-layers, objects inside the group may be dragged out and restored to free-standing items by dragging their Layers palette entries outside the <Group> sub-layer. Similarly, new objects may be inserted into the group simply by dragging them into the sub-layer. Reorder sub-layers of the <Group> sub-layer to change the stacking order of objects inside the group.

Stacking Order

Also called the *z-order*, referring to the z-axis, which runs front-to-back in the third dimension, the *stacking order* is the front-to-back arrangement of objects—which objects overlap and which underlap. With path-based artwork, stacking order is important; when working with transparency, it is vital.

Figure 18.2
Within the <Group> sub-layer are sub-layers for all the constituent objects in the group.

Each new object created is higher in the stacking order than—and on top of—other objects on the same layer or sub-layer. Reorder objects by dragging their Layers palette entries up or down, by menu commands, or by keyboard shortcuts.

By choosing commands from the Object, Arrange submenu, you can tell one or more objects, including grouped objects, to do the following:

- **Bring to Front:** Move the selected object(s) to the top of the stacking order on the current layer or sub-layer.

- **Bring Forward:** Move the selected object(s) one step closer to the top of the stacking order on the current layer or sub-layer.

- **Send Backward:** Move the selected object(s) one step closer to the bottom of the stacking order on the current layer or sub-layer.

- **Send to Back:** Move the selected object(s) to the bottom of the stacking order on the current layer or sub-layer.

- **Send to Current Layer:** Move the selected object(s) from whatever layer or sub-layer it may be contained in to the layer currently selected in the Layers palette.

Arrange commands are relative to other objects; if the selected object is already the top object on the layer or sub-layer, Bring to Front and Bring Forward are grayed out and disabled.

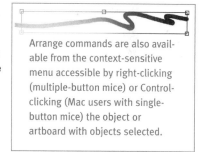

Arrange commands are also available from the context-sensitive menu accessible by right-clicking (multiple-button mice) or Control-clicking (Mac users with single-button mice) the object or artboard with objects selected.

Similar to the Arrange commands are the Select commands to select objects with different places in the stacking order without actually changing the stacking order. Available from either the Select menu or the right-click or Control-click context menu, the Select submenu includes the following commands:

- **First Object Above:** Select the top object above the currently selected one.

- **Next Object Above:** Select the next object above the currently selected one.

- **Next Object Below:** Select the next object beneath the currently selected one.

- **Last Object Below:** Select the bottom object beneath the currently selected one.

Alignment and Distribution

With Alignment commands, the near impossible task of perfectly lining up objects by hand is unnecessary. Alignment commands can align any surface or plane of objects as well as distribute them relative to each other and/or the artboard.

Though most of the alignment commands appear on the Control palette automatically when more than one object is selected, this is a subset of the commands available on the Align palette (see Figure 18.3). To access all the alignment and distribution commands, open the Align palette from the Window menu and select Show Options from the Align palette menu.

Figure 18.3
The Align palette after selecting Show Options from the Align palette menu.

The Align palette contains three rows of command buttons: Align Objects, Distribute Objects, and Distribute Spacing.

Here are descriptions of the Align Objects buttons (see Figure 18.4):

Figure 18.4
Three aligned objects, left to right: Horizontal Align Left, Horizontal Align Center, Horizontal Align Right; Vertical Align Top (top), Vertical Align Center (center), Vertical Align Bottom (bottom).

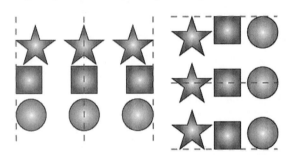

- **Horizontal Align Left:** Align the left edges of all objects to match the left selected object.

- **Horizontal Align Center:** Align the horizontal middles of all objects to the midpoint between the left and right edges of the selection.

- **Horizontal Align Right:** Align the right edges of all objects to match the right selected object.

- **Vertical Align Top:** Align the top edges of all objects to match that of the top selected object.

- **Vertical Align Center:** Align the vertical middles of all objects to the midpoint between the top and bottom edges of the selection.

- **Vertical Align Bottom:** Align the bottom edges of all objects to match that of the bottom selected object.

Here is what the Distribute Objects buttons do (see Figure 18.5):

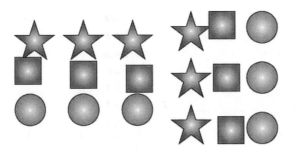

Figure 18.5
Three objects distributed, left to right: Vertical Distribute Top, Vertical Distribute Center, Vertical Distribute Bottom, Horizontal Distribute Left, Horizontal Distribute Center, Horizontal Distribute Right.

- **Vertical Distribute Top:** Equidistant vertical spacing of the top edges of all objects. If objects are of disparate sizes, this command may result in overlapping objects or uneven spacing between objects.

- **Vertical Distribute Center:** Equidistant vertical spacing of the vertical centers of all objects. If objects are of disparate sizes, this command may result in overlapping objects or uneven spacing between objects.

- **Vertical Distribute Bottom:** Equidistant vertical spacing of the bottom edges of all objects. If objects are of disparate sizes, this command may result in overlapping objects or uneven spacing between objects.

- **Horizontal Distribute Left:** Equidistant horizontal spacing of the left edges of all objects. If objects are of disparate sizes, this command may result in overlapping objects or uneven spacing between objects.

- **Horizontal Distribute Center:** Equidistant horizontal spacing of the horizontal centers of all objects. If objects are of disparate sizes, this command may result in overlapping objects or uneven spacing between objects.

- **Horizontal Distribute Right:** Equidistant horizontal spacing of the right edges of all objects. If objects are of disparate sizes, this command may result in overlapping objects or uneven spacing between objects.

Here is what the Distribute Spacing buttons do (see Figure 18.6):

Figure 18.6
Three objects with distributed spacing. Vertical Distribute Spacing (left) and Horizontal Distribute Spacing (right).

- **Vertical Distribute Spacing:** Equidistant vertical spacing of all objects, regardless of their dimensions. Uses the distance specified in the Spacing measurement field, or, if the Spacing field is set to Auto, distributes all objects evenly between the top and bottom objects among the selected objects.

- **Horizontal Distribute Spacing:** Equidistant horizontal spacing of all objects, regardless of their dimensions. Uses the distance specified in the Spacing measurement field, or, if the Spacing field is set to Auto, distributes all objects evenly between the left and right objects among the selected objects.

- **Spacing Measurement Field:** Specifies the distance between objects created by the Vertical or Horizontal Distribute Spacing commands.

To align or distribute objects or spacing relative to the artboard—to center an object on the artboard, for example—select Align to Artboard from the Align palette menu and then use the appropriate palette button command.

Override the default behavior of the alignment and distribution commands by choosing a *key object*. For example, rather than aligning all objects to the left object when clicking Horizontal Align Left, all objects may be left-aligned to the center object or any other. After selecting all candidates for alignment or distribution, click once on the desired object to make it the key object. All alignment and distribution commands involving the key object will thereafter be relative to the position of the key object.

Restore nonrelative alignment and distribution by choosing Cancel Key Object from the Align palette menu.

Alignment and distribution are relative to the path, which, with certain appearance attributes, may not equal the correct object dimensions. To make all such actions relative to the full object and not the path, choose Use Preview Bounds from the Align palette menu.

BLENDING AND WARPING OBJECTS

Blending and warping, among other uses that will become apparent, can quickly distort and reshape objects without permanent alteration to the objects' paths.

Blending Objects

Blending is the process of morphing one object into another, creating intermediary objects called *steps*. Blending can be used for the purposes of creating smooth color transitions between objects, for creating interceding shapes between two unequal paths, and for creating transformation steps between two objects—for example, blending a small object with a large object fills in the sizes between (see Figure 18.7).

To create a blend, select two or more open or closed path objects and choose Object, Blend, Make. Between the two objects appear intermediary steps using the default blend options.

An alternative to using the Object, Blend, Make command is the Blend tool. Located on the Tools palette beside the Eyedropper tool, the Blend tool has the same effect as the menu command, but with the added benefit of specifying the origin point for the blending. When making a blend using the menu command, objects are blended relative to their center points (both vertically and horizontally). However, selecting any anchor point on the source and destination objects with the Blend tool causes all blend steps to form from the perspective of morphing the source anchor point into the destination's anchor point, including shape and location.

Figure 18.7
Different blends: Smooth color (top), morphing shapes (upper middle, lower middle), and transformation steps (bottom).

Either by double-clicking the Blend tool or choosing Object, Blend, Blend Options, blends may be modified by setting the Spacing and Orientation. Spacing options include Smooth Color (the number of steps is calculated by Illustrator to ensure a smooth color transition between different fill and/or stroke colors), Specified Steps (a number is entered for the quantity of blend steps to create), and Specified Distance (the distance between the corresponding edges of each step determines the number of steps—for example, if a blend is 10 inches across from start to finish, setting a Specified Distance of 1 inch creates 10 blend steps. Orientation is whether the blend steps align to the page regardless of the curvature of the *spine*, the path followed by the blend, or rotate in response to the direction of the spine (see Figure 18.8).

Figure 18.8
Two blends created from pairs of instances of the same object: the first (top) oriented to the page; the second (bottom) oriented to the spine.

Between the blended objects is the spine, which determines the path steps follow when blending. The spine may be manipulated and shaped with the Bézier tools—Direct Selection, Pen, Add Anchor Point, Delete Anchor Point, and Convert Anchor Point—like a normal path. Selecting the blend with the Selection or Direct Selection tools reveals the spine running between the blended objects and through blend steps.

18

To edit the spine, select an end point with the Direct Selection tool or convert an end point from a corner to a smooth point with the Convert Anchor Point tool. Use the Pen and other tools to add or remove anchor points, and edit their angle and curvature as desired with the Direct Selection tool. However the spine is reshaped, the blend steps follow. For more on working with the Bézier tools and editing paths, see Chapter 16, "Understanding and Drawing Paths in Illustrator."

As hinted at in Figure 18.8, the steps in a blend are not objects unto themselves. They do not have anchor points and cannot be edited unless expanded into separate, unblended objects using the Object, Blend, Expand command. Until that time, steps reshape, reiterate, and recalculate based on any changes to the paths or spine of the blended anchor objects.

Also on the Object, Blend submenu are the following commands:

- **Replace Spine:** To replace the spine of a blend with another path, draw the path as a separate object, select both the path and the blend, and select the Replace Spine menu option. The old spine disappears, and the blend now follows the contour of the new path.

- **Reverse Spine:** Reverse the order of blend along the spine.

- **Reverse Front to Back:** Invert the order of blend. For example, if the left blended object is higher in the stacking order than the right, the blend moves backward behind the left object until it meets the front of the right object. This command reverses that.

Remove the blend and restore the original objects to independence by selecting Object, Blend, Release.

Placed images and type may not be used in a blend, though type may be converted to outlines then blended.

Warping

The Warp command distorts objects with 15 different, highly customizable effects (see Figure 18.9). It is a *live effect*, meaning that it applies as an appearance attribute and does not alter the path or the original object. Additionally, multiple warp styles, each building on the results of the previous one, may be applied to the same object for complex effects.

Figure 18.9
Warp effects in action. From top to bottom: Arc (left), Arc Lower (right); Bulge (left), Flag (right); Rise (left), Squeeze.

From the Effect, Warp submenu select which warp style to apply. In the Warp Options dialog change the warp style, choose whether to bend horizontally or vertically, choose the bend amount, and choose the horizontal and vertical distortion. Turn on Preview to see the effects in real time.

Edit applied warp styles by double-clicking the appearance attribute in the Appearance palette.

WORKING WITH 3D OBJECTS

Illustrator includes a trio of basic but powerful 3D effects. Like any effects, these are live appearance attributes that may be saved in graphic styles.

3D Extrude & Bevel

Instantly turn any path, shape, or text into a 3D object with the Extrude & Bevel command. This Illustrator effect *extrudes*, or gives depth to, objects in addition to, or in place of, *beveling* or chiseling their edges (see Figure 18.10).

Figure 18.10
The word Illustrator has been extruded, and CS2 has a bevel.

Accessed from the Effect, 3D submenu, the 3D Extrude & Bevel Options command includes everything needed for basic three-dimensional work (see Figure 18.11). In the Position pop-up menu choose a preset position from which to begin the extrusion, or manually set the position by clicking on and dragging the track cube in three dimensional space. The track cube rotates smoothly through all three axes, the rotation of which may also be specified numerically in the x, y, and z axes measurement fields. To create perspective, as if some surfaces of the object are farther away, set Perspective to a degree between 0 and 160.

In the Extrude & Bevel section set the Extrude Depth, the depth or thickness of the object, and whether the object is solid or hollow (via the two Cap options).

To create a chiseled or mitered face, select a Bevel and set its height and whether the bevel is added to the exterior of the object or carved away from the interior.

The options in the Surface section define the type of light reflection in four modes (see Figure 18.12):

- **Wireframe:** Draw a wireframe or skeletal object with no fill and no shading. Surface lighting options are unavailable with this mode.

- **No Shading:** Fill the object. Using this option does not shade the object according to dimensionality, but merely results in flat-color artwork common to comic book and pop art styles. Surface lighting options are unavailable with this mode.

- **Diffuse Shading:** Fill the object and reflect light softly, as if it had a matte surface.

- **Plastic Shading:** Fill the object and create a shiny surface that reflects light.

18

Figure 18.11
The 3D Extrude & Bevel Options dialog (with More Options shown).

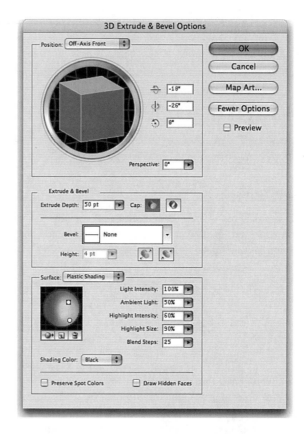

Figure 18.12
3D Revolved objects in the four shading modes: Wireframe, No Shading, Diffuse Shading, and Plastic Shading.

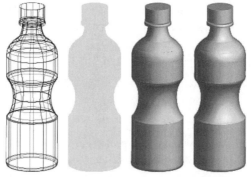

Clicking the More Options button reveals numerous other options in the Surface section. Most prominent is the lighting sphere, which displays at least one light. A light is represented by a white circle on the lighting sphere, and when selected is encased in a box. This is the object's light source(s), from which highlights and shading are calculated (see Figure 18.13). Click and drag on the light to move it around relative to the 3D object.

Figure 18.13
Three variations of the same object, with one (left), two (center), and three (right) light sources defined. The third light source was moved to the back to create backlighting.

Beneath the lighting sphere are three buttons:

- **Move Light Back/Front:** Move the selected light behind or in front of the 3D object.

- **New Light:** Add another light source to the lighting sphere and object.

- **Delete Light:** Remove the selected light.

Also in the Surface area are several measurement fields and other options that appear depending on the selected shading mode:

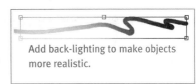

Add back-lighting to make objects more realistic.

- **Light Intensity:** Set the brightness of the currently selected light, from 0% (off) to 100% (pure white).

- **Ambient Light:** Set the amount of light shining on the whole object. Changes here affect all surfaces of the object uniformly.

- **Highlight Intensity:** Set the amount of light reflecting from the object; the higher the percentage, the shinier the object.

- **Highlight Size:** Set the diameter of the selected light source.

- **Blend Steps:** Set the number of steps used in creating smooth shading. The more steps used, the smoother the shading, but the longer it takes to render and print.

- **Shading Color:** Set the color of shadows.

- **Preserve Spot Colors:** Leave spot colors in the object unchanged (otherwise they convert to RGB or CMYK, depending on the document color mode). This feature does not function if the shading is a custom color.

- **Draw Hidden Faces:** By default, Illustrator does not render nonvisible surfaces of a 3D object to save rendering time. Checking this option draws those hidden faces, making them available to shine through transparency in the object.

3D Revolve

3D Revolve takes an open path and revolves it in three-dimensional space to create a solid object. To create a 3D Revolve object, draw a *contour path*, an open path forming the shape of the object's side (optionally include path segments to define the radius, or half the diameter, of its top and bottom surfaces) (see Figure 18.14). With the contour path selected, choose Effect, 3D, Revolve.

Figure 18.14
The open contour path (left),
revolved into a solid 3D object.

In the 3D Revolve Options dialog are Position and Surface sections identical to those in the 3D Extrude & Bevel Options dialog. In place of the Extrude & Bevel section is the Revolve section. Options in the Revolve section are

- **Angle:** Define how far around the path is revolved—360° is a full revolution, creating a solid object; anything less is a partial revolution.

- **Cap:** Set whether the revolved object is solid or hollow, as revealed at the ends if top and bottom surfaces were not drawn in the contour path.

- **Offset:** Enter a value between 0 and 1,000 points to push the sides of the object out from the axis of revolution.

- **From:** Determine from which edge revolution occurs. If the object looks inside out or a curvaceous object becomes a nearly solid cylinder (see Figure 18.15), swap the From edge to the opposite.

Figure 18.15
When revolved along the wrong
edge (left), unpredictable artwork
develops. The same object (right)
revolved from the correct edge.

Try this exercise:

1. With the Pen tool, draw a curvaceous, roughly vertical open path.

2. Set a fill color but no stroke color.

3. Select the path with the Selection tool.

4. Choose Effect, 3D, Revolve.

5. Leave all options at their defaults and check the Preview button. The path should now appear to be a reflective 3D object. If it does not look as expected, switch the setting for the From edge from Left to Right.

Like the other 3D effects, Revolve is a live effect. Revolved objects are still open paths, and can be edited like any other path, with instantaneous reapplication of the 3D effect. To understand the concept of a live effect, try the following exercise:

Under some circumstances, white gaps may appear between surfaces or blend steps in 3D objects. These are *artifacts*, or screen glitches, and neither print nor export.

1. Complete the previous exercise to create a revolved object on the artboard.

2. Select any smooth point on the revolved object with the Direct Selection tool.

3. Using the direction handles, change the curvature of the smooth point and its corresponding path segment. The revolved object will rerender to reflect the changes in the path.

Because the 3D Revolve Options dialog, as well as the other 3D effects dialogs, include full rotation capabilities on all three axes plus perspective, basic transformation of 3D objects' underlying paths is minimized. Though the default revolution is along either the x or y axis (horizontally or vertically), the track cube or axes measurement fields may be employed to rotate an object in any direction (see Figure 18.16). 3D rotation while revolving enables light sources to match across multiple objects when building a scene—something not possible when the Transform palette accomplishes the transformation.

18

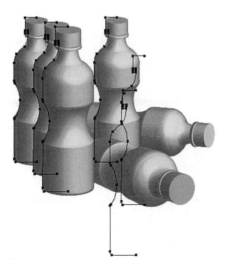

Figure 18.16
All six bottles are exact duplicates of the same path (the rear bottle paths have been scaled down 5%–10% for proper perspective). Note that even the overturned bottles' paths (the dark lines) are still vertical, and that, because they were rotated entirely in the 3D Revolve Options dialog, their highlights and shadows fit the scene.

3D Rotate

Rotate is the 3D effect with a unique and simple purpose: to transform objects in three dimensions without making them *look* like 3D objects (see Figure 18.17).

Figure 18.17
Original point type object (top) and three copies, each with different 3D Rotate effect settings. The shadow instance of the 3D rotated text is also feathered with the Effect, Stylize, Feather command, and its blending mode and transparency are adjusted for context.

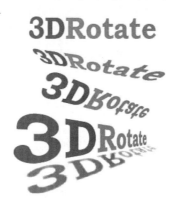

The 3D Rotate Options dialog (accessible by choosing Effect, 3D, Rotate) is, for all intents and purposes, merely the Position section from the 3D Extrude & Bevel options dialog and the 3D Revolve Options dialog. It includes the Position presets, track cube, and measurement fields for the x, y, and z axes as well as Perspective. The Surface area includes a subset of the other 3D tools, with options limited to No Shading and Diffuse Shading.

Despite being 3D rotated, the type in these objects is editable at all times—just like the path in the 3D Revolve section of this chapter. Because 3D objects are effects, their contents always remain editable.

Mapping Artwork to 3D Objects

In the 3D Extrude & Bevel Options and 3D Revolve Options dialogs is the Map Art button, which enables *mapping* or painting symbol artwork on to the surfaces of 3D objects (see the section "Understanding Symbols," later in this chapter). Map Art can apply any symbol to any surface of an extruded, beveled, or revolved object (see Figure 18.18).

Figure 18.18
The 3D revolved bottle with simple mapped art.

To map art to a 3D object, create symbols from the art to be mapped to each surface. Then create a 3D object, and, in the 3D Extrude & Bevel Options or 3D Revolve Options dialog, click the Map Art button.

The Map Art dialog box (see Figure 18.19) shows each of the surfaces created by the 3D effect. With a box, for example, there would be six surfaces for each face of the 3D box. The total number of surfaces, as well as First Surface, Previous Surface, Next Surface, and Last Surface navigation buttons, is at the top of the dialog. In the main window section below it is the surface preview. Light gray areas in the surface preview are surfaces visible in the 3D object as it is currently positioned; dark gray areas are hidden surfaces. As each surface becomes active in the Map Art dialog, that surface in the 3D object is outlined in red in the document window.

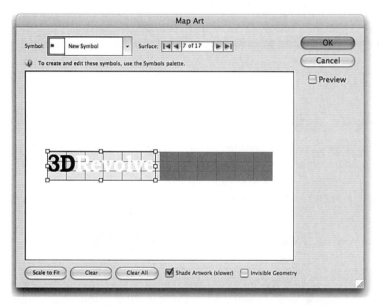

Figure 18.19
The Map Art dialog box.

From the Symbol menu choose the artwork to be mapped to the surface. It appears in the surface preview with a bounding box. The bounding box enables resizing and rotating (move the cursor just outside a corner control point) of the artwork. Arrange the artwork to fit within the desired area. Use the surface navigation buttons to cycle through the various surfaces, applying artwork as needed. Each surface may have the same or a different symbol mapped to it.

At the bottom of the Map Art dialog box are three buttons and two check boxes:

- **Scale to Fit:** Resize artwork nonproportionately to fill the entire surface, including both visible and invisible areas.

- **Clear:** Clear the artwork from the current surface.

- **Clear All:** Clear the artwork from all surfaces.

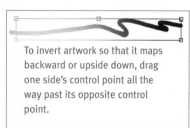

To invert artwork so that it maps backward or upside down, drag one side's control point all the way past its opposite control point.

- **Shade Artwork:** Shade the mapped artwork according to the 3D Extrude & Bevel or 3D Revolve shading mode and options. This option can significantly increase rendering and redraw time.

- **Invisible Geometry:** Hide the 3D object while still drawing the mapped artwork—this is useful, for example, in creating a 3D effect for mapped artwork without having an object or background in 3D.

If the geometry of the 3D object changes, mapped art may alter as well, either to change position or, in the case of adding or subtracting surfaces, to disappear.

Because symbols exist outside of 3D objects, and the Map Art dialog only references symbols, making changes to a symbol on the Symbols palette automatically updates the 3D object's mapped art.

UNDERSTANDING SYMBOLS

Symbols are reusable artwork stored only once in Illustrator, in the Symbols palette or a symbol library. They can make sweeping changes as simple as editing a single object.

Creating and Working with Symbols

After an object is converted to a symbol, unlimited instances of the symbol may be inserted into the document without the increased file size and system RAM overhead associated with multiple copies of an object (see Figure 18.20). Moreover, symbol instances retain their links to the original symbol artwork—changing the content of one changes them all.

Figure 18.20
A package design using symbols. Each object, including the background raster image, vector logo, 3D revolved can, and all other elements on each panel are instances of symbols. Thus each object is stored in the file only once, reducing a 43MB document to 6MB.

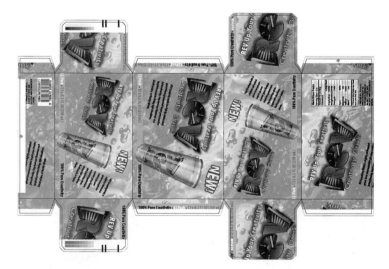

Create a symbol by drawing artwork—paths, shapes, text, meshes, compound paths, embedded images, and almost anything else—and dragging it into the Symbols palette (choose Window, Symbols to display the palette). Hold the Shift key while dragging into the Symbols palette to create a new symbol while simultaneously converting the original artwork to an *instance* of, or reference to, that symbol.

Try this:

1. Draw an object or collection of objects to be turned into a symbol.

2. Select all the objects to comprise the symbol.

3. Drag the object(s) into the Symbols palette—hold Shift after beginning to drag. A new symbol appears in the palette, and the object(s) commute into an instance of that new symbol, no longer editable as individual objects.

4. On the Symbols palette, double-click the new symbol thumbnail to access the Symbol options.

5. Rename the symbol to something meaningful and click OK.

Create instances by dragging the symbol from the Symbols palette into the current document. Dragging a symbol from one document's Symbol palette or artboard into another document automatically adds the symbol to the second document's local Symbols palette.

Symbol instances may be individually transformed and manipulated without breaking their links to the original symbol—one instance may be rotated, for example, and another reflected and resized up to 300% of its original size. Most effects may also be applied to symbol instances to create 3D objects, drop shadows, glows, path offsets, and other effects. Transparency and blending mode changes may also be applied, though access to the actual content and appearance attributes of objects within the instance is not possible without breaking the link to the symbol, thus converting the instance into a standalone object.

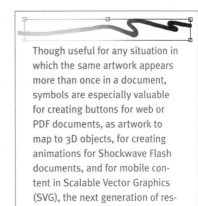

Though useful for any situation in which the same artwork appears more than once in a document, symbols are especially valuable for creating buttons for web or PDF documents, as artwork to map to 3D objects, for creating animations for Shockwave Flash documents, and for mobile content in Scalable Vector Graphics (SVG), the next generation of resolution-independent artwork for online and mobile publishing.

Try this:

1. Create a new symbol.

2. Drag the symbol onto the artboard from the Symbols palette to create an instance.

3. Using the Transform palette or the Selection tool, resize, rotate, skew, or distort the instance.

4. Drag a second instance of the same symbol onto the artboard.

5. Apply an effect from the Effects menu (see the section on effects in Chapter 20, "Working with Placed Graphics and Filters in Illustrator").

When access to the content of a single instance is necessary, the link to the original symbol must be broken. This converts the symbol instance back into a standalone object; any changes made to either the symbol or the broken instance do not affect the other. With the instance selected on the artboard, choose Break Link to Symbol from the Symbols palette menu or press the Break Link to Symbol button at the foot of the Symbols palette. The symbol converts to a normal object group, which may be edited as such or ungrouped into its constituent elements.

To redefine or edit a symbol, simultaneously altering all instances of that symbol, place a single instance of the symbol and break the link to the symbol. Make the necessary changes, select the modified symbol, and choose Redefine Symbol from the Symbols palette menu.

Try this:

1. Create a new symbol.

2. Place two instances of that symbol onto the artboard.

3. With one instance selected, choose Break Link to Symbol from the Symbols palette menu.

4. Ungroup the resulting object and modify it in some way—change fills, paths, or any other change.

5. Reselect all the objects comprising the symbol.

6. On the Symbols palette, ensure that the correct symbol is selected, and choose Redefine Symbol from the Symbols palette menu. The second, unmodified instance of the symbol should instantly update to reflect the changes made to the first edited symbol.

Create symbol libraries from the content of the Symbols palette. After all desired symbols have been added to the Symbols palette, remove those undesired ones (the default symbols, for instance) and select Save Symbol Library As from the Symbols palette menu. The resulting file is an Illustrator document containing nothing but the symbol library, which may be shared with any other Illustrator CS2 user, on either the Windows or Macintosh platform.

Copy symbols by dragging them from the Symbols palette onto the New Symbol button at the bottom of the palette or by selecting Duplicate Symbol from the Symbols palette menu.

Rearrange symbols by dragging them from their original location in the Symbols palette to any other location.

At the bottom of the Symbols palette are five buttons:

The Adobe Studio Exchange website (http://studio.adobe.com) features numerous downloadable and free symbol libraries created by Adobe and other Illustrator users. Upload and share yours!

- **Place Symbol Instance:** Equivalent to dragging a symbol from the Symbols palette, use this button to insert an instance of the selected symbol onto the artboard. The insertion happens at the center of the view.

- **Replace Symbol:** Replace the selected symbol instance on the artboard with an instance of the symbol selected in the Symbols palette.

- **Break Link to Symbol:** Break the link between the instance and the symbol, converting the instance to a free-standing group.

- **New Symbol:** Create a new symbol from the selected object(s).

- **Delete Symbol:** Delete the symbol(s) selected in the Symbols palette.

Included with Illustrator are 25 prebuilt symbol libraries, including the libraries loaded into the Symbols palette upon the creation of new RGB or CMYK color mode documents. Access these preinstalled libraries from the Window, Symbol Libraries submenu, or from the Open Symbol Library submenu on the Symbols palette menu. Each new library loaded appears onscreen in its own palette (multiple libraries form a tabbed palette group). To make any symbol library load automatically with Illustrator, thus making it accessible to all new documents, choose Persistent from that library's palette menu.

Using the Symbol Sprayer

In addition to placing a single instance of symbols by dragging out of the Symbols palette or using the Place Symbol Instance button, the Symbol Sprayer tool sprays many instances onto the artboard at one time in a random fashion (see Figure 18.21). The result is a single object called a *symbol set*, which acts much like a group in that it may be transformed and modified as a single object or edited with the Symbolism tools (see the section "Symbolism Tools," later in this chapter).

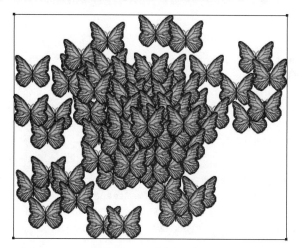

Figure 18.21
Randomly grouped symbols in a symbol set after using the Symbol Sprayer tool.

To create a symbol set, select the Symbol Sprayer tool on the Tools palette and click, drag, or click and hold to begin spraying symbols.

Instances in a symbol set interact with one another as if they had volume. Clicking and holding with the Symbol Sprayer tool progressively pushes symbol instances outward from the center of the nozzle. Though they also overlap one another and grow into a dense stacking order, they also push each other out of the way. Selecting a different symbol on the Symbols palette and continuing to spray into the same symbol set adds instances of the new symbol into the existing symbol set, causing the instances already there to react to the volume of new instances as well.

Hold the Alt key (Windows users) or the Option key (Mac users) while spraying to delete instances.

To create an additional symbol set instead of adding to an existing one, lock the symbol set in the Layers palette or by choosing Object, Lock from the menu bar before spraying.

Double-clicking the Symbol Sprayer opens the Symbolism Tools Options dialog (see Figure 18.22), where the following options are set:

18

Figure 18.22
The Symbol Sprayer tab of the
Symbolism Tools Options dialog.

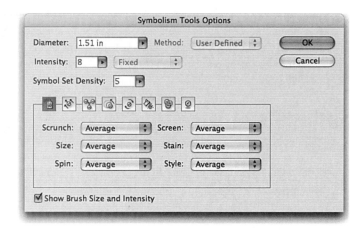

- **Diameter:** Specify the brush or nozzle size for the Symbol Sprayer tool.

- **Method:** Specify how, if at all, the Symbolism tools affect new instances. The User Defined option adjusts instances in relation to the cursor (drag quickly to space out effect, drag slowly or hold in place to intensify the effect). The Select Random option randomizes the effect of the Symbolism tools. The Average option evaluates the effects of existing instances in the set and creates new instances based upon the average effect—for example, if the average instance in a set is rotated 45°, new objects will, typically, be rotated 45° as well.

- **Intensity:** Specify the rate of change between instances, as defined by scrunch, size, spin, and so on. The Fixed option equals the intensity value set in the measurement field, and the Use Pen Pressure option uses the pressure from an electronic tablet and stylus to vary intensity in place of the value in the measurement field. This pop-up menu option is unavailable if Illustrator does not register the presence of a tablet and stylus installed on the system.

- **Symbol Set Density:** Define how densely packed are the instances in a set. Higher values equal greater density or instance bunching; lower values push instances further apart.

The other options on the Symbol Sprayer tab are relative to the settings of the various Symbolism tools (see the next section), which may be applied while spraying by changing any of the values in the pop-up menus to User Defined. By default, each is set to Average, which has the same effect as the Average setting of the Method pop-up menu at the top of the dialog.

Symbolism Tools

In addition to the Symbol Sprayer tool, which creates symbol instances in a symbol set, seven other Symbolism tools control various effects and transformations of the instances within sets by clicking with the tool and dragging across the set. The tools are (see Figure 18.23)

Figure 18.23
The Symbolism tools in action. The original symbol set is in the upper left.

- **Shifter:** Move instances in a symbol set. Hold the Shift key to bring affected instances to the front and Shift+Alt (Windows users) or Shift-Option (Mac users) to send them behind.

- **Scruncher:** Pull instances closer together. Hold Alt or Option to push instances apart.

- **Sizer:** Resize instances within a symbol set because they cannot be modified directly with the Selection tool. Instances are sized up by default. Hold Alt or Option to size down. Resized instances interact with other instances, pushing them away or pulling them closer to fill the space. Hold Shift while sizing to maintain density.

- **Spinner:** Rotate instances. While spinning, instances display arrows indicating their directions of appearance and travel.

- **Stainer:** Color instances with the active fill color like applying a semitransparent stain (not like opaque paint). The longer the left mouse button is depressed over instances, the more pronounced the staining. Staining varies the amount of color applied as the mouse drags across instances. Hold the Shift key while dragging to create a uniform stain effect. Hold the Alt or Option key to reduce color staining.

- **Screener:** Alter the opacity of instances by making them more transparent. Hold the Alt or Option key to reverse the effect and make transparent instances more opaque.

- **Styler:** Apply styles and appearance attributes to instances. To use, deselect all objects and choose a graphic style or set appearance attributes. Select the Symbol Styler tool and begin clicking or clicking and dragging across instances in the set. The effect varies as the mouse drags across instances. Hold the Shift key while dragging to style uniformly. Hold Alt/Option to reduce the amount of styling.

> As with any painting tool in Illustrator, easily change the brush size from the keyboard without the need to use an options dialog. Just press the left bracket key ([) to decrease the size of a brush or nozzle, and the right bracket key (]) to increase the size—even in the middle of a stroke.

If the symbol set contains instances from multiple symbols, the Symbolism tools affect only the symbol or symbols highlighted in the Symbols palette. This enables isolation of effects to specific symbols' instances. To affect other instances in the set, select their symbol(s) in the Symbols palette.

Double-click any one of the Symbolism tools to change its options in the Symbolism Tools Options dialog. Pay particular attention to the Diameter setting because the Symbolism tools affect all instances beneath their nozzle—the effect is more profound at the center—which could lead to unexpected results.

USING LIVE PAINT

New in Illustrator CS2 is Live Paint, a unique but more natural way of painting. By taking the focus away from objects and stacking order and concentrating on coloring within the lines, Live Paint seeks to bridge the gap between vector drawing and raster painting. For this reason, Live Paint is especially freeing when used in conjunction with the Pencil tool.

Creating and Using Live Paint Groups

Create a Live Paint group by drawing shapes or open or closed paths with any of the drawing, shape, or line tools. Select all paths and objects, and choose Object, Live Paint, Make. Then all the paths and objects in the Live Paint group are treated like equal areas for coloring—stacking order is negated. When paths and objects overlap, their overlapping areas are treated as areas equal with non-overlapping areas—even if not all the parts of paths and objects are visible (see Figure 18.24).

Figure 18.24
In this 1-minute drawing of the chapter author, the original paths (left) overlap in various places. When converted to a Live Paint group, each overlapping and non-overlapping area created by the paths is separately filled to create the final Live Paint drawing (right).

In a Live Paint group are *faces* (fillable areas) and *edges* (strokable areas dividing faces). Fill faces with the Live Paint Bucket by choosing a color, gradient, or pattern from the Swatches palette, mixing a new color on the Color palette, or creating a gradient on the Gradient palette. As the Live Paint Bucket cursor moves over a Live Paint group, each face in the group highlights individually in red; clicking floods the highlighted face with the fill. Drag the Live Paint Bucket across multiple faces to fill them all. Hold the Shift key to change the Live Paint Bucket into stroke painting mode and fill strokes with the active stroke color.

Try this:

1. Create a drawing with several overlapping (open or closed) paths and shapes.

2. Select all paths and shapes with the Selection tool.

3. Choose Object, Live Paint, Make.

4. Select the Live Paint Bucket and begin filling in areas of the Live Paint group.

Use the Live Paint Selection tool to select faces and edges for coloring. Selecting a face brings the fill swatch to the front on the Tools palette; selecting an edge brings the stroke swatch to the front. Shift-click to select multiple faces or edges. Double-click the Live Paint Selection tool on a face or edge to select it and all faces and edges connected to it. Triple-click the Live Paint Selection tool on a face or edge to select it and all other faces or edges of the same color.

Paths in Live Paint groups remain editable at all times. Adjust paths with the Direct Selection, Pen, Pencil, and Bézier path editing tools. Faces and edges dynamically adapt to match path modifications. Paths and shapes may be deleted from Live Paint groups. Any faces or edges that were previously divided but combine as a result of path or shape deletions, adopt the fill and stroke of the largest adjoining faces and/or edges.

Additionally, new paths and shapes may be added to the Live Paint group at any time—for example, to further divide a face for coloring. There are four ways to add paths or shapes to an existing Live Paint group:

- Draw the paths and/or shapes desired, and, with the Selection tool, select the paths and shapes as well as the Live paint group. Choose Object, Live Paint, Add Paths.

- Draw the paths and/or shapes desired, and, with the Selection tool, select the paths and shapes as well as the Live paint group. On the Control palette, choose Add Paths.

- Double-click the Live Paint group with the Selection tool. The group is bordered by a gray frame, indicating that the group is now being edited. Draw the desired paths or shapes. To exit Live Paint group editing mode, deselect the group by double-clicking the artboard or pasteboard outside the group.

- On the Layers palette, drag existing or new paths and shapes inside the Live Paint group sub-layer.

To convert a Live Paint group into individual objects that mirror the constituent faces and edges (to export to other applications, for example), select the Live Paint group and choose Object, Live Paint, Expand. Each face and edge becomes a separate filled object.

Double-click the Live Paint Bucket to access the Live Paint Bucket Options where the highlight color and width may be changed or disabled and where whether to paint fills (faces), strokes (edges), or both may be decided. Choosing to paint strokes with the Live Paint Bucket tool eliminates the need to first select an edge with the Live Paint Selection Tool or to Shift-click with the Live Paint Bucket.

18

Locating Live Paint Gaps

When objects and paths don't line up or overlap gaps can occur. Live Paint stops filling faces and edges when it encounters the edge of an object or a gap between objects. This can result in unpainted areas of the artwork. Large gaps should be filled by editing paths or creating new paths to cover them, but smaller gaps can be handled automatically with Live Paint Gap Detection.

First, make sure Live Paint Gaps are viewable by choosing View, Show Live Paint Gaps.

Set the way Illustrator handles gaps in the Gap Options dialog available by choosing Object, Live Paint, Gap Options with the Live Paint group selected (see Figure 18.25):

Figure 18.25
The Live Paint Gap Options dialog.

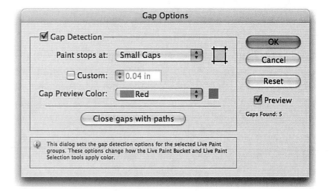

- **Gap Detection:** Determine whether paint "leaks" through to paint small gaps between paths.

- **Paint Stops At:** Set whether paint stops at Small, Medium, or Large Gaps. The actual values of Small, Medium, or Large Gaps are shown in the Custom measurement field when you change the Paint Stops At setting.

- **Custom:** Enter a custom size for gaps at which paint should stop. The Custom field displays measurements in the units specified during document creation, but it accepts any measurement unit Illustrator supports—px (pixels), in (inches), " (inches), p (pica), mm (millimeters), and cm (centimeters).

- **Gap Preview Color:** Change the preview color of gaps with a predefined color. Choose a custom color by selecting Custom Color from the pop-up menu or by clicking on the color swatch.

- **Close Gaps with Paths:** Close gaps detected with the previous settings by inserting new paths into the Live Paint group.

Under the Preview check box is the number of gaps detected using the active settings.

Understanding the Limitations to Live Paint

Because Live Paint groups are special objects unto themselves, some of the features and commands that work with many or all other Illustrator objects do not work with Live Paint groups.

Certain objects cannot be made into Live Paint groups, including type, placed images, and brush strokes. For these objects, though, there are ways to work around the limitation:

- **Type:** Convert to outlines first (see the section on Creating Outlines in Chapter 19, "Working with Type in Illustrator").

- **Placed Images (linked or embedded):** Trace the image with Live Trace first (see the section on Live Trace in Chapter 20).

- **Objects with Brushes:** Expand the brushes and brushed objects into paths.

The following do not work on Live Paint faces, edges, or groups:

- Brushes

- Effects menu effects

- Envelope Distort

- Flare objects

- Gradient meshes

- Graphs

- Magic Wand tool

- Making a clipping mask from

- Making a crop area from

- Making an opacity mask from (makes the opacity mask from the entire group, not selected faces or edges)

- Making auto-slices from

- Making blends from

- Making guides from

- Multiple strokes and fills

- Object, Slice, Make (applies to entire group, not selected faces or edges)

- Pathfinder commands and effects

- Rasterize (applies to entire group, not selected faces or edges)

- Selecting Same (commands)

- Stroke alignment options

- Symbols

- Text wrap (applies to entire group, not selected faces or edges)

- Transparency and blending modes (applies to entire group)

18

FINAL THOUGHTS

Working with objects in Illustrator is, first and foremost, about creativity—if you can imagine it, you can draw it. But it's also about efficiency and reducing repetitive tasks.

In the old days, Illustrator required you to draw everything by hand. Multiple sizes of objects needed to be drawn individually. If you needed duplicates of objects, you copied and pasted and lived with the increased file size and the higher processor and RAM overhead. When the duplicate objects needed to be modified, you edited them one by one or copied, pasted, and positioned them all over again. Warped objects were hand drawn, with tedious tweaking of paths and careful adjustment of direction handles. Lining up and spacing objects required guides and temporary boxes used as spacers. If you wanted 3D—well, you didn't do it in Illustrator.

Illustrator's 3D effects aren't the end-all and be-all of 3D work—they still don't compare to dedicated applications such as Maya, Bryce, and Lightwave—but do they need to measure up to those applications? Most 3D work is of the simple nature of extrusion or rotation. Why use an entirely different 3D rendering application, with a completely new user interface to learn, for simple work? Those applications have valuable roles in the modern creative workflow, but when only simple dimensionality is needed, you can do it more conveniently within the familiar environment of Illustrator. From there, Illustrator's tight Creative Suite integration enables rapid deployment of the 3D objects to InDesign, Photoshop, or GoLive.

Even the way in which Illustrator fills objects is improving. What more natural, more familiar way to color is there than simply coloring between the lines? Live Paint in particular is a huge productivity enhancer when used judiciously. With the right artwork, it takes your mental focus off the objects and places it where it belongs—in the artwork.

As Illustrator matures, more and more of the menial tasks are becoming automated. You'll find that you spend less time working the mechanics of a drawing and more time being creative.

18

19

WORKING WITH TYPE IN ILLUSTRATOR

When Adobe released InDesign 2.0 to the public in January 2002 it featured revolutionary type handling and typography controls never before available on the desktop. InDesign CS further expanded type freedom and control in October 2003. Now, all of InDesign's type-handling power is in Illustrator CS2.

UNDERSTANDING TYPE OBJECTS

Almost as often as it's used for illustration, Illustrator is called upon to create type-heavy documents like flyers, menus, labels, and packaging. There are four kinds of type objects: Point Type, Area Type, Type on a Path, and Legacy Type.

Point Type and Area Type Objects

Of all the methods for entering type, Point Type is the simplest to work with. It is so named because it begins with a single end point and no path segments (see Figure 19.1).

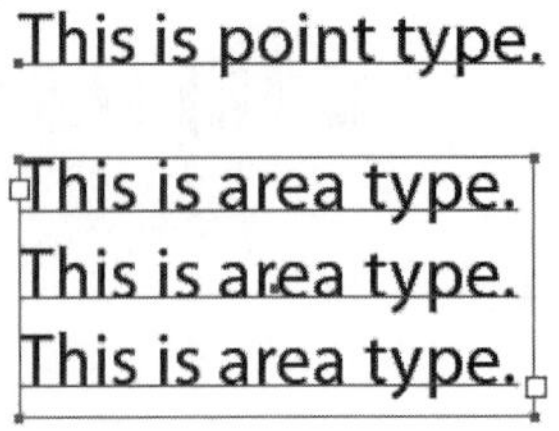

Figure 19.1
Point type (top) is click-and-type from a single point. Area type (bottom) is text flowing within an area.

This is point type.

This is area type.
This is area type.
This is area type.

To create point type, choose the Type tool from the Tools palette, click and release on the artboard, and begin typing. Text flows from the inception point outward—either left, right, or to both sides, depending on the alignment set in the Paragraph palette. Point type does not *wrap*, or automatically break and flow to the next line, as does area type. To create a new line of text in the same point type object, press Return or Enter.

Try this:

1. Select the Type tool from the Tools palette.

2. Click and release on the artboard.

3. Begin typing anything—**Hey diddle diddle, the cat and the fiddle** works. Note how the text grows outward to the right.

4. Press Return or Enter and type another line—for example, **The cow jumped over the moon**.

In point type, the type *is* the object. Area type is *contained* within an area, creating a container-content relationship. To create area type, click with the Type tool and drag to define the area for the type. This area becomes what InDesign calls a *text frame*.

Area type may also be created from a preexisting shape—for instance, a star—and text flows in the shape of a star (see Figure 19.2).

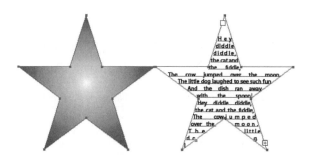

Figure 19.2
The star shape (left) converted (right) to a type area (with forced justification).

Try this:

1. Create a closed path or shape with the drawing or shape tools.

2. Select the Type tool from the Tools palette.

3. Click along the object's path. Its fill and stroke, if active, disappears.

4. Begin typing. Type several lines to observe how the type wraps into the shape of the original path. That path is now the shape of the area type or text frame.

Either the Type or Area Type tool (or Vertical Type or Vertical Area Type tool) may be used to convert a shape or path to area type.

A major difference between point type and area type is the way each relates to the bounding box. Clicking on either object with the Selection tools reveals its bounding box. In area type, changing the shape of the bounding box changes the *area* into which type flows—making more or less room for text to flow; using the control points to change the bounding box on point type distorts the text itself.

To edit existing type of any kind, choose the Type tool and click along the *baseline*, the bottom line, of text.

There are six type tools (click and hold on the Type tool to find the other tools):

- **Type tool:** Edit type of any kind. Click to create point type. Click and drag to create area type. Click an existing closed path to convert it to a type area.

- **Area Type tool:** Click an existing closed path to convert it to a type area.

- **Path Type tool:** Click an existing open or closed path to type along the path (not within its area).

- **Vertical Type tool:** Creates vertical type, where each character or glyph entered appears below the prior glyph. Click to create point type. Click and drag to create area type. Click an existing closed path to convert it to a vertical type area.

- **Vertical Area Type tool:** Click an existing closed path to convert it to a vertical type area.

- **Vertical Path tool:** Click an existing open or closed path to type vertically along the path (not within its area).

> **Caution**
>
> If you miss the baseline of text when clicking with the Type tool, Illustrator creates a new, empty point type instance, which unnecessarily complicates the document.

19

Type Areas

In addition to the features shared with point type, area type offers some special functions of its own. Among them are your ability to create multiple columns in a type area, include insets, and flow text between multiple, otherwise independent, areas.

With a type area selected, choosing Type, Area Type Options accesses the Area Type Options dialog:

- **Width:** Set the overall width of the type area.

- **Height:** Set the overall height or depth of the type area.

- **Number:** Set the number of rows or columns in the type area. Setting columns to a number higher than 1 creates columnar text; adding more than a single row turns the type area into a table.

- **Span:** Set the width of columns or height of rows.

- **Fixed:** Toggles whether rows or columns resize when the type area resizes, or whether more columns or rows are added (or subtracted) in response to resizing the type area.

- **Gutter:** Set the width of the space between columns or rows.

- **Inset Spacing:** *Insets* are internal margins that push content inward from the edges of the container. Thus the Inset Spacing is the width and depth of the margin between the text and the path of the type area. One measurement sets all sides equally.

- **First Baseline:** Set the alignment of the baseline, or bottom, of the first line of text relative to the top of the type area. Options are

  - **Ascent:** The top of characters with ascenders (for example, *f*) are contained within the type area.

  - **Cap Height:** The top of capital letters (for example, *F*) are flush with the top of the area.

  - **Leading:** The baseline of type is the same distance from the top of the area as it is from the baseline of the next line of text.

  - **x Height:** The top of lowercase letters without ascenders (for example, *x*) are flush with the top of the area.

  - **Em Box Height:** For use in Asian fonts (and available if Show Asian Options is checked in the preferences), the top of the em box in Asian fonts is flush with the top of the area.

  - **Fixed:** Use the value of the Min measurement box to define baseline spacing.

  - **Legacy:** Use the first baseline option from text created in previous versions of Illustrator.

- **Text Flow Options:** Set in which direction text flows across multicolumn or multirow text areas, either left-to-right and then top-to-bottom, or top-to-bottom and then left-to-right.

Type that does not fit entirely in a given type area is called *overset*, and overset text is invisible. A red plus sign in the lower-right corner of a type area (or at the end of point or path type) indicates the presence of overset text. There are several ways to resolve the situation of overset text:

- Delete the extra text.

- Reduce the type or leading size.

- Reduce paragraph spacing.

- Increase or decrease the number of columns in a text area.

- Reduce the text area inset.

- Resize the text area.

- Create additional threaded text areas.

Threading is the process of linking one text area to another so that text flows freely between them—text that does not fit in one area moves automatically and dynamically to the next, the one beyond that, and so on (see Figure 19.3). Threading may be created between one type area and another empty type area, a closed path that is converted to a type area, and another type area drawn and threaded in one step.

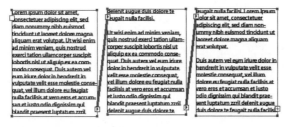

Figure 19.3
Threaded text areas, connected by the threading indicators.

To thread text into an existing object, either another type area or a closed path, click the red plus sign in the lower-right corner (this plus sign is located within the *out port*), of the first type area. The cursor changes to a loaded cursor, which, when clicked somewhere inside the destination area, threads the two areas and enables the overset text from the first to flow into the second. Threading may occur between text areas of any shape and size as well as to type on a path.

To thread text into a new type area that does not yet exist, click the red plus sign in the out port of the first type area. With the loaded cursor, click and drag to define the shape of the destination type area. Upon releasing the mouse button, the new area is created and threaded with the first, and overset text flows into the new area. Create additional text areas as needed.

Selecting any text area in a thread indicates the direction in which text is threaded by displaying lines connecting the out port(s) of source areas to the upper left in ports of destination areas. The threading indicators may be hidden by selecting View, Hide Text Threads.

To disable threading and return text to an overset status, delete the second or subsequent text areas; the text itself is not deleted.

Type on a Path Objects

Used primarily for short passages of text and special effects, type on a path is the third of four types of text objects. Point type flows outward on a straight plane. Area type fills a specific volume. Type

19

on a path follows a path, causing text to flow in whatever direction a path might take, including around corner points, through the curves of smooth points, and all the way around shapes (see Figure 19.4).

Figure 19.4
Examples of type on a path objects.

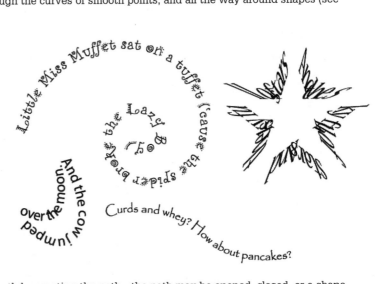

Begin creating type on a path by creating the path—the path may be opened, closed, or a shape. Draw the path and click on it with the Type tool or Type on a Path tool. For vertical type, where each subsequent glyph appears below the prior glyph, use either the Vertical Type tool or the Vertical Type on a Path tool. Clicking a path with any of these tools causes three things to happen: the object is converted to a type on a path object; the original fill, stroke, and any other appearance attributes are removed; and the I-beam text cursor is inserted at the point of click, ready for you to type.

Clicking on a closed path with the Type or Vertical Type tool turns it into a type area. Use the Type on a Path or Vertical Type on a Path tool to convert a closed path to a type on a path object. Any of the four may be used on open paths.

Typing (or pasting text from the Clipboard) causes text to follow along the path until it reaches the end of the path, at which point it oversets (see the previous section on Type Areas for a definition of overset text and how to work with it).

Try creating type on a path:

1. With any of the drawing, line, or shape tools, create a path.

2. Select the Type on a Path tool from the Tools palette (click and hold on the Type tool to reveal it).

3. Click on the path, which should become an unfilled, unstroked path outline regardless of any prior appearance attributes, with a flashing I-beam.

4. Type a favorite nursery rhyme—for example, `Little Miss Muffet sat on a tuffet ('cause the spider broke the La-Z-Boy)`. The text flows around the path.

Select the text with one of the Type tools, or select the entire object with the Selection tool, and apply the desired styling. Type on a path may be styled with the Character, OpenType, Color, and Swatches palette like any other text object (see the sections on the Character palette and the

OpenType palette in this chapter). Most of the options on the Paragraph palette are also applicable, but because type on a path does not allow carriage returns, the Space Before and Space After a Paragraph options have no effect (see the sections on the Paragraph palette in this chapter). The alignment buttons along the top of the Paragraph palette are especially useful when working with type on a path because they affect where the text begins its journey around the path.

To raise or lower type relative to the path—for example, to put type *inside* the path area rather than its default exterior—use the Baseline Shift option on the Character palette. Alternatively, choose Type, Type On a Path, Type On a Path Options. The same options are also available by double-clicking the Type on a Path tool in the Tools palette.

The Type On a Path Options dialog includes four Align to Path options (see Figure 19.5):

Figure 19.5
Align to Path options (from top to bottom): Ascender, Descender, Center, and Baseline.

- **Ascender:** The top of characters with ascenders (for example *f*) align flush with the path. This option has the effect of putting the type below the path (or inside shapes and closed paths).

- **Descender:** Align relative to the bottom portions of type, using descenders (for example *g*). This option places all portions of text outside the path, leaving a space equal to the descender height between the path and the baseline.

- **Center:** Align the vertical center of the type to the path. Because the center is the midpoint between the ascender and descender, such aligned type often appears off center on the path. Adjust with the Character palette Baseline Shift.

- **Baseline:** (Default) Align the text to the path relative to its baseline (for example, the bottom of characters like *x* that do not have descenders).

Also in the Type on a Path Options dialog are the following options:

- **Effect:** (Also accessible from the Type, Type on a Path menu.) Define how the individual characters of type on a path react to the path (see Figure 19.6).

- **Flip:** Flip the text so that it follows the opposite side of a path.

- **Spacing:** Set the amount of padding between the end of the text and the beginning.

Figure 19.6
Type on a Path effects (from top to
bottom): Rainbow, Skew, 3D
Ribbon, Stair Step, and Gravity.

When a type on a path object is selected with the Selection tool, additional, otherwise invisible, structures appear. Specifically, brackets appear at either end of the path, a center point bar appears in the middle, and in and out ports similar to area type show on the ends (see Figure 19.7).

Figure 19.7
End brackets (A and B), the center
point bar (C), and in and out ports
(D and E) appear when the object
is selected with the Selection tool.

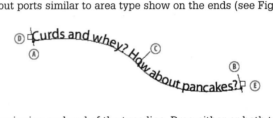

End brackets control the beginning and end of the type line. Drag either or both to indent the text.

The center point bar is exceptionally useful. Not only does dragging it change the center point of the text, moving the text to a different place on the path, but it can also flip type to the other side of the path. Click on and drag the center point bar to the opposite side of the path to flip type—which has the same effect as the Flip check box in the Type on a Path Options dialog.

Just as with type areas, type on a path may be threaded. If text oversets on a single type on a path object, you can thread it to another or even between type areas and type paths. Click the overset red plus sign in one or the other object's out port, and then click in another object's in port or use the loaded cursor to initiate a new type on a path (from a preexisting path) or area type object.

A common question is whether type on a path can be converted to point type or area type—or vice versa. Strictly speaking, no. However, text may be copied from and pasted into and between any of the three editable type objects.

Despite the fact that the path is unfilled and unstroked, type on a path is still on a path. It has anchor points and path segments like any other path, and it may be edited like any other path with the Bézier, drawing, and Direct Selection tools. Any changes to the path instantly affect the flow of type.

Legacy Text Objects

In Illustrator CS the way type is handled in the application changed dramatically. Text created in Illustrator 10 or earlier is not the same kind of object as it is in CS or CS2. This older type is called *legacy text*. Legacy text can be identified on the artboard as having an *X* through its bounding box, much like the way placed and linked images appear.

Legacy text *does* print, contrary to popular misconception. It can even be moved. However, to edit the text or apply live effects, it must be updated to the newer type format pioneered with Illustrator CS.

There are a few ways to update legacy text:

- Click the Update button when Illustrator prompts to update the legacy text upon opening a document that includes legacy text.

- Click the legacy text with one of the Type tools, as if it were directly editable. A warning appears asking whether the legacy text should be updated. Click Update to make the text a modern type object.

- Select the legacy text object with the Selection tool and choose Type, Legacy Text, Update Selected Legacy Text.

- Update all legacy text in a document in one sweep with the Type, Legacy Text, Update All Legacy Text menu command. In order for the command to update legacy text objects, they must all be unlocked.

The Type, Legacy Text menu command is grayed out and disabled if the document does not contain any instances of legacy text.

Because type handling has completely changed in recent versions of Illustrator, converting from legacy text introduces a risk of text composition differences. Glyphs in all type objects (point, area, and path type) may change how they relate to one another with respect to kerning, tracking, and other compositional aspects. Changes are usually most obvious, however, in area type where Illustrator's new paragraph composer may change the way lines of type hyphenate and wrap in paragraphs, resulting in the possible introduction of extra space at the bottom of the area, or even in oversetting of type that previously fit within the area.

> Unlock legacy type or any object by selecting it and choosing Object, Unlock. Unlock all locked objects with Object, Unlock All. Additionally, objects can be (and layers *must* be) unlocked by clearing the padlock beside the layer or sub-layer entry on the Layers palette.

WORKING WITH TYPE

After type objects have been created, they should be formatted and styled.

The Character Palette

All character level formatting is handled on the Character palette (see Figure 19.8). Open the Character palette from the Window, Type menu. Choose Show Options from the Character palette menu to see all options. With any type object selected with the Selection tool or highlighted with the Text tool, set any character-level options:

Figure 19.8
The Character palette (with options showing).

- **Font Family:** The type or font family. Illustrator displays on this list all functioning OpenType, TrueType, and Type1 PostScript fonts installed on the system. Fonts listed at the bottom of the list, below the divider line, are those that Illustrator believes contain errors or are not functioning properly.

- **Font Style:** The particular style of font or typeface available within the selected font family. Typical styles, which vary with each font family, include Roman, Normal, Regular, Bold, Italic, Bold Italic, Medium, Light, Caption, Display, and hundreds of other possible styles.

- **Font Size:** The size of type in points. Most fonts are drawn by designers at slightly different sizes; therefore, 12-point glyphs from one typeface will not necessarily be the same height as 12-point glyphs from another. A list of common sizes is available via the pop-up menu, or the measurement field accepts input in whole points or hundredths of point increments (for example, 12.56 pt).

- **Leading:** The amount of space between lines. A list of common sizes is available via the pop-up menu, or the measurement field accepts input in whole points or hundredths of point increments (for example, 16.25 pt). Setting leading to Auto automatically creates a leading of 120% of the font size. Auto leading is indicated by the presence of parentheses around the measurement.

- **Kerning:** Use to adjust two letters at a time to make the space between them more optically correct. For example, the *A* and *V* shown in the icon; when paired, the slanting of the capital *A* and capital *V* cause unsightly white space. Negative kerning values are used to bring the characters physically closer together so they *appear* to be as far apart as most other glyph pairings. A list of common sizes is available via the pop-up menu, or the measurement field accepts input in whole numbers. Setting kerning to Auto uses information that may be encoded within the font to determine kerning pairs. Using Optical allows Illustrator to read the text and adjust kerning pairs based on its observations. Only Auto and Optical are accessible if any glyphs are highlighted (a single glyph holds the kerning changes, which affect its distance to the next glyph on its right). To set kerning, insert the cursor between the two glyphs to kern and then use the Character palette kerning options.

- **Tracking:** The horizontal spacing between all selected glyphs. Tracking respects kerning; thus if *A* and *V* are kerned for appearance, tracking spaces them out slightly less than it would blocky pairings like an *H* followed by an *M*. A list of common sizes is available via the pop-up menu, or the measurement field accepts input in whole numbers.

- **Horizontal Scale:** Adjusts in percentages the horizontal scaling of glyphs. A list of common sizes is available via the pop-up menu, or the measurement field accepts input in whole percentage or hundredths of a percent increments (for example, 98.25%).

- **Vertical Scale:** Adjusts in percentages the vertical scaling of glyphs. A list of common sizes is available via the pop-up menu, or the measurement field accepts input in whole percentage or hundredths of a percent increments (for example, 98.25%).

- **Baseline Shift:** Modifies the baseline of selected text, raising it up (positive values) or down (negative values) beyond the expected baseline. A list of common sizes is available via the pop-up menu, or the measurement field accepts input in whole points or hundredths of a point increments (for example, 5.25 pt).

- **Character Rotation:** Rotates selected characters individually. This option is useful, for example, in creating a haphazard or "ransom note" seesawing of text in a single point or area type line. A list of common sizes is available via the pop-up menu, or the measurement field accepts input in whole percentage or hundredths of a percent increments (for example, 45.25%).

- **Underline:** New in Illustrator CS2, click this button to underline the selected text.

- **Strikethrough:** New in Illustrator CS2, click this button to place a horizontal line through the selected text.

- **Language:** Specify the language of the selected text on a character level to facilitate Illustrator's built-in multilingual spell-checking and hyphenation features.

On the Character palette menu are other useful options, including changing the case of selected text; creating superscript or subscript type; and the No Break command, which prevents highlighted words from hyphenating or, in the case of multiple highlighted words, wrapping onto different lines from one another. For example, it is incorrect to wrap a proper name in the middle to another line unless absolutely unavoidable.

The Paragraph Palette

After character-level formatting is paragraph-level formatting, which controls everything that happens between the beginning of a paragraph and pressing Return or Enter. This includes alignment, indents, spacing, and hyphenation. These options and more are set on the Paragraph palette (see Figure 19.9). Open the Paragraph palette from the Window, Type menu.

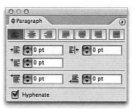

Figure 19.9
The Paragraph Palette (with options showing).

Along the top row of the Paragraph palette are the alignment buttons, which control the horizontal alignment of text (see Figure 19.10):

Figure 19.10
Text areas aligned (from left to right): Left, Center, Right, Justify with Last Line Aligned Left, and Justify All Lines.

Lorem ipsum dolor sit amet, consectetuer adipiscing elit, sed diam nonummy nibh euismod tincidunt ut laoreet dolore magna aliquam erat volutpat. Ut wisi enim ad minim veniam, quis nostrud exerci tation ullamcorper suscipit lobortis nisl ut aliquip ex ea com-

Lorem ipsum dolor sit amet, consectetuer adipiscing elit, sed diam nonummy nibh euismod tincidunt ut laoreet dolore magna aliquam erat volutpat. Ut wisi enim ad minim veniam, quis nostrud exerci tation ullamcorper suscipit lobortis nisl ut aliquip ex ea com-

Lorem ipsum dolor sit amet, consectetuer adipiscing elit, sed diam nonummy nibh euismod tincidunt ut laoreet dolore magna aliquam erat volutpat. Ut wisi enim ad minim veniam, quis nostrud exerci tation ullamcorper suscipit lobortis nisl ut aliquip ex ea con-

Lorem ipsum dolor sit amet, consectetuer adipiscing elit, sed diam nonummy nibh euismod tincidunt ut laoreet dolore magna aliquam erat volutpat. Ut wisi enim ad minim veniam, quis nostrud exerci tation ullamcorper suscipit lobortis nisl

Lorem ipsum dolor sit amet, consectetuer adipiscing elit, sed diam nonummy nibh euismod tincidunt ut laoreet dolore magna aliquam erat volutpat. Ut wisi enim ad minim veniam, quis nostrud exerci tation ullamcorper suscipit lobortis nisl

- **Left:** Align text flush left, with a right *rag*, or uneven edge.

- **Center:** Center text horizontally.

- **Right:** Align text flush right, with a left rag.

- **Justify with Last Line Aligned Left:** Align text to both the left and right edges, leaving no rag. If the last line of the paragraph is shorter than the whole paragraph, it aligns flush left.

- **Justify with Last Line Aligned Center:** Align text to both the left and right edges, leaving no rag. If the last line of the paragraph is shorter than the whole paragraph, it aligns to the center.

- **Justify with Last Line Aligned Right:** Align text to both the left and right edges, leaving no rag. If the last line of the paragraph is shorter than the whole paragraph, it aligns flush right.

- **Justify All Lines:** Align text to both the left and right edges, leaving no rag. If the last line of the paragraph is shorter than the whole paragraph, it is stretched by increasing (first choice) word spacing or (secondary choice) letter spacing to force the last line flush with both the left and right.

Also on the Paragraph palette are the following options:

- **Left Indent:** Indent selected paragraphs the specified amount from the left. This option accepts positive and negative values, the latter pushing text outside the text area.

- **Right Indent:** Indent selected paragraphs the specified amount from the right. This option accepts positive and negative values, the latter pushing text outside the text area.

- **First Line Indent:** Indent only the first line of the paragraph. This option accepts positive and negative values, the latter pushing text outside the text area.

- **Space Before Paragraph:** Insert vertical spacing before the beginning of each new paragraph.

- **Space After Paragraph:** Insert vertical spacing after a return at the end of each paragraph.

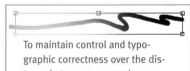

To maintain control and typographic correctness over the distance between paragraphs, use the Space Before Paragraph and/or Space After Paragraph options instead of a blank line (double-Return) for the paragraph type.

- **Hyphenate:** Specify whether to allow hyphenation to occur in the selected text. How words hyphenate is determined by Illustrator's built-in and user dictionaries according to the language(s) assigned to the selected text on the Character palette.

The OpenType Palette

With the exception of Stylistic Sets and Slashed Zero, Illustrator's support for, and options for using, OpenType fonts is identical to InDesign's support for OpenType fonts. However, whereas InDesign's OpenType options are hidden two levels deep on the Character palette menu, Illustrator has push-button OpenType options. Choose Window, Type, OpenType to open the OpenType palette (see Figure 19.11).

OpenType
Figure: Default Figure
Position: Default Position

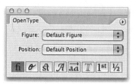

Figure 19.11
The OpenType palette.

OpenType fonts are the new generation of font technology, with the possibility in each font for many glyph variations, including multilingual accented letters, stylistic alternates, swashes, ligatures, and several types of numerals. Whether a given font contains these and other OpenType features is entirely dependent on whether the type designer built them in. If an OpenType font does not contain a particular feature, that feature's button or menu item is grayed out in the OpenType palette. All options are grayed out when using fonts that are not OpenType.

The following options are available, depending on the font, on the OpenType palette:

- **Figure:** Four possible styles of numbers (see Figure 19.12):

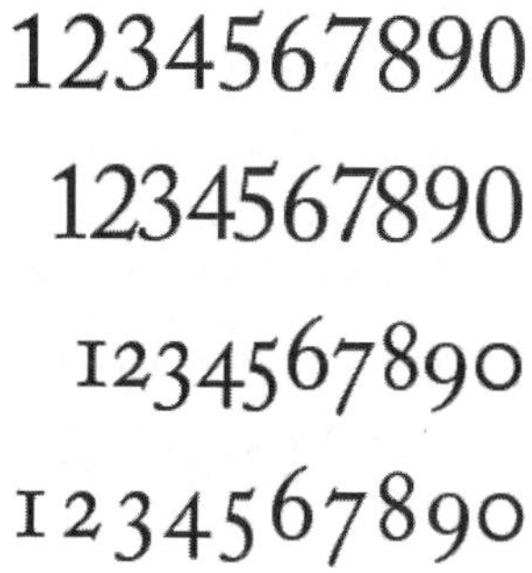
1234567890
1234567890
1234567890
1234567890

Figure 19.12
The four possible OpenType figures (set in the Adobe Caslon Pro Regular typeface, from top to bottom): Tabular Lining, Proportional Lining, Proportional Oldstyle, Tabular Oldstyle.

  - **Default Figure:** Whichever of the following style of numerals the type designer specified as the default figure style.
  - **Tabular Lining:** Squarish numbers that share a common baseline are all as tall as the capitol letter *X*, and all occupy the same amount of horizontal space—for example, the number 1, though the glyph itself is narrower than 9, occupies horizontal space equal to 9. Used for lining up numbers vertically or horizontally, such as in tables or price lists.

- **Proportional Lining:** Numbers that share a common baseline are all as tall as the capital letter *X*, but have variable widths (for example, the number 1 is narrower than the number 9, as is the space it occupies). Used in text with capital letters.

- **Proportional Oldstyle:** Numbers whose baselines, heights, widths, and horizontal spaces vary according to the correct or old-style shape of numerals. Used for numbers that appear with mixed-case text.

- **Tabular Oldstyle:** Numbers whose baselines and heights vary, but that all occupy the same amount of horizontal space—for example, the number 1, though the glyph itself is narrower than 9, occupies horizontal space equal to 9. Used for lining up numbers vertically in columns but with more elegant height and proportion variance than Tabular Lining.

- **Position:** The location and size of type relative to the baseline.

  - **Default Position:** Whichever of the following positions of the glyphs that the type designer specified as the default. Nearly always this is the normal, full-size type aligned to the baseline.

  - **Superscript/Superior:** Smaller glyphs about half the height of the lowercase *x* and whose tops are aligned to the cap height, the tops of the capital *X*.

  - **Subscript/Inferior:** Smaller glyphs about half the height of the lowercase *x* and lowered below the baseline.

  - **Numerator:** Numerals drawn specifically to be used as numerators in fractions.

  - **Denominator:** Numerals drawn specifically to be used as denominators in fractions.

- **Standard Ligatures:** Replace pairings of letters universally recognized as awkward with standard ligatures. For example, when typed beside each other, the teardrop loop of the lowercase *f* crowds the dot on the lowercase *i*; to compensate, a specially drawn *fi* glyph replaces the two individual letters. Standard ligatures include *fi, ff, ffl,* and *ft,* among others.

- **Contextual Alternates:** Replace some glyphs with variations drawn for readability or aesthetics in certain contexts (see Figure 19.13).

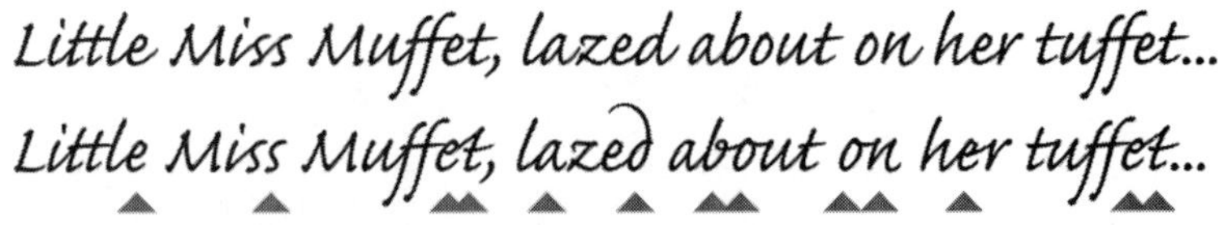

Figure 19.13
Contextual Alternates in action in the OpenType typeface Caflisch Script Pro.

- **Discretionary Ligatures:** Replace optional pairings of letters such as *ct* or *st* with specially drawn glyphs combining the letters in a more stylistic or aesthetically pleasing way.

- **Swash:** Replace some glyphs with variations drawn with extra flourishes, such as a long-tailed capital *Q* or an *L* with a long and curvaceous leg (see Figure 19.14).

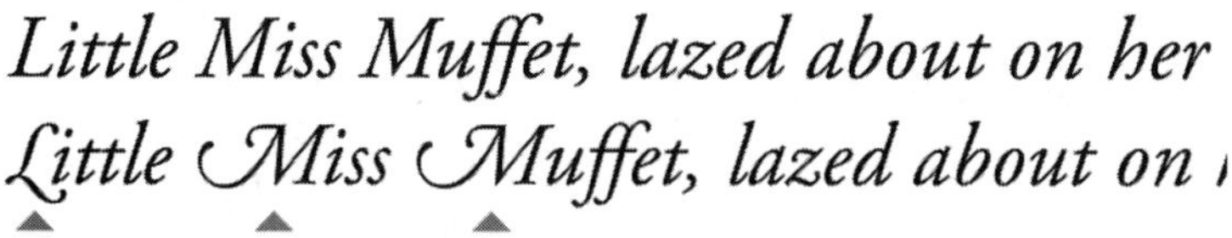

Little Miss Muffet, lazed about on her

Little Miss Muffet, lazed about on

Figure 19.14
Swash in action in the OpenType typeface Adobe Garamond Pro (Italic).

- **Stylistic Alternates:** Replace some glyphs with alternate versions drawn to be used in certain contexts for aesthetics or variety. For example, in a single word Stylistic Alternates may change some of several instances of the lowercase *e* to alternate drawings for the lowercase *e* (see Figure 19.15).

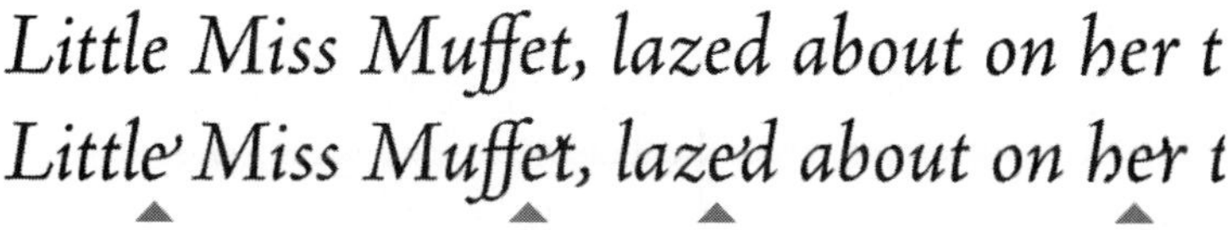

Little Miss Muffet, lazed about on her t

Little Miss Muffet, lazed about on her t

Figure 19.15
Stylistic Alternates in action in the OpenType typeface Adobe Jenson Pro (Italic).

- **Titling Alternates:** Replace some glyphs with variations drawn to be used specifically for titles (usually at larger sizes) for the purposes of aesthetics and/or readability. Often the variations take the form of thinner, more delicate strokes in the capital letters (see Figure 19.16).

LITTLE MISS MUFFET...

LITTLE MISS MUFFET...

Figure 19.16
Titling Alternates in action in the OpenType typeface Adobe Garamond Pro.

- **Ordinals:** Replace notations in ordinal numbers with superscripts. For example *1st* becomes 1st.

- **Fractions:** Numbers separated by a slash (/) are turned into proper fractions and the slash (a *virgule*), which is not the correct character to separate the numerator and denominator of a fraction, transforms into the correct character, a solidus (/).

Special Characters

To access all the glyphs in any font, including OpenType fonts, or to insert special characters that are difficult or impossible to type with the keyboard, use the Glyphs palette (see Figure 19.17). Open the Glyphs palette by choosing Window, Type, Glyphs.

Within the grid of the Glyphs palette are all the letters, numbers, punctuation, special characters, accents, and other glyphs drawn into the selected font. With a Type tool inserted into a type area, point type line, or type path, double-clicking any glyph in the Glyphs palette inserts the glyph into the type object at the position of the cursor.

At the bottom of the Glyphs palette are four devices:

- **Font Family:** Change the font family of the displayed font.

- **Font Style:** Change the displayed glyphs to those available in the particular style within the chosen font family.

19

Figure 19.17
The Glyphs palette.

Font Family   Font Style   Zoom In

Zoom Out

- **Zoom Out:** View the glyphs smaller.

- **Zoom In:** View the glyphs larger.

To see only available alternates for a specific glyph in an OpenType font, highlight the glyph on the artboard. Then, on the Glyphs palette, choose Alternates for Current Selection from the show menu.

USING CHARACTER AND PARAGRAPH STYLES

Just as graphic styles store and apply to other objects *appearance* attributes of an object, character and paragraph styles store the *formatting* attributes of type, enabling the rapid and facile application and modification of all settings on the Character, Paragraph, and OpenType palettes. Any character formatting can be saved in character styles, and any character and paragraph attributes can be saved in paragraph styles.

Styles are saved to, used from, and managed on, the Paragraph Styles and Character Styles palettes (see Figure 19.18). Open these palettes from the Window, Type menu. By default, both palettes contain a single style, Normal, the default for all newly created type, though they can hold as many as needed.

Paragraph styles define formatting on a paragraph level—all text between the beginning of a paragraph and a hard return (created by pressing Enter or Return on the keyboard) receives the same styling from an applied paragraph style. Conversely, character styles apply to text on a character, word, sentence, or paragraph level. Whatever text is highlighted when a character style is chosen is styled with the attributes stored in the style.

Figure 19.18
The Paragraph Styles (left) and Character Styles (right) palettes.

The easiest way to create text styles is to first set up the type as desired. Create a text area or point type, style it with the Character, Paragraph, Open Type, Color, and Swatches palettes. Then highlight the styled text and click the New Style button at the bottom of either the Paragraph or Character Styles palettes (depending on the type of styling employed, paragraph level or character only).

Try this:

1. Create a new area type object.

2. Type your name and press Return or Enter.

3. Type your address.

4. With the Type tool, highlight your name and change its fill color (using the Swatches or Color palette) and its font family, font style, and size on the Character palette.

5. On the Paragraph Styles palette, click the New Style button at the bottom. A new style entry, `Paragraph Style 1`, appears in the list above it.

6. Click or Alt-click (Windows users) or Option-click (Mac users) once on Paragraph Style 1 to assign it to your name. Your type does not change, but it is now tied to that paragraph style and adopts any changes made to the style.

7. Highlight your address and style it as well, but also indenting it 10 points from the left using the Paragraph palette's Left Indent measurement field.

8. On the Paragraph Styles palette, click the New Style button at the bottom. Paragraph Style 2 is created.

9. Click or Alt-click (Windows users) or Option-click (Mac users) once on Paragraph Style 2 to assign it to your address. Again, your type does not change, but it is now tied to that paragraph style and adopts any changes made to the style.

10. Press Return or Enter and type your phone number. By default, the text you type inherits the paragraph style from the previous paragraph—in this case, Paragraph Style 2.

11. Highlight your phone number with the Type tool and click the Paragraph Style 1 on the Paragraph Styles palette. Your phone number should reformat to match your name.

Only the attributes actually set in the style affect text. If the type fill color is not specified in the style, for instance, the style can be applied to any color of type without changing the fill color. This is why attributes in the Style Options dialogs may be completely cleared out.

19

Character styles augment paragraph styles without causing overrides. For example, applying a character style whose only attribute is to change the fill color to red in a passage of text with a paragraph style will turn the selected text red, but will not cause an override plus sign to appear beside the paragraph style in the Paragraph Styles palette.

After completing the above exercise, try working with a character style:

1. Using the name, address, and phone number type area, highlight your first name.

2. Change the fill color to one chosen from the Swatches palette. On the Paragraph Styles palette a plus sign should appear next to Paragraph Style 1, indicating that something (the color) is different than what is stored within the style definition.

3. On the Character Styles palette click the New Style button at the bottom. A new style, Character Style 1, appears in the list.

4. Click or Alt-click (Windows users) or Option-click (Mac users) once on the style to apply it to your first name. The plus sign beside Paragraph Style 1 should disappear.

5. With the Type tool, highlight the street name in your address.

6. Click on Character Style 1 in the Character Styles palette to apply it. The street name should become the same color as your first name—again, without triggering an override plus sign in the Paragraph Styles palette.

Apply styles by selecting text and then by clicking the desired style on the relevant palette. Styles may be applied to text selected by any of the following means:

- Highlight with one of the Type tools (paragraph styles apply to whole paragraphs, regardless of whether the selection is only part of a paragraph).

- Select the entire type object—area type, point type, or type on a path—or multiple objects with the Selection, Direct Selection, or type tools.

- Use the Select menu's Select or Same commands.

- Click on the target circles on the Layers palette to select type objects.

- Place the cursor inside the text without highlighting (applies paragraph styles only).

Perhaps the most powerful function of text styles is the fact that a change to the style instantly updates all text assigned to it—a single modification can save quite a bit of time and effort. If, for example, your layout contains 10 blocks of type, and all need to change from using the Times New Roman font family at 9.5 points to Adobe Jenson Pro at 11 points, making the change *once* in the style updates *all* 10 instances—assuming, of course, that the text was all assigned to the same style. Styles may be updated by using the Style Options dialog box or by redefining the style in context.

To redefine in context, make the needed change to type on the artboard. With the changed text selected, click once on the style entry in the appropriate Styles palette and then choose Redefine Paragraph Style from the Paragraph Styles palette menu or Redefine Character Style from the Character Styles palette menu (whichever is applicable).

19

Try this:

1. With the Selection tool, select the type area created and styled in the previous exercises.

2. Choose Edit, Copy.

3. Choose Edit, Paste. A new copy of the type appears in the center of the view. Move it with the Selection tool so that it is next to the first text area.

4. Highlight some or all of the text in the new text area and change its font family on the Character palette.

5. At the same time, increase the text size to, say, 20 points.

6. With the Type tool, highlight your last name.

7. On the Paragraph Styles palette click once on Paragraph Style 1, which should already be active and include a plus sign indicating the use of overrides.

8. From the Paragraph Styles menu choose Redefine Paragraph Style. The text in the first type area should update to match the changes made in the second and now saved in the paragraph style.

In the Paragraph Style Options are collected all the type and paragraph styling attributes from the Character, Paragraph, OpenType, Color, and other palettes and menus. Such a unified interface often makes multiple style changes more convenient than doing them in context and redefining.

Access the Paragraph Style Options dialog from the Paragraph Styles menu or by double-clicking a style in the palette; access the Character Style Options dialog the same ways on the Character Styles palette.

The General panel of the Paragraph Style Options dialog shows a summary of all attributes set on subsequent panels. Add, change, or clear any attribute to include it in the style. For example, on the Basic Character Formats tab (see Figure 19.19), set the same options that appear on the Character palette (additional Character palette options appear in the Paragraph Style Options dialog under Advanced Character Formats).

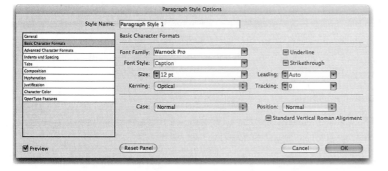

Figure 19.19
The Basic Character Formats panel in the Paragraph Style Options dialog.

On this or any panel in either the Paragraph Style Options dialog or Character Style Options dialog, any value may be set, changed, or cleared. Use the various pop-up menus, measurement fields, check boxes, and radio buttons to set or change options. To clear pop-up menus and measurement fields so that those attributes are no longer part of the style, highlight their content and press the Delete key on the keyboard. To clear check boxes, click the boxes until they are either empty (when the style is applied, the attribute is cleared from the text) or filled with a gray rectangle (in Windows) or a minus sign (on the Mac), which ignores the presence of the attribute in styled text—if styled text includes the attribute, it is neither applied nor removed.

The Character Style Options dialog, because it defines only character-level formatting and not paragraph-level formatting, includes fewer but nearly identical panels to the Paragraph Style Options dialog (see Figure 19.20).

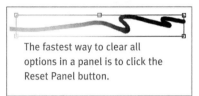

The fastest way to clear all options in a panel is to click the Reset Panel button.

Figure 19.20
The Basic Character Formats panel in the Character Style Options dialog.

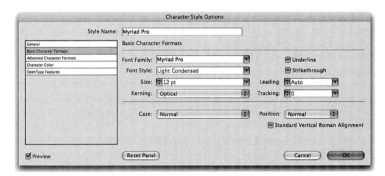

A plus sign beside the style name in either Styles palette indicates that the selected or active text contains an *override* to the style. Overrides are any applied formatting attributes not specifically contained within the style or defined differently between the style and the selected text. For example, assigning the Normal Paragraph Style to a paragraph of text and then making a single word bold registers the bold font style as an override when that word is selected.

When overrides are present, the following options are available:

- Create a new style to account for the differences between the overridden attributes and the original style. Many Illustrator users create character styles for bold, italic, and other font styles. Such styles leave Font Family and all other fields blank, setting only the Font Style, thus enabling bold or italic to be applied to any font that has a bold or italic font style. Because paragraph styles overridden by character styles are not really overrides, styling a single word or a few words in a paragraph with a bold character style does not register an override in either Styles palette.

- Manually clear the overridden attribute.

- Force the reapplication of the style, eliminating any overrides, by Alt-clicking (Windows users) or Option-clicking (Mac users) the style with the override text selected.

- Redefine the style to incorporate the overrides into the style itself, updating all other text assigned to the style to match. With the override text selected, click once on the style entry in the relevant Styles palette and then choose Redefine Paragraph Style from the Paragraph Styles palette menu or Redefine Character Style from the Character Styles palette menu (whichever is applicable).

Highlighting or placing the cursor within text to which a text style is already assigned highlights that style in the Paragraph or Character Styles palettes.

Change style names by double-clicking the style in the Paragraph or Character Styles palette and typing a new name at the top of the Options dialog. A good practice is to name styles based on their usage; even if Paragraph Style 1 and Character Style 9 make perfect sense now, will they still make sense in 6 months if the document needs to be edited again or used as the basis for a new design?

By default, all new text is created with the document default Normal Paragraph Style and Normal Character Style—Myriad (font family) Roman (font style) 12 pts (size) on auto (120%) leading and filled with 100% black and a stroke of none (all other settings are 100% or 0 pts).

To change the default text styles for new documents, begin a new blank RGB document. Double-click each of the Normal styles on their respective palettes. Make the necessary changes, and save the blank document as **Adobe Illustrator Startup_RGB.ai** to the folder C:\Program Files\Adobe\Adobe Illustrator CS2\Plug-ins (in Windows) or Applications/Adobe Illustrator CS2/Plug-ins (on the Mac). Replace the existing file. Do the same with a new CMYK document, and save it as **Adobe Illustrator Startup_CMYK.ai** to the same location.

WORKING WITH TEXT WRAP

To create visual interest or adhere to a document layout grid, it's often necessary and desired to place artwork within the boundaries of a text area, forcing the text to wrap around it (see Figure 19.21). In QuarkXPress, a layout competitor to InDesign, this process is referred to as *runaround*; in all the Adobe applications, including Illustrator, InDesign, InCopy, and PageMaker, it's called *text wrap*.

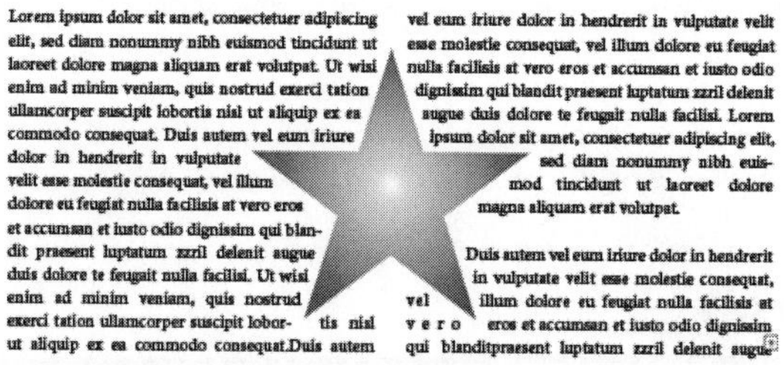

Figure 19.21
Text in the type area dynamically wraps around the shape.

Create text wraps by selecting the *wrap object*, the object around which text should wrap, and choosing Object, Text Wrap, Make. After the text wrap is created, control the distance between the wrap object and surrounding text through the Text Wrap Options dialog (choose Object, Text Wrap, Text Wrap Options); set the offset to the desired distance between the object and text on all sides. The Invert Wrap option makes text flow *inside* the wrap object, but not out to the sides. To remove the text wrap, choose Object, Text Wrap, Release.

Try creating a text wrap:

1. Create an area type object and fill it with text—nursery rhymes are excellent if nothing else comes to mind.

2. Draw a path or shape atop the type area with any of the drawing or shape tools.

3. With the path or shape selected, choose Object, Text Wrap, Make. Instantly, text flows around the object instead of under it.

One or more text areas may wrap around any object, even as other text areas overlap it. Because text wrap is relative to the stacking order of objects—the wrap object must be above the text—it's a simple matter of changing stacking order to have some text wrap around an object while other text overlaps. This is useful, for example, when inserting a photograph into columnar type (see Figure 19.22). The type should wrap around the photograph, but the caption and photo credit should not; merely place the caption and photo credit text area(s) higher in the stacking order than the photo.

Any Illustrator object may wrap text—even other type objects.

Figure 19.22
Note how the main flow of type wraps around the photo, but the caption does not. The caption type area itself is a text wrap object.

Lorem ipsum dolor sit amet, consectetuer adipiscing elit, sed diam nonummy nibh euismod tincidunt ut laoreet dolore magna aliquam erat volutpat. Ut wisi enim ad minim veniam, quis nostrud exerci tation ullamcorper suscipit lobortis nisl ut aliquip ex ea commodo consequat. Duis autem vel eum iriure dolor in hendrerit in vulputate velit esse molestie consequat, vel illum dolore eu feugiat nulla facilisis at vero eros et accumsan et iusto odio dignissim qui blandit praesent luptatum zzril delenit augue duis dolore te feugait nulla facilisi. Ut wisi enim ad minim veniam, quis nostrud

"Old Image", from Photoshop Samples

CREATING OUTLINES

Type in Illustrator is a special kind of object. It accepts many effects, including all Illustrator effects (see Chapter 20, "Working with Placed Graphics and Filters in Illustrator"), but it is not as editable as a shape. Though within fonts, glyphs are merely paths, they also have the added duty in Illustrator of conveying language. Therefore Illustrator does not allow direct editing of glyphs' paths while they are treated as text.

To modify the shape of glyphs—to create a unique effect for a logo, for example—select the type object with the Selection tool and choose Type, Create Outlines (see Figure 19.23). This action converts the type into paths that are no longer considered text. From there, anchor points and path segments may be edited like any other path.

After type has been converted to outlines there is no going back. Outlines cannot be made back into type, nor can their fonts be changed or used with paragraph or character styles. Additionally, outlines are invisible to text functions such as Check Spelling, Change Case, and Find Font.

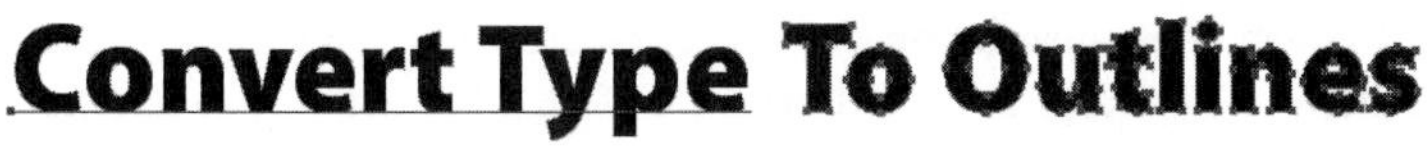

Convert Type To Outlines

Figure 19.23
Point text (left) displays only the point of the type path. After conversion to outlines (right), however, the actual paths that draw the glyphs are accessible.

In addition to the access to paths made possible by converting type to outlines, the process is often employed to negate font embedding and to eliminate the risk of font substitution (the computer choosing a different font) if the document is opened or printed from a system that does not have the same fonts installed as the creator.

EMBEDDING FONTS

Adobe Illustrator files (`.ai`) are actually PDF files. You may have noticed that the Illustrator Options dialog (see Figure 19.24) that appears after a Save As is similar to, but far simpler than, the Export To PDF or Save As PDF dialogs found throughout the Creative Suite.

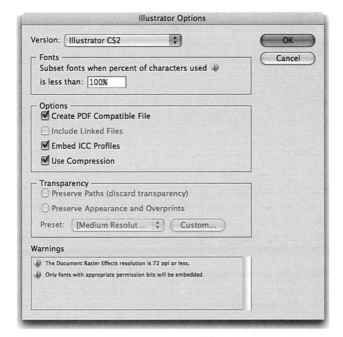

Figure 19.24
After choosing File, Save As, the Illustrator Options dialog appears.

Like PDF files created in almost any other fashion, Illustrator files may embed the fonts used in the document to style text. Embedding ensures that others who try to print the document can print it, even if they don't have the same fonts installed on their computers. In most cases, others will also be able to edit the type without the need to install the font.

Without font embedding, trying to print or edit a document without the correct fonts installed causes font substitution—the computer chooses a different (often hideously different) font to show in place of a missing one. As you might expect, font substitution can lead to recomposing of your type, including oversetting type that previously fit within its area, and, with some substituted fonts, even render the text completely unreadable.

Fonts embedded in Illustrator documents are, by default, *subsetted*. Subsetting is the process of including in the file only the glyphs or characters in use. For example, a document including every letter from *A–Y* may be edited without the need to install the font as long as *Z* is not required for editing, because the outline necessary to draw the *Z* in that font was omitted during subsetting.

When fonts are embedded, that additional data is included in the document, increasing its file size on disk. The primary purpose of embedding is to facilitate output and collaboration; the primary purpose of subsetting is to reduce file size and complexity. The setting for the Subset Fonts When Percent of Characters Used Is Less Than option in the Illustrator Options dialog determines the percentage of glyphs that must be used before Illustrator embeds the outlines and information necessary to print *all* glyphs in the font, used or not. The lower the percentage, the more likely the entire font(s) will be embedded, increasing file size and potentially complicating printing or other operations.

Regardless of the percentage of subsetting, entire fonts are not embedded in either Illustrator native files or PDFs. Only their outlines and certain other information needed to draw the fonts on screen and print them to a high-resolution output device are included as part of the document; most of the computer code and font structure information that actually comprises a font are left out. Therefore it is impossible to extract sufficient data from an Illustrator native or any PDF file to reconstruct a working font. The safety this brings to type foundries (font designers and manufacturers) is what has enabled the widespread adoption of font embedding in native Illustrator and PDF files.

Checking Spelling

Because Illustrator has the capability of typesetting large quantities of type, it also needed a way to check spelling. On the Edit menu is the Check Spelling command. Select it and up pops the Check Spelling tool (see Figure 19.25).

The spell checker reads and evaluates all visible and editable text in the document, whether point type, area type, or type on a path. It operates similarly to a word processor's spell check tool, showing an unrecognized word, that word in context, and replacement suggestions. Check Spelling also highlights the unrecognized word on the artboard.

In the Check Spelling dialog is the context area, in which the unrecognized word appears along with several of the words surrounding it for context. Below that is the list of suggestions for the current unrecognized word. The following buttons and check boxes are also available (if Options are shown):

- **Start:** To initiate a spell check, click the Start button.

- **Ignore:** Ignore the current instance of the unrecognized word and move on to the next unrecognized word or instance.

- **Ignore All:** Ignore all instances of the current unrecognized word and move on to the next unrecognized word.

- **Change:** Replace the unrecognized word with the currently highlighted suggestion.

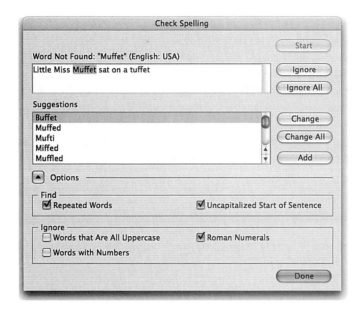

Figure 19.25
Illustrator's Check Spelling tool (with options shown).

- **Change All:** Replace all instances of the unrecognized word with the currently highlighted suggestion.

- **Add:** Add the unrecognized word to the dictionary, making it a recognized word.

- **Repeated Words:** Flag repeated words—for example, `the the red fire engine`.

- **Uncapitalized Start of Sentence:** Have Check Spelling alert you if it finds a sentence that begins with a lowercase letter.

In the Ignore section, tell Illustrator what not to check—Words that Are All Uppercase, Words with Numbers (in them), and Roman Numerals (for example, *XXII*).

When the spell check is complete, click the Done button.

FINAL THOUGHTS

John Warnock, co-founder of Adobe, father of Illustrator, and half the reason we have digital typography and desktop publishing, once said: "Good typography is something everybody sees but nobody notices."

Of course, he was referring to the function of typography and, ultimately, the reason Illustrator contains all of its amazing typesetting features. Decorative type objects aside, the function of typography is to convey language. In this book, for example—indeed, in this very passage of text—you should not notice the typeface (font) chosen, how well the letters of the words are kerned together, or the thickness of the em dashes (—). All you should see are the meanings of my words. My words, the information conveyed by the marks of black ink on this page, are what really matter.

You are reading this book to obtain information, and the typography of the book is only the vehicle to convey that information to you. The function of typography is to support the written word.

Shown up only by its Creative Suite pal InDesign, Illustrator contains some of the most advanced typographic tools ever accessible on a desktop computer. With control over kerning, tracking, leading, hyphenation, and paragraph composition, and with its Open Type features, you may set type in Illustrator with greater precision than has been possible since the advent of desktop publishing.

Yet the real purpose of all this control, all this freedom and power, is ultimately to be unseen. Its job is to merely make words, and then sentences, and then paragraphs first visible, and then legible, and then readable. If the typography is noticed, the book designer has failed the job.

Typography is an ironic practice; in a world where creativity is noticed and creative people strive to be unique, the goal of typography is to be unnoticed. The more robust the application's typesetting functions and the more skilled a designer is with those functions, the closer to invisible the designer becomes.

The better you are with Illustrator's type tools, the less your work will be noticed. And that is the way it should be.

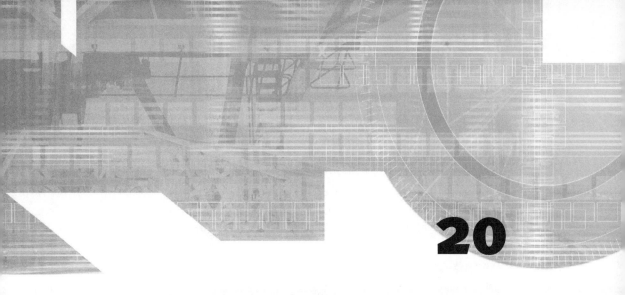

WORKING WITH PLACED GRAPHICS AND FILTERS IN ILLUSTRATOR

Though Illustrator is a vector drawing program, it can make good use of placed raster images, including incorporating them into vector drawings, applying filters and live effects, and even masking opacity.

WORKING WITH PLACED GRAPHICS

Although Illustrator can open and edit Photoshop documents—as well as accept raster (and vector) objects copied from Photoshop or InDesign and pasted into Illustrator—to work with a raster image as a single, flat object in an Illustrator document, you must *place* the file.

Placing Graphics

On the File menu is the Place command, which opens a dialog very similar to the one displayed with the File, Open command (see Figure 20.1). Instead of opening a file, however, the Place dialog inserts the external file on the current document's artboard. Placed files, even other Illustrator documents, are not directly editable when inserted via the Place command. In other words, constituent objects in the placed graphic cannot be manipulated independently of the whole.

Figure 20.1
The Place dialog.

In the Place dialog are three options:

- **Link:** Link to the original file (checked) or embed (unchecked) the graphic in the Illustrator document (see the "Linking and Embedding Placed Images" section, later in this chapter).

- **Template:** Check to insert the image and automatically set the image's layer to Template mode (see the section on the Layers palette in Chapter 15, "Understanding Illustrator Palettes and Menus").

- **Replace:** Active only if another image is selected in the document prior to using the Place command. Check to replace the selected image with the one currently chosen in the Place dialog.

Illustrator can place the following file formats into an active document; in the case of textual documents (text, Rich Text Format, and Microsoft Word), the text of the file is placed as editable type within a selected text object or as a new type area if no object is selected:

- Adobe Illustrator documents and templates (*.ai, *.ait, *.pdf)
- Adobe PDF files (*.pdf)
- AutoCAD Drawing and Interchange files (*.dwg and *.dxf)
- BMP (*.bmp, *.rle, *.dib)
- Computer Graphics Metafile (*.cgm)
- CorelDRAW versions 5–10 files (*.cdr)
- Encapsulated PostScript (*.eps, *.epsf, *.ps)
- Enhanced Metafile (*.emf)
- FreeHand versions 4, 5, 7, 8, and 9 files (*.fh*)
- GIF89A (*.gif)
- JPEG (*.jpg, *.jpe, *.jpeg)
- JPEG2000 (*.jpf, *.jpx, *.jp2, *.j2k, *.j2c, *.jpc)
- Macintosh PICT (*.pic, *.pct)
- Microsoft Word (*.doc)
- PCX (*.pcx)
- Photo CD (*.pcd)
- Photoshop (*.psd, *.pdd)
- Pixar (*.pxr)
- PNG (*.png)
- Rich Text Format (*.rtf)
- SVG (*.svg)
- SVG Compressed (*.svgz)
- Targa (*.tga, *.vda, *.icb, *.vst)
- Text (*.txt)
- TIFF (*.tif, *.tiff)
- Windows Metafile (*.wmf)

When placing some of these formats, an additional options dialog appears (see Figure 20.2). In some cases—with PDF and Illustrator files, for example—the dialog asks where to crop the artwork or, if the original is a multipage document, which page to place. In such cases, only one page may be placed at a time, although the same file may be placed multiple times, with each instance displaying a different page.

Figure 20.2
When placing a PDF or Illustrator file, the Place PDF dialog appears, with Crop To box and page navigation features.

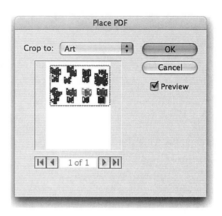

In addition to the Place command, supported graphic and text file formats may be placed as linked assets into the Illustrator document by dragging and dropping one or multiple files from

- Adobe Bridge

- The Desktop

- An Explorer (Windows) or Finder (Macintosh) window

- iPhoto (Macintosh)

Using Photoshop Layer Comps

In Photoshop CS and CS2, layers are augmented by the addition of the Layer Comps feature. *Layer comps* are snapshots of the state of layers in a document—which image, vector, type, and adjustment layers are turned on or off, as well as certain layer transformations (see the section on layer comps in Chapter 6, "Working with Layers in Photoshop"). Saved in Photoshop documents, layer comps may be taken advantage of when such Photoshop documents are placed into Illustrator (or InDesign).

When placing a Photoshop document that includes layer comps, the Photoshop Import Options dialog appears after you finish with the Place dialog (see Figure 20.3).

At the top of the Photoshop Import Options dialog is a pop-up menu of layer comps saved in the Photoshop document. Below that is a preview of the selected layer comp (the Show Preview option is unchecked by default), as well as any comments written into the layer comp in Photoshop. The When Updating Link pop-up menu includes two options: Keep Layer Visibility Overrides, which tells Illustrator to preserve the layer comp as chosen regardless of any layer and layer comp changes made in the original document in Photoshop, and Use Photoshop's Layer Visibility, which ignores the chosen layer comp settings and updates the asset in the Illustrator document if changes are made in Photoshop.

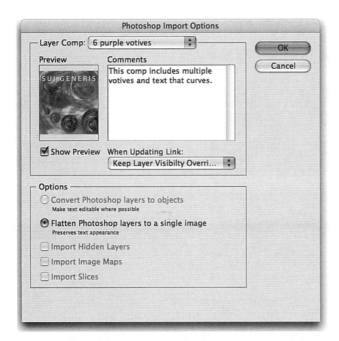

Figure 20.3
The Photoshop Import Options dialog displaying a document with layer comps.

The options, which affect only how the Photoshop document is handled inside Illustrator and not the original asset in any way, include

- **Convert Photoshop Layers to Objects:** If available, convert layers in the Photoshop image to Illustrator-editable objects, layers, and sub-layers in the Illustrator document. This option also attempts to make text in the Photoshop document editable within Illustrator as text.

- **Flatten Photoshop Layers to a Single Image:** If available, does not add Photoshop layers or objects to the Layers palette, but instead it creates a single, solid image like other raster image formats placed into Illustrator.

- **Import Hidden Layers:** Available if Convert Photoshop Layers to Objects is chosen. Import layers even if they were deactivated or hidden in Photoshop.

- **Import Image Maps:** Available if Convert Photoshop Layers to Objects is chosen. If the Photoshop document contains image maps created in Photoshop or ImageReady, they are preserved.

- **Import Slices:** Available if Convert Photoshop Layers to Objects is chosen. If the Photoshop document contains slices created in Photoshop or ImageReady, they are preserved and may be manipulated with Illustrator's Slice tool and Slice commands.

Try this exercise:

1. Begin a new Illustrator document.

2. Choose File, Place.

20

3. In the Place dialog, navigate to the Photoshop sample files. On Windows that would be `C:\Program Files\Adobe\Adobe Photoshop CS2\Samples`. On the Mac that location would be `Applications/Adobe Photoshop CS2/Samples`.

4. Place the `Layer Comps.psd` sample file and check the Link option.

5. In the Photoshop Import Options dialog, turn on Preview and select the 6 Purple Votives layer comp.

6. Set the When Updating Link pop-up menu to Keep Layer Visibility Overrides and click OK.

The only way to change the active layer comp for a placed Photoshop document is to relink it:

1. Select the `Layer Comps.psd` file with the Selection tool.

2. With a linked image selected, the Control palette updates to reflect information relevant to that type of object. On the far left of the Control palette is a rather wide button with an arrow on it. Click this button to access a menu of linked file options.

3. Choose Relink, which opens the Place dialog again.

4. Choose the same file (`Layer Comps.psd`) and click the Place button.

5. In the Photoshop Import Options dialog select a different layer comp and click OK.

The commands on the Control palette's (unofficially named) Linked File menu are also available on the Links palette menu, and some also appear as buttons on the Links palette (see "Linking and Embedding Placed Images," later in this chapter).

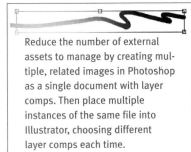

Reduce the number of external assets to manage by creating multiple, related images in Photoshop as a single document with layer comps. Then place multiple instances of the same file into Illustrator, choosing different layer comps each time.

Linking and Embedding Placed Images

Placed images may be either linked or embedded, with advantages and drawbacks to both.

Linking merely stores a reference to the placed graphic in the Illustrator document, not the placed graphic itself. Changes made to the original graphic file outside of Illustrator prompt Illustrator to ask whether you want to update the placed reference. In this way, a common image asset like a logo or photograph used in multiple projects may be changed across all documents simultaneously. Another pro is that the asset's file size is not added to the Illustrator document.

One drawback to linking is that, when transporting the Illustrator document, all image assets must be transported as well (or the document cannot print with high quality) and editing is severely restricted. Additionally, many effects and filters (Drop Shadow, for example) may be applied only to embedded images; applying them to linked images has no visible effect.

Linked placed graphics appear on the artboard with an X through them (see Figure 20.4).

Figure 20.4
This placed graphic is linked, as denoted by the x across the picture.

Embedding stores the placed copy of the original image directly within the Illustrator document and disassociates it with the external file. Embedding has two major advantages: A greater range of filters and effects are available for application to the embedded graphic, and additional assets need not be located and transported when moving the Illustrator document. If an asset is embedded in the Illustrator document, changes to the original file do not affect the placed copy, and Illustrator is totally unaware of changes made to the original. Additionally, the entire original asset is embedded in the Illustrator document, increasing the latter's file size on disk accordingly.

The Links palette (choose Window, Links to display the palette) tracks and manages linked and embedded assets (see Figure 20.5). Each linked asset has an entry on the Links palette, and various icons appear beside the entry's name to communicate important information:

- **Embedded Artwork:** Indicates that the asset is embedded in the document.

- **Modified Artwork:** Indicates that the linked asset has been updated outside of Illustrator.

Figure 20.5
The Links palette.

20

- **Missing Artwork:** Indicates that the linked asset has been moved or deleted, or that the Illustrator document is no longer in the same location relative to the location of the asset. Printing with missing artwork results in low resolution output of the asset.

- **Transparency Interaction:** Indicates that the linked asset has or is touching another object that has some form of transparency active.

Embed images in one of three ways: by clicking the Embed button that appears on the Control palette when the image is selected, by unchecking the Link box in the Place dialog, or by selecting a linked asset entry on the Links palette and then Embed Image from the Links palette menu.

At the bottom of the Links palette are four buttons that become active depending on the highlighted asset in the Links palette:

- **Relink:** Open a dialog to link to a missing asset from a new location to replace an asset with another; to relink to the same image, change its options—for example, to choose a different layer comp for display in placed Photoshop PSD files that include layer comps.

- **Go To Link:** Navigate the document window to display the linked asset.

- **Update Link:** If a linked asset has been modified outside of Illustrator, this re-reads the original file, updating the reference on the artboard.

- **Edit Original:** Open the linked asset in its source application—for example, a linked PSD document opens in Photoshop. Upon saving the asset in the source application, Illustrator instantly updates it on the artboard without the need to click the Update Link button.

Working with Live Trace

New in Illustrator CS2 is Live Trace, an automated utility to vectorize or trace raster images into vector objects (see Figure 20.6).

Figure 20.6
Raster image before tracing (left) and the same image after Live Trace with different tracing presets. From left to right: Grayscale, Color 6, and Photo High Fidelity.

When a raster image is selected in the Illustrator document, the Control palette displays the Live Trace button. Clicking the Live Trace button instantly traces the image with the last used or default Live Trace options. The down-pointing black arrow beside the Live Trace button is the Tracing Presets and Options menu. On the menu are all the default and user-created tracing presets, as well as the last item, Tracing Options.

In the Tracing Options dialog, default and user-created presets appear in a menu at the top. Often, a preset provides exactly the right settings for a particular tracing. When it doesn't, the options in the Adjustments and Trace Settings sections provide precise tracing control (see Figure 20.7).

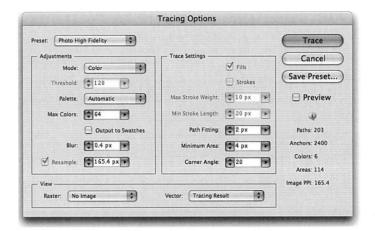

Figure 20.7
The Tracing Options dialog.

The Adjustments section contains various options that are enabled or disabled by the choice of Mode:

- **Mode:** Select the color mode of the desired tracing, either color, grayscale, or black and white.

- **Threshold:** (Black and White mode) Set the limit among the possible 256 levels of gray (including black at 0 and white at 255) to convert from black to white. Any pixel lighter than the threshold value is converted to white; all others are black.

- **Palette:** (Color or Grayscale mode) Determine the colors used for fills and/or stroke when tracing. To create a tracing in a particular color library—for example, in spot colors—open the needed library from the Window, Swatch Libraries command *before* using Live Trace. After it is opened, the library appears in the list of palettes.

- **Max Colors:** Determine the maximum number of colors allowed in the resulting trace. More colors equals richer detail but more paths.

- **Output to Swatches:** Choose whether to create swatches from the colors Live Trace picks from the traced image and uses to paint the tracing paths.

- **Blur:** Blur the traced image prior to tracing to limit the effects of pixelation and raster image artifacts—for example, dirt, scratches, or noise in color areas.

- **Resample:** Resample or change the resolution of the raster image prior to tracing.

Also dependent on the Mode, the Trace Settings options control to the fidelity of the tracing result:

- **Fills:** Determine whether Live Trace should fill traced paths or leave them unfilled.

- **Strokes:** Determine whether Live Trace should draw strokes or leave paths unstroked.

- **Max Stroke Weight:** (Available only if Strokes is checked.) Define in pixels the maximum weight or thickness of strokes in traced paths.

20

- **Min Stroke Length:** (Available only if Strokes is checked.) Define the minimum length of a traced stroke. The higher the number, the fewer paths resulting from the trace but the lower detail.

- **Path Fitting:** Determine how close to the pixels in the raster image vector paths should be drawn. The lower the number, the more closely paths follow the pixel shapes in the image.

- **Minimum Area:** Determine the minimum area in pixels to be traced. For example: an area 1- by 1-pixel is ignored and not traced if the value of Minimum Area is higher than 1.

- **Corner Angle:** Determine the angle that corners in the raster image must be before requiring a corner anchor point instead of a smooth anchor point.

The View section controls whether and how the raster image and vector tracing results are displayed in the Live Trace object.

Also in the Tracing Options dialog, on the right side, are counts of the number of paths, anchors, colors, and areas of the tracing result; the pixels per inch of the raster image; and the Save Preset button, which creates new presets for the Preset menu from the current settings.

Try this:

1. Place a raster graphic.

2. From the Control palette, click on the Tracing Presets and Options menu (the black arrow beside the Live Trace button).

3. Choose the Color 6 preset. Within seconds (if that long) the raster image is traced into six colors of vector objects, making it look much like a screen print on a t-shirt or soda can.

4. From the Tracing Presets and Options menu select Photo High Fidelity. The image retraces with more realistic options.

As the name implies, Live Trace is a live effect. Tracing settings can be tweaked at any time. Unless and until the Live Trace object is expanded, the tracing is always tied to the raster image and the level of detail, colors, and fidelity may be altered in real time.

Although Live Trace is a marvelous tool capable of stellar results, it isn't perfect. For example, when tracing an image with a white or even transparent background, Live Trace draws the background as white-filled paths. If the desired result is to have the traced object placed atop other objects that show through the negative space, those extraneous background paths must be deleted.

Moreover, Live Trace is not always the last step in working with traced objects.

To answer both (and other) scenarios in which the paths resulting from a trace must be accessed directly, you must expand the Live Trace object. With a Live Trace object selected, the Control palette displays the Expand button. Clicking it converts the object into a grouped collection of paths. From there, ungroup using the Object, Ungroup command to access each of the individual paths Live Trace drew and work with them as with any other path object.

After a placed image has been converted to a Live Trace object, modify it with the Object, Live Trace submenu, which enables a return to the Tracing Options dialog, as well as the following:

- Release the Live Trace and convert the object back to a placed image.

- Expand to break the live aspect of the Live Trace and expand it into a separate raster image and the tracing result.

- Expand as Viewed, which has the same essential functionality as Expand, but does not restore any hidden aspect of the Live Trace object, such as the original image if it is not shown.

- Use various settings from the View section of Tracing Options and Convert to Live Paint, which converts the Live Trace paths to a Live Paint object (see the Live Paint section of Chapter 18, "Working with Objects in Illustrator").

Working with Clipping Masks

Illustrator does not have the capability of erasing parts of a raster image like Photoshop, nor does it need that capability. It has clipping masks. Clipping masks hide portions of images, text, paths, shapes, or groups without changing them.

To create a clipping mask, place or draw the artwork to mask. Using any of the shape or drawing tools, draw a closed path in the shape of, and on top of, the portion of the artwork to remain visible. Select both the artwork and the mask object, and choose Object, Clipping Mask, Make. The mask object disappears, clipping away all areas of the artwork falling outside it (see Figure 20.8).

Try this:

Figure 20.8
Before masking (left) and after masking (right).

1. Choose File, Place.

2. Select any image and check the Link option in the Place dialog.

3. On top of the placed image, draw a closed path or shape—for example, an ellipse, using the Ellipse tool. This is the mask object.

4. With the Selection tool, select the mask object and Shift-click to select the placed image.

5. Choose Object, Clipping Mask, Make. Any fill or stroke the mask object had disappears, and the placed image is clipped to take its shape.

When an object or objects are contained within a clipping mask, any transformation made to the clipping mask object equally transforms the mask and the object(s) within. To transform just the contents without affecting the clipping mask, deselect the object, then select it with the Direct Selection tool.

To release a clipping mask, choose Object, Clipping Mask, Release. Both the artwork and the mask object are restored and separated, though the mask object returns as an unfilled, unstroked path.

Working with Opacity Masks

Clipping masks are all or nothing—the masked artwork either shows fully or not at all. When you want a semitransparent state—a soft-edged vignette, for example—use opacity masks (see Figure 20.9).

Create an opacity mask in the same way as a clipping mask, with existing artwork and a mask shape. The difference is in the fill. Whereas the fill is irrelevant to a clipping mask, it is the basis for

Figure 20.9
Before opacity mask (left) and after (right). The mask object was a gradient-filled circle.

an opacity mask. Fill the mask object with shades of gray to define transparency; black is completely transparent, white completely opaque. Set the opacity percentage or blending mode for the final masked artwork on the *mask object*. Select both the mask and the artwork, and choose Make Opacity Mask from the Transparency palette menu. The thumbnail preview of the artwork is joined by, and linked to, an opacity thumbnail resembling the mask object (see Figure 20.10).

On the Transparency palette, the Clip option turns any areas of the artwork that appear outside the mask object to black (invisible). In other words, if a circle is used to mask a square, the corners of the

Figure 20.10
An opacity mask shows two thumbnails in the Transparency palette, the masked artwork and the mask object.

square not overlapped by the circle are rendered invisible by the Clip option. Disable the Clip option for special effects like creating a window through artwork.

The Invert Mask option flips the black and white points, making what was completely invisible opaque and vice versa.

Try this:

1. Choose File, Place.

2. Select any image and check the Link option in the Place dialog.

3. On top of the placed image, draw a closed path or shape—for example, an ellipse, using the Ellipse tool. This is the mask object.

4. Fill the circle with the black-to-white radial gradient swatch on the Swatches palette.

5. With the Selection tool, select the mask object and Shift-click to select the placed image.

6. On the Transparency palette menu, choose Make Opacity Mask. The image should clip to fit the circle, and it should seem to fade out from a solid center.

In addition to making opacity masks from the Transparency palette menu, you can also choose the following options:

- **Release Opacity Mask:** Restore the mask and masked artwork to separate, unmasked objects.

- **Disable Opacity Mask:** Turn off the opacity mask without releasing it.

- **Unlink Opacity Mask:** Keep the mask applied to the artwork, but allow independent transformation of both the mask and the masked artwork.

USING FILTERS WITH PLACED IMAGES

Filters (on the Filter menu) either create new objects and paths when applied (as in the case of Drop Shadow), or, more commonly, permanently alter the object. To change the filter options after they're applied, the result must be deleted and the filter reapplied to the source object. Filters do not create appearance attribute entries in the Appearance palette and are therefore not able to be saved and applied via graphic styles. For filters to apply to placed images, the images must be embedded.

Dimmed or unavailable filters are not applicable to one or all of the currently selected objects.

Illustrator Filters

The Colors filters are discussed in Chapter 17, "Working with Color in Illustrator"); the following are the rest of the Illustrator Filters:

- **Crop Marks:** (On the Create submenu) Add crop marks around the selected object(s) (see Figure 20.11).

- **Object Mosaic:** (On the Create submenu) Create a grid or mosaic of solid color rectangles from the artwork. In the Object Mosaic dialog set the tile spacing, size, and quantity, and whether the result is color or gray.

- **Free Distort:** (On the Distort submenu) *Vector only*. Reshape objects by manipulating four control points. Drag points around the Free Distort dialog to skew, flip, stretch, squish, or create false perspective (see Figure 20.12).

- **Pucker & Bloat:** (On the Distort submenu) *Vector only*. Push the object's anchor points outward while curving path segments inward with Pucker; push path segments outward with Bloat.

20

Figure 20.11
Create Filters: Crop Marks (left)
and Object Mosaic (right).

- **Roughen:** (On the Distort submenu) *Vector only*. Convert the object's path segments into random angles. In the Roughen dialog specify the percentage of distortion, whether the center point is relative or absolute, the amount of detail to preserve, and whether the new anchor points created by the filter are corner points or smooth points.

- **Tweak:** (On the Distort submenu) *Vector only*. Suck in or push out path segments randomly. In the Tweak dialog specify the percentage of distortion horizontally and vertically, whether the center point is relative or absolute, and whether to distort anchor points, control points leading into anchor points, and control points leading out from anchor points.

- **Twist:** (On the Distort submenu) *Vector only*. Distort the artwork by twisting it to a provided angle.

- **Zig Zag:** (On the Distort submenu) *Vector only*. Push out the object's path segments uniformly. In the Zig Zag dialog specify the size of distortion, whether the center point is relative or absolute, the number of ridges per path segment, and whether the anchor points are smooth or corner points.

- **Add Arrow Heads:** (On the Stylize submenu) *Vector only*. Add arrowheads or other shapes to the ends of open paths (see Figure 20.13).

Figure 20.12
Distort Filters, from left to right:
(top row) Original shape, Free
Distort, Pucker, Bloat; (bottom
row) Roughen, Tweak, Twist, and
Zig Zag.

20

- **Drop Shadow:** (On the Stylize submenu) Create a drop shadow on the selected object(s). In the Drop Shadow dialog specify the blending mode, opacity, X and Y offsets (how far away the shadow casts) in positive (right and down, respectively) or negative (left and up, respectively) measurements, the amount of blur, the color (click on the color swatch to access the Color Picker), and whether to create separate shadow (raster) objects for each of the selected artwork objects or to create a unified shadow for all selected objects.

- **Round Corners:** (On the Stylize submenu) *Vector only.* Round the corners of angled shapes such as rectangles.

Figure 20.13
Stylize Filters, from left to right:
Add Arrow Heads, Drop Shadow,
and Round Corners.

Filter Gallery

The Filter Gallery provides a single interface for 47 of the Photoshop filters in six groups (see Figure 20.14). Dominating the Filter Gallery window is the preview, showing the selected object and any applied filters. At the bottom are zoom controls. In the center column, grouped in expandable sections, are the filters.

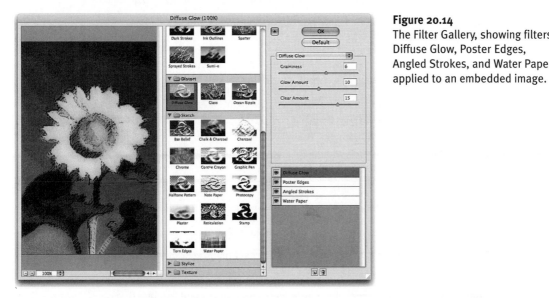

Figure 20.14
The Filter Gallery, showing filters
Diffuse Glow, Poster Edges,
Angled Strokes, and Water Paper
applied to an embedded image.

20

Expand filter groups by clicking the expansion arrow; close them by clicking the expansion arrow again. Each group demonstrates its filters by using preview thumbnails. Click a thumbnail to apply the effect with default settings to the selected artwork. The preview updates to show the effect of the filter on the artwork. For a larger view of the artwork preview, hide the filters column by clicking the arrow (it's a double-arrow on Windows machines) next to the OK button.

If the selected filter has options, they appear to the right. Enter changes or adjust sliders and watch the changes in real time in the preview pane. The pop-up menu at the top of the right column is another way to access all the filters; it is enabled when any filter layer is selected below it.

Below the filter options are filter layers. Like layered transparency or blending modes, each filter layer builds on the ones below it. For example, applying the Water Paper filter textures the image. Adding the Angled Strokes filter atop the Water Paper smoothes some of Water Paper's texture while creating the distinctive look of oil paint on a rough canvas. Creating a new filter layer and selecting the Poster Edges filter applies that filter's edge-enhancement and posterization effect to the oil painting composite image, not to the original artwork. Adding yet another filter—Diffuse Glow, for example—applies *its* effects to the result of Poster Edges of Angled Strokes of Water Paper.

Add and delete filter layers with, respectively, the New Filter Layer and Delete Filter Layer buttons below the filter layers pane.

Preview the composition without specific filters by clicking the eye icon to render the filter temporarily invisible. Change the layer order, and thus the relationship of the filters, by dragging filter entries above or below one another in the filter layers pane.

Photoshop Filters

Though most of the Photoshop filters are accessible within the Filter Gallery, for different reasons, several are not. These must be selected individually from the Filter menu, and include

- **Gaussian Blur:** (On the Blur submenu) Uniformly blur artwork via a precisely adaptable interface (see Figure 20.15).

- **Radial Blur:** (On the Blur submenu) Blur artwork by spinning or zooming. Drag the pattern in the proxy preview to change the center of the blur.

- **Smart Blur:** (On the Blur submenu) Blur artwork by color and contrast. Radius defines the area in which dissimilar pixels must be before being affected. Threshold specifies how different pixels must be. Mode choices include Normal (the entire image is examined for blur), Edge Only (draws white on black edges for contrasting colors), and Overlay Edge (adds white edges for contrasting colors over the original artwork).

- **Color Halftone:** (On the Pixelate submenu) Convert the artwork to a colored halftone reminiscent of the Pop Art style and approximating the results of halftone printing (see Figure 20.16).

- **Crystallize:** (On the Pixelate submenu) Fragment artwork into irregularly shaped cells of colors.

- **Mezzotint:** (On the Pixelate submenu) Create a random mezzotint effect in dots, lines, or strokes, and three sizes of each.

- **Pointillize:** (On the Pixelate submenu) Approximate the pointillism painting style by converting the artwork to overlapping, round dots with white space between.

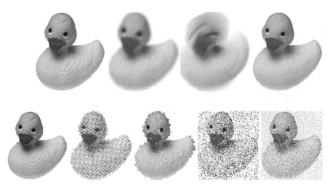

Figure 20.15
Blur Filters, from left to right:
Original image, Gaussian Blur,
Radial Blur (on spin), and Smart
Blur.

Figure 20.16
Pixelate Filters, from left to right:
Original image, Color Halftone,
Crystallize, Mezzotint, and
Pointillize.

- **Unsharp Mask:** (On the Sharpen submenu) Sharpen edges between contrasting colors by adjusting contrast and by lightening and darkening the pixels on either side of the edge.

- **De-Interlace:** (On the Video submenu) Remove interlace lines in still images captured from video.

- **NTSC Colors:** (On the Video submenu) Change colors to fit within the reduced RGB-derived gamut of television display.

WORKING WITH EFFECTS ON PLACED IMAGES

Effects (on the Effects menu) are similar to filters in visual result, with the difference being that effects are *live*. They do not create new objects or paths, are not necessarily permanent, and automatically update to reflect changes in the source object. Effects create appearance attribute entries in the Appearance palette and are therefore able to be saved and reapplied in graphic styles. Additionally, they may be removed simply by deleting their attribute entries in the Appearance palette, leaving the source object intact. Effects may also be nested, one applied atop another, with each one reacting to the others.

Moreover, you don't have to apply effects to entire objects—you can (and often will) apply effects to individual appearance attributes. For example, in an object with three different fills, one fill may have the Offset effect and Inner Glow applied, the second fill may have the Roughen attribute, and the third fill may be distorted using Free Transform and the Gaussian Blur effect applied solely to the distorted fill. Filters, on the other hand, may be applied only to entire objects, not to individual appearance attributes.

To edit effects, do not reselect them from the Effects menu. Instead double-click the effect's attribute entry in the Appearance palette. Choosing the effect from the Effects menu will apply a second instance of the effect.

20

To convert Effects results to separate, editable paths and objects, select the effected object and choose Object, Expand.

The Document Raster Effects Settings dialog (see Figure 20.17) determines the resolution, color model, background, and other important options used when converting objects to raster by using the Rasterize command on the Object menu as well as all raster-based effects such as drop shadow, inner glow, outer glow, feather, the SVG filters, and all the Photoshop effects. Raster effects on the Effects menu render as pixels instead of paths, though they retain their live status. Set the correct resolution for the output device prior to using any raster effects to prevent improper-quality (which is usually lower-quality) output.

Figure 20.17
The Document Raster Effects Settings dialog.

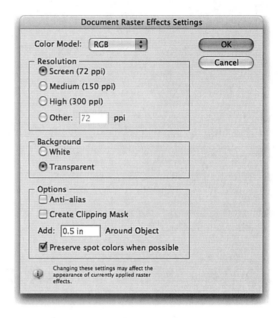

Dimmed or unavailable filters are not applicable to one or all of the currently selected objects.

Illustrator Effects

The Illustrator 3D effects and Warp effects are discussed in Chapter 18; the following are the rest of the Illustrator effects:

Caution

Effects take longer to draw and redraw every time objects or the document view changes. Waiting time for several effects to render on even a few objects could become significant. If an effect is to be permanent, consider using instead the equivalent filter, which typically requires less time to render to the screen.

- **Rectangle:** (On the Convert to Shape submenu) Convert the selected shape(s) to a rectangle while retaining the original shape of the path. Options include setting absolute dimensions and dimensions relative to the size of the original shape (see Figure 20.18).

- **Rounded Rectangle:** (On the Convert to Shape submenu) Convert the selected shape(s) to a rounded-corner rectangle while retaining the original shape of the path. Options include setting absolute dimensions, dimensions relative to the size of the original shape, and corner radius.

- **Ellipse:** (On the Convert to Shape submenu) Convert the selected shape(s) to an ellipse while retaining the original shape of the path. Options include setting absolute dimensions and dimensions relative to the size of the original shape.

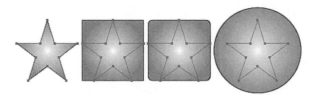

Figure 20.18
Convert to Shape Effects, from left to right: Original image, Rectangle, Rounded Rectangle, and Ellipse.

- **Free Distort:** (On the Distort & Transform submenu) Reshape objects by manipulating four control points. Drag points around the Free Distort dialog to skew, flip, stretch, squish, or create false perspective (see Figure 20.19).

- **Pucker & Bloat:** (On the Distort & Transform submenu) Push the object's anchor points outward while curving path segments inward with Pucker; push path segments outward with Bloat.

- **Roughen:** (On the Distort & Transform submenu) Convert the object's path segments into random angles. In the Roughen dialog specify the percentage of distortion, whether the center point is relative or absolute, the amount of detail to preserve, and whether the new anchor points created by the filter are corner points or smooth points.

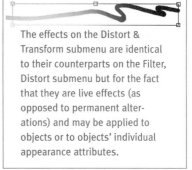

The effects on the Distort & Transform submenu are identical to their counterparts on the Filter, Distort submenu but for the fact that they are live effects (as opposed to permanent alterations) and may be applied to objects or to objects' individual appearance attributes.

- **Transform:** (On the Distort & Transform submenu) Precisely transform the selected object(s) or appearance attribute by adjusting the horizontal or vertical scale, moving horizontally or vertically, and rotating or reflecting. Create multiple instances of the effect by using the Copies text box to apply the Transform Effect to each progressively.

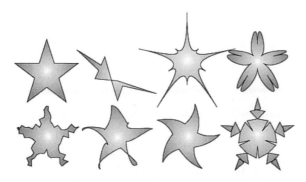

Figure 20.19
Distort & Transform Effects, from left to right: (top row) Original shape, Free Distort, Pucker, Bloat; (bottom row) Roughen, Tweak, Twist, and Zig Zag.

20

- **Tweak:** (On the Distort & Transform submenu) Suck in or push out path segments randomly. In the Tweak dialog specify the percentage of distortion horizontally and vertically, whether the center point is relative or absolute, and whether to distort anchor points, control points leading into anchor points, and control points leading out from anchor points.

- **Twist:** (On the Distort & Transform submenu) Distort the artwork by twisting it to a provided angle.

- **Zig Zag:** (On the Distort & Transform submenu) Push out the object's path segments uniformly. In the Zig Zag dialog specify the size of distortion, whether the center point is relative or absolute, the number of ridges per path segment, and whether the anchor points are smooth or corner points.

- **Offset Path:** (On the Path submenu) Offset the object's path (and corresponding fill and stroke) by specifying the distance to offset relative to the actual path, the type of path segment joins, and the miter limit (see Figure 20.20).

Figure 20.20
Path Effects, from left to right: Original object, Offset Path (demonstrated by offsetting additional fills), Outline Object, and Outline Stroke.

- **Outline Object:** (On the Path submenu) Outline the selected object(s). When used on type, this option has the same result as Type, Create Outline, but in live effect form that keeps type as live, editable text.

- **Outline Stroke:** (On the Path submenu) Outline the stroke of the selected object(s), creating the effect of turning strokes into filled, closed paths.

- **SVG Filters:** *Raster Effect.* Use various XML-based effects with images that you intend to export in Scalable Vector Graphic format.

- **Add:** (On the Pathfinder submenu) *Requires multiple object selection.* Combine the shapes of all selected objects. The resulting compound shape has the fill and stroke settings of the top object (see Figure 20.21).

- **Intersect:** (On the Pathfinder submenu) *Requires multiple object selection.* Clip or mask all selected objects to only the area of overlap. The resulting compound shape has the fill and stroke settings of the top object.

Figure 20.21
Pathfinder Effects, from left to right: (Row 1) Original artwork, Add, Intersect, and Exclude; (Row 2) Subtract, Minus Back, Divide, and Trim; (Row 3) Merge, Crop, Outline, and Hard Mix; (Row 4) Soft Mix and Trap.

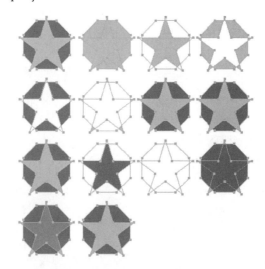

20

- **Exclude:** (On the Pathfinder submenu) *Requires multiple object selection.* Clip or mask all selected objects to omit all areas of overlap. The resulting compound shape has the fill and stroke settings of the top object.

- **Subtract:** (On the Pathfinder submenu) *Requires multiple object selection.* Cut out the shape of all other selected objects from the bottom object.

- **Minus Back:** (On the Pathfinder submenu) *Requires multiple object selection.* Knock all shapes overlapping the top object out of the area of the top object.

- **Divide:** (On the Pathfinder submenu) *Requires multiple object selection.* Divide all shapes by each other, resulting in new paths from each visible section of the originals, broken into new shapes at any overlap point.

- **Trim:** (On the Pathfinder submenu) *Requires multiple object selection.* Remove all overlapping areas from each shape. Also remove strokes assigned to any of the objects.

- **Merge:** (On the Pathfinder submenu) *Requires multiple object selection.* Combine the paths of any overlapping objects of the same fill color (and without strokes). Objects not of the same color are trimmed to remove overlap.

- **Crop:** (On the Pathfinder submenu) *Requires multiple object selection.* Remove all portions of the selected shapes that fall outside the area of the top objects. Also remove strokes assigned to any of the objects.

- **Outline:** (On the Pathfinder submenu) *Requires multiple object selection.* Divide the selected objects to their non-overlapping path segments. Fills are removed and strokes are preserved.

- **Hard Mix:** (On the Pathfinder submenu) *Requires multiple object selection.* Display the highest value colors present in any of the select objects.

- **Soft Mix:** (On the Pathfinder submenu) *Requires multiple object selection.* Specify a mixing rate percentage.

- **Trap:** (On the Pathfinder submenu) *Requires multiple object selection.* Create *traps*, or areas in which colors overlap to eliminate gaps caused by slight misregistration on press. In the Pathfinder Options dialog specify the trap thickness, relative height and width, tint reduction, and precision.

- **Rasterize:** *Raster Effect.* Convert the selected object(s) to raster (pixel-based) format. Choose resolution, background color, anti-aliasing, clipping mask, and outset.

- **Add Arrowheads:** (On the Stylize submenu) Add arrowheads or other shapes to the ends of open paths (see Figure 20.22).

- **Drop Shadow:** (On the Stylize submenu) *Raster Effect.* Create a drop shadow on the selected object(s). In the Drop Shadow dialog specify the blending mode, opacity, X and Y offsets (how far away the shadow casts) in positive or negative measurements, the amount of blur, and the color (click on the color swatch to access the Color Picker).

- **Feather:** (On the Stylize submenu) *Raster Effect.* Soften the edges of the selected object(s) by introducing transparency-blur to the outside edges.

20

Figure 20.22
Stylize Effects from left to right: (first row) Add Arrowheads, Drop Shadow, and Feather; (second row) Inner Glow, Outer Glow, and Round Corners.

- **Inner Glow:** (On the Stylize submenu) *Raster Effect.* Create a glowing effect inside the object's fill. Specify the color, blending mode, opacity, blur amount, and whether the glow moves from the center outward or the edge inward. Click the color swatch to access the Color Picker.

- **Outer Glow:** (On the Stylize submenu) *Raster Effect.* Create a glowing effect exterior to the object. Specify the color, blending mode, opacity, and blur amount. Click the color swatch to access the Color Picker.

- **Round Corners:** (On the Stylize submenu) Round the corners of angled shapes such as rectangles.

- **Scribble:** (On the Stylize submenu) Create hand-drawn or sketched effects to varying degrees. In the Scribble Options dialog choose among several presets or mix new settings. Set the angle of scribble lines, path overlap (how far within or beyond the path edge scribble lines may go), variation (how different scribble lines may be from one another), stroke width, curviness and variation of curviness of scribble strokes before reversing direction, and spacing (how far apart scribble lines are from one another) (see Figure 20.23).

Figure 20.23
Examples of the Scribble effect in action.

Photoshop Effects

The Effect Gallery, and the Photoshop effects within it, function exactly like the Filter Gallery and its Photoshop filters (see the "Filter Gallery" section earlier in this chapter). Also, as you might guess, other Photoshop effects on the Effects menu replicate the functions of their non-live counterparts, the Photoshop filters, but with the strengths and unique applications of live effects.

IMPORTING, EXPORTING, AND SAVING IN ILLUSTRATOR

21

There are a lot of times you won't use Illustrator to create an entire document; you'll use it to create graphics you will use in InDesign. In addition, there are often times when you want to bring other, previously created documents into Illustrator to work with its unique vector graphic tools. In this chapter, you take a look at some of the file formats you can import, as well as some of the ways you can export and save your Illustrator documents to use them in other applications. Finally, you explore the options for printing Illustrator files.

IMPORTING OPTIONS

When you select File, Place to bring an object into Illustrator, you have the option to link the placed file by clicking the Link check box in the Place dialog. If you select Link, the image you are placing is linked to its original file. If you uncheck Link, the file you are placing is embedded in the Illustrator document.

When files are linked, remember that if you send this current Illustrator file to be printed, you need to send the linked file along with it. You also have fewer options for editing the items in the file you placed. If you embed the file, your Illustrator file is larger because the file you are placing is stored inside.

If you are working with a file and you are not sure whether it is linked or embedded, choose Window, Links and check the Links palette. All linked files are listed in the palette.

To see a list of the type of files Illustrator allows you to place, see Chapter 13, "Understanding the Illustrator Environment," or select File, Place, and look at the Files of Type pop-up menu. In certain cases, you have additional options when you import.

Importing Adobe PDFs

When you import a PDF as a linked file, you can transform the image but you cannot edit it. If you embed the file, you can edit individual parts of the PDF.

If you choose to import a multiple-page PDF, you must choose which page you want to import. You can also specify how you want to crop the object (see Figure 21.1).

Figure 21.1
The PDF import options are listed in the Place PDF dialog.

In the Crop To pop-up menu in the Place PDF dialog, select from the following options:

- **Bounding Box:** Crop to the smallest area that encloses everything on the page, including page marks.

- **Art:** Crop to a rectangle specified in the PDF as artwork.

- **Crop:** Place what is displayed in Acrobat.

- **Trim:** Place the final produced page as it will be trimmed if trim marks are present.

- **Bleed:** Place a representation of where the page is trimmed if a bleed area has been set up.

- **Media:** Place the original PDF size on the InDesign page, including page marks.

Importing Bitmap Files

Remember that *bitmap* refers to any resolution-dependent file format, most notably digital images. The same rules about resolution apply when you place a bitmap file in Illustrator, meaning that the resolution of the image must be sufficient for its use (that is, higher for printing, lower for display only). The resolution of the original file is preserved when it is placed. You should not enlarge the image a great deal or do anything that might compromise the final printed quality of your file.

Importing Encapsulated PostScript (EPS) Files

EPS is a common format for vector files. You can open an EPS created in another program in Illustrator, or you can place an EPS in an Illustrator document. Like most file formats, you can edit an EPS if you embed it in your Illustrator document, but information can be lost if you place a file that contains effects Illustrator does not support. If you place a file that contains a color with the same name as a color in your Illustrator file, you are asked which color to use.

Importing Photoshop (PSD) Files

When you place native Photoshop files with multiple layers as embedded objects in Illustrator (that is, the Link check box is not checked), you have quite a few options as to how the files are displayed. When you select the file and click Place, a Photoshop Import Options dialog appears with the following options (see Figure 21.2):

- **Layer Comp:** If the Photoshop file contains layer comps, select the version of the image you want to import. Select Show Preview to display a preview of the layer comp. The Comments text box displays any comments saved with the Photoshop file.

- **When Updating Link:** Select from the following options for layer visibility settings when a linked Photoshop file that includes layer comps is updated:

  - **Keep Layer Visibility Overrides:** Show the layer you chose when you first placed the file.

  - **Use Photoshop's Layer Visibility:** Show the layer that is currently visible in the Photoshop file.

21

Figure 21.2
The Photoshop Import Options dialog.

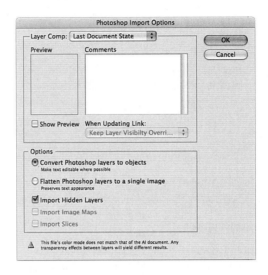

- **Convert Photoshop Layers To Objects:** Select this option and the application does everything it can to keep a file's appearance and text editability intact when it's placed. If there are effects applied that Illustrator doesn't support, it merges and rasterizes layers to preserve the appearance of the file.

- **Flatten Photoshop Layers To A Single Image:** Check this option and the file imports as a single bitmap that is not editable at all, unless a clipping path has been added. In that case, you can edit the clipping path only.

- **Import Hidden Layers:** Import all layers that exist in the Photoshop file, even those that are not visible.

- **Import Image Maps:** When available, select this option to preserve all image maps that exist in the Photoshop file.

- **Import Slices:** When available, select this option to preserve any slices that exist in the Photoshop file.

EXPORTING OPTIONS

Illustrator also gives you numerous options for exporting files that you can import into other applications, such as InDesign. To export your work, select File, Export and select the appropriate format in the Format pop-up menu before clicking Export. The following are those document formats, as well as other options the export selection gives you:

- **AutoCAD Drawing and AutoCAD Interchange File:** AutoCAD Drawing is the file format created when you use vector graphics in AutoCAD. AutoCAD Interchange File is the format used when you export AutoCAD drawings, or for importing drawings into AutoCAD.

- **BMP (Bitmap):** This is a general format used by Windows. Options when exporting bitmaps include color model, resolution and anti-alias settings, the Windows format (Windows or OS/2), and a bit depth, which determines the number of colors used.

- **Enhanced Metafile:** This is a file format used by Windows applications for vector graphics. Some Illustrator graphics may be rasterized when you export to this format.

- **JPEG (Joint Photographic Experts Group):** Usually used for photos (see Figure 21.3), JPEG is a lossy format, meaning the file is compressed by discarding image information. JPEGs are also often used on web pages:

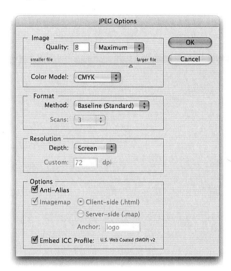

Figure 21.3
The JPEG Options dialog.

- **Quality:** Choose a number between 0 and 10 to select the quality level for your JPEG. The higher the number, the larger the file size.

- **Color Model:** Set the color space of the file.

- **Method and Scans:** Select Baseline (Standard) to export to a format recognized by most web browsers; select Baseline Optimized to optimize color and a smaller file; select Progressive to display a specific number of scans as the image downloads. If you save for the web, optimized and progressive JPEG images are not supported by every web browser.

- **Depth:** Select from Screen (low), Medium, or High. If you want to enter a specific resolution, choose Custom.

- **Anti-Alias:** Smooth out the edges of line art.

- **Imagemap:** Create code for web image maps. Select either Client-side (.html) or Server-side (.map) to choose the type of code created.

- **Embed ICC Profiles:** Save the ICC profile present in the JPEG file.

21

- **Macintosh PICT:** This is a general format used by Macintosh.

- **Macromedia Flash:** This format is used mostly for interactive, moving web graphics (see Figure 21.4):

Figure 21.4
The Flash Export Options dialog.

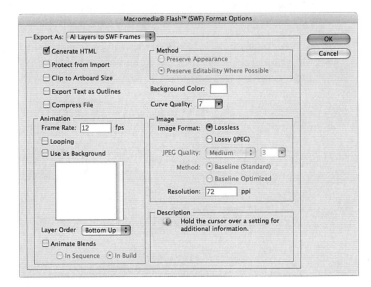

- **Export As:** First, choose how you want the Illustrator file's layers to export to SWF frames. The AI File to SWF File option exports your file to a single frame. The AI Layers to SWF Frames option exports each layer to a separate SWF frame. This creates an animated SWF file. The AI Layers to SWF Files option exports the artwork on each layer to an individual SWF file. Each SWF file contains a single frame corresponding to the Illustrator file's layers.

- **Generate HTML:** Check this box to create HTML code for the SWF file. A separate HTML file is exported with the SWF, and this code is then available so you can add the SWF file to a web page.

- **Protect from Import:** Ensure the file cannot be edited or changed.

- **Clip to Artboard Size:** Export everything within the edges of the artboard.

- **Export Text as Outlines:** Convert type to vector paths. This option ensures your text will not appear differently in the Flash player.

- **Compress File:** Create a smaller file. Note that these files cannot be used in Flash Player 5 and lower.

- **Method:** You have two choices when you select AI File To SWF File: Preserve Appearance or Preserve Editability Where Possible. The Preserve Appearance option flattens artwork to a single layer when it is exported. The Preserve Editability Where Possible option gives you as much layer editing control as possible.

- **Background Color:** Click the square to open a Color Picker and choose a background color for the SWF file.

- **Curve Quality:** This option, which can be set from 0 to 10, refers to the quality of Bézier curves. Lower numbers make the file size smaller, but can cause a loss of curve quality. Higher numbers give more accurate curves, but create larger files.

- **Animation:** Under Animation, there are several selections that are available only if you have chosen to export AI Layers to SWF Frames. The *Frame Rate* refers to the rate at which the animation is played in the Flash viewer. *Looping* causes the animation to play over and over, as opposed to playing once and then stopping. *Use As Background* sets one or more layers or sub-layers as static content in the SWF frames that are exported. This content shows in every SWF frame.

  - **Layer Order:** Set up the animation order. Bottom Up exports layers starting with the lowest layer in the Layers palette. Top Down exports layers starting with the uppermost layer in the Layers palette.

  - **Animate Blends:** Select to animate blended objects. Blends are always animated from start to end no matter the layer order. If you select Animate Blends, you have two options for exporting the blend: In Sequence, which exports each object in the blend to a separate frame, or In Builds, which creates a sequence of objects that build on each other.

- **Image Format:** Choose Lossless or Lossy to determine how the artwork is compressed. Lossless compression does not degrade the image at all and results in a larger file. Lossy compression creates smaller files that can contain artifacts. Adobe recommends that you select Lossless if you will continue to work on the files in Flash; select Lossy if this is the final SWF file you are exporting.

- **JPEG Quality:** Available only if you select Lossy compression above, use this option to indicate how much detail remains in the exported image. The file size grows relative to the quality selected.

- **Method:** Available only if you select Lossy compression, choose Baseline (Standard) for standard compression or Baseline Optimized for optimized compression.

- **Resolution:** Indicate the screen resolution for bitmap images. Resolution can range from 72 to 2400 pixels per inch. Again, the higher the resolution, the higher the quality and the larger the file. The smaller the resolution, the smaller the file and the lower the quality.

- **Photoshop:** Create a standard PSD, or Photoshop document (see Figure 21.5). Depending on whether Photoshop supports the effects as exported, Illustrator may flatten or rasterize the file:

  - **Color Model:** Choose either Grayscale, RGB, or CMYK. When you export a color file, the safest choice here is always to export with the same color mode you have been working in. Changing the color mode here flattens the image and may cause some items to display differently from how you intended.

  - **Resolution:** Choose the resolution of the exported file: Screen (low), Medium, High, or Other (in which you enter your own resolution).

21

Figure 21.5
The Photoshop Export Options dialog.

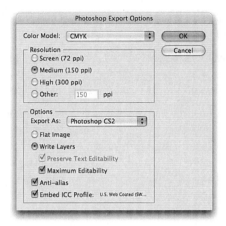

- **Export As:** Choose Photoshop CS2 or Photoshop 5.5. The Photoshop CS2 format enables you to edit text objects of all types (point text, area text, and path text), and the Photoshop 5.5 format enables you to edit only point text objects.

- **Flat Image:** Create a flattened, rasterized image that preserves the appearance of the file.

- **Write Layers:** Export the Illustrator layers to separate Photoshop layers as much as possible without degrading the appearance of the file. If Maximum Editability is checked, nested layers are not flattened into their parent layer. If Preserve Text Editability is selected, horizontal and vertical point type is exported into an editable Photoshop layer if it does not compromise the design.

- **Anti-Alias:** Smooth out the edges of line art.

- **Embed ICC Profiles:** Save the ICC profile present in the Illustrator file.

- **PNG (Portable Network Graphic):** This is a lossless compression format used for web graphics. Although PNGs have better display than a format such as GIF, for example, they are also not supported by every web browser (see Figure 21.6):

  - **Resolution:** Choose Screen (low), Medium, High or Other, which enables you to enter your own resolution. If you know the application in which your PNG file will be viewed, you should open the file in it to check your resolution choice. Some applications display PNGs at only 72 ppi, so a file saved at 300 ppi displays more than four times larger than the size you intended.

There are many variables that can occur between layers and nested layers, and between the versions of Photoshop you export to. For the most part, these should be variables you will not encounter, such as Illustrator files with more than 100 layers not being supported in Photoshop 5.5. If you are creating extremely complex Illustrator documents, check out the Photoshop Export Options entry in the Adobe Help Center for Illustrator to ensure you are creating files that export as you intend.

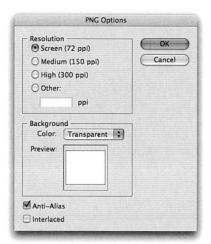

Figure 21.6
The PNG Export Options dialog.

- **Background:** Choose Transparent, White, Black or Other, which enables you to choose your own color. Your selection here fills in the background of your document as indicated in the preview.

- **Anti-Alias:** Smooth out the edges of line art.

- **Interlaced:** Create files that gradually display low-resolution previews as the file loads in a web page. Although it makes files load faster, it also creates larger documents.

- **Targa:** This is a format used on Truevision video board systems.

- **Text Format:** Export the text in an illustration.

- **TIFF (Tagged Image File Format):** This format is best used in cross-platform, cross-application situations. Most applications support TIFFs (see Figure 21.7):

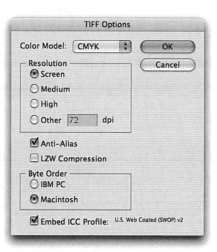

Figure 21.7
The TIFF Export Options dialog.

21

- **Color Model:** Choose either Grayscale, RGB, or CMYK.

- **Resolution:** Choose Screen (low), Medium, High or Other (in which you to enter your own resolution).

- **Anti-Alias:** Smooth out the edges of line art.

- **LZW Compression:** Apply a lossless compression, producing a smaller file.

- **Byte Order:** Choose either IBM PC or Macintosh, based on the platform in which the file will be used. If you are working with updated software versions, this is usually not a problem because more modern applications and operating systems are capable of translating either platform.

- **Embed ICC Profiles:** Save the ICC profile present in the Illustrator file.

- **Windows Metafile:** Used by Windows applications for vector graphics, this format generally displays files better than the Enhanced Metafile option.

SAVING OPTIONS

When you save your Illustrator files, you also have various options, not only in the Save dialog, but also other choices in the File menu. The format options available when you choose File, Save are called *native formats*, because they preserve all Illustrator data. These options are detailed in the following sections.

Adobe Illustrator Document (`.ai`)

The AI format is the standard Adobe Illustrator format, which can be placed in Photoshop and InDesign files within the Creative Suite. When you choose to save as an Illustrator document, you have the following options (see Figure 21.8):

Figure 21.8
The Illustrator Options dialog when saving a file.

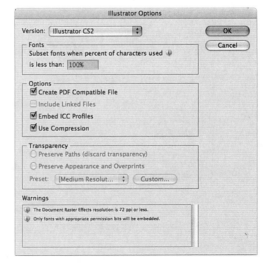

- **Version:** Choose from CS versions or legacy versions of Illustrator. As always when you are saving back, certain features that didn't exist in previous versions will not be available. The Warnings area at the bottom of the dialog alerts you to any of these nonsupported features.

- **Fonts:** Choose at what point the font should be embedded in the document. If you enter 75% in the field, if less than 75% of the individual characters in that font are used in the document, the font is subset—that is, only those characters used are included in the document. If 75% of the characters or more are used, the entire font is embedded, which increases your file size.

- **Create PDF Compatible File:** Save a PDF representation of the file with the Illustrator file.

- **Include Linked Files:** Embed any linked files.

- **Embed ICC Profiles:** Save the ICC profile present in the Illustrator file.

- **Use Compression:** Compress the PDF data in the file. Checking this option can make saving your file very slow, so uncheck it if you are experiencing save times of more than 8 minutes.

- **Transparency:** Select among the following options, which are available when you have used transparency in your document and are saving to a legacy version of Illustrator, where transparency is not supported in the same way: Choose Preserve Paths to discard any transparency in the document and Choose Preserve Appearance and Overprints to preserve overprints that don't interact with transparent objects. Overprints that interact with transparent objects are flattened. When you choose this option, you can also select a transparency flattener preset or create your own.

The Warnings section of the dialog alerts you to any issues within your document that may cause it to reproduce incorrectly, such as resolution or fonts that cannot be embedded.

PDF

When you save a file as a PDF, you create a compact document that contains everything you need to view the file exactly as you create it, with all fonts, colors, and graphics preserved. Because of that, the options to save a PDF are more complicated than the average graphic format. When you select PDF, a dialog opens with multiple panes, accessed by clicking in the list at the left (see Figure 21.9). The following is an overview of the various PDF options.

At the top of the dialog is an area to choose a preset. Illustrator is preloaded with several PDF presets, including High Quality Print, Press Quality, and Smallest File Size. PDF/X-1a: 2001 and PDF/X-1a: 2003 are also available presets. These settings refer to specific standards for graphic compliance that help eliminate problems with colors, fonts, and trapping. If you are preparing a file for output at a printing facility, check with the printer to see which setting is best for your document. In general, if you are preparing a document for viewing only, you should choose Smallest File Size when exporting.

The Standard pop-up menu should stay at None unless you are working to specific PDF/X-1a:2001, PDF/X-1a:2003, PDF/X-3:2002, and PDF/X-3:2003 standards for color-managed documents.

In the Compatibility pop-up menu, choose the version of Acrobat to which your document should conform, from version 4 (PDF 1.3) through version 7 (PDF 1.6). If you are exporting the document for

21

viewing only, you should work to the lowest version that your audience might have; however, different versions of Acrobat have varying levels of support for some of Illustrator's features. See the end of this section for specific information on what is supported by the various PDF versions.

Figure 21.9
The General pane of the Save Adobe PDF dialog.

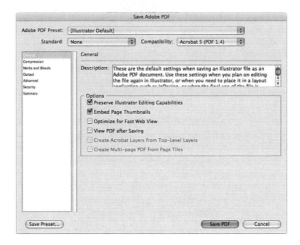

General PDF Options

Preserve Illustrator Editing Capabilities maintains all the Illustrator data in the file so it can be edited. Checking this option can create large file sizes:

- **Embed Page Thumbnails:** Create a preview of the PDF's pages that travel with the document and can be viewed if you try to import the PDF into another document, for example. Including thumbnails increases the file size of the PDF.

- **Optimize for Fast Web View:** Compress the objects in the file and reduce the size of the PDF so it loads quickly in a web browser.

- **View PDF after Saving:** Automatically open the PDF in Acrobat as soon as it is finished exporting.

- **Create Acrobat Layers from Top-Level Layers:** Export items on top-level layers in Illustrator into a layered PDF, accessible in Acrobat 6.0 and later. You see this option only if you select Acrobat 6 or 7 in the Compatibility pop-up menu. The layers can be shown and hidden to create different looks for your document depending on what's placed on which layer.

- **Create Multi-page PDF from Page Tiles:** Separate tiles in the Illustrator document into individual pages in the PDF. This is the only way to create a multipage document from Illustrator.

PDF Compression Options

The PDF Compression panel of the Save Adobe PDF dialog (see Figure 21.10) enables you to select how to deal with color, grayscale, and monochrome images. If you are creating documents for viewing onscreen or on the Web only, it's a good idea to choose a downsampling option for the different types of images, because it's going to result in smaller file sizes without causing the images to lose visual quality. If you are printing these documents, however, this is an important place to check with your service provider and get advice on how to prepare the document.

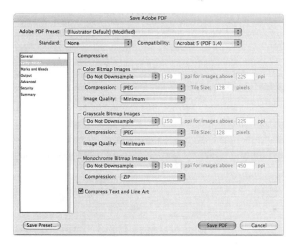

Figure 21.10
The Compression pane of the Save Adobe PDF dialog.

Your choices for downsampling include

- **Average Downsampling:** Replace specific pixels in the image with the average pixel color in a sample area.

- **Subsampling:** Pick a pixel in the center of a sample area and use it as the color for the entire area. This results in the fastest conversion time, but the least smooth look.

- **Bicubic Downsampling:** Use a weighted average to sample pixel color. This results in the slowest conversion time, but has the smoothest appearance.

Compression options include

- **None:** Select for no compression.

- **Automatic (JPEG):** Select for the best quality for color and grayscale images. This option is available only for documents exported to Acrobat 6 and later.

- **Automatic JPEG 2000:** Automatically determine the best quality for image reproduction.

- **JPEG:** Reduce file size with the least amount of lost information.

- **JPEG 2000:** Set progressive display (enter the number of tiles in the field to the right). This is the international standard compression format and is available only in documents set to export to Acrobat 6 or higher.

- **ZIP:** Determine whether this downsampling will be lossless or lossy, depending on whether the resolution is set at or below the image's original resolution.

The Image Quality pop-up menu determines the amount of compression.

21

For monochromatic images, the compression options include CCITT, which is good for black-and-white images. Group 4 is a general-purpose compression method; Group 3 is used by fax machines and compresses the bitmaps one row at a time. Run Length compression works well for images with large solid areas of black or white.

The Compress Text and Line Art check box applies a Flate compression algorithm, which compresses without degrading detail or quality.

PDF Marks and Bleed Options

Based on your choices in check boxes on the Marks and Bleeds pane of the Save PDF Options dialog (see Figure 21.11), various printer's marks are applied to your page. Again, you might want to check with your printer to see whether any of these marks are required. You do not want to select any options in this panel if you are creating a PDF for the Web or onscreen viewing only.

Figure 21.11
The Marks and Bleeds pane of the Save Adobe PDF dialog.

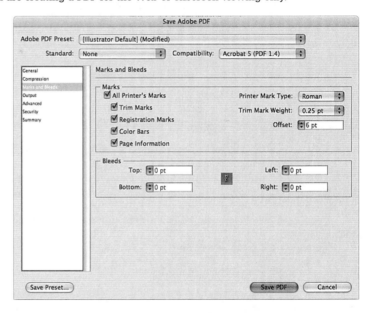

Setting up a bleed area helps ensure that your bleeding page objects actually extend off the page, as opposed to printing with a white line between the bleed element and the page edge.

PDF Output Options

The Output panel of the Save Adobe PDF dialog (see Figure 21.12) gives you options for handling color management within your document. Choices vary depending on whether you have color management turned on for the document, whether you have applied a color profile to the document, and which PDF standard has been selected. To get more information about the individual settings, hold your mouse over the selection; a brief explanation appears in the Description field.

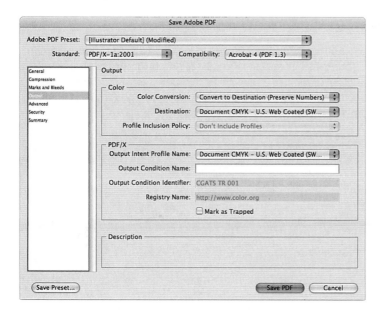

Figure 21.12
The Output pane of the Save Adobe PDF dialog.

For most PDFs, you have the option to choose No Conversion, Convert to Destination, or Convert to Destination (Preserve Numbers). For the last two choices, you can select the destination color space that objects with embedded profiles convert to—make sure your printer or output agency makes you aware of the best choice to make. If you choose to preserve numbers, any object without an embedded profile keeps the color settings applied to it.

You can choose whether to include destination profiles in the next pop-up menu; this determines whether a color profile is included in the document. Again, based on other color choices you make, your options differ:

- **Don't Include Profiles:** Set to not include destination profiles.

- **Include All Profiles:** Create color management in the document. Make sure you turn on color management in the document and set up a profile.

- **Include Tagged Source Profiles:** Choose to include settings that have been specifically created for output on calibrated devices.

- **Include All RGB and Tagged Source CMYK Profiles:** Choose to include profiles for these items.

- **Include Destination Profile:** Assign the profile to all page elements.

If you have specified to export to a PDF/X format, you can choose the output profile in the next section. If color management is on, the output intent device is the same profile as selected previously, in the Destination area. If not, the selections match the destination color space.

Enter your own information in the Output Condition Name field.

The Output Condition Identifier field enables you to type the name of the Output Condition if one is not entered automatically from the ICC profile. Similarly, the Registry Name may be filled in, or you can use the field to type the URL of the output condition.

21

Advanced PDF Options

The Advanced pane of the Save Adobe PDF dialog is shown in Figure 21.13. The Fonts section enables you to choose at what point the font should be embedded in the document. The default setting is 100, which means that if less than 100% of the individual characters in that font is used in the document, the font is subset—only those characters used are included in the document. If 100% of the characters is used, the entire font is embedded, which increases your file size.

Figure 21.13

The Advanced pane of the Save Adobe PDF dialog.

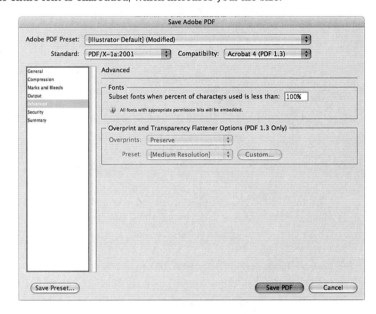

If you select an export version of Acrobat 5 or higher, the options in the Overprint and Transparency Flattener Options (PDF 1.3 only) section are not available because overprinting (the process of printing colored elements on top of another color) and transparency is automatically supported and preserved in documents.

Overprint enables you to preserve or discard overprint settings, which refer to colors that overlap each other and are set to overprint. With version 4 (Acrobat 1.3), you can also choose to simulate overprinting by flattening.

For transparencies, you can choose High, Medium, or Low Resolution options that flatten all transparent objects. The flattening process takes the area where transparency has been applied and breaks it into individual vector or raster areas. You can set up transparency flattening presets to specify how this should take place.

To customize your transparency flattening options, click the Custom button. In the Custom Transparency Flattener Options dialog that opens, choose from the following settings:

- **Raster/Vector Balance:** Determine to what point artwork is rasterized. Rasterization converts vector graphics, or those created with curves and lines, to dots. The higher the setting, the less the graphics are rasterized. This means your page objects are smoother, but they take longer to load and print.

21

- **Line Art and Text Resolution:** Determine the resolution for those objects that are rasterized when you flatten. If you are outputting to low-resolution devices, this number can equal the output resolution. If you are outputting to a high-resolution device, you should check with your printer or the device manual for resolution suggestions.

- **Gradient and Mesh Resolution:** Determine the resolution for gradients and drop shadows or feathers when flattened. Adobe recommends keeping this setting between 150 and 300. Higher resolutions cause slower printing and exporting and larger file sizes, without any equivalent return in quality.

- **Convert All Text to Outlines:** On spreads with transparency, convert all type to outlines and discard glyph information for that font. It helps ensure text retains its proper width during flattening, but small type sizes may appear thicker when these documents are viewed onscreen or printed on low-resolution output devices.

- **Convert All Strokes to Outlines:** Convert all strokes to filled paths on spreads with transparency to ensure the stroke width stays consistent when flattened. As with the fonts discussed in the previous option, thin lines may appear thicker onscreen or when printed on low-resolution output devices.

- **Clip Complex Regions:** Reduce stitching that can result where vector and raster objects meet. Stitching shows up as blocky areas where colors don't exactly match. If you check this box, you also create complex paths that might make your document harder to print.

PDF Security Options

Security options are available only for files exported for Acrobat 5 and higher (see Figure 21.14).

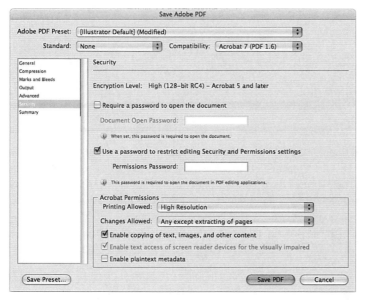

Figure 21.14
The Security pane of the Save Adobe PDF dialog.

If you want to require users to enter a password when they open the file, click in the Document Open Password check box and enter the password you want them to use.

In the Permissions area, you can set up various degrees of protection for your document. Click in the first check box to restrict printing, editing, and other document changes, and enter a password. Then choose whether to allow high-resolution, low-resolution, or no printing, and whether to allow various page and form tasks. You can also check the box to enable page elements to be copied.

With high security settings, you also have the option to allow users to access the document with software that reads the document for the visually impaired.

PDF Summary

The final panel of the PDF Export dialog is a summary (see Figure 21.15). You can drill down through the various PDF settings to see the choices that were made for this document. This is especially useful if you use a PDF preset and want to access information about the document quickly. Click Save Summary to save a text file of this information.

Figure 21.15
The Summary pane of the Save Adobe PDF dialog.

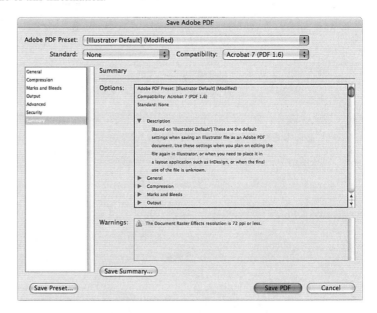

Before you click the Export button, notice the Save Preset button in the lower left of the dialog. If you are creating multiple documents with the same settings, or will always have to export with the same options for a specific printer, you can save these settings and quickly load them for use with various documents. Click the Save Presets button, name the preset, and click OK. From that point on, the preset you saved is available if you go to File, Adobe PDF Presets, [preset name]. After you load your preset, you can click Export and know that everything is being saved exactly as you set it up.

21

How Do I Know What PDF Version to Export To?

As stated earlier, always work to the lowest common denominator. If you think there is a chance your audience might still be using an outdated version of Adobe Reader, save to the lowest version that still supports your design. It's also a good idea to keep as many versions of Reader installed as you can, so you can open documents on specific versions and test them. The following is an overview of what is supported by various versions of Acrobat:

- **Acrobat 4 (PDF 1.3):** Files can be opened with version 3 and later. ICC color management is supported. Artwork that uses transparency must be flattened before it can be exported to PDF 1.3. Layers are not supported. DeviceN color space with eight colorants is supported. Pages can be up to 45 inches by 45 inches. Double-byte fonts can be embedded. 40-bit RC4 security is supported.

- **Acrobat 5 (PDF 1.4):** Files can be opened with version 3 and later, but certain features may not be available. ICC color management is supported. Transparent artwork is supported. Layers are not supported. DeviceN color space with eight colorants is supported. Pages can be up to 200 inches by 200 inches. Double-byte fonts can be embedded. 128-bit RC4 security is supported.

- **Acrobat 6 (PDF 1.5):** Files can be opened with version 4 and later, but certain features may not be available. ICC color management is supported. Transparent artwork is supported. Layers are preserved when imported into applications that support their use. DeviceN color space with up to 31 colorants is supported. Pages can be up to 200 inches by 200 inches. Double-byte fonts can be embedded. 128-bit RC4 security is supported.

- **Acrobat 7 (PDF 1.6):** Files can be opened with version 4 and later, but certain features may not be available. ICC color management is supported. Transparent artwork is supported. Layers are preserved when imported into applications that support their use. DeviceN color space with up to 31 colorants is supported. Pages can be up to 200 inches by 200 inches. Double-byte fonts can be embedded. 128-bit RC4 and 128-bit AES security is supported.

Illustrator EPS

EPS is an Encapsulated PostScript file, and one of the most common graphic formats used today for print. When you save as an EPS, you have the following options (see Figure 21.16):

- **Version:** Choose from CS versions or legacy versions of Illustrator. As always when you are saving back, certain features that didn't exist in previous versions will not be available. The Warning window at the bottom of the dialog alerts you to any of these nonsupported features.

- **Format:** This option refers to the preview that is saved with your EPS. It is always good to save a preview because some applications in which you might place this file cannot display EPS files. Therefore, the preview enables you to see your EPS in these applications. Choose None if you do not want to save a preview, or choose black-and-white or color.

   If you choose TIFF (8-bit Color), you can make the background for your preview Transparent or Opaque (that is, solid). If you will place the EPS in a Microsoft Office application, choose Opaque.

21

Figure 21.16
The EPS Options dialog when you save an Illustrator file.

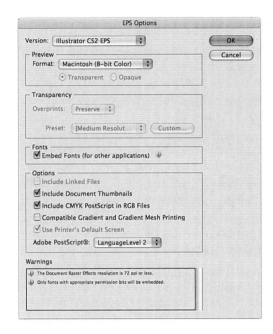

- **Transparency:** Your options in this section vary depending on the version you chose earlier. If you chose a CS version, choose the Transparency Flattening Preset you want to use, or click Customize to create your own. If you chose a legacy version, select Preserve Paths to discard any transparency in the document. Choose Preserve Appearance and Overprints to preserve overprints that don't interact with transparent objects. Overprints that interact with transparent objects are flattened. When you choose this option, you can also select a transparency flattener preset or create your own.

- **Embed Fonts (For Other Applications):** It is usually a good idea to embed fonts as long as you have the appropriate permissions for the font(s). When fonts are embedded, your file is sure to display the way you intended. If the file is opened or placed on another computer, where the font is not installed, another font is substituted. Embedding fonts increases file size.

- **Include Linked Files:** Embed any placed graphics that are linked.

- **Include Document Thumbnails:** Create a thumbnail preview that displays in the Open and Place dialogs.

- **Include CMYK PostScript In RGB Files:** Allow files in RGB color modes to print on CMYK printers. Choosing this option does not change the color mode of the original document.

- **Compatible Gradient And Gradient Mesh Printing:** Convert gradients and gradient meshes to JPEG format for older printers and PostScript devices that might not support these effects. Select this option only if you have problems printing these effects; otherwise, it slows printing.

- **Adobe PostScript:** Select PostScript Language Level 2 or 3. This determines how the file is saved for output on PostScript devices. The main difference is in how gradient meshes are printed. If your file contains a gradient mesh, you should choose PostScript Language Level 3.

The Warnings section of the dialog alerts you to any issues within your document that may cause it to reproduce incorrectly, such as resolution or fonts that cannot be embedded.

Illustrator Template (`.ait`)

Selecting this option in the Save dialog saves a document that opens as Untitled every time you open it, to help preserve document settings and characteristics. When you save as a template, you do not have the options that you see when you save as a standard Illustrator file.

SVG and SVGX

SVG stands for Scalable Vector Graphic (see Figure 21.17). An SVGX file is a compressed SVG. SVG is a fairly recent development in file formats, with the files mostly being used for web graphics at this time. There are, however, numerous cell phones on the market that support the use of SVG graphics in their display, as well as PDAs and other mobile devices. There are many benefits to the use of SVG graphics, including their small file size, their animation abilities, and the fact that they can be used or displayed at any size without losing resolution (hence, *scalable* and *vector* graphics).

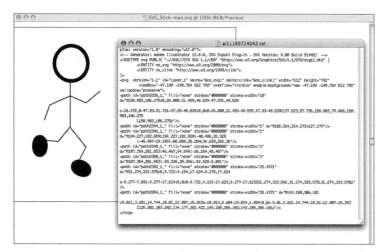

Figure 21.17
An example of an SVG in Illustrator and the code it produces.

But be aware that although the use of SVG should explode within the next few years, it is still not fully supported by all web browsers. Internet Explorer, for example, requires the download of a plug-in from Adobe to display SVG. Mozilla browsers, including the popular Firefox, were still developing SVG support as of this writing. As with any graphic, you should make sure it is accessible to your users before you start to create it as a standard. The w3.org site is the best source of information about SVG and its current use and support; you can access it directly at www.w3.org/Graphics/SVG.

SVG and SVGX Options

Figure 21.18 shows the SVG Options dialog; the following are options you have when you choose to save an SVG or SVGX file:

21

Figure 21.18
The SVG Options dialog.

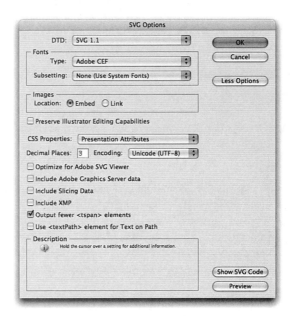

- **DTD:** Choose the Document Type Definition for the file. SVG 1.0 and SVG 1.1 should be used for files that will be viewed on a desktop computer. SVG Tiny 1.1 and SVG Tiny 1.1 Plus should be used for files that will be viewed on small mobile devices like cell phones. SVG Basic 1.1 can be used for larger mobile devices, like PDAs. Some SVG formats do not support all Illustrator effects, so check the Adobe Help Center for information on specific file options.

- **Font Type:** Choose how fonts are exported. Adobe CEF gives a better display of small fonts, but is supported by only Adobe's SVG Viewer. SVG is supported by all SVG viewers, but may degrade the look of your text. Convert To Outlines is the safest choice because it preserves the look of text by converting it to vector graphics.

- **Font Subsetting:** Choose how fonts are embedded in the file. None assumes that your end users have all of the fonts you used installed on their systems. Only Glyphs Used embeds only those characters used in the file. Common English, Common English + Glyphs Used, Common Roman, Common Roman + Glyphs Used, and All Glyphs are better choices if the text in the graphic is interactive and can be changed by the end user or is automatically generated for display.

- **Image Location:** Choose how raster images are handled in the file. Linking images creates smaller files, but the links must be available to the end user to display properly. Embedding the images makes the file size larger but preserves your display for all users.

- **Preserve Illustrator Editing Capabilities:** Check this box if you will be opening the file and editing it again in Illustrator.

The following options are available when you click the More Options button on the SVG Options dialog. Click Less Options to hide these choices:

- **CSS Properties:** Choose how style attributes are saved in the file. Presentation Attributes gives you the most flexibility for editing style attributes. Style Attributes results in larger files, but gives the best display. Style Attributes <Entity References> creates smaller files and faster load times. Style Elements should be chosen if you are sharing these files with HTML documents, because you can create styles that can be referenced in HTML code. These files are slower to render, however.

- **Decimal Places:** Choose a value from 1 to 7 to determine how precisely vector data is displayed. A higher value gives you better quality but a larger file.

- **Encoding:** Choose how characters are encoded in the file. Unicode Transformation Format (UTF-8 and UTF-16) is supported by all XML processors. Choosing ISO 8859-1 and UTF-16 may result in the loss of metadata.

- **Optimize For Adobe SVG Viewer:** Give the file the highest level of editability.

- **Include Adobe Graphics Server Data:** Include variable data information in the file.

- **Include Slicing Data:** Include slice locations and optimization settings.

- **Include XMP:** Keep any XMP metadata with your file.

- **Output Fewer <tspan> Elements:** Keep your file editable and compact by ignoring any automatic type kerning settings in the document. Use this for graphics without a lot of text or without auto-kerning.

- **Use <textPath> Element For Text On Path:** Export text on a path as a <textPath> element. Note that there is no way to guarantee that the text on a path will appear the same in the SVG file as it does in Illustrator.

- **Show SVG Code:** Show the code for your file in a browser window.

- **Preview:** Show the SVG file in a browser window.

Save for Web

Selecting File, Save for Web opens a dialog that gives you many options for saving your web graphics. This section provides a brief overview of the Save for Web dialog (see Figure 21.19).

Your file is displayed in its original format. Click the Optimized tab at the top of the dialog to show the file in a web-optimized format. You can see the optimization that has taken place under the display; in this case, our graphic has been reduced from 1.85MB to 4.079KB when it is displayed as a GIF. If you want to compare your optimized graphic side by side with your original file, click the 2-Up tab; to compare several versions of optimization, click the 4-Up tab.

The tools to the left of the window enable you to move the graphic around, select individual slices for optimization, zoom in or out of your file, sample color with the Eyedropper tool to add it to the color table (the box below shows the current color), and turn slice visibility on and off.

21

Figure 21.19
The Save for Web dialog. Notice the optimization view of the file in its original format and as a GIF.

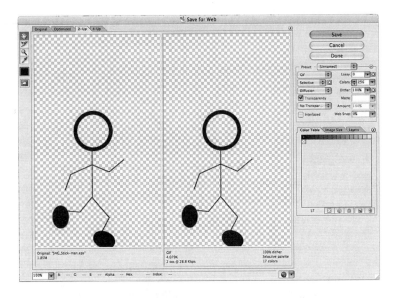

To the right of the display, the Color Table tab shows the colors that are used in your graphic if you are exporting to GIF or PNG-8 formats. The Image Size tab enables you to adjust the size of your image, and the Layers tab enables you to use the layers in your graphic to generate CSS layers for special effects in your web document.

You can also select from several formats, including GIF, JPEG, PNG, SWF, SVG, and WBMP. See the Adobe Help Center for complete information on these file types and the options available when you choose them for saving web graphics.

SHARING VECTOR GRAPHICS

As you save and export files, it's important to keep your final audience in mind. If you use Illustrator to create a whole document, you generally need to make sure only your output agency and/or printer can open and work with your file.

If you use Illustrator to create a corporate logo, however, there are many more people you need to please. Do some research. Does everyone who needs to place the logo work in page layout software? Or do some users need to have a logo they can place in Microsoft Word, for example? Are they Mac users, or do they have Windows computers? Even though platform is becoming less and less important as graphic options standardize, it can still be important with certain formats.

Keep in mind that you might have to save several different versions of your graphic to take care of everyone who will be using it. You might even be forced to simulate certain effects that may not be supported in other applications. Know your audience so you can minimize your issues.

Understanding SWF Animation

There are several options within Illustrator to export graphics that are appropriate for the Web, but only one—SWF—is appropriate for animation. The Flash animation format is supported by all web browsers, usually through the use of a plug-in (see Figure 21.20).

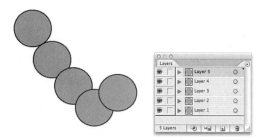

Figure 21.20
A simple example of a layered Illustrator document that could be exported as Flash animation.

There are several ways to create Flash animations. You can use the Symbolism tools to create regular occurrences of your graphic and create an animation from that. You can also place various versions of a graphic on different layers within Illustrator and export each layer as a separate animation frame. See the SWF Export Options dialog earlier in this chapter for complete information about the options available for SWF creation.

Understanding SVG Interactivity

You can add interactive features to a web page, such as movement of a page element created by a mouse event, through the SVG Interactivity palette. Prior to creating the interactive event, you must have a JavaScript action saved and defined that represents the action you want to create.

To create an interactive event, first open the palette by choosing Window, SVG Interactivity (see Figure 21.21). From the Event pop-up menu, select the event that you want to trigger the action. These are simple, standard events like click or mouseover.

Figure 21.21
In the SWF Interactivity palette, choose the action and script with which to create the interactivity.

Associate your JavaScript with the action by selecting JavaScript files from the palette menu. Browse to a file, select it, and click Open. Click Add to continue to associate JavaScript files, or click Done.

Type the name of your file in the JavaScript field on the palette and click Enter. When you export and view the SVG file, the interactivity associates with it.

PRINTING

When you are ready to print your document, select File, Print. You can select a print preset if one has been created, or use the default. Select the printer you want to print to and the PPD for that printer. In most cases, the PPD is preloaded, but there might be instances in which you need to select another PPD file for the document. See the information about PPDs in the PostScript Printing section that follows.

Use the left pane to navigate through your printing options.

21

General Options

The following options (such as number of copies and paper size) found in the General pane of the Print dialog (see Figure 21.22) enable you to choose how the document prints from your output device.

Figure 21.22
The General pane of the Print dialog.

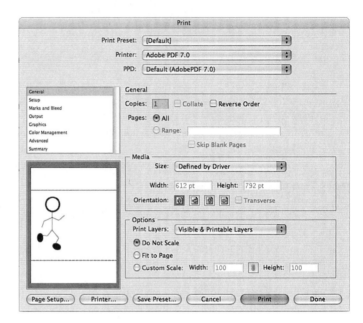

- Enter the number of copies.

- If you are printing multiple copies of tiled documents, you can select to collate the documents.

- Click the Reverse Order check box to print the pages in reverse order.

- Select to print all pages, or enter a range of pages.

- If you are printing a range of pages, click the check box if you'd like to skip any blank pages.

- Under Media, select the page size. It can either be defined by the print driver, a custom size (in which you enter the width and height of the document), or a predefined standard page size. Select the orientation of your document using the graphic buttons. If your PPD supports transverse printing—that is, automatic rotation to 90°—click in the Transverse check box.

- Under Options, choose to print Visible and Printable Layers, Visible Layers only, or All Layers. You can choose not to scale your document and print it at its current size, to fit the document to the page, or to custom scale the document. Enter percentages for width and height. If the chain between the width and height entry fields is linked, the artwork will be scaled proportionally. Click the link to break it, and enter different percentages in the two fields.

Setup Options

The following options, found in the Setup pane of the Print dialog (see Figure 21.23), enable you to choose how and where your document prints on the paper.

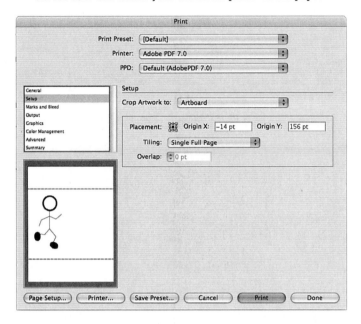

Figure 21.23
The Setup pane of the Print dialog.

- Choose to crop your artwork to the artboard, the artwork bounding box, or a specific cropped area.

- The Placement section enables you to position your artwork exactly where you want for printing. To change the orientation, click on one of the points in the placement proxy and enter the x and y coordinates where you want that portion of the page to lie. You can also drag the document in the preview window to position it.

- For Tiling, you can print as a single full page, or you can choose to tile full page or tile printable areas. If you tile your document, it prints on as many pages as necessary to fit the artwork. The preview shows you the number of pages the tile will occupy. If you choose Tile Full Page, you can set up an overlap amount to duplicate that amount of space between pages and help with assembling tiled pages.

Marks and Bleed Options

The Marks and Bleed pane (see Figure 21.24) enables you to specify printer's marks for the page, as well as set up a bleed area.

21

Figure 21.24
The Marks and Bleed pane of the
Print dialog.

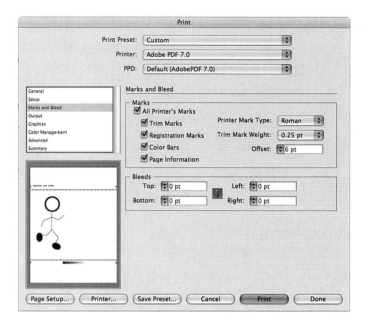

Output Options

From the Mode pop-up menu on the Output pane of the Print dialog (see Figure 21.25), select Composite, which prints all color plates on the same page, or Separations, either Host-Based or In-RIP. The average user generally prints only Composites or occasionally Host-Based Separations to check color coverage and to test the need for trapping in a document. If you are required to set up print presets to this level of detail, you should check with your output agency or the specifications of your output device to get the best settings for your document.

Graphics Options

The following options, found in the Graphics pane of the Print dialog (see Figure 21.26), enable you to choose how images and color print from your output device.

- In the Paths setting, move the Flatness slider to indicate whether you would like to print your paths at a higher quality or a faster speed. In most cases, keeping the settings at Automatic is sufficient. Uncheck the box and use the slider only if you have problems with either printing speed or the quality of the paths that are printing.

- Under Fonts, Download, choose None if your fonts are installed in the printer's memory. Choose Complete to download all fonts when the document is printed. Choose Subset to download only the characters used in the document.

- Under PostScript, choose the PostScript level that most closely matches your printer for the best output.

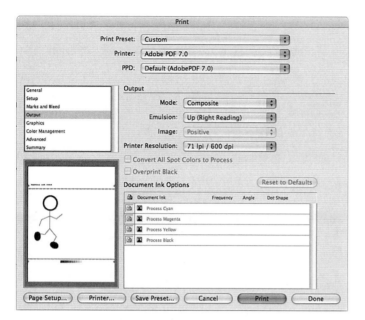

Figure 21.25
The Output pane of the Print dialog.

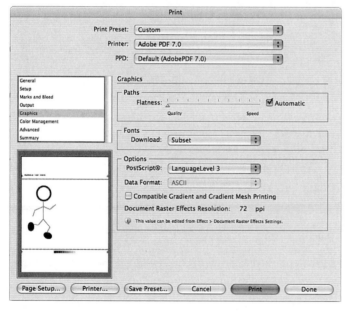

Figure 21.26
The Graphics pane of the Print dialog.

- Data Format refers to how InDesign sends image data to the printer, either as ASCII (more common) or Binary (smaller).

- If you have problems with gradients or gradient meshes printing correctly, click the Compatible Gradient and Gradient Mesh Printing check box to rasterize gradients and gradient meshes.

21

Color Management Options

The color space of your document is listed at the top of the Color Management pane of the Print dialog (see Figure 21.27).

Figure 21.27
The Color Management pane of the Print dialog.

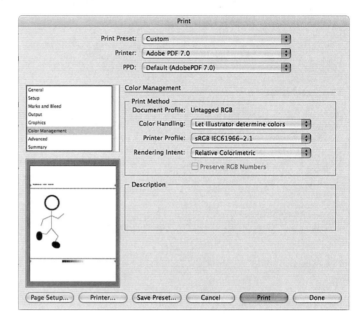

Choose to let Illustrator or the attached PostScript printer determine your document color. If you choose to let Illustrator determine your color, choose the Printer Profile from the pop-up menu.

The Rendering Intent pop-up menu determines how color is printed, based on where it falls in the gamut and how it is converted from one color space to another. The Description window gives details about each choice and how that rendering intent is determined.

Advanced Options

Figure 21.28 shows the Advanced pane of the Print dialog, If your printer supports bitmap printing, you can select Print As Bitmap to rasterize your artwork during printing, creating more reliable output.

Select to Preserve, or Discard any overprinting you have applied in the Overprints pop-up menu. If you are printing a composite, or have specified overprinting with a transparent object, you can make the selection to Simulate Overprinting.

If your document contains transparency, you can select from the Low, Medium, or High resolution transparency flattening presets under Overprint and Transparency Flattener Options. You can also create your own preset by clicking Custom.

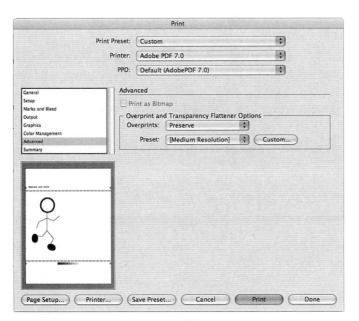

Figure 21.28
The Advanced pane of the Print dialog.

Summary

The Summary pane of the Print dialog (see Figure 21.29) enables you to drill down into your print settings and see each one.

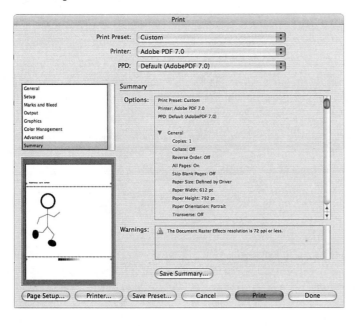

Figure 21.29
The Summary pane of the Print dialog.

21

USING PRINT PRESETS

If you will be printing the same type of document many times, or if your print settings often need to be the same, you can create print presets that help you quickly apply the settings you need without having to enter them continually.

After you enter all your print settings, click the Save Preset button on the Print dialog. Enter a name for your preset. Click OK.

The next time you want to print with that preset, select it from the Preset pop-up menu at the top of the Print dialog.

PRINTING WITH POSTSCRIPT

PostScript is a language that tells the printer how to output the file you are sending to it. PostScript is the de facto standard in the printing industry and is preferable because of its high-quality output of even complicated documents.

If you have printed a document from any Adobe program, not just Illustrator, you have experienced PostScript printing without really thinking about it. This goes for printing to high-end devices at an output agency or printing to the laser printer in your office. For the most part, you shouldn't have to put a lot of thought into PostScript, unless you suddenly have problems printing your documents and generate the dreaded PostScript error.

If you do have problems with PostScript printing, the following are some things to try to get through the issue:

- Make sure you are using the most updated PostScript Printer Description (PPD) for your printer. A PPD should have loaded with your printer driver. (Check the PPD pop-up menu when you go to File, Print. You should be printing by default to a PPD that matches your printer.)

  Check your printer manufacturer's website from time to time for updated PPDs. Sometimes issues and errors are found after a printer driver has been released, and an updated PPD that can solve your problem might be available for download.

- In the previous section, you learned about Output settings in the Print dialog that are available to simplify your document. If you have trouble printing a very complicated document, go back to the Output pane and change some of the settings to simplify the file.

- Long, complex paths that are drawn on the page might need to be split into smaller paths to help with PostScript printing. Use the Scissors tool to split paths at various locations and simplify the document.

Know that when you are preparing documents to be output, your printer may supply you with a special PPD that prepares your document for output, especially if you are creating PDFs. To load a specialized PPD, select Other from the PPD pop-up menu in the Print menu and then browse to the provided PPD and click Open.

21

OVERPRINTING

Recall that overprinting is the process of printing colored elements on top of another color, as opposed to knocking them out. If you're scratching your head a little at that, let's take a look at what this means.

When color documents are printed on a four-color press, four separate plates lay down the various colors of ink. The plates are created based on separations of each color.

If you were to place 100% black text on a 100% cyan background, the separations would look like the example in Figure 21.30; one plate would have the cyan square with the text knocked out of it, and the other plate would have the black text. You can see how the slightest bit of slipping causes a registration problem.

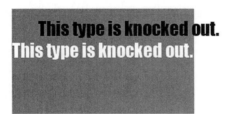

Figure 21.30
An example of how colors are printed; ink is placed on the paper only where it is placed on the artboard. One layer of ink is "knocked out" where the other ink prints.

When you overprint the text, it gives you the 100% cyan square, with the text printing in 100% black on top of it, therefore avoiding registration issues.

Which makes it seem pretty simple, right? Just overprint everything, and you won't have registration problems, right? Not so fast. There are other variables at play here.

When ink colors are laid on top of each other, mixing occurs (see Figure 21.31). Print 100% magenta text on top of a 100% cyan box, and you get violet text, not the magenta you want. Therefore, think about overprinting in a couple of different ways.

Figure 21.31
A simulation of two ink colors overprinting, which might not give you the result you are looking for.

First, if you are working with colors other than black on top of the color, think about trapping them instead of overprinting them (see the next section for more information on trapping). If anything, trapping creates a slight overlap if the printing doesn't register correctly, rather than the white line.

If you do choose to overprint non-black colors, do the following:

1. Select the object(s) you want to overprint.

2. Open the Attributes palette (choose Window, Attributes to display the palette).

3. Select Overprint Fill, Overprint Stroke, or both options in the palette (see Figure 21.32).

21

Figure 21.32
Overprint settings in the
Attributes palette.

With black ink, overprinting can be an easier decision because it's not as likely to react negatively with the colors under it. Select overprinting all blacks in the Print dialog:

1. Select File, Print.

2. Click Output in the left pane.

3. Choose Separations under Mode.

4. Click the Overprint Black check box.

You can also use a filter if you want to overprint items with a specific percentage of black:

1. Select the object(s) you want to overprint.

2. Choose Filter, Colors, Overprint Black to display the Overprint Black dialog (see Figure 21.33).

3. Make sure Add Black is selected.

4. Enter the percentage of black you want to overprint.

5. Choose to overprint fill, stroke, or both.

Figure 21.33
The Overprint Black filter enables
you to choose to overprint only
when certain percentages of ink
are specified.

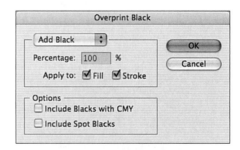

6. If you also want to overprint colors that contain cyan, magenta, and yellow with the specified black percentage, select Include Blacks with CMY.

7. To overprint spot colors that contain the equivalent to the specified percentage of black, select Include Spot Blacks.

8. Click OK.

Always check out your overprint before you commit to it. Go to View, Overprint, Preview to see a simulation of how your overprint will look on the page.

You should also talk to your printer about overprinting before you make a decision. Based on the printer's experiences with his or her equipment, you might receive recommendations and guidelines to help you get the best out of your printed documents.

21

TRAPPING

From time to time you might have a document printed and find that two objects of different colors that were set to print next to each other have a thin line separating them. This *misregistration* isn't uncommon, nor does it mean your printer isn't doing a good job. In any given printing situation, paper can slip or stretch on the press, as can the plates being used to print. When you see a slight misregistration, it most likely happened because you didn't set up trapping in your document.

Trapping is a process by which objects of different colors are created with a slight overlap to avoid any issues with misregistration on the press (see Figure 21.34). To create trapping, you must be working with a document in CMYK mode.

Figure 21.34
A simulation of how trapping works by overlapping page elements of different colors.

To create a trap:

1. Select the objects you want to trap.

2. Open the Pathfinder palette (choose Window, Pathfinder to open the palette).

3. Select Trap from the palette menu.

The trap settings dialog opens. The options in this dialog determine how much overlap is created by the trap. Talk to your printer before specifying trap options; in most cases, the printer takes care of trapping at the RIP stage of output, and you don't have to concern yourself with it. Trapping settings are determined by ink colors, press type, and paper type among other things. Also know that the colors you are using might mean you don't have to trap at all. If the two elements share similar percentages of cyan, magenta, yellow, or black, you might not see or notice if items misregister. Your printer is best qualified to give you an idea of the most appropriate choices here, if you have to make these choices at all.

SPEEDING UP ILLUSTRATOR AND DATA FUNCTIONALITY

IN THIS CHAPTER

As you can see, this twelfth version of Illustrator fits in perfectly with the rest of the Creative Suite. Adobe has continued to build on the features and functions of previous versions to create a vector graphic program that can help serve nearly all of your illustration needs. Paired with Photoshop, the two programs can add amazing graphics to your publications—publications you can create in InDesign.

In addition, the robust web graphic creation features meld seamlessly with GoLive to help you build awesome websites.

There are a handful of other things you should know about Illustrator, features and tricks that can make the program more accessible and user friendly. The end of this chapter follows up with some tips on how to make sure Illustrator works for you, instead of the other way around.

AUTOMATING TASKS WITH ACTIONS

Much like Photoshop, Illustrator gives you a way to automate tasks you might perform over and over, through the use of *actions.* Although creating actions can sometimes involve trial and error, they are completely worth the time. Have you ever worked on a project where creativity took a back seat to tedium because you had to perform the same tasks over and over? That would have been the perfect time for an action.

Choose Window, Actions to open the Actions palette (see Figure 22.1). Notice that Illustrator offers numerous actions that have already been created and loaded. You take a look at one of these as an introduction, to get more detailed information about how actions work and how to work with them.

Figure 22.1
The Illustrator Actions palette comes preloaded with several actions you might find useful. Click the arrows next to each step of the action to see the steps the action will perform.

Notice that each action has an arrow next to it. Click the arrow to expand the action and see its individual steps. In this case, let's look at Save for Web JPG Medium.

When you expand the arrow, there is an entry for Save for Web. This is the command that this action performs. When you expand that arrow, you see the various choices that the Save for Web action makes.

To the left of the action name, there is a box with three dots in it. Notice that some of the actions have these and some don't. This icon indicates that there is a stop in the action, or a place where you can customize the action, where all of your choices are not made for you. In the case of this action, that step is choosing where your file is saved.

An empty box next to the action name means there is a dialog that comes up somewhere within the action where a stop could be inserted. If you want to insert a stop, just click in the empty box to turn it on.

Clicking the check box at the far left of the action name enables you to turn a certain step in the action on or off. This is helpful in complicated actions that have certain steps you might want to skip from time to time.

To play an action, simply click the object you will be modifying, if necessary, and then click the action name in the palette. Click the Play button at the bottom of the palette to start the action. It plays, stopping if necessary so you can adjust a setting.

Now that you know how actions work, it's time to learn how to create your own. Before you start, think about how to approach the action. Sometimes it's helpful to write down the steps before you begin so you're sure to cover everything you need to do.

When you're ready to start recording, have your document open, or have the object selected that you're going to be working with. Start in whatever mode you are going to be starting when you're ready to use the action.

Click the Create New Action button on the Actions palette (see Figure 22.2). Name your action.

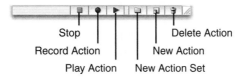

Stop | Delete Action
Record Action | New Action
Play Action | New Action Set

Figure 22.2
Use the buttons at the bottom of the palette to create new actions, delete actions, and play and record actions.

When you click OK, the action starts recording. Perform the steps you want to record. Don't worry about dialogs where you may want to change your entries when you are working with different files. You can add a stop there later. When you're finished, click the Stop button on the Actions palette.

Now test the action on another file or object. Again, if there are certain dialogs within the action where you might want to change the settings when you use it again, click in the box to the right of that step in the Actions palette to create a stop.

If your action doesn't work the way you intended, just drag the action name from the palette to the trash icon at the bottom of the palette to delete it.

If you plan to share your actions and help your co-workers relieve their drudgery, create a new action set. Click the folder icon at the bottom of the palette. Name your action set and click OK. When you create another action, choose to save it in that set. To export a set of actions, click the folder and select Save Set from the palette menu. You can browse to a location to save the set (see

Figure 22.3). To load a saved set of actions, choose Load Actions from the palette menu and browse to the location of the saved set. Select it and click Open. The action set loads into the palette.

Figure 22.3
When you save a set of actions, it can be shared with others. Save the actions file (.aia) in a location that is accessible so others can load the actions you create.

Batch Processes

If you have a number of different files you want to perform an action on, select Batch from the Action palette menu. In the Batch dialog (see Figure 22.4), take the following steps:

Figure 22.4
A batch process can run an entire folder of files through the steps of an action, one file after the other.

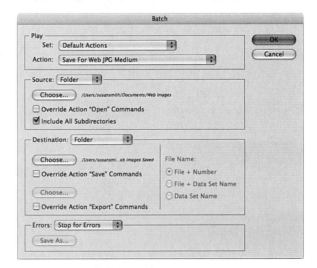

1. Select the set the action is in and the action you want to perform.

2. From the Source pop-up menu, select Folder. You can also select Data Sets, which can be used with data-driven graphics.

3. Click the Choose button and browse to the folder that contains the files on which you want to perform the action.

4. Enable the Override Action "Open" Commands check box to work with the files in the folder, and ignore any open commands that are part of the action.

5. Enable the Include All Subdirectories check box to perform the action also on files within sub-folders of the original folder.

6. From the Destination pop-up menu, select None, Save and Close (to save the files in their current location) or Folder (to specify another folder to save the files in after the action is performed).

   If you choose to save to another folder, you can choose to override any save commands in the original action. You can also choose to override any export commands in the action.

7. If errors occur during the action process, choose either to stop the action or to save an error log to a specific location by choosing the desired response from the Errors pop-up menu.

8. Click OK when you are ready to perform the batch process.

WORKING WITH ILLUSTRATOR SCRIPTS

You can also automate Illustrator tasks through the use of *scripts*. Illustrator supports scripts written in Visual Basic, AppleScript, and JavaScript.

The benefit to scripting, which is like writing a mini computer program, is that you can create scripts to perform everyday or not-so-everyday tasks for you. As with actions, after you work in Illustrator for a while you start to recognize the types of things that scripting might help with. In addition, remember that SVG interactivity relies on JavaScript to perform actions.

For more information on scripts and how they can help make Illustrator easier to work with, check out http://partners.adobe.com/public/developer/illustrator/sdk/index_scripting.html.

CREATING DATA-DRIVEN GRAPHICS

Another handy automation within Illustrator is your ability to create graphics with variable data. This prevents you from having to create numerous versions of the same file over and over.

To better understand this feature, let's look at an example. Say you work for a company that produces a product sold in different countries. The company has a website in each country's native language, so the graphic you produce will vary based on the site on which it appears. Rather than creating a number of different graphics, you can create a single ad with fields for the variable data. References to the variable data are stored in the Variables palette (choose Window, Variables to display the palette, as shown in Figure 22.5).

22

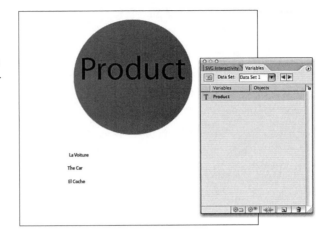

Figure 22.5
Illustrator creates data-driven graphics using the Variables palette to define the graphic areas and link them to the variable information.

A note about data-driven graphics: They must be saved in SVG format. As previously mentioned, SVG is not completely supported by all web browsers, or wasn't at the time of this writing. Displaying SVGs in Internet Explorer, for example, requires a plug-in from Adobe. Support in Mozilla browsers, including Firefox, was still in development. Depending on when you read this, you may or may not be giggling at the antiquity of this reference because SVG does look poised to take off, but you're better safe than sorry. Check it out before you commit a lot of time to creating these graphics.

The first step is to create your graphic with all of the information in place. Then, tag each element based on its variable type.

There are four types of variables that can be created. Graph data is created from existing graphs, linked files display from Illustrator links, text strings are created from text, and visibility variables can be shown or hidden by your choice. You can also create a variable without assigning a specific type to it:

- To create a graph data variable, select a graph and click the Make Object Dynamic button on the Variables palette.

- To create a linked file variable, select a linked file and click the Make Object Dynamic button on the Variables palette.

- To create a text string variable, select a type frame and click the Make Object Dynamic button.

- To create a visibility variable, select the object you want to show and hide and click the Make Visibility Dynamic button.

- To create a variable without assigning it to an object, click the New Variable button on the Variables palette. If you later want to assign the variable, select the object, as well as the variable in the palette, and click either Make Object Dynamic or Make Visibility Dynamic button.

To specify multiple variables in the same graphic, you can import information from a database using XML. You can also import and export variable data using scripts and XML. For more information on scripting, go to http://share. studio.adobe.com/ and select Scripting in the Illustrator area.

After you identify your variables, you can define specific pieces of information as data sets, which can then be associated with the variables in your piece of artwork. To do this, create a type frame, for example. Select it and then select Capture Data Set in the Variables palette menu. To associate a data set with a variable, select the defined variable object on your layout, and then use the Data Set pop-up menu at the top of the palette to scroll through your defined data sets.

For visibility objects, toggle the visibility of specific objects using the Layers palette.

WORKING WITH GRAPHS

Illustrator's graph tools enable you to create a number of different types of graphs (see Figure 22.6). The graphs you create here are superior to those you can create in common spreadsheet applications, because the graphic file formats supported by Illustrator reproduce more accurately when you place them in your page layout application.

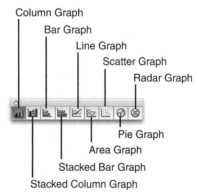

Column Graph
Bar Graph
Line Graph
Scatter Graph
Radar Graph

Pie Graph
Area Graph
Stacked Bar Graph
Stacked Column Graph

Figure 22.6
You can create nine different types of graphs with Illustrator, depending on the tool you use to define the graph area.

Illustrator offers the tools to create nine different types of graphs: column graphs, stacked column graphs, bar graphs, stacked bar graphs, line graphs, area graphs, scatter graphs, pie graphs, and radar graphs.

To create a graph, select one of the graph tools and then click and drag with it on the artboard to define the graph area. This is the area that contains the graph itself; the graph legend and the labels for the graph may extend outside the area you draw.

After you draw a frame for your graph, the Graph Data window opens. You can copy and paste graph data from an application like Excel, import it as tab-separated text from a word-processing program, or enter it yourself. Different types of graphs require different types of information. The following sections give you a brief overview of entering data for each type of graph.

Setting Up Your Graph and Graph Labels

First, here are some tips for creating your graph labels (see Figure 22.7):

- If you want to label your graph with a legend, do not enter any information in the upper-left corner of the Graph Data window. Enter row descriptions in the left column and column headings in the first row.

- If you accidentally enter your row and column headings in the wrong places, click the Transpose button at the top of the Graph Data window to switch the column and row information.

- If you want a label to consist of a number, you must enter the number in quotation marks—for example, "2005"—so Illustrator does not think it is data as opposed to a label.

- If your graph labels need to break or continue to the next line, type a vertical bar (|) between the words you want to break.

Figure 22.7
Graph labels are created based on where you enter the graph information in the Graph Data window.

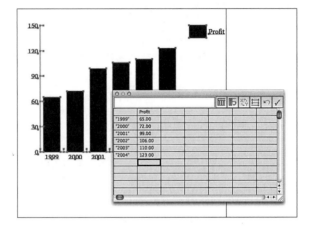

Next, enter the graph data. Again, you can enter the data in the fields, or copy and paste it from a spreadsheet application. To import data formatted as tab-separated text, click the Import button on the Graph Data window. Browse to the file, select it and click Open. The data you import should be straight numbers and decimals only; do not import numbers that contain commas, for example.

Entering Data for Column, Stacked Column, Bar, Stacked Bar, Line, Area, and Radar Graphs

The column, stacked column, bar, stacked bar, line, area, and radar graphs all track changes in information along axes. For column, stacked column, bar, and stacked bar graphs, enter the information you are tracking in a single data column. Each entry creates a separate column in the graph. If you create more than one data column, another column is displayed in the graph; these types of graphs compare information (see Figure 22.8).

For line graphs, each data column represents a different line in the graph. Area graphs do the same, but each subsequent data column is added to the one before. And for radar graphs, each column creates a line that is tracked around the circle.

Entering Data for Scatter Graphs

Scatter graphs are different; there are no categories of data; they simply compare sets of data along x and y axes.

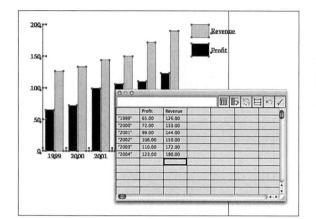

Figure 22.8
If you enter a single column of graph data in the window, each row creates a separate column or bar in the graph. Two columns of information create two columns or bars for each category.

To enter data, first create labels for the sets of data you are comparing. Enter the first label in the first cell of the first row and then enter the second label in the third cell of the first row. Continue entering your data set labels in every other cell (see Figure 22.9).

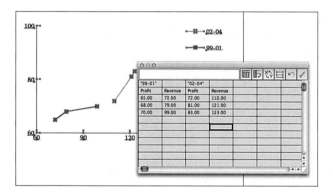

Figure 22.9
Create data labels for the two sets of information you are comparing in every other cell of the first line in the Graph Data window.

Then, enter the information you want to track along the x axis in the first column and the information you want to track along the y axis in the second column. Continue entering information for all the data sets you are tracking.

Entering Data for Pie Graphs

Pie graphs combine the information entered into a whole. For each row of data you enter, another pie graph is created. To create a single pie graph, you should enter a single row of data. To create a legend that labels the data, enter the categories in the first row of the Graph Data window.

Creating Graphs

To generate your graph, click the Apply button on the Graph Data window. The graph is created but the window does not close. Move the window out of the way to make sure your graph looks the way you want and then close it if you're satisfied with how your data is displayed. If you need to change any data, enter the proper information and click Apply again.

After your graph is created, you can make any changes to the information. Use the Type tool to select text and change it. Use the Direct Selection tool to select individual parts of the graph to alter them.

In addition, you can add effects and color to your graphs. Change the fill and stroke of graph parts to add color or patterns to it, or add drop shadows or transparency. You can even create graphics to serve as columns or bars, making your own infographics. You can find great information in the Adobe Help Center.

For more graph inspiration check out the Cool Extras folder in the Illustrator application folder. Open the Sample Files folder and then the Graphs folder (see Figure 22.10).

Figure 22.10
The documents in the Graphs folder of Illustrator's Cool Extras give examples of different ways to customize the graphs you create, including graph markers that can be used for infographics.

WORKING WITH VERSION CUE

If you read the other sections of this book, you know that all the Creative Suite programs use Version Cue to help track changes, manage projects, and browse file thumbnails and information. You explored Version Cue further in other sections of the book; this section introduces the basics of using it with Illustrator.

If you're ready to create a file in Illustrator that you want to save as a Version Cue project, select File, Open. Make sure you use the Adobe version of the Open dialog (see Figure 22.11).

In the left panel, click Version Cue. From the Project Tools menu, select New Project. Choose where you want to save the project in the Location pop-up menu. Enter a project name and a project description.

If you want this project to be available to others, enable the Share This Project with Others check box. Click OK.

If a project is shared, two users can work on it at the same time. Version Cue does not allow one user's editing to overwrite the other's. After users save their document to the Version Cue workspace, they are alerted to another version and given the opportunity to either download the new changes or continue. You can also save your version of a file as an alternate. Files are marked with icons that indicate whether they are open, in use, or have conflicting copies.

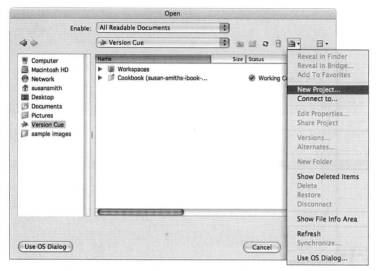

Figure 22.11
The Adobe Open dialog enables you to create and save documents as Version Cue projects.

You can save a document by selecting File, Save from the application's menu bar, which overwrites all the changes you made, or you can select File, Save a Version to save a version of the document in Version Cue, adding comments to indicate the particular changes that this version represents. Saving a version enables you to go back later and work with the document in a particular state, as represented by the version you saved.

If you want to turn Version Cue off for any reason, you can choose Edit, Preferences, File Handling & Clipboard (Windows users) or InDesign, Preferences, File Handling &Clipboard (Mac users) and uncheck the Enable Version Cue check box.

WORKING WITH PHOTOSHOP

As it has with all the programs in the Creative Suite, Adobe has made it easy to move files between Photoshop and Illustrator. Although there are many similarities between the programs, and many tools and features they share, there are still things you can do only in Illustrator and things you can do only in Photoshop.

There are four ways to exchange documents between Illustrator and Photoshop: export, import, copy and paste, and drag and drop.

Exporting

In Chapter 21, "Importing, Exporting, and Saving in Illustrator," you learn the options you have when exporting an Illustrator document to a Photoshop document (.psd). These settings give you various degrees of control after you open the document in Photoshop. Make sure you know what you want to do in Photoshop before you export a file to it from Illustrator; for example, choose to export

22

to Photoshop CS2 if you know you need to edit all the text in your Illustrator file. Flatten the image if you know you won't need to work with the Illustrator layers.

Importing

You can import native Photoshop documents into Illustrator using the File, Place command. As with exporting documents to Photoshop, there are numerous settings that help you determine how much control you have over the Photoshop document after it's placed in Illustrator. So again, know in advance whether you need to work with Photoshop's layers in your Illustrator file or whether they can be flattened, whether you should import hidden layers, and what layer comps to work with.

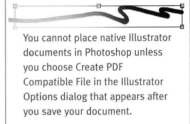

You cannot directly open native Illustrator documents in Photoshop unless you choose Create PDF Compatible File in the Illustrator Options dialog that appears after you save your document.

Copying and Pasting

You can copy and paste from Illustrator to Photoshop and vice versa. When you copy, objects are placed on the Clipboard, a kind of holding spot for information you cut and copy from one spot to another.

Illustrator's Preferences window enables you to choose how artwork is stored in the Clipboard (See Figure 22.12). You have two choices: PDF and AICB. PDF enables you to preserve transparency in the objects you copy. AICB enables you to choose between preserving the overall appearance of the selection or copying the selection as a set of paths. Because you can select both PDF and AICB in the Preferences dialog, selecting Preserve Paths with AICB discards transparency, and Preserve Appearance and Overprints flattens transparency and preserves overprints.

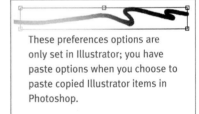

You cannot place native Illustrator documents in Photoshop unless you choose Create PDF Compatible File in the Illustrator Options dialog that appears after you save your document.

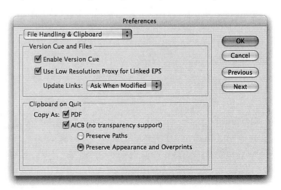

These preferences options are only set in Illustrator; you have paste options when you choose to paste copied Illustrator items in Photoshop.

To access the Illustrator preference, choose Edit, Preferences, File Handling & Clipboard (Windows users) or Illustrator, Preferences, File Handling & Clipboard (Mac users).

Figure 22.12
Illustrator's File Handling & Clipboard Preferences window determines how Photoshop files are pasted into Illustrator.

Dragging and Dropping

When you drag and drop from Illustrator to Photoshop, there are two ways to get the items from one spot to another. You should have your Illustrator document and your Photoshop document open and visible before you begin.

To copy the object(s) from Illustrator into Photoshop as a bitmap object, drag the selection into the Photoshop window until the edges are highlighted in black, and then release. The object(s) are copied to the active layer in the Photoshop document.

You can also drag and drop Photoshop objects into an Illustrator document.

To copy vector object(s) into Photoshop as path(s), hold down Ctrl (Windows users) or ⌘ (Mac users) as you drag the selection from Illustrator into the Photoshop window. Release the mouse button, and the item is placed as a Photoshop path.

THINGS TO KNOW

You covered a lot of ground in the chapters about Illustrator, and gained a good introduction to Illustrator and its capabilities. Following are some things to keep in mind when you use the program to help you be as successful as you can with Illustrator.

Organize Your Workspace

With so many palettes—and many having multiple states—quickly finding the tools and commands you need can be daunting. Keep your workspace as uncluttered as possible—it's one of the hall-marks of an efficient designer.

Use the techniques in Chapter 15, "Understanding Illustrator Palettes and Menus," not only to arrange, group, and stack palettes for your comfort, but also to build task-specific workspaces containing all—and only—the palettes you need to work efficiently in Illustrator on different projects.

Know the Shortcuts

Another way to save time is to learn Illustrator's keyboard shortcuts. Memorizing the Illustrator key-board shortcuts won't happen overnight, but the more you use the program, the more you learn. Mouse trips to the menus are tedious and inefficient—learning the shortcuts help you avoid those trips.

Learn the single-key keyboard shortcuts for all the tools in the Tools palette first, and then build on your efficiency by learning the shortcuts for your most commonly used commands, such as Save (⌘-S on the Mac and Ctrl+S in Windows), Print (⌘-P on the Mac and Ctrl+P in Windows), Zoom to Fit (⌘-0 on the Mac and Ctrl+0 in Windows), and so on.

If a command you frequently use doesn't have a keyboard shortcut, give it one. On the Edit menu choose Keyboard Shortcuts. Then select the command or tool for a new shortcut, click inside the Shortcut column beside it, and press the desired keys on your keyboard. Save your keyboard short-cut set.

Back Up and Share Your Customizations

If you work on multiple computers or just want the added security of being able to get back up and running quickly with your workspaces and customizations in the event of a reinstall of the application, make backup copies of your important customization files.

You will find Keyboard Shortcut sets (`*.kys` files), Print Presets, and Transparency Flattener Presets in the following locations:

- **Windows**: `Documents and Settings\[username]\Application Data\Adobe\Adobe Illustrator CS2 Settings`

- **Macintosh**: `[username]\Library\Preferences\Adobe Illustrator CS2 Settings`

Your workspaces are saved in the Workspaces folder inside the Illustrator CS2 Settings folders.

Reuse Styles and Elements and Automate Tasks

Aside from, and ahead of, organizing and customizing your workspace, getting into the habit of expeditiously reusing elements and automating common tasks is critical to working efficiently in Illustrator or any application.

Take advantage of Illustrator's reusable content elements like paragraph and character styles for quickly formatting and modifying text; graphic styles to format, reformat, and modify the appearance attributes of objects; and symbols for multiple instances of identical or nearly identical objects.

Styles, symbols, and swatches can all also be reused between documents. Instead of loading a preexisting swatch library, for example, from the Swatches palette menu, choose Other Swatch Library. In the Open dialog that follows, navigate to and select another Illustrator document you created. Instead of opening the document, Illustrator opens just the swatches (or symbols, graphic styles, paragraph styles, or character styles) contained in that document.

Make use of the automation features built into Illustrator by using actions, batch operations, and scripting. If you perform the same sequence of steps more than once, automate it. Don't waste precious creative time and energy doing *anything* repetitive manually if it can be done automatically.

Import placed assets as links rather than using copy and paste or other embedding methods. Not only is linking a safer practice than embedding (if one document becomes corrupted, it is much faster to rebuild if all its assets don't die with it), but a single linked image can be used in numerous documents, with each instantly updating to reflect changes to the original image.

Swatches, symbols, and graphic styles loaded from another Illustrator document appear in their own free-floating palettes. Paragraph or character styles merge into the main Paragraph Styles or Character Styles palettes.

Investigate external automation utilities as well. Numerous applications, applets, and widgets are available by way of a well-phrased Google search to perform such common creative workflow tasks as batch numbering, renumbering, or renaming of files; organization functions; file format conversions (for example, converting Microsoft Office EMF files into EPS or changing the compression level on a folder full of JPEG files); duplication of files; and hundreds of other time-saving functions.

Work Safely

The mantra of computer work of any kind is *save often*. Train your fingers to press ⌘-S (Mac users) or Ctrl+S (Windows users) every time you rise from your chair at the bare minimum, and preferably every few minutes as you work.

Employ the functions of Version Cue and Adobe Bridge to save versions and backups of your documents—particularly those that are created over the course of days or weeks, or that are built by a team. Although all the Creative Suite 2 applications have multiple undo capability, undo can't save you from a mistake after the file has been closed.

Although backups and versions use more hard drive space, it is only temporary. Delete the backup and version files when a project is complete. If you have to sacrifice safety for space, your priorities are out of order.

When viewing thumbnails in the Adobe Bridge, press ⌘-D (Mac users) or Ctrl+D (Windows users) to duplicate the selected file(s) quickly, thus creating backups. This works even while files are open in Illustrator, Photoshop, InDesign, GoLive, Acrobat, or any application!

Know Your Audience

The most important part of any creative project is the pre-design planning stage. Before putting Pen tool to artboard, *know* what and for whom you are drawing.

Ask yourself questions such as these:

- What is the goal of this project? Is it to sell something? Is it to build a brand? Is it a call to action, inspiring the audience to *do* something?

- What am I trying to evoke with this project? Emotion? Thought? Action? What, specifically, is the intended audience reaction?

- Who is the audience for this project? What do they care about? What appeals to the audience's average sense of humor, piety, adventure, or whatever emotion or emotion-based action I'm trying to elicit?

- How will this project be communicated to the audience? Will it be a logo to appear on numerous media, in as many situations? Will it be a sign or banner? Will the audience choose to expose itself to the results of the design, or will the design be placed before the audience?

- In what media will the project appear? What are the limitations to be wary of, and the strengths to take advantage of, inherent in that or those media?

- How will the project move from my software to its final form(s) and media?

- Who will do all of the work involved in this project? Can I do it all alone, or do I need help?

Answer these questions—and any that logically arise from them—before beginning a project. If your project is for a client, in-house or external, discuss your answers with the client. In many for-hire assignments, the questions *cannot* be answered without input from the client. Whenever possible and appropriate, talk to your audience (the client's clientele) not only to ascertain the answers to the planning questions, but also for reactions to your sketches and concept proofs. Creative work is not about the creator; it is about—and can only succeed if it receives the intended reaction from—the audience.

Know Your Media

Illustrator is an industry standard tool in all forms of graphic communication. It is used to create illustrations and layouts for printing on a commercial printing press; for flyers, menus, and business graphics to print from a standard laser or inkjet desktop printer; to design, slice, and create website graphics; for building animations to be used online or in video; for titling and initial effects creation for television, film, and DVD; and in dozens of other workflows and media. Each media has its strengths and limitations. Nowhere is that more true than with color.

Work to be printed, for example, must be in CMYK process colors, which has a much more limited gamut or range of color than a monitor's RGB color space. To print from an office color laser or inkjet printer, colors are limited to only CMYK—spot colors may not be used. When sending Illustrator artwork to press, however, spot colors can be used, but there is typically an increase in cost associated with each spot ink. On the Web, RGB is the color space, but some experts still limit their color use to the 216 Web-safe colors. In broadcast media, a whole other set of colors are used; called the NTSC Safe color palette, highly saturated colors like pure red, green, or blue cause television and other screens to "fuzz" the color or "blow out" subtle shading.

Talk to your output vendor—your printer, effects department, video producer, or whomever—about the limitations and requirements for the output media specific to your project. It would be useless—and irresponsible—for us to give you specific information and settings in this book. Every project is different, and workflows vary wildly between vendors even in the same industry. Ask questions specific to *your* project and *your* vendor. Vendors don't mind answering questions that help ensure that their collaboration with you runs smoothly.

Use What's There

Adobe gave you a lot of great resources when you installed Illustrator. In the Illustrator application folder is a folder called Cool Extras. Open it up. Explore. In the Sample Files folder you find examples of graphs and graph markers, data-driven graphics, SVG files and other documents that use some of Illustrator's best features. In the Templates folder (also accessible when you choose File, New from Template), you find a variety of document types that you can work with and customize. These documents can serve as an inspiration, but they are also a great source of information about Illustrator. Open a document that contains a special effect you're interested in duplicating. All the objects in the files can be selected, moved around, and deconstructed so you can see how it was done. In addition, don't discount the wide selection of blank templates, which can give you a quick setup on items like CD cases, DVD menus, and business cards (see Figure 22.13).

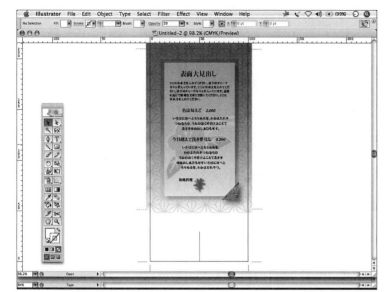

Figure 22.13
Illustrator's templates are not only a great base for your designs, they can also help you learn how various techniques are applied.

Let Others Help You

There are a ton of great resources at the Adobe Studio site, not just for Illustrator, but for all of the Creative Suite components. You can download scripts, plug-ins, actions, and other items that have been developed, many of them free of charge. Just go to http://share.studio.adobe.com/ and browse through the options for each application; you might be surprised at what's out there.

Every application in the Creative Suite serves a specific purpose. Although there is often overlap, no other program gives you the power over vector graphics that Illustrator does. Although it might seem like there are a million options to learn, concentrate on using those you need and then go from there. The more you use the program, the more you learn about it, and the better your designs will be.

III

INDESIGN

IN THIS PART

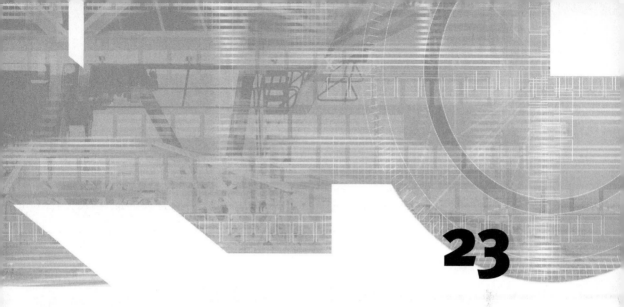

UNDERSTANDING THE INDESIGN WORK AREA

IN THIS CHAPTER

When the first version of InDesign was introduced in 1999, it was immediately dubbed a potential "Quark-killer" by the technology press. Although version 1.0 lacked many of the features that would vault InDesign to the top of the page layout heap, three versions later Adobe has a powerful product that, combined with the other products in the Creative Suite, gives you incredible production flexibility and resources.

InDesign is the perfect solution for any page layout needs. From the most basic newsletter to a fully designed publication with table of contents, footnotes and index, InDesign's capabilities can be harnessed by any user.

BEST PRACTICES

But be careful. Although InDesign contains many familiar Photoshop and Illustrator features, don't be fooled into thinking it can actually replace those programs. If you are working with simple page layout projects, you may find you're able to do much of the design in InDesign alone, including adding some visual effects to type, graphics, and images. But most digital image manipulation will still have to be done in Photoshop, many complicated graphic elements will still have to be created in Illustrator, and you'll still need GoLive to make your project web-ready.

With that in mind, this section of the chapter takes an overall look at InDesign and how it can fit into your creative workflow.

The first thing you notice when you open InDesign, especially if you've previously worked in other programs of the Creative Suite, are the similarities in the tools and palettes. This should make moving to InDesign from many of those programs much easier. If you started out in InDesign and are interested in moving to Illustrator or Photoshop, for example, the same is true; tools, menus, palettes and even keyboard shortcuts are the same.

Information for QuarkXPress Users

If you are just starting in InDesign after having used QuarkXPress, you'll be impressed with how Adobe has taken some of the best features of that program and integrated them into its own page layout process. In fact, InDesign contains a set of keyboard shortcuts that correspond to those you used in QuarkXPress (see Figure 23.1). You can also open your QuarkXPress documents and save them as InDesign files. Most features of your original QuarkXPress documents are retained, such as links, type styles, master pages, and layers. Other features may be changed to reflect the InDesign option most closely related to your original effect. To get an overview of exactly how QuarkXPress files are converted, check out the Opening QuarkXPress Files in the InDesign section of the Adobe Help Center.

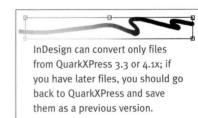

InDesign can convert only files from QuarkXPress 3.3 or 4.1x; if you have later files, you should go back to QuarkXPress and save them as a previous version.

Information for PageMaker Users

If you're upgrading to InDesign after being a PageMaker user, fear not. Along with a set of PageMaker keyboard shortcuts, Adobe has also ported over familiar PageMaker features, such as the toolbar. And like QuarkXPress, you can open your PageMaker files from version 6.0 and later and convert them to InDesign documents. Most items convert correctly, but text flow and other elements are often affected in the conversion. For full details on PageMaker-to-InDesign conversion issues, see the Common PageMaker Conversion Issues entry in the Adobe Help Center. The Help Center also contains a convenient set of entries comparing PageMaker's menu commands with its InDesign counterparts.

Pages palette

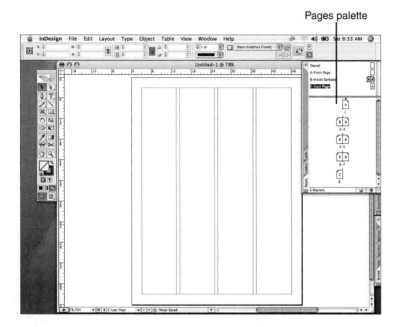

Figure 23.1
The Pages palette is a good example of how Adobe has made InDesign accessible to QuarkXPress users.

23

WHY USE INDESIGN OVER ILLUSTRATOR?

So what's the big deal? Especially if you are an Illustrator user, you may be wondering why you would choose to design documents using InDesign rather than the program you're most comfortable in. And the answer, for certain documents, might be that you wouldn't.

InDesign's strength is definitely in the category of page layout. Although its graphic tools are similar if a little less robust than Illustrator's, the biggest plus is its ability to handle larger documents. Illustrator is still, at its heart, a graphics program. It might be the perfect way to create a one-off document, like a poster or label—after all, you can still draw vector objects, create and edit text, and import images. But if you need a resource for magazines, newsletters, or more involved documents, it's easy for Illustrator users to move straight into InDesign.

Because it serves as more of a production workhorse, you might find that InDesign has some interface features that are different from those in Illustrator. Palettes can dock along the side of the InDesign workspace, giving you more room to maneuver, although most of the palette options are the same. You will find that more flexibility with text exists in InDesign, and more complicated design effects can be created in Illustrator.

All in all, although there is some overlap between Illustrator and InDesign, just as there is with the other programs in the Suite, both have a place for the designer and can peacefully coexist on the same hard drive while you take advantage of their unique strengths.

SAVING AND EXPORTING FILES

InDesign gives you many options for saving and exporting your files. When you create a new document, it starts out Untitled. When you select File, Save or File, Save As, you can choose to save your file as an InDesign document (.indd) or as a template (.indt).

Save your document as a template when you want it to serve as a consistent starting point for other files. An example would be if you were creating a newsletter that will always have the same masthead in the same location, the same footer information, and be four pages long. You can design the original newsletter and then save it as a template. The template will always open as Untitled documents, forcing you to save it continually with a different name but still preserve the original settings.

To save as a template:

1. Select File, Save As. The Save As dialog box opens (see Figure 23.2).

2. Name your file.

3. Select InDesign Template from the Save As Type (Windows) or Format (Mac) pop-up menu.

4. Click Save. Your file will be saved with the extension .indt, indicating it is an InDesign template.

Figure 23.2
Saving your file as a template gives you a convenient starting place.

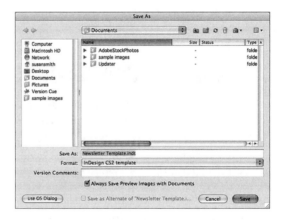

InDesign documents can also be exported in a variety of file types, accessible through the File, Export menu command (see Figure 23.3). The following is an explanation of each of the file types available for export and common reasons for choosing that file type:

Figure 23.3
There are many different file formats in which you can export your InDesign document.

23

- **Adobe PDF:** This selection exports a PDF using preset or custom specifications. If you are designing a document to be printed, PDF is a great format because it can embed all graphics, images, and fonts used, making it unnecessary to gather those items for submission to your printer. PDFs can also be opened and read by any user who has downloaded the free Adobe Reader program. You learn more about exporting PDFs and the various settings in Chapter 31, "Exporting, Saving and Printing with InDesign."

- **EPS:** This exports an Encapsulated PostScript File of a selection, certain pages, or an entire file. Use this option if you need to export to a PostScript file type or if you create an element that you'd like to use later as a graphic.

- **InDesign Interchange (.inx):** The .inx file type saves InDesign CS2 documents for use in InDesign CS. This is obviously a great convenience to those who are working in the previous version of InDesign and comes as a huge relief to anyone who struggled with the lack of backward compatibility in the first version of InDesign CS. To open an InDesign Interchange document, your copy of InDesign CS must have been updated to 3.0.1. Any CS2 features that are not available in CS, such as footnotes or object styles, will not be saved in the document, although if an object style has been applied, its characteristics will stick to objects in the new file.

- **JPEG:** JPEG (Joint Photographers Expert Group) is a file format that uses lossy compression to discard similar color pixels. You can choose to save a selection, an entire page or spread, or your whole document. Each page of a multiple-page document will save with a different name. This file format should be used only when you want to create a small, low-quality preview of your page or if you are saving part of a page that doesn't contain type. The JPEG produced by InDesign, at maximum quality, is only 72 dpi in its full-size view. Saving as a JPEG also rasterizes type, which makes it blurry.

23

- **SVG and SVG Compressed:** SVG is Scalable Vector Graphic format; the compressed format is SVGX. Text, vector, or raster graphics (images) can be saved as SVG. These are mostly used in XML layout.

- **XML:** XML (Extensible Markup Language) is a way of setting up files that tags page elements so they can be used in multiple locations and in different types of files. The XML tags do not describe the formatting of an element as an HTML tag does; they describe the type of content. You can use either XML that is already created and import it into your InDesign document, or you can export a tagged InDesign document and use the XML file generated to create a different type of file. The beauty of XML is its flexibility; information about the page element is contained within the tags, so you can drag and drop them in any location and know what information you are placing on your page. Chapter 32, "Speeding Up InDesign and Data Functionality," contains further information about using XML within InDesign.

WHAT'S NEW?

If you've used InDesign in the past or own a previous version of the Creative Suite, here is a quick overview of the changes and new features you'll find in CS2, specifically with InDesign and how it interacts with the other programs. Most of these categories are covered in greater detail in later sections of this book.

Graphics

New graphics features include the following:

- Layered Photoshop documents and PDFs are supported when they are placed in InDesign, meaning you can show and hide the layers or layer comps (PSDs only) as you choose. You can also import multipage PDF documents page by page or all at once.

- The Pathfinder palette is a new addition and contains buttons to convert one shape to another—for example, changing a rectangle to a triangle.

- Transparency options, such as feather and drop shadow, now include spread and noise settings.

- Snippets are a new InDesign feature that take advantage of its powerful handling of XML. Like library elements with a twist, you can export snippets from your InDesign file and make them available not only to be placed in InDesign but also to be dragged and dropped in the Bridge, on your desktop, or in other types of documents.

- To maintain consistency in text, you use character or paragraph styles. To maintain consistency with page elements, you can now create object styles, which can be assigned to any type of frame (see Figure 23.4).

Object styles

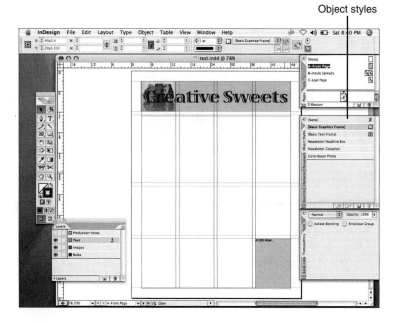

Figure 23.4
Object styles enable you to
assign quickly specific characteristics, such as transparency
effects, to your page elements.

23

Copy

New copy features include the following:

- Adobe has incorporated the popular InCopy program into InDesign CS2. InCopy is a resource that helps collaboration between writers and designers; writers can "check out" text in the file and make edits to it without affecting the overall design of the document.

- Text that you paste in InCopy is stripped of any formatting from the previous application and automatically takes on the type characteristics specified where it's pasted.

- When copy is imported from Microsoft Word, InDesign enables you to map styles from the origi-nal document to its counterparts in your InDesign file, as well as take care of any style name conflicts.

- Creative Suite 2 offers more options for porting styles from other InDesign documents and more convenient ways to sort and apply the styles you create.

- InDesign has taken on many more word processor–like features, including autocorrection, drag and drop text, and support for multiple dictionaries (see Figure 23.5).

Integration

New integration features include the following:

- You learned about the Adobe Bridge in Chapter 1, "Creative Suite 2 Basics." One specific benefit of Bridge when it comes to InDesign is Bridge's use of document previews. If you save your InDesign files with document previews, you can quickly identify the file in Bridge by its preview.

Figure 23.5
If you choose, InDesign automatically alerts you to misspelled words.

A wavy underscore marks misspellings

- More presets for PDF exports have been added, and the custom settings you create can be saved and used by others.

- Quickly package your publication for use with GoLive through a simple export function.

- Color can now be synchronized across applications within the Creative Suite (see Figure 23.6).

Figure 23.6
Color synchronization can be applied across every application in the Creative Suite.

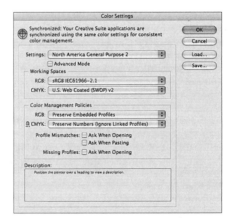

- Save documents in the InDesign Interchange Format so they can be opened in InDesign CS.

XML

New XML features include the following:

- XML formatting can now be applied to tables in InDesign.

- When XML is placed, a link is created. When the source code is updated, the XML in your InDesign document can be quickly updated as well.

- The new Tags palette makes it easier to apply XML within the document.

23

GETTING FAMILIAR WITH THE INDESIGN WORK AREA

When you open InDesign for the first time and create a new document, it's helpful to get oriented to the work area. Your blank page is in Fit In Window view, which shows the entire page as well as the pasteboard. The *pasteboard* is the area you can see in the workspace that is not part of the page itself. The pasteboard can be used to hold items like graphics and page elements you want to "store" off the page as you work with your design.

Scrollbars are on the right and bottom of the page to help you move around your page. *Rulers* are at the top and left of the page. At the bottom of your document window, you see the current *display percentage,* a pop-up menu, arrows that enable you to navigate from page to page, and information about the current Version Cue state.

The *Tool palette* is open at the upper-left corner of the workspace. This is the one palette you will most likely always have open—you learn more about the tools in the next chapter. The *Control palette* is docked to the top of the window, below the menus. This is another important palette with many uses that will probably always be open in your workspace.

Finally, you see numerous *tabs* to the right of the workspace; these are palettes that are collapsed along the side. The *Pages palette* opens by default, with the *Layers palette* and *Info palette* grouped in the same space. Click a palette tab to expand it and/or bring it to the front of a group of palettes. Click again to collapse the palette back to the right side of the screen.

Now that you've had a brief introduction to InDesign, you're ready to take a look at its features and functions in the chapters that follow.

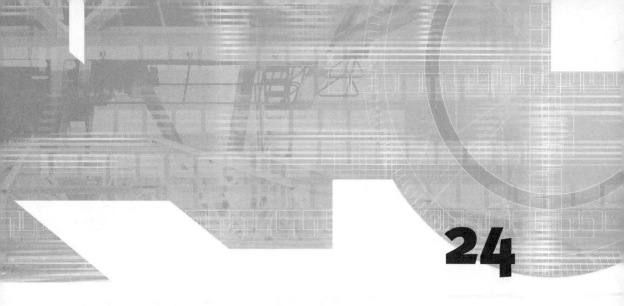

24

UNDERSTANDING THE INDESIGN
INTERFACE AND TOOLS

IN THIS CHAPTER

This chapter serves as a reference and overview for how InDesign works. It provides very little step-by-step instruction; instead, this chapter takes a high-level look at all the tools, palettes, and menu options available in the program. The last sections of this chapter, dealing with keyboard shortcuts and application preferences, lay a foundation for setting up the program to start creating files and working on actual documents.

In the following chapters, you will see these tools, palettes, and menu commands at work as you go through the various aspects of document creation and modification. For that reason, you might want to scan this chapter for basic information and then use it as a reference as you work, whenever you need more information about a specific tool, palette, or menu command.

THE INDESIGN TOOL PALETTE

The InDesign Tool palette (see Figure 24.1) is central to the creation process. Before you start to examine it, though, it's helpful to know a couple things about InDesign.

Figure 24.1
The Tool palette is the starting point for all page element creation.

First, every page element in InDesign is considered a frame. Type, images, and graphics are all placed in frames. When you are working with elements in InDesign, you will often be able to work with the contents independently of the frame, and vice versa.

Also, every line is considered a path and can be altered as such. Points can be added or subtracted, direction can be changed, and type can be placed along the path.

Following is a brief description of each of InDesign's tools:

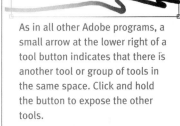

As in all other Adobe programs, a small arrow at the lower right of a tool button indicates that there is another tool or group of tools in the same space. Click and hold the button to expose the other tools.

- **Selection tool:** Use the Selection tool to select or move and resize page elements. Use the Selection tool to alter an object's frame.

- **Direct Selection tool:** Use the Direct Selection tool to select or move and resize the contents of a frame.

- **Position tool:** When the contents of a frame, such as an image, are selected, this tool (located under the Direct Selection tool) works like a cropper to move the contents within the frame.

- **Pen tool:** Click with the Pen tool to create anchor points. Clicking multiple times creates straight lines between anchor points. Clicking and then dragging creates a Bézier curve. To close a frame created with the Pen tool, click again on the first point of the frame.

Under the Pen tool, there are three additional tools:

- **Add Anchor Point tool:** This tool creates additional points along any path.

- **Delete Anchor Point tool:** This tool deletes points when you click with it. Deleting a point joins the two points on either side.

- **Convert Direction Point tool:** If you have created curves with the Pen tool, you can click with the Convert Direction Point tool to reverse the direction of the curve.

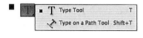

- **Type tool:** Click, hold, and drag the Type tool to create a text frame on-the-fly. You can also click inside any previously created frame to add type.

Under the Type tool, the Type on a Path tool allows you to type along any previously created path. Hold the tool over the path until a plus sign (+) appears and then click and type.

- **Pencil tool:** The Pencil tool is a freehand drawing tool that you can use to create a continuous path or a closed shape. You can use the Add Anchor Point tool, the Delete Anchor Point tool, or the Convert Direction Point tool to work with the points along the path. Several tools beneath the Pencil tool help you work with its paths:

- **Smooth tool:** Dragging this tool over a path smoothes out angles or corners. This may remove anchor points from the path.

- **Erase tool:** You remove portions of a path with the Erase tool. This may erase anchor points or break the path if you drag over more than one point. The Erase tool only works with paths created by the Pencil tool.

- **Line tool:** Use the Line tool to draw straight lines. Hold down the Shift key while using this tool to constrain the line to 45- and 90-degree angles.

- **Rectangle Frame tool:** The Rectangle Frame tool draws four-sided frame shapes. Click, hold, and drag to draw frames. Hold down the Shift key while using this tool to draw square frames. With any of the frame tools selected, click the page, and a dialog opens, allowing you to enter exact measurements of the frame you wish to draw. Under the Rectangle Frame tool are two other tools:

- **Ellipse Frame tool:** This tool draws circular frames. Click, hold, and drag to draw, or hold down the Shift key while using this tool to draw perfect circles.

- **Polygon Frame tool:** This tool draws multisided frames when you click, hold, and drag. Hold down the Shift key while using this tool to draw polygons with sides having equal measurements. Double-click the tool to open a dialog that allows you to set the number of sides of the polygon you draw, as well as the star inset, if you wish.

- **Rectangle tool:** The Rectangle tool works like the Rectangle Frame tool, except that it draws four-sided *shapes*. Click, hold, and drag to draw the shape. Hold down the Shift key while using this tool to draw a square. With any of the tools selected, click the page, and a dialog opens, allowing you to enter exact measurements of the item you wish to draw. Under the Rectangle tool are two other tools:

  - **Ellipse tool:** This tool draws round shapes. Click, hold, and drag to draw, or hold down the Shift key while using this tool to draw perfect circles.

  - **Polygon tool:** This tool draws multisided shapes when you click, hold, and drag. Hold down the Shift key while using this tool to draw polygons with sides having equal measurements. Double-click the tool to open a dialog that allows you to set the number of sides of the polygon you draw, as well as the star inset, if you wish.

Question and Answer

Q: **What's the difference between the frame tools and the standard shape tools?**

A: At the heart of it, nothing. Any shape you draw is still a frame and can be used as a container for text or graphics. Using the tools is a matter of preference. Most professional designers prefer to use the frame tools because the *X* in the frame serves as a reminder that the shape is a container.

The next set of tools work to transform any page element. Before you can transform an element, you must select it by clicking with the Selection tool. After you click with one of the transform tools, you see a crosshairs, which indicates the point from which the item will be transformed. You can freely move the crosshairs by clicking and dragging it. The following are the tools you can use to transform page elements:

- **Rotate tool:** The Rotate tool rotates objects when you click, hold, and drag. This is a manual rotation, but you can use the Control palette or the Transform palette to see your angle of rotation.

- **Scale tool:** Use the Scale tool to resize elements. Click and drag any anchor point or the side of the object to resize. The item is resized from the crosshairs, which can be moved at any time. Hold down the Shift key while using this tool to resize proportionally.

- **Shear tool:** With an item selected, use the Shear tool to skew page elements. The element skews from the crosshairs.

- **Free Transform tool:** The Free Transform tool performs several functions, including rotating, scaling, and shearing. With the item selected, when you position the tool at the corner of the frame, you see a double-ended, curved arrow. Click, hold, and drag to rotate. Scale by clicking and holding an anchor point. Hold down the Option or Alt key while scaling to scale from the center of the object. To shear an element, click, hold, and drag a side anchor point while holding down Ctrl+Alt (Windows users) or ⌘+Option (Mac users).

- **Eyedropper tool:** The Eyedropper tool samples either color or type style to apply to another element. Click the color you want to sample with the Eyedropper tool and then click the element to which you want to apply the sampled color. To sample text, click the type frame with the tool. Position the Eyedropper tool over the unformatted text until a small I-beam appears with the eyedropper and then drag the I-beam across the text. Color, font, and size of the sampled text are all applied to the unformatted text.

  - The Measure tool measures straight lines or angles.

- **Gradient tool:** Select an object with the Selection tool and then click, hold, and drag the Gradient tool across it to apply a gradient. Drag with the Gradient tool in different locations and with different starting points to alter the flow and direction of the gradient.

- **Button tool:** The Button tool creates elements that can be used to perform actions in an HTML or PDF document.

- **Scissors tool:** Use the Scissors tool to click any part of a selected path to cut the path. To break a closed path into two parts, you must cut the path in two places. You cannot cut a frame that contains text.

- **Hand tool:** The Hand tool works the same way in every Adobe program, allowing you to scroll around the currently open page.

- **Zoom tool:** Like the Hand tool, the Zoom tool is an Adobe standard. Click to zoom into an area of the page, or click and drag a marquee around an area on the page to zoom to that specific area. Click and hold down Option (Mac users) or Alt (Windows users) to zoom out of an area.

There are several important controls below the tools. The first is the Fill and Stroke control. The outline box controls the stroke of the selected object. Click the outline box to make the stroke active. The solid box controls the fill of the selected object. Click the solid box to make the fill active. Click the curved arrow to switch the application of fill and stroke. Click the fill and stroke proxy to return to the defaults.

The icons below the Fill and Stroke controls allow you to set where to apply the fill and stroke. The Container button applies fill and stroke characteristics to a frame, and the Text button applies fill and stroke characteristics to individual text characters.

Below these controls, the Apply Color button applies the last-selected color to the fill or stroke, the Apply Gradient button applies the last-selected gradient to the fill or stroke, and Apply None switches the color choice to none.

Finally, InDesign offers several View modes to help you preview your document. The Normal View mode shows the document with all frames and guides showing.

The Preview Mode button shows the document as it will print, with guides, the edges of unselected frames, and any nonprinting items hidden. Two other view buttons beneath the Preview mode are Bleed Mode, which shows the document as it will print with bleed area showing, and Slug Mode, which shows the document as it will print with the slug area showing. See the section on document setup in Chapter 25, "Understanding Document and Page Setup in InDesign," for more information about creating a document with bleed and slug areas.

INDESIGN PALETTES

Like other Adobe programs, InDesign also features numerous palettes that help make common tasks more convenient. This section contains a brief description of each palette. As with the previous descriptions of the tools, other chapters in this section go into more detail about the specific functions of the palettes.

InDesign makes it very convenient to work with the palettes and arrange them in your workspace. The following are some things you should know about palettes that will help you arrange and work with them:

- Most palettes contain palette menus, which you access by clicking the arrow in the top-right or top-left corner of the palette. These menus offer additional features and choices for the palette you're working with.

- All palettes can be collapsed to the right or left side of the workspace. When a palette is collapsed, you can see its title tab only. You can click the tab to expand the palette and make all selections visible. You can click again to collapse the palette back into the side of the workspace (see Figure 24.2). The only tabs that cannot be collapsed to the side of the workspace are the Tool palette, the Control palette, the Tabs palette, and the PageMaker toolbar. To move a palette elsewhere on the workspace, you click and drag it from the side of the workspace by the tab.

Figure 24.2
Grouped palettes expanded from the right side of the workspace.

- In their default state, many palettes are grouped together, such as the Character palette, the Paragraph palette, and the Transform palette. To group or ungroup a palette, click the palette tab and drag it on top of the palette to group it or away from the palette to ungroup it. You can group palettes you use often to help clean up the workspace for maximum accessibility and convenience.

- You can also *dock* palettes to each other, which is convenient when you need to work with palettes as a group. For example, it's helpful to have both the Color palette and the Gradient palette open when you're creating gradients. To dock one palette to another, you drag one palette's tab over the bottom of the palette you want to dock it to until the bottom of the second palette highlights. When palettes are docked, they move as a unit when you drag the title bar. You can click and drag one tab to separate docked palettes.

- Palettes with double arrows on the palette tab can be abbreviated or collapsed. Abbreviated palettes show some, but not all, of the palette features. You know that a palette has additional features when there is a More Options selection in the palette menu. In collapsed mode, only the title bar and palette tab show. To cycle through a palette's full, abbreviated, and collapsed views, you click the double arrow on the palette tab.

As you work more and more with InDesign, you'll start to see a pattern to how you tend to arrange and use palettes. This will help you figure out your optimal workspace arrangement. If you share a computer, it can be irritating to come back to your workspace and find it arranged in someone else's optimal way. Or maybe you have your own favorite arrangements that change, depending on what type of project you're working on. In these cases, you can set up a custom workspace that will automatically snap to your preferences when you want it to:

1. Choose Window, Workspace, Save Workspace from the menu bar. The Save Workspace dialog opens (see Figure 24.3)

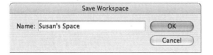

Figure 24.3
You can set up a custom workspace.

2. Give your space a name and click OK.

3. When you want to get back to your preferred workspace, select Window, Workspace, *<Workspace Name>*. Everything goes back the way you like it.

The following sections provide an overview of InDesign's palettes.

The Attributes Palette

You can use the Attributes palette to set your preferences for how specific objects are printed. Check boxes allow you to choose Overprint Fill or Stroke, to select Overprint Gap, or to set a selected item as Nonprinting.

Automation Palettes

Several palettes are grouped together as Animation palettes.

The Data Merge Palette

If you want to import information from a tab-separated or comma-delimited text document, the Data Merge palette allows you to specify records and prepare a document.

The Scripts and Script Label Palettes

InDesign supports automation of tasks using JavaScript, AppleScript, or Visual Basic. You can run or edit your scripts from the Scripts palette and use the Script Label palette to edit scripting labels.

The Color Palette

The Color palette (see Figure 24.4) works as a color mixer. You choose your Color mode from the palette menu and then use sliders or enter specific percentages to create the color you want. A fill and stroke control, a container button, and a text button allow you to control where the color you create is placed. The color ramp at the bottom allows you to sample colors with an eyedropper. When you mix a color you like, you can choose Add to Swatches from the palette menu to add it to the Swatches palette for further use.

Figure 24.4
The Color palette.

The Control Palette

The Control palette does just what its name promises: It gives you additional control over the location and appearance of page elements.

The Gradient Palette

The Gradient palette (see Figure 24.5) allows you to mix gradients with the colors of your choice. You can also use this palette to specify the gradient type, location, and angle. This is the place to mix gradients for one-off use; you can create and save a gradient as a swatch by using the New Gradient Swatch command in the Swatches palette so that you can preserve your gradient for later use in the document. You can find more information on gradients in Chapter 29, "Working with Color in InDesign."

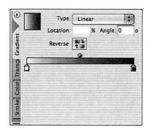

Figure 24.5
The Gradient palette.

The Info Palette

The Info palette (see Figure 24.6) has a wealth of information about any element on a page, including color, location, and measurements. When placed images are selected, the Info palette gives detailed information about the images. When text frames are selected, the Info palette shows character, word, line, and paragraph counts.

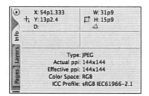

Figure 24.6
The Info palette.

Interactive Palettes

The Interactive palettes are used to work with the hyperlinks and button features that can help you navigate through your InDesign document or the resulting PDF file.

The Bookmarks Palette

You can mark any headings in a document that you want to use in a table of contents by using the Bookmarks palette. The bookmarks will be saved as such when you export a document to PDF.

The Hyperlinks Palette

InDesign allows you to specify text or graphics as hyperlinks and then point them to documents or to locations within documents or URLs. As with bookmarks, the hyperlinks are also saved in any PDF file that is exported.

The States Palette

The States palette works with the Button tool to define the appearance of a button based on the action performed.

The Layers Palette

The Layers palette in InDesign gives you control over the placement of objects (see Figure 24.7). You can hide or lock layers to help with object location and visibility.

Figure 24.7
The Layers palette.

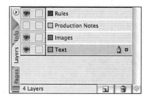

The Links Palette

The Links palette tracks all files placed in the document. From this palette you can edit your original document and then update it, or you can embed the link in your file.

Object and Layout Palettes

The Object and Layout palettes give you one-touch access to moving and altering page objects.

The Align Palette

You can use the Align palette to line up page elements as well as maintain consistent internal margins through distribution and distribution spacing. You simply select the objects you want to align and then click the alignment button that matches what you want to do. If you are choosing how the objects are distributed or setting spacing, you can select the Use Spacing check box and enter the measurement you want to use.

The Navigator Palette

The Navigator palette shows a thumbnail of your layout, with a viewing proxy you can move to change the display of the document and a magnification slider to zoom in and out.

The Pathfinder Palette

You can work with compound paths in the Pathfinder palette, or you can quickly transform selected shapes into the shapes shown on the palette. The options in the lower right of the palette allow you to close, open, or reverse the direction of paths.

The Transform Palette

The Transform palette tracks the location and size of page elements and allows you to resize, skew, or rotate selected items to specific degrees or percentages.

The Object Styles Palette

Object styles work much like character or paragraph styles, helping you add consistency to page elements as well as text. If you have a specific color scheme or drop shadow, for example, that you want to add to numerous page elements, you can save those specifications as an object style and then apply them to another element through this palette.

Output Palettes

The Output palettes enable you to access commands that help prepare a document for printing.

The Flattener Preview Palette

The Flattener Preview palette gives you options to highlight objects on your page that will be flattened when you export or print the file.

The Separations Preview Palette

The Separations Preview palette gives you options to display a document with certain swatches turned on or off, to preview things like special varnishes, rich blacks, and ink coverage.

The Trap Presets Palette

The Trap Presets palette lets you set up trap presets for documents or pages within a document.

The PageMaker Toolbar Palette

The PageMaker Toolbar palette mimics the PageMaker toolbar for users who are unfamiliar with InDesign's interface. Buttons on the toolbar give you quick access to common document functions as well as one-button entry to the other programs in Adobe CS2.

The Pages Palette

Using the Pages palette is the best way to navigate through a document. You can use it to create and apply master pages, page numbering, and sections.

The Stroke Palette

The Stroke palette is the where you set stroke weight and appearance (see Figure 24.8). InDesign comes with a variety of stroke types already created, as well as start and end options, such as arrows. If you are using a variety of strokes multiple times, you can also set up stroke styles that can be used and applied throughout a document.

Figure 24.8
The Stroke palette.

The Swatches Palette

The Swatches palette is a holding area for color chips that can be applied to any page element (see Figure 24.9). These chips can be any kind of color mix, including gradients and tints.

Figure 24.9
The Swatches palette.

The Tags Palette

The Tags palette shows XML tags and allows you to quickly apply them to page elements.

The Text Wrap Palette

You can control offset styles and amounts to wrap text around any page object by using the Text Wrap palette.

The Tools Palette

The Tools palette (not surprisingly) contains tools to create and alter page objects.

The Transparency Palette

The options in the Transparency palette (see Figure 24.10) should be familiar to Photoshop or Illustrator users. The Opacity slider and entry box let you choose the degree of transparency you want to apply, and a pop-up menu contains a selection of Blending modes that alter the appearance of items that are layered on top of each other. The Isolate Blending option displays blending in grouped items, while Knockout Group knocks out those items rather than blending them.

Figure 24.10
The Transparency palette.

Type and Tables Palettes

These palettes enable you to access commands for altering the appearance of text and tables on a page.

The Character Palette

You can select fonts, type size, leading, kerning, and letter and font characteristics in the Character palette.

The Character Styles Palette

You can use the Character Styles palette to apply character styles to single letters and to control most aspects of type appearance. See Chapter 27, "Working with Type in InDesign," for specific information on the Character Styles palette.

The Glyphs Palette

The Glyphs palette displays every available character for the chosen font. At a text entry point—that is, when you see a blinking cursor in a text frame—you can double-click a character in the Glyphs palette to "type" it on the page.

The Index Palette

The Index palette shows all entries in the document that have been marked for the index, and it also allows you to edit them without changing the entry in the document itself.

The Paragraph Palette

You can select paragraph alignment, indents, spacing, and hyphenation in the Paragraph palette.

The Paragraph Styles Palette

You can use the Paragraph Style palette to apply paragraph styles to entire paragraphs of text and to control most aspects of type appearance. See Chapter 27 for specific information on the Paragraph Styles palette.

24

The Story Palette

One function of the Story palette is to turn on optical margin alignment, which aligns text in the document based on actual letters instead of hanging punctuation, such as quotation marks. You can also set the font size on which to base the alignment.

The Table Palette

You can quickly set table specifications such as the number and size of rows and columns as well as content alignment, offset, indent, and direction, by using the Table palette.

The Tabs Palette

You can define tab style, stops, and location in a text frame by using the controls in the Tabs palette.

The Control Palette

The most ever-present and arguably the most useful palette InDesign offers is the Control palette. By default, the Control palette is docked to the top or bottom of the workspace; it can also float on the workspace. You can change its location by selecting Dock to Bottom or Float from the palette menu.

What makes the Control palette so powerful is its flexibility. The palette changes with your selection and page action (see Figure 24.11). If you're working in a text frame, the Control palette displays options found in the Character and Paragraph palettes. You can also quickly change from Character Formatting view to Paragraph Formatting view. If you have a frame or line selected, the selections displayed are similar to those you find in the Transform palette. The Control palette menu also changes depending on your selection.

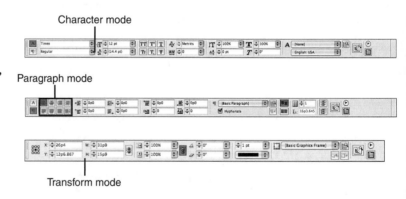

Figure 24.11
The Control palette in Character, Paragraph, and Transform modes, respectively.

The Control palette provides a quick jump to Bridge, as well as a button to toggle all palettes other than the Tool palette. Again, you can find more details about the Control palette as it pertains to text and page elements in Chapters 26, "Working with Objects in InDesign," and 27.

THE PAGEMAKER TOOLBAR

Adobe has included a number of features in InDesign to make former PageMaker users more comfortable. The PageMaker toolbar is one such feature (see Figure 24.12). This toolbar mimics a feature of PageMaker that puts many common application features at your fingertips. The selections should also be familiar to Microsoft Office users. Each button represents a different action; they are listed here as they appear across the toolbar from left to right:

- New Document
- Open Document
- Save
- Print
- Find/Change
- Check Spelling
- Open Character Palette
- Increase Font Size
- Decrease Font Size
- Open Swatches Palette
- Open Paragraph Palette
- Open Tabs Palette
- Bulleted List
- Numbered List
- Decrease Left Indent
- Increase Left Indent
- Insert Pages
- Remove Pages
- Text Frame Options
- Open Text Wrap Palette
- Update Link
- Place

- Open Photoshop

- Open Illustrator

- Package for GoLive

- Export Adobe PDF

- Zoom In

- Zoom Out

- Actual Size

- Fit Spread in Window

- Open Adobe Help Center

Figure 24.12
The PageMaker toolbar.

INDESIGN MENU COMMANDS

Using menus is an easy way to access commands that help you work in applications. You'll notice as you work with InDesign that many menu commands are duplicated in palettes, giving you a choice of how you perform an action.

You'll also notice that many menu commands are the same throughout Adobe CS2; this is another nice bit of consistency that makes the programs easier to pick up. Keyboard shortcuts for the menu commands are listed beside the commands themselves, and as you get more familiar with the program, you'll find yourself relying on those shortcuts more than the menus themselves.

The following sections list the various menu selections, along with a brief description of the action each performs. More details about some of these commands are included in subsequent chapters.

The File Menu

The File menu has commands that, in general, help you create, open, close, print, or place other files in your document:

- **New, Document:** You use this command to create new documents.

- **New, Book:** You use this command to create new books.

- **New, Library:** You use this command to create new libraries.

- **Open:** You use this command to open a dialog that allows you to browse for the document you want to open.

- **Open Recent:** You use this command to obtain a list of the most recently opened InDesign documents.

- **Close:** This command closes the currently open window.

- **Save:** This command saves the currently open document. The first time you save a document, a dialog allows you to name the document and specify how to save it.

- **Save As:** This command allows you to rename and save the currently open document.

- **Save a Version:** This command saves the current changes as a version, which is then accessible through Version Cue.

- **Save a Copy:** This command saves a copy of the currently open document but leaves the first document active.

- **Revert:** This command takes the document back to its last-saved state. It is available only if a document has been saved at least once.

- **Place:** This command allows you to browse for text or images to be imported into the document.

- **Import XML:** This command allows you to browse for XML files to be imported into the document.

- **Adobe PDF Presets:** This command allows you to choose any PDF presets, either in the program or that you have set up, with which to export PDFs.

- **Export:** This command enables you to choose from PDF, EPS, InDesign Interchange, JPEG, SVG, SVG compressed, and XML formats.

- **Document Presets:** This command enables you to choose from any document presets you have created, opening files that are set up with your settings (such as page size and margins) already applied.

- **Document Setup:** This command opens a dialog where you can access several important page specification features, including page size, margins, columns, text frame options, and the number of pages in the document.

- **File Info:** This command allows you to enter information about the document that may be helpful for others who are using or printing it. The metadata you enter here helps you find files through Bridge. You can also save the metadata as an XMP template and assign it to any other document.

- **Preflight:** This command checks a document's fonts, links, colors, print settings, and associated plug-ins for conflicts that may cause problems in printing.

- **Package:** This command copies your file with all necessary fonts, links, and other information into a folder so it can be easily gathered for a printer.

- **Package for GoLive:** This command packages your file for use in GoLive.

- **Print Presets:** This command allows you to set up presets by using the options in the Print dialog.

- **Print:** This command opens the Print dialog, which allows you to print the currently open file.

- **Quit/Exit:** (Windows only; this command is found under the InDesign menu on Mac systems.) This command closes the InDesign application.

24

The Edit Menu

The Edit menu has commands that, in general, help you work with page objects of all types and customize an application:

- **Undo:** This option allows you to undo the last action you took. You can undo up to 300 moves in an InDesign document, up to the last save.

- **Redo:** When Redo is available, it allows you to redo a step that you have undone with the Undo command.

- **Cut:** This command removes a selected object and stores it in the Clipboard to be pasted.

- **Copy:** This command duplicates a selected object and stores it in the Clipboard to be pasted.

- **Paste:** This command places a cut or copied object on the page.

- **Paste without Formatting:** This command pastes formatted text copied from a source such as a Word document, without styles.

- **Paste into:** This command pastes a cut or copied object into a selected frame.

- **Paste in Place:** This command pastes an object at the same coordinates from which it was cut or copied.

- **Clear:** This command deletes the selected object.

- **Duplicate:** This command duplicates a selected object and places the duplicate at a slight offset from the original location. It does not use the Clipboard, so any object that has previously been cut or copied remains there to be pasted.

- **Step and Repeat:** This command opens a dialog that allows you to create multiple duplicates of an object at a specified offset from each other.

- **Select All:** This command selects every object on the current page/spread.

- **Deselect All:** This command deselects every object currently selected on the current page/spread.

- **Edit Original:** When a graphic or an image is selected, this command allows you to edit the original document in the program it's associated with.

- **Edit in Story Editor:** This command opens the Story Editor, a word processor within InDesign.

- **Quick Apply:** This command opens the Quick Apply menu from the Control palette. This palette helps you easily navigate documents that have many styles; you just type the first few letters of the style you're searching for in the field at the top of the palette, and you jump through the styles.

- **Find/Change:** This command allows you to search for text or text characteristics and change all occurrences as you choose. You enter the appropriate information in the Find and Change fields, and then you choose to make the changes all at once or one at a time.

- **Find Next:** This command finds the next occurrence of a find request.

- **Spelling, Check Spelling:** This command checks the spelling in all text frames of a document.

- **Spelling, Dynamic Spelling:** This command turns on the dynamic spelling feature, which checks your spelling as you type and underlines words that are thought to be misspelled.

- **Spelling, Autocorrect:** This command turns on the autocorrect feature, which automatically corrects commonly misspelled words as you type (for example, *teh* will automatically be changed to *the*).

- **Spelling, Dictionary:** You use this command to specify how InDesign handles hyphenation and dictionaries.

- **Transparency Blend Space:** This command allows you to select Document RGB or Document CMYK. You make this choice based on the color space of your document.

- **Transparency Flattener Presets:** This command allows you to create or load Transparency Flattener presets, which determine how transparency effects are flattened, based on how you save or export the document. See Chapter 31, "Exporting, Saving, and Printing with InDesign," for more information on transparency flattening.

- **Color Settings:** This command allows you to change or load the color profiles for the document. See Chapter 1, "Creative Suite 2 Basics," for more information about color management with Adobe CS2. You use this option when you have to set up color management for your Creative Suite documents.

- **Assign Profiles:** This command allows you to assign RGB or CMYK profiles to the document. You use this option when you are setting color management for your document on-the-fly or within InDesign only. The Assign Profiles dialog enables you to use the current working space, assign a working space as defined by Creative Suite color settings, or assign a different profile for this application only.

- **Convert to Profile:** This command allows you to convert from the currently assigned color profile to another.

- **Keyboard Shortcuts:** This command allows you to view basic keyboard shortcuts for the application and set up customized keyboard shortcuts. See "InDesign Keyboard Shortcuts," later in this chapter, for more information on keyboard shortcuts.

- **Preferences:** (Windows only; this command appears under the InDesign menu on Mac systems.) This command allows you to customize various document and application properties, including Text, Composition, Units & Measurements, Grids, Guides, and Dictionary. See the section "InDesign Application Preferences," later in this chapter, for a complete explanation of InDesign preferences.

The Layout Menu

The Layout menu has commands that, in general, enable you to set options for guides and page numbering:

- **Pages:** You use the Pages submenu to add, insert, or move pages; duplicate or delete spreads; or quickly assign master pages.

- **Margins and Columns:** This command sets margin and column guides for the document.

- **Ruler Guides:** This command allows you to choose the color of guides you drag from InDesign's rulers.

- **Create Guides:** This command allows you to automatically place guides in rows and columns, setting the amount of space you want in between. You can also clear guides from the dialog this command opens.

- **Layout Adjustment:** This command automates how objects on the page interact with guides.

- **First Page, Previous Page, Next Page, Last Page, Next Spread and Previous Spread; Go Back, Go Forward:** These commands allow you to navigate through the document with more precision and speed than by simply dragging the scrollbars.

- **Numbering & Section Options:** This command opens a dialog that you can use to change the starting page number of the document or set up document sections.

- **Table of Contents:** This command allows you to specify currently existing styles for headings and entries in your table of contents.

- **Update Table of Contents:** As long as you use styles and mark items for your table of contents, you can automatically update with this menu selection if page numbering changes, for example.

- **Table of Contents Styles:** This command allows you to set up presets for your table of contents.

The Type Menu

The Type menu has commands that enable you to alter the appearance of text and text frames on a page:

- **Font:** This command opens a submenu to select a typeface. You see a preview of all available fonts.

- **Size:** This command opens a submenu to select a type size.

- **Character:** This command opens the Character palette, allowing you to set options for specific type characters.

- **Paragraph:** This command opens the Paragraph palette, allowing you to set options for the appearance of a paragraph.

- **Tabs:** This command opens the Tabs palette, allowing you to set tabs and indents.

- **Glyphs:** This command opens the Glyphs palette, allowing you to see all possible characters for a given font.

- **Story:** This command opens the Story palette, allowing you to turn Optical Marginal Alignment on or off.

- **Character Styles:** This command opens the Character Styles palette, allowing you to create and apply character styles.

- **Paragraph Styles:** This command opens the Paragraph Styles palette, allowing you to create and apply paragraph styles.

- **Create Outlines:** This command allows you to convert text to a graphic. The text itself then becomes a frame that you can alter by using its anchor points.

- **Find Font:** This command shows a list of all fonts being used in the currently open document. You can use this dialog to see which fonts you have used or to substitute other fonts for fonts that have been used in the document.

- **Change Case:** You can select text and then use this command to change the text to all lower-case, all uppercase, proper case (where the first letter of each word is capitalized), or sentence case (where the first letter after a period is capitalized).

- **Type on a Path, Options:** The dialog this command opens allows you to apply different effects to text on a path, including how it appears and how it aligns.

- **Type on a Path, Delete Type from Path:** This command deletes type from a selected path.

- **Insert Footnote:** This command automatically inserts a numbered reference in the spot where a cursor is blinking. A footnote is then inserted at the bottom of the page, where you can type your footnote information.

- **Document Footnote Options:** This command lets you set preferences for how footnotes are numbered and how they appear in the layout.

- **Insert Special Character:** This command opens a submenu with various frequently used marks and characters, allowing you to insert them at the current spot.

- **Insert White Space:** This command opens a submenu with various space options.

- **Insert Break Character:** This command opens a submenu with various text break options.

- **Fill with Placeholder Text:** This command fills the currently active text frame with dummy text.

- **Show/Hide Hidden Characters:** This command turns on hidden characters so you can see characters that are not usually shown, such as spaces, text breaks, or hard returns.

The Object Menu

The Object menu has commands that help you alter or add effects to objects on a page:

- **Transform:** This command opens a submenu that allows you to move, scale, rotate, or shear a selected page element by entering specific measurements.

- **Transform Again, Transform Again Individually:** This command duplicates the previous transformation, either to all selected objects as a group or to each object individually.

- **Transform Again, Transform Sequence Again Individually:** This command duplicates the last sequence of transformations, either to all selected objects as a group or to each object individually.

- **Arrange:** This command opens a submenu that allows you to control the layering of page elements (Bring to Front, Send to Back, Bring Forward, Send Backward).

- **Select:** This command opens a submenu that allows you to select a layered page element (First Object Above, First Object Below, and so on).

- **Group/Ungroup:** With multiple objects selected, Group turns those objects into a single entity for easy movement. You can select a grouped object and choose Ungroup to work with each component individually.

- **Lock Position/Unlock Position:** The Lock Position command locks the position of a selected object(s). Unlock Position allows you to move or alter a locked object.

- **Text Frame Options:** The dialog that this command opens allows you set specifications for the selected text frame, including columns in the frame, text inset, and vertical justification.

- **Anchored Object, Options:** This command allows you to select the defaults for how an anchored object frame is set up.

- **Anchored Object, Insert:** This command sets defaults for anchored objects.

- **Anchored Object, Release:** This command releases an anchored object from its position with a text frame.

- **Fitting:** This command opens a submenu that allows you to fit a frame to its contents or the contents of a frame to the frame.

- **Content:** This command opens a submenu that allows you to specify or change the content of the selected frame, either graphic, text, or unassigned.

- **Drop Shadow:** This command opens a dialog in which you can assign drop shadows to any selected frame. If a text frame is selected, a drop shadow is applied to the individual text characters in the frame.

- **Feather:** This command applies a feathered edge to the content of a selected frame. You can set the amount of feathering and the feathering appearance.

- **Corner Effects:** This command designs the corners of any frame that has a stroke applied to it.

- **Object Layer Options:** This command sets visibility and layer composition options for layered Photoshop or PDF files that are placed in InDesign.

- **Clipping Path:** This command makes clipping paths that have been applied to images active, or it detects the edges of an item that is in stark contrast to its background.

- **Image Color Settings:** This command selects color profiles and rendering options for specific images within the document.

- **Interactive, Movie Options:** This command enables you to change the settings for movies you can embed in a PDF created from your InDesign document. These options include how the movie is played and how it appears in the document.

- **Interactive, Sound Options:** This command enables you to change the settings for sound files you can embed in a PDF file created from your InDesign document. These options include what sound is played, when it plays, and any text that should appear if it can't be played.

- **Interactive, Button Options:** This command enables you to specify how buttons should appear in PDF documents created from your InDesign document, as well as how they should behave.

- **Interactive, Convert to Button:** With an object selected on your page, you can choose this command to convert the object to a button.

- **Interactive, Set Tab Order:** You use this command to set the order in which buttons are activated when the user presses the Tab key in a PDF file created from your InDesign document.

- **Compound Paths:** You use this menu command to create compound paths, which result when overlapping page elements are combined to create one element. You can select Create or Release to make or undo compound paths.

- **Paths, Open Path; Paths, Close Path; Paths, Reverse Path:** These commands do exactly what they say to selected paths: open, close, and reverse them, or fill a hole in a subpath, respectively. You can find more information about paths in Chapter 26.

- **Pathfinder:** This command gives you access to the commands found in the Pathfinder palette, which you can use to create shapes out of compound paths.

- **Convert Shape:** You use this command to change a selected shape to another shape, as listed in the submenu: Rectangle, Rounded Rectangle, Beveled Rectangle, Inverse Rounded Rectangle, Ellipse, Triangle, Polygon, Line, or Orthogonal Line.

- **Display Performance:** This command sets the display performance of individual items on the page. Setting items to Optimized Display uses less memory to display photos and graphics. Setting the level to High Quality displays images as clearly as possible, but it may also slow down performance.

The Table Menu

The Table menu has commands that help you create and set up tables in a document:

- **Insert Table:** When you click in a text frame, this option allows you to create a table that has a specific number of rows and columns.

- **Convert Text to Table:** This command converts selected text to a table, based on defined separators that indicate where one cell's data ends and the next cell's begins.

- **Convert Table to Text:** This command takes text in tables out of the table format.

- **Table Options:** This command opens a submenu that gives you access to different table setup options, such as stroke, fill, headers, and footers.

- **Cell Options:** This command allows you to set specifications for selected cells.

- **Insert:** This command allows you to quickly insert blank rows or columns.

- **Delete:** This command allows you to quickly delete selected rows, columns, or an entire table.

- **Select:** This command allows you to quickly select specific parts of a table.

- **Merge Cells/Unmerge Cells:** This command combines or unmerges two or more selected cells in the same row or column.

- **Split Cell Horizontally/Vertically:** This command splits a single selected cell either vertically or horizontally.

- **Convert Rows:** This command converts existing table rows to header or footer rows, as you choose.

- **Distribute Rows/Columns Evenly:** This command makes the selected columns or rows the same width or height, respectively.

- **Go to Row:** This command is like a search feature for your table; when you select Go to Row, you can enter the row number you want to jump to.

- **Edit Header/Footer:** This command gives you options to edit the header or footer information for a table.

The View Menu

The View menu has commands that affect your view of a document in the open window:

- **Overprint Preview:** This command shows a preview of the document so you can see how overprinting will appear on the final output.

- **Proof Setup:** This command allows you to choose or create a custom proof setup to print a more accurate proof of the final output.

- **Proof Colors:** This selection toggles on and off to show a soft proof of the color output.

- **Zoom In/Zoom Out:** This command increases or decreases the amount of magnification to a specific amount.

- **Fit Page in Window:** This command shows the entire current page in the window.

- **Fit Spread in Window:** This command shows the entire current spread in the window.

- **Actual Size:** This command shows your page at 100%.

- **Entire Pasteboard:** This command shows the document and the entire pasteboard area.

- **Screen Mode, Normal:** This command shows the page in Normal View mode, with all frame edges and guides.

- **Screen Mode, Preview:** This command allows you to preview the page with all guides and frame edges hidden.

- **Screen Mode, Bleed:** This command allows you to preview the document with the bleed area.

- **Screen Mode, Slug:** This command allows you to preview the document with the slug area.

- **Display Performance, Fast Display:** This option hides all the images and graphics placed on the page to make InDesign work faster.

- **Display Performance, Typical Display:** This option displays low-resolution views of all images and graphics placed on the page. It is the default display setting.

- **Display Performance, High Quality Display:** This option displays images and graphics at the highest quality possible. Choosing this option can lead to reduced performance.

- **Display Performance, Allow/Clear Object-Level Overrides:** These options allow you to specify how you want objects to appear if they have been individually selected with a different display applied.

- **Structure, Hide/Show Structure; Structure, Hide/Show Tag Markers; Structure, Hide/Show Tagged Frames:** These commands allow you to toggle the visibility of XML information.

- **Hide/Show Hyperlinks:** This command toggles the display of hyperlinks that are tagged as such within the document.

- **Hide/Show Text Threads:** This command hides or shows arrows that illustrate how text threads are linked.

- **Hide/Show Frame Edges:** This command hides or shows the outside lines of any text or image frames on the page.

- **Hide/Show Rulers:** This command hides or shows the rulers at the top and left of the workspace.

- **Grids & Guides, Hide/Show Guides:** This command hides or shows any guides that are dragged out of the rulers.

- **Grids & Guides, Lock Guides:** When this command is activated, ruler guides are locked and cannot be moved.

- **Grids & Guides, Lock Column Guides:** When this command is activated, column guidelines on the page cannot be moved.

- **Grids & Guides, Snap to Guides:** When this command is turned on, text or graphics automatically snap to guides that are on the page.

- **Grids & Guides, Hide/Show Baseline Grid:** This command hides or shows the Baseline Grid view, which consists of horizontal lines that help align columns of text.

24

- **Grids & Guides, Hide/Show Document Grid:** This command hides or shows the page grid used to align page elements.

- **Grids & Guides, Snap to Document Grid:** When this command is activated, text or graphics automatically snap to the document grid.

- **Story Editor:** This command opens a submenu that gives options for what is displayed in Story Editor view.

The Window Menu

The Window menu has commands that affect what you see in the workspace and how you see it:

- **Arrange, New Window:** This command opens another window of the same document. You can zoom into specific page elements in one window while maintaining a full-page view in the other.

- **Arrange, Cascade:** This command staggers all open windows across the screen from left to right for easy access.

- **Arrange, Tile:** This command lines up all open windows within the screen area, allowing you to have a full view of every window.

- **Arrange, Minimize (Mac only):** This command hides the currently open window, sending it to the Dock.

- **Arrange, Bring All to Front (Mac only):** This command brings your InDesign windows to the front of the workspace, in front of any open windows in other applications.

- **Workspace:** This command allows you to save the current palette arrangement or restore a previously saved arrangement.

The rest of the Window menu commands call up or hide specific InDesign palettes. See the "InDesign Palettes" section, earlier in this chapter, for a complete overview of InDesign palettes.

The Help Menu

The Help menu gives you information about InDesign—the application itself, its activation and registration, product updates, and the plug-ins installed:

- **InDesign Help:** This command opens the Adobe Help Center.

- **Welcome Screen:** This command opens the first screen you see when you open InDesign.

- **About InDesign:** This command gives credit information for the application. (This command is found under the InDesign menu on Mac systems.)

- **Configure Plug-ins:** This command lists all installed plug-ins and allows you to enable or disable specific plug-ins or create plug-in sets. (This command is found under the InDesign menu on Mac systems.)

- **Activate:** If you haven't yet activated your software, you do so by using this command.

- **Transfer Activation:** You use this selection if you need to transfer the software license to another computer.

- **Online Support:** This command automatically connects to www.adobe.com for InDesign support.

- **Updates:** This command automatically connects to www.adobe.com for available updates to InDesign.

- **Registration:** This command opens registration information.

- **InDesign Online:** This command goes to the Adobe InDesign website.

INDESIGN KEYBOARD SHORTCUTS

As with any application, in InDesign, keyboard shortcuts make your work faster and easier. InDesign's keyboard shortcut list is extensive and covers almost any conceivable task you might want to perform. It also provides a lot of flexibility.

As mentioned earlier, PageMaker and QuarkXPress users can choose keyboard shortcut sets that match those programs they are used to working with. Do that by following these steps:

1. To choose application preference sets, choose Edit, Keyboard Shortcuts. The Keyboard Shortcuts dialog opens (see Figure 24.13).

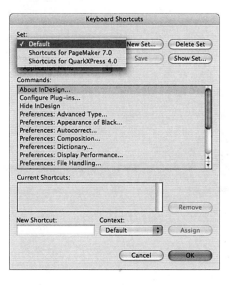

Figure 24.13
Specify the keyboard shortcut set for another application if you're most used to that program.

2. In the Set pop-up, select either Shortcuts for PageMaker 7.0 or Shortcuts for QuarkXPress 4.0.

3. Click OK.

After you follow these steps, shortcuts for the entire application are changed. For example, QuarkXPress users who are used to using Ctrl+E (Windows users) or ⌘+E (Mac users) to place images, as opposed to using Ctrl+D (Windows users) or ⌘+D (Mac users), will find that the File, Place keyboard shortcut is now set to Ctrl+E (Windows users) or ⌘+E (Mac users).

You can also view keyboard shortcuts, and even customize them, in the Keyboard Shortcuts dialog by following these steps:

1. Choose Edit, Keyboard Shortcuts. The Keyboard Shortcuts dialog opens (see Figure 24.14).

Figure 24.14
You can set up your own keyboard shortcuts to make it easier to perform specific functions.

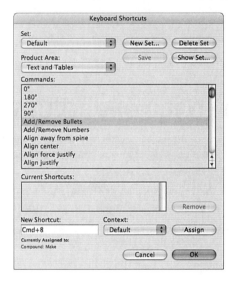

2. To view the keyboard shortcuts, select the appropriate product area from the pop-up. A list of keyboard shortcuts for that product area appears in the Commands pane.

3. Select the action for which you want to see the shortcut. The shortcut (if one has been assigned) appears in the Current Shortcuts window.

4. If you want to change a shortcut to one that is easier for you to remember, select the shortcut in the Current Shortcuts window and click the Remove button.

5. Click in the New Shortcut field and then press the key combination you want to assign to that shortcut. If that key combination is already assigned, it appears below the field. You can type another key combination or overwrite the one currently assigned.

6. The Context menu lets you choose how you want the shortcut to function. Most should be set in the Default context; select another if you want to assign the same shortcut to another type of command.

7. Click Assign.

8. Click OK.

If you want to customize quite a few shortcuts and share your computer with another person, you might want to create your own set of shortcuts that can be easily accessed and changed on-the-fly. Here's what you do:

1. Choose Edit, Keyboard Shortcuts.

2. Click the New Set button.

3. Name your set and choose the set it should be based on.

4. Click OK.

Now follow the earlier instructions for customizing shortcuts to assign your own.

INDESIGN APPLICATION PREFERENCES

Before you start creating documents, you'll find it helpful to go through InDesign's preferences and set them up in a way that makes sense to you.

You should set preferences with no documents open so that they take effect applicationwide. If you set preferences with a document open, those preferences apply only to the document you have open.

To access the Preferences dialog, choose Edit, Preferences, General (Windows users) or InDesign, Preferences, General (Mac users). It's helpful to start with the General preferences and work your way through the panes using the window to the left, although the submenu also gives you easy access to the other selections within the dialog.

General Preferences

Table 24.1 lists the options found on the General page of the InDesign Preferences window (see Figure 24.15):

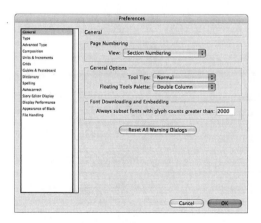

Figure 24.15
General preferences.

Table 24.1   Options Found on the General Page of the InDesign Preferences Window

Option	Description
Page Numbering	You can set up your InDesign documents with sections that can be numbered separately. The View pop-up lets you choose between section numbering and absolute numbering, which will stay in consecutive order no matter how many sections you create or how you number them.
General Options	ToolTips can be set to Normal, None, or Fast. Fast ToolTips appear immediately upon hovering your mouse over the object, without the usual delay. The Tools palette can be displayed in a double column (the default) or as a single column or single row.
Font Downloading and Embedding	This option indicates the number of characters a font may contain before fonts are automatically subset when you export the file—to PDF, for example. Fonts with fewer characters are embedded, which can increase file size. Remember that this is a general preference; when you export the file, you have another chance to specify whether to subset or embed fonts, based on the percentage of characters used.
Reset All Warning Dialogs	Click this button to display all warning dialogs, even if you've checked not to display them. Upon their appearance, you can check to not display them again.

Type Preferences

Table 24.2 lists the options found on the Type page of the InDesign Preferences window (see Figure 24.16):

Figure 24.16
Type preferences.

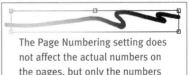

The Page Numbering setting does not affect the actual numbers on the pages, but only the numbers that appear in the status bar at the bottom of the workspace and in the Pages palette. For example, if you create a document that starts on page 43, the starting page number will be 1 in the Pages palette if you have set the view to absolute numbering.

Table 24.2 Options Found on the Type Page of the InDesign Preferences Window

Option	Description
Type Options	You can check to choose the following: ■ Use Typographer's Quotes toggles between curly quotes and straight quotes. ■ Automatically Use Correct Optical Size refers to Multiple Master fonts, whose characteristics, such as serif weights, can differ based on the size at which they are used. ■ Triple Click to Select a Line controls selections. If this option is disabled, triple-clicking selects an entire paragraph. ■ Adjust Text Attributes when Scaling controls whether type or page element settings are adjusted in a palette when the text frame is scaled. ■ Apply Leading to Entire Paragraphs applies leading changes to every line of a paragraph, not just selections. ■ Adjust Spacing Automatically When Cutting and Pasting Words refers to whether InDesign will naturally place spaces before and after a word that is pasted between two others in a sentence, while not placing a space after a word that's pasted in front of a period. ■ Font Preview Size adjusts the font preview in the Type menu, Character palette, and Control palette.
Drag and Drop Text Editing	You can check to enable or disable this option in the Layout view or the Story Editor.
Links	You can choose whether to create links when text and spreadsheet files are placed.
Paste	You can choose whether to paste formatting features when you paste text and tables from other applications.

Advanced Type Preferences

Table 24.3 lists the options found on the Advanced Type page of the InDesign Preferences window (see Figure 24.17):

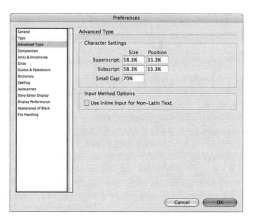

Figure 24.17
Advanced Type preferences.

Table 24.3 Options Found on the Advanced Type Page of the InDesign Preferences Window

Option	Description
Character Settings	You can choose the percentage of size and/or position for superscript, subscript, and small caps.
Input Method Options	You can toggle this option to use Inline Input for Non-Latin Text.

Composition Preferences

Table 24.4 lists the options found on the Composition page of the InDesign Preferences window (see Figure 24.18):

Figure 24.18
Composition preferences.

Table 24.4 Options Found on the Composition Page of the InDesign Preferences Window

Option	Description
Highlight	These selections let you choose whether to highlight the following text issues in documents: ■ **Keep Violations:** This option keeps parts of the paragraph together when headings, as specified in Paragraph Styles, are separated from the paragraph that follows them. ■ **H&J Violations:** This option highlights text when the hyphenation and justification settings create rivers of white in documents. The tint of the highlight indicates the seriousness of the problem. ■ **Custom Tracking/Kerning:** This option highlights places where you have altered the standard tracking and kerning. ■ **Substituted Fonts:** This option highlights text that appears in a font you do not have installed. ■ **Substituted Glyphs:** This option highlights when certain characters of an installed font are not available for display.

Table 24.4   Continued

Option	Description
Text Wrap	This option gives you choices for how text wraps behave: ■ **Justify Text Next to an Object:** This option automatically sets text to justify when it wraps. ■ **Skip by Leading:** This option adjusts text so it lines up with the next leading increment after it wraps around an object. This helps type stay even with type in other columns or text frames. ■ **Text Wrap Only Affects Text Beneath:** This option wraps type around objects only when the object is placed on the text, not when a text frame is placed on the object.

Units & Increments Preferences

Table 24.5 lists the options found on the Units & Increments page of the InDesign Preferences window (see Figure 24.19):

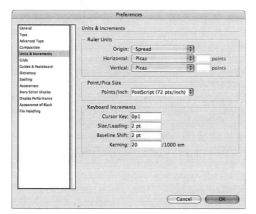

Figure 24.19
Units & Increments preferences.

Table 24.5   Options Found on the Units & Increments Page of the InDesign Preferences Window

Option	Description
Ruler Units	The Origin setting allows you to decide where ruler measurements begin: at the spread, each page, or from the spine. You can also set the measurement units for both the horizontal and vertical rulers with common choices, or you can set up a custom selection, in points.
Point/Pica Size	You can choose the way to measure points and picas.
Keyboard Increments	These options set the tolerance when keyboard shortcuts are used to move or alter the size of objects: ■ Cursor Key refers to how much the selected object moves when you press one of the arrow keys on your keyboard. ■ The Size/Leading, Baseline Shift, and Kerning entries control how much these options are changed when you use the keyboard shortcut to increase or decrease size.

Grids Preferences

The settings in the Grid Preferences window (see Figure 24.20) control the baseline grid and document grids available under the View menu. You can set the color for each.

Figure 24.20
Grids preferences.

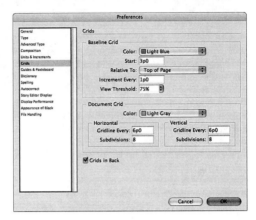

The Baseline Grid options allow you to choose where the baseline grid starts, relative to either the top of the page or the margins. You can choose the measurement between lines and at what percentage you want the view to be visible.

The document grid is customizable in terms of the gridlines themselves; you can set the increment and number of subdivisions for gridlines. For example, if you set a gridline every 6 picas, with 6 subdivisions, you see a heavier line every inch, with a fainter line for every pica.

You can use the Grids in Back check box to toggle grids in front or back of objects on the page.

Guides & Pasteboard Preferences

Table 24.6 lists the options found on the Guides & Pasteboard page of the InDesign Preferences window (see Figure 24.21):

Figure 24.21
Guides & Pasteboard preferences.

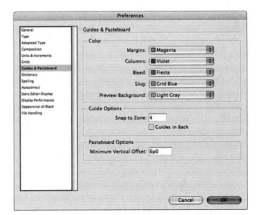

Table 24.6   Options Found on the Guides & Pasteboard Page of the InDesign Preferences Window

Option	Description
Color	You can use the options in this section to choose colors for margin lines, column guides, bleed lines, slug lines, and the background when you are in Preview mode.
Guide Options	This entry lets you specify the tolerance of the Snap To zone and whether guides should move to the back or in front of page elements.
Pasteboard Options	The Minimum Vertical Offset entry lets you specify how far the pasteboard extends from the page edge, bleed area, or slug area.

Dictionary Preferences

Table 24.7 lists the options found on the Dictionary page of the InDesign Preferences window (see Figure 24.22):

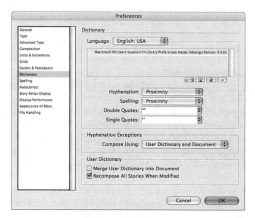

Figure 24.22
Dictionary preferences.

Table 24.7   Options Found on the Dictionary Page of the InDesign Preferences Window

Option	Description
Language	You can choose the language you will be working in.
	The default dictionary path is shown. The buttons below allow you to add, delete, or relink other dictionaries. You can set hyphenation and spelling as you wish. You can also choose how to display quotes in these pop-ups.
Hyphenation Exceptions	These options allow you to choose to use either the settings specified in the current document, user dictionary settings, or both.
User Dictionary	You can choose whether to merge the selected user dictionary into the document and whether to recompose stories if the dictionary is modified.

Spelling Preferences

Table 24.8 lists the options found on the Spelling page of the InDesign Preferences window (see Figure 24.23):

Figure 24.23
Spelling preferences.

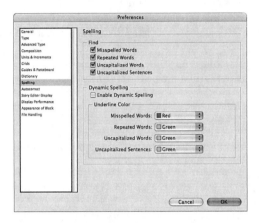

Table 24.8 Options Found on the Spelling Page of the InDesign Preferences Window

Option	Description
Find	You can enable or disable the check boxes to turn on or off the options to find misspelled words, repeated words, uncapitalized words, or uncapitalized sentences.
Dynamic Spelling	When this feature is enabled, you can choose the color with which the previous issues are highlighted.

Autocorrect Preferences

The Autocorrect page of the InDesign Preferences window is shown in Figure 24.24. When the Enable Autocorrect option is checked, you can choose to autocorrect capitalization, as well as spelling errors. Based on the language choice, commonly misspelled words and their misspellings are listed in the window. You can add to that list if you have specific errors you know you make frequently, and you can delete any you do not wish to autocorrect.

Figure 24.24
Autocorrect preferences.

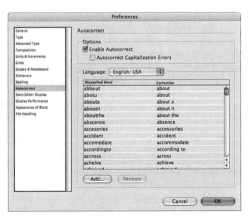

Story Editor Display Preferences

The Story Editor Display page of the InDesign Preferences window is shown in Figure 24.25. The Story Editor is like a built-in word processor for InDesign, and this page of the Preferences window gives you options for how text is displayed in the Story Editor. You can select font, size, spacing, and color. You can also choose from various preset color themes. You can choose to enable anti-aliasing of your type. There are four cursor options, and you can choose whether the cursor should blink. The Terminal theme with a block cursor and blinking turned on gives you a great flashback to old CRTs (see Figure 24.26)—very retro.

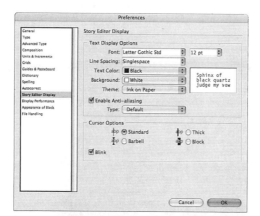

Figure 24.25
Story Editor preferences.

24

Figure 24.26
InDesign's Story Editor can even take you back in time.

Display Performance Preferences

Table 24.9 lists the options found on the Display Performance page of the InDesign Preferences window (see Figure 24.27):

Table 24.9   Options Found on the Display Performance Page of the InDesign Preferences Window

Option	Description
Default View	This option allows you to set how the file should display by default. The Fast display shows graphics and images as gray frames, while the High Quality display shows print-quality views but slows down redraw when you resize or scroll through the document. Options in the Object menu allow you to set the view for selected page elements—for example, if you want to see only certain images as high quality. You can enable the Preserve Object-Level Display Settings check box to preserve any object-level display settings you've selected.

Table 24.9 Continued

Option	Description
Adjust View Settings	In this portion of the dialog you can customize the different level of view settings and how each one deals with raster images, vector graphics, and transparency. You can check the boxes to enable anti-aliasing of fonts and enter your size preference for greeked type, referring to the zoom point at which text appears as individual letter forms or gray bars. Clicking the Use Defaults button returns all these settings to their original states.
Scrolling	You can choose what is most important to you when you use the Hand tool: high-quality display or better performance.

Figure 24.27
Display Performance preferences.

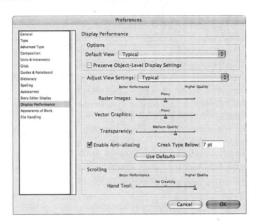

Appearance of Black Preferences

The Appearance of Black page of the InDesign Preferences window (see Figure 24.28) gives you options for how blacks display and output on RGB devices. 100 K black refers to black with a CMYK setting of 0, 0, 0, 100. Rich Black contains percentages of all four colors.

Figure 24.28
Appearance of Black preferences.

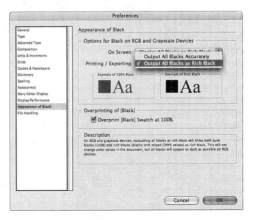

The Overprint [Black] Swatch at 100% check box toggles between overprinting a 100 K black swatch and knocking it out when it is placed on other colors in PostScript and PDF documents.

File Handling Preferences

The File Handling page of the InDesign Preferences window is shown in Figure 24.29. The Document Recovery Data section gives the path where copies of document changes are stored in case of application crash or failure. You can browse to change the default location.

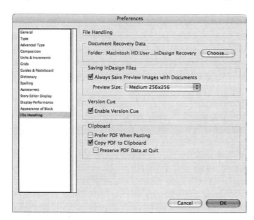

Figure 24.29
File Handling preferences.

Table 24.10 lists the options found on the File Handling page of the InDesign Preferences window:

Table 24.10 Options Found on the File Handling Page of the InDesign Preferences Window

Option	Description
Saving InDesign Files	This section lets you choose whether to save previews with documents, as well as their size.
Version Cue	This section allows you to toggle between enabling and disabling the feature.
Clipboard	In this section, the Prefer PDF When Pasting check box refers to how items from other applications are pasted into InDesign. If this option is enabled, a graphic pasted from Illustrator, for example, would be pasted as a PDF and would not be editable.
Copy PDF to Clipboard	This option refers to the way objects are referenced when they are copied.
Preserve PDF Data at Quit	This option determines when Clipboard items are deleted.

SUMMARY

Now that you've had an overview of the InDesign application, and hopefully set some preferences that will make the program easier and more productive for you, it's time to get started using InDesign. Chapter 25 deals with documents and how to set them up.

25

UNDERSTANDING DOCUMENT
AND PAGE SETUP IN INDESIGN

IN THIS CHAPTER

After InDesign's workspace is set up to your specifications, you're ready to start creating documents. This chapter takes you through the process of creating a new document and setting it up for production.

DOCUMENT SETUP

Start your InDesign document by choosing File, New, Document. The New Document dialog appears, as shown in Figure 25.1. If you will be creating many documents with a specialized page size or setup, you can save a document preset here that will be available every time you work in the program.

To do that, first set up the document as you want:

- Set the number of pages. The Facing Pages check box indicates a document that is set up in two-page spreads if it is checked, or as single pages if it is not. You can also use the Master Text Frame check box to indicate whether you want a text frame automatically placed on each page you create.

- InDesign offers the standard choices for the Page Size option, or you can choose Custom to enter your own page dimensions and orientation.

- Set up columns with the appropriate amount of space between them.

- You can also adjust the default margin settings for your page. Click the chain link icon between the margin entries to make them all equal; click to break the link and enter different measurements in each field.

> If you don't see the bleed and slug areas in the New Document dialog, click the More Options button at the right of the dialog.

- Finally, set up bleed and slug areas for your document if you want. The *bleed area* gives you a visual reference of how far you should extend page elements you want to "bleed"—that is, to extend completely off the page. The *slug area* is extra space where you can type instructions for your printer, for example. It doesn't actually add space to the document; that area is trimmed when your document is printed.

Before you click OK, save these settings as a document preset if you will be creating other files with these same specifications:

1. Click the Save Preset button. The Save Preset dialog opens (see Figure 25.2).

2. Type a name for your preset, for example, **Newsletter**.

3. Click OK to close the Save Preset dialog and return to the New Document dialog.

4. Click OK in the New Document dialog to create the document.

When you're ready to open your preset, choose File, Document Preset, *Preset Name*, and a blank document with the settings specified by the document preset you created opens. Alternatively, choose File, New and select the preset from the pop-up menu at the top of the dialog.

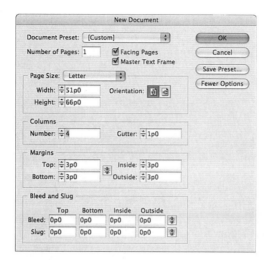

Figure 25.1
The New Document dialog gives you options for how your page is set up.

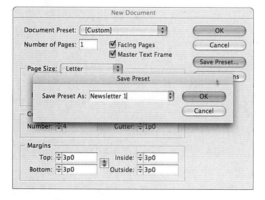

Figure 25.2
Save a document preset if you'll be creating many documents with the same general page specifications.

25

GRIDS AND GUIDES

Once your file is open, you can set it up as you want to start your design. Most of the page setup options are found under the Layout menu. Let's take a look at several of the selections here and how they can help make designing your document easier:

- **Margins and Columns:** Choose Layout, Margins and Columns to display the Margins and Columns dialog (see Figure 25.3). This is the same information you can set in the New Document dialog. The Preview check box enables you to see your page before you commit to your choice and click OK.

- **Ruler Guides:** Ruler guides are dragged from the rulers at the top and left side of the InDesign workspace to help with object placement. You can change various guide settings by selecting Layout, Ruler Guides. View Threshold indicates the magnification at which ruler guides will no longer be visible. If this is set too high, individual guides will be indistinguishable when you are zoomed out of the document. Choose the color you want those guides to be.

Figure 25.3
Use the Margins and Columns dialog to create even column guides on your page.

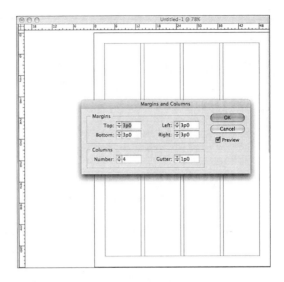

- **Create Guides:** Choose Layout, Create Guides and set horizontal and vertical guides here (see Figure 25.4). Vertical guides are similar to column guides; adding horizontal guides helps you create modular designs. You can fit the guides to the entire page or just to the area within the margins, based on how you want to divide the page. If you'd like to get rid of guides you've already placed on the page, check the Remove Existing Guides box. Again, enable the Preview check box to see the guides before you accept them.

- **Layout Adjustment:** Choose Layout, Layout Adjustment to access InDesign's automatic adjustment feature, which can be helpful if you are designing a piece that might change size or shape or that will need to be revamped while still using a lot of the same elements. When elements such as page size, margins, or columns are changed, layout adjustment makes your document conform to the original settings and object placement as much as possible.

  Click the Enable Layout Adjustment check box. You then have choices that will help you control the degree of layout adjustment. The measurement in the Snap Zone field

Any time you see a Preview check box in a dialog, click to enable it. When the Preview box is checked, you see whatever action you're performing on the page. If you like it, you can click OK. If you don't, you can click Cancel or change your settings. You may have to move the dialog out of the way to get a good view, but the Preview check box can keep you from committing to something you don't really want to do.

refers to the point at which items will adjust. For example, if your Snap Zone measurement is set to 0p2, everything within two points of the guide that changes will snap to the guide's new location. Check boxes give you options to Allow Graphics and Groups to Resize, which will keep these items with the guides as they change; Allow Ruler Guides to Move, which will move ruler guides along with the other guides; or Ignore Ruler Guide Adjustments, which adjusts based on layout guides like margins and columns, not ruler guides; and to Ignore Object and Layer Locks, which will adjust locked items or items on locked layers.

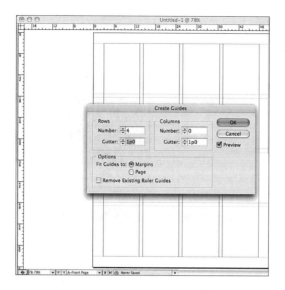

Figure 25.4
The Create Guides dialog not only enables you to set up column guides, but it also creates regularly spaced horizontal guides on your page for the ultimate control over modular designs.

Other options to help set page grids can be turned on under the View menu:

- **View Baseline Grid:** The baseline grid corresponds to how text is spaced on the page. The default baseline grid is set to 1 pica; alter this depending on your preference. Choosing this option only puts a visual representation of the baseline grid on the page. See Chapter 27, "Working with Type in InDesign," for more information on the baseline grid.

- **View Document Grid:** The document grid places horizontal and vertical guides on your page. There are two weights of gridlines; if you were measuring in picas on your document, for example, you could set a gridline every 6 picas (to signify an inch) with 6 subdivisions (to signify picas).

The settings for both of these features, including gridline color, are found in the Grids pane of the Preferences window.

RULER MEASUREMENTS

Rulers appear at the top and left of the InDesign workspace. The default ruler setting is in picas, but you can change it to the measurement units of your choice in the Units and Increments pane of the Preferences window. You can also change measurements on the fly by right-clicking (Windows users) or Control-clicking (Mac users) on the ruler itself and selecting the measurement unit.

The rulers also control the document's zero point, which determines where measurement numbering will start (see Figure 25.5). The zero point's default location is to start numbering at the upper-left corner of each page. In the Units and Increments panel you can change where the zero point starts in the Preferences window. Under Ruler Units, use the Origin pop-up to specify rulers to start numbering at the Spread (puts the zero point for both pages of a double-page spread at the top left of the left page), at the Page (starts numbering at zero at the top left of each page in the document), or at the Spine (the zero point is at the intersection of the right and left pages in a spread, with numbering increasing as you go to the right or left on the ruler).

Zero point

Figure 25.5
The zero point is controlled where the page rulers meet.

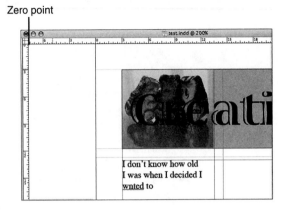

To change the zero point's location as you work, click in the upper left of the workspace, where the two rulers intersect. Click, hold, and drag from the perpendicular dotted lines to move the zero point to the location of your choice.

If you want to lock the zero point, right-click (Windows users) or Control-click (Mac users) where the rulers intersect and select Lock Zero Point from the context menu.

As mentioned previously, guides can be dragged out of the rulers and placed on the page to help with object alignment. When you drag a guide from the top ruler, it will appear only on the page to which you drag it. If you drag the ruler into the pasteboard, or the area outside of the page itself, or hold down the Ctrl or ⌘ key while you drag, the guide will extend across the entire spread.

Ruler guides are selectable objects in InDesign, so you can click to select one guide, Shift+click to select multiple guides, and move selected guides incrementally by pressing the arrow keys on your keyboard.

THE PAGES PALETTE

A good source of navigation throughout your document is the Pages palette (see Figure 25.6). This palette shows your document and its arrangement as thumbnail pages. Because this palette is such an important part of the InDesign workspace, it's important to arrange it on your workspace the way you like. Select Palette Options from the palette menu to specify how it should appear on your workspace.

Figure 25.6
Many document controls can be found in the Pages palette and its menu.

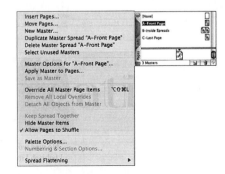

Double-click on individual pages or spreads in the Pages palette to navigate to them. Pages can also be dragged and dropped in the palette to rearrange your document easily. If you don't want that to happen, just uncheck the Allow Pages to Shuffle option in the palette menu. If you would like to allow page shuffling but don't want to break up spreads, select the spread by double-clicking on the page numbers, and then select Keep Spread Together in the palette menu.

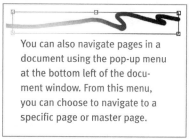

You can also navigate pages in a document using the pop-up menu at the bottom left of the document window. From this menu, you can choose to navigate to a specific page or master page.

The Power of Selection

There is some rhyme and reason to selecting pages, spreads, master pages, and master spreads in the Pages palette. This becomes important when you select just certain pages to delete, duplicate, or apply master pages to:

- Click on a page icon to select just that page. Double-click to go to that page.

- Click the page numbers below the icon to select a spread. Double-click to navigate to that spread.

- To select a master page, click on the icon for that page. Double-click to navigate to the master page.

- To select a master page spread, click on the master spread name. Double-click to view the entire master spread.

- Drag a master page icon over a page icon to apply it to just that page.

- Drag a master page icon below the spread until both page icons are highlighted to apply master pages to an entire spread (see Figure 25.7).

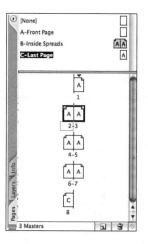

Figure 25.7
Make sure the entire spread is highlighted in the Pages palette to apply a set of master pages to the spread.

Select Insert Pages from the Pages palette menu to add pages to your document, or click the Create New Page button at the bottom of the palette to add pages. To delete pages, drag a page icon to the trash can icon, or select a page or spread and click the trash can icon.

If you want to duplicate a spread (as well as the items on the pages), select Duplicate Spread from the Pages palette menu. Choose Delete Spread from the palette menu to get rid of a spread as well as the items on the pages.

Master Pages in the Pages Palette

The Pages palette also displays the master pages for the document. InDesign enables you to create numerous master pages that can be created independently or based off each other. To access the master pages, double-click on the A-Master icon in the Pages palette. Select Master Options for A-Master from the palette menu and rename your master if you want. You can also use the palette menu to duplicate, delete, or add new master pages.

Anything you place on master pages appears on every page of the document to which that master is applied. The master pages can be used for guides or grids, or for folios or other design elements that should be duplicated on many pages. Items placed on the master pages are also locked to a certain extent; that is, if you are working on a page, you cannot select a master page element and alter it, unless you hold down Ctrl+Shift (Windows users) or ⌘+Shift (Mac users) as you click. At that point, the object will no longer be a master page item and can be freely moved or altered on the page itself. To detach it from its association with the master page, select Detach Selected Object from Master in the Pages palette menu. If you want to take an item back to its original nonselectable state, choose Remove All Local Overrides from the Pages palette menu.

You can also automatically override all elements on a master page. Select Override All Master Page Items from the Pages palette menu to make all master elements that display on the current page selectable.

To hide the elements from the applied master page, select Hide Master Items from the palette menu.

To apply a master page to a page in your document, click the master page name and drag it to the page to which you want to apply it. The alpha character assigned to that master will appear on the page icon itself.

You can apply a master page to a range of pages by selecting the master and then choosing Apply Master To Pages in the palette menu. Enter the page range to which you want to apply the master and click OK.

Each master is assigned an alpha character prefix based on the order of creation. You can change it by selecting Master Options for [*master name*] from the Pages palette menu. Note that your pre-fix does not have to be a letter, but can be any four-character pre-fix that is meaningful to you.

To duplicate a master page, select it and then choose Duplicate Master Spread from the palette menu. To delete that master page, choose Delete Master Spread instead. If you've created several masters and want to see which ones you haven't used, choose Select Unused Masters in the palette menu.

If you design a page and then decide you would like to use it as a master page, make sure the page or spread is selected in the Pages palette and then select Save as Master in the Pages palette menu.

The Pages palette also contains spread-flattening options that help you deal individually with those spreads that contain complex transparency features. InDesign transparencies must sometimes be flattened to help with page output. To apply flattening to specific spreads, select Spread Flattening from the palette menu and choose Default, which preserves the flattening settings for the entire document; None (Ignore Transparency), which ignores the transparency on the specific spread; or set Custom flattening options, which opens the Spread Flattener Settings dialog for that particular spread. For detailed information about transparency flattening, see the "Transparency Flattening" section of Chapter 31, "Exporting, Saving, and Printing with InDesign."

Finally, the Numbering and Section Options command in the palette menu displays the New Section dialog (see Figure 25.8), which gives you some beneficial control over your file, especially if it is a long document, or part of one.

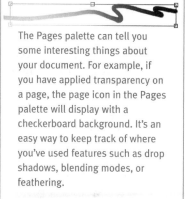

The Pages palette can tell you some interesting things about your document. For example, if you have applied transparency on a page, the page icon in the Pages palette will display with a checkerboard background. It's an easy way to keep track of where you've used features such as drop shadows, blending modes, or feathering.

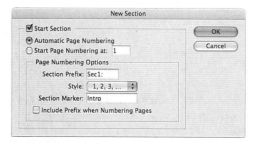

Figure 25.8
The Numbering and Section Options command controls just that: how your document is numbered and any sections you want to include.

25

First, you can set your document's starting page number in the New Section dialog. To change the starting page number, click the Start Page Numbering At radio button and enter your starting page number in the field. Choose your numbering style from various letters and Roman numerals in the Style pop-up list.

If this is a long document, you may want to set up sections to help with page numbering. When a page other than the first page of the document is selected, the Start Section check box is available. You can continue with Automatic Page Numbering, or you can start page numbering over at that point—for example, if you have set up the Intro to your document to number in lowercase Roman numerals, you can start numbering over at the second section with regular numerals.

A *section prefix* serves as a label for your section. The section prefix appears with the page number in the navigational pop-up menu at the bottom left of the document area. Check the Include Prefix When Numbering Pages option, and it will also appear with your table of contents, index, or in any situation where you are using automatic page numbers. The prefix characters also appear on any page that displays the page number. As an example, use the prefix if you want to number pages with the chapter number—for example, if in Chapter 10, the pages are numbered 10-1, 10-2, and so on.

If you use section names in your document—for example, if the folio area of your document contains both the page number and the section name—enter that information in the Section Marker field. Then choose Type, Insert Special Character, Section Marker in any text frame, and your Section Marker will be automatically inserted.

THE BOOK FEATURE

If you are creating a large document, it may be easier to work on it in smaller sections, especially if several designers are collaborating. But you'll still want to share styles, table of contents, index information, and color swatches across those documents.

InDesign's Book feature gives you that option. By adding files to a book, you can synchronize items such as character and paragraph styles, the contents of the Swatches palette, and page numbering.

The book appears like a palette on your workspace. To set up a book, select File, New, Book. Name your book document and choose its location. The book will be created with the extension .indb.

Add documents to your book by clicking the + sign at the bottom of the Book palette (see Figure 25.9), or select Add Document from the palette menu. Add multiple documents by holding down the Shift key as you select and then click Open.

Figure 25.9
The Book palette.

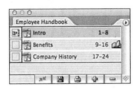

To open book documents, double-click the document name in the Book palette. To delete a document from the Book, select the file name and click the – sign at the bottom of the palette, or select Remove Document from the palette menu.

Icons designate the status of documents within the book:

- No icon indicates the document is closed.

- An open book icon indicates the document is open.

- A question mark means the document was moved, renamed, or deleted.

- An exclamation mark indicates the document was changed or repaginated.

- A lock indicates the document is in use by someone else.

If you have selected documents saved in previous versions of InDesign, they will automatically update to CS2 when you add them to the book. You will be given the option to save and rename these documents when they are added unless you select Automatic Document Conversion in the palette menu, at which point the previous versions will be overwritten.

If a document is missing and you want to replace it with another, click the document name and select Replace Document from the palette menu. Browse to the replacement document and click Open.

For more detailed information, or to relink a missing document, select the document name and then choose Document Information from the palette menu.

If necessary, you can rearrange the documents in the Book palette by dragging and dropping them.

If you have styles or swatches you want to share between book documents, you should set up one document as your style source. The book will automatically use the first document added to the book as the style source, but you can choose any document at any time. Just click the box to the left of the document name to make that document the style source.

If you have added new documents to your book that need to be synchronized with the style source, select Synchronize Book from the palette menu. If you want only to synchronize certain documents, first select the document(s) and then select Synchronize Selected Documents.

To choose the items you want to synchronize, select Synchronization Options from the palette menu and use the check boxes to indicate the items you want to update.

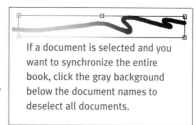

If a document is selected and you want to synchronize the entire book, click the gray background below the document names to deselect all documents.

The book will honor the numbering specifications you choose in the Numbering and Section Options dialog. If you choose Automatic Page Numbering, the documents will automatically number based on their location in the book—for example, the first document will number starting with page 1.

Finally, the book is a good way to output or check all included documents automatically. Select to Preflight, Package, Print, or Export either the selected document or the entire book from the palette menu (see Figure 25.10). The Preflight option checks the documents for common problems that might cause issues with printing; The Package option gathers all documents, linked files, and fonts and places them in a folder for easy submission to a printer; and the Export option enables you to gather the documents in the book and save them in the file format of your choice, such as PDF, or EPS.

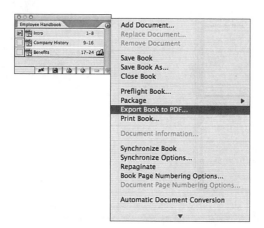

Figure 25.10
Print, preflight, or export all documents in your book from the palette menu.

25

Now that you're familiar with setting up your InDesign documents, it's time to move on to the nuts and bolts of the program—how to create page elements and text, and how to take advantage of the great creative options InDesign has to offer.

WORKING WITH OBJECTS
IN INDESIGN

IN THIS CHAPTER

26

After you have your document set up, you're ready to dig into InDesign in earnest. The program has an almost mind-boggling number of controls that you can use in the document creation process. The next step is learning how to use them.

In the next three chapters, you take a look at creating and working with various types of page elements. This chapter gives an overview of creating and modifying all types of objects. In Chapter 27, "Working with Type in InDesign," you explore text specifically, and then in Chapter 28, "Working with Graphics in InDesign," you look at various types of graphics.

CREATING OBJECTS

In Chapter 24, "Understanding the InDesign Interface and Tools," we gave you some general information about how to use all of InDesign's tools. Now let's talk about objects and how to use those tools to create them.

Paths

The simplest object type is a *path*. Any object created in InDesign is a path of some sort, except for text. The frame that contains the text, however, has a path surrounding it. A closed path, where the starting and ending points are connected, is a *shape*. An unclosed path is a *line* (see Figure 26.1).

Figure 26.1
Paths drawn with the Line tool,
Pencil tool, and Pen tool

Line tool   Pencil tool   Pen tool

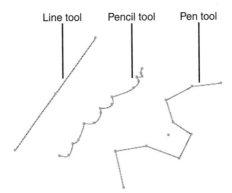

You can draw paths with a variety of tools. Use the Line tool by clicking at the spot where you want to start your straight line and then dragging and releasing the mouse where you want the line to end. If you hold down the Shift key while you draw the line, the line is constrained to increments of 45°. If you hold down the Alt key (Windows users) or Option key (Mac users), you can draw your straight line from the center out.

Use the Pencil tool to draw freehand lines. Click and hold to start the line and then move your mouse to continue it in any direction. A dotted line appears, and when you finish the path and release the mouse, the line takes on the fill and stroke characteristics chosen.

Use the Pen tool to draw more controlled lines. When you click once with the Pen tool, a point is created. Click again and a line appears—you have created a line segment. Continue to click to create straight-line segments.

If you drag with the mouse after creating the first point with the Pen tool, as opposed to clicking and releasing to create a straight-line segment, a direction line appears, and a Bézier curve forms when you click the second time. Depending on the direction you drag, the curve changes shape when you click again. Drag toward the first point to create a C-shaped curve. Drag away from the first point to create an S-shaped curve (see Figure 26.2). When you're ready to end the path (without creating a closed shape), hold down the Ctrl key (Windows users) or ⌘ key (Mac users) as you click.

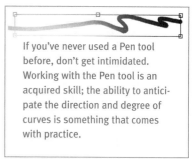

If you've never used a Pen tool before, don't get intimidated. Working with the Pen tool is an acquired skill; the ability to anticipate the direction and degree of curves is something that comes with practice.

Figure 26.2
A path with connected straight segments drawn with the Pen tool and a path consisting of Bézier curves.

Shapes

Simple shapes, like rectangles, ellipses, and polygons, are created with the Rectangle, Ellipse, and Polygon tools. Any of these tools can be used by clicking and dragging to create the shape. If you select one of the three shape tools and then click on the page, a shape dialog opens. In it, enter the desired height and width of your shape and it is drawn based on that information.

If you click with the Polygon tool, you can also enter the number of sides (between 3 and 100) you want the shape to have and a percentage of inset if you are creating a star (see Figure 26.3). Double-click the tool to set the sides and inset before you draw on the page.

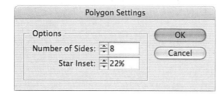

Figure 26.3
Double-click with the Polygon tool to see a dialog in which you enter the number of sides and star inset for your polygon.

26

The Rectangle, Ellipse, and Polygon Frame tools work the same way. When you draw a frame on your page, the shape you draw has an X through it, showing that it is an empty container. As you will see, however, the normal shape tools can also serve as frames. Which type of tool to use is your choice.

For any of the six shape tools, hold down the Shift key as you draw to constrain the shape proportionally. As with the Line tool, you can hold down the Alt key (Windows users) or the Option key (Mac users) as you draw to create your shape from the center out, as opposed to from a corner out.

To draw freehand shapes, use the Pencil tool. Again, drag to draw the path you want, but hold down the Alt key (Windows users) or Option key (Mac users) as you draw. When your shape is finished, release the mouse button and then release the Alt or Option key. The path closes.

To draw a closed shape with the Pen tool, click or drag to draw the shape. When you are ready to close the shape, hold your mouse over the first anchor point you created with the Pen tool. A small circle appears beside the Pen. Click on the point, and the path closes.

Remember, any shape you create, regardless of the tool you use to create it, can be used as a frame. That is, as long as the path is closed, regardless of the shape of the object, you can place type or a graphic inside it or fill it with a color or gradient.

Other Types of Objects

Boiling everything in InDesign down to paths and shapes is a rather simplistic way of looking at page elements, but it is the easiest way to start talking about the objects you create in InDesign. The rest of this chapter deals with how to work with the objects you create.

In subsequent chapters, including Chapter 27, which gives an overview of type, and Chapter 28, which gives an overview of graphics, you learn more about these specialized types of page elements and how to create and format them.

EDITING AND RESHAPING OBJECTS

After you draw a page element, you also have a variety of tools at your disposal to edit and reshape them. For the most part, the tools available to reshape objects are found in the same palette space as the tool used to create the object, although most tools can be used on any kind of path.

The two tools at the top of the Tools palette can also be used to alter any kind of shape. It's important to learn the difference between the Selection tool (the black arrow) and the Direct Selection tool (the white arrow) early in your InDesign experience (see Figure 26.4).

Figure 26.4
A shape selected with the Selection tool and the Direct Selection tool. Notice the differences in the bounding box and selection and anchor points.

Selected with Selection tool

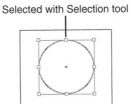

Selected with Direct Selection tool

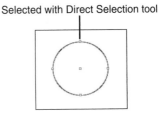

When you click an object with the Selection tool, a bounding box appears. This box shows the area around the shape you selected. It is always a four-sided shape with eight *selection points*. For any object with a bounding box, the resulting selection points can be dragged to resize the object.

When you click an object with the Direct Selection tool, the *anchor points* of the object appear. You will see as many anchor points as were used to create the shape. Any of the anchor points can be dragged to alter the shape of the object.

The tools under the Pen tool in the Tools palette deal with a shape's anchor points:

- Click on an existing path with the Add Anchor Point tool, and an anchor point is added where you click.

- Click on an existing anchor point with the Delete Anchor Point tool. The point is deleted, and the path is joined between the two points on either side of the deleted point.

- Click on a point between curved path segments with the Convert Direction Point tool to change it to a corner point. Click on a corner point and drag to change it into a curve point. You can also click on a direction handle at a curve and drag to turn the curve point into a combination point.

Under the Pencil tool on the Tools palette are the Smooth tool and the Erase tool. The Smooth tool can be used to make jagged paths smooth, which generally involves deleting points on the path. To use the Smooth tool:

1. Select the Pencil-drawn path with the Direct Selection tool.

2. Drag the Smooth tool over the part of the path you want to be smooth.

3. You will see fewer points on the line. Continue this process until the path looks the way you want it (see Figure 26.5).

Before   After

Figure 26.5
A path before and after being smoothed with the Smooth tool.

The Erase tool removes parts of paths. To use the Erase tool, drag over the part of the path you want to remove. The area you drag over is deleted, and anchor points are added to the resulting ends of the path(s).

The Scissors tool is used to cut paths at their anchor points. Select the Scissors tool and click on an anchor point to cut and then use one of the Selection tools to move the anchor point (see Figure 26.6). Click on two anchor points and then click the path segment between the two cut points with one of the Selection tools to remove the area you cut.

Finally, if you want to join two separate paths to create a continuous path or a closed shape, you can use the Pencil tool:

1. Hold down the Shift key and click to select the paths you want to join.

Although we're not dealing with these types of objects yet, you cannot use the Scissors tool to divide a text frame containing text, although you *can* use it to reshape the frame. If you use the Scissors tool to split a frame that contains a graphic, creating two frames, both frames will contain the same graphic. Select one copy of the graphic with the Direct Selection tool and delete to get rid of it.

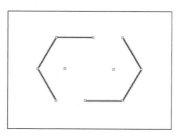

Figure 26.6
A six-sided polygon after being separated by the Scissors tool.

26

2. Select the Pencil tool and start dragging at the end of one path.

3. Hold down the Ctrl key (Windows users) or the ⌘ key (Mac users). A small diamond next to the Pencil indicates that the paths will be merged.

4. Drag until you have connected the paths. Release the mouse button and then release the Ctrl/⌘ key.

Figure 26.7
Two paths joined by the Pencil tool.

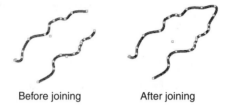

Before joining   After joining

TRANSFORMING OBJECTS

After you have your objects on your page, there are a number of ways to transform those objects. You can use tools, palettes, or menu commands to accomplish the transformations.

Transforming with Tools

The Tools palette contains a variety of tools that can be used to transform your page objects. In fact, an entire group of tools are referred to as *transformation tools*. These are the Rotate, Scale, Shear, and Free Transform tools.

Before you use any of the transforming tools, you must select the object you want to transform with the Selection tool. When you click on a transformation tool, crosshairs appear in the center of the shape.

The crosshairs represent the point from which the object is transformed. Move the crosshairs wherever you would like to transform from that point (see Figure 26.8).

Figure 26.8
All of the transformation tools use crosshairs to indicate where the object is transformed from. You can move the crosshairs anywhere on the page by dragging them.

Crosshair

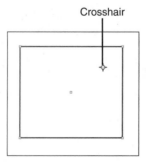

The Rotate tool does just what you think. When you see the crosshairs, click anywhere and drag to rotate the object.

The Scale tool changes the size and potentially the shape of the object. Again, drag the crosshairs to the point from which you want to scale the object. Click and drag anywhere on the page, moving across or down, to scale the object either horizontally or vertically only. Click and drag diagonally to scale the object both horizontally and vertically. As with other tools, holding down the Shift key scales the item proportionally.

The Shear tool skews page objects. Drag the crosshairs to the point from which you want to skew. Click anywhere on the page and drag to skew the object.

The Free Transform tool is multifunctional, enabling you to perform any transformation. As with the other tools, drag the crosshairs to the desired location:

- Move objects by clicking anywhere on the object and dragging.

- Scale objects by dragging until the item is resized. Hold down the Shift key to scale proportionally.

- Rotate objects by moving the mouse outside the object until it turns to a curved double arrow. Click and drag the arrow to rotate.

To transform items to specific sizes or percentages, you have several options. Double-click on any of the transformation tools except the Free Transform tool and a dialog appears enabling you to enter specific transformation numbers:

- Double-click on the Rotate tool to enter a rotation degree. If the object is a frame with contents, click the check box to rotate the contents as well.

- Double-click on the Scale tool to enter a scale percentage. Choose to scale proportionally or enter a different number for horizontal and vertical scale percentages. If the object is a frame with contents, click the check box to scale the contents as well.

- Double-click on the Shear tool to enter a shear degree. Choose to shear vertically or horizontally, or enter a specific degree to shear from. If the object is a frame, click the check box to shear the contents as well.

Transforming with Palettes

You can also use the Control palette or the Transform palette to perform transformations on objects. Choose Window, Object & Layout, Transform to open the Transform palette. Choose Window, Control to open the Control palette. Because the options in both palettes are the same, we refer to them only once (see Figure 26.9).

Figure 26.9
The Transform palette and the Control palette can be used to accomplish many of the same transformations.

Each palette shows a proxy of the selected object with nine selectable points. Click the point that represents the part of the shape you want to transform from:

- The X and Y entry fields enable you to enter the location on the page to which you would like to move the object.

- The W and H fields (width and height) enable you to enter specific measurements. Click the chain link beside these fields to either constrain the entries (enter a measurement in one field and the other automatically updates to keep the measurements proportional) or enter each measurement independently.

- The Scale X Percentage and Scale Y Percentage fields can be used to enlarge or reduce your object by a specific percentage. Again, the chain link works to either constrain the entries or enable you to enter each one individually.

- Use the Rotation Angle or Shear X Angle to enter a degree of rotation or shear.

When you enter X and Y values in the Control or Transform palette, the location is determined based on the zero point of the page rulers at the top and left of your workspace. The ruler measurements and the width and height are calculated based on the measurement units you chose in InDesign's Units and Increments pane of the Preferences window (choose Edit, Preferences, Units & Increments on Windows or choose InDesign, Preferences, Units & Increments on the Mac to open the Preferences window).

Transforming with Menu Commands

All the transformation commands are also available under the Object, Transform submenu: Move, Scale, Rotate, and Shear. These choices open the same dialogs you see when you double-click on the transformation tools, enabling you to enter specific transformation amounts.

Also under the Object menu are selections to Transform Again. If you apply a transformation or a series of transformations to an object, you can select another object and choose Object, Transform Again to apply those same transformations to the new object. The Transform Again submenu commands work as follows:

- **Transform Again:** Apply the last single transformation to the selected element.

- **Transform Again Individually:** Apply the last single transformation to each selected element individually, rather than as a group.

- **Transform Sequence Again:** Apply the last sequence of transform operations to the selection.

- **Transform Sequence Again Individually:** Apply the last sequence of transformations to each selected element individually.

Flopping Objects

You can flop any page object so it becomes a reflection of itself. Click to select it and then drag a corner handle up or down over the object, or left or right over it, to flop the object (see Figure 26.10).

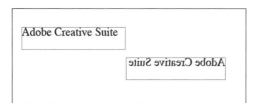

Figure 26.10
A text frame before and after being flopped horizontally. Flop any object by dragging a handle over the object.

APPLYING FILL AND STROKE

Adjusting fill and stroke is another way to alter the look of a page element. You can apply a fill or stroke to nearly every type of page element you create.

Fill refers to what you see inside a page object, although it shouldn't be confused with *content*. A frame can contain a graphic or text (content), but it can also be filled with a color or tint, even at the same time.

The *stroke* is what you see around a page object, like a keyline around an image. You can apply a stroke to any frame, but you can also apply a stroke to individual text characters.

There are a couple of places to set stroke and fill. There are stroke and fill controls on the Tools palette, the Color palette, and the Swatches palette. Like the options in the Control and Transform palette, the options in the Tools and Swatches palettes are the same, so we'll hit them only once (see Figure 26.11).

Figure 26.11
Find fill and stroke controls on the Tools palette as well as the Swatches palette.

26

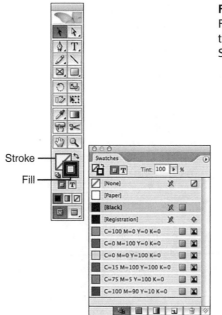

Stroke

Fill

The fill and stroke icons sit on top of each other. The fill icon looks like a solid square, and the stroke icon looks like an empty square. Click on the appropriate icon to bring it to the front and make it active.

When you open InDesign after installation, the default setting is a solid black fill and no stroke (indicated by a white stroke box with a red line running through it). Let's assume those settings are active throughout this session; however, if you have applied a color or gradient, the solid fill will default to the last chosen swatch. You can learn more about color swatches and gradients in Chapter 29, "Working with Color in InDesign."

A small, double-ended arrow sits to the upper right of the fill and stroke icons. Clicking on this icon swaps the current fill with the current stroke, whether they are set to colors, gradients, or none. If an object is selected, click this icon to swap the fill and stroke of the selected item.

A small fill-and-stroke graphic also sits to the lower left of the fill and stroke icons on the Tools palette. Click this icon to return to the default setting of solid black fill and no stroke.

As mentioned earlier, a fill and stroke can also be applied to individual type characters. When you have specific type highlighted (or selected with the Type tool), changing the fill and stroke automatically applies to the text characters (see Figure 26.12). If you have a text frame chosen, you can use the buttons on the Swatches palette and the Tools palette to select either the square (Formatting Affects Container) or the T button (Formatting Affects Type), depending on where you want to apply your fill and stroke.

Figure 26.12
An example of text with a black stroke and no fill.

And, on the Tools palette, you can select exactly what type of fill or stroke you want to apply: solid (defaults to the last-selected color or black), a gradient (defaults to the last-selected gradient or a white-to-black gradient), or none.

The Stroke palette gives you control over the stroke of any item (see Figure 26.13). When you work with the Stroke palette, remember that these options apply to any type of path, including lines drawn with the Pen, Pencil or Line tools. (You look at colors—the most common type of fill—in Chapter 29.)

To open the Stroke palette, choose Window, Stroke:

- The *weight* of the stroke is its width. Click the appropriate Cap option for how you want your line to end.

Figure 26.13
The Stroke palette with all options shown.

- The Miter Limit option controls the bevel of the corner point on a frame when a Join option is selected. Miter Join, Round Join, and Bevel Join are the three Join corner point options.

- Align Stroke indicates where the stroke is located in relation to the anchor points.

- The Type pop-up menu enables you to choose different predefined stroke styles. The Start and End pop-up menus add arrows, circles, and squares to the lines.

- If you choose a dashed or dotted line, the Gap Color and Gap Tint fields enable you to choose how the line fills in.

In the Stroke palette menu, you can select Stroke Styles to choose from predefined styles or create your own. Click New to open the New Stroke Style dialog and set up striped, dotted, or dashed lines to very exacting specifications.

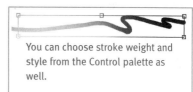

You can choose stroke weight and style from the Control palette as well.

We refer to this fact several times throughout this chapter, but it bears repeating: Any closed path in InDesign is considered a *frame*, and as such, can serve as a holder for graphics or type. Every type of object creation and transformation we've talked about to this point can be applied to any type of frame, whether it's a graphic frame or a type frame. You learn more about type frames specifically in Chapter 27, and about graphic frames in Chapter 28.

GROUPING OBJECTS

From time to time you create something on your InDesign page and think, "Wow, I could use that somewhere else." If it's a single element, it's easy to move or copy that item and paste it on another page or in another document. But if it's several items that you want to stay together, you might want to group them to keep them intact. Follow these steps to group multiple objects:

1. Select all the items you want to stay together. Hold down the Shift key while you click to select more than one item at a time.

2. After all the items are selected, choose Object, Group.

3. All the different selection points you saw in step 1 disappear. A dotted line with eight selection points now appears to show the boundaries of the entire grouped object (see Figure 26.14).

Figure 26.14
Items before and after being grouped.

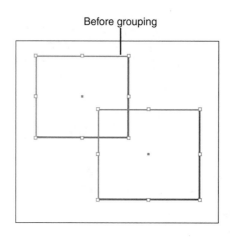

Before grouping

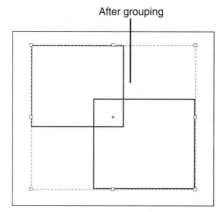

After grouping

After your page objects are grouped, you can move them or transform them as a group, but you still have control over the individual items in the group. Use the Direct Selection tool to select individual grouped items and apply transformations. Use the Type tool to click in grouped text frames and alter text.

To ungroup, select the group and choose Object, Ungroup.

USING OBJECT LIBRARIES

Object libraries serve as holders for objects or groups of objects that you want to use regularly throughout a single or multiple documents. Libraries can hold any type of page object.

To create a library, choose File, New, Library. Name your library and save it in your chosen location. Click Save. The library is now saved like a document and can be opened from any computer, enabling you to share your libraries with others working on the same projects.

After saving, a Library palette opens. You can now add page elements and work with the library.

To add page elements to the object library:

1. Select the item(s) you want to add as a library entry. Shift-click to select more than one page element.

2. Click the New Library Item button on the Library palette.

3. The selected item(s) are added to the library (see Figure 26.15).

4. For maximum organization, double-click on the library entry immediately and name the element. You can also enter a Description in the Item Information dialog. This name and description can be used for keyword searches.

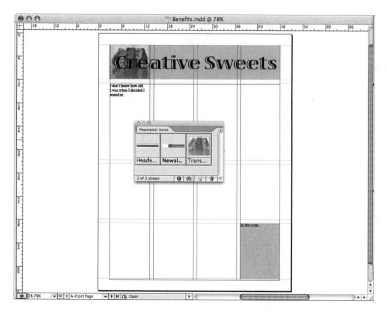

Figure 26.15
A library with page elements added.

You can also access the Item Information dialog by selecting it from the palette menu or by clicking the Item Information icon at the bottom of the Library palette (see Figure 26.16).

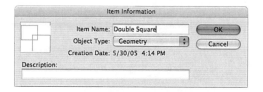

Figure 26.16
Enter item information for an object you're adding to the library so that you can do keyword searches and add labels.

Other options to add elements to library are found in the Library palette menu:

- **Add Item:** Add the selected object to the library.

- **Add Items on Page:** Add everything on the page as one library element.

- **Add Items on Page As Separate Items:** Add every page object as an individual library element.

To place a library element on your page, click and drag it from the Library palette onto the document or select the library element and choose Place Item from the palette menu.

26

To delete an item from the library, drag it to the trash can icon on the Library palette, or select it and then choose Delete Item from the Library palette menu.

To search for an item using the name, creation date, object type, or a keyword from the item description you assigned it when you added the item to the library, choose Show Subset from the palette menu or click the Search button on the palette. After you perform a search, choose Show All in the palette menu to view all items in the palette.

If you change a library item and want to update it, or want to replace one item with another, click to select the item, click on the item you want to update or replace in the palette, and choose Update Item from the palette menu.

It might be a good idea to group items you're adding to the library before you add them: doing so makes it easier to select all the items you want to add to the library, and it helps ensure that the items maintain their proportions and size in relationship to each other when you place the group in a document.

WORKING WITH OBJECT EFFECTS

One of the big appeals to InDesign is the ability it gives you to apply object effects to page elements that you previously would have had to create in Photoshop or Illustrator. One reason for this is InDesign's transparency features.

Transparency Overview

You can set the transparency of an object using the Transparency palette (choose Window, Transparency to display the palette). Transparency can be applied to any page element, and it enables you to create great layered effects with color photos, type, and other objects with color applied (see Figure 26.17).

26

Figure 26.17
A photo with a transparency effect applied.

The Transparency palette enables you to set the percentage of transparency for the item. If objects are layered, you can also create different effects with blending modes, which are different ways for the colors of layered objects to be combined. The concept of blending modes may be familiar to you from Photoshop or Illustrator. Here is a brief overview of the various blending modes available in InDesign, but words don't really do them justice; this is another place where it's best to experiment until you get the effect you're looking for:

- **Normal:** There is no interaction between the selection and the base color.

- **Multiply:** Make the base color darker by adding the selection color to it. This color is always darker than the other colors.

- **Screen:** The opposite of multiply. Lighten the base color by adding the inverse of the selection color to it. This color is always lighter.

- **Overlay:** Depending on the colors involved, either multiply or screen. The blend color reflects either the lightness or darkness of the base color.

- **Soft Light:** Darken or lighten the colors, depending on the blend color. If the blend color is lighter than 50% gray, it lightens the artwork. If the blend color is darker than 50% gray, it darkens the artwork.

- **Hard Light:** Multiply or screen the color, depending on the blend color. If the blend color is lighter than 50% gray, it screens the artwork and adds highlights. If the blend color is darker than 50% gray, it multiplies the artwork and adds shadows.

- **Color Dodge:** Make the base color brighter to reflect the blend color.

- **Color Burn:** Make the base color darker to reflect the blend color.

- **Darken:** Select the darker of the base and blend colors and use it as the resulting color.

- **Lighten:** Select the lighter of the base and blend colors and use it as the resulting color.

- **Difference:** Depending on whether the base color or the blend color is brighter, subtract one from the other.

- **Exclusion:** Similar to Difference, but with less contrast.

- **Hue:** Create a color from the base and blend color.

- **Saturation:** Create a color from the base and blend color.

- **Color:** Create a color from the base and blend color. Especially useful with black and white.

- **Luminosity:** Use like Color, but create the inverse of the blend and base color.

> In the previous definitions, the term *selection* refers to the top layered object, *base color* refers to the color of the bottom layered object, and *blend color* refers to the color created when the selection and base colors are blended.

Most effects that can be applied to objects are found—yes—under the Object menu. In the next sections you look at a few of these features in detail.

Drop Shadows

Drop shadows add a dimensioned look to type or page elements. To add a drop shadow, select the item and follow these steps:

1. Choose Object, Drop Shadow. As always, check the Preview box; it helps you see your drop shadow before you click OK.

2. Click the Drop Shadow check box.

3. Select a blending mode from the Mode pop-up menu.

4. Set the percentage of opacity for the drop shadow. A higher opacity means the drop shadow is denser; a lower opacity means it is more transparent.

> If you add a drop shadow to type, for example, you must select the text frame instead of the text itself.

5. Set the X and Y offset. Higher numbers move the drop shadow further from the object. Positive numbers move the drop shadow to the right and bottom of the object; negative numbers move it to the top and left of the object.

6. Set the Blur amount. A larger number makes a softer shadow.

7. The Spread percentage moves the drop shadow further out.

8. The Noise percentage controls the graininess of the drop shadow.

9. If you want your drop shadow to be a color other than black, select RGB, CMYK, or LAB from the Color pop-up menu to enter percentages and mix your own color. Choose Swatches to pick a predefined color from the Swatches palette.

10. Click OK to apply your drop shadow (see Figure 26.18).

Figure 26.18
The Drop Shadow dialog gives you lots of options for creating a great dimensional effect.

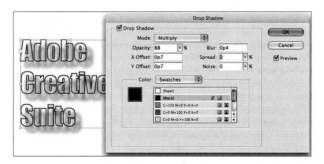

Feathering

Feathering is another transparency feature that gradually blends out the edges of images, type, and other page elements. Follow these steps to add a feathering effect to an object:

1. Select the object you want to feather.

2. Choose Object, Feather.

3. Click the Feather check box and select Preview.

4. Set the width of the feather effect. The larger the number, the further in to the selected object the feathering extends.

5. Select the option for Sharp, Rounded, or Diffused Corners.

6. Increase the noise for a grainier feather.

7. Click OK to apply the feather (see Figure 26.19).

Sharp feather corners   Diffused feather corners

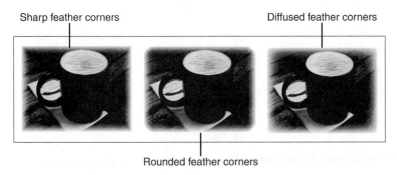

Figure 26.19
Images with sharp, rounded, and diffused feather effects.

Rounded feather corners

Corner Effects

The corner effects option adds different looks to an object's corners. Start by selecting the object, and then follow these steps:

1. Choose Object, Corner Effects. Click the Preview button.

2. Select from Fancy, Bevel, Inset, Inverse Rounded, or Rounded corners.

3. Enter the size of the inset. The measurement of the inset is based on your choice in the Units & Increments pane of the Preferences dialog (choose Edit, Preferences, Units & Increments in Windows or choose InDesign, Preferences, Units & Increments on the Mac).

4. Click OK to apply the effect (see Figure 26.20).

Fancy corners   Bevel corners   Inset corners

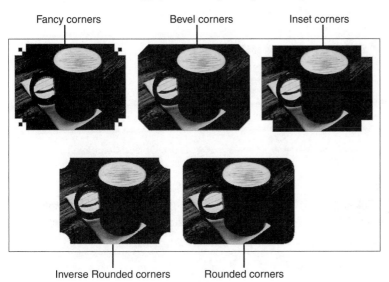

Figure 26.20
Examples of various corner effects.

26

Inverse Rounded corners   Rounded corners

UNDERSTANDING THE COPY/PASTE OPTIONS

Almost every application affords you the opportunity to copy and paste items from one place in a document to another, or from one document to another. InDesign has the same Cut, Copy, and Paste options as any other Create Suite program, and it also gives you a number of other paste options that can help make document design easier.

All of the copy and paste options are found under the Edit menu. Cut deletes the selected item(s) and places it on the Clipboard, and Copy leaves the selected item(s) and makes a copy on the Clipboard. The Paste command pastes the cut or copied object on the page.

The Paste Without Formatting command is active when you are pasting text from another application, such as a word processor. It pastes "clean" text into your document; that is, any type styles applied in the other application are wiped out when you paste it in InDesign.

When you cut or copy content and then select a frame, the Paste Into command pastes the content in the frame you select.

When you select the normal Paste command, the object you cut or copy is pasted in the center of the document window. Paste in Place pastes the object in the same coordinates as the original. For example, if you copy something from one page of your document and want it to appear in exactly the same place on another page, select Paste in Place.

Closely related to copying and pasting are the Duplicate and Step and Repeat commands. Duplicate copies and pastes the selected object at an offset over the original object in one step. You can also duplicate an object by selecting it and then dragging with the Alt (Windows users) or Option (Mac users) key held down.

Select Step and Repeat to copy and paste multiple copies of a selected item at a specific offset. Select your object and then choose Edit, Step and Repeat. Enter the number of items you want to paste and the horizontal and vertical offset at which you want the duplicated items to be placed.

WORKING WITH COMPOUND PATHS

A *compound path* occurs when you combine more than one path or object. You can apply compound paths to objects that are layered, and different effects will be seen depending on the order of the objects, the colors, and the objects themselves. Wherever a path overlaps with another object, a hole is created (see Figure 26.21).

To create a compound path, select the overlapping objects and choose Object, Compound Path, Make.

To break up a compound path, select the item and choose Object, Compound Path, Release.

This is a pretty simplistic explanation of compound paths. In Chapter 30, "Creating and Modifying Paths in InDesign," you delve more deeply into compound paths and the various ways you can edit and change them.

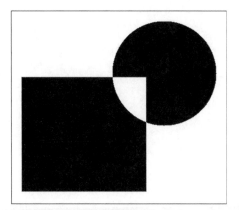

Figure 26.21
When two objects that overlap are made into a compound path, the top item is punched out of the other object.

CONVERTING SHAPES

If you draw a shape on your page and want to convert it quickly to another shape, use the options in the Object, Convert Shapes submenu. You can convert the selected shape into any of the following:

- Rectangle

- Rounded Rectangle

- Beveled Rectangle

- Inverse Rounded Rectangle

- Ellipse

- Triangle

- Polygon (if you choose this option, it defaults to the last type of polygon you specified. If you have a certain shape in mind, double-click on the Polygon tool in the Tools palette to open the Polygon Settings dialog and enter specifics about the number of sides and star inset before you choose this menu option).

- Line

- Orthogonal Line

USING OBJECT STYLES

If you have several objects to which you would like to add the same object effects, Object Styles gives you the option to save the effects as styles that you can quickly add to another page element.

Choose Window, Object Styles to open the Object Styles palette (see Figure 26.22).

26

Figure 26.22
The Object Styles palette.

To create a new style, select New Object Style from the palette menu. You can set multiple types of object effects in this dialog using the selections in the left pane. All these options have either been explained previously in this chapter or will be covered in Chapter 27. The following is an overview of the options you can apply in your Object Style:

- **Fill:** Set color, tint, or gradients.

- **Stroke:** Select color options and stroke type.

- **Stroke and Corner Effects:** Set stroke effects and corner effects.

- **Transparency:** Select the transparency percentage and blending mode.

- **Drop Shadow and Feather:** Select from the same options previously mentioned for these two effects.

- **Paragraph Styles:** Choose from defined paragraph styles.

- **Text Frame General Options and Text Frame Baseline Options:** Define how the text appears in a type frame.

- **Story Options:** Choose whether to apply Optical Marginal Alignment.

- **Text Wrap and Other:** Choose text wrap type and non-printing options.

- **Anchored Object Options:** Choose how to deal with anchored objects.

If you have already created and modified an object and then decide you'd like to save that effect as an object style, select the object and click the New Style button at the bottom of the Object Styles palette.

Again, those options in this dialog that deal with text are covered in Chapter 27.

Object styles can also be imported from another document. Choose Load Object Styles from the palette menu to browse for a document that contains the object style(s) you want to bring into the current document.

WORKING WITH SNIPPETS

Snippets use XML to save page items so that you can use those items in other InDesign documents or in other applications. When you save something as a snippet, you are also saving all the styles, formatting, and XML tags and structure applied to it. To create a snippet, first create the items you want to save, then follow these steps:

1. Choose File, Export.

2. Name the item you're saving.

3. Select InDesign Snippet (.inds) from the Save As Type (Windows users) or Format (Mac users) pop-up menu.

You can also drag and drop snippets onto the desktop (see Figure 26.23). A new file will appear; simply rename it and add the extension .inds.

Figure 26.23
Save a snippet file to the most convenient place or drag it on the page.

26

To use a snippet on an InDesign page, either choose File, Place and import the snippet, or drag the snippet from its location and drop it on the InDesign page.

Why a snippet? Why not a library or an Object Style? Because of the XML tagging that's supported in snippets. We go into a little more detail in Chapter 32, "Speeding Up InDesign and Data Functionality," about XML and why it's so powerful.

27

WORKING WITH TYPE IN INDESIGN

Creating text in your InDesign document is as simple as drawing a frame with either the Type tool or any frame tool. Click in the frame with the Type tool to get a blinking cursor, at which point you can start typing.

When you select a text frame with the Selection tool, you see the standard eight boundary box handles, as well as two larger squares at the top left and bottom right of the frame. These are the in port and out port, respectively (see Figure 27.1). The in port and out port may contain symbols that give you information about the text frame.

Figure 27.1
With text frames, you see in and out ports as well as the normal selection handles.

In port

Out port

A red plus symbol in the out port indicates *overset text*—that is, more text than is able to fit in the text frame (see Figure 27.2). To place overset text, you can click on the red plus symbol and then either click the resulting loaded text cursor elsewhere on the page to create another text frame or click in an existing frame to place the overset text there. The text in the second frame is *linked* to the first frame, so if you change the size of the first frame, the text reflows in the second frame.

Arrows in the in port or out port indicate that the text either flows from or to another text frame. To see how text is linked, choose View, Show Text Threads. As long as one of the text frames is selected, you see a line from one text frame to the next (see Figure 27.3).

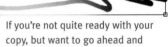

If you're not quite ready with your copy, but want to go ahead and design your document, InDesign's placeholder text feature will put dummy text in place that can later be replaced. To place the dummy text, click in a text frame with the Type tool and select Type, Fill with Placeholder Text. Instant copy— just make sure you replace it with the real thing.

Figure 27.2
A red plus in the out port indicates overset text, meaning there is more copy in the frame than can be seen.

Ming eum il ilisi bla
feuisci ex el utem quisi.
Iquamet wisciduipit lum-
sandre ero deliquam inci
eum nonsed minim vent ⊞—— Overset text symbol

Commod mincipis nos delent at, sequat. Ut lorperi usciliquat, quamconse tin erciduis ent elit ut init utpate core magna feum et dolor iriureet at, venisl ex eugait dum ent praessed ting exerat. Putat ercinci tat. Wisi. Er sit loreet utat veliquat. Ut aci blaortie delesed te mod tatum delisim dipit vendip et utatet iure tat. Vel utat praestrud modolob ex

essed dit num ex ercillu ptatum vulla racip esecte min ulput nummodit amet, velit, si tie veleniat, sit venim ipis nisci et volorerat. atum volorer sectet dunt atie do corem in venim exeratis alit nummolor iril irillummy niat. Duisciduis at lore faccum dipit, vent ute magniamcor adiat. Bor ilit eu feu feum vendrem iure el irit

Linked text symbols

Figure 27.3
When text is linked, arrows appear in the in and out ports. The Show Text Threads option shows the link between the text frames.

USING THE CHARACTER PALETTE

Many options for changing the appearance of your text are found in the Character palette (choose Type, Character to display this palette). Here you can select your font and the font style (see Figure 27.4). InDesign does not allow you to stylize type artificially; only those type styles that are installed with your fonts are available from the top two pop-up menus in this palette.

The next section of the palette enables you to set type size (the size of text in points; there are 72 points in an inch), *leading* (the amount of space between lines of type), *kerning* (the amount of space between letters), and *tracking* (the tightness or looseness of horizontal lines of type).

In the next section of the Character palette, select the percentage of the text height and width if you want the text to appear wider or taller than the default for the font size you've chosen. Enter a baseline shift amount (the amount you want the selected text to be placed above or below the baseline on which the text rests). You can also enter a degree of *skewing* for your type—that is, the degree to which the type leans. Positive numbers create type that leans to the right; negative numbers create type that leans to the left.

Finally, use the pop-up menu at the bottom of the palette to select your language for spelling options.

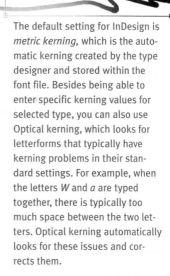

The default setting for InDesign is *metric kerning*, which is the automatic kerning created by the type designer and stored within the font file. Besides being able to enter specific kerning values for selected type, you can also use Optical kerning, which looks for letterforms that typically have kerning problems in their standard settings. For example, when the letters *W* and *a* are typed together, there is typically too much space between the two letters. Optical kerning automatically looks for these issues and corrects them.

Figure 27.4
The Character palette.

27

In the palette menu, select to view OpenType Options for OpenType fonts. More information about OpenType fonts can be found later in this chapter.

The Character palette menu also enables you to set the desired case of your type—choose from all caps, small caps, superscript, or subscript. Select to underline or strike through your text. If the selected font supports it, you can turn ligatures on or off (see Figure 27.5). (*Ligatures* refer to the connections you sometimes see between letters like ff, fi, and so on.)

Figure 27.5
Some fonts display ligatures you can turn on in the Character palette menu.

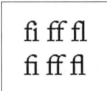

The Underline and Strikethrough Options on the palette menu give you control over the stroke of the underline and strikethrough.

If there are certain places where you do not want text to break like a URL or phone number in a line, paragraph, or column, highlight the text and select No Break from the Character palette menu.

USING THE PARAGRAPH PALETTE

The Paragraph palette (choose Type, Paragraph to display it) also gives you options for adjusting the appearance of your text, but on a paragraph basis as opposed to individual characters (see Figure 27.6).

Figure 27.6
The Paragraph palette.

The first set of buttons across the top of the Paragraph palette enables you to choose from left-aligned, centered, or right-aligned text; justified text with the last line left-aligned, centered, or right-aligned; force-justified text, in which all lines are justified regardless of length; and align toward spine or away from spine.

The next set of fields deals with indents. Enter specific values to indent your type to the left or right, and left-indent the first line or right-indent the last line.

If you want a specific amount of space before or after each paragraph, enter that measurement in the next set of fields. Create a drop cap (an initial letter that drops above or below the baseline a set number of lines) by entering the number of *lines* you want the first letter of the paragraph to drop or rise. If you prefer, specify the number of *characters* you want the drop cap to drop above or below the baseline in the last field.

Click the Hyphenate check box to hyphenate text automatically based on dictionary settings. Use the buttons in the lower-right portion of the palette to choose to align or not align your text to the baseline grid automatically.

In the palette menu, select a composition method. Adobe Paragraph Composer looks at an entire paragraph to help avoid unattractive breaks in text. Adobe Single-Line Composer takes only single lines of type into consideration for appearance and breaks.

Based on how you want your text to appear, select Only Align First Line to Grid (ignores grid alignment for subsequent lines of type) or Balance Ragged Lines (when Adobe Paragraph Composer is selected, this balances ragged headlines or pulled quotes when you click in the paragraph you want to balance) from the palette menu.

The Justification selection enables you to choose the word spacing, letter spacing, and glyph scaling (the size of individual characters in the font) for justified text. Changing these percentages can help improve the appearance of justified text and minimize the *white river* effect you sometimes see. Note, however, that adjusting these settings with too-large swings between the maximum and minimum settings can result in characters that are noticeably wider or thinner.

The Keep Options entry in the palette menu enables you to set specific lines of type that should stay with the lines that follow or precede them—for example, the last item in a list that you do not want to flow to another page or column. You can set how many lines to keep together, or whether to keep an entire paragraph together, either all of the lines, or a certain number of lines at the beginning and end of the paragraph. You can also choose where to start the paragraph when it does break.

The Hyphenation option in the Paragraph palette menu contains specific settings for how words should be hyphenated, and enables you to choose a degree of hyphenation between fewer breaks and better spacing.

Paragraph styles, which you explore later in this chapter, can normally be applied only to a specific paragraph, not to individual words or characters. The Drop Caps and Nested Styles selection gives you the ability to set up nested styles, which are applied to only certain characters within the paragraph. For example, if you are creating a directory and want the name to appear in a certain style but all the following information to appear in another style, you can create a nested style for the person's name and set the style to end after the colon that separates the name from the information that follows.

Paragraph rules are lines you can specify to always follow or precede a paragraph. Turn them on or off from the Paragraph palette menu.

In the Bullets and Numbering dialog (choose Bullets and Numbering from the Paragraph palette menu to display the dialog), choose to create bullets or numbers from the pop-up menu at the top of the dialog. For bullets, select the available glyphs for your font. For numbering, select the numbering style, the separator, and the starting number for a specific font. Both options give you the chance to select your desired position for the bullet or number. You can also select a different font and font size for the bullet or number without changing the font and size of your text (see Figure 27.7).

If you later change your mind about bullets and numbering, you can select Convert Bullets and Numbering to Text from the Paragraph palette menu to change it back to normal text.

27

Bullets   Numbers

Figure 27.7
Choose the appearance and style of bullets and numbering in the Bullets and Numbering dialog.

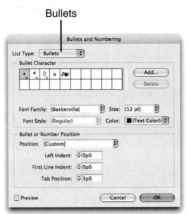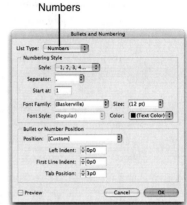

USING THE TYPE MENU COMMANDS

We've covered most of the commands from the Type menu in our discussion of the Character and Paragraph palettes in the first part of this chapter; Chapter 24, "Understanding the InDesign Interface and Tools," offers an overview of the Type menu. Here is a more detailed look at some of the options that are in the Type menu:

- **Glyphs:** The Glyphs command opens the Glyphs palette, which shows all available characters for the chosen font. To insert a character in your text, insert the text cursor where you want the character to appear and then double-click the glyph in the Glyphs palette.

- **Story:** The Story palette has only one option: turning on Optical Margin Alignment. This option creates hanging punctuation in your document; that is, if a line starts with a quote mark or any other character that is not a letter, the line is moved out so the letters align more closely on a vertical line (see Figure 27.8).

Figure 27.8
An example of a paragraph with the Optical Margin Alignment feature turned on.

"From the first taste, I
always knew my future
would include coffee."
— Michelle Schofield,
owner

- **Insert Special Character, Insert White Space, Insert Break Character:** These selections open submenus of various non-keyboard characters, enabling you to insert them in your document quickly.

27

WORKING WITH TYPE STYLES

InDesign gives you an option to set both character and paragraph styles for your document. Many of the options are the same for the two types of styles, so how do you decide which to use?

First, use this section as an overview of the types of characteristics you can apply with the styles. But also consider how styles are applied. Character styles can be applied to individual characters, and paragraph styles are applied to an entire paragraph at a time.

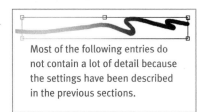

Most of the following entries do not contain a lot of detail because the settings have been described in the previous sections.

Character Styles

Both the New Character Style and New Paragraph Style dialogs, accessed by selecting New Character Style or New Paragraph Style from their respective palette menus, are set up to show various selections in the left pane; based on what you select from the left pane, options in the main part of the dialog change. The following are selections in the left pane of the New Character Style dialog:

- **General:** Name your style in this pane (see Figure 27.9). If the style is based on another, select that style from the Based On pop-up menu. You can create a keyboard shortcut to apply the style quickly.

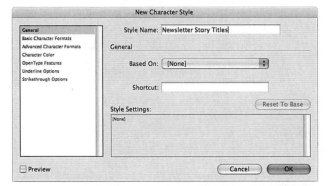

Figure 27.9
The General page of the New Character Style dialog.

- **Basic Character Formats:** Set the font, style, size, leading, kerning, tracking, case, and position here (see Figure 27.10). Use the check boxes to select underline, strikethrough, ligatures, or break controls.

- **Advanced Character Formats:** Enter specific information for horizontal and vertical scale, baseline shift, and skew (see Figure 27.11). Select the language for this text.

- **Character Color:** Set fill and stroke, and choose colors from the Swatches palette (see Figure 27.12).

27

Figure 27.10
The Basic Character Formats page of the New Character Style dialog.

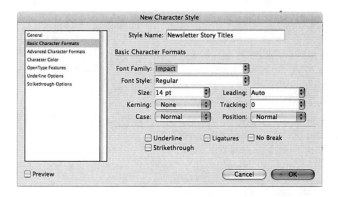

Figure 27.11
The Advanced Character Formats page of the New Character Style dialog.

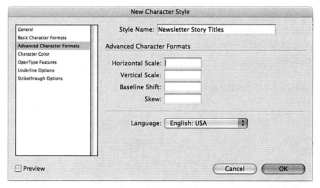

Figure 27.12
The Character Color page of the New Character Style dialog.

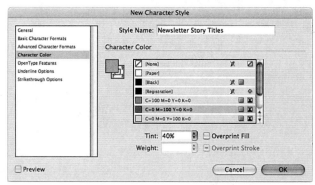

■ **OpenType Features:** If you've specified an OpenType font, select from the various options available with it (see Figure 27.13). See the "Working with OpenType Fonts" section later in this chapter for more information on the options offered with this font type.

■ **Underline Options and Strikethrough Options:** Choose the stroke specifics for these settings (Figure 27.14 shows the Underline options page).

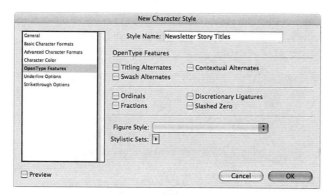

Figure 27.13
The OpenType Features page of the New Character Style dialog.

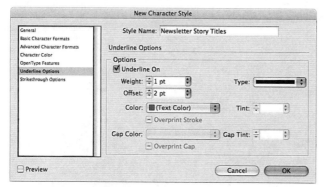

Figure 27.14
The Underline Options page of the New Character Style dialog.

Paragraph Styles

Like the New Character Style dialog, the New Paragraph Style dialog shows a list of options in the left pane; based on what you select from the left pane, the options in the main part of the dialog change. The following are selections in the left pane of the New Paragraph Style dialog:

- **General:** Name your style in this pane. If the style is based on another style, select that style from the Based On pop-up menu. You can create a keyboard shortcut to apply the style quickly.

- **Basic Character Formats:** Set the font, style, size, leading, kerning, tracking, case, and position here. Use the check boxes to select underline, strikethrough, ligatures, or break controls.

- **Advanced Character Formats:** Enter specific information for horizontal and vertical scale, baseline shift, and skew. Select the language for this text.

- **Indents and Spacing:** Specify text alignment, left, right, first line, and last line indents, spaces before or after each paragraph, and how to align to the grid (see Figure 27.15).

- **Tabs:** Set up tabs and indents based on the text frame ruler. Use the double-triangle to set the specific alignment: Move the top triangle to indent the first line, the bottom triangle to indent all subsequent lines, and both to indent the entire paragraph (see Figure 27.16). To insert a new tab, click on the ruler where you want the tab to be located. Click the buttons at the top for left-, centered-, right-, or decimal-aligned tabs. Enter a character or characters in the Leader field to create a line of characters for the tab (such as a period or a dash). If you choose a decimal-aligned tab, type in the character to align on.

- **Paragraph Rules:** Set lines you can specify to always follow or precede a paragraph (see Figure 27.17).

Figure 27.15
The Indents and Spacing page of the New Paragraph Style dialog.

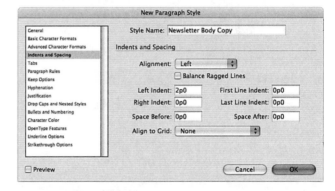

Figure 27.16
The Tabs page of the New Paragraph Style dialog.

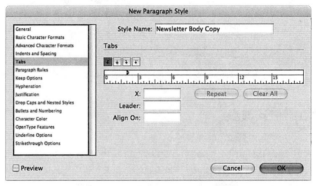

Figure 27.17
The Paragraph Rules page of the New Paragraph Style dialog.

27

- **Keep Options:** Set specific lines of type that should stay with the lines that follow or precede them (see Figure 27.18).

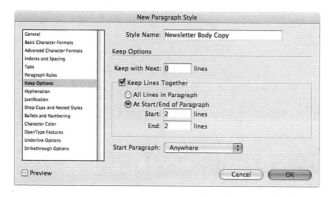

Figure 27.18
The Keep Options page of the New Paragraph Style dialog.

- **Hyphenation:** Set how words should be hyphenated and choose a degree of hyphenation between fewer breaks and better spacing (see Figure 27.19).

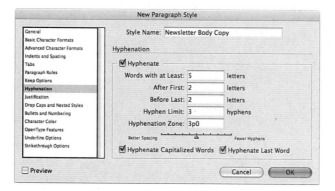

Figure 27.19
The Hyphenation page of the New Paragraph Style dialog.

- **Justification:** Choose the word spacing, letter spacing, and glyph scaling for justified text.

- **Drop Caps and Nested Styles:** Set up nested styles, which are applied to only certain characters within the paragraph (see Figure 27.20).

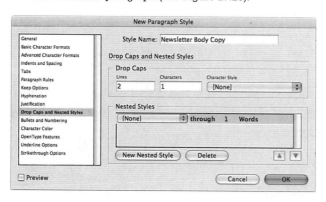

Figure 27.20
The Drop Caps and Nested Styles page of the New Paragraph Style dialog.

27

- **Bullets and Numbering:** Choose to create bullets or numbers. For bullets, select the available glyphs for your font. For numbering, select the numbering style, the separator, and the starting number for a specific font. Both options give you the chance to select your desired position for the bullet or number.

- **Character Color:** Set fill and stroke, and choose colors from the Swatches palette.

- **OpenType Features:** If you specified an OpenType font, select from the various options available with it. See "Working with OpenType Fonts" later in this chapter for more information.

- **Underline Options** and **Strikethrough Options:** Choose the stroke specifics for these settings.

UNDERSTANDING TEXT FRAME OPTIONS

The Text Frame Options dialog, found under the Object menu, has several options that make working with entire text frames easier (see Figure 27.21):

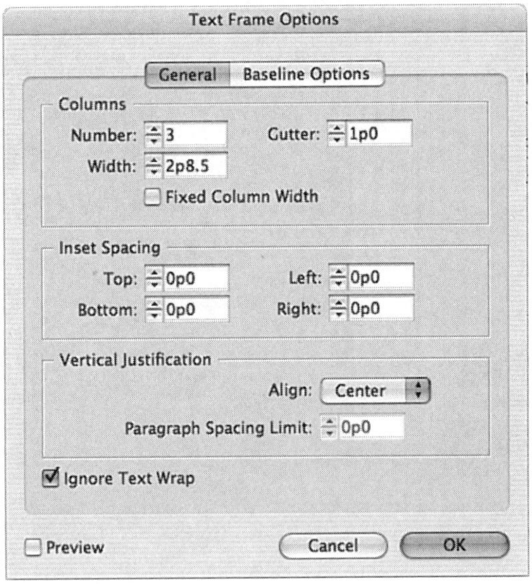

Figure 27.21
The Text Frame Options dialog.

- **Columns:** Set a number of columns that your text frame should contain, as well as the *gutter* (the amount of space that should appear between the columns). If you want your columns to be a specific width, click Fixed Column Width and enter the desired measurement.

- **Inset Spacing:** Set an inset spacing amount for the top, bottom, left, and/or right side of the text frame. *Inset spacing* refers to the amount of space that should be left between the type and the edge(s) of the text frame.

- **Vertical Justification:** Set the vertical alignment for the text in the frame. If you choose Justify, you can enter a maximum paragraph spacing amount.

- **Ignore Text Wrap:** If you want this text frame to ignore any text wrap, click the check box.

- **Baseline Options:** Click the tab in the Text Frame Options dialog to set how the text should sit on the baseline and the minimum measurement. Click the check box to create a custom baseline grid, and set your starting point, where it should start, the grid increments, and the grid color.

WORKING WITH OPENTYPE FONTS

OpenType fonts are a specific type of scalable font developed by Microsoft and Adobe that contain numerous glyphs and characters with swashes or discretionary ligatures. InDesign has a number of built-in features that provide additional support for OpenType fonts.

To see additional OpenType glyphs, open the Glyphs palette (choose Type, Glyphs) and select an OpenType font from the pop-up menu. Any character with additional glyphs displays an arrow in the lower-right corner of each character's display square (see Figure 27.22). To add any of these characters to your page, select it from the Glyphs palette.

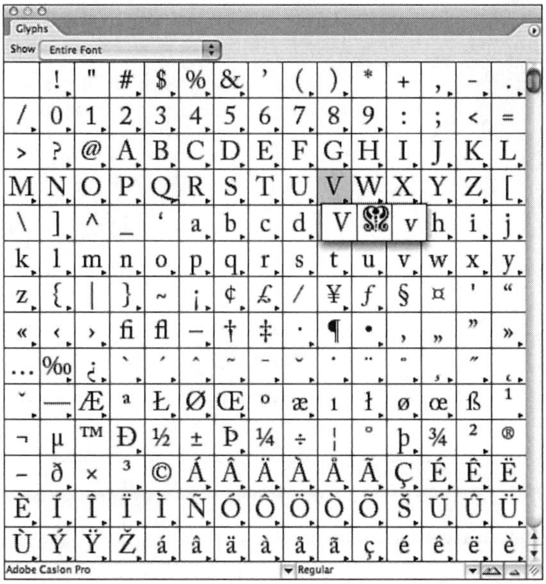

Figure 27.22
An OpenType font displays multiple options for various characters in the Glyphs palette.

To turn on the optional font characteristics, like swashes and discretionary ligatures, select the OpenType font in the Character or Control palette. Select OpenType in the palette menu and choose the option you want to turn on. Any option that is not available with that particular font will appear in square brackets ([ ]).

USING THE STORY EDITOR

When InDesign was first released, it quickly became obvious that as a page layout program, this was a step up from PageMaker. And lots of people jumped over to gain more control and more creativity for their documents. But one of the most common complaints heard was the lack of a Story Editor. Adobe corrected that oversight in the first version of InDesign CS.

The Story Editor is the word processor that lives within InDesign. It can help you see your text a little more clearly, especially if you are working with a decorative font or are trying to view type's effect on the entire page as opposed to being zoomed in on your copy only. It also enables you to see everything you are typing in a single font and size (selected through InDesign's Preferences window) without having to view formatting.

To use the Story Editor, first click in a frame with the Type tool. Choose Edit, Edit in Story Editor, and the Story Editor window opens (see Figure 27.23).

Figure 27.23
The Story Editor makes it easier to type text without having to view styles or zoom in to see your copy.

You can enlarge or reduce the Story Editor window as you want. Type your copy in the window, and it appears in the text frame however you have it formatted there.

The Story Editor displays any style applied to your type in the left frame, as well as the vertical depth of the story based on the text frame. It also shows you whether your type is overset, and by how much.

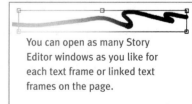

You can open as many Story Editor windows as you like for each text frame or linked text frames on the page.

Certain text tags, such as footnotes, index markers, tables, XML tags, hyperlink sources or anchors, and inline objects are marked in the Story Editor with various nonprinting markers.

For example, text that has been marked for the index displays with a caret (^) beside it, **XML-tagged** text is enclosed in red brackets, and hyperlinked text is enclosed in a rectangle.

After you finish working in the Story Editor, close it. All type appears in the text frame with which you were working.

MANAGING TABLES

Designing documents can sometimes be fun, but there's always a certain amount of drudgery to some of the things you might be asked to do, such as design tables of financial data. So there was much rejoicing in the page layout world when InDesign 2.0 came out with its table features, meaning the days of painstakingly drawing columns and rows and then setting up tabs to put information in those fields were over.

The best part of the table feature is that you can import Excel spreadsheets directly into the document by choosing File, Place; you can copy and paste data into a table; you can convert tabbed text into a table; or you can set up your own tables and enter the information. However you choose to do it, you'll be happy the table features are there.

To create a table on the fly, first create a text frame on your page. Click in it with the Type tool so you have a blinking cursor. Choose Table, Insert Table and in the Insert Table dialog shown in Figure 27.24, enter the number of rows, columns, header rows and header columns you want in your table.

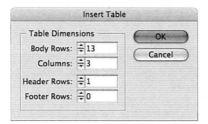

Figure 27.24
To create a custom table, first set up the number of rows and any header information.

Insert text by typing at the blinking cursor within a cell. The cell's size expands horizontally to hold as many lines of text as needed. To move from cell to cell, press the Tab key.

You can place a graphic file within a table cell by choosing File, Place and choosing your graphic. If the graphic does not fit in the cell, you might see an overset text symbol, indicating you need to enlarge the frame. To avoid an overset graphic in a cell, place your graphic file on the page and then choose Edit, Copy or Edit, Cut. Use the Type tool to click the cell in which you want to place your graphic and then choose Edit, Paste. The cell expands to fit the graphic.

Importing Table Data

To import table data, you must first draw a text frame on your page. Either draw the frame with the Type tool or draw a frame and then click in it with the Type tool to turn it into a text frame. Then follow these steps:

1. Choose File, Place. Find the table document you want to import. You can import Microsoft Excel documents, tab-delimited text, or plain text. If you want to see how the table will import, select View Import Options in the Place dialog.

2. The Import Options dialog enables you to choose which sheet of the document you want to import (see Figure 27.25). The name that was given to the sheet shows up in the pop-up menu.

If you set up a view with specific cells in Excel you can choose that or type in the cell range you want to import.

Figure 27.25
If you view import options for your table, you can choose exactly what is imported and how.

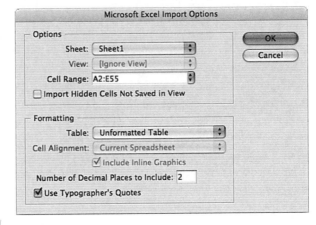

3. Use the Import Hidden Cells Not Saved in View check box to import cells that do not appear in the view of the file you selected in the original document.

4. In the Formatting area, choose Formatted Table, Unformatted Table, or Unformatted Tabbed Text from the Table pop-up menu. Any option enables you to choose the number of decimal places you want to import and whether to use typographer's quotes (also called *smart quotes*).

5. If you choose Formatted Table, you can also choose whether to leave the cell alignment as it is in the file or bring it in as left-, right-, or center-aligned text. Click the check box to import inline graphics that are in the Excel spreadsheet.

6. Click OK to import the table into the text frame.

Copying and Pasting in Tables

To get table information into your InDesign document as a table, you have to place it; you cannot copy information from an Excel file, for example, and then paste it into an InDesign table.

There are a couple of things to know, however, about copying and pasting when you're working with tables in InDesign:

- If you copy several cells' worth of information and then paste at a blinking cursor within a single table cell, all the information copied is pasted into the selected cell. You have essentially pasted a table within a single table cell.

- To paste the information in individual cells, drag your cursor across the appropriate number of cells needed to paste the information and then choose Edit, Paste.

Formatting Tables

InDesign gives you many options for formatting the tables you place or create. You can use the commands under the Table menu, or you can use the Table palette. In this section, you concentrate on going through the Table palette, but understand that the menu commands are named the same and perform the same functions:

- When you click in your table, the Table palette displays the number of rows and number of columns. Use the Number of Rows and Number of Columns entry boxes or arrows to change the number of either.

- Row height can either be determined by a fixed measurement or automatically adjusted to fit the content. For automatic row height, select At Least in the Row Height pop-up menu and enter the smallest height the row should have. To set a fixed height for the row, select Exactly from the pop-up menu and enter the exact measurement in the Row Height entry field.

- Enter the specific width for the columns in the Column Width field.

- The next two sets of buttons (Align and Rotate) enable you to align your text vertically and set the direction your type should run.

- Set top, bottom, left, and right cell insets in the Cell Inset fields at the bottom of the palette.

The first selection in the Table palette menu is for Table Options, Table Setup. The other selections in the Table Options submenu are available through the Table Setup dialog, so you can either pick a specific dialog through the menu, or open the Table Setup dialog and pick what you want to change by clicking on one of the five tabs. Again, make sure that you use the Preview check box:

- **Table Setup:** Set table dimensions, specifications for the table border stroke, table spacing, and options for how your table strokes are drawn (see Figure 27.26).

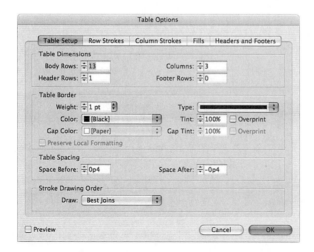

Figure 27.26
The Table Setup tab of the Table Options dialog.

27

- **Row Strokes:** Use the Alternating Pattern pop-up menu to choose how you want strokes to alternate (see Figure 27.27). For easier reading, you might want to set up different strokes on every other row, if there are several different categories of information being displayed, for example. These options enable you to set alternating stroke weights, type, color, tint, and gap color if you have specified dotted or dashed lines. You can also choose to skip numbers of the first or last rows.

Figure 27.27
The Row Strokes tab of the Table Options dialog.

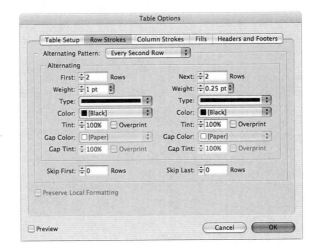

- **Column Strokes:** Like Row Strokes, these options enable you to decide whether you want alternating column strokes. These are the same options as in the Row Strokes tab (see Figure 27.28).

Figure 27.28
The Column Strokes tab of the Table Options dialog.

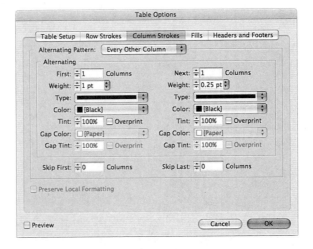

- **Fills:** To make large tables easier to read you might want to alternate the fill of rows or columns (see Figure 27.29). Choose your Alternating Pattern and then choose the color (the list of available colors is pulled from the Swatches palette) and tint. You can also choose to skip rows.

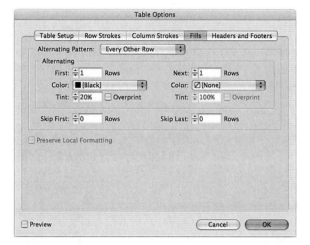

Figure 27.29
The Fills tab of the Table Options dialog.

- **Headers and Footers:** Header and footer rows enable you to define the information in your table (see Figure 27.30). If you have a table that spans several columns or pages, you might want to set the header or footer to repeat for ease of reading. Enter the number of header and footer rows the table contains, and then choose from the pop-up menus how often you want your header and/or footer to repeat. Use the check boxes to skip the first header or the last footer.

Figure 27.30
The Headers and Footers tab of the Table Options dialog.

The next selection in the Table palette menu is Cell Options, Text. Again, the other selections in the Cell Options submenu are available through the Text dialog, so you can either pick a specific dialog through the menu, or open the Text dialog and pick what you want to change by clicking on one of the four tabs. As always, use the Preview check box:

■ **Text:** You can set Cell Insets for the Top, Bottom, Left, and Right (see Figure 27.31). Use the pop-up menu to select the vertical text alignment. If you choose Justify, you can select a limit for the paragraph spacing. Choose the Offset, or how you want your type to align to the baseline, and a minimum offset number. Click the check box to clip the contents to the cell and select your text rotation angle in increments of 90 degrees.

Figure 27.31
The Text tab of the Cell Options dialog.

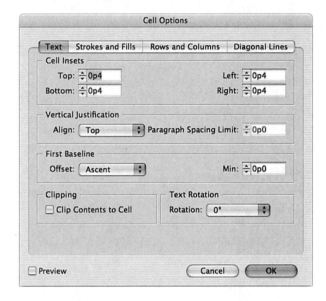

■ **Strokes and Fills:** This tab enables you to choose the stroke and fill for the selected cell(s). A preview window at the top shows a preview of the cell(s) you selected (see Figure 27.32).

Figure 27.32
The Strokes and Fills tab of the Cell Options dialog.

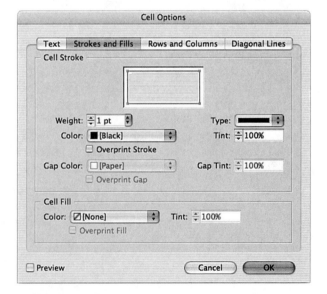

- **Rows and Columns:** Choose At Least to set a minimum and maximum size for row height (see Figure 27.33). The rows change size based on content, but they are never larger or smaller than the amount you enter here. Select Exactly to enter a set height that will not change. Set Column Width. Keep Options refers to how the selected cell(s) will break. You can choose to flow the table to the next frame, next column, or next specific page, or let it break anywhere. Click the Keep with Next Row check box if you want the row in which you clicked to stay with the row that follows.

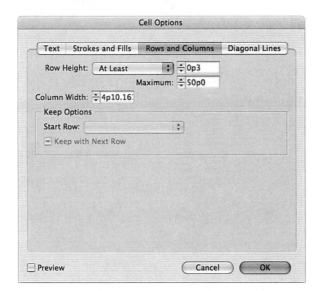

Figure 27.33
The Rows and Columns tab of the Cell Options dialog.

- **Diagonal Lines:** If you want selected cells to contain diagonal or crossed lines, click to select the type of diagonal you want to put in the cell(s), and then set the line stroke characteristics and whether you want the cell's content or the diagonal to be in front (see Figure 27.34).

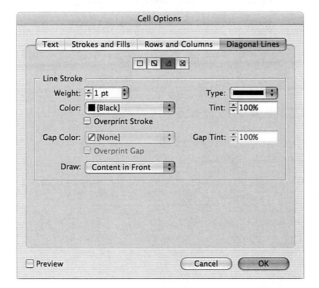

Figure 27.34
The Diagonal Lines tab of the Cell Options dialog.

27

The next selections in the Table palette menu enable you to insert rows or columns, and to delete rows, columns, or the entire table:

- Select Merge Cells from the palette menu to combine two or more selected cells into one cell (see Figure 27.35). Select Unmerge Cells to separate merged cells back to individual cells.

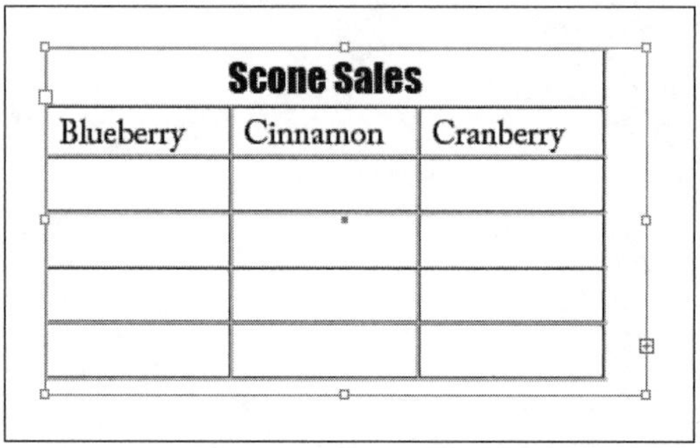

Figure 27.35
Merged cells can create a heading for a number of columns.

- Split Cell Horizontally and Split Cell Vertically enable you to create multiple cells in one cell (see Figure 27.36). The commands under Convert Rows convert the selected row to a header, a footer, or a body row.

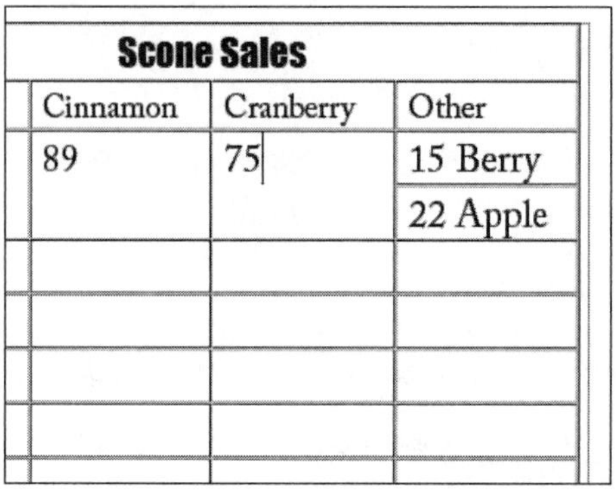

Figure 27.36
Table cells can be split vertically or horizontally.

- Distribute Rows Evenly and Distribute Columns Evenly make the selected rows or columns the same size.

- When you have a defined header or footer row, Edit Header and Edit Footer jump to the first cell in the row to enable you to edit the information quickly.

Again, the majority of the commands under the Table menu give you the same options as provided by the Table palette menu. There are, however, a few differences:

- **Convert Text to Table:** If you placed tab- or comma-delimited text in a document and later want to convert it to a table, select it and then use this command to open a dialog specifying how to separate rows and columns.

- **Convert Table to Text:** This command does just the opposite, converting a table to regular text. You can select how rows and columns should be separated in the resulting text.

- **Go to Row:** Enter a row number to jump there quickly.

PLACING TEXT

If you prefer to create text in another program, such as a word processor, you can import that text file into InDesign using the Place command.

Choose File, Place. Search for the file you want to import and select it. InDesign supports importing many types of text files, including Microsoft Word documents, plain text, and rich text files.

Select Show Import Options in the Place dialog to prepare your text for importing if you choose. Depending on the type of file you are importing, the import options are different.

Importing Text Files

If you are importing a plain text document, saved with the extension .txt, the Place dialog offers the following options:

- Plain text files (.txt) enable you to specify character set, platform, and the dictionary to use with the imported text.

- The Extra Carriage Returns option deals with hard returns in your document. If you choose, InDesign can remove these extra returns at the end of lines or between paragraphs.

- Under Formatting, choose the number of consecutive spaces that should be replaced with a tab and whether to use typographer's, or "curly," quotes in the placed text.

Importing Word or RTF Files

InDesign offers extra support for Microsoft Word or rich text (.rtf) files (see Figure 27.37). After you choose your import options, you can save these choices as a preset by clicking Save Preset and naming your import style. This enables you to choose the same options quickly if you are importing many similar documents:

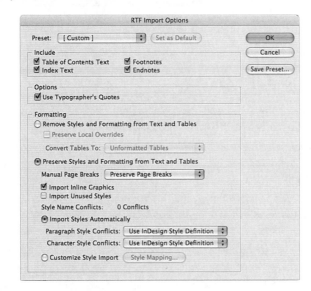

Figure 27.37
When you place Microsoft Word or rich text files in your InDesign document, you have many options for formatting text or matching styles.

27

- In the Include section you can choose to include Table of Contents Text, Index Text, Footnotes, and Endnotes.

- You can choose to use typographer's quotes.

- In the Formatting area, select the option to either remove or include the styles and formatting applied in the original program. If you choose to remove them, any styles such as color, font, and type are stripped, although you can check a box to preserve local overrides or styles that are applied to parts of paragraphs.

- If you choose to preserve styles, you have the following options:

  - When dealing with manual page breaks, you can choose to preserve page breaks, convert them to column breaks or include no breaks.

  - Click the check box to import any inline graphics or graphics that are attached within the text.

  - Click the check box to import any styles that were created in the document but not applied to any text.

- InDesign alerts you to any style name conflicts—that is, styles that are named the same but have different characteristics.

- You can choose to import styles automatically and resolve any character or paragraph style conflicts by choosing to use the InDesign style definition, to redefine the InDesign style, or to rename the style automatically.

- You can also choose to customize the style import. Click the Style Mapping button to see the style in your text document and the InDesign styles. Use the pop-up menu to choose the InDesign style to which you want to map the document style.

- When you place your text on the page, the styles are preserved as you specified in the import options, and any styles you chose to preserve are available in the Character or Paragraph Styles palettes.

WORKING WITH AUTOFLOW

When you place a text file on a page that already has column guides applied, you can choose from various autoflow options to place the text within the columns automatically.

Without specifying autoflow, after you select the file you want to place, you see a loaded text icon on your page. If you click in a column, the text flows into that column and an overset text symbol shows, enabling you to click and reload the text icon.

If you hold down the Alt key (Windows users) or Option key (Mac users) when you click the loaded text icon in the first column, the text flows into the column and then automatically reloads so you can click and flow it into the next column.

If you hold down the Shift key when you click in the first column, the text automatically flows into the columns set up on the page and adds pages to place all of the text in the file.

If you hold down Shift+Alt (Windows users) or Shift-Option (Mac users) while you click, Fixed Page Autoflow is activated, and text is flowed onto that page only, without adding pages or columns. All unplaced text is overset.

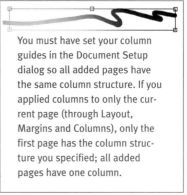

You must have set your column guides in the Document Setup dialog so all added pages have the same column structure. If you applied columns to only the current page (through Layout, Margins and Columns), only the first page has the column structure you specified; all added pages have one column.

WRAPPING TEXT

The Text Wrap palette (choose Window, Text Wrap to display it) enables you to create text frames that flow around other page elements, such as photos, graphics, or even other text frames (see Figure 27.38):

Figure 27.38
The Text Wrap palette enables you to specify how the text contained in type frames wraps around objects on the page.

1. Drag your text frame into position as you want it to appear in relation to the wrap object. Select the object you want it to wrap around.

2. Choose how you want the text to wrap around your object.

The Wrap Around Bounding Box option gives you a rectangular text wrap, regardless of the shape of the object inside the bounding box (see Figure 27.39).

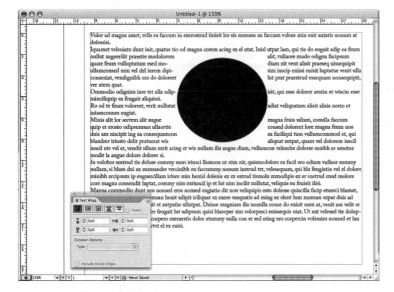

Figure 27.39
A text wrap around an object's bounding box.

27

The Wrap Around Object Shape option automatically detects the path of the object, including clipping paths applied in Photoshop (see Figure 27.40).

Figure 27.40
A text wrap around an object's shape.

Jump Object places text above and below the item.

Jump to Next Column ends the type at the top of the object and continues in the next available column.

The Invert check box makes the text wrap inside the path as opposed to outside.

3. In the next four fields set the amount of offset you want between the type and the object, above, below, and to the left and right of the object.

4. If you select to wrap around object shape, you can also select from the contour options, which are to wrap around the bounding box, detect the edges of the object, wrap around an alpha channel or Photoshop path, wrap around the graphic frame, or wrap around the clipping path.

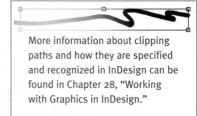

More information about clipping paths and how they are specified and recognized in InDesign can be found in Chapter 28, "Working with Graphics in InDesign."

5. Check Include Inside Edges to apply type inside "holes" in an object, like a tire.

6. After your text is wrapped around the object, you can select the object with the Direct Selection tool to see the path. Use the Direct Selection tool to move points on the path and reshape the wrap, or the Add or Subtract Anchor Points tools to adjust the anchor points on the path.

PUTTING TYPE ON A PATH

Under the Type tool on the Tool palette lives the Type on a Path tool. This tool enables you to type on any path, whether it is a path created by the Pen or Pencil tool or around a frame created by the Rectangle or Ellipse tool.

To place type on a path, hover the Type on a Path tool over the path. A small plus sign appears by the I-beam. Click, and begin typing. The words you type adhere to the path (see Figure 27.41).

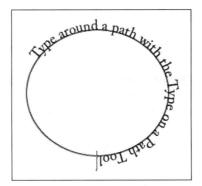

Figure 27.41
Type adheres to any path when it's placed with the Type on a Path tool.

If you end up with overset text, first use the Direct Selection tool to lengthen your path. A bar shows the end of the type. Click and drag it to expose the overset text.

You can adjust the display of your type on a path by selecting Type, Type on a Path, Options. This dialog gives you a choice of various skew types, alignment, and text spacing (see Figure 27.42). Use the Flip check box to flip the type to the other side of the path.

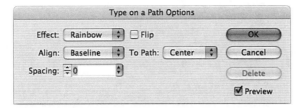

Figure 27.42
The Type on a Path Options command enables you to create different effects with your path text.

Select Type, Type on a Path, Delete Type From Path to remove the text.

27

WORKING WITH GRAPHICS IN INDESIGN

IN THIS CHAPTER

Graphics, which in this chapter serves as a catch-all term for all digital image files or imported art-work, are an important part of most designs. InDesign supports importing most standard graphics formats, including native Illustrator and Photoshop documents and PDFs.

The application includes numerous options and effects for using graphics in your InDesign document. This chapter deals with how to get your graphics into your InDesign document and the things you can do with them after they're there.

PLACING IMAGES

You have several options for importing graphics into InDesign. Items can be copied and pasted from other applications, such as Photoshop or Illustrator, or they can be placed in your document using the File, Place command.

You should decide between placing and pasting graphics based on several factors. When you paste graphics, you embed a full copy of the graphic in your file and have more options for editing the graphic. Embedded graphics make your file larger, however. Placing graphics often means you have to make your choices of how the graphic should display in the Place dialog, and you will not have many editing options after it's on the InDesign page. Linked files are low-resolution proxies placed in your document; linking graphics makes your file sizes smaller.

When you choose File, Place, you see the Place dialog. There are a couple of ways to view the Place dialog. When you place graphics, it's usually best to use the Adobe version of the Place dialog because it's going to give you more information about your graphics (see Figure 28.1). Switch to the Adobe dialog by clicking the Adobe dialog button in the lower-left corner of the Place dialog. If the button says OS dialog, you are already viewing the Adobe dialog. Although the OS version of the dialog enables you to browse to file locations, search for files, create a new folder, and check boxes Show Import Options and Replace Selected Item, the Adobe dialog gives you all of those options and more.

Figure 28.1
The Adobe Place dialog gives you many options for viewing and working with the files you are importing.

First, you can view previews of all available images by selecting Thumbnails from the View pop-up menu (the last button on the right at the top of the dialog).

Use the Project Tools pop-up menu to do the following:

- **Reveal in Finder/Reveal in Bridge:** Open the chosen folder in a Windows Explorer or Finder window or from the Bridge.

- **Add To Favorites:** Add the current folder to your favorites, after which it will display in the Favorites pane of Bridge.

- **New Project:** Automatically create a new Version Cue project.

- **Connect to:** Connect to an existing Version Cue project by entering the network path that leads to the project.

- **Edit Properties:** Edit the properties of a project.

- **Share Project:** Mark a project to share or unshare.

- **Versions:** Go to other versions of the project or to files that have been saved as alternates.

- **New Folder:** Create a new folder.

- **Show Deleted Items:** Change the view to show items that have been deleted.

- **Delete/Restore:** Delete selected items, or restore deleted items.

- **Disconnect:** Disconnect from a project.

- **Show File Info Area:** Show the File Info area at the left of the Place dialog, which tells you the file name, creation, and modification dates and the file's size, status, and location.

- **Refresh:** Refresh the view or synchronize the project or selected file.

- **Use OS Dialog:** Switch back to the OS dialog, which is simpler, but doesn't give you the previously mentioned options of the Adobe dialog.

Despite the version of the dialog you use, you always have the option to View Import Options when you select to place a file. When you click Open, the dialog that appears will show a preview of the file if you choose and enable you to set certain image and color settings. Standard image options include applying a Photoshop clipping path to the image or choosing an alpha channel you have created out of a selection in Photoshop to use like a clipping path.

The selections in the Import Options dialog will change based on the type of image you are placing. There isn't enough room in this book to go into every option offered for every file format, but it's easy to get more information about the selections. Open the Adobe Help Center and search in the InDesign CS2 Help for Import Options. Information for all importable file types will appear in the left pane and you can quickly find your information.

28

Standard color options include setting the image's color profile, which should be based on the source profile of your document. If a color profile is embedded in your document, that profile is automatically selected in the pop-up menu.

You can also choose a rendering intent for your graphic. You should leave this at the default setting, which is based on the document's color profile and has been tested by Adobe to meet printing standards.

There are a couple of ways to place a graphic on your page. If you've designed the document and drawn frames that will hold your graphics, select the frame prior to choosing File, Place. In the Place dialog, you have the option to Replace Selected Item. If the frame is empty, you're not exactly replacing it; the program simply places the item in the frame.

If you haven't selected a frame, after you click the Open button you'll have a loaded graphic cursor. There are three ways to place your graphic:

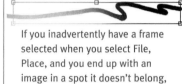

- Click, hold, and drag a frame; the graphic is placed inside the frame at full size. This means a portion of the graphic may be hidden, depending on how large it is in relation to the frame you drew.

- Hover the mouse over a frame you've drawn. The right angle of the graphic cursor will change to curves, indicating the graphic will be placed inside the frame. Click.

- Click anywhere on the page. The graphic will place at 100 percent, with a frame around it.

If you inadvertently have a frame selected when you select File, Place, and you end up with an image in a spot it doesn't belong, undo it: Choose Edit, Undo or press Ctrl+Z (Windows users) or ⌘+Z (Mac users), and you'll get a loaded graphic cursor you can place in the right spot.

UNDERSTANDING LINKS

One of the benefits of using the File, Place command to import graphics is that a link is created for every graphic you place with this command. A *link* is an internal document reference to the location of the original file. If the placed file moves, the link can become broken.

Links are important because they help keep InDesign documents small while still retaining all the resolution and features of the graphics files you place. When a graphic is placed but a link is not created (for example, when you copy a graphic from one application and paste it into InDesign), a low-resolution proxy of the file is pasted and you may find it does not print or display the way you wanted.

When you export a file to PDF or prepare a document for a service bureau or printer, all the links to files in the InDesign document must be available. If not, InDesign has only the low-resolution version of the graphics files to work with, and you end up with a document that has low-resolution, pixelated graphics. The Links palette (shown in Figure 28.2) gives you at-a-glance information about the graphics you've placed in the document and whether they are linked files (like the first two files listed) or embedded (like the last one).

28

Figure 28.2
The Links palette tells you all graphics that have been placed in your document and whether they are embedded.

It is possible to embed graphic files in your document. Graphics that are embedded are still linked, but they are actually stored within the document instead of just having a reference to them, like a normal linked file. A benefit of embedding graphic files is that you do not have to have the original file, or link, to print or export the file correctly. The downside of embedding links, however, is that storing graphics within the file can make the file very large. Depending on the complexity of the file and what you're trying to do, it can really bog down your computer. Embedded graphics are also static; they cannot be edited and relinked working through InDesign. See the information that follows about the Links palette for more about embedding and working with links.

UNDERSTANDING PLACED IMAGE RESOLUTION

We've talked a little about issues with low-resolution images and why it's important to maintain links to the original graphics files. Part of the assumption there is that you will want to output the documents you are preparing in InDesign. But output them where? And how?

These are questions you'll have to answer yourself, and some a commercial printer will have to answer for you. Before you send a document to print, it's important to know what your printer expects from you and needs to print your document as you want. One specification you will need to know is *resolution*.

Resolution is communicated in terms of pixels per inch, or ppi. The measurement is literally how many pixels are contained within an inch of display on your page. Lower numbers mean fewer pixels. Fewer pixels mean less information being displayed. Depending on your output device—a computer monitor for web pages, a laser printer for interoffice communications, a printing press for your corporate magazine—you need more or less resolution for your images to print correctly.

In general, commercial printers need anywhere from 150–300 ppi to print an image at high quality. If you are printing documents on a desktop printer, you may print documents with images from 72 ppi or higher, depending on the output resolution of your printer. Most monitors do not display images higher than 72 ppi or 96 ppi, so any document being created for strictly onscreen display can contain lower-resolution images without losing display quality. Figure 28.3 shows an image that does not have enough resolution to display properly; you can see the jagged edges along the curves of the water droplets.

When you create graphics or save images in Illustrator or Photoshop, you'll be able to set the resolution of the file. Resolution is closely tied to image size: a 1- by 1-inch image at 100 ppi displays at 50 ppi when enlarged to 2 by 2 inches. Wherever you set the resolution in your graphic-editing program, know that you must keep the image at 100% or smaller when you place it in InDesign. If you enlarge the graphic, you lose resolution.

Fortunately, InDesign gives you a good tool to track image resolution within the program. The Info palette displays the actual ppi and effective ppi of a selected graphic (see Figure 28.4). The *actual ppi* tells you the resolution at which the graphic was originally saved. The *effective ppi* tells you the resolution of the image as it prints or displays. Watch the effective ppi of graphics in your document to ensure you get the output you want.

28

Figure 28.3
Images that are placed without sufficient resolution for the output device will be pixelated when they print in your final document.

Figure 28.4
The Info palette is a good source of information about items in your document, including resolution of placed images.

WORKING WITH PSD FILES

One of InDesign's strengths has been its support for placing native Photoshop documents. When you don't export your Photoshop document to another file format, you're able to preserve many of the Photoshop settings.

Here are some of the things you should know about how InDesign deals with Photoshop PSD files:

- You have a choice when you place images with embedded ICC color profiles. InDesign will read the color profile, or you can choose to overwrite it with the color profile of your choice on the Color tab of the Import Options dialog. Changing the color profile upon import does not alter the color profile of the original Photoshop document. Remember that you must have the Show Import Options check box selected in the Place dialog when you place the file to choose another color profile.

- Alpha channels, masks, or paths applied to Photoshop images are preserved in InDesign. These can then be used to create text wraps around objects or delete backgrounds after they are placed.

- Any spot color channels in the original Photoshop document creates that spot color swatch in InDesign's Swatches palette after the graphic is imported. The spot color must be one InDesign recognizes, or it will display as a gray in the document. In that case it will not print correctly on composites (on your office's color laser printer, for example), but the color will separate correctly when film or plates are made by a commercial printer.

- PSD files are not flattened when they are imported—a new feature in InDesign CS2. Because layers are preserved, you can hide layers or view layer comps in InDesign.

To work with layered Photoshop documents:

1. Choose File, Place.

2. Choose your document. Make sure that the Show Import Options check box is selected in the Place dialog.

3. In the Import Options dialog, check Show Preview so you can see the effects of your choices (see Figure 28.5).

4. Toggle the eye icon next to a specific layer under Show Layers to show or hide the layer.

5. If your PSD graphic contains layer comps, use the Layer Comp pop-up menu in the Image Import Options dialog to select the layer state you want to import.

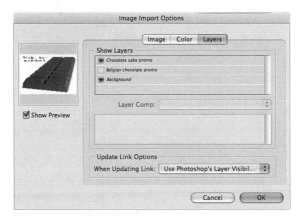

Figure 28.5
Layers and layer comps in placed PSD files can be shown or hidden based on your import option choices.

If you want to work with the layer options after you import the file instead of during the placing process, select the graphic on your page and choose Object, Object Layer Options to display the Object Layer Options dialog.

USING CLIPPING PATHS IN INDESIGN

Based on paths or channels you may have created in Photoshop, InDesign can create text wraps or recognize paths in images that are placed in it and apply a *clipping path*, which cuts out unwanted areas of the image.

28

To apply a clipping path to an imported image, first select the image. Then choose Object, Clipping Path and turn on the Preview feature.

The Clipping Path dialog offers several options for clipping paths:

- Choose Detect Edges from the Type pop-up menu for images that have not had paths applied in Photoshop. It creates a clipping path based on pixel color, so the part of the image you want to clip should be in stark contrast to its background—for example, a dark object on a white background. Selecting Detect Edges cuts out the background (see Figure 28.6).

Figure 28.6
The Detect Edges option in InDesign's Clipping Path dialog will look for color differences between the subject and background to help cut the subject out from the background.

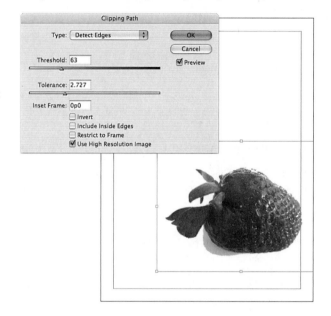

- The Alpha Channel and Photoshop Path options (available in the Type pop-up menu) look for alpha channels or paths applied in Photoshop and clip based on those. The User-Modified Path option is available when a clipping path has already been created (either in Photoshop or when using Detect Edges in InDesign) and then manually edited.

- The Threshold slider enables you to control how closely the clipping path is applied, based on the color of the pixels. Zero is white, so the higher the Threshold number, the darker the pixels that will be removed.

- Tolerance refers to how likely a pixel is to be hidden when its color is close to being clipped, based on the Threshold setting. If the Tolerance is set to a high number, fewer pixels will be hidden, but the path will be smoother. If the Tolerance is low, the pixels will be clipped much closer to the object.

- Inset Frame makes the clipping path closer based on a uniform number.

- Invert reverses the clipping path, clipping dark pixels from around light ones.

28

- The Include Inside Edges option can punch out "holes" in objects that are clipped. For example, if you clip a tire, this option clips not only the area around the tire but also the area inside the hole of the tire.

- The Restrict to Frame option creates a path that stops at the edges of the frame.

- The Use High Resolution Image option sets the clipping path based on the true resolution of the object, not on the screen resolution. This option provides a more precise clipping path but takes longer to render onscreen.

CROPPING IMAGES

Many times when you place an image, you don't want the entire image to be displayed. Every shape in InDesign can serve as a frame, and when you place an image, the image is placed inside a frame, regardless of whether you've drawn a frame on the page or not.

To crop an image, or make the frame smaller, click on the frame with the Selection tool. You will see the object's bounding box, the frame that shows its dimensions. Eight handles appear around the bounding box. Click a handle and drag to resize the frame, hiding part of the image (see Figure 28.7). You can also use the Position tool to drag a handle after a frame has been selected.

Figure 28.7
Use the Selection tool to resize the frame of an image and crop, or hide, part of the subject matter.

If you have a specific point from which you want to resize, like the center, take advantage of the Scale tool and its crosshairs to scale your frame. Select the frame with the Selection tool, then switch to the Scale tool. Crosshairs will appear. Position the crosshairs at the point from which you want to scale the frame. Now, use the Scale tool to drag a handle (or just drag from any point on the page) and resize. Corner handles resize from all four corners; side handles resize either vertically or horizontally, depending on which side handle you use.

If you have a specific size in mind for your frame, select the frame and then use the Control palette or Transform palette to enter the width and height for the frame, or enter a percentage in the Scale X and Scale Y fields. Click to join the chain link if you want either set of fields to enlarge or reduce proportionally.

28

After your frame has been resized, you may need to reposition the image within the frame to show only the area you want to see. To do this, use the Position tool or the Direct Selection tool. When you click on the frame contents with one of these tools, you will see the edges of the image within the frame, again with eight handles. This frame is a different color, however, to indicate that you've selected the image itself.

You can crop graphics in other programs—cropping the background out of a large digital image in Photoshop, for example—before you place them in InDesign. If you have a lot of graphics in your document, it might be a good idea to crop the image before placing it in InDesign, because getting rid of excess information in the image makes the graphic file smaller. Smaller graphic files mean smaller document files, which are easier and faster to print and export.

When you hold the Direct Selection tool or the Position tool over the image, it turns into a hand. Click, hold, and drag to reposition the image within the frame. And take it easy! If you immediately start moving the hand after you click, you have to guess where your content is in relation to the frame. If you hold for a second with the hand, you see the rest of your graphic ghosted outside the frame (see Figure 28.8). This can help you as you reposition to see exactly what you're hiding and what will show through the frame.

Figure 28.8
If you wait a second before trying to reposition an object with the Direct Selection or Position tool, you will see a ghosted version of the hidden parts of the image to help with cropping.

RESIZING GRAPHICS

If you want to make an image larger or smaller after you place it on the page, you have several options for resizing. This section starts out dealing with the content only, and then you learn about resizing both the frame and the content.

Select the content of a frame by clicking with the Direct Selection or the Position tool until you see the selection handles of the graphic itself. To resize on the fly, use the Selection tool, the Direct Selection tool, or the Position tool to grab a handle and drag. Hold down the Shift key while you drag to resize the graphic content proportionally.

You can also use the Scale tool to resize graphic contents from a specific point, by positioning its crosshairs and then dragging a selection handle (or just dragging anywhere on the page) in the direction you want to resize. Again, use the Shift key to resize the graphic proportionally.

If you want to enlarge or reduce to a specific size or percentage, use the Width and Height fields or X scale percentage and Y scale percentage information in the Control or Transform palette. Using the chain link button to enlarge or reduce proportionally becomes very important here, because entering unequal percentages or disproportionate measurements can skew your image and distort its appearance (see Figure 28.9).

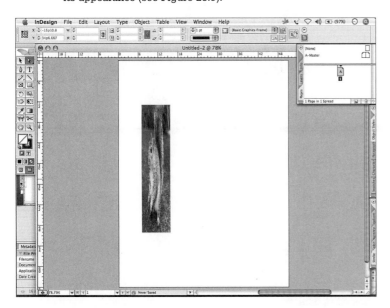

Figure 28.9
Always resize images proportionally or they will be distorted on the page.

And always remember to be careful when you enlarge graphics. Watch the Effective ppi number in the Info palette to make sure you're not blowing the resolution of your image.

FITTING GRAPHICS

InDesign gives you several options for more automatic graphics fitting. To see fitting options, select either the frame or the contents and then choose Object, Fitting. You can also right-click (Windows users) or Control-click (Mac users) to bring up a context menu and select Fitting, or use the Fitting buttons on the Control palette (see Figure 28.10). You then have five options:

- **Fit Content to Frame** sizes the content to fit the frame exactly. This can result in distorted images if the frame and the contents are not of proportional sizes.

- **Fit Frame to Content** automatically resizes the frame to fit the graphic content exactly. The entire graphic is displayed.

- **Center Content** automatically centers the content in the frame, regardless of fit. That is, neither element changes size; the content and the frame are just centered with each other.

- **Fit Content Proportionally** looks for the first proportional fit, either height or width, and sizes the content to that point. In this case, the frame might still be larger than the content and have to be resized.

28

■ **Fill Frame Proportionally** resizes the graphic to fill the frame. In this case, the content might still be larger than the frame and may need to be repositioned within the frame.

Figure 28.10
Use InDesign's Fitting options to resize graphics or frames quickly.

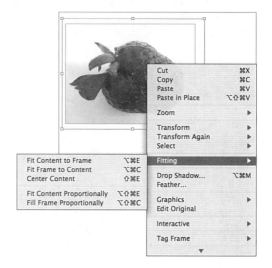

USING THE LINKS PALETTE

The Links palette helps you keep track of the graphics that are placed within your document. Graphics that are copied and pasted into InDesign are not listed in the Links palette, so with those graphics you do not have any of the control that the Links palette affords.

To show the Links palette, choose Window, Links. Your placed graphics are listed (see Figure 28.11).

Figure 28.11
The Links palette shows all graphics that have been imported into your document.

Double-click on a linked filename to see more information, including file size, modification dates, color space, file type, and the path to that file, as well as Version Cue and layer information if appropriate. You can use the Link Information dialog to update or replace with another image by clicking the Relink button and browsing for the new or updated file.

Use the Prev and Next buttons in the Link Information dialog to move from image to image in the Links palette and click Done to close the dialog.

There are also many options in the Links palette menu when you select a specific listed graphic:

You may also see references in the Links palette to text files or spreadsheets you've placed in your document. This is an option in InDesign's Preferences window, found at Edit, Preferences, Type, under the Links category. See the "Placing Text" section in Chapter 27, "Working with Type in InDesign," for more information on this option.

- **Relink** enables you to search for the image again or browse to another image.

- **Go to Link** takes you to the spot in the document where that file was placed and selects the graphic on the page.

- **Edit Original** opens the original placed file in its native application.

- **Update Link** is available when a link has been modified (the link name will have a yellow question mark icon next to it). Choosing this option replaces the graphic with the new version.

- **Copy Links To** enables you to specify a place to copy all linked files. When you choose this option, the link is actually connected to the file in the new location, not the original location.

- **Save Link Version** enables you to save the current version of the Version Cue graphic.

- **Versions** gives you access to the various saved versions of the graphic.

- **Alternates** gives you access to the various alternates you may have saved in Version Cue.

- **Purchase This Image** is available for Adobe Stock Photos comps when you are ready to buy the image.

- **Reveal in Explorer** (Windows) or **Reveal in Finder** (Mac) and **Reveal in Bridge** show the graphic file in the chosen program.

- **Unlink** breaks the document link. If you break a link, you are not warned about links that have moved or changed when you open the document. This may be helpful if you are sharing your document with someone who does not have access to your links; breaking the links can help avoid warning dialogs.

- **Link File Info** shows the XMP File Information dialog for the selected graphic.

- **Link Information** shows the same file info you see if you double-click the graphic name in the Links palette.

- **Sort by Name** and **Sort by Page** enables you to see linked files easily in alphabetical or page order; **Sort by Status** floats any missing or modified links to the top of the palette.

- **Small Palette Rows** changes the size of the linked file name display.

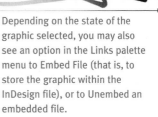

Depending on the state of the graphic selected, you may also see an option in the Links palette menu to Embed File (that is, to store the graphic within the InDesign file), or to Unembed an embedded file.

There are several indicators InDesign uses in the Links palette to warn or inform you of issues with your graphic. Various icons show embedded graphics (a square and triangle icon), modified links (a yellow caution triangle), missing links (a question mark), whether a layer in the graphic has been hidden, or whether the graphic used is an Adobe Stock Photos comp (see Figure 28.12).

The four buttons at the bottom of the palette enable you to Relink, Go To Link, Update Link, or Edit Original.

28

Figure 28.12
Icons alongside the placed images listed in the Links palette show various information about those files.

Relinking

If a graphic has become unlinked because either its location or the location of the original file is different, there are some simple options for relinking the file. Click the missing link icon in the Links palette and select Relink from the palette menu or click the Relink button at the bottom of the Links palette. Either option takes you to the folder where the linked graphic was stored when it was placed.

You can also double-click on the link name in the Links palette to see the specific path from which the file was placed and click the Relink button in the Link Information dialog (see Figure 28.13).

Relinking a file preserves any changes that were made to it in InDesign. For example, if you resized and then rotated the first linked graphic, the relinked file comes in scaled to the same size, with the same rotation degree applied.

Figure 28.13
The Link Information dialog shows the path to the graphic's original location.

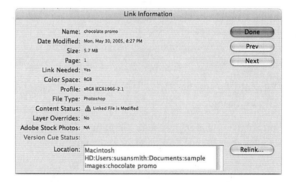

COPYING AND PASTING FROM ILLUSTRATOR

As mentioned previously, it is generally best to use the File, Place command to bring any graphic into InDesign. The program does, however, support copying graphics from Illustrator and pasting them into InDesign. There are some things you should be aware of, however, before you do this.

In Illustrator's File Handling and Clipboard Preferences window, make sure you have selected the AICB and Preserve Paths option. This option does not support transparencies in Illustrator, nor will you have access in InDesign to layers.

When the Illustrator graphic is pasted in InDesign, it comes in as a grouped object. You can choose Object, Ungroup to work with the individual points and parts and alter the image as you want.

28

WORKING WITH PLACED PDFS

Adobe Portable Document Format files can be placed in InDesign like any other type of text or graphic file. You cannot, however, edit PDFs after they have been placed, other than choosing the pages you want to place or toggling the visibility of layers within the PDF.

When you're ready to place your PDF, make sure you've selected the Show Import Options check box in the Place dialog. If you don't, you will place only the first page of the selected PDF.

In the Import Options dialog, make sure that the Show Preview option is selected. A dotted line shows how the PDF will be cropped when it's placed on the page. You can scroll through all pages in the view and choose to place the previewed page only. You can also choose to place all pages or a specific range of pages.

In the Options pop-up menu, choose your Crop option:

- **Bounding Box** crops to the smallest area that encloses everything on the page, including page marks.

- **Art** crops to a rectangle specified in the PDF as artwork.

- **Crop** places what is displayed in Acrobat.

- **Trim** places the final page as it is trimmed, if trim marks have been placed on the page.

- **Bleed** places a representation of where the page is trimmed if a bleed area has been set up.

- **Media** places the original PDF size on the InDesign page, including page marks.

Check the Transparent Background option if you want to place your PDF without a background; if you uncheck this option, a white background is placed with the file (see Figure 28.14).

The Layers tab enables you to toggle the visibility of layers that were created in your PDF. Click the eye icon to turn the layer visibility on and off.

The Update Link Options section refers to what happens if you update or relink to the PDF if it changes. If you choose to use the PDF's layer visibility, any changes in the PDF layers are reflected in the placed PDF. If you choose to keep layer visibility overrides, the choices you make here are preserved after the PDF is updated.

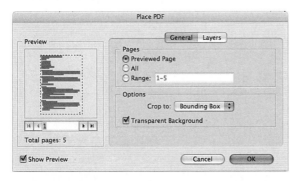

Figure 28.14
InDesign gives you multiple options for importing PDFs into your documents.

28

You can also select the placed PDF graphic on the page and then choose Object, Object Layer Options to work with the PDF's layers.

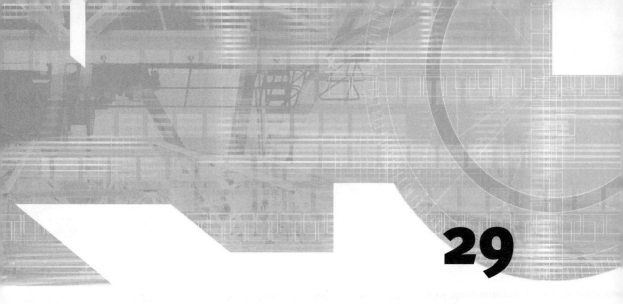

WORKING WITH COLOR IN INDESIGN

29

29

Color is one of the easiest ways to add more excitement and interest to your document. It is also one of the most misunderstood processes, and it can be one of the main causes of dissatisfaction with the final printed document.

This chapter gives a brief introduction to color and using color in InDesign. It is not, however, an exhaustive color resource. Check out the information in the other parts of this book for instructions on saving graphics and images with the proper color space for your document, as well as a description of the Creative Suite's color management system in Chapter 1, "Creative Suite 2 Basics," which enables you to more closely match colors throughout the different applications (see Figure 29.1).

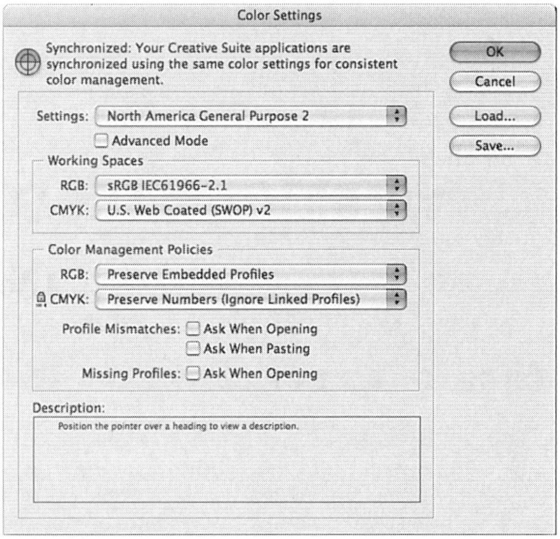

Figure 29.1
The Creative Suite enables you to create a color space that can be applied and used in every program in the suite.

UNDERSTANDING COLOR BASICS

Before you explore colors and the various ways to create and apply them in your InDesign document, it helps to have an understanding of exactly how color works, both when you print it and how it displays on your monitor. It's important to know the difference between the various color modes, like CMYK and RGB, and how selecting one type over another can help or hurt your project.

Color Printing

There are two main types of color used in commercial printing: spot color and process color. *Spot colors* are single-color inks. You may hear a printing project that uses spot color referred to as a "two-color job," with the two colors being black and the spot color (see Figure 29.2).

Process colors are created by mixing specific percentages of cyan, magenta, yellow, and black, the four ink colors used in color printing. You may hear this referred to as *CMYK*. The colors in printed photographs, for example, are duplicated based on how cyan, magenta, yellow, and black dots are laid down on a sheet of paper (see Figure 29.3).

29

Coffee of the Week

This week's blend was imported from Jamaica's Blue Mountain, one of the richest coffee areas of the world.

Figure 29.2
Use spot colors to add a single color to your document as an accent. In this example, our headline is printed in a coffee-brown, giving extra visual emphasis to the subject matter.

Figure 29.3
When cyan, magenta, yellow, and black inks are laid down on top of each other, the four colors combine to create full-color printing. This example displays the cyan, magenta, yellow, and black plates that are combined to create a four-color image.

Spot colors are usually used as accent colors, and spot color printing can often be less expensive than full-color printing, since you are printing with only two plates instead of four. (Note that new printing technologies and the use of specialty spot colors can make an exception to that rule.) Spot colors can also be used at the same time as process colors if you are trying to duplicate a specific shade that cannot be replicated with a CMYK mix, or if you are creating a special effect with the spot color, as with the use of a metallic ink.

If you are using a service bureau or printing company to print your documents, it's always a good idea to have a conversation about color before you send in your documents. They can show you specific samples of both four-color and spot color jobs they have printed and give you advice on preparing your documents for their specific output devices.

Color Display

Another thing to keep in mind when creating your documents is color display and how what you see on your screen matches up to the printed piece. If you are creating a document that will be viewed primarily on a computer monitor, such as a website or an e-book, you can feel confident that what you see is what your final viewer will see, give or take some variance between displays. If you are creating a document to be printed, however, what you see on your screen can be wildly different from the final printed piece.

The simple explanation is that your monitor displays color completely differently from how color is printed. As stated, the printing process uses CMYK to produce full-color documents. Your monitor displays documents and graphics with an RGB color setup, using red, green, and blue light (see Figure 29.4). The RGB color space's capability of displaying colors is greater than the CMYK's. Therefore, if you're trying to duplicate in print a specific printed color you see onscreen, you should either use a spot color or use a process color from a color library that you have picked from a swatch booklet, for example. Mixing your own process colors can work for you, but is often a chancy proposition because what you see on the screen might not be exactly what prints in your document.

Figure 29.4
This illustration shows the difference between how subtractive color (CMYK, on the left) and additive color (RGB, on the right) mixes and displays.

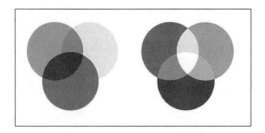

The final type of color you will run into in InDesign is Lab color. Like CMYK and RGB, Lab colors are displayed as mixes, although in Lab color the different hues are based on the brightness of the various components. You may run into Lab colors when you use colors from Pantone, Toyo, or other color libraries.

An option in InDesign's Preferences window enables you to choose how blacks are displayed in your document (see Figure 29.5). You might be wondering what that's all about. *Rich black* refers to the color created when red, green, and blue are set to zero. *Pure black* refers to the color created when the K setting in CMYK is set to 100%. When displayed onscreen, pure black looks more like a dark gray. Use the Appearance of Black pop-up menus to set which black you want to use onscreen and when printing.

Figure 29.5
Use InDesign's Preferences window to determine how pure black and rich black appear in your documents.

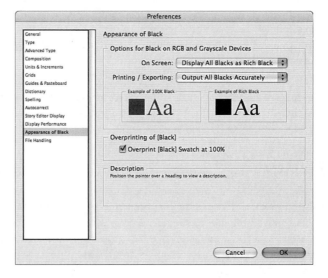

USING THE COLOR PALETTE

If you want to apply or mix colors on the fly, you can use the Color palette (choose Window, Color to display the palette). Before you start, use the palette menu to select the color space you want to work in: RGB, CMYK, or Lab. Select the Show Options menu command to see the color sliders on the Color palette (see Figure 29.6).

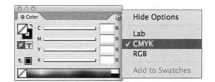

Figure 29.6
The Color palette menu should always be used to choose the type of color you're trying to create.

Notice the stroke and fill selector on the Color palette, as well as the buttons that specify formatting for either a container or type. Make the appropriate selections there based on where you want to apply the color (see Chapter 24, "Understanding the InDesign Interface and Tools," for more about setting fill and stroke colors).

To pick a color quickly, position your mouse over the color spectrum at the bottom of the palette and click. Click None to deselect any color. The color where you click will be sampled and applied to the selected item. It will also become the last-used color and will display in the Tools palette. If you select another page element and click the Apply Color button, the last-used color is the color that will be applied to the new element, and that color remains the last-used color until you use another color.

You can also select a color using the Color Picker. Double-click the fill or stroke indicator on either the Tools palette or the Color palette. The Color Picker opens (see Figure 29.7). You can pick your color in one of three ways:

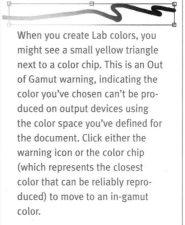

When you create Lab colors, you might see a small yellow triangle next to a color chip. This is an Out of Gamut warning, indicating the color you've chosen can't be produced on output devices using the color space you've defined for the document. Click either the warning icon or the color chip (which represents the closest color that can be reliably reproduced) to move to an in-gamut color.

- Click in the Color Picker display window. Crosshairs show the color you selected. Drag the crosshairs to change your selection.

- Drag the triangles on the vertical color slider to the right of the display window and click in the color slider or the display window to select a color.

- Enter specific percentages of RGB, Lab, or CMYK.

If you want to create a swatch of this color—more on the Swatches palette later—click the Add CMYK Swatch, Add Lab Swatch, or Add RGB Swatch button (the button changes names based on the current document's specified color space). Click OK to exit the Color Picker and apply the color to the selected item.

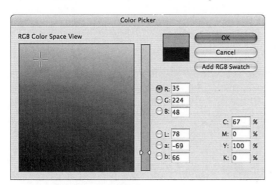

Figure 29.7
The Color Picker enables you to choose a color from the display window or enter percentages to mix a color with known values.

After selecting your color type from the Color palette menu, you can also use the sliders or entry fields to mix colors. If you want a swatch of the color you created, select Add to Swatches from the Color palette menu.

USING THE SWATCHES PALETTE

A more reliable and consistent way of choosing and creating colors in your document is the Swatches palette (choose Window, Swatches to display this palette). You can use this palette to pick swatches from various color libraries, as well as to mix your own colors (see Figure 29.8). The most convenient thing about it is that the swatches are saved with the document, so they can be used again and again for reliable color duplication.

Figure 29.8
The Swatches palette holds the colors you create so they can be applied to numerous objects in the document without having to be mixed on the fly.

Like the Color palette and the Tools palette, the Swatches palette has a fill and stroke selector, located at the top of the palette, as well as buttons to apply your selection to either the container or text. Select your page element, make sure you made the proper choice for fill, stroke, container or text, and then click a swatch to apply the color to your selected item.

The default Swatches palette contains 100% cyan, magenta, and yellow, as well as CMYK mixes of red, green, and blue. If you want to get rid of these colors, you can drag them to the trash icon at the bottom of the palette or select a color and then choose Delete Swatch from the Swatches palette menu. If you use the color you're deleting on a page object, InDesign asks whether you want to replace the color with a defined swatch—pick it from the pop-up menu—or use it as an unnamed color. The color remains applied to the page element, but it no longer appears in the Swatches palette.

The Swatches for None, Black, and Registration always appear in the palette and cannot be deleted or edited. The Paper swatch cannot be deleted, but it can be changed to help you design for printing on a colored paper stock. To change the color of the Paper swatch, follow these steps:

1. Double-click on Paper in the Swatches palette. The Swatch Option dialog opens (see Figure 29.9).

2. You cannot change the name of the swatch, but you can change its appearance. Use the Color Mode pop-up menu to select the color mode in which you want to work (RGB, CMYK, and Lab are your only selections).

3. Use the sliders and/or entry boxes to create a color that simulates the color of paper you will be printing on. Click OK.

The fill of the page in your document will change to the paper color.

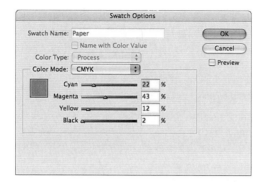

Figure 29.9
Change the values of your Paper swatch to help you see how your design will print on a colored paper stock.

29

If you are creating color separations or printing to a composite printer, the colors used to create the Paper swatch are not included. It is simply a tool to help make working on your design as realistic as possible. For that reason, you should never use the Paper swatch to apply a color to an object that you want to be the same color as the page itself; apply None instead for a completely transparent effect.

To create a color and add it to the Swatches palette, select New Color Swatch from the Swatches palette menu; the New Color Swatch dialog opens (see Figure 29.10). Follow these steps:

1. By default, the swatch is named with the percentages used to create the color. If you want to create a name for the color, uncheck the Name with Color Value box and enter your color name.

2. In the Color Type pop-up menu, select Spot or Process, depending on how you plan to print the current document.

3. In the Color Mode pop-up menu, select RGB, CMYK, or Lab. (You explore the list of color libraries in the next section.)

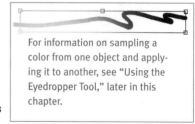

For information on sampling a color from one object and applying it to another, see "Using the Eyedropper Tool," later in this chapter.

4. Use the sliders or entry boxes to specify the mix of colors that will create your swatch.

5. Click Add to put the defined swatch into the palette and continue creating color swatches or click OK to exit the New Color Swatch dialog.

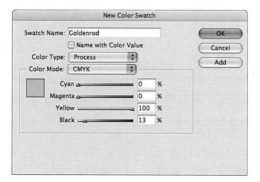

Figure 29.10
Create specific swatches to add to your Swatches palette.

Colors you create have various icons in the Swatches palette to indicate color type and color mode. A four-color swatch displays as a square with four colors; an RGB swatch displays as a square with red, green, and blue stripes; and a LAB swatch displays as a square with six colors. Spot colors are identified with a circle inside a square; process colors are identified with a tinted gray square. Mixed inks are displayed with two droplets.

As on the Color palette and Tools palette, the Swatches palette has a stroke and fill indicator that enables you to select where you want to apply a color and to apply it to either a container or type. Select the page element, choose how you want to apply the swatch, and then click the swatch to apply it to the page element.

> If you import PDF or EPS files into your InDesign document that use spot colors, those colors are added to your Swatches palette. The same is true for the spot color channels in imported Photoshop or TIFF files. These swatches can be applied to other items in the document, but they can't be edited, and they can't be deleted unless the imported graphic is deleted.

Working with Tints

After a color swatch is defined, you can use it to create a *tint* of that color. For one-time use, apply a swatch to a page element and then use the Tint slider or entry box on the Swatches palette to choose the percentage of color you want to apply (see Figure 29.11).

Figure 29.11
A pop-up menu at the top of the Swatches palette enables you to create tints of any color.

To create a swatch of a particular tint, select the swatch for which you want to create the tint. Select New Tint Swatch from the Swatches palette menu and use the Tint slider at the bottom of the dialog to specify the percentage of color. Click OK to add the swatch to the palette, or if you want to create additional tints of that color, click the Add button, continue creating and adding swatches, and then click Done.

Working with Mixed Inks

Because the gamut of colors that can be produced by mixing CMYK inks is limited, there may be times when you need to mix one or more spot colors, or mix spot colors with CMYK mixes to create a specific shade. This is referred to as a *mixed ink*.

To create a mixed ink, you must first add a spot color to your Swatches palette. If you want to use more than one spot color in your mixed ink, make sure all spot colors are in the Swatches palette as well. Then, select New Mixed Ink from the palette menu.

Choose to add any of the four-process colors and any defined spot color by clicking in the box to the left of the color name. Use the slider to define the percentage of that color you want to add to your mixed ink. Click Add to add the color and continue creating mixed inks, or click OK to finish.

You can also create groups of mixed ink swatches that are almost like *increments* of colors or different tints of colors that are mixed together:

1. Select New Mixed Ink Group from the Swatches palette menu to display the New Mixed Ink Group dialog (see Figure 29.12). Name your group in the dialog.

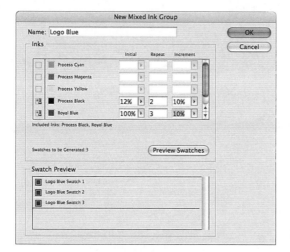

Figure 29.12
Mixed ink groups enable you to create various tints of colors that you have created from mixing spot and process colors.

2. Click in the box to the right of the color name to mark a color you want to add to your group.

3. Enter the percentage of the color(s) you want to start by adding to the mixed ink under the Initial column, for example, 12% process black and 100% Royal Blue.

4. Indicate the number of times you want to add an increment to that color to increase the number of colors in your group, for example, two increments of black and three increments of blue.

5. Select the percentage of each increment, for example 10%.

6. The dialog indicates the number of swatches that will be added to your group (in this example, it is 3 increments because we're adding three increments of Royal Blue). Click the Preview Swatches button to see the swatches you are adding.

7. Click OK to finish your group and add it to the Swatches palette.

The Load Swatches menu command brings in *all* swatches from another document. You can also pick and choose the swatches you want to import; select New Color Swatch and choose Other Library from the Color Mode pop-up menu. Browse to the InDesign document that contains the swatches you want to add and click Open. Click in the dialog on a color swatch and click Add. Add all the colors you want and then click Done.

The Swatches palette menu offers several other options, as shown in Figure 29.13:

- Select **Duplicate Swatch** from the palette menu to create a duplicate copy of the selected swatch.

29

29

Figure 29.13
Numerous options in the Swatches palette menu enable you to define and work with your colors.

- Choose **Load Swatches** to bring swatches from another InDesign document into this document. Browse to your file and click Open, and the swatches are added.

- To export the swatches in this document for use in another InDesign document—as well as any Photoshop, Illustrator, or GoLive file—select **Save Swatches for Exchange** from the Swatches palette menu. Specify a location for the .ase file and click Save. You can then load that file into the Swatches palette of another document.

- If you have numerous extra swatches in your document, you can choose **Select All Unused** in the Swatches palette menu to highlight those colors so you can drag them to the trash to delete them.

- If you have applied color to an item without defining a swatch, select **Add Unnamed Colors** from the palette menu to add that color to the Swatches palette.

- Select **Swatch Options** to change the name, mix, or color type of a particular swatch.

- **Name, Small Name, Small Swatch** and **Large Swatch** change the display of the Swatches palette.

- The **Ink Manager** option is generally used by service providers in preparing documents for output. See the Adobe Help Center for more information about this function.

Another way to swap colors between InDesign documents is to drag items or swatches, or copy and paste items from one document to another. To swap with page elements, copy a page element (that has the color you want applied to it) from one document to another, and the color will be added to the Swatches palette. You can also drag the element from one document and drop it into another. Or, drag a swatch from one document's Swatch palette into the other document. The swatch will not be applied to any element, but will appear in the Swatches palette.

USING COLOR LIBRARIES

The most reliable way to specify color for your document is through a color library. Color libraries are based on swatch booklets, which give you a more accurate representation of how your color will appear as ink on paper, as opposed to how it appears on your computer screen. The color library you choose to use can depend on several things, including your corporate standards, the type of paper you're printing on, the color libraries supported by your prepress provider, even the country you're printing in.

Below is a list of the color libraries that come preloaded with InDesign and what they contain. You can access these libraries by selecting New Color Swatch from the Swatches palette menu (see Figure 29.14):

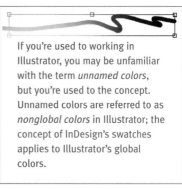

If you're used to working in Illustrator, you may be unfamiliar with the term *unnamed colors*, but you're used to the concept. Unnamed colors are referred to as *nonglobal colors* in Illustrator; the concept of InDesign's swatches applies to Illustrator's global colors.

Figure 29.14
Choose a swatch from a specific color library in the New Color Swatch dialog to add to your Swatches palette.

- **DIC Color:** 1280 CMYK spot colors from Dainippon Ink & Chemicals, Inc.

- **Focoltone:** 763 CMYK colors that help you get predictable results when you overprint colors or layer inks on top of each other to help prevent misregistration in printing.

- **HKS:** A color library commonly used in Europe.

- **PANTONE:** Probably the most commonly used color system in the world. Pantone offers more than 1000 spot colors, as well as thousands of specific process color combinations. Best of all, Pantone swatch booklets are printed on different types of paper, giving you a much better way to visualize how your color will print based on the paper you're using.

29

- **System (Windows)** and **System (Macintosh):** Contains the 256 RGB colors found in the 8-bit palette of the Windows and Mac operating systems, respectively.

- **Toyo Color Finder:** With more than 1000 colors, this library is most commonly used in Japan.

- **Trumatch:** An accurate CMYK color-matching system that contains more than 2000 colors.

- **Web**: The 216 RGB colors used by web browsers to display 8-bit images. The items you create with these colors display the same on either Mac or Windows systems.

There is also a selection for **Other Library**. Earlier you learned that this option can be used to browse for other InDesign documents from which you'd like to import colors, but you can also use it if you have a color library that is not included with InDesign. Simply browse to the library, select it, and click Open.

After your color library is loaded, scroll through the available swatches. Click to select swatches you want to add to the Swatches palette; hold down the Ctrl key (Windows users) or ⌘ key (Mac users) to select more than one color. Holding down the Shift key on either platform enables you to select a range of contiguous swatches. Click the Add button and continue browsing for colors, or click OK to add the selected colors only.

WORKING WITH GRADIENTS AND GRADIENT SWATCHES

A color effect that is easy to create in InDesign is a *gradient*—two or more colors that gradually blend from one to the next. You can create gradients using anywhere from one color fading into white to 256 colors, although restraint is a good thing. Nothing screams "Look at me, I'm just learning to use InDesign!" like the overuse of gradients. Gradients can be applied to text, shapes or any other page elements.

First, let's talk about how to apply gradients. The default gradient when you first start with InDesign is a basic white-to-black gradient. To apply a gradient, create the page element you want to apply it to and make sure the fill or stroke is properly selected in the Tools palette. Click to select the Gradient tool and drag it across the selected page object in the direction you want the gradient to flow. Anytime you want to adjust your gradient by changing direction or changing the point at which it starts and/or ends, click with the Gradient tool to select the point at which it should start, and release the mouse button at the point where you want it to end (see Figure 29.15).

To apply gradients across multiple objects instead of just one, make sure all the elements are selected and then drag across the multiple selection.

You can also apply gradients to text. Make sure the Formatting Affects Text option is selected in the Tools palette when you drag the Gradient tool across your text frame, by clicking the small T icon under the fill and stroke controls. If you want to apply the gradient to only certain characters, you can highlight them with the Type tool and drag the Gradient tool across your selection.

Gradient tool

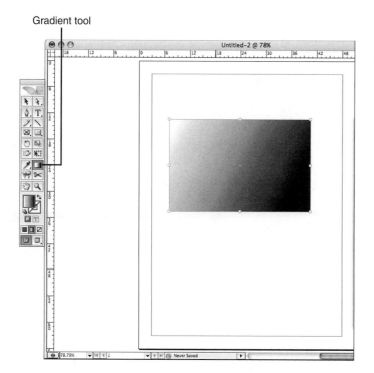

Figure 29.15
You can quickly change the angle and direction of a gradient by dragging across your page element with the Gradient tool.

29

To get more creative, open the Gradient palette (select Window, Gradient) (see Figure 29.16). Make sure all options in the palette are showing by selecting Show Options from the palette menu. Use the Type pop-up menu to choose between a linear gradient (which flows across the object) and a radial gradient (which starts in the center and extends outward).

Figure 29.16
The Gradient palette gives you more choices for setting specific gradient options

To change the direction of your gradient, click the Reverse button. The colors switch.

Colors in the gradient are controlled by the squares, called *color stops*, below the gradient ramp. If you click the left color stop in its default location, you see 0% in the Location field. Enter another percentage and tab out of the field to move the color stop to a specific point. The same options apply to the other color stops on the gradient. The right color stop is located by default at 100%. You can also drag the stops to various locations on the gradient ramp.

If you have created a linear gradient, you can also enter a specific degree in the Angle field to change the angle to which it flows. Slide the diamond at the top of the gradient ramp to change the midpoint of the gradient between the two colors represented by the stops on either side of it.

Now that you have a basic overview of how gradients work, let's look at two ways of creating gradients: on the fly with the Color palette or with defined colors in the Swatches palette.

To create a gradient using the Color palette:

1. Create the page element to which you want to apply the gradient and select it.

2. Open both your Color and Gradient palettes (choose Window, Color and Window, Gradient to display these palettes). If the two palettes are in the same space, click on the tab of one and drag it away from the other palette (see Figure 29.17).

3. To apply a gradient, either use the Gradient tool to drag across your page element or select the page element and click on the Apply Gradient button at the bottom of the Tools palette.

4. To change the colors of your gradient, click on one of the color stops below the gradient ramp on the Gradient palette.

5. Make sure you have the proper color mode selected in the Color palette menu.

> When gradients are applied to only certain characters in a text frame, only the portion of the gradient that corresponds to that area of the text frame is applied. That is, applying a white-to-black gradient to only half of the type in a text frame does not apply the entire white-to-black range to that text; it applies only the white-to-halfway-to-black range. The same idea is at work when you apply a gradient to text that does not extend fully across a frame. You see only the portion of the gradient that is the same size as the text.

6. Either use the sliders and entry boxes on the Color palette to mix a specific color or click in the color spectrum at the bottom of the Color palette. The color you create or sample will be applied to the selected color stop.

Figure 29.17
Create colors in the Color palette and apply them to the gradient color stops in the Gradient palette.

7. Repeat steps 4–6 to apply a different color to the other color stop.

8. To apply a gradient of more than two colors, add color stops to the gradient bar by clicking on it. Follow steps 4–6 to apply a color to each color stop. To delete a color stop, drag it away from the gradient ramp.

Remember, you can also slide the color stops around on the gradient ramp for different effects; move the diamond at the top of the gradient ramp to vary the angle at which the gradient is applied.

If you decide you want to add this gradient to your Swatches palette, make sure the object you apply the gradient to is selected and then choose New Gradient Swatch from the Swatches palette menu. Name the swatch and click OK.

To create a gradient from a predefined color (using the Swatches palette), you must first add the colors you want to use to create the gradient to the Swatches palette. Follow the instructions earlier in this chapter to add swatches to the Swatches palette.

To create a gradient:

1. Select New Gradient Swatch from the Swatches palette menu.

2. In the New Gradient Swatch dialog, you may want to name your gradient (see Figure 29.18). Select either Linear or Radial as the gradient type.

3. Click on one of the color stops on the gradient ramp.

4. In the Stop Color pop-up menu, select Swatches.

5. The colors in the Swatches palette become available in the New Gradient Swatch dialog. Select the color you want to use for that stop.

6. Continue adding colors to your gradient by clicking on the stops and then selecting the color you want to use from the Swatches list.

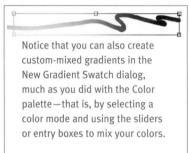

Notice that you can also create custom-mixed gradients in the New Gradient Swatch dialog, much as you did with the Color palette—that is, by selecting a color mode and using the sliders or entry boxes to mix your colors.

7. Remember that you can add stops to your gradient by clicking at the bottom of the gradient ramp or delete stops by dragging them away from the gradient ramp. You can also change the angle of the gradient by dragging the diamond(s) on top of the gradient ramp.

8. When your gradient looks the way you want, click OK. A gradient swatch will be created in your Swatches palette.

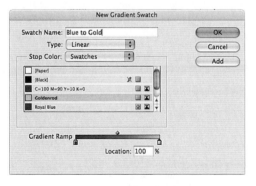

Figure 29.18
Create defined gradients with existing color swatches for more control over the gradient's appearance.

Using the Swatches palette to create a gradient is convenient because the swatch is then available for use throughout your document, or for importing into other documents.

29

USING THE EYEDROPPER TOOL

Consistent color can create eye-catching designs. Think of layouts you've seen, for example, that contained text that matched a color used in the dominant photo of the page. InDesign's Eyedropper tool enables you to sample color from a photo or graphic and apply it to any other object on your page (see Figure 29.19).

Figure 29.19
For color consistency, use the Eyedropper tool to sample and apply colors that already exist in your document.

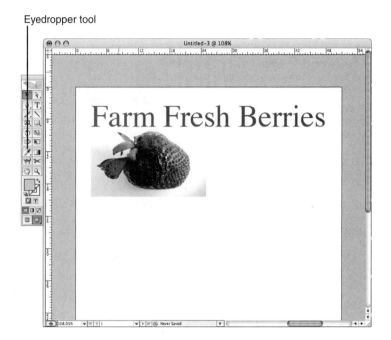

Eyedropper tool

After the graphic containing the color you want to sample is placed on the page, select the Eyedropper tool and click on the color you want to match. The Eyedropper becomes loaded with the color; you'll know this because it switches directions and is filled with black.

To apply the sampled color to a page object, click on it with the Eyedropper tool. To apply the sampled color to type, hold the Eyedropper over the text until an I-beam appears next to the tool. Drag the I-beam over the text to apply the color.

The Eyedropper stays loaded with the color until you sample another color or switch tools.

To make a sampled color into a swatch, select Add Unnamed Colors from the Swatches palette menu. Any color(s) that were not created through the New Color Swatch dialog are added to the Swatches palette and named with the percentage of colors that comprise them.

CREATING AND MODIFYING
PATHS IN INDESIGN

InDesign makes great use of tools and other options to create vector graphics. Before we get into detail about those options, it's helpful to understand the two types of graphic information you can display on your page. A *vector graphic* is any object on the page created with lines and curves that does not depend on resolution to display correctly. If you draw a shape or path with the Pen tool, that's an example of a vector graphic. No matter how much you enlarge that shape or path, it will still print or display correctly on your page (see Figure 30.1).

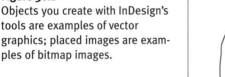

Figure 30.1
Objects you create with InDesign's tools are examples of vector graphics; placed images are examples of bitmap images.

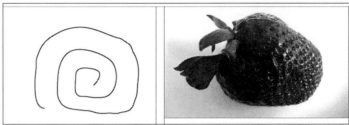

The other type of graphic is a bitmap image. *Bitmap images* are resolution dependent; you cannot enlarge them freely as you can vector objects, because their appearance depends on a fixed number of pixels. An example of a bitmap image is a digital image you place on the page. There's a certain point at which enlarging the image will cause it to lose so much resolution it becomes unusable.

Let's take a look at some of the options InDesign gives you for working with vector objects.

WORKING WITH OBJECTS

In Chapter 26, "Working with Objects in InDesign," you explored the different ways to create InDesign page objects. This section serves as a brief review of some of that information, with special attention paid to paths and how to work with them.

Generalities

Following are some general pieces of information to remember about selecting page objects:

- No matter what the shape, you can select it with either the Selection tool or the Direct Selection tool (see Figure 30.2).

- When you select an object with the Selection tool, you see the eight handles that make up the bounding box. The bounding box enables you to see the outside edges of any item quickly.

- When you select an object with the Direct Selection tool, you see its *anchor points*. The anchor points control the shape of the object. If you move any of the anchor points of an object, you can change the shape of the object itself.

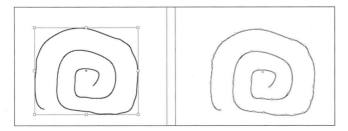

Figure 30.2
Depending on which tool you use to select an object, you will either see the bounding box (left) or anchor points (right).

Anchor Points

Following are some things to know about anchor points:

- Every object that you create has anchor points.

- The more anchor points that are included along a path, the more complicated that object is, and the longer it will take to print and display.

- Tools under the Pen tool give you options to add or delete anchor points from a path. Adding anchor points can give you more control over the path and how it is drawn.

- There are two types of anchor points: *corner points,* where a line abruptly changes direction, and *smooth points,* which connect curves.

Curves

Following is important information about creating and working with curves:

- The Pen tool is used to create a type of curve referred to as a *Bézier curve* (see Figure 30.3).

- When a curve is created, in addition to the anchor points at either end of the path, you also see direction lines.

- The direction lines appear at the anchor points where the curves were created and can be dragged from either end to change the shape of the curve. Drag a direction line close to the path to create a sharper curve. Drag the direction line away from the path to create a rounder curve.

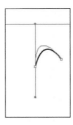

Figure 30.3
Direction lines, which appear on curved paths drawn with the Pen tool, give you the ability to change the shape of the curve.

- If you have drawn straight segments with the Pen tool, you can use the Convert Direction Point tool to click on a corner point and change it into a curve, or vice versa.

WORKING WITH COMPOUND PATHS

A *compound path* is the shape created when two or more objects are selected to create one continuous object. The most common reason to create a compound path is when you want to punch one shape out of another shape it is overlapping (see Figure 30.4). To create a compound path, select the objects with which you want to create the path and then choose Object, Compound Paths, Make.

Figure 30.4
An example of a compound path.

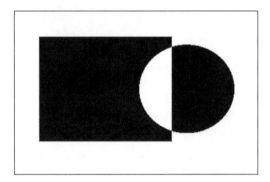

In this example, a circle overlaps a rectangle. When you select the two shapes and choose Object, Compound Paths, Make, the resulting shape (the path) is the circle punched out of the rectangle shape. The areas where the objects overlapped create a hole. You can now place text or an image or apply a stroke and fill to the two overlapping shapes (the compound path).

If we want to alter the compound path, we can select it with the Direct Selection tool and move anchor points to create whatever shape we want.

To fill in the hole that was left in the overlapping area, select the subpath with the Direct Selection tool and choose Object, Paths, Reverse Path. In the case of this example, you click with the Direct Selection tool on the circle. This selects the shape as well as the hole that is created when you combine these objects into a compound path. When you choose Object, Paths, Reverse Path, the hole fills in with black, but the rectangle and circle are still combined into one shape.

> Don't be confused by the use of the word *path*. Although compound paths can be created by lines, which we normally think of as paths, they are also created by overlapping shapes. The resulting shape, which combines the selected objects into a single shape that takes on the fill and stroke characteristics of the object that is furthest back, is a compound path.

Even though compound paths are most often created with overlapping paths, you can create a compound path with multiple non-overlapping shapes. Again, you can place text or an image, or apply a stroke and fill to the compound path.

To *release* a compound path (that is, to turn the elements used to create the compound path back into separate, editable objects), select the item and choose Object, Compound Paths, Release.

A few notes about releasing compound paths:

- If you've placed an image in the compound path you created, when you release it the image will snap to the first object in the group, and the other object(s) will be empty frames.

- If you alter the fill and stroke of the objects when they are grouped as a compound path, all items will retain those fill and stroke characteristics when the path is released.

- If you have placed text in the compound path, you cannot release it.

USING THE PATHFINDER PALETTE

After you draw a shape on your page, no matter what tool you use, you have a vector object that you can alter. The Pathfinder palette is one source for altering those objects.

The Pathfinder palette (choose Window, Object & Layout, Pathfinder to display the palette) has two main areas: the Pathfinder options at the top of the palette and the Convert Shape options at the bottom of the palette (see Figure 30.5).

Figure 30.5
Pathfinder options in the Pathfinder palette.

Pathfinder Options

There are five buttons at the top of the Pathfinder palette that can be used to combine paths; Figure 30.6 shows the results of combining a black rectangle and a black circle with the following five path options:

- **Add:** This option combines the selected paths. It does not create a compound path because it does not punch out the overlapping areas; rather, it puts them together.

- **Subtract:** This option cuts the top object(s) out of the bottom object. If the top object completely overlaps the bottom object, it creates a hole in the bottom object.

- **Intersect:** This option cuts out everything except the area where the two objects overlap. If a fill and stroke are applied, the resulting object, which may be a compound path or a compound shape, will have the characteristics of the top object.

- **Exclude Overlap:** This is a traditional compound path as described previously: two or more objects are combined into one and any overlap is punched out of the resulting object.

- **Minus Back:** This is the opposite of subtract; it cuts the bottom objects out of the top object. The resulting object may be a compound path or a compound shape.

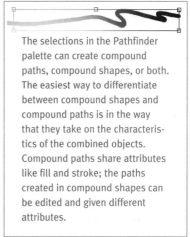

The selections in the Pathfinder palette can create compound paths, compound shapes, or both. The easiest way to differentiate between compound shapes and compound paths is in the way that they take on the characteristics of the combined objects. Compound paths share attributes like fill and stroke; the paths created in compound shapes can be edited and given different attributes.

30

Figure 30.6
The circle and square combination from above, altered with the Pathfinder palette, using the Add, Subtract, Intersect, Exclude Overlap, and Minus Back commands.

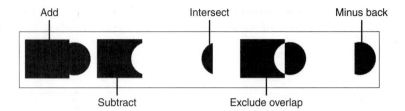

Add   Intersect   Minus back

Subtract   Exclude overlap

Convert Shape Options

The bottom portion of the Pathfinder palette has one-button access to shape-changing features. No matter what type of shape is selected, press the buttons on the Pathfinder palette to change it into one of the following shapes:

- Rectangle

- Rectangle with Rounded Corners

- Beveled Rectangle

- Inverse Rounded Rectangle

- Ellipse

- Triangle

- Polygon

- Diagonal Line

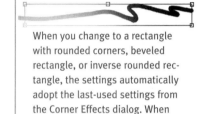

When you change to a rectangle with rounded corners, beveled rectangle, or inverse rounded rectangle, the settings automatically adopt the last-used settings from the Corner Effects dialog. When you change to a polygon, the settings automatically default to those of the last-drawn polygon.

- Orthogonal Line (one that is perfectly horizontal or vertical; the length of the orthogonal line can be changed, but not the angle)

The last three buttons in the Pathfinder palette deal with object paths:

- **Open Path** opens the path of a selected closed object. After you click Open Path, use the Direct Selection tool to drag an anchor point and open the object. You can also select the page element and choose Object, Paths, Open Path to achieve the same effect.

- **Close Path** closes the path of a selected open object, for example, a path drawn with the Pencil or Pen tool that has not been closed. Again, you can select the path and choose Object, Paths, Close Path as well.

- **Reverse Path** fills a hole created by a compound path when the associated subpath is selected, for example, a compound path that cuts one circle out of another, resulting in a tire shape. If you select the object with the Direct Selection tool, reversing the path fills the hole in the center, but the paths are still combined.

CREATING OUTLINES

The Create Outlines command takes text and converts the outlines of each individual letter shape to a path. Essentially, this command turns a letter form into a closed path that you can then fill, drag to edit the shape of, or treat as a container. This can be useful if you want to place an image inside the text, place other text inside a letter shape, or alter the paths of individual letters to create a special effect of custom letter shapes.

To create path outlines, select your text using the Type tool to highlight it, or select the text frame itself. Choose Type, Create Outlines.

Your text will look the same, but the in port and out port have disappeared from the bounding box of the resulting frame. If you select the text with the Direct Selection tool, you see anchor points around each letter (see Figure 30.7). Your text has ceased to exist as type and has been converted to paths—a phrase that might sound familiar to you if you've ever worked with the Illustrator or Freehand application. Converting to paths takes away all text characteristics, meaning you cannot edit the type you've converted (you can't change or add letters). So make sure you're happy with your spelling and font choices before you create outlines, or you'll have to start the process over by retyping your text and converting it to outlines again.

Figure 30.7
Outline text with an image and text placed inside. Notice the anchor points on the individual letters, which can be used to alter the shapes of those letters.

You can use any of the appropriate tools to alter the anchor points and paths created by the Create Outlines command:

- The Direct Selection tool moves anchor points and changes the shape of the path.
- The Add and Delete Anchor Point tools do just that.
- The Convert Direction Point tool changes the characteristics of corner and smooth points.
- The Smooth tool deletes anchor points to simplify the path.
- The Erase tool erases anchor points.

PLACING IMAGES AND TEXT IN PATHS

As mentioned previously, any closed path can be used as a container for an image, type (text), or a stroke and fill. This includes paths like those you can create with text following the instructions in the earlier section "Creating Outlines."

To place an item in a path, choose File, Place. In the Place dialog, browse to your image and click Open. If your path was selected before you choose File, Place, the item will automatically be placed in the path. If a path was not selected, position the mouse over the closed path. The lines around the loaded graphic or loaded text cursor will curve, indicating your item will be placed in the path. Click to place.

If you place text, you may need to adjust the size, font, tracking, kerning, or leading to help its appearance within the path. As long as the path's shape is open without numerous twists and turns, your text's appearance should be fine. If you have a complicated path, however, such as the paths that can be created when you use the Create Outlines command, it may become necessary to do more adjusting to your text.

If you place images, use the Direct Selection tool to select them for resizing or cropping. Reposition the image within the path using the Position tool. Remember to click and hold for a moment before you attempt to move the image so you can see how it will appear within the frame.

To make any changes to the appearance of the text you have placed inside a path, just use the Type tool along with the Control palette, or Character and Paragraph palettes to adjust font, size, alignment, kerning, and so on. If you need to make changes to the copy itself, the easiest way is to open the Story Editor by clicking in the text with your Type tool and then choosing Edit, Edit in Story Editor. You will get a good look at your text in the Story Editor window, which is helpful if the text on your page is very small, or the shape it is placed in is complicated.

A reminder about using the Scissors tool to split frames with text and image placed in them: First, you cannot split the path of a text frame using the Scissors tool. If you split a path containing a graphic, a copy of the graphic stays with each resulting frame. Simply delete any graphic you do not want to stay there

31

EXPORTING, SAVING, AND PRINTING WITH INDESIGN

Despite the many web-based features Adobe has added to InDesign in the last few versions, it is still above all else, a page layout program. Your ability to deal with long documents and create multiple-page printable files using InDesign makes it perfect for publication design. Because there is so much integration between the various applications in the Creative Suite, creating PDFs from your documents makes it easier for you to ensure that everything prints as you intend it.

And if you're not creating PDFs? InDesign's preflight and package services make it easier to gather your files for remote printing or publishing.

Why PDF?

Later in this book, you get an introduction to Adobe Acrobat and its capabilities. Acrobat is the default program for creating and reading PDFs. The benefits of PDF are numerous, but its greatest strength is that a PDF naturally contains all the items you need to print or view a document remotely. That is, if you send a correctly prepared PDF to your printer or service bureau, you do not have to send any fonts, graphics, or linked images, because those items are all embedded in the PDF file. What you see onscreen should look essentially the same as what comes out when ink is put on paper.

Sounds easy, right? It can be, but there are a couple of things to keep in mind when you create a PDF, especially if it is to be output. First, because all the peripheral files are embedded in the PDF, you still need to know where everything is. If you have a lot of problems losing links or not sending the correct fonts with your job, you might still have problems when creating PDFs. It's still important to be organized.

The other thing to be aware of is how the PDF fits into your commercial printer's workflow. As you will see, there are many options when creating PDFs, and most commercial printers have their own set of preferred specifications. Therefore, don't send a PDF to your printer without first making sure you prepared it correctly for them. If not, what you see may be completely different from what you get.

What if you're not printing documents, but you just want to share them with a wider audience while still preserving their appearance? This is a little easier because you don't have to worry about output. The compact PDF files are a great way to share information via the Internet, or they can also serve as an archive—one that is fully searchable and retains all the formatting of the original document.

EXPORTING TO PDF

To export your document to a PDF file, select File, Export and choose Adobe PDF in the Format pop-up. Name your file and navigate to the spot where you want to save it. Click Save.

A dialog opens with numerous export options, all of which you explore in the next section.

If you work with several small documents that make up a larger whole, you can join those documents together by creating a book, as described in Chapter 25, "Understanding Document and Page Setup in InDesign." Then, you can export either the entire book or just selected book documents by selecting the Export to PDF option from the Book palette menu (see Figure 31.1).

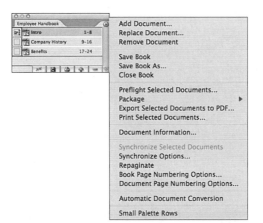

Figure 31.1
Export PDFs from the Book
palette to create a PDF that contains all documents in the book.

PDF Settings

After you name your PDF and choose its location, you have quite a few options for exporting your PDF. Again, these options are very important if you will be printing your document with a commercial printer because the settings you choose have to fit into the workflow of your service bureau and/or printer.

One place to start with your PDF settings is by choosing a PDF Preset. InDesign is preloaded with several PDF presets, including High Quality Print, Press Quality, and Smallest File Size. Based on where and how your document will be read and output, choosing one of these options might be a good starting point for creating your PDF. The text in the Description box gives you a good idea of the best use for each setting (see Figure 31.2).

PDF/X-1a:2001 and PDF/X-3:2002 are also available presets. These settings refer to specific standards for graphic compliance. Check out Part V, "Acrobat, Distiller, and Designer," later in this book for more detailed information.

The Standard pop-up menu should stay at None unless you are working to specific PDF/X-1a:2001, PDF/X-1a:2003, PDF/X-3:2002 and PDF/X-3:2003 standards for color-managed documents.

In the Compatibility pop-up menu, choose the version of Acrobat to which your document should conform, from version 4 through version 7. Especially if you are exporting the document for viewing only, you should work to the lowest version that your audience may have. Lower versions of Acrobat do not support some features of InDesign documents, such as transparency. The Adobe Help Center contains a great chart, titled PDF Compatibility Levels, which details the features supported by various versions.

The Export Adobe PDF dialog has seven categories of options. When you select a category from the pane on the left, the options on the right change to reflect the selected category. The following sections describe the options in each of the categories in this dialog.

Figure 31.2
You can choose from various PDF presets—they are often a good starting point for document export.

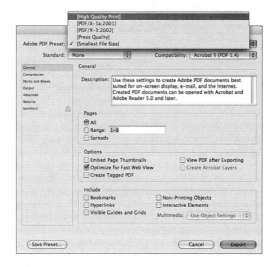

General Options

In the Pages area, choose All or enter a range of pages. If you prefer to export your document in spreads (left and right facing pages) as opposed to single pages, click the Spreads check box.

The Options area of the General page contains various settings:

- **Embed Page Thumbnails:** Create a preview of the PDF's pages that will travel with the document and can be viewed if you're trying to import the PDF into another InDesign document, for example. Including thumbnails increase the file size of the PDF.

- **Optimize for Fast Web View:** Compress the objects in the file and reduce the size of the PDF so it loads quickly in a web browser. It also restructures the file so it downloads page by page.

- **Create Tagged PDF:** Export structure tags for various text properties like paragraphs, lists, and tables so they can be used for other things. The tags are supported to various degrees depending on your version of Acrobat.

> Enabling the Spreads check box keeps facing pages together, which means your output provider cannot change the order of the pages for printing, also known as *imposition*. Therefore, do not check this box if you are sending your document to an outside vendor.

- **View PDF after Exporting:** Automatically open the PDF in Acrobat as soon as it is finished exporting.

- **Create Acrobat Layers:** Export items on different layers in InDesign into a layered PDF, accessible in Acrobat 6.0 and later. You see this option only if you have selected Acrobat 6 or 7 in the Compatibility pop-up menu. The layers can be shown and hidden to create different looks for your document depending on what's placed on which layer.

The Include area contains options that can help with the navigation and view of your document. You can include Bookmarks, specified in the Bookmarks palette, for table of content entries; Hyperlinks, which are clickable links created by hyperlinks, table of contents, and index entries; Visible Guides and Grids, which show all guides and grids visible on the InDesign page; Non-Printing Objects, which are items you've specified as nonprinting in the Attributes palette; and Interactive Elements, or all movies, sounds, and buttons embedded in the document.

The Multi-media pop-up menu becomes active when you work with Acrobat 6 or higher documents because you can choose either to link or embed interactive items in the document. For Acrobat 4 and 5, you must embed sounds and link movies, which doesn't give you a choice in this area.

Compression Options

The Compression panel of the Export Adobe PDF dialog enables you to select how to deal with color, grayscale, and monochrome images (see Figure 31.3). If you are creating documents for viewing onscreen or on the web only, it's a good idea to choose a downsampling option for the different types of images, because it's going to result in smaller file sizes without causing the images to lose visual quality. If you are printing these documents, however, this is an important place to check with your service provider liaison and get advice on how he or she would suggest you prepare the document.

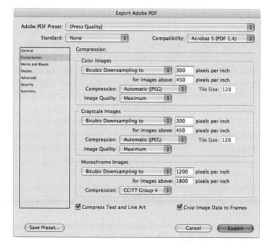

Figure 31.3
PDF Compression options.

Without going into too much detail about each individual setting (that comes later in this chapter), let's take a look at what the various options mean.

In the Color Images area of the panel, the pop-up menu that refers to downsampling determines how pixels within the images are deleted and blended with neighboring pixels to create a smooth display. Choosing Subsampling results in smaller images files and smaller documents. Choosing Bicubic Downsampling results in smooth, high-quality images but larger document sizes.

The Compression pop-up menu gives you options that help make your images smaller and faster to load. Automatic (JPEG) gives you the highest quality.

The Image Quality pop-up menu refers to how much compression you apply. Minimum gives you smaller images with less quality; Maximum gives you better quality but larger images.

The Tile Size option is available for files compatible with Acrobat 6 and higher and set with JPEG 2000 compression. It enables you to choose the size of tiles when you load images with progressive display—think of this as how images load in web pages, one part at a time.

The Compress Text and Line Art check box at the bottom of the dialog applies compression to those items without loss of quality.

The Crop Image Data to Frames option, also at the bottom of the dialog, deletes any extra image information that falls outside the frame in which it's displayed and reduces file size.

Marks and Bleeds Options

Based on your choices in the check boxes in the Marks and Bleeds panel of the Export Adobe PDF dialog (see Figure 31.4), various printer's marks are applied to your page. Again, you may want to check with your printer to see whether any of these marks are required. You would not want to select any options in this panel if you are creating a PDF for the web or onscreen viewing only.

Figure 31.4
PDF Marks and Bleed options.

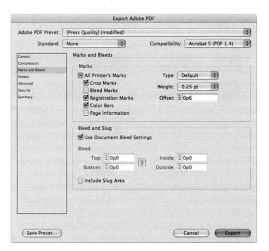

If objects bleed off your page or extend all the way to the page edge, you have two chances to set up a bleed area. The first is when you create your document in the Document Setup dialog. If you set up your bleed there, click the Use Document Bleed Settings check box on the Export Adobe PDF dialog. If not, you can specify your bleed area here. Setting up a bleed area is just a safety net for bleeds; you can make them extend past the crop marks to ensure you don't have a white line between your image and the edge of your page.

If you set up a *slug* area to provide printing or output instructions, enable the Include Slug Area check box.

Output Options

The Options panel of the Export Adobe PDF dialog gives you options for handling color management within your document (see Figure 31.5). Choices vary depending on whether you have color management turned on for the document, whether you have applied a color profile to the document, and which PDF standard has been selected. To get more information about the individual settings, hold your mouse over the selection and a brief explanation will appear in the Description field. There is also an explanation of PDF color later in this chapter.

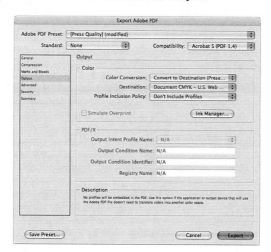

Figure 31.5
PDF Output options.

31

Advanced Options

The Font section of the Advanced panel of the Export Adobe PDF dialog enables you to choose at what point the font should be embedded in the document (see Figure 31.6). Say you enter 75% in the field. If less than 75% of the individual characters in that font are used in the document, the font will be a subset, or only those characters used are included in the document. If 75% of the characters or more are used, the entire font will be embedded, which increases your file size.

The Omit for OPI option enables you to select various graphic types used in your document that can be omitted, making a smaller file. A low-resolution version of the graphic will be used for display only, and the high-resolution graphic will be swapped in when the file is output. You must send the high-resolution graphic with your file so it can be included with output. If a graphic is embedded, this choice will not apply to it.

If you select an export version of Acrobat 5 or higher in the Compatibility pop-up menu, the Transparency Flattener option is not available because transparency is automatically supported and preserved in documents in later PDF versions (see Figure 31.7). You can choose High, Medium, or Low Resolution options that apply to all pages in the document with transparency applied. A complete explanation of transparency flattening is found later in this chapter.

31

Figure 31.6
Advanced PDF options.

Figure 31.7
Transparency Flattening options for your PDF.

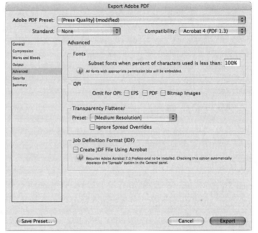

If you have set up in your document to apply a flattening preset on certain spreads, you can click the Ignore Spread Overrides check box to maintain the choice you make in this panel throughout the document.

If you have Acrobat 7 installed, the Advanced panel also gives you an option to create a JDF, (Job Definition Format) file that will travel with your document. The JDF contains file references and instructions for prepress creation.

Security Options

Security options are available only for files exported for Acrobat 5 and higher (see Figure 31.8).

If you want to require users to enter a password when they try to open the file, click in the Document Open Password check box and enter the password you want them to use.

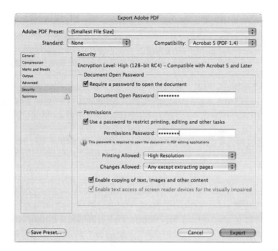

Figure 31.8
Security options for your PDF.

In the Permissions area, you can set up various degrees of protection for your document. Click in the first check box to restrict printing, editing, and other document changes, and enter a password. Then choose whether to allow high-resolution, low-resolution, or no printing, and whether to allow various page and form tasks. You can also check the box to enable page elements to be copied.

With high security settings, you also have the option to allow users to access the document with software that reads the document for the visually impaired.

Summary Options

The final panel of the PDF Export dialog is a summary (see Figure 31.9). You can drill down through the various PDF settings to see the choices that were made for this document. This is especially useful if you are using a PDF preset and want to access information about the document quickly. Click Save Summary to save a text file of this information.

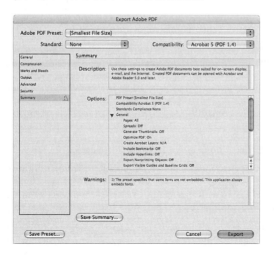

Figure 31.9
The PDF Summary panel.

Before you click the Export button, notice the Save Preset button in the lower left of the dialog. If you are creating multiple documents with the same settings or will always have to export with the same options for a specific printer, you can save these settings and quickly load them for use with various documents. Click the Save Preset button, name the preset, and click OK. From that point on, the preset you saved will be available if you go to File, Adobe PDF Presets, [preset name]. After you load your preset, you can click Export and know that everything is being saved exactly as you set it up.

DEFINING PDF PRESETS

You can also create a preset by choosing File, Adobe PDF Presets, Define, and then clicking New. You see the same dialogs we went through in the preceding section, and after you finish customizing them you can name your preset and keep it available every time you open InDesign.

If you set up presets in a previous version of InDesign, click the Load button in the PDF Presets dialog. Select Previous Version PDF Settings Files from the Files of Type pop-up menu and then search for the settings file (.pdfs) you created in the past. Select it and click Open to load.

Finally, if you work with a particularly PDF-savvy commercial printer, that printer might actually supply you with a PDF preset file to load to make sure you create everything according to printer specifications. PDF preset files for InDesign CS2 have the extension .joboptions. Browse to the preset file your printer has provided, select it, and click Open to load.

TRANSPARENCY FLATTENING

When you use any type of transparency in a document, including feathering, drop shadows, or an effect applied through the Transparency palette, the document has to be flattened to be printed or exported.

The flattening process takes the area where transparency has been applied and breaks it up into individual vector or raster areas. You can set up transparency flattening presets to specify how this should take place.

Select Edit, Transparency Flattener Presets. InDesign comes preloaded with low-, medium- and high-resolution flatteners. Select each one and read the description in the Preset Settings window to see how the flattener will affect your document.

If you export a PDF to Acrobat 5 or higher, the transparency effects do not have to be flattened.

If you saved a flattener preset, or someone has provided you with one, click the Load button, browse to its location and click Open.

Select any preset and click the Edit button to change any settings.

To create your own preset, click the New button. Name your preset (see Figure 31.10). The options that you set in this dialog are as follows:

- **Raster/Vector Balance:** Determine to what point artwork is rasterized. Rasterization converts vector graphics, or those created with curves and lines, to dots. The higher the setting, the less the graphics will be rasterized. This means your page objects are smoother, but they take longer to load and print.

- **Line Art and Text Resolution:** Determine the resolution for those objects that are rasterized when you flatten. If you are outputting to low-resolution devices, this number can equal the output resolution. If you are outputting to a high-resolution device, you should check with your commercial printer or the device manual for resolution suggestions.

- **Gradient and Mesh Resolution:** Determine the resolution for gradients and drop shadows or feathers when flattened. Adobe recommends keeping this setting between 150 and 300. Higher resolutions cause slower printing and exporting and larger file sizes, without any equivalent return in quality.

- **Convert All Text to Outlines:** On spreads with transparency, convert all type to outlines and discard glyph information for that font. It helps ensure that text retains its proper width during flattening, but small type sizes may appear thicker when these documents are viewed onscreen or printed on low-resolution output devices.

- **Convert All Strokes to Outlines:** Convert all strokes to filled paths on spreads with transparency, to ensure the stroke width stays consistent when flattened. As with the fonts mentioned in the last bullet, thin lines may appear thicker onscreen or when printed on low-resolution output devices.

- **Clip Complex Regions:** Reduce stitching that can result where vector and raster objects meet. *Stitching* shows up as blocky areas where colors don't exactly match. If you enable this check box, know that it also creates complex paths that might make your document harder to print.

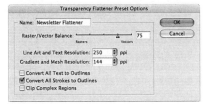

Figure 31.10
Specify how transparencies should be flattened in your printed or exported documents.

Transparency flattening options are also found in the Export Adobe PDF dialog (described earlier in this chapter) if you want to apply these options as you export.

Using the Transparency Flattener Preview Palette

Choose Window, Output, Flattener Preview to display the Flattener Preview palette (see Figure 31.11). This palette highlights transparency flattening in your document. Choose from the following highlight options in the pop-up menu:

- **None**.

- **Rasterized Complex Regions** shows those areas that will be rasterized due to overlap or nearness of raster and vector objects. To prevent stitching problems, use the Clip Complex Regions option in the Transparency Flattener Presets dialog.

- **Transparent Objects** shows the items that use transparency.

- **All Affected Objects** shows items involved in transparency, either transparent objects or those they overlap.

- **Affected Graphics** shows those placed graphics that are affected by applied transparency.

- **Outlined Strokes** shows strokes that are either transparent or all strokes if you select the Convert All Strokes to Outlines option in the Transparency Flattener Preset Options dialog.

- **Outlined Text** shows transparent text or all text if you select the Convert All Text to Outlines option in the Transparency Flattener Preset Options dialog.

- **Raster-Fill Text and Strokes** shows text and strokes that are rasterized when the file is flattened.

- **All Rasterized Regions** shows all rasterized objects, including those that are forced to rasterize because of complexity or because there is no other way to output them.

Figure 31.11
The Flattener Preview palette enables you to see the areas of your page where transparencies will be flattened.

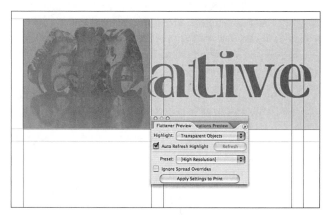

Click the Refresh button to refresh the view after every change in selection, or check the Auto Refresh Highlight box to do it automatically.

You can also select a predefined Transparency Flattener Preset in the pop-up menu if you want to Ignore Spread Overrides or to Apply the preset settings to the document's print options.

Overriding Transparency Flattening Options

If you have a document with various types of images and page elements, you might want to select certain spreads to which your transparency flattening presets will not apply:

1. Navigate to the particular spread.

2. Go to the Pages palette menu and select Choose Spread Flattening.

3. The dialog that opens contains options to choose the default flattening presets, no flattening preset, or custom options that you can set for these pages only.

4. After you make your flattening selections, click OK.

After you set an override, you can choose to ignore it in the Print or Export Adobe PDF dialog.

WORKING WITH PDF COLOR

PDFs have very specific options for setting up colors and color management. These options are found in the Output panel of the Export Adobe PDF dialog (see Figure 31.12).

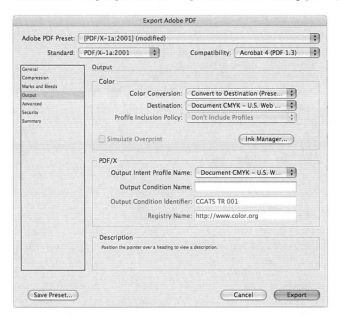

Figure 31.12
Use the Output panel of the export Adobe PDF dialog to specify exactly how color should be managed in the PDF.

Depending on various selections you can make in this dialog and others, your options are going to vary. This discussion serves as an overview only, to show how the options interact.

For most PDFs, you have the option to choose No Color Conversion, Convert to Destination, or Convert to Destination (Preserve Numbers). For the last two choices, you can select the destination color space that objects with embedded profiles will be converted to—make sure that your printer or output agency makes you aware of the best choice to make here. If you choose to preserve numbers, any object without an embedded profile will keep the color settings applied to it.

You can choose whether to include Destination Profiles in the next pop-up menu; this determines whether a color profile is included in the document. Again, based on other color choices you make, your options here differ:

- **Don't Include Profiles**.

- **Include All Profiles** creates color management in the document. Make sure you turn on color management in the document and set up a profile.

- **Include Tagged Source Profiles** refers to settings that have been specifically created for output on calibrated devices.

- **Include All RGB and Tagged Source CMYK Profiles** includes profiles for these items.

- **Include Destination Profile** assigns the profile to all page elements.

The Simulate Overprint option shows how separations are printed by simulating overprint for process color objects on a composite document.

The Ink Manager button controls the conversion of spot color to process equivalents. This setting is not saved with the PDF preset.

If you have specified to export to a PDF/X format, you can choose the output profile in the next section. If color management is on, the output intent device is the same profile as selected previously, in the Destination area. If not, the selections match the destination color space.

Enter your own information in the Output Condition Name field.

The Output Condition Identifier enables you to type the name of the Output Condition if one is not entered automatically from the ICC profile. Similarly, the Registry Name may be filled in, or you can use the field to type the URL of the output condition.

SPECIFYING PAGE MARKINGS

31

In the Export Adobe PDF or Print dialog, you can choose to have printer's marks print on your documents (see Figure 31.13):

- **Crop Marks:** Show the page edge at the top, bottom, left, and right of the document. Crop marks can help you ensure that items are falling exactly where you want them compared to the page edge.

- **Bleed Marks:** Print marks a specific distance from the crop marks, based on what you enter in the Document Setup dialog. Certain printers may have specific bleed measurements they want you to set up. Bleeds marks show if the items that you want to bleed off the page have been extended far enough past the edge of the page.

Figure 31.13
Page markings on your printed or exported document tell you and your printer a lot about how the document is trimmed and printed.

- **Registration Marks:** Line up documents printed as color separations.

- **Color Bars:** Test the density of CMYK inks, including tints of gray. These bars are used by printers.

- **Page Information:** Print the filename, page number, current date and time, and separation name in the lower-left corner of each sheet.

WORKING WITH IMAGE COMPRESSION

In the Output panel of the Export Adobe PDF dialog, you have certain options for compressing the images in your document to help with file size. As mentioned earlier, compression can be applied to color, grayscale, and monochrome images (see Figure 31.14).

Your choices include

- **Average Downsampling**, which replaces specific pixels in the image with the average pixel color in a sample area.

- **Subsampling**, which picks a pixel in the center of a sample area and uses it as the color for the entire area. This results in the fastest conversion time, but the least smooth look.

- **Bicubic Downsampling**, which uses a weighted average to sample pixel color. This results in the slowest conversion time, but has the smoothest appearance.

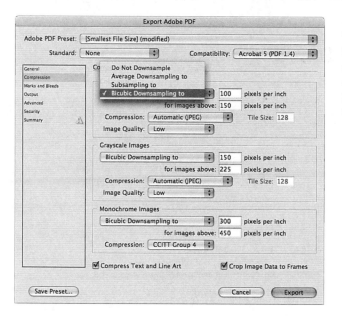

Figure 31.14
Take care when compressing images in your PDF; this can make the file smaller, but it can also degrade image quality if you print to a high-resolution output device.

Choose from the following compressed image formats:

- **Automatic (JPEG)**, which is the best quality for color and grayscale images. This option is available only for documents exported to Acrobat 6 and later.

- **JPEG**, which tries to reduce file size with the least amount of lost information.

- **ZIP**, which can be lossless or lossy, depending on whether the resolution is set at or below the image's original resolution.

- **JPEG 2000**, which is the international standard compression format. This option enables you to set progressive display (enter the number of tiles in the field to the right) and is available only in documents set to export to Acrobat 6 or higher.

- **Automatic JPEG 2000**, which automatically determines the best quality for image reproduction.

The Image Quality pop-up menu determines the amount of compression.

For monochromatic images, the compression options include CCITT, which is good for black-and-white images. Group 4 is a general purpose compression method; Group 3 is used by fax machines and compresses the bitmaps one row at a time. Run Length compression works well for images with large solid areas of black or white.

The Compress Text and Line Art option applies a flat compression without degrading detail or quality.

The Crop Image Data to Frames option deletes image areas that are hidden outside the frames in which they are placed.

EXPORTING TO GOLIVE

Most people use InDesign to set up files for printing, but there are obviously many options that deal with document navigation in a way that is very web-like. Because of that, you might want to design documents in InDesign and then repurpose them for the web by exporting them to GoLive.

First, let's look at what happens to your documents when you package them for GoLive:

- Text stories are converted to XML files and saved with the extension `.incd`.

- Character and paragraph styles are converted to CSS (Cascading Style Sheets).

- Linked objects are packaged with the file—if they are placed images or graphics, they are converted to TIFFs.

- Nonprinting objects are not included in the package.

To package a file, select File, Package for GoLive. Browse to the location where you want to save the package, name it, and click Package. You can also select Package for GoLive from the Book palette menu if you'd like to package an entire book. The dialog shown in Figure 31.15 opens.

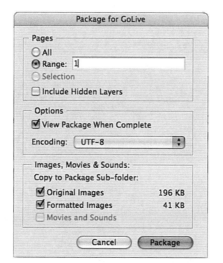

Choose from the following options in the Pages section of the Package for GoLive dialog:

- **All** packages everything in the document.

- **Range** enables you to enter a range of pages to package.

- **Selection** packages anything you have selected on the page.

- **Include Hidden Layers** packages items on hidden layers.

If you want to view the package after it is exported, select the View Package When Complete option.

Choose how the file should be encoded. This choice must match how your GoLive web page is encoded.

Choose to package Original Images to copy graphics files as they are, or select Formatted Images to copy them as they are in the InDesign document. An example of a formatted image is including only the cropped area of a placed image.

If you placed movies or sounds in your document, you can choose to copy them with your files.

The package that's created contains a file with the extension .idpk—an XML file that tells GoLive how the page should be created. A PDF shows the layout of the document, and con-

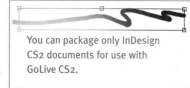

You can package only InDesign CS2 documents for use with GoLive CS2.

tent can be dragged from the PDF to the GoLive page. An Assets folder contains folders for stories, images, formatted images, movies, and sounds.

PRINTING YOUR DOCUMENT

To print your file to a connected printer, choose File, Print. Choose a print preset if one has been defined, the name of your printer, and the PPD that drives that printer.

Use the tabs on the left side of the dialog to set the options in various categories.

General Print Options

The General panel of the Print dialog provides the most common printing options (see Figure 31.16):

Figure 31.16
General print options.

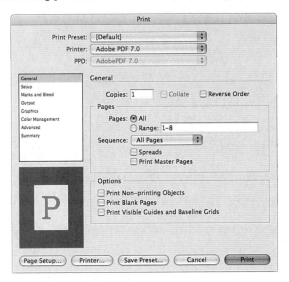

- Set number of copies.

- Check Collate if you are printing more than one copy of a multiple page document, to keep the pages together.

- Check Reverse Order to print the pages backwards.

- Choose to print All pages or a specific Range.

- Choose your Sequence: All Pages, Even Pages, or Odd Pages.

- Check to print in Spreads and/or to print Master Pages.

- Check to choose whether or not to print Non-printing Objects, Blank Pages, and/or Visible Guides and Baseline Grids.

Setup Print Options

The Setup panel of the Print dialog enables you to choose your paper size and specify the size at which the pages should be printed and arranged on the sheet (see Figure 31.17):

- Choose your page size. Select Custom to enter your own width and height.

- Choose your page orientation.

- Offset refers to how much space is left between the print area and the left side of the page.

- Gap refers to how much space is left between pages if you are printing on continuous media, such as a roll of paper.

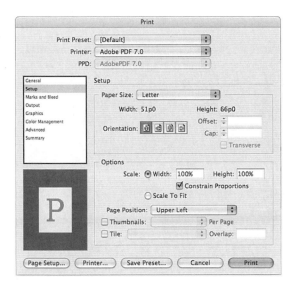

Figure 31.17
Print Setup options.

- Transverse rotates the pages by 45°.

In the Options area are several additional setup choices you can specify:

- Choose a different percentage for the width and height of your document to change the scale. Use the Constrain Proportions check box to keep the width and height equal.

- Click the Scale to Fit radio button to shrink or enlarge your print area automatically to fit the page.

- Choose how the print area should align on the page.

- If you want to print thumbnails of multiple pages in your document, check the check box and enter the number of thumbnails that should print per page.

- Tile your document to print a large-format file on multiple pages. Tile options include Auto, which automatically prints the number of tiles as necessary, including overlap. Auto Justified increases the amount of overlap as necessary so the right edges of the right tiles align to the right edge of the page, and the bottom edges of the bottom tiles align to the bottom edge of the page. Manual prints a single tile based on the location of the zero point on the page.

- For Overlap, type the minimum amount of duplicated information you want printed with each tile. Overlap helps make it easier to arrange your final document from the tiles.

Marks and Bleeds Print Options

This panel of the Print dialog enables you to specify printer's marks for the page, including whether to use the document's bleed information or enter your own.

Output Print Options

On the Output panel of the Print dialog (see Figure 31.18), you can choose how to deal with color in your document. You can choose Composite Gray (for black-and-white printers), Composite RGB, Composite CMYK, or Composite Leave Unchanged, or you can choose to print Separations.

Figure 31.18
Print Output options.

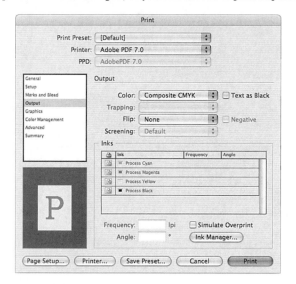

What's the difference? A composite prints all colors in the document on the same page, simulating how it will look when it is printed on a press. Printing separations result in a separate page for each color used on the page. A CMYK page printed as separations, for example, results in four printed pages: one that shows cyan ink placement, one that shows magenta, one that shows yellow, and one that shows black.

If you choose to print separations, use the Inks window to turn certain ink colors on and off.

Graphics Print Options

The Graphics print options panel (see Figure 31.19) enables you to choose how graphics are handled when you print your document. If you do not necessarily need to see your graphics at their highest resolution in your printout, printing no graphics or proxies can help speed up the printing process:

The Images, Send Data pop-up menu offers the following options:

- **All** prints all graphics at the appropriate resolution.

- **Optimized subsampling** prints the graphic at the best resolution supported by the output device.

- **Proxy** prints a low-resolution image suitable for checking placement.

- **None** prints a gray box in place of all graphics for faster printing.

The Fonts, Download pop-up menu offers these options:

- Choose **None** if your fonts are installed in the printer's memory.

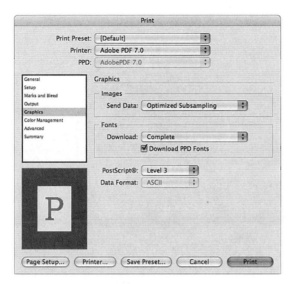

Figure 31.19
Graphic print options.

- Choose **Complete** to download all fonts when the document is printed.

- Choose **Subset** to download only the characters used in the document.

The Download PPD Fonts option download fonts even if they are installed in the printer's memory, for more reliable reproduction.

From the PostScript pop-up menu, choose the PostScript level that most closely matches your printer for the best output.

The Data Format pop-up menu, refers to how InDesign sends image data to the printer: either as ASCII (more common) or Binary (smaller).

Color Management Print Options

The choices in the color management print options pane (see Figure 31.20) refer to the color profiles used to print your document and how colors should be simulated based on your printer:

- Choose whether you are printing a document or a proof.

- Choose to let either InDesign or the PostScript printer determine your colors. If you choose to let InDesign determine colors, choose the printer profile from the list.

- Preserve the CMYK or RGB numbers if your document uses color in images, for example, that do not have color profiles applied to them.

- If you have set up a paper color other than white, you can choose to simulate that color here.

Advanced Print Options

The Advanced Print Options dialog (see Figure 31.21) gives you choices for omitting or keeping graphics, as well as how transparencies should be printed:

Figure 31.20
Color management options
for printing.

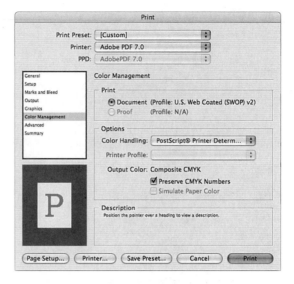

Figure 31.21
Advanced printing options.

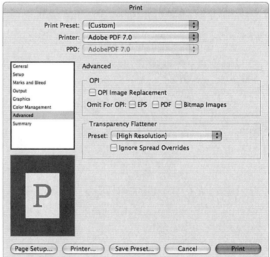

- The Omit for OPI option enables you to select various graphic types used in your document that can be omitted, making a smaller file.

- Choose your Transparency Flattener preset.

- Click the Ignore Spread Overrides check box to maintain the transparency flattening choice you make in this panel throughout the document.

Summary Print Options

The Summary panel of the Print dialog shows a summary of your printing choices:

- Click Save Preset to name and save this printing profile.

- Click Setup to access the printer's setup options directly.
- Click Print to print your document.

PREPARING YOUR DOCUMENT FOR A SERVICE PROVIDER

The Preflight and Package features are valuable tools when you are trying to pull files together for a service bureau or printer. Not only do the options check your document for any issues that might keep it from printing as you want, it also pulls all linked graphic files and the fonts you've used into one convenient folder.

Using Preflight

The Preflight dialog, which opens when you select File, Preflight, contains several panes containing information about your document. In most of the panes, you have the option to select a Show Problems Only check box, which alerts you only if there are issues that will keep the document from printing as you expect:

- **Summary:** This panel shows the number of fonts and images used, color usage, external plug-ins associated with the file and pagination options (see Figure 31.22).
- **Fonts:** This panel shows the fonts used, as well as alerts if fonts are missing, embedded, incomplete, or protected. If a font is missing, click the Find Font button to substitute a font.

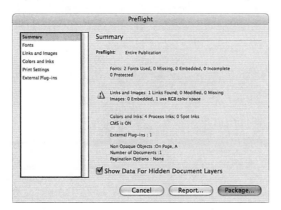

Figure 31.22
The Summary panel of the Preflight dialog.

- **Links and Images:** This panel shows a complete list of the links included in the document. Select a link name in the list to see file information. Click Update to relink a file.
- **Colors and Inks:** This panel shows all color and names of inks used in the document.
- **Print Settings:** This panel shows all print options chosen in the Print dialog.
- **External Plug-ins:** This panel shows any third-party plug-ins used in the creation of the document. External plug-ins can sometimes prevent you from opening documents if you do not have the same plug-ins installed as the person who created the document.

31

Click the Report button to save a text file with your page information.

Click the Package button to gather the related files for printing.

Using Package

Click the Package button at the bottom of the Preflight dialog. If your document has not been saved, you are prompted to do so.

The first screen of the packaging process is an information screen; enter your contact information and any special instructions in this screen. This information is saved in a text file and gathered along with your documents. Click Continue.

You are prompted to name a folder and browse to the location where you want to save it (see Figure 31.23). Add any comments for Version Cue. Use the check boxes to

- Copy Fonts (except CJK) (copies all used font files but not the entire typeface).

- Copy Linked Graphics.

- Update Graphic Links in Package (changes graphic link paths to the new package folder location).

Figure 31.23
Choose the items you want to package with your document.

- Include Fonts and Links from Hidden Document Layers.

- View Report (opens a preflight and package report after the process is completed).

- Click Save to package your file(s).

InDesign gives you numerous options for saving and outputting your document, depending on your final audience or output device. Give some thought to these things when you set up your document so that making your print choices will be easier.

SPEEDING UP INDESIGN AND DATA FUNCTIONALITY

IN THIS CHAPTER

Ready for some more? Believe it or not, the chapters in this section have only scratched the surface of InDesign's capabilities. Hopefully the preceding chapters gave you a good overview of InDesign and how you can take its many creative features and use them to make your own documents more exciting.

This chapter briefly mentions some of InDesign's other functions and features, potentially piquing your interest and leading you to learn more about them. And as always, the Adobe Help Center is a great start for more information. In addition, this chapter ends with some hints and tips to help you get the most out of InDesign.

UNDERSTANDING XML

Recall that XML stands for Extensible Markup Language, a programming language that works like HTML to tag items on a page. HTML is used to describe how items should be formatted, and XML is used to define the items themselves. XML is beneficial because it enables you to use information in different documents in different ways, without having to retype it or copy and paste it each time.

An XML tag, or the XML reference to a specific item, can be mapped to particular styles in your document so that when you apply the tag, the item takes on the proper formatting. You can also store XML text in a database so it can be easily accessed and repurposed for any document.

The best way to talk about XML is to use a specific example and walk through how to use it.

Let's say I'm creating a newsletter for my business, a bakery. In each issue of the newsletter, I publish a recipe for one of the items I sell. I've been hired to bake and serve several types of cookies for a wedding shower. As a courtesy, I would like to create recipe cards for the cookies, and I'm looking for an easy way to get the information from my newsletter onto a recipe card, the template of which I already have created.

To use XML to make this job easier, I'll first open an issue of the newsletter that contains a recipe. I then perform these steps:

1. Open the Tags palette (choose Window, Tags).

2. Create a new tag by clicking the New Tag button at the bottom of the palette.

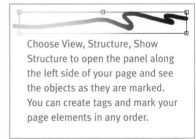

Choose View, Structure, Show Structure to open the panel along the left side of your page and see the objects as they are marked. You can create tags and mark your page elements in any order.

3. The tag name is highlighted when it is created; type a new name describing the item it will be associated with, for example, **BakingInstructions**. Your XML tag names cannot contain spaces.

4. Highlight the text or select the item that you want this tag to apply to. In this example, we select the recipe instructions.

5. Click the tag in the palette to mark it—with the recipe instructions highlighted, we click the BakingInstructions tab in the Tags palette to mark it (see Figure 32.1).

Figure 32.1
Tag the items in your file that you want to export as XML.

6. Continue creating tags and naming them for the objects in your document, then tagging page elements until all the information you want to use is marked.

7. Select File, Export. Name your file and choose XML as the Format. Click Save.

8. Open a new file or a template you've created for the new file. In this case, we open the template for our recipe card.

9. Go to File, Import XML. Browse to the XML file you saved in step 7, select it and then click Open.

10. The Structure pane opens at the left of your new document. Make sure you have created frames for the different page elements in the new document and drag and drop each tag into the proper frame.

All information from the original document is placed in the frame in which you drag and drop the tags (see Figure 32.2).

Again, this is a very simplistic explanation of XML; there are many more options available for importing and exporting using this language. A good source of additional information is found on the Adobe website, at http://www.adobe.com/products/indesign/indepth.html.

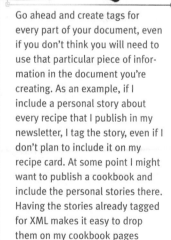

32

Go ahead and create tags for every part of your document, even if you don't think you will need to use that particular piece of information in the document you're creating. As an example, if I include a personal story about every recipe that I publish in my newsletter, I tag the story, even if I don't plan to include it on my recipe card. At some point I might want to publish a cookbook and include the personal stories there. Having the stories already tagged for XML makes it easy to drop them on my cookbook pages when the time comes.

Figure 32.2
Drag and drop tags from the Structure pane into your new document to place the page objects.

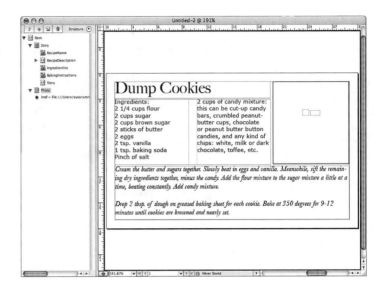

USING DATA MERGE

The Data Merge function takes information from a tabbed text or comma-delimited file and imports it into InDesign to create documents with specific, different information. Again, I'll use an example.

My bakery newsletter has become very popular, so not only do I hand out copies in my shop, I also mail it to customers who can't make it in regularly. I've tried creating mailing labels with label software, but it's hard to line those darned things up, and besides, I'd like the name and address information printed right there on the newsletter.

If you have character or paragraph styles already set up in your end document (that is, the document you are dropping the tags into), you can map the tags you import to those styles. In the fly-out menu on the Structure pane, select Map Tags to Styles. A dialog opens that enables you to select a style for each tag you are placing.

I have an Excel file with all of my subscribers' names and addresses typed in it. I set up my Excel file so that the subscriber's first name is in the first column, the last name is in the second column, the street address is in the third column, city is in the fourth, state is in the fifth, and ZIP code is in the sixth. In Excel, I select File, Save As and, in the Format pop-up menu, I choose Text (Tab delimited) or CSV (Comma delimited). I can now import the text into my InDesign document. To do this, I use the following steps:

1. In InDesign, choose Window, Automation, Data Merge to open the Data Merge palette.

2. Choose Select Data Source from the Data Merge palette menu and browse to the file you saved from Excel. Select the file and click Open. The field names appear in the Data Merge palette, along with an icon specifying whether this is a text or an image field.

3. Make sure your target document, that is, the newsletter file, is open. If you are placing text, you should have a text block in the proper location on your file, waiting for the data.

4. Drag each field from the Data Merge palette to its proper location in the document. If you have a text frame, for example, the field name appears in the text frame, offset by brackets (see Figure 32.3).

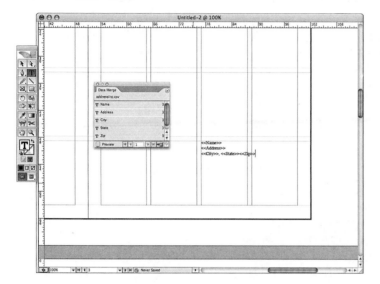

Figure 32.3
The Data Merge feature enables you to import information from a tab- or comma-delimited file and place fields in your document to print files with variable data.

5. Click the Preview button to scroll through the pages at the bottom of the palette and see the addresses displayed on the file.

6. When you are ready, click the Create Merged Document button.

7. Choose how many records to merge, among other options in the Create Merged Document dialog. Click OK.

The information in the Excel file is merged into the newsletter file, and you can now save and print the InDesign document with all data in place.

CREATING TABLES OF CONTENTS, FOOTNOTES, AND INDEXES

If you are creating long documents, it may be helpful for your readers if you include an index or table of contents with the document. InDesign gives you options that help you easily add and format these references, as well as footnotes. To make it easier, let's look at each one individually, even though many of the steps and processes are similar.

As with all of the sections in this chapter, these instructions are written to explain the basic process. You can check out the Adobe Help Center for more detailed instructions and explanations of all available options.

Tables of Contents

To create a table of contents, you must first create a document to hold your table of contents. If you are creating a table of contents for multiple documents, you should add the documents to a *book* so they can all be referenced. Refer to Chapter 25, "Understanding Document and Page Setup in InDesign," for more information about creating and working with book documents. Make sure you save your table of contents document and add it to the book as well.

InDesign creates tables of contents by scanning the documents included in the book for heading styles that are defined as table of content styles. When it finds type that has been marked with these styles, it pulls that text for the table of contents.

Next, define the information in your document that should be included in the table of contents. To do this, you tell InDesign what styles should be associated with entries in the table of contents:

1. Choose Layout, Table of Contents Styles. The Table of Contents dialog opens (see Figure 32.4).

2. Name the Table of Contents in the Title field. If you want to apply a style to that title, select it in the Style pop-up menu.

3. In the Other Styles list, click on the style name(s) that represent content you want to appear in the table of contents. Click the Add button to add them to the Include list.

4. For each style in the Include list box, select the style you want to apply to those items in the table of contents from the Entry Style pop-up menu.

> You should not perform these steps until your document(s) has been created and paragraph styles have been applied to the headings and other information you want to use to create the table of contents. You must define table of content styles and mark your text with them to create a table of contents.

5. If your documents have been gathered into a book, make sure you click the Include Book Documents check box so all entries from all documents are included.

6. Click OK and then click OK again.

Figure 32.4
Create styles and apply them to headings you want to appear in your Table of Contents.

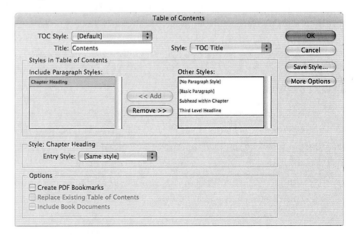

To generate the table of contents text, choose Layout, Table of Contents. Make sure all the options in the dialog are the way you want them—for example, the entry style; where the page number should appear relative to the chapter/section name and the style, if any, that should be applied to it; and what character, if any, should appear between the chapter/section name and the page number. You can also choose to sort the entries alphabetically. Click OK. A loaded text cursor appears; click it to place the table of contents on the page.

Footnotes

To insert a footnote in your document, click with the text cursor where you want the footnote to appear. Choose Type, Insert Footnote. A number automatically is inserted where you click, and your text cursor will move to the bottom of the page, enabling you to type your footnote. As you add footnotes on a page, the footnote area at the bottom of the page automatically expands as needed to fit the footnote information (see Figure 32.5).

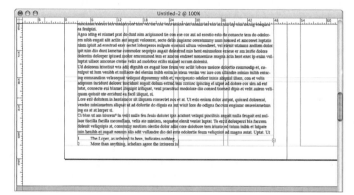

Figure 32.5
Inserting footnotes in your InDesign document is very easy.

32

Indexes

An *index* is text that appears, usually at the end of your document, as an alphabetical list of references within the document that people might want to look up easily.

To create an index, you must do three things: mark all names or references that you want to index, create a book file with the empty file that will contain your index and all marked documents, and then generate your index.

To mark references, follow these steps:

1. With a document open, choose Window, Type and Tables, Index to open the Index palette (see Figure 32.6).

2. Use the Type tool to highlight the phrase you want to mark.

3. Click the New Index Entry button at the bottom of the Index palette.

4. The New Page Entry dialog opens. If you want to add a subtopic below the one that has been marked, type it here. You can add up to four levels of subtopics.

5. Click OK to add the topic or click Add All to add the topic and subtopics you've entered.

6. Continue marking references in this way throughout the document.

Figure 32.6
The Index palette enables you to see a reference to all the marked text in your document.

Many of your index entries may be single words or phrases that you want to appear in the index as they appear on your page. This may not be the case for proper names. You have two choices when you mark names:

- When you click the button to mark the entry for the index, you can enter the last name in the Sort By field in the New Page Entry dialog. This makes sure that the name is sorted by last name instead of first.

- You can also use a keyboard shortcut to mark names in last name, first name order: use Shift+Alt+Ctrl+] (Windows users) or Shift+Option+⌘+] (Mac users).

To set up a book file for the index, follow these steps:

1. Choose File, New, Book. Name your book file and save it in an appropriate location.

2. Add all marked documents to the book.

3. Create a new document and save it as your index. Make sure this file is added to the book as well.

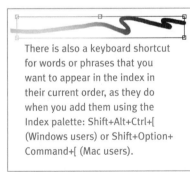

There is also a keyboard shortcut for words or phrases that you want to appear in the index in their current order, as they do when you add them using the Index palette: Shift+Alt+Ctrl+[(Windows users) or Shift+Option+ Command+[(Mac users).

To generate your index, follow these steps:

1. With your index file open, select Generate Index from the Index palette menu.

2. Make all necessary formatting choices in the Generate index dialog. Make sure the box for Include Book Publications is checked, and the book file listed is the appropriate one to reference.

3. Click OK.

4. A loaded text cursor will appear; click on your page to place it.

WORKING WITH SCRIPTING, PLUG-INS, AND INCOPY

One of the benefits of Adobe products has always been how well they can be extended to do the things you need. Scripting and plug-ins are two examples of ways you or others can add to InDesign's functionality to make the program work harder for you, not the other way around.

Scripting

InDesign supports scripts written in Visual Basic on the Windows side and AppleScript for Mac users. Both are programming languages, but they are very easy to pick up and start working.

The benefit to scripting, which is like writing a computer miniprogram, is that you can create scripts to perform everyday or not-so-everyday tasks for you. After you work in InDesign for a while, you find there are certain tasks associated with certain types of documents that you have to perform over and over, ad nauseam. Sometimes these tasks can get so mundane that they can overwhelm the creativity you have and make your project feel like drudgery.

It's worth it to get your programming feet wet and write a script to automate processes like these. Check out http://www.adobe.com/products/indesign/scripting.html for more information about creating scripts, as well as a link to the InDesign Scripting guide, a PDF of scripting instructions. You can also jump to the Adobe Studio Exchange site, where you can view scripts that have been written and shared—and maybe even download one that can help you.

Plug-ins

When Adobe decided to develop InDesign and move away from PageMaker as its default layout program, it also made a huge fundamental change to the way the application was coded. Not to get too detailed about programming, but under the hood InDesign is composed of hundreds of plug-ins held together by a basic application framework.

This is actually a really good thing for users, because it makes it easier for third-party vendors to create plug-ins that can extend InDesign's functionality in very specific ways. There are a number of vendors out there who have programmed ways for InDesign to perform tasks such as imposing your InDesign documents into printers' spreads or batch-converting PageMaker or QuarkXPress files into InDesign. And that functionality can be yours by simply ordering and installing a plug-in.

A *plug-in* is a program that works within an application to perform a specific function.

For more information on some of the companies who work with Adobe to add functionality to InDesign, visit http://www.adobe.com/products/plugins/indesign/main.html or do an Internet search for *InDesign plug-ins*. You'll find a wealth of information and potentially some ways to save yourself time and effort.

32

InCopy

One of the most-used InDesign plug-ins is InCopy. InCopy was originally developed by a third-party provider, but has, with this version of InDesign, been taken over by Adobe and is available for sale through the Adobe website.

InCopy adds text editing functionality to InDesign by enabling users to open files and make text changes—but only that. For example, if you have a document you have designed, but there is also a copywriter and editing group who will be working on the text, it's usually not a very appealing idea to turn the application file over to the word people and let them have at it. Letting another person change the text also means you run the risk of someone accidentally moving or changing something that has nothing to do with copy.

InCopy creates a workflow that enables specified users to open a file and make any changes to text, but not to styles or any other items on the page. If overset text is created by adding copy, for example, you as the designer are the only person who can make a change to deal with that overset text. It's a great way to give copy control to those who need it—really, don't you have better things to do with your time than add commas and correct misplaced hyphens?—while still maintaining your control over the ultimate appearance of the document.

For more information about InCopy, visit http://www.adobe.com/products/incopy/main.html.

WORKING WITH VERSION CUE AND INDESIGN

If you've read the other sections of this book, you know that all the Creative Suite programs use Version Cue to help track changes, manage projects, and browse file thumbnails and information. We've explored Version Cue in other sections of the book; this section explores the basics of using it with InDesign.

If you're ready to create a document in InDesign that you want to save as a Version Cue project, select File, Open. Make sure you're using the Adobe dialog and not the OS version of the Open dialog (see Figure 32.7).

In the left panel, click Version Cue. If you have not yet created and saved your project, click on the Project Tools menu and select New Project. In the New Project dialog, choose where you want to save the project in the Location drop-down. Enter a project name and a project description and then click OK. After your project is created, you can save and assign individual files to that project.

If you want this project to be available to others, click Share this project with others. Click OK.

Remember, there is a button on many of InDesign's dialogs that enables you to switch between the OS version of the dialog and the Adobe version. If you see a button in the lower-left corner that says Use Adobe Dialog, you're in the OS version. If you see a button that says Use OS Dialog, you're in the Adobe version.

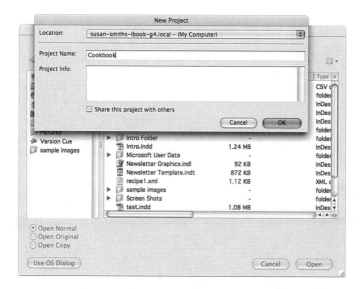

Figure 32.7
Create projects in Version Cue
that you can share with others
and easily manage.

If a project is shared, two users can work on it at the same time. Version Cue will not let one user's editing overwrite another's. After users save their document to the Version Cue workspace, they are alerted to another version and given the opportunity either to download the new changes or continue. You can also save your version of a file as an *alternate*. Files are marked with icons that indicate whether they are open, in use, or have conflicting copies.

You can save a document by selecting File, Save in the application, which overwrites all the changes you made, or you can select File, Save a Version to save a version of the document in Version Cue, adding comments to indicate the particular changes that this version represents. Saving a version enables you to go back later and work with the document in the particular state represented by the version you saved.

If you want to turn Version Cue off for any reason, choose Edit, Preferences, File Handling (Windows users) or InDesign, Preferences, File Handling (Mac users) and disable the Enable Version Cue check box.

USING OTHER RESOURCES

When you install the Creative Suite 2, you not only get a great collection of software, you also install files and fonts that can help you create great-looking documents. InDesign's templates and the OpenType fonts Adobe provides are both helpful in creating knock-out designs.

Templates

InDesign comes with a variety of templates and documents that can help you get started, or help you practice some of the skills we've discussed throughout this section.

To view or open the templates, click the New From Template button on the InDesign Welcome screen, which appears when you open the application for the first time. You can also access the screen at any time by selecting Help, Welcome Screen.

When you click New From Template, Bridge launches (see Figure 32.8). You see previews of various templates that you can double-click to open. Any of these templates can be used as a starting point for your own documents, and there are lots of great effects applied in them that can help add excitement to your document. You can also use them as inspiration for your own creations.

Figure 32.8
InDesign's included templates can help jump-start your own designs.

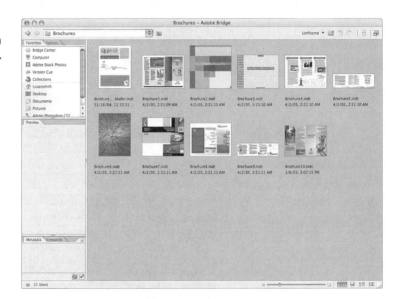

Typography Resources

In Chapter 27, "Working with Type in InDesign," we talked about some of the great effects you can add to your InDesign documents using nothing more than typography. One great resource that comes with InDesign is a collection of OpenType fonts, including several Chinese and Japanese fonts. Use the Glyphs palette to compare an OpenType font to the average TrueType font (see Figure 32.9)—you'll see quite a difference in the number of characters and therefore the amount of information you can communicate!

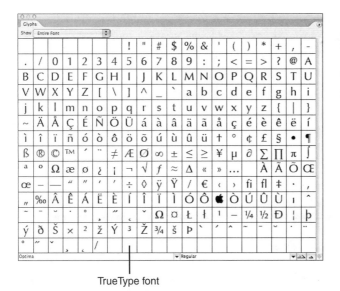

Figure 32.9
Compare the average TrueType font with an OpenType font. The number and variety of characters that OpenType fonts provide is staggering.

TrueType font

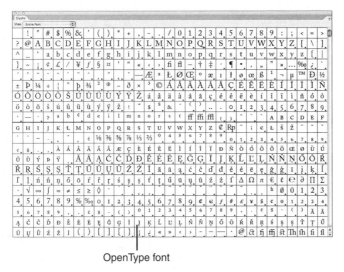

OpenType font

MASTERING THE PROGRAM

As with any software application, the quickest way to master InDesign is to use it regularly, if not daily. If you're in a situation where you are used to using another page layout program, but you've upgraded to InDesign, stay strong. Don't backslide; use InDesign to create all documents from this point forward.

If you're new to page layout software in general—perhaps you only used office-type software in the past—again, force yourself to use InDesign. Even if you're just writing a letter, write it in InDesign. It may feel inconvenient and clunky, but it helps you get used to working in the program. Plus, think of how impressed everyone will be if you start using transparency in your correspondence!

That being said, there are a handful of things—a top ten, if you will—you should know or think about to make working with InDesign the most pleasant experience possible:

- Keyboard shortcuts are one of the best ways to save time when you're creating documents. There's nothing worse than being in the middle of some great creative flow and having to hunt around in a menu for a command. It's not like you should sit around studying keyboard shortcut charts and memorizing them—just make sure you pay attention when you are working. Keyboard shortcuts for all menu commands are shown in the menus themselves. Take a look at them as you're making selections, and pretty soon you'll be shortcutting with the best of them.

- Speaking of keyboard shortcuts, you should learn the best InDesign keyboard shortcut ever: starting the program and then holding down Ctrl+Alt+Shift (Windows users) or ⌘+Option+Shift+Control (Mac users) to delete preferences. Why would you want to do this? Even the best of programs act wonky from time to time. A feature like InDesign's nearly limitless undos is very cool, but it can also add a lot of overhead to the application. If things start getting weird for you, try this trick. You'll lose some of the settings you might have added, but you'll gain speed and functionality and InDesign happiness back in one fell swoop.

By the way, the second coolest InDesign shortcut ever? Highlight text and then press Ctrl+Shift+, (Windows users) or ⌘+Shift+, (Mac users) to increase the font size incrementally.

- Speaking of wonkiness, if you're having problems with files that are corrupting or freaking out in any way, there are some things you can do to help. First, instead of performing simple saves (File, Save)—and we know you're doing that regularly to ensure you don't lose any of your hard work, right? *Right?*—try choosing File, Save As. Every time you save, you're adding extra overhead to the document. Every time you choose Save As, you're wiping out the document and creating a fresh new copy. If you're still having problems, try exporting your document to the InDesign Interchange format (`.inx`) and then reopening it.

- "All this talk about documents freaking out and getting wonky has me worried. What's up with all of this?" Nothing you're not going to find with any application. Why do things like this usually happen? A lot of problems are caused by networks. If you're opening files directly from a server, working on them, and then saving them back to the server, you could be contributing to the problem. Because InDesign documents tend to be large and complicated, with a lot of placed images and extra effects, any lags or drops in the process of working over those network cables can create weak spots in your document and make them vulnerable to corruption. Your best bet? Copy any file—as well as any links or associated files—you'll be working on to your hard drive, make changes, save and close, and copy the file(s) back to the server. Have your network administrators closed off access to the hard drive, or otherwise kept you from following this practice? Have a talk with them. Point them to Adobe's tips for working with InDesign documents at

http://www.adobe.com/support/techdocs/324687.html

This site includes a blurb about working off of servers as opposed to the local drive. Been working off your server for months or years and never had a problem? Good for you. Just be warned that even the best systems can sometimes go awry.

- Remember that InDesign gives you plenty of options for streamlining your workflow when you'll be using similar page elements for different documents. Use the Layout Adjustment feature to snap page elements into place automatically when you change a document's size and use XML to tag page elements and share information between documents. Start small and experiment. Soon you'll find plenty of uses for these types of features.

- As mentioned earlier in this chapter, InDesign comes with a number of templates that can help you come up with document ideas. Even better, some great special effects have been added to some of these documents, such as the folded page simulation pictured in Figure 32.10. Dig in. Take the documents apart and learn how these effects were created. In this instance, you'll find a triangle with a gradient applied, placed at the corner of the document. Very cool, very easy.

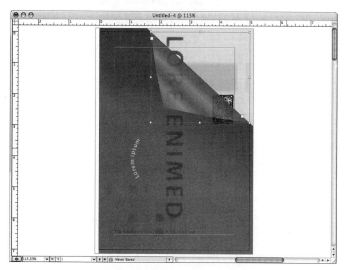

Figure 32.10
Besides serving as inspiration, InDesign's templates can also show you how to create some great special effects.

32

- You might have noticed that there are a lot of places in InDesign where you can set up presets. Take advantage of this. Saving document presets and customizing workspaces for specific users or document types can help make document creation easier. Creating print presets and PDF presets make outputting documents simple as well. If you have more than one person working on a specific project or type of project, share your presets with them. You'll save a co-worker some time, potentially make your company's documents better and more correct, and create good karma for yourself.

- InDesign's transparency features are among its strongest attributes. But they can also be among the most likely to fail when it comes to printing a document. Use the Flattener Preview palette to highlight possible problem areas when your document is actually printed. And talk to your commercial printers. Find out how much they've worked with InDesign transparencies and any problems they may have encountered. The first time you get a proof back that is nothing like what you sent in, you'll realize that you had to have this conversation eventually.

- If you're working with long documents, like books, there are compelling reasons for breaking up the book into smaller files—less memory being used, faster performance, the ability to have more than one person work on the files, less of a loss if something does go wrong. The solution? Create a book file. The best thing about books is the ability to share styles and formatting across the documents that are included. It creates less work for you, as well as a safer workflow. Plus, being able to print and create PDFs from the book can also make that part of the process easier.

- Communication is key. We mentioned it a couple of steps ago but it bears repeating, not just for transparency, but for everything. Talk to your commercial or offset printer. Especially if you're creating PDFs, quiz these people. Are there certain settings that need to be applied? How should you compress images? How should you handle color? There are a million things that can go wrong in printing—don't set yourself up for failure. Plan ahead, have a conversation, and make sure it's done right. The first time.

InDesign is most definitely the standard-bearer in page layout software. Combined with the other applications in the Creative Suite, your designs are sure to be a knock-out.

IV

GOLIVE

IN THIS PART

33

UNDERSTANDING THE GOLIVE WORK AREA

GoLive is primarily a web development application with available features that address pretty much every scenario you can think of when it comes to building a website. If all you want to do is create beautiful web pages, GoLive is the program for you. Conversely, if you want to go crazy and include video, animation, cascading style sheets, interactive forms; manage your website's assets; create active server pages; or even create content for mobile devices like cell phones, GoLive is also the program for you. GoLive is designed so you can do as much or as little as you like. This chapter introduces the things you need—and want—to know.

NEW FEATURES

This latest version of GoLive offers some great new features and some nifty improvements and enhancements to existing features. Many of the newer features are geared toward the development of web content for mobile devices because that's what's hot these days. If you haven't explored this booming segment of web development, you might want to peruse some of the tools and features in GoLive. If you're already into creating content for mobile devices you'll probably jump for joy at all the feature-rich additions to GoLive.

If you're a person who likes to have visual input and accurate visual representation, you'll really appreciate GoLive's visual tools, such as visual CSS (Cascading Style Sheets) layout, CSS prebuilt block objects, and enhanced live rendering. Transferring assets from InDesign and even using InDesign layers makes integrating your print design with your web design easier than ever. If you work in a team, this version of GoLive offers some powerful new additions that make team-creation and versioning easier to manage than ever before. Here's a quick look at all the new features—learn more about them in the upcoming chapters.

Tools and Features for Mobile Web Development

In this version of GoLive, Adobe has added a number of features and tools that enable you to develop content for mobile devices. Not only can you make your code conform to established standards for mobile authoring, GoLive also offers a rich visual interface where you can preview what your content will look like on a particular mobile device:

- **Visual CSS Authoring.** Generate CSS content that conforms to current standards for mobile devices using new visual tools that enable you to preview how your CSS formatting will look before you even create the actual content. See Chapter 37, "Using Cascading Style Sheets in GoLive."

- **Visual Content Development for a Variety of Interfaces.** Visually generate content for a variety of mobile devices and formats.

- **Convert Existing Web Content to Mobile Content.** Automatically convert your existing table-based web content to a mobile CSS layout.

- **Mobile Video Editing Tools.** Add interactivity and optimize video components with mobile video editing tools that support MPEG-4 and 3GPP (Third Generation Partnership Project) standards. MPEG-4 is a compression algorithm for video and graphics that enables the transmission of video, text, graphics, and even 2-D and 3-D animation over narrow bandwidth connections.

3GPP has established worldwide standards for the creation and delivery of all types of multimedia over high-speed wireless networks. The standards for MPEG-4 and 3GPP are fairly complex and detailed. You can find out more about MPEG-4 compression at http://www.apple.com/mpeg4. To learn more about 3GPP, visit www.3gpp.org.

- **Mobile Device Emulation.** Preview your sites as they will appear on mobile devices from Sony Ericsson and Nokia. You can even automatically update the skins for these devices to keep up to date with the latest models of phones and handheld units.

- **Blog Authoring Tools.** If you're a blogger, or maybe a wanna-be blogger, GoLive's blog tools that support Six Apart's TypePad service and Movable Type servers make creating a weblog site easier than ever. If you use the TypePad weblogging service and the Movable Type server, create the required elements using the draggable TypePad Blog Objects or draggable Movable Type 3.x Objects in the Objects palette. To learn more about Six Apart's software and services visit its website at www.sixapart.com.

- **Check for CSS Compliance.** Automatically check your mobile web content for compliance with version one of CSS (CSS1) and the most recent version of CSS (CSS2) standards. Visit www.w3.org/TR/REC-CSS1 and www.w3.org/TR/REC-CSS2 for detailed specs.

- **SMIL (Synchronized Multimedia Integration Language) Support.** Create content for SMIL (pronounced *smile*) applications using an object-based interface. SMIL content plays back as a RealMedia file in RealPlayer and can include anything from a simple slide show using the RealPix window in GoLive, to an elaborate interactive multimedia presentation incorporating the Timeline editor, SMIL Objects in the Objects palette, and the RealPlayer Editor. Get specific information about SMIL from Real's website at http://service.real.com/realplayer.

- **OMA, W3C, and 3GPP Development Environment.** The three main bodies for establishing standards and practices for the creation of mobile content are the Open Mobile Alliance (OMA), the World Wide Web Consortium (W3C), and the Third Generation Partnership Project (3GPP). GoLive enables you to check your code and design for compliance using one or all of these standards. Develop compliant code using CSS, XHTML, SVG-t, SMIL, MPEG-4, and others.

33

Improved Visual Tools for Web Design and Layout

This version of GoLive includes some improved visual tools along with some new ones that make creating content easier and the expected results more dependable when you view your pages in a browser:

- **CSS Layout Window.** Use the visual CSS Layout window to create CSS content that works correctly on web browsers and mobile devices. You can now preview a greater majority of CSS features from within the GoLive interface with a much improved design interface for formatting content with CSS.

- **Integrate InDesign content.** If you use InDesign for page layout and design, you can easily transfer assets from Adobe InDesign to GoLive, enabling you to repurpose your printed content for use on the web. Flow tagged InDesign pages to CSS templates, include graphics and URLs, and maintain your overall design style.

- **CSS Prebuilt Block Objects.** GoLive provides you with some prebuilt CSS block objects that help you standardize your websites. You can even create your own prebuilt CSS blocks and incorporate them into your GoLive working environment.

- **Enhanced Live Rendering.** Preview web and mobile content from within GoLive using a preview engine built on the Opera browser with support for Small-Screen Rendering (SSR). The Opera browser has long supported the most current CSS and DTD standards. Visit Opera's website at www.opera.com where you can download a browser for any platform, including your mobile phone.

- **Improved Layer Selection.** Select and Manipulate CSS layers easier than ever with new layer selection features.

- **Favicon Creation.** *Favicons* stands for *Favorites Icons* and are those tiny little icons you sometimes see next to a URL in the address bar of the browser and next to the bookmarked site in your Favorites or Bookmarks menu. Drag-and-drop favicons come with GoLive, or create your own and easily add them to your web pages.

Website Administration and Development Features

If you're a website administrator or manager, you probably have a specific way you like to work. Whether it means working mostly with raw code, or working with an advanced versioning system or staging server, GoLive enables you to work the way you want to:

- **Code Only Developer Mode.** Open GoLive in a code-only mode where you can still take advantage of GoLive's powerful site-management tools.

- **Split-view CSS.** View your CSS source code in a side-by-side mode with either CSS visual content or a live-rendering window. This feature is especially useful when you want to review a number of pages on your site to examine changes you make to an external CSS file.

- **Batch Convert HTML to XHTML.** Easily convert existing HTML content into the more flexible XHTML (Extensible HyperText Markup language) encoding.

- **Secure WebDAV and Secure FTP Client.** Update and manage your site on a remote server that supports SSH (Secure Shell) or SSL (Secure Sockets Layer) connections. These two common connection protocols are in use for most web servers these days and enable, among many other things, the connection and file transfer between you and your server. If you need details, visit www.openssl.org or openssh.org.

- **Versioning Support for Team Development.** Track and manage team-based websites using versioning systems such as Perforce, CVS, or Version Cue. You can also use Local/Network File System Directory Versioning.

- **Improved Software Development Kit (SDK).** Customize every aspect of GoLive, including the creation of CSS prebuilt objects using the SDK tools.

FILE FORMATS

Adobe GoLive has to be the most versatile web design program when it comes to file formats. Of course, GoLive supports all the file formats necessary to create and save web content, but GoLive does conversions for you on the fly, adding Smart Objects to your web content. For example, let's say you have a Photoshop image in Photoshop format (.psd) and you want to incorporate it in your web page. Insert it on your web page and GoLive prompts you to convert it to a usable format and enables you to scale the image and choose the appropriate format and compression. After it's inserted into your document as a Smart Object, you can simply double-click the image to edit it in its native format and then save it to update the web page content. Source files supported include BMP, PCX, Pixar, Amiga IFF, TIFF, TARGA, PDF, EPS, JPEG, JPEG 2000, PNG, and PICT (Mac OS only). The following are some of the formats GoLive supports:

- **HTML (HyperText Markup Language).** The language of the web since the beginning, HTML codes are now the most basic building blocks for web pages. Whether you want to hand-code your own HTML or use GoLive's tools to create HTML content, GoLive accommodates you in this endeavor and even helps you check the syntax of your code, along with its compliance to established standards.

- **XHTML (Extensible HyperText Markup Language).** The successor to HTML, XHTML extends the capabilities of HTML to include encoding for CSS and mobile devices and is entirely XML (Extensible Markup Language) compatible, which makes the code usable by any system capable of interpreting XML. GoLive automatically formats web pages for XHTML 1.0 Transitional, though you can easily convert it to other subsets of XHTML by choosing Convert under the Special menu. There are three basic DTDs (Document Type Definitions) widely specified for XHTML:

  - **XHTML 1.0 Strict.** This method is used when you desire the cleanest structural markup without any markup for layout formatting. Use CSS to handle the layout and formatting in this case.

  - **XHTML 1.0 Transitional.** If you're creating web pages for the general public and want to include support for older browsers, this is probably the best and most common method. You can still take advantage of the benefits of XHTML, but this method also supports some of the more traditional HTML methods of doing things, such as the attributes for the body tag and link tag.

  - **XHTML 1.0 Frameset.** Use this DTD when you want to use frames in your web pages.

To view the complete XHTML specification, visit http://www.w3.org/TR/xhtml1. You can also take advantage of the W3C's markup validation service by going to http://validator.w3.org/ (see Figure 33.1). You can enter a URL address or validate by file upload if you haven't published your pages yet. Your pages must have a DOCTYPE declaration in the head section for the validator to report on your pages accurately. See Chapter 35, "Creating Web Page Layouts with GoLive," for details.

33

Figure 33.1
The W3C Markup Validation Service can be very helpful in determining whether your web pages conform to established standards.

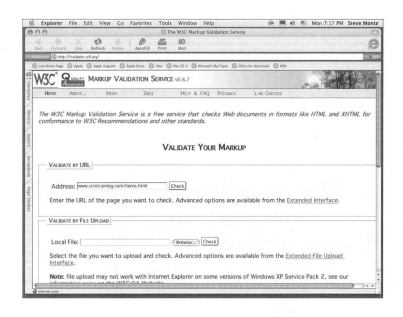

ASP, JSP, and PHP Pages

GoLive can create, edit, and save Active Server Pages (ASP), Java Server Pages (JSP), and Hypertext Preprocessor pages (PHP). If your server supports any of these web page-processing methods, you can easily create the content using GoLive tools and features.

File Formats for Mobile Web Authoring

Create Synchronized Multimedia Integration Language (SMIL) documents for the Multimedia Messaging Service (MMS). Create documents using the Wireless Markup Language (WML). MMS documents are saved with the `.smil` extension and WML documents are saved with the `.wml` extension. See Chapter 35 for more information on authoring web content for mobile devices.

Other Formats

GoLive can also open, edit, and save a number of file formats that are external components of websites. GoLive can open and save plain text documents and has scripting help built in to enable you to create such helpful text files as `robots.txt`, which tells search engine robots which files to download. If you need to set up password access on your site and your service provider supports `.htaccess`, you can easily create the `.htaccess` file along with the `.htpasswd` file when you choose File, New in GoLive.

Image File Formats

GoLive enables you to import and incorporate all the image file formats supported by browsers. These formats include GIF (Graphic Interchange Format), JPEG (Joint Photographic Experts Group), and PNG (Portable Network Graphic). In addition, the more recent additions of SVG (Scalable Vector Graphics) and the SVG-Tiny format for mobile devices are entirely supported by GoLive. For mobile devices, the WBMP format, which is strictly 1-bit color (black-and-white pixels only), is also supported. The SWF format also supports scalable vector graphics and can be imported into GoLive, although the SWF format is more frequently seen in sites that implement Macromedia Flash content (.swf being the file extension of Flash movies).

Multimedia Formats

GoLive offers the most support for the QuickTime file format. Aside from the ability to insert and implement QuickTime movies on your web pages, GoLive has an entire QuickTime editing suite built in to the GoLive application. The QuickTime editor is also able to create and edit 3GPP movies for 3G mobile devices. GoLive enables the insertion of multimedia elements using a series of plug-in modules. In the Basic Objects palette, you can drag and drop objects to insert Flash SWF, QuickTime, Real, SVG, and Windows Media file formats. Java applets and other generic plug-in formats can also be added using this method.

THE GOLIVE INTERFACE

If you have been using previous versions of GoLive, you will find the overall interface largely unchanged. If you are new to GoLive, the interface can, at first glance, be a bit daunting. There's a lot going on onscreen, but after you get a feel for where things are located it all makes sense. As shown in Figure 33.2, the GoLive interface is broken up into four main components—the Main toolbar, the Tools and Objects palette, the document window, and the various floating palettes.

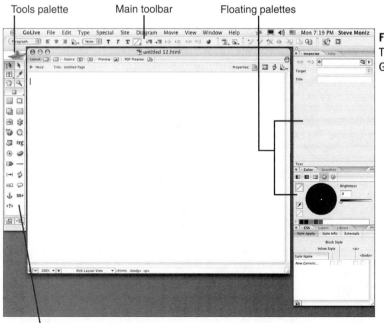

Figure 33.2
The four main components of the GoLive interface.

33

The Main Toolbar

The Main toolbar, shown in Figure 33.3, contains the standard HTML markup along with access to the CSS and the little bug icon that enables you to show link warnings in the document and code. The Document toolbar, Adobe Services toolbar, and Version Control toolbar are also shown in Figure 33.3, although these can be displayed separately by clicking and dragging the vertical bar to the left of the tools (see Figure 33.4).

Figure 33.3
The main GoLive toolbar.

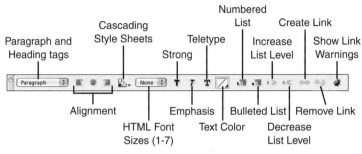

Figure 33.4
Separate and rearrange the tool-bars by clicking and dragging the vertical bar when a toolbar is docked.

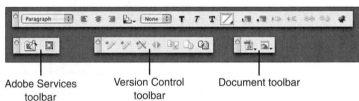

The Document Toolbar

The Document toolbar shown in Figure 33.4 enables you to switch between open documents and also provides a list of available browsers you can use to preview your web pages. Click the Select Window button (left icon) to display a list of open windows. Click on a window in the list to bring it to the front. Click and hold the Preview in Browser button (right button) to display a list of available browsers. Click the browser you want to use to preview the web page.

Preferences for the Preview in Browser Button

If you click the Preview in Browser button without holding it to display the list of browsers, your web page opens in every bolded browser in the list. To reduce the number of browsers in the list and select which ones automatically launch, click and hold on the Preview in Browser button and then select Edit to display the Browsers Preferences window shown in Figure 33.5. Check only the browsers you want to launch when you click the Preview in Browser button. Click OK to close the Preferences window.

The Adobe Services Toolbar

The Adobe Services toolbar provides buttons that link to other Adobe services, such as the Adobe Bridge and Adobe Stock Photos (refer to Figure 33.4). Chapter 1, "Creative Suite 2 Basics," has more information about these nifty features.

The Version Control Toolbar

The Version Control toolbar contains tools that enable you to take advantage of versioning features such as file check-in and check-out. The tools appear grayed out when you have not set up a versioning server. See Chapter 1 for more information about Version Cue.

The Site Management Interface

When the Site window is displayed, the buttons in the Main toolbar change to correlate with the functions needed to manage your website. Additionally, the buttons in the Main toolbar change based on which tab in the Site window is selected. In Figure 33.6, the buttons in the Main toolbar reflect the available options when the Files tab is selected. If you click through the other tabs in the Site window, you see some of the buttons in the Main toolbar change. You'll learn about these options in Chapter 40, "Creating a Website with GoLive."

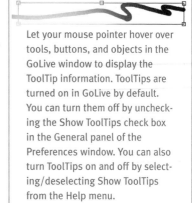

Let your mouse pointer hover over tools, buttons, and objects in the GoLive window to display the ToolTip information. ToolTips are turned on in GoLive by default. You can turn them off by unchecking the Show ToolTips check box in the General panel of the Preferences window. You can also turn ToolTips on and off by selecting/deselecting Show ToolTips from the Help menu.

33

Figure 33.6
When the Site window is displayed, the buttons in the Main toolbar reflect the options for the various tabbed panels.

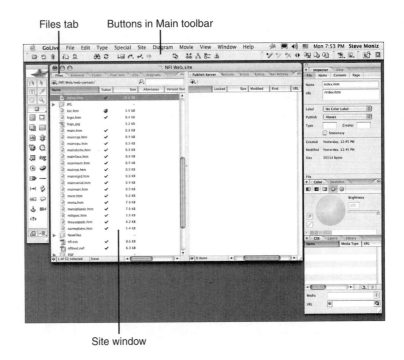

Files tab   Buttons in Main toolbar

Site window

DISPLAYING TOOLBARS AND PALETTES

All the GoLive toolbars, palettes, and windows are available under the Window menu, as shown in Figure 33.7. Select an option from the Toolbars submenu in the Window menu to activate the toolbars when they have been closed. You can't toggle the toolbars off using the menu, but if you intentionally or inadvertently close a toolbar, this is where you turn them on again.

Setting Up Your Workspace

GoLive's Workspace feature can come in quite handy when you're working on sites with different specifications or if you're sharing your computer with others who use different palettes than you do. For example, I like to have the History palette open all the time and the Layers palette open along with the CSS palette rather than having them grouped in the same palette group. The Window, Workspace submenu is shown in Figure 33.8.

To save your workspace after you arrange it to your liking, follow these steps:

1. Open and arrange the palettes the way you like.

2. Choose Window, Workspace, Save Workspace from the menu bar to display the Save Workspace dialog shown in Figure 33.9.

3. Type a name for your workspace, or select a workspace name from the pop-up menu to overwrite an existing workspace, and then click OK.

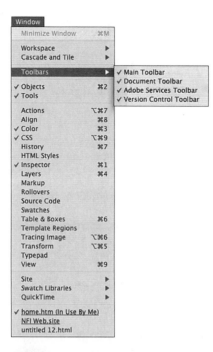

Figure 33.7
The Window menu enables you to control what is displayed on your screen.

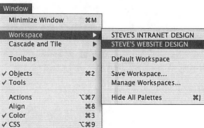

Figure 33.8
Select the Workspace options under the Window menu.

33

Figure 33.9
Assign a name to your workspace
in the Save Workspace dialog box.

You can have as many workspaces defined as you like and switch between them at any time. If you notice yourself going to the Window menu numerous times to turn palettes on and off, consider creating workspaces for them. Select Manage Workspaces to rename workspaces, delete them, or add new sets to be assigned at a later time:

1. Choose Window, Workspace, Manage Workspaces to display the Manage Workspaces dialog box shown in Figure 33.10.

2. Highlight an existing workspace name to edit its name.

3. Click the trash button to delete the highlighted workspace name.

4. Click the page button to create a new workspace.

5. Click OK when you finish managing your workspaces.

Figure 33.10
Add, delete, and edit Workspaces.

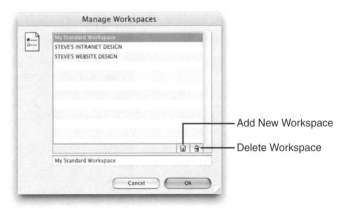

THE DOCUMENT WINDOW

The Document window is where your web pages are displayed when they're open in GoLive. The Document window contains a number of tabs along the top that enable you to view your document in a variety of ways.

The Layout Editor is enabled by clicking the Layout tab of the Document window, and it is the visual editing environment for web pages, as shown in Figure 33.11. At the top of the Layout Editor window, the Head information for your document can be displayed by clicking the right-pointing triangle next to the word *Head*, as shown in Figure 33.12. All the head elements are displayed as icons in the Head section. You can easily edit the information in the Head section by double-clicking the appropriate icon and editing the settings in the corresponding palette, such as the Inspector palette shown in Figure 33.13.

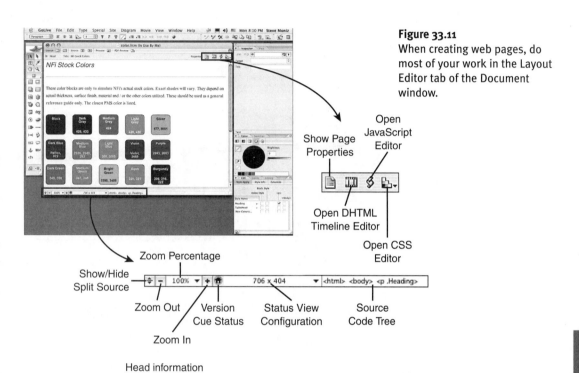

Figure 33.11
When creating web pages, do most of your work in the Layout Editor tab of the Document window.

Open JavaScript Editor

Show Page Properties

Open DHTML Timeline Editor

Open CSS Editor

Zoom Percentage

Show/Hide Split Source

Zoom Out

Version Cue Status

Status View Configuration

Source Code Tree

Zoom In

Head information

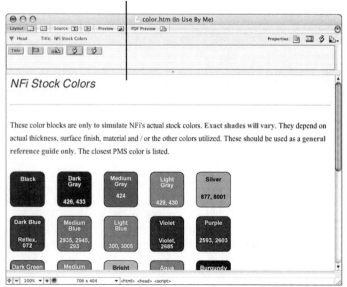

Figure 33.12
The Head section of your HTML code is depicted as icons at the top of the Layout Editor window.

Figure 33.13
Double-clicking the Title icon in the Head section displays the Page Inspector palette where the title can be edited.

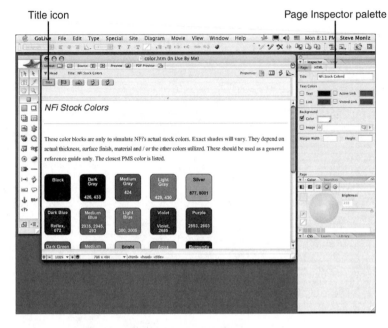

The buttons in the upper-right corner of the Layout Editor window enable you to access some of the features in GoLive quickly. The Page Properties button displays the Page Inspector palette in the Inspector palette group where you set the page attributes, such as title, colors, margins, and background images. The filmstrip button opens the DHTML Timeline Editor where you can animate layers. The Script button opens the JavaScript Editor where you can create and edit JavaScript code. The stair-step button opens the CSS editor.

> You can edit the HTML title of your page by clicking the title name to the right of the word *Title* at the top of the Layout Editor window.

At the bottom of the Layout Editor window are a number of helpful features that enable you to work more efficiently (refer to Figure 33.11):

- In the bottom-left corner, click the button to toggle split source code view, as shown in Figure 33.14. In Split Source view, the source code appears along with the layout to enable you to see how the changes in one affect the other.

- Click the + or − button to zoom in or out; alternatively, select a zoom percentage from the pop-up menu between the + and − buttons.

- The Version Cue status icon depicts the current status of your document when you're using a Version Cue server.

- You can change the information that appears in the Status View Configuration section by clicking the downward pointing triangle, as shown in Figure 33.15. Select from the Show submenu to determine what is displayed. If you choose View Configuration, the current view is displayed, such as `Web Layout View`. If you choose Version Cue Status, the Version Cue Status is displayed, such as `Only Copy`. Choose Page Dimensions to display the current width and height (in pixels) of the current document. Select Document Statistics to display the size of the current file in Bytes. All of these options are strictly informational and do not affect your pages.

Show/Hide Split Source

Figure 33.14
The Split Source view of the Layout Editor window.

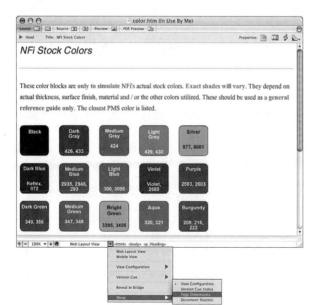

Figure 33.15
Explore the settings for the Status View Configuration.

33

The Frame Editor

The Frame Editor enables you to create, edit, and manage framesets and frames (see Figure 33.16). All the attributes for the frames and framesets are edited using the Frame Inspector and FrameSet Inspector palettes, respectively. You can double-click inside a frame to open the corresponding page in the Layout Editor, or click the Preview Frame button in the Frame Inspector palette to preview the frame content, as shown in Figure 33.17. Preview the entire frameset by clicking the Preview Set button in the FrameSet Inspector palette, as shown in Figure 33.18.

Figure 33.16
Create, edit, and manipulate framesets and frames using the Frame Editor.

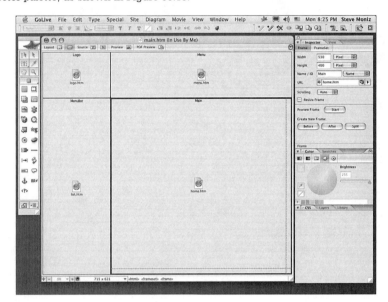

Preview frame content

Figure 33.17
Use the Frame Inspector palette to set the attributes for your frames.

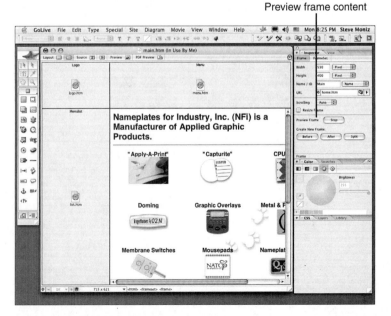

Preview entire frameset

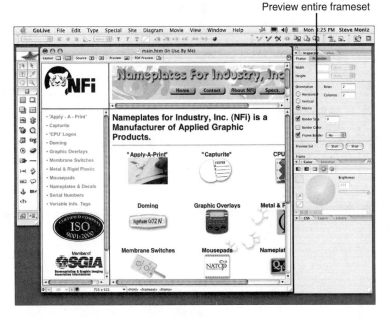

Figure 33.18
Use the FrameSet Inspector palette to set the attributes for the frameset.

The Source Code Editor

The Source Code Editor enables you to navigate the source code used in an open document easily. The buttons and pull-down menu along the top of the Source Code Editor window determine how the source code is displayed (see Figure 33.19). See Chapter 38, "Working with Source Code in GoLive," to learn more about the source code window.

The Outline Editor

The Outline Editor offers an interactive outline view of the source code where you can expand or contract any section of the code selectively (see Figure 33.20). The Outline Editor is a handy tool for getting an overall view of the basic structure of your code, especially if your pages contain lots of DIV tags.

If you want to familiarize yourself with HTML code, create elements in the Layout Editor. Select an element in the Layout Editor and click the Source Code tab to see the highlighted corresponding HTML code.

Simply click the triangles to expand and contract the sections of code. You can even edit the code and web content by clicking first and then editing. If you prefer to reduce the amount of code by showing only the opening tag of HTML tags that have both opening and closing tags, click the Toggle Unary/Binary Tags button in the Main toolbar to hide or show the closing tags. The Main toolbar changes to contain buttons that help you edit your HTML code in the Outline Editor, as shown in Figure 33.21.

33

Figure 33.19
The Source Code Editor window.

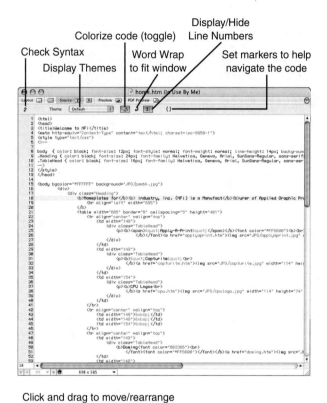

Figure 33.20
The Outline Editor makes working with long pages of code a breeze.

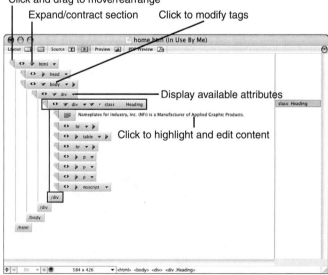

Add New Text

Add New
Element

Add New
Generic Item

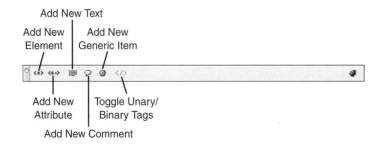

Add New
Attribute

Toggle Unary/
Binary Tags

Add New Comment

Figure 33.21
The Main toolbar changes to display the editing tools for the Outline Editor.

The Layout Preview

Preview your web pages in the Layout Preview window by clicking the Preview tab, as shown in Figure 33.22. The Layout Preview window uses the GoLive Browser Profile to emulate the latest browsers. You can click links to navigate through your site in the Layout Preview window as well.

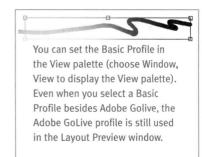

You can set the Basic Profile in the View palette (choose Window, View to display the View palette). Even when you select a Basic Profile besides Adobe Golive, the Adobe GoLive profile is still used in the Layout Preview window.

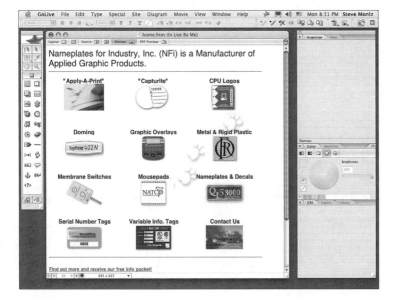

Figure 33.22
The Layout Preview window is great for doing a quick check of your web pages and the links on the pages.

33

The PDF Preview

The PDF Preview tab enables you to preview your layout as an Acrobat PDF file (see Figure 33.23). The Main toolbar changes to display buttons to save, print, or email the PDF file. These features offer a quick way to proof a web page for client approval, or to help build a presentation to present to the clients. Settings for the PDF file and navigation aids are found at the bottom of the PDF Preview window.

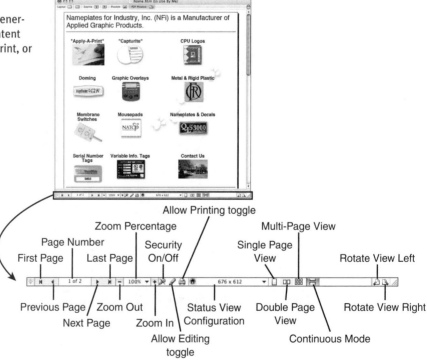

It's a good idea to always check your web pages on multiple platforms and in multiple browsers—and even multiple versions of browsers, depending on your target audience. Install as many of them as you can on your computer and then add them to the Browser list in the Preferences window.

As you can see, the GoLive interface is a very well-structured adaptable environment. When you become accustomed to the basic way things work, you'll find your way around with ease. Many of the basic interface features are also found in other Adobe applications, making it easier to adapt to one program when you already know another. Try to stick with all Adobe applications for every aspect of web development, and you will find that you work faster and more efficiently. Don't forget to check Adobe's online help (look in the Help menu) and visit the Adobe website often for the latest cool stuff.

Figure 33.23
The PDF Preview window generates a PDF of your web content and enables you to save, print, or email the PDF.

34

WORKING WITH GOLIVE TOOLS AND PALETTES

GoLive provides tools and objects for just about every possible need, including specialized tools for working with web pages and websites, and even tools for editing QuickTime movies. Thankfully, the tools are broken down into logical categories and arranged in the Tools palette and Objects palette. The Tools palette contains some standard editing tools, and the Objects palette contains the elements needed to build web pages, manage websites, edit QuickTime movies, and add dynamic features to your web pages.

THE TOOLS PALETTE

The Tools palette is located above the Objects palette by default (see Figure 34.1), though depending how you like to work, you could separate the Objects palette from the Tools palette (as shown in Figure 34.2) by clicking the Separate Palettes button at the bottom-left of the Objects palette. Click the same button again to put the Objects palette back with the Tools palette. The Tools palette contains the following seven tools used to edit web pages. You can use the shortcut key (the letter in parentheses) to access the tools; note that many of the same shortcuts are used in other Adobe products, such as Photoshop and Illustrator:

Figure 34.1
The Tools in the Tools palette.

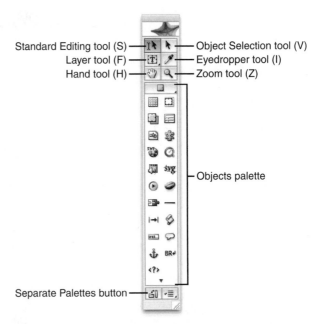

Standard Editing tool (S) — Object Selection tool (V)
Layer tool (F) — Eyedropper tool (I)
Hand tool (H) — Zoom tool (Z)

Objects palette

Separate Palettes button

Figure 34.2
Separate the Tools and Objects into individual palettes.

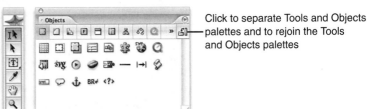

Click to separate Tools and Objects palettes and to rejoin the Tools and Objects palettes

- **Standard Editing tool (S):** You use the Standard Editing tool the most; this tool is selected by default. Use the Standard Editing tool to edit your web content and to select and edit text.

- **Object Selection tool (V):** The Object Selection tool makes it easier to select objects on your web pages, such as images, layers, tables, and frames. The only thing you can't select with the Object Selection tool is text—use the Standard Editing tool for that.

- **Layer tool (F):** The Layer tool enables you to draw and position layers on a page.

- **Grid Text Box tool (Shift+F):** The Grid Text Box tool is located in the same position on the Tools palette as the Layer tool. Click and hold the Layer tool to reveal the Grid Text Box tool or press the shortcut key (Shift+F) to select it. Use the Grid Text Box tool to draw and position text boxes on a layout grid.

- **Eyedropper tool (I):** Use the Eyedropper tool to pick up a color from text or any object on your web page.

- **Zoom tool (Z):** Zoom in and zoom out on specific areas of your documents. This Zoom tool works like all Adobe Zoom tools. Click and drag to draw a box around the area you want to zoom in on, hold down the Option key (on a Mac) or the Alt key (in Windows) as you drag to zoom out. Double-click the Zoom tool in the Tools palette to return your page to 100%. You can also zoom in and out using the + and – buttons at the bottom of the document window or choosing a magnification value from the Zoom Values menu at the bottom of the document window.

To access the Hand tool when you have any other tool selected, hold down the Control-Option keys (on a Mac) or Ctrl+Alt keys (in Windows). You can click and drag after the Hand tool is selected to move your work inside the window. This approach is especially helpful when you've zoomed in to the page or when your web page is wider than the document window.

- **Hand tool (H):** When your document is larger than the document window, use the Hand tool to move the work around inside the window.

THE OBJECTS PALETTE

The Objects palette contains all the draggable objects that you use to create content for your web pages and documents. The Objects palette is separated into 11 sections or categories, as shown in Figure 34.3. Each section contains objects for a specific purpose. For example, use the objects in the QuickTime Objects palette to create and edit QuickTime movies, or use the objects in the Form Objects palette to add form elements to your web page. You can access the different Objects palettes in a number of ways:

34

- When the Objects palette is joined with the Tools palette, click the Object button at the top of the Objects palette to display a list of available palettes and then select the Objects you'd like to display (see Figure 34.4).

Figure 34.3
The 11 Object palettes, shown when the Objects palette is separated from the Tools palette.

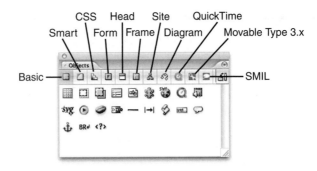

Figure 34.4
The Objects palettes are also accessible in list form.

- You can also display and select Objects palettes from the palette options menu of the Objects palette, as shown in Figure 34.5.

- When the Objects palette is separated from the Tools palette, click the tabbed icons along the top of the palette to switch between Objects palettes.

All the objects in the Objects palettes are draggable and must be dragged onto your page before you can access them. If you want to insert an object, for example, right-click (in Windows) or Control-click (on the Mac) at the location where you want to insert the object and choose Insert Object from the context menu, as shown in Figure 34.6. You can also choose Special, Insert from the menu at the top of the screen.

Click the GoLive star icon at the very top of the Tools palette to access the GoLive web page on Adobe's website:

(http://www.adobe.com/ products/golive/main.html).

Figure 34.5
The Objects palette options menu.

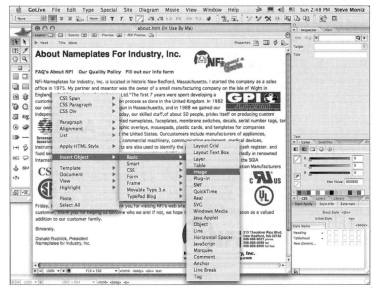

Figure 34.6
Insert objects using the context-sensitive menu.

GOLIVE'S MENUS

As with all Adobe products, the GoLive menus are logical and well thought-out to make it as easy as possible for you to find what you're looking for. You will find menus in a number of places in GoLive. The application menus are located along the top of the screen and contain access to nearly all of GoLive's features. Take a second to click each of the application menus and examine the contents of each menu:

- The **GoLive** menu is available on the MacOS only and contains Web Settings and Preferences, as well as the About GoLive option. On the Windows operating system, Preferences and Web Settings are found under the Edit menu, and the About GoLive option is under the Help menu.

- The **File** menu enables you to open, close, import, and export files as well as set some file-related settings.

- The **Edit** menu contains the standard editing features in addition to selections for finding elements; checking spelling and code syntax; and settings for PDFs, colors, and keyboard shortcuts.

- The **Type** menu contains HTML text formatting options along with access to some cascading style sheet (CSS) features.

- The **Special** menu contains a variety of submenus to help you work with everything from JavaScript to tables to dynamic HTML (DHTML) timelines. You can also set the page properties from this menu and view document statistics such as character count and word count.

- The **Site** menu contains options specific to the management and editing of your site using the GoLive site window.

- The **Diagram** menu offers options for diagramming a website, setting up a staging server, and creating a table of contents.

- The **Movie** menu contains features for editing QuickTime movies.

- The **View** menu enables you to specify how things appear on the screen. It's also where you go to show or hide the rulers, grid, and smart guides.

- The **Window** menu is where you go to display palettes and toolbars. All open windows and documents are listed at the bottom of this menu, making it easy to see what's open and to switch between the listed items.

- The **Help** menu provides, as its main feature, access to GoLive help. There is a lot to know about GoLive, and Adobe's help files are comprehensive and easy to navigate. Before you spend time paging through the documentation, check the help files. This is also the menu where you can turn Tool Tips on or off, control how you want to check for software updates, and transfer the activation code if you need to install GoLive on a new computer.

34

Palette and Window Menus

Most of the palettes in GoLive contain some sort of palette menu that offers features and options for that particular palette. The site window and document window also contain minimenus of their own. The palette menus and window menus are indicated by a triangle pointing to the right, as shown in Figure 34.7.

Button Menus, Object Menus, Tool Menus, and Status Menus

You may also encounter menus attached to buttons, objects, and status displays. Button menus are indicated by downward pointing triangles and typically display a list of options for a particular button. For example, the Open CSS Editor button in the upper-right corner of the document window will open the CSS Editor if you click it. If you click and hold on the button, however, other options are also available.

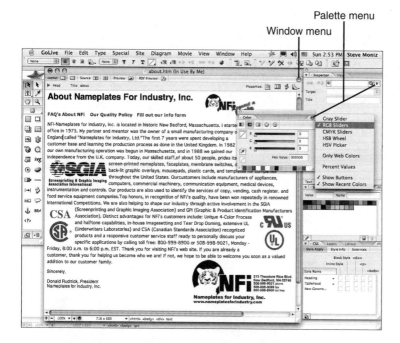

Palette menu

Window menu

Figure 34.7
Window menus and palette menus.

Object and tool menus are represented by a tiny angled triangle in the lower-right corner of the object or tool's icon in the Objects or Tools palette. Click and hold for a second on a tool to display its underlying tools. Simply click the object buttons to display their options. Status menus are indicated by downward-pointing triangles to the right of some status area, such as the Zoom Value located in the lower-left corner of the document window. Clicking on the arrow displays a list of options for displaying status information or, as shown in Figure 34.8, changing the view percentage.

You'll also find menus sprinkled throughout the various palettes and indicated by right-pointing triangles.

Context-Sensitive Menus

I always say, "When in doubt, check the context menu." If you're not sure whether an editing feature is available, or if you know it exists but just don't know where to find it, check the context menu. As with all Adobe products, you can access the context-sensitive menu by right-clicking (in Windows) or Control-clicking (on the Mac). A context menu will appear, displaying options for the thing you were pointing at when you clicked (see Figure 34.9).

> Take note of buttons that contain button menus and examine the contents of the menu before clicking the button. In some cases, clicking the button may produce results you are not expecting. For example, if you click the Preview in Browser button located in the Document toolbar, your web page may launch and display in a number of browsers specified in the button menu.

34

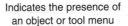
Indicates the presence of
an object or tool menu

Figure 34.8
Click the little downward-pointing
triangle to display options for display and status.

Figure 34.9
The context menu shown here displays the various text-editing
options available.

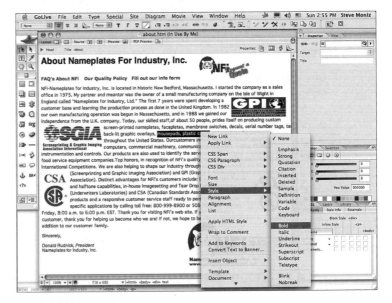

KEYBOARD SHORTCUTS

There are keyboard shortcuts for most of the frequently used features of GoLive and even shortcuts
for some not-so-frequently used features. The menus in GoLive display corresponding shortcut keys
to the right of the menu option where applicable. If you're familiar with other Adobe products, you'll

find most of the keyboard shortcuts are the same for corresponding features. Some keyboard shortcuts are not found anywhere in the menus or in the program, so you have to look those up separately using the Adobe Help Center. Choose GoLive Help from the Help menu and search for the word shortcuts. Table 34.1 lists some of my favorite undocumented shortcuts (feel free to copy this page and stick it up near your computer).

Table 34.1 Keyboard Shortcuts

Result	Windows	Mac OS
Keyboard shortcuts not found in menu commands or ToolTips.		
Suppress confirmation dialog when deleting items.	—	Option
Close the Web Settings window without saving changes.	Alt	Option
Maintain proportions of objects when resizing.	Shift+drag	Shift-drag
Create a new link with text or objects.	Alt+drag	⌘-drag
Select a word.	Double-click	Double-click
Select a line of text.	Triple-click	Triple-click
Select a paragraph.	Quadruple-click	Quadruple-click
New line instead of new paragraph (inserts).	Shift+Enter	Shift-Return
Nonbreaking space.	Shift+Spacebar	Option-Spacebar
Move boxes on a layout grid in 1-pixel increments.	Ctrl+Alt+Arrow	Option-Arrow
Duplicate a selected object.	Ctrl+drag	Option-drag
Delete a file in the Site window without a confirmation dialog.	Ctrl+click the delete icon	Option-click the delete icon
Display source code as a ToolTip.	Alt+Shift	Option-Shift

You can edit the existing keyboard shortcuts or create your own using GoLive's Shortcut Editor. In the Shortcut Editor you can create new sets of keyboard shortcuts and apply them individually to different workspaces that you've set up in the Window, Workspace submenu.

Changing the Current Shortcut Set

Choose Edit, Keyboard Shortcuts to display the Edit Keyboard Shortcuts dialog box and select a shortcut set from the Select Set menu, as shown in Figure 34.10. Click OK.

Creating a New Shortcut Set

Choose Edit, Keyboard Shortcuts and click New Set. Type a name for the new set in the Set Name field and select a shortcut set from the Copy From menu, as shown in Figure 34.11. Click OK.

34

Figure 34.10
Select a shortcut set to make it
the current active set.

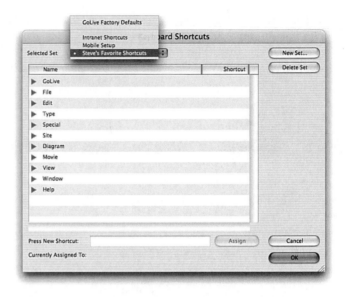

Figure 34.11
Create a new shortcut set.

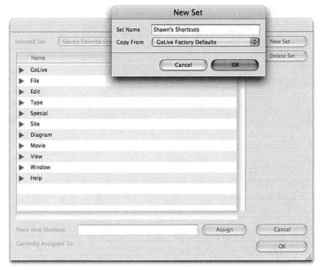

Creating or Editing a Shortcut

It's a good idea to create a new shortcut set before making any edits to the default set. Follow the
instructions for creating a new set, then perform the following steps:

1. Choose Edit, Keyboard Shortcuts to display the Keyboard Shortcuts dialog.

2. Select an existing shortcut set (not the GoLive Default set) from the Selected Set menu or create
a new set.

3. In the list of menu items, expand the list for the menu item that contains the command you want to edit and then select the command.

4. Click in the Press New Shortcut field and press the keys for the new keyboard shortcut. If the shortcut already exists, it appears in the Current Assigned To area below the shortcut field. If this happens, try a different shortcut or change the shortcut for the other command and come back to this command and use the shortcut you want.

5. Click Assign to create a new shortcut or click Replace to replace an existing shortcut.

6. Repeat these steps for all shortcuts you want to change and then click OK.

WORKING WITH COLOR

GoLive offers excellent tools and features for creating, editing, and managing color. You can specify colors in any of a variety of color spaces, save your colors, create color swatch libraries, define site colors, and even manage color workflow to correspond with other Adobe applications in the Creative Suite. You can apply color to objects on your pages using a combination of the Color palette, Swatches palette, Swatch Library palettes, and the Color Picker.

The GoLive Color Palette

The GoLive Color palette contains color models based on CMYK, RGB, HSV, HSB, and Grayscale. Color swatches at the bottom of the Color palette reflect the most recently used colors. The Hex value field in the Color palette displays the hexadecimal color value for the current color (see Figure 34.12).

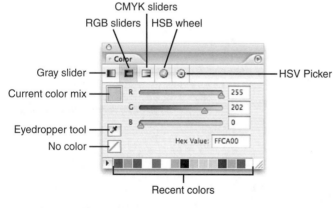

Figure 34.12
The GoLive Color palette.

The Swatches Palette

The Swatches palette contains colors swatches that you create, edit, and manage as shown in Figure 34.13. You can add colors to the Swatches palette by mixing a color using the Color palette, copying a color from an existing swatch library, or sampling a color with the Eyedropper tool. When you select a swatch in the Swatches palette, the color mix is displayed in the Color palette.

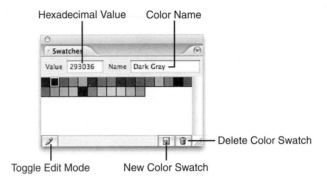

Figure 34.13
The GoLive Swatches palette.

Choose from the following options:

- **Add a New Color Swatch:** Mix a color using the Color palette or click a color with the Eyedropper tool, and then click the Create New Swatch button in the Swatches palette.

- **Delete Color Swatch:** Select the color swatch in the Swatches palette and click the Delete Swatch button in the Swatches palette.

- **Edit the Color Name:** Click the Toggle Edit Mode button in the bottom-left corner of the Swatches palette to switch to Edit mode and then type a name in the Name field of the Swatches palette.

- **Adjust or Change a Swatch Color:** Click the Toggle Edit Mode button in the bottom-left corner of the Swatches palette to switch to Edit mode, select a color swatch to adjust, and then adjust the color in the Color palette.

- **Search for a Color in the Swatches Palette:** Click the Toggle Edit Mode button in the bottom-left corner of the Swatches palette to turn Edit mode off. Type a color name or hex value in the search fields at the top of the Swatches palette and press Enter/Return to search for the color swatch. You type only the first few letters of the color name to find the first color that matches that text string.

- **Change the Display of the Swatches Palette:** To change the display of the Swatches palette between List view and Small Thumbnail view, select the desired setting from the Swatches palette menu (click the arrow in the upper-right corner of the Swatches palette, as shown in Figure 34.14).

Figure 34.14
Use the Swatches palette menu to set options for the Swatches palette.

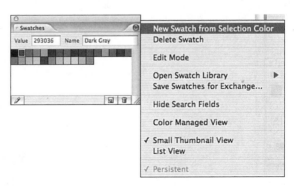

■ **Save Swatches:** To save swatches for use later, choose Save Swatches for Exchange from the Swatches palette menu. Save your swatches in a location you'll remember. Saved swatches can be opened from other Adobe Creative Suite applications when the colors are synchronized. See "Color Settings in GoLive," later in this chapter, for more information on synchronized color. Choose Open Swatch Library from the palette menu and select Other Library at the bottom of the list to navigate to your saved color library and open it.

Swatch Libraries

You can load a number of different swatch libraries as separate palettes in GoLive. Simply choose a swatch library from the palette menu of the Swatches palette, as shown in Figure 34.15. The Swatch Library palettes contain the same options and settings as the Swatches palette, except that you cannot add colors, delete colors, or edit colors.

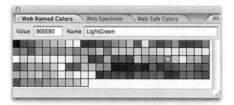

Figure 34.15
Open as many swatch libraries (which appear onscreen as palettes) as you need.

COLOR SETTINGS IN GOLIVE

GoLive's Color Settings dialog box enables you to specify which color profile you'd like to use to display color in GoLive. For most folks, the default settings work fine. However, if you're working in an environment where an active effort is being made to manage color, you may want to customize the color settings used in GoLive. A dissertation on color management systems (CMS) is beyond the scope of this book, but you can find instructions on how to use the Adobe Creative Suite's color synchronization in Chapter 1, "Creative Suite 2 Basics."

Follow these steps to work with the Color Settings dialog:

1. Choose Edit, Color Settings to display the Color Settings dialog, as shown in Figure 34.16.

2. Select color settings from the Settings pop-up list. Choose Custom from the list if you want to create your own settings.

   If you selected Custom from the Settings list and indicated your own settings using the options in the Color Settings dialog, your color settings are no longer synchronized with the rest of the Creative Suite applications (see Figure 34.17).

3. Click OK after you set your color settings.

34

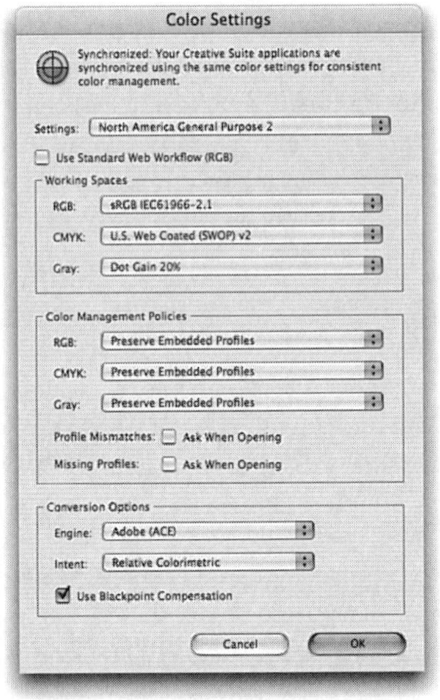

Figure 34.16
The GoLive Color Settings dialog.

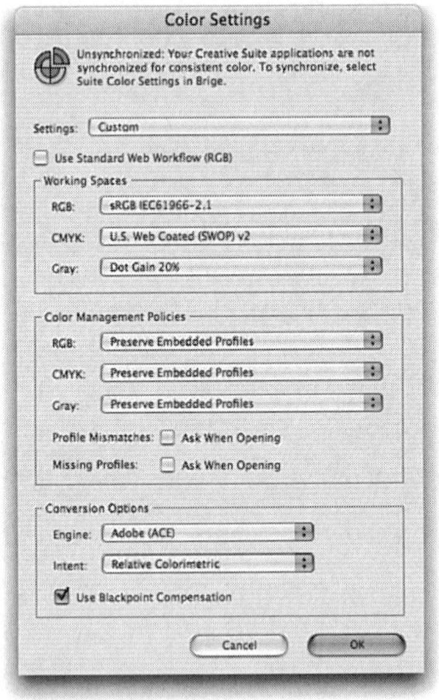

Figure 34.17
Custom color settings must match those for all the other Creative Suite applications to be synchronized.

SITE COLORS

Collect and organize all the colors for your site in one central location and then apply them to the text and objects on your website. When you set the colors of text and objects using the site colors, the colors are linked to the site colors. That means that when you edit a site color, the color changes everywhere it was previously used on your site. Use the Colors tab in the Site window to define colors individually or as part of groups of colors organized in folders (see Figure 34.18). When you create a site color, you assign a color name to it, and it is displayed in the Site window with the name you assign, in addition to its hex value and HTML color name when available.

Colors tab of the Site window
Color group | Color used in site

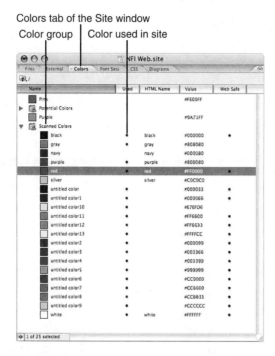

Figure 34.18
The site colors are found in the Site window.

Adding Site Colors

You can add site colors in a number of ways. Do any of the following to add site colors:

- Select text in the color you want to add to the site in the document window and drag it onto the Site Colors window. If you select text that contains more than one color, all colors are added to the Site window.

- Drag colors into your Site Colors window from another site window.

- Select the Colors tab in the Site window and choose Get Colors Used from the Refresh button menu in the Main toolbar to load all the colors currently used in your site in the Scanned Colors group.

- Drag the Color object onto the Site Colors window from the Objects palette and then use the Inspector palette to select a new color from the Color palette, as shown in Figure 34.19.

- Click the Create New Color button in the Main toolbar, enter a name for your color, and then use the Color palette to specify the color values (see Figure 34.20).

34

The Site Objects palette

Set color values

Color in Inspector palette

Figure 34.19
Drag and drop the Color object onto the Colors tab of the Site window.

The Color object

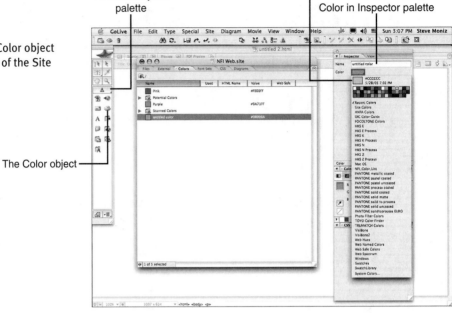

Create New Color Group

Create New Color

Delete Selected Item

Get Colors Used/Remove Unused Colors

Figure 34.20
Use the tools in the Main toolbar to add and remove colors in the Colors tab of the Site window.

34

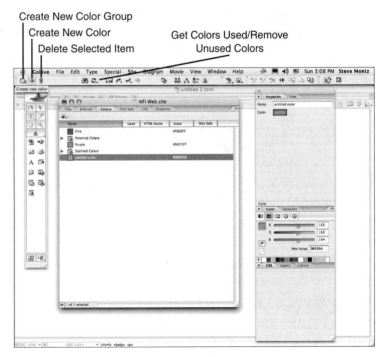

Applying Site Colors to Objects and Text

Select the text or objects on your web page that you want to color and then drag and drop the site color from the Colors tab of the Site window onto the selected object(s) on your page. You can also load the site colors as a swatch library and select your colors that way. Choose Open Swatch Library from the Swatches palette menu and select Site Colors to load the Site Colors Library.

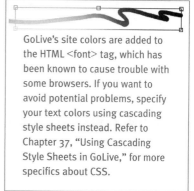

GoLive's site colors are added to the HTML <font> tag, which has been known to cause trouble with some browsers. If you want to avoid potential problems, specify your text colors using cascading style sheets instead. Refer to Chapter 37, "Using Cascading Style Sheets in GoLive," for more specifics about CSS.

Editing Site Colors and Updating Pages

When you change a site color that is used on the pages of your website, GoLive can automatically apply the change throughout your site. To change a site color, select it in the Colors tab of the Site window and change the color using the Swatches palette or Color palette. If other pages besides currently open pages use the same color, the Change Link dialog appears as shown in Figure 34.21. Select the pages that you want to update and click OK.

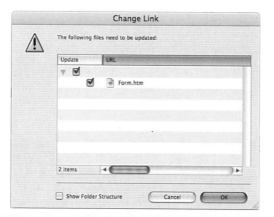

Figure 34.21
The Change Link dialog enables you to update the colors on your entire site.

Organizing Site Colors into Groups

Create a new group in the Color tab of the Site window by either dragging the Color Group object from the Objects palette onto the Site Color window or by clicking the Create New Color Group button in the Main toolbar. Give your folder a name and drag any existing colors you want to add to the group into the folder. To add new colors, be sure the group folder is selected before creating a new color. Color groups are strictly organizational and can be quite helpful when you're working on a particularly large site.

35

CREATING WEB PAGE LAYOUTS WITH GOLIVE

IN THIS CHAPTER

GoLive enables you to create new web pages in a variety of ways, including the use of predesigned web page templates. We'll get to those features momentarily, but first let's have a look at how to do the most basic of things—create a plain old blank web page. When you first launch GoLive a Welcome screen appears offering options to create or open a new document, as shown in Figure 35.1. Deselect the check box to show the Welcome screen at startup if you don't want to encounter this screen every time you launch GoLive. You can always turn this feature back on in the GoLive Preferences window.

This latest version of GoLive introduces a new dialog that's actually called the New dialog. The New dialog is where you create new stuff like web pages, sites, and scripts, as shown in Figure 35.2. To display the New dialog box, choose New from the File menu. It may look confusing at first glance, but it's actually quite an organized way to present all the options for creating new files and sites.

Figure 35.1
The Welcome splash screen offers you the opportunity to create or open files.

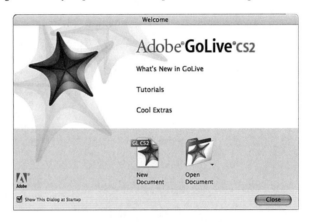

Figure 35.2
The New dialog.

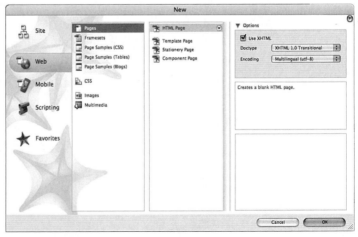

The New dialog offers categories for Site, Web, Mobile, and Scripting. You can use the Favorites category to add files such as HTML pages, Cascading Style Sheets, Images, and QuickTime movies. When you select a category on the left, a list of file types or site types is displayed. You have the option of creating new pages using a variety of methods, as shown in Figure 35.3. To create a new basic blank web page do the following:

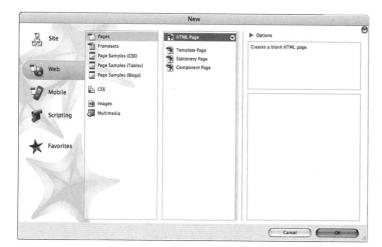

Figure 35.3
Create a basic blank HTML page.

1. Choose New from the File menu to display the New dialog.

2. Click on the Web category in the left pane to display the various options for creating web pages.

3. Select Pages from the column to the right of the categories. When you select Pages, four options are displayed: HTML Page, Template Page, Stationery Page, and Component Page. When you click on any of these, a description of what they do is displayed in a box in the right column, as shown in Figures 35.3 and 35.4.

4. Select HTML Page in the next column to create a blank HTML page.

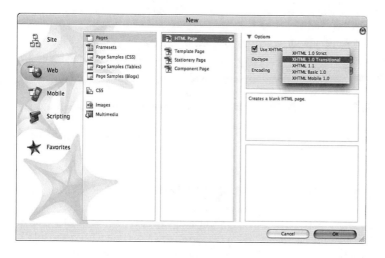

Figure 35.4
The document options enable you to set the Doctype and Encoding for your new blank document.

35

5. Click the triangle to the left of the word Options in the right column to display the options for Doctype and Encoding, as shown in Figure 35.4. The choice you make here inserts the `!DOCTYPE` tag at the top of your document and depends largely on the kind of web page you're creating and what set of standards you want the code for your web page to conform to. See "Understanding Doctypes and Encoding" later in this chapter for more information.

6. Click OK and a new blank document is created.

UNDERSTANDING DOCTYPES AND ENCODING

When creating web pages and pages for mobile devices, it's a good idea to include a Doctype declaration in your files to ensure compliance with established standards. When it comes to web browsers, they'll pretty much display your web pages regardless of whether you include this information or not, but the same is not so true of mobile devices which have adopted stricter guidelines. If you want to use an online HTML validator, you must include a `!DOCTYPE` declaration at the beginning of the HTML code, as shown in Figure 35.5, so the validator knows what to check your code against. The GoLive syntax checker also checks your document against the doctype you specify.

Figure 35.5
The `!DOCTYPE` declaration tells validators and browsers that your code is conforming to that particular Document Type Description (DTD).

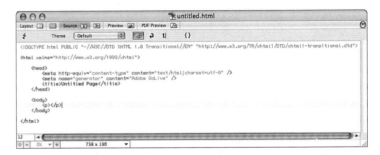

By indicating a document's doctype, you are specifying that the document complies with a particular Document Type Description (DTD). The DTDs can sometimes limit the type of code allowed. For example, the HTML 4.0 Strict DTD does not allow the use of frames, and you can't use font tags in the XHTML Basic DTD. Many cell phone manufacturers require the XHTML Basic doctype for all mobile content. Eventually all browsers will likely require compliance with some DTD, so it's a good idea to familiarize yourself with them now. You can find everything you need to know about DTDs at the World Wide Web Consortium website (www.w3.org). Other good sources of information for web developers on the web also offer great explanations of DTDs, such as www.alistapart.com/articles/doctype/ or www.webmonkey.com. Visit these sites and use their search engines to search for DTD.

UNDERSTANDING PAGE LAYOUT METHODS

The method for laying out web pages using GoLive is pretty much the same regardless of the type of content you're creating. The Layout Editor in the document window is where you build pages, bringing in the content as objects from the Objects palette and Site window. Tables, layers, and GoLive's layout grid and its text boxes provide the containers for text, images, animations, and movies. It's a good idea to spend some time setting up your site in GoLive so you can gather the assets you want to incorporate on your website. See Chapter 40, "Creating a Website with GoLive," for details on setting up your site.

The following are available designs:

- **Basic HTML Design:** You can still build web pages using basic HTML top-down design, as shown in Figure 35.6. Simply type text into the layout editor's window and insert elements like images, links, and horizontal lines from the Basic Objects palette.

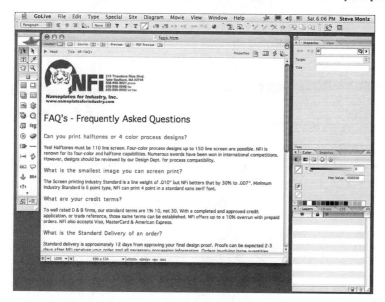

Figure 35.6
A basic HTML page in a top-down design.

- **Table-based Design:** Tables are commonly used to create web pages because nearly all web browsers support them. In GoLive you can build your pages with tables using two methods. Use the standard HTML table format to input your page content into table cells, rows, and columns, as shown in Figure 35.7, or use GoLive's layout grid, as shown in Figure 35.8. The GoLive layout grid creates a table for all intents and purposes, but it enables you to create the table by positioning grids on your page and then adding embedded grids, text boxes, images, and other media by freely positioning them on the grid. See "Using the Layout Grid" later in this chapter for details.

- **Layer-based Design:** You can use DHTML layers to position content on your page freely without the use of tables or grids. Layers are positioned based on the CSS DIV tag coordinates and can be overlapped to create special effects, as shown in Figure 35.9. You can incorporate layers with tables to create those cool rollover effects, making layers show and hide based on what your cursor is over. See "Using Layers" later in this chapter for more information.

35

Figure 35.7
Create a web page by adding content to table cells, rows, and columns.

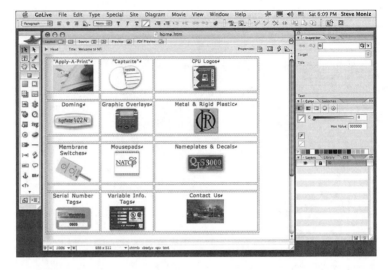

Figure 35.8
Use the layout grid to position your page elements in a table layout without the restrictions of tables.

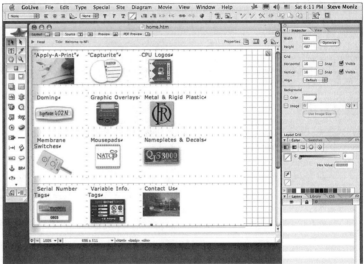

- **Photoshop, Imageready, InDesign, and Illustrator Design:** You can easily incorporate web pages designed with the other applications in the Adobe Creative Suite. GoLive will arrange sliced Photoshop, ImageReady, and Illustrator graphics into tables, as shown in Figure 35.10, and even enable you to import Photoshop and InDesign layers into GoLive's layers, as shown in Figure 35.11. Drag any of the Creative Suite native files from the Site window onto your layout and GoLive automatically imports them as Smart Objects enabling you to modify and update your content easily. See Chapter 36, "Working with Images and Multimedia in GoLive."

35

Figure 35.9
Layers lend themselves well to some forms of web design. In this example, a number of layers are positioned on top of each other with only a single layer visible at any time. Moving the cursor over the list on the left changes the content on the right by hiding one layer and showing another.

Figure 35.10
GoLive automatically places sliced images into table cells.

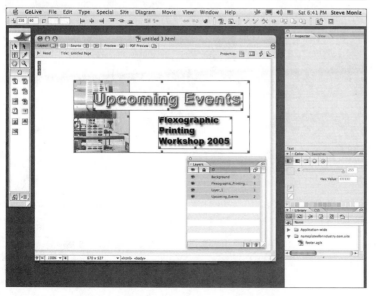

Figure 35.11
Photoshop layers, shown here, are imported into separate layers in GoLive.

35

■ **Frames-based Design:** Another form of web page design that is used less and less frequently these days is frames-based design, as shown in Figure 35.12. Page layouts are designed using a series of frames gathered together by a *frameset*. GoLive offers all the tools and features needed to create frame-based content effectively. Creating frames and framesets is not covered in this book, but you can learn all you need to know about frames using GoLive's help files.

■ **CSS-based Design:** You can incorporate Cascading Style Sheets (CSS) in any of the various GoLive design methods. Using external CSS files along with some internal CSS styles is the most effective method for creating a consistent layout and design format for your web pages. See Chapter 37, "Using Cascading Style Sheets in GoLive," to learn how to implement CSS in your work.

> Most web developers stay away from frames because many search engines ignore content using frames and frames pages cannot be bookmarked for later reference. Another drawback is the lack of support for framesets in applications that read web pages to users who are visually impaired.

Figure 35.12
In this example of a frames-based page, there are four frames, three of which contain scrollbars.

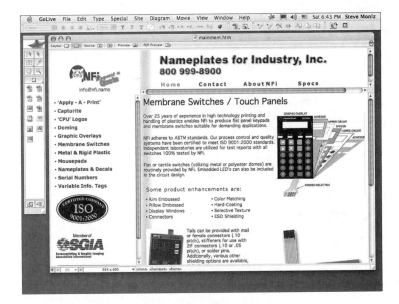

ADDING CONTENT TO YOUR WEB PAGES

There are two basic methods for adding content to your web pages. You can drag object placeholders onto your page and use the Inspector palette to link in the content, or you can drag and drop the content from a variety of places:

1. Start by choosing the type of container for your content from the Basic Objects palette, such as a layer, layout grid, or table. Drag the container onto your web page.

2. Drag an object from one of the Object palettes into your container or onto the web page.

3. Use the Inspector palette to import the object's content.

4. Add content by optionally dragging the content from the Site window onto the page.

   - Drag image and media files directly from the Site window into the layout editor.

   - Photoshop and Illustrator images are automatically brought in as Smart Objects.

   - Drag HTML files, URLs, or email addresses from the site window to create a hypertext link automatically with the name of the file used as its label. You can highlight some text before dragging to use the highlighted text as the label.

   - Drag other site assets such as components to incorporate common elements like navigation bars and contact links.

USING THE LAYOUT GRID

GoLive's layout grid simplifies the process of creating web content using tables. Instead of formatting tables with cells, rows, and columns to position your content, use GoLive's layout grid to drag and drop elements onto a grid that ends up a table as far as browsers are concerned. Layout grids can contain tables, although it's not advisable to put layout grids inside layout grids. Layout text boxes—which serve as containers for most of your content—and images and multimedia elements can be positioned directly onto the grid.

GoLive inserts special source code to enable the use of layout grids. This code can be stripped out of your HTML documents when you publish the pages to your web server, or you can convert layout grids to standard HTML tables, which also strips out the code. It doesn't affect the way browsers interpret your tables to leave the code in, but some folks like to keep their code as clean as possible.

Adding a Layout Grid

You can design your web pages with one large layout grid that represents the entire page, or you can implement a number of layout grids on a single page to create more complex layouts:

1. Drag the Layout Grid object from the Basic set on the Objects palette onto the page or double-click the object to place it at the blinking insertion point, as shown in Figure 35.13.

2. Choose Window, Inspector to display the Layout Grid Inspector if it isn't already on the screen, as shown in Figure 35.14.

3. Resize the layout grid either by dragging its handles or by setting the width and height values in the Layout Grid Inspector. If the layout grid has a background image, you can select Use Image Size in the Layout Grid

Hold down the Shift key when you click the Optimize button in the Layout Grid Inspector to reduce only the width. Hold down the Alt key (Windows users) or the Option key (Mac users) while clicking the Optimize button to reduce only the height.

35

Inspector to make the layout grid automatically the same size as the image. After you place all the content on your layout grid, you can click the Optimize button in the Layout Grid Inspector to make the grid conform to the size of your content.

Figure 35.13
Create a layout grid.

Layout Grid object

Layout grid

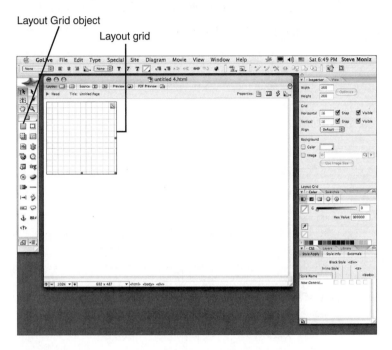

Figure 35.14
The Layout Grid Inspector.

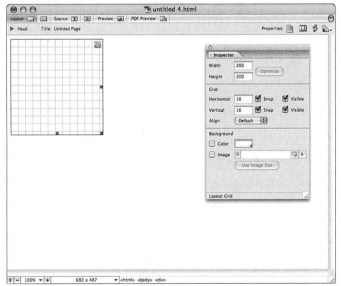

Adjusting Settings in the Layout Grid Inspector

The Layout Grid Inspector contains a number of options that affect how you work in a layout grid:

- Select Snap for Horizontal and Snap for Vertical to make the objects on your grid snap to the grid lines. If you use the arrow keys to move objects on the grid, the objects automatically snap to the closest grid line.

- Deselect Snap for Horizontal and Snap for Vertical to move your objects freely in 1-pixel increments regardless of the spacing of the grid.

- To change the spacing of the grid, enter a size in pixels for both the Horizontal and Vertical fields.

- To turn off the grid lines, deselect the Visible check box for both the Horizontal and Vertical options.

- To set the position of the grid in relation to the page, choose an alignment from the Align pop-up menu. Choose Default to align the grid with the upper-left corner of the page. Choose Right or Left to wrap other web content around the layout grid.

Set the top margin and left margin values to o in the Page Properties Inspector to position your layout grid in the very top left corner of the web page. To see the page properties in the Inspector palette, click the Page Properties button at the top of the Layout Editor window.

Adding Layout Text Boxes to the Grid

Layout text boxes act as containers for text you want to add to the grid as well as any images or other media elements you want to encapsulate, as shown in Figure 35.15. Layout text boxes have their own attributes you can set using the Inspector palette.

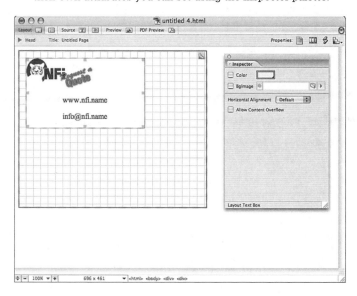

Figure 35.15
A layout text box containing text and an image.

35

- Drag the layout text box object from the Basic Objects palette onto the grid.

- Adjust the size of the layout text box by dragging its handles or by setting the Width and Height values in the Layout Text Box Inspector.

- You can set the background of the layout text box to contain a color or an image. Choose Color in the Layout Text Box Inspector and then select a color or choose BgImage, and then select an image file. See Figure 35.16.

Figure 35.16
Layout text boxes can have background colors and background images.

Adding Images and Other Objects to the Layout Grid

You can drag images or other media files from the Site window directly onto the layout grid or into a layout text box on a Layout Grid. You can alternatively drag an object from the Objects palette onto the grid to create a placeholder and then use the Inspector palette to link to the desired object, as shown in Figure 35.17.

Setting the Background of a Layout Grid

You can set the background of a layout grid to a color or to contain a tiled image much like a web page would, as shown in Figure 35.18:

1. Select the layout grid.

2. Choose Background Image in the Layout Grid Inspector and then browse to select an image file.

3. To set the layout grid to the same size as the image, click the Use Image Size button.

4. Select Background Color in the Layout Grid Inspector and set the color.

> You can click an empty area anywhere on the grid to put the blinking insertion bar there and then paste layout text boxes, images, and other objects that have been previously copied.

35

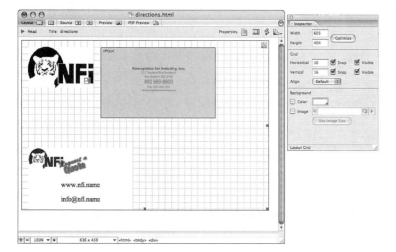

Figure 35.17
Place images and media objects directly on the grid or put them inside layout text boxes with other content.

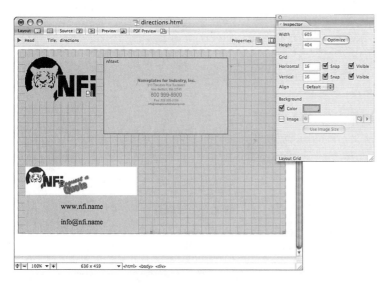

Figure 35.18
Set the background of a layout grid.

Grouping and Ungrouping Objects on a Layout Grid

You can group only objects contained on a layout grid. The advantages to grouping objects on a layout grid are obvious and make rearranging your layout much easier:

1. Select the objects on your layout grid that you want to group or ungroup, holding down the Shift key to select multiple objects.

2. Click the Group Selection button or the Ungroup Selection button in the toolbar, as shown in Figure 35.19. You also find the same buttons in the Transform palette.

35

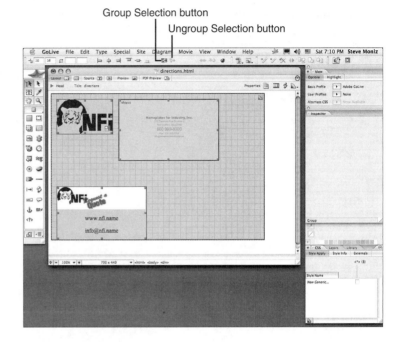

Group Selection button

Ungroup Selection button

Figure 35.19
Group your content to make it
easier to rearrange the page.

Positioning Elements on a Layout Grid

Position the elements on a layout grid by dragging the objects around or by precisely specifying the
x and y pixel coordinates of the selected object or group. Set the x and y coordinates using the toolbar or Transform palette, as shown in Figure 35.20.

Distributing and Aligning Objects on a Layout Grid

Use the Align palette to align and distribute objects within the layout grid. You can align a selection
of objects to each other or align an object to its parent layout text box, as shown in Figure 35.21. To
distribute objects, select them all and click one of the distribute buttons in the Align palette, as
shown in Figure 35.22. Click the Distribute Spacing button to distribute the *space* instead of the
objects, as shown in Figure 35.23. If you want to specify the exact number of pixels between
objects, check the Use Spacing check box and enter a value in the corresponding field, as shown in
Figure 35.24.

35

X coordinate

Y coordinate

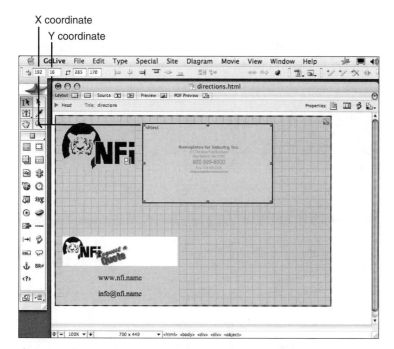

Figure 35.20
Position elements precisely on
the layout grid.

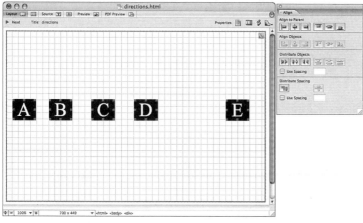

Figure 35.21
Align objects to each other or to a
parent object.

Figure 35.22
Distribute objects evenly.

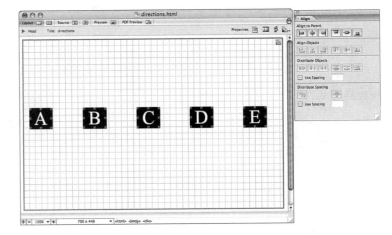

Figure 35.23
Distribute all spacing evenly.

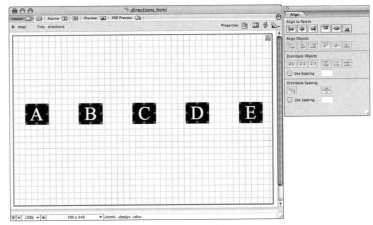

Figure 35.24
Distribute with specific pixel spacing.

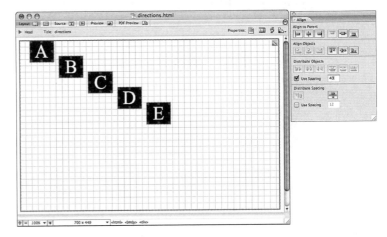

35

Converting a Layout Grid to a Table

You don't have to convert your layout grids to standard HTML tables, but you can if you want to because layout grids are really just tables with a little extra code that makes them work like grids in GoLive. When you convert a layout grid to a table, the special code that makes the layout grid work is stripped out:

1. Select the layout grid you want to convert and then choose Special, Convert, Layout Grid to Table.

2. In the Convert dialog shown in Figure 35.25, the following options are presented:

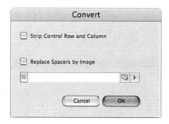

Figure 35.25
Options for converting a layout grid to a table.

- Select Strip Control Row and Column to remove the 1-pixel empty control row and column GoLive inserts at the bottom and right of the table, respectively.

- Deselect Strip Control Row and Column, and then select Replace Spacer by Image to replace the Netscape Spacer elements with a transparent spacer GIF file that GoLive automatically inserts for you. The Spacer element and the spacer GIF serve the purpose of enabling empty cells in a table for Netscape browsers. The Spacer elements are ignored by Internet Explorer browsers.

3. Click OK.

Converting a Table to a Layout Grid

You can convert a table to a layout grid by selecting Special, Table, Convert to Layout Grid, or by simply clicking the Convert button in the Table Inspector, as shown in Figure 35.26.

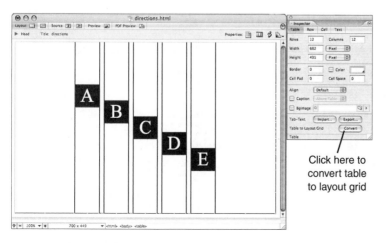

Figure 35.26
Convert any table into a layout grid.

Click here to convert table to layout grid

35

USING LAYERS

Layers are a pretty versatile way to create web page content because you can position layers any way you want on the page, even overlap them. Layers, however, are supported only by version 4 and later browsers and can result in some messy-looking web pages if you don't use CSS text formatting to keep the content of the layers consistent between browsers and platforms. Layers can be made visible and invisible using the Show/Hide Layers mouse action in GoLive and can be animated using the DHTML Timeline Editor in GoLive.

Adding Layers to the Page

When you add a layer to a page, GoLive inserts a small yellow marker at the insertion point where the layer is added. Because layers are essentially floating boxes, the yellow marker can appear in one place while the actual layer is someplace else. The yellow marker always shows where the source code for the layer is in relation to the rest of the document, as shown in Figure 35.27.

Yellow layer marker

Figure 35.27
The source code for the layer is located where the yellow markers are.

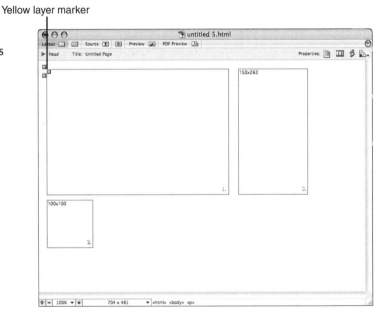

To add a layer to a page:

1. Drag the Layer object from the Basic Objects palette onto the page to add a layer. If you point to a specific point in the text and the insertion icon appears, the yellow marker appears in this location as does the corresponding DIV source code. You can alternatively position your cursor in the text and then click the New Layer button in the Layers palette, as shown in Figure 35.28.

Layer object   Selected layer

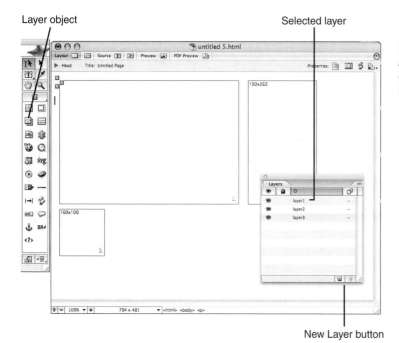

Figure 35.28
Add a new layer by dragging the object or clicking the New Layer button.

2. Assign a name to your layer in the Layer Inspector or in the Layers palette.

3. You can set the background color or background image of a layer in the Layer Inspector. Select BgImage and then select a file to insert a background image. Select Color, click the color field, and then select a color to set the background color of the layer.

4. Add content to your layer the same way you add content to a web page. Avoid, however, using tables and layout grids inside layers.

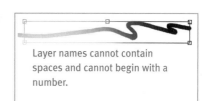

Layer names cannot contain spaces and cannot begin with a number.

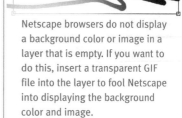

Netscape browsers do not display a background color or image in a layer that is empty. If you want to do this, insert a transparent GIF file into the layer to fool Netscape into displaying the background color and image.

Selecting, Positioning, and Resizing Layers

To select a layer you can either click the layer name in the Layers palette or position your cursor over the top edge of the layer until the hand icon appears and then click. After the layer is selected you can position it by clicking and dragging the top edge of the layer. To resize the layer, select it and drag the handles that appear. You can also precisely position the layer using the Layer Inspector. With the layer selected, use the Layer Inspector to set the following options:

35

■ Enter the x and y coordinates of the layer from the top-left corner of the web page by entering pixel values in the Left and Top field of the Layer Inspector, as shown in Figure 35.29.

Figure 35.29
Enter the coordinates of your layer.

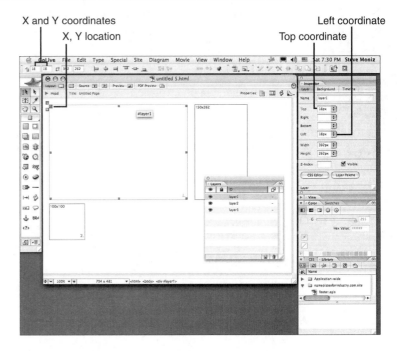

■ Enter the dimensions of your layer in pixels using the Width and Height fields in the Layout Inspector.

■ Select Auto from the Width or Height menus to make the layer fit its content automatically.

■ Choose Percent from the Width and Height menus to size the selected layer automatically in relation to the percentage of the window width or height.

Setting the Layer Order

The stacking order of layers is controlled by a value called the Z-index. The Z-index is simply a number that determines which layers are under or over other layers. The lower the number, the further down in the stacking order the layer. The highest number will be on top and the lowest on the bottom. Use the Layer Inspector to set a layer's Z-index, as shown in Figure 35.30.

To turn on the grid lines for positioning the layer, choose Layer Grid Settings from the Layers palette menu and then define the page grid values. Choose Prevent Overlapping to prevent the layers from overlapping, especially if you intend to convert the layers to a table later.

Z-index of 1   Z-index of 27

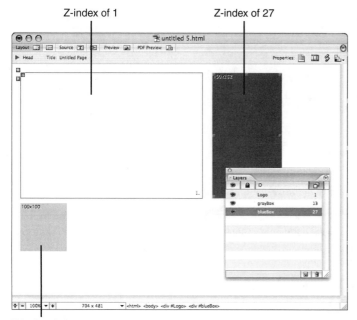

Figure 35.30
Set the stacking order of your lay-
ers using the Z-index value in the
Layer Inspector.

Z-index of 13

Managing Layers with the Layers Palette

Use the Layers palette to manage the layers in your document, as shown in Figure 35.31. You can
lock, hide, or show layers while you work. Use the Layers palette to assign names to your layers, and
adjust the Z-index of your layers by dragging within the Layers palette. Use the Set Stacking Order
button in the upper-right corner of the Layers palette to change the layering to either lowest to highest or vice-versa based on the Z-index number.

Lock/Unlock Layer
Hide/Show Layer   Layer name

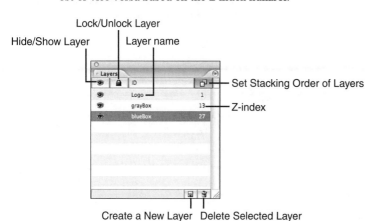

Set Stacking Order of Layers

Z-index

Create a New Layer   Delete Selected Layer

Figure 35.31
The Layers palette.

35

Use these options in the Layers palette to manage the layers in your document:

- Click on the eye icon inside the first column to hide or show layers temporarily.

- Click in the padlock column to lock or unlock a layer temporarily.

- You can click the name of a layer, even if it's hidden or locked, to bring it to the foreground.

- Click the icon at the top of the Z-index column to change the stacking order to either ascending or descending order.

- To change the name of a layer, click once on the name to highlight the layer and then click again to select the name and type to edit it.

- To change the Z-index value, click once to select the Z-index number and then click again and type to edit the number.

You can have more than one layer with the same Z-index number. In this case layers are layered based on which was created first, then second, then third, etc. Because the Z-index value comes into play only when layers are overlapped, you don't have to worry about the numbers when none of your layers overlap.

To hide all layers or show all layers, hold down the Ctrl key (in Windows) or the ⌘ key (on the Mac) and then click an eye icon in the Layers palette. This same technique works on the lock icons as well: Ctrl-click or ⌘-click on a lock icon to lock all layers or unlock all layers.

Nesting Layers

Layers can be nested inside other layers to create a parent-child relationship. Nesting layers together can help keep groups of items together and facilitate minilayouts that can be moved and formatted together or even animated using the DHTML timeline. Existing layers can be easily nested using the Layers palette, and you can nest layers when you first create them by dragging a new layer onto an existing layer. To view nested layers in the Layers palette, the Hierarchic option must be selected in the Layers palette menu, as shown in Figure 35.32:

Figure 35.32
The options in the Layers palette menu.

1. Create a layer by dragging the Layer object from the Basic Objects palette onto the page, or double-click the Layer object in the Basic Objects palette.

2. Use the Layer Inspector to specify the settings for the new layer and assign a name to your layer using the Layers palette.

35

3. Drag a new layer onto your page, this time positioning the new layer over an existing layer until the edge of the existing layer is highlighted. Release the new layer to nest the new layer inside the highlighted layer. Remember, the nesting won't be visible in the Layers palette unless you select Hierarchic from the palette menu.

4. When the hierarchic option is selected for the Layers palette, you can nest and un-nest layers by dragging them inside the Layers palette, as shown in Figure 35.33. Nested layers appear indented under their parent layer in the Layers palette.

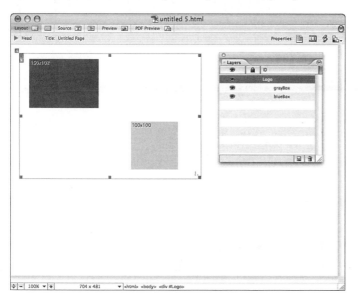

Figure 35.33
Nested layers in the Layers palette.

Using the Show/Hide Layer Action

One of the really neat things you can do with DHTML layers is to show and hide them on your web pages using a text, object, or graphic trigger. For example, you can create a list and set a trigger action for each item in to the list to show and hide layers, making things pop on and off the screen as you move your mouse over the items in the list. This is also an effective way to create pop-up menus as a navigation aid on your site:

1. Start by creating some layers and adding content to them. If you want all your layers to appear in the same place on the page, stack them on top of each other. Be sure to name the layers to make them easier to select later. Uncheck the Visible check box in the Layer Inspector to make a layer initially invisible when the web page loads.

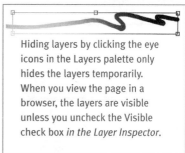

Hiding layers by clicking the eye icons in the Layers palette only hides the layers temporarily. When you view the page in a browser, the layers are visible unless you uncheck the Visible check box *in the Layer Inspector.*

2. Select the text, image, or object that you want to have act as the trigger for hiding and showing a layer. Click the New Link button in the toolbar or in the Link tab of the Inspector to create a

link. Type the number symbol (#) in the Link field of the Inspector palette, as shown in Figure 35.34 to create a null link. A *null link* doesn't go anywhere, it just makes the text, image, or object act like a link. If you want the trigger to also *link to* someplace, you can enter the URL for the link here instead of the null link. There must be one or the other in the link field to enable assigning an action.

New Link button   Null link

Figure 35.34
Create a link for the trigger text,
graphic, or object.

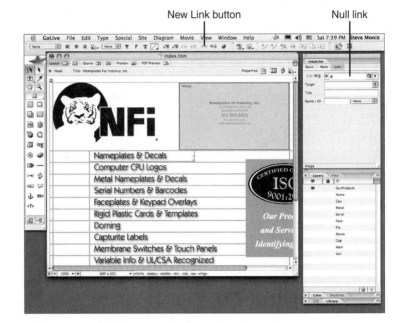

3. Choose Window, Actions to display the Actions palette, as shown in Figure 35.35.

Figure 35.35
The Actions palette.

4. In the Actions palette, select the mouse event called Mouse Enter and then click the Create New Action button.

5. From the Action pop-up menu in the Actions palette, select ShowHide from the Multimedia sub-menu, as shown in Figure 35.36.

6. From the Layer menu in the Actions palette, select a layer from the list.

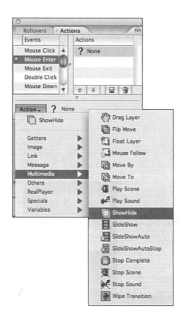

Figure 35.36
Choose the ShowHide action.

7. From the Mode menu, select the action you want to take place when you put your mouse pointer over the trigger. Select Show or Hide to show or hide the selected layer, or select Toggle to show and hide the layer based on its current status.

8. Save and preview your page in a web browser. You can also preview this action in the Preview tab of GoLive.

CREATING AND EDITING TABLES

Tables are widely used these days to format and control the layout of web pages. If you're going to use tables as a layout tool for your web pages, you'd be best served to learn how to use the layout grid to create these tables (refer to "Using the Layout Grid," earlier in this chapter). You can, however, still use the Table object in the Basic Objects palette to create inline tables:

1. Drag the Table object from the Basic Objects palette onto your page or double-click the Table object to add a 3 by 3 table to your page, as shown in Figure 35.37.

2. With the table selected, indicate the number of columns and rows in your table, as well as the width and height of the overall table using the Table Inspector. You can also indicate whether the table has a border, background image, caption, or background color, as shown in Figure 35.38.

3. Type the data for your table directly into the table cells. Use the HTML text formatting options under the Type menu or format your table data using Cascading Style Sheets (CSS).

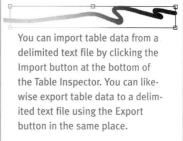

You can import table data from a delimited text file by clicking the Import button at the bottom of the Table Inspector. You can likewise export table data to a delimited text file using the Export button in the same place.

35

Figure 35.37
Insert a new blank table on your page.

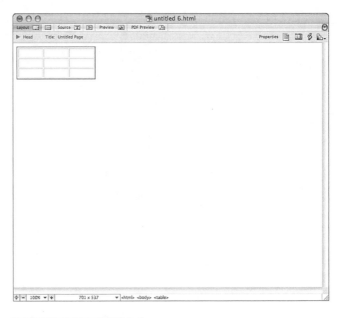

Figure 35.38
Specify the basic setup of your table in the Table Inspector.

4. Click and drag the table and cell walls to resize your table. You can indicate the individual cell and row attributes using the Cell and Row tabs of the Table Inspector.

GoLive enables you to create your web pages using any of a variety of methods. The method you choose for your pages is based largely on the look you're trying to achieve and also based on the users you're trying to reach. A good rule of thumb, especially if you're trying to build pages for a very broad range of visitors, is to keep it simple. Always consider your potential audience and consider whether your site is primarily providing information or entertaining users with all the latest bells and whistles. Always test your website and web pages on as many browsers as you can and on as many computer platforms as you can.

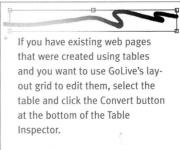

If you have existing web pages that were created using tables and you want to use GoLive's layout grid to edit them, select the table and click the Convert button at the bottom of the Table Inspector.

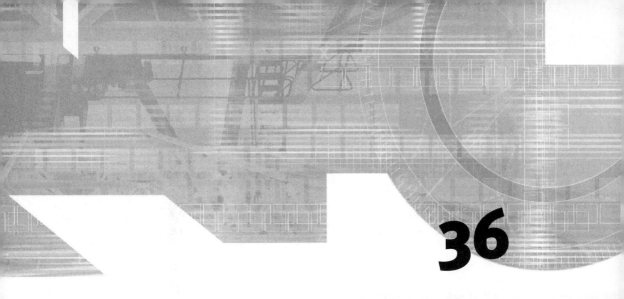

36

WORKING WITH IMAGES AND MULTIMEDIA IN GOLIVE

GoLive enables you to import pretty much every type of image and multimedia element supported by browsers and mobile devices. Whether you need to insert JPEG and GIF images on your web pages or you want to incorporate Quicktime or Flash movies, GoLive has an object for you to use in the Objects palette and a place for you to set the attributes and properties in the Inspector palette.

ADDING IMAGES

GoLive enables you to add images to your pages in two primary ways. You can add images that have already been optimized and formatted, like GIFs, JPEGs, PNGs, and WBMPs. You can also add images as Smart Objects, where you perform the optimization options in GoLive when you import the image. If you're using the Adobe Creative Suite of applications, Smart Objects make it easy to integrate your Photoshop, Illustrator, and InDesign work. To insert an image on your web page, use one of the following methods:

- Drag the image file from the Site window onto the Layout Editor.

- Drag the Image object from the Basic Objects palette onto the Layout Editor, as shown in Figure 36.1, or double-click the Image object. Use the Inspector palette to link to the image file in the Source field of the Inspector palette.

Image in the site window   URL of image

Figure 36.1
Adding images to your pages.

Image object —

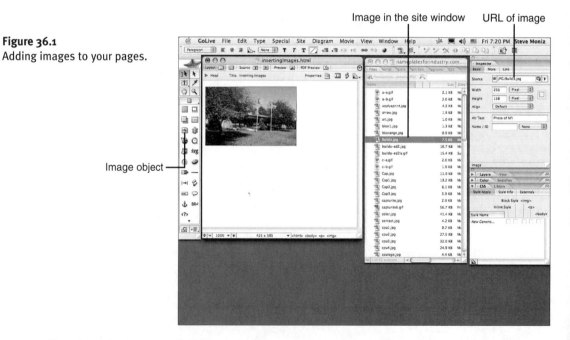

If you have the Site window visible somewhere on your screen, even if most of it is hidden by your document window, use the Fetch URL (point-and-shoot) button to link to your file. All you have to do is drag it onto any visible part of the Site window and the Site window comes to the foreground enabling you to select an image, as shown in Figure 36.2.

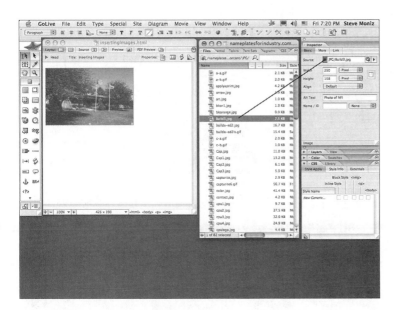

Figure 36.2
Point and shoot with the Fetch URL button.

Setting Image Attributes

Use the Image Inspector to set all the attributes available for images. You can scale images by dragging one of the three handles that appear on the right, bottom, and bottom-right corners. Hold down the Shift key while scaling to constrain the image proportions. You notice a scaling icon in the lower-right corner of images that have been resized, as shown in Figure 36.3. If you want to return an image to its original size, click the Set to Original Size button in the Image Inspector, as shown in Figure 36.4.

Setting Image Alignment Options

The alignment options for images determines how the image interacts with the rest of the content surrounding it. In the Image Inspector there is an Align pop-up menu that contains all the HTML alignment attributes, as shown in Figure 36.5:

- Choose Top to align text vertically with the top of the image. The alignment is based on the height of the tallest character in the font. In most browsers TextTop works exactly the same way as Top, though GoLive does not preview TextTop correctly. See Figure 36.6.

> When enlarging or reducing the size of imported images, keep in mind that the image is probably optimized to be used at its 100% size. If you scale an image by only a small amount, you shouldn't have to worry about image quality. However, if you scale an image up, it's likely that the image quality will suffer. If you find yourself scaling images down significantly, you end up with images on your website that take longer to download than they have to. In either case, you should edit the images and resize them in an image editing program like Photoshop or ImageReady.

36

Figure 36.3
The scaling icon in the lower-right corner of the image indicates that an image has been resized.

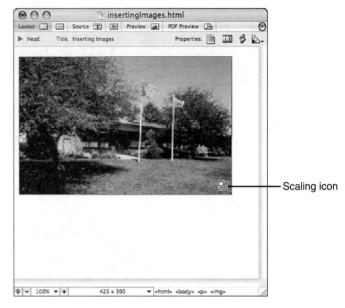

Scaling icon

Figure 36.4
Set a resized image back to its original dimensions.

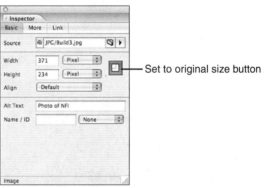

Set to original size button

Figure 36.5
Image alignment options in the Image Inspector.

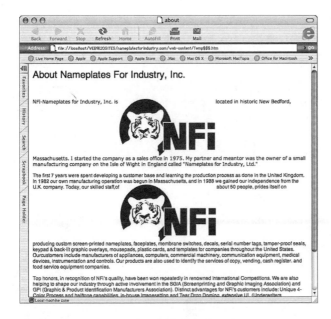

Figure 36.6
Top and TextTop alignment attributes shown in Internet Explorer.

- Most of the newer browser versions treat Middle and AbsMiddle the same way, aligning the vertical center of the text with the vertical center of the image. Older versions of the browsers, however, aligned the baseline of the text with the middle of the image when Middle was selected. Use AbsMiddle to cover your bases. See Figure 36.7.

Figure 36.7
Middle and AbsMiddle alignment attributes shown on images inserted within paragraphs of text and previewed in Internet Explorer.

- Bottom and Baseline align the bottom of an image with the baseline of the text (the descenders in the text hang below the bottom of the image). AbsBottom takes the descenders into account and aligns the bottom of the image with the bottom of the descenders in the text. Keep in mind that if you use all capital letters with AbsBottom, the text appears higher than the bottom of the image to allow for descender depth. See Figure 36.8.

Figure 36.8
Bottom and AbsBottom alignment attributes.

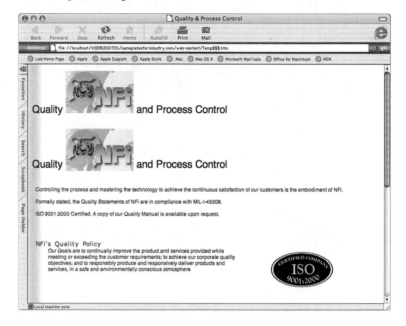

- Use the Left and Right alignment options when you want text to wrap around the image, as shown in Figure 36.9. Control the amount (in pixels) of space around the image using the HSpace and VSpace fields in the More tab of the Image Inspector, as shown in Figure 36.10.

Figure 36.9
Left and Right alignment attributes.

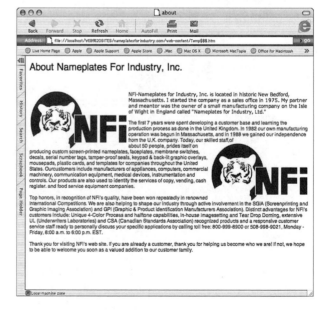

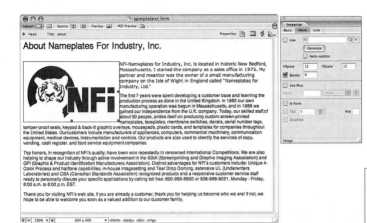

Figure 36.10
Set the amount of space to offset the text runaround.

When you add space around your left-aligned and right-aligned images using the HSpace and VSpace attributes, the extra space is added to *all sides* of the image. The problem with this is that images that are left-aligned appear to be inset from the left side of the web page as well. You can easily solve this problem by adding a border in the same color as your background around the images before importing them. Just add a border to the top, right, and bottom sides for a left-aligned image. If you're willing to convert your images to GIF format, you can add a transparent border to the right, bottom, and top of your left-aligned images.

Adding Borders to Images and Setting Alt Text

You can add a border around your image by entering a value in the Border field of the More tab in the Image Inspector. By default, the Border value is set to zero because borders automatically appear around images that contain links, unless, of course, the border is set to zero. Type some text in the Alt Text field of the Image Inspector, as shown in Figure 36.11. The Alt (alternative) text appears in the place of the image when the web page is loading or if browsers have images turned off, and the text is read aloud by web page–reading software for the visually impaired. It's good form to include Alt text for all your images, as shown in Figure 36.12, even if the text simply says what the image is. In some Windows browsers, the Alt text is displayed like a ToolTip when the cursor hovers over an image that contains Alt text.

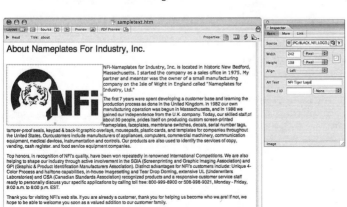

Figure 36.11
Include Alt Text for your images by typing it in the Image Inspector.

Figure 36.12
Alt text displays in the place of missing images.

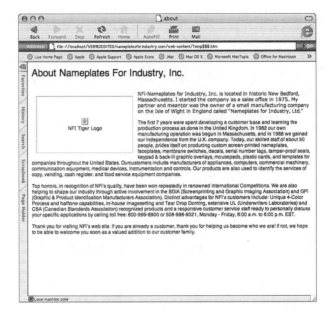

Creating a LowSrc Image

LowSrc images are typically black-and-white images that are much smaller in file size than their color counterparts. The LowSrc attribute loads the lower resolution, black-and-white image first, so the user has something to look at white the larger color image is downloading on a slow connection, as shown in Figure 36.13. GoLive enables you to create LowSrc images on the fly and will even automatically regenerate the LowSrc image if you make changes to the original.

To create a LowSrc image:

1. Import an image that you want to use on your web page.

2. With the image selected, click the Generate button in the More tab of the Image Inspector, as shown in Figure 36.14 to automatically create a low-res black-and-white GIF of your image in the same location as the original image.

3. Click the Auto-update check box to update the LowSrc file automatically when the original is modified.

The border color is controlled by the text color. If you want to change the color of a border around an image, select the image by clicking and dragging from the left of the image to the right of the image, in the same way you would select text. Choose a color from the Color palette.

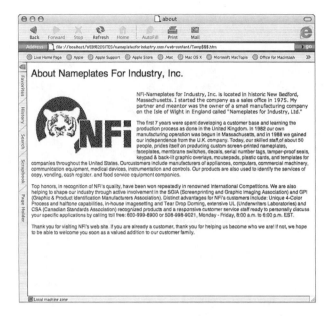

Figure 36.13
LowSrc images load first, followed by the full-color images.

Figure 36.14
Generate a LowSrc image.

Creating an Image Map

Image maps are useful when you have an image that contains different areas that you want to link to different places. Using GoLive's image mapping tools, you can define *hot zones* on an image and create links for each of these zones:

1. Import an image that you want to use with an image map.

2. Click the Use Map check box in the More tab of the Image Inspector, as shown in Figure 36.15.

3. Assign a name for the image map by typing it into the Name field or use the name that GoLive suggests. From the pop-up menu to the right of the Name field choose Name if you are going to assign a JavaScript action to the hotspots, ID if you are only going to use the hotspots as hypertext links, or Name and ID if you think you'll be using both—the latter is usually the best choice.

36

Figure 36.15
The Image Map option in the Inspector palette.

4. Use the tools in the main toolbar to draw shapes for the hotspots of your image. Choose from the Rectangle, Ellipse, or Polygonal Map-area tools, as shown in Figure 36.16. Click and drag with the Rectangle and Ellipse tools. Point and click with the Polygonal tool to set the anchor points of your polygon. Use the Select Map-area Tool to move and adjust the mapped areas.

Figure 36.16
Creating image maps with the Image Map tools.

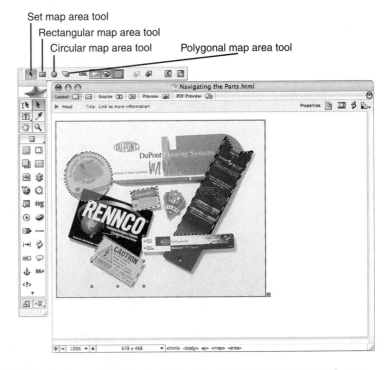

5. Click the Display URLs button in the main toolbar to display the URLs inside the mapped areas, as shown in Figure 36.17. Use the three buttons to the right of the URL button to further indicate how you want to view the mapped areas in GoLive.

36

Colorize map area tool
Display URLs toggle
URL button
Select map area color

Figure 36.17
URLs can be displayed in the mapped regions.

6. Use the Inspector palette to create the links for your mapped areas. You can also assign separate Alt text for each mapped area.

USING SMART OBJECTS

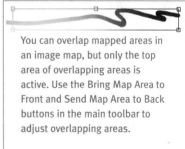

You can overlap mapped areas in an image map, but only the top area of overlapping areas is active. Use the Bring Map Area to Front and Send Map Area to Back buttons in the main toolbar to adjust overlapping areas.

Smart Objects enable you to import web content from any of Adobe's Creative Suite applications, such as Photoshop and Illustrator. There are many benefits to using Smart Objects in GoLive aside from the obvious convenience of being able to import an image from anywhere. The biggest advantage of using Smart Objects is probably your ability to edit your images in their native applications and have the web images automatically generated and updated in GoLive, eliminating the process of exporting images separately. Here are some of the cool things you can do with Smart Objects:

- Smart Objects are automatically reoptimized when you resize them in GoLive.

- You can have multiple Smart Objects that link to a single source file. This means that you can use the same image at multiple sizes and even cropped differently while still maintaining a single source.

- When you double-click a Smart Object in GoLive, the source file opens in its original application.

36

- Using the variable feature you can set layers to be variable and type your own text to be formatted in the manner of the source file. This feature is great for creating buttons, menu items, and page headers that change from time to time.

- Crop your Smart Objects in GoLive and retain the option to uncrop at any time.

- Change the matte color to make the backgrounds of your images match your web page background.

Inserting a Photoshop Smart Object

Photoshop Smart Objects are probably the most popular kind of Smart Object because Photoshop's image creation and editing features lend themselves so well to creating web content. Of course, you can also use the features of ImageReady to edit and manipulate Photoshop images, so the Photoshop Smart Object is quite powerful.

To insert a Photoshop Smart Object, follow these steps:

1. Drag the Smart Photoshop Object from the Smart Objects palette onto the Layout Editor or double-click the Smart Photoshop Object to insert the image at your cursor location. You can optionally drag any Smart Object compatible file from the Site window onto the Layout Editor.

2. Specify the Source file for your Smart Photoshop Object using the Inspector palette, as shown in Figure 36.18.

Figure 36.18
Choose a Source file from the Smart Object Inspector.

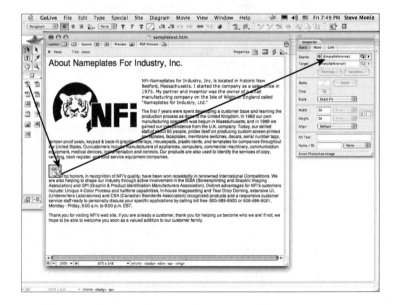

3. ImageReady's Save for Web dialog appears, as shown in Figure 36.19. Choose the optimization settings for your image and click the Save button to save a target file. Refer to Chapter 12, "Building Web Graphics in ImageReady," for specific information on how to use the Save for Web dialog.

Figure 36.19
The Save for Web dialog.

4. After you save the target file, your image appears in GoLive, as shown in Figure 36.20. You can always use the Settings button in the Basic tab of the Inspector to optimize your image differently.

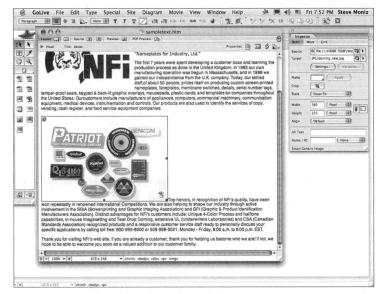

Figure 36.20
The Smart Photoshop Object in GoLive.

Inserting an Illustrator Smart Object

Illustrator Smart Objects behave like Photoshop Smart Objects in most ways, but you have more options for optimizing the content. Not only can you optimize Illustrator Smart Objects in the usual bitmap formats offered by ImageReady's Save for Web dialog, you can also import them in SVG or

36

SWF format, retaining the vector outlines. Refer to Chapter 21, "Importing, Exporting, and Saving in Illustrator," for details on SVG and SWF formats.

To insert an Illustrator Smart Object, follow these steps:

1. Drag the Smart Illustrator Object from the Smart Objects palette onto the Layout Editor or double-click the Smart Illustrator Object to insert the image at your cursor location. You can optionally drag any Smart Object compatible file from the Site window onto the Layout Editor.

2. Specify the Source file for your Smart Illustrator object using the Inspector palette.

> If you choose an Adobe Illustrator EPS (encapsulated Postscript) file for a source file for the Illustrator Smart Object, you do not have the options to create an SVG or SWF file and are taken directly to the Save for Web dialog.

3. If you choose an Illustrator native file, the Conversion Settings dialog appears, as shown in Figure 36.21. Choose a destination format from the pop-up menu. Select the Bitmap Formats option to display ImageReady's Save for Web dialog box, or choose SVG, SVG compressed, or SWF to display dialog boxes for these formats, as shown in Figure 36.22 and Figure 36.23.

Figure 36.21
The Conversion Settings dialog for Illustrator Smart Objects.

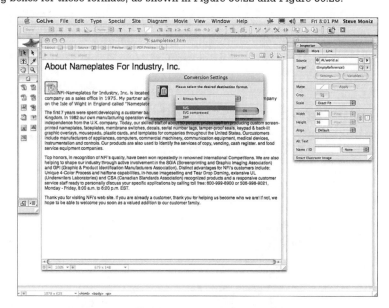

Figure 36.22
The SVG Options dialog.

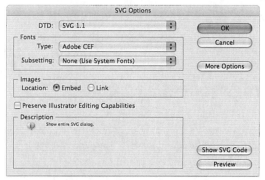

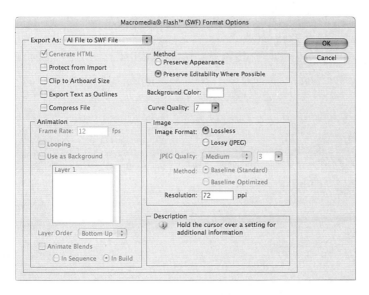

Figure 36.23
The SWF Format Options dialog.

4. After you save the target file, your image appears in GoLive, as shown in Figure 36.24. You can always use the Settings button in the Basic tab of the Inspector to optimize your image differently or change the SVG or SWF options.

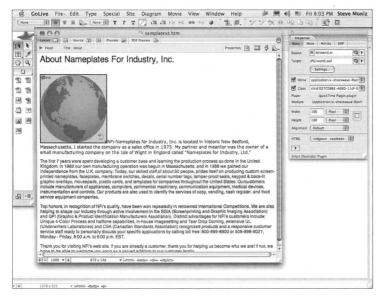

Figure 36.24
The Smart Illustrator Object in GoLive.

Inserting a Smart PDF Object

When inserting an Acrobat Smart PDF Object into GoLive, you can select from multiple page PDFs or single page image PDFs made in Photoshop or Illustrator. So much graphical content is provided in PDF format these days that the ability to import images directly from a PDF file can be a big time saver:

36

1. Drag the Smart PDF Object from the Smart Objects palette onto the Layout Editor or double-click the Smart PDF Object to insert the image at your cursor location. You can optionally drag any Smart Object–compatible file from the Site window onto the Layout Editor.

2. Specify the Source file for your Smart PDF Object using the Inspector palette, as shown in Figure 36.25.

Figure 36.25
Choose a Source file from the Smart Object Inspector.

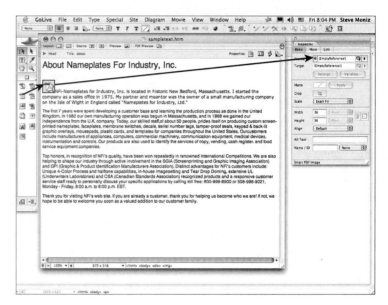

3. The PDF Options dialog appears, as shown in Figure 36.26. Choose a page from the PDF file if it contains more than one page and click OK to display ImageReady's Save for Web dialog box, as shown in Figure 36.27.

Figure 36.26
The PDF Options dialog.

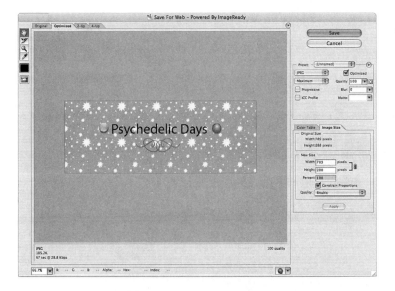

Figure 36.27
The Save for Web dialog.

4. After you save the target file, your image appears in GoLive, as shown in Figure 36.28. You can always use the Settings button in the Basic tab of the Inspector to optimize your image differently or choose a different page from the source PDF file.

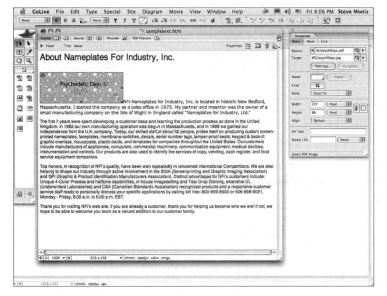

Figure 36.28
The Smart PDF Object in GoLive.

Inserting a Smart Generic Object

The Smart Generic Object supports the following file formats: BMP, PCS, Pixar, Amiga IFF, TIFF, TARGA, PDF, EPS, JPEG, JPEG 2000, PNG, and PICT (Mac only). Most high-end artwork and imagery

36

is saved in TIFF and EPS format, so the ability to convert TIFF and EPS files on the fly in GoLive is great:

1. Drag the Smart Generic Object from the Smart Objects palette onto the Layout Editor or double-click the Smart Generic Object to insert the image at your cursor location. You can optionally drag any Smart Object compatible file from the Site window onto the Layout Editor.

2. Specify the Source file for your Smart Generic object using the Inspector palette, as shown in Figure 36.29.

Figure 36.29
Choose a Source file from the Smart Object Inspector.

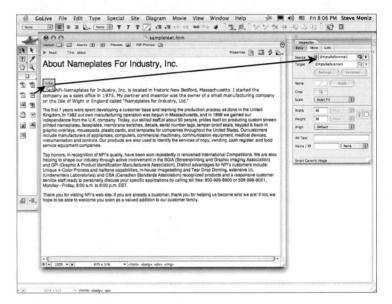

3. The ImageReady Save for Web dialog appears. High resolution images usually need to be scaled down for use on web pages. Use the Image Size tab of the Save for Web dialog to scale the image while importing, as shown in Figure 36.30.

4. After you save the target file, your image appears in GoLive, as shown in Figure 36.31. You can always use the Settings button in the Basic tab of the Inspector to optimize your image differently.

Cropping Smart Objects in GoLive

You can crop any Smart Object you place in the GoLive Layout Editor. When you choose to crop a Smart Object, the Layout Editor window becomes masked and only the cropped area appears in full brightness, as shown in Figure 36.32. The tools to handle cropping are located in the main toolbar and you can revert to the uncropped image at any time, even after you've cropped the image.

To crop Smart Objects, follow these steps:

1. Select a Smart Object and click the Crop Image button in the Inspector palette shown in Figure 36.33.

Image Size tab

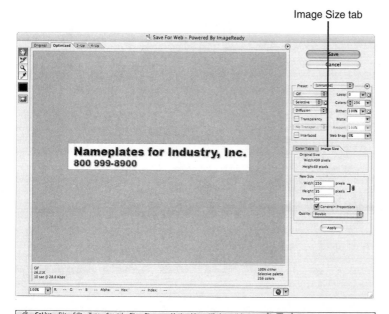

Figure 36.30
The Image Size options in the Save for Web dialog.

36

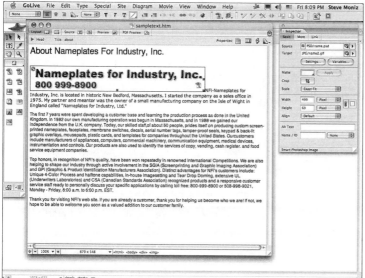

Figure 36.31
The Smart Generic Object based on a TIFF file in GoLive.

36

Figure 36.32
The Layout Editor is dimmed by a
mask when cropping.

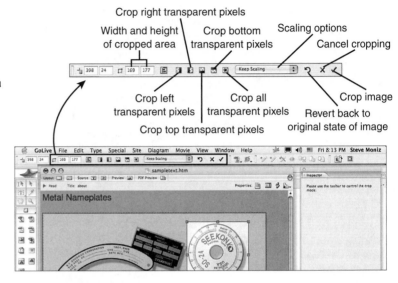

Figure 36.33
The Smart Object Inspector.

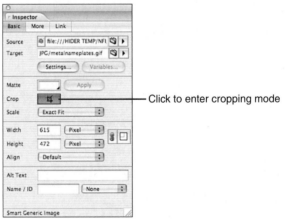

Click to enter cropping mode

2. Click and drag to create a rectangle over the area you want to crop. Adjust the cropping area by dragging the handles that appear around the rectangle.

3. If you want to get out without making any changes to the image, click the Cancel button in the main toolbar or press the Escape key.

4. To finalize your adjustments and crop the image, as shown in Figure 36.34, click the Crop Image button in the main toolbar, double-click inside the cropping area, or press the Return/Enter key.

There really isn't any visual cue that a Smart Object has been cropped, but if you know you've cropped an image and want to revert it back to its uncropped state, simply click the image, click the Crop button in the Inspector, and click the Revert button in the main toolbar.

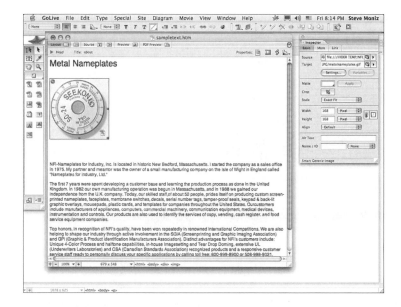

Figure 36.34
The cropped image.

36

Inserting Favicons for GoLive Pages

Favicons are those tiny little icons that sometimes appear next to a website's URL in the URL field of the browser. Some browsers display them in other places as well, like in Netscape's tabs, as shown in Figure 36.35, or Explorer's Favorites menu. The code for favicons is inserted in the Head section of web pages.

Favicon

Figure 36.35
Favicons appear in various places on browsers as in the Netscape tab and URL address field.

To insert a favicon, follow these steps:

1. Start by creating images that are relatively small, using Photoshop or Illustrator, as shown in Figure 36.36. Note that 16- by 16-pixel images are typical for favicons.

Figure 36.36
Create a small square image to use as a favicon.

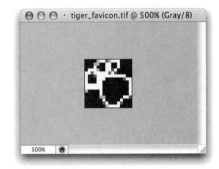

2. Expand the Head section of the document by clicking the triangle next to the word Head in the upper-left corner of the Layout Editor.

3. Drag the Smart Favorite Icon Object from the Smart Objects palette into the Head section of your document or double-click the Smart Favorite Icon Object in the Smart Objects palette to insert the favicon code, as shown in Figure 36.37.

Figure 36.37
Insert the favicon code in the Head section of the document.

Head section

Smart Favorite Icon (favicon) Object

Favicon code object

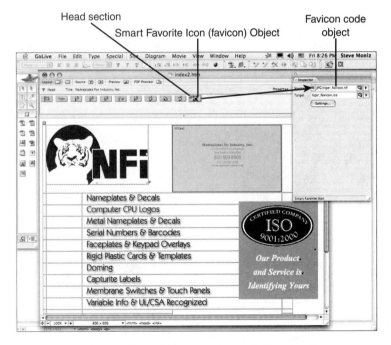

4. Use the Inspector palette to link to the Source file in the same way you do for other Smart Objects.

5. When the Settings dialog appears, choose which formats you want to save your favicon in. You can select one or more of the color options to create favicons for specific browser settings.

6. Click OK and GoLive prompts you for a location to save the `.ico` file. Save the file and preview your page in a browser to view the favicon. You may have to try different browsers to find one that displays favicons.

IMPORTING MULTIMEDIA FILES

GoLive can import any type of multimedia file commonly used on web pages and some not-so-commonly used ones. Creating content for mobile devices is gaining popularity, and GoLive offers a number of ways to include multimedia objects for mobile pages. The scope of this book does not enable us to delve too deeply into the finer points of creating multimedia files, but you will take a look at how to import them onto your pages. GoLive's tutorials on working with the Quicktime tools, and setting up multimedia files is helpful in gaining a better understanding of what is required if you are not already familiar with it.

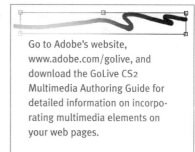

Go to Adobe's website, www.adobe.com/golive, and download the GoLive CS2 Multimedia Authoring Guide for detailed information on incorporating multimedia elements on your web pages.

GoLive offers objects in the Basic Objects palette to import SWF, QuickTime, RealOne, SVG, Windows Media, and a generic Plug-in to cover other types of media.

Inserting Multimedia Objects

If you are inserting SWF, QuickTime, RealOne, SVG, or Windows media files, most of the settings in the Inspector palette are already set up for you. If you are inserting a media format that does not have a specific object with the generic Plug-in object, you have to know the specific MIME type for the object along with any other Class information required:

1. Drag a plug-in object such as SWF or QuickTime onto the Layout Editor, as shown in Figure 36.38.

2. In the Basic tab of the Plug-In Inspector select a MIME type from the pop-up menu if you're inserting a generic Plug-in object. Otherwise, leave the MIME information as it is set by the Plug-in object.

3. Enter width and height values to indicate the size you want a media clip to occupy and play back in.

4. Set the align options the same way you do for images and Smart Objects.

5. From the HTML menu, choose which HTML code to use. Both object and embed work for most media types, though you must specify a plug-in class in the Class text box if you are embedding a generic plug-in file.

6. In the More tab of the Plug-In Inspector shown in Figure 36.39, type a unique name for the plug-in element in the Name field.

Figure 36.38
Use the Plug-in Inspector's Basic tab to set the basic settings for multimedia objects.

Figure 36.39
The More tab of the Plug-In Inspector.

7. Check the Page check box and insert a link to an instruction page for the media file. If you insert any of the media types that have objects in the Objects palette, the link is inserted for you.

8. For RealOne and SVG plug-ins, check the Code check box and indicate a link for the code base. The SWF code base, for example, indicates the location of the Macromedia Flash player installer. The code base is provided for you when you insert SWF or QuickTime media files.

9. Select Default from the Palette pop-up menu to place the plug-in in the background.

10. Set the HSpace and VSpace values the same way you do for images and Smart Objects. Enter a pixel value to offset the surrounding text from the media element.

11. Check the Is Hidden check box if you don't want any of the controllers for the media file to appear on the page.

12. The Attribs tab of the Plug-in Inspector shown in Figure 36.40, lists the current attributes set for the media file. Add additional attributes if necessary.

Figure 36.40
The Attribs tab of the Plug-in Inspector.

13. Some of the plug-ins, such as the SWF plug-in shown in Figure 36.41, have an additional tab in the Inspector palette that contains specific controls and attributes for the plug-in. Check here first for attributes instead of typing them into the Attrib tab.

Figure 36.41
The SWF tab of the Inspector palette.

14. After you finish inputting the settings for the media file, you can click the Play button in the bottom of the Inspector palette to play the media file inside GoLive.

GoLive has always done a great job of incorporating multimedia elements, and this latest version of GoLive supports even more live previewing, making the development process easier than ever. Incorporating multimedia objects on your websites can be quite an involved process, especially considering the time required to produce movies and animation before you can incorporate them on your site. As always, investigate the specific requirements for the media types you want to incorporate on your site to be sure they are well supported by the browsers before investing the time in developing multimedia content.

37

USING CASCADING STYLE SHEETS IN GOLIVE

IN THIS CHAPTER

Cascading Style Sheets (CSS) offer many advantages over standard HTML formatting when creating web pages. In its simplest and most widely used form, CSS is used for text formatting and for creating a uniform style sheet for your website. In its more complex forms, CSS is used to build and position floating layers and to format not only the text, but the entire layout, including background colors, background images, paragraph formats, and even printing. Every browser from version 4 on supports some level of CSS. As a matter of fact, the first rendition of CSS was referred to as CSS1 for Cascading Style Sheets Level 1. We are currently, at the time of this writing, at CSS2 and probably won't see a CSS3 because XML is going to take over in the near future. GoLive offers an easy-to-use, graphical interface, that makes creating cascading style sheets easier than ever. If you're creating websites and want complete control over the formatting of your pages, use CSS.

Using CSS over tables is preferable because CSS uses a fraction of the code that is necessary when building tables. Even with today's high-speed connections, bandwidth economy is still an issue and still needs to be considered when developing websites. One of the most appealing aspects of CSS is the ability to apply text formatting to selections of text, paragraphs of text, or entire blocks of text, much as you would in InDesign or Illustrator. Also, because CSS can be saved as an external style sheet and then be called up on web pages throughout the site, you can control the formatting of your site from one or more external style sheets instead of editing every page when you want to make a change.

CASCADING STYLE SHEET BASICS

CSS enables you to format the text on your website using three fundamental methods: redefining HTML code with element styles, creating class styles, and creating ID styles that apply to unique elements such as floating layers. After you create CSS styles, you can then apply them to your content based on HTML tags such as the paragraph tag or use inline styles to format selected text. After you assign the CSS styles to your text, you can then change the styles and watch the text change on your page, visually formatting your page. If you are familiar with hand-coding CSS styles, view the source code in the CSS Editor's source code tab or split the view and look at source code at the same time you create your styles. The latter option is great if you want to learn about the code, or if you want to break down existing code you didn't create. Whether or not you create internal or external style sheets depends on whether you want your formatting to be applied to a single page or to multiple pages in your site. Internal style sheet code appears in the Head section of your document, and external code is saved in an external text document. See "Creating External Style Sheets," later in this chapter, for more information.

Working with the CSS Editor

The CSS Editor is where you define and control all the cascading style sheets in your document, as shown in Figure 37.1. The CSS Editor contains many tabs when you are defining styles, each tab containing a number of options for formatting your web content. The choices you make in the various tabs of the CSS Editor insert the appropriate code in the Head section of your document when creating internal style sheets:

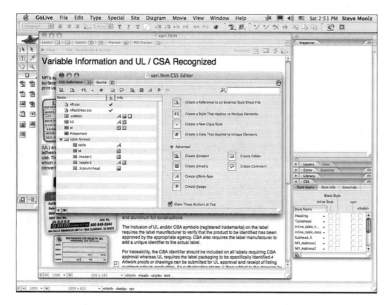

Figure 37.1
The CSS Editor enables you to define CSS elements selectively.

To create a CSS style, follow these steps:

1. Click the Open CSS Editor button in the upper-right corner of the Layout Editor to open the CSS Editor, as shown in Figure 37.2.

Create a Folder button

View Source Code of CSS button

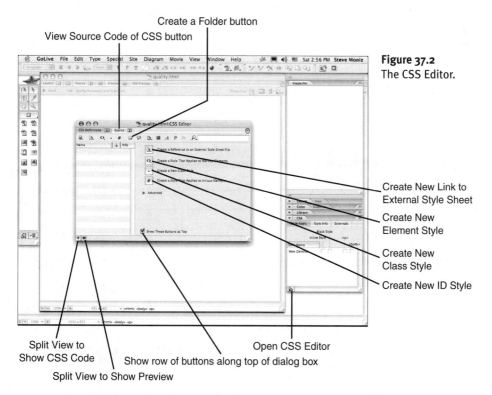

Figure 37.2
The CSS Editor.

Create New Link to External Style Sheet

Create New Element Style

Create New Class Style

Create New ID Style

Split View to Show CSS Code

Show row of buttons along top of dialog box

Open CSS Editor

Split View to Show Preview

2. Click either the Create New Element Style button, the Create a New Class button, or the Create a New ID style to create a new CSS style, as shown in Figure 37.3.

- Choose Create New Element Style if you want to redefine the formatting for an existing HTML tag. For example, if you want to make text formatted with the <h1> tag bold and red, use this method.

- Choose Create a New Class if you want to define the formatting for text and use your own unique names for the style. For example, create a class style called **subhead** and then you can select text and click the subhead style in the CSS Styles palette to format it.

- Choose Create a New ID if you want to create a style that can be used only once in a document. The ID styles are also used by Layers to define their properties, so if your document contains layers, you will also find CSS ID Styles defined.

Figure 37.3
Create a new Style (the H1 Element Style is shown here).

3. Under the Name column in the large window on the left side of the CSS Editor, enter the HTML code you want to redefine if you're redefining an element style, such as the H1 tag shown in Figure 37.4. If you're creating a Class style, enter a name of your choosing for the style. If you're creating an ID style, enter a name of your choosing.

4. Click the Font Properties tab of the CSS Editor to define the font properties, as shown in Figure 37.5. The following are the options available on the Font Properties tab:

- **Color:** Set the text color.

- **Back Color:** Set the background color of the text based on the Margin and Padding settings in the Margin and Padding Properties tab.

- **Size:** Set the size of the text using a variety of measurement units available in the pop-up menu to the right of the text field.

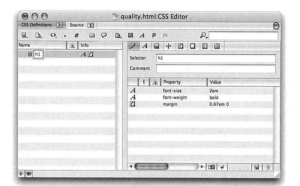

Figure 37.4
Enter the name of the HTML code you want to redefine.

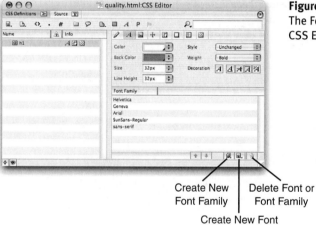

Figure 37.5
The Font Properties tab of the CSS Editor.

Create New Font Family | Delete Font or Font Family

Create New Font

- **Line Height:** Set the distance vertically between baselines of text.

- **Style:** Select italic or oblique text.

- **Weight:** Make text bold or select from a series of numeric weight values between 100 and 900. The numeric values are not supported by all browsers and work only for some fonts, so it's not recommended to use them unless you're developing an internal (intranet) site where you have control over the computing environment.

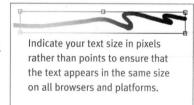

Indicate your text size in pixels rather than points to ensure that the text appears in the same size on all browsers and platforms.

- **Stretch:** Set values for condensing and expanding text. Be sure to test this feature in multiple browsers because different fonts yield different results on the various browsers.

- **Decoration:** Set the type of text decoration you want to apply, including the dreaded blinking text. Click the first button to turn off all text decorations. This is where you can turn off the underlines for your links when redefining the a:link, a:hover, a:visited, and a:active HTML tags. The a:link option defines the attributes of link text on your web page. The a:hover option defines the attributes of link text on your web page when you hover over it with your cursor. The a:visited option defines the attributes of link text when the link has already been clicked and the linked page or site already visited. The a:active option defines the attributes for link text on your website when you are clicking on it. Using these options you could make your text appear one way when it's a new link, change its appearance when you hover over it, change again when you click it, and change when you've already visited the linked page.

- **Font Family:** Select a font family from the Create New Font Family pop-up menu, or define your own font family in the same pop-up menu and then select it. Click the Create New Font button to add fonts one at a time.

5. Click the Text Properties tab of the CSS Editor to define the text properties, as shown in Figure 37.6. The following list explains the options available on this tab:

Figure 37.6
The Text Properties tab of the CSS Editor showing the source code in split view.

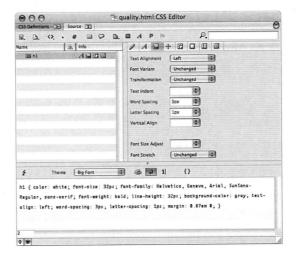

- **Text Alignment:** Select standard alignment values of Left, Center, Right, or Justify.

- **Font Variant:** The only variant you can set is Small Caps, and this feature doesn't always work with certain fonts and certain browsers.

- **Transformation:** Transform the text to all uppercase, all lowercase, or with the first letter of each word capitalized.

- **Font Size Adjust:** Control whether the HTML + or – size values affect the text. For example, if the HTML code contains a font size of +1 and you set this value to 10, the font size increases by 10 of whatever unit you set your font size. This is useful only for existing code because the use of the font tag isn't necessary when coding with CSS.

> You can view the source code for the CSS styles by clicking the Source tab in the CSS Editor or by clicking the Source Code toggle in the lower-left corner of the CSS Editor.

- **Text Indent:** Indent the first line of text in a paragraph by whatever value you enter here. Stick to pixel values for the most consistent results across platforms and browsers.

- **Word Spacing:** Indicate an extra amount of space to be inserted between words. Use this value in concert with the Letter Spacing value to make letter-spaced words easier to read.

- **Letter Spacing:** Insert extra space between each character. This feature, along with the Word Spacing feature is most useful for headlines and subheads.

- **Vertical Align:** Vertically align text within a paragraph of mixed type sizes. This feature applies only to inline Class styles or to HTML tags that are used inline like the (b)old, (i)talic, or font tags.

> You can view sample text that depicts how your styles will work in the Inspector palette by clicking the eye icon in the lower-left corner of the CSS Editor to show the sample text in split view.

6. You can set block properties to define a block of a specific width and height. *Blocks* enable you to define a section of your page by indicating a width and height, as well as other features like background colors and borders. Making the block float left or right can create static left and right blocks with content that flows between the two, as shown in Figure 37.7. The Block Properties are also used to control specifically ID styles for floating layers. See the section titled "Creating ID Styles," later in this chapter, for details. The following list explains the options available on this tab:

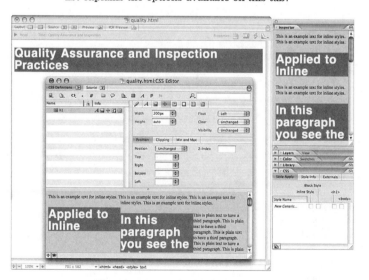

Figure 37.7
Block Properties can create stationery blocks on your web page as well as floating layers.

- **Width** and **Height:** Use to set the width and height of the block that contains your CSS elements. These values are typically set in pixels, but you can choose from any of the available measurement units in the pop-up menu.

- **Float:** Choose Left or Right from the pop-up menu to align your block with the left or right margins. Text that follows this CSS style automatically flows around the block.

- **Clear:** The Clear option doesn't work with all browsers. It emulates the `clear` attribute of the BR tag when used with images that are left and right aligned. The Clear feature makes anything that follows the block appear below it depending on whether the block is set to left or right and whether the stuff that follows it is aligned left or right.

- **Visibility:** The default visibility is visible for all browsers. If you want the content of the block to be invisible, choose hidden. The space that the block occupies is still accounted for when you choose hidden, as shown in Figure 37.8.

Figure 37.8
Visibility set to Hidden as it appears in a browser.

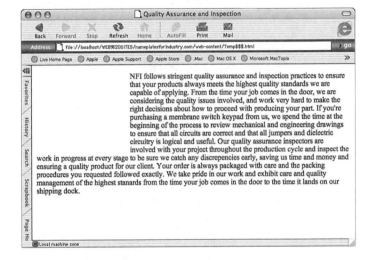

- **Position, Clipping, Min and Max:** Unless you're really feeling adventurous, leave the Position, Clipping, and Min and Max settings unchanged. The Position settings can be changed in the Layers Inspector when you're creating layers. The Clipping and Min and Max settings are not well-supported in all the browsers and produce varying results.

7. Use the Margin and Padding Properties tab of the CSS Editor to set the margins and padding values for your CSS style, as shown in Figure 37.9. The following list explains the options available on this tab:

Figure 37.9
The Margin and Padding Properties tab of the CSS Editor.

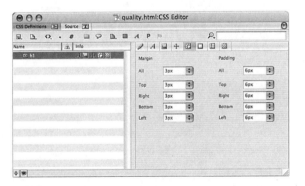

- **Margin:** Set the outset from the text to the edge of the block width and height set in Block Properties, effectively creating an offset for your block when it is set to float left or right, as shown in Figure 37.10.

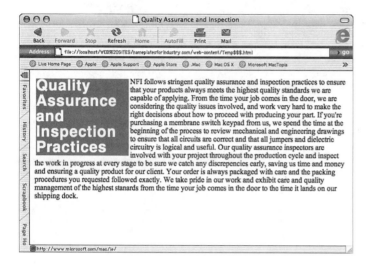

Figure 37.10
The Margin setting keeps the flowing content away from the block.

- **Padding:** The Padding values control the amount of space inside the block (inset), from the block edge to the content of the block, including background color, as shown in Figure 37.11.

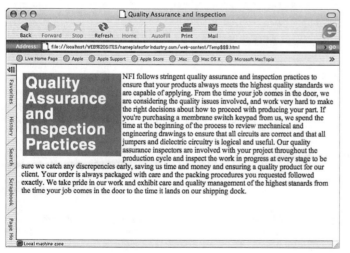

Figure 37.11
The Padding setting insets the content within the block.

8. Set the Border and Outline properties to add a unique border to your block, as shown in Figure 37.12. The Border setting adds a border inside your block, and the Outline setting adds a border outside the block in the padding area specified in the Margin and Padding Properties tab. At this writing the Outline feature is not supported by the latest browsers, though GoLive displays it in the Inspector palette and preview split view:

37

Figure 37.12
Add borders and outlines to your blocks.

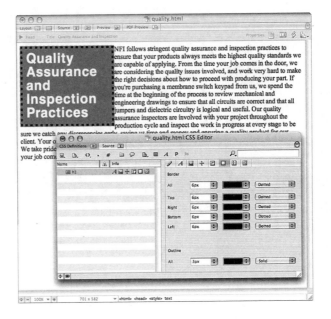

- **Border:** Enter a value for the thickness of your line, along with a color and line style from the pop-up menus.

- **Outline:** Enter a value for thickness and specify a color and style from the pop-up menus.

9. The List Item and Other Properties tab of the CSS Editor contains a hodgepodge of styles that don't necessarily fit into any of the tab categories. List items are the `<li>` tags used in ordered and unordered lists to insert hanging numbers or bullets. You can use the List Item choices to customize the way these lists appear, as shown in Figure 37.13:

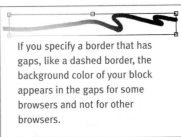

If you specify a border that has gaps, like a dashed border, the background color of your block appears in the gaps for some browsers and not for other browsers.

- For bulleted lists, select a **List Image** from the pop-up menu by first selecting **URL**; then browse to link to a small image that you want to act as a bullet. You can apply this CSS style to the OL or UL tag.

- From the **List Style** pop-up menu, select a typical list item for either the bulleted or numbered list.

- **List Position:** Choose Inside if you don't want the bullet or number to hang outside the left margin. Choose Outside to hang the list element outside the left margin.

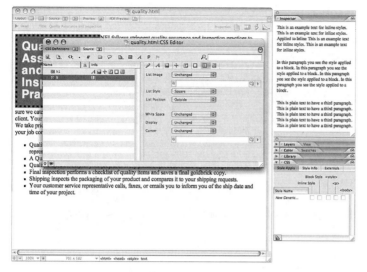

Figure 37.13
Customize the appearance of bulleted and numbered lists.

- **White Space:** White space is one of those CSS attributes that's never quite worked the way it was supposed to, and that's still the case, unfortunately. When you choose Preformatted from the pop-up menu, it's supposed to let you keep the extra spaces in your text, as the PRE tag does in HTML. If you choose No Wrap, it should work just like the NOWRAP table tag attribute and prevent your text from wrapping the width of the browser window.

- **Display:** The display property defines whether an element includes line breaks above and below, is included inline with other elements, is treated as part of a list, or is displayed at all. Choose None from the pop-up menu to make an element not display, such as an image.

- **Cursor:** The cursor property changes the cursor to one you specify from the pop-up menu when your cursor hovers over the text that is formatted with the CSS style defined.

Use the None setting for the Display property in the CSS Editor to preload images. Insert some images that you want to appear on subsequent pages on a page of your website. Define a Class style called something like noshow. Set the Display attribute to None and then apply the noshow style to the images you want to preload. The images load when the first page loads and remain in the cache for subsequent pages, making your site appear faster.

10. Change to the Background Properties tab in the CSS Editor to set the background of your web page by applying the style to the body tag. You can also set the background properties of individual elements on your page, such as table cells, layers, and text elements, as shown in Figure 37.14:

   - Choose **URL** from the **Image** pop-up menu and then select an image to use as a background image.

   - **Color:** Set the background color using the pop-up menu.

   - **Horizontal:** Inset the background image from the left side.

Figure 37.14
The Background Properties tab in the CSS Editor.

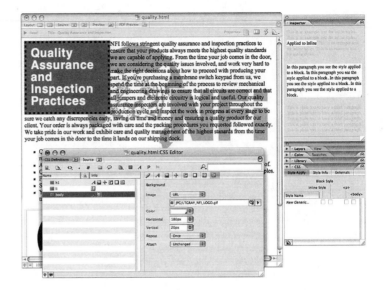

- **Vertical:** Inset the background image from the top.

- **Repeat:** The default for background images is to repeat in both the x and y direction. You can select just the x or just the y direction from the pop-up menu, or select Once to display a single instance of the image in the background.

- **Attach:** Choose Scroll to provide scrollbars for background images that are larger than the block containing them. Choose Fixed, the default setting, to display only the portion of the image that will fit.

11. Close the CSS Editor when you finish setting all the formatting for your styles.

REDEFINING HTML CODE WITH CSS

You can redefine HTML tags to be formatted to precise text specifications. For example, you can make all the <h1> tags in your document 34 point Arial Black in red with a silver background. The ability to redefine HTML tags enables you to reformat your website quickly without having to edit every page of code or select every element. Simply add some CSS styles to your page and, voila—instant formatting.

USING CLASSES TO FORMAT WITH CSS

Define Class CSS styles when you want the ability to select text and apply formatting. Class styles always appear in the code with a period (.) preceding the class name. GoLive automatically inserts this period for you if you fail to do so when naming your style. The CSS palette contains all the Class styles defined internally and any imported external style sheets. Use the CSS palette to apply styles to your text, as shown in Figure 37.15:

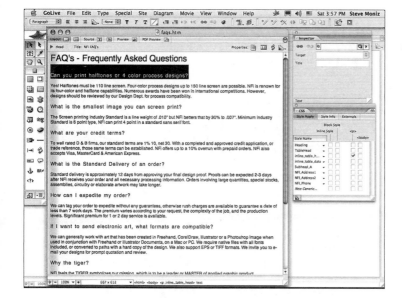

Figure 37.15
Use the CSS palette to apply styles.

1. Select some text or other items on your page that you want to format with a CSS style.

2. Choose from the following options in the CSS palette to apply styles:

   - **Inline Style:** Format the text inline, applying only to the selected text.

   - **Block Style:** Create a separate division from the regular flow of the HTML text.

   - **<p>:** Although this applies to entire paragraphs, you don't have to select the entire paragraph. Click somewhere in the paragraph to apply this style.

   - **<body>:** Apply the style to the entire page.

   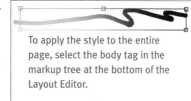

   To apply the style to the entire page, select the body tag in the markup tree at the bottom of the Layout Editor.

   - **Specific Tags:** Depending on what you select, the CSS palette displays different options. For example, if you have your cursor inside a table cell, the <td> tag is available.

CREATING ID STYLES

ID styles, unlike Class styles, can be applied only to a specific style once in a document. ID styles are rarely used these days, but you can use them to specify a unique occurrence of text within your documents like caution, warning, or news flash text, for example. ID styles are used by default by GoLive to define layers, so you can use the CSS Editor to perform additional edits on your layers that may not be available in the Layers Inspector or Layers palette. The biggest drawback to using ID styles is that you have to code them in the HTML code, as shown in Figure 37.16.

The ID style is applied to a paragraph

Figure 37.16
Insert ID styles inside the HTML code.

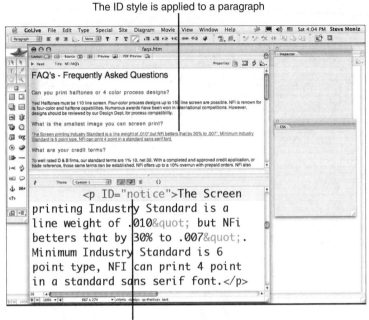

The ID style entered in the source code, applied to a paragraph with the <p> tag

CREATING EXTERNAL STYLE SHEETS

Create external sheets to centralize the formatting for your website, enabling you to make global changes at any time. If you've ever built a large website, you know that the formatting of pages is an evolving thing, changing as you incorporate more content. You use the same techniques as those for internal style sheets described earlier in this chapter to specify the settings for external style sheets:

1. Select File, New to display the New dialog, as shown in Figure 37.17, and choose Web from the first column, CSS from the second column, and Basic CSS from the third column; then click OK. Notice that the title of the CSS Editor dialog box, as shown in Figure 37.18, represents an untitled.css file. You name this external style sheet when you save it.

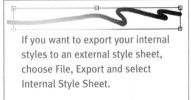

If you want to export your internal styles to an external style sheet, choose File, Export and select Internal Style Sheet.

2. Define any styles you want to include in the external style sheet only and then choose File, Save As.

3. Assign a name with a .css extension and click Save.

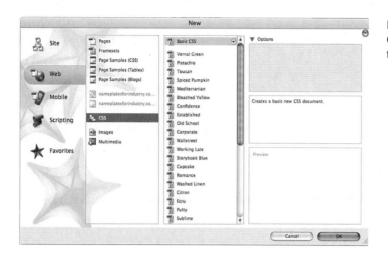

Figure 37.17
Create new external CSS files in the New dialog.

37

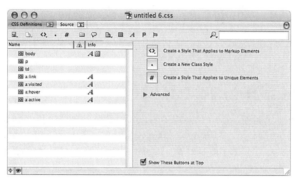

Figure 37.18
The new `untitled.css` file contains some typical styles that you can keep, edit, or delete.

IMPORTING AND USING AN EXTERNAL STYLE SHEET

After you create one (or more) external style sheet you can implement it by first importing it on your pages. You can even specify an external style sheet for your site to be used whenever you create a new page. The CSS tab of the Site window enables you to manage your external style sheets and to drag and drop them onto your pages to import them. After they're imported, the styles contained in the external style sheet appear in the CSS palette along with any internal styles you created. The reason cascading style sheets cascade is because they are applied in a cascading fashion starting with external style sheets, followed by internal styles, followed by ID styles, followed by HTML formatting. This means that if you define the <h1> tag to be red text in your external style sheet, but then redefine the <h1> tag to be blue in the internal style, the text appears blue. The internal style supersedes the external style:

Text formatted with HTML tags overrides any settings in your CSS styles on most browsers. If you notice that your text stays red, even though you defined it as green in a CSS style, it's probably formatted as red with the HTML font tag. Remove the formatting, and the CSS style will apply.

1. Click the Open CSS Editor button in the upper-right corner of the Layout Editor to display the CSS Editor, as shown in Figure 37.19.

Figure 37.19
Use the CSS Editor to import external style sheets.

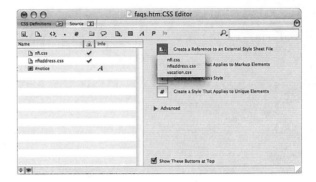

2. Click the Create a Reference to an External Style Sheet File button in the CSS Editor and locate a file with a `.css` extension. If you hold down the button, all the available CSS files on your site appear and you can select one from there.

3. The external style sheet name appears in the list; the styles and the external styles are now available in the CSS palette.

USING ADVANCED CSS FEATURES

You may have noticed the Advanced section of the CSS Editor in Figure 37.20. If you can't see the Advanced options, click in the empty space on the left side of the CSS Editor and then click the triangle next to the word Advanced to display the options. These Advanced features enable you to link to one external style sheet from another, apply specific styles for print, and apply specific styles, depending on the type of media device:

Figure 37.20
The Advanced options in the CSS Editor.

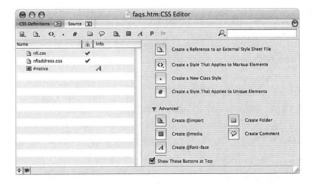

- **Create @import:** Reference an external style sheet from another external style sheet, as shown in Figure 37.21. Click and hold the button to display a list of existing external style sheets to select from, or click the button and click the New button to create a new external style sheet. If the external style sheet is designed for certain media, choose it from the Media pop-up menu.

Click Edit to edit the external style sheet. Click In & Out Links to display the In & Out Links palette, as shown in Figure 37.22.

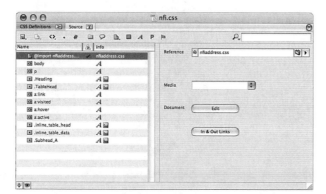

Figure 37.21
Link to an external style sheet from an external style sheet.

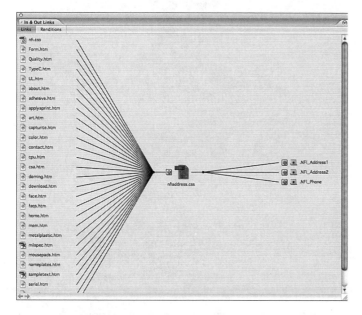

Figure 37.22
The In & Out Links palette displays all of the web pages using the external CSS file on the left, and which styles are in use on those pages.

- **Create @media:** Define styles for specific types of media, such as Braille, Print, and Aural (spoken word). Click the Create @Media button to display the @media rule in the left column of the CSS Editor and then select a media type from the Media pop-up menu, as shown in Figure 37.23. Create CSS styles as usual and then drag them onto the @media rule to add them, as shown in Figure 37.24.

- **Create @font-face:** Download fonts on the fly for your web pages. This feature doesn't work with all browsers and you must be using OpenType fonts at this point. Click the Create @font-face button to display the Font Styling options, as shown in Figure 37.25. Select a font or font family from the Font-Family pop-up menu and indicate the settings for the font, including specific sizes in the Size field. Click the Font Source tab and then click the Create New Item button to specify the URL for the font, or indicate whether the font is available locally.

37

Figure 37.23
Select a media type.

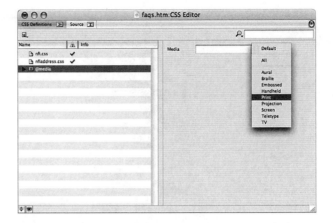

Figure 37.24
Add CSS styles to the @media rule.

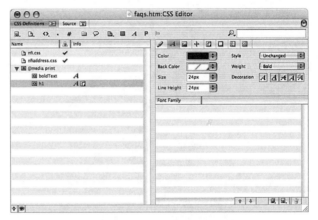

Figure 37.25
Font Styling options for the @font-face rule.

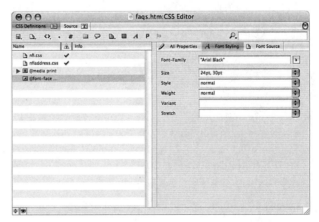

- **Create @page:** Set the dimensions, orientation, and margins of a page box for printing. In the Selector section, leave the field empty (unchanged) to apply to all pages. Choose :first to apply to the first page, or choose :left to apply to pages left of the binding or :right to apply to pages right of the binding. Indicate page marks, margin values, and size values, as shown in Figure 37.26.

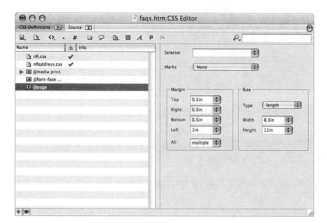

Figure 37.26
The @page settings in the CSS Editor.

37

SPECIFYING A DEFAULT CSS STYLE SHEET FOR YOUR SITE

You can specify an external CSS style sheet to be used every time you create a new page on your site. Click the CSS tab in the Site window to display the CSS information, as shown in Figure 37.27. The CSS tab of the Site window tells you how many times a style is defined and how many times it's been used. To set an external style sheet as the default for all new pages, expand the CSS Files section and right-click (in Windows) or Control-click (on the Mac) the filename, and then select Set as Default CSS from the context menu. If the external style sheet is already the default, the context menu displays Is Default CSS, as shown in Figure 37.28. The default CSS style sheet appears in bold in the list.

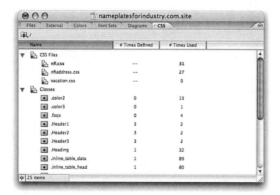

Figure 37.27
The CSS tab of the Site window.

Figure 37.28
Use the context menu on a
selected external style sheet to
set it as the default.

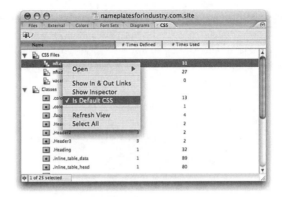

USING GOLIVE'S CSS LAYOUT OBJECTS

GoLive now offers support for using prebuilt, drag-and-drop CSS block objects, which define a style
for an entire page, controlling the flow of text into columns and sections on your page. The prebuilt
blocks are especially useful if you're new to CSS or if you want to implement some of the more complex CSS styles and features. The particular layouts offered
in GoLive are those popular layout styles so often found on
web pages these days: a static left and right column with a
liquid center that adjusts as the page size is adjusted. This
technique is particularly useful when you create content for
mobile and portable devices that have very small screen
areas. The CSS Layout Objects are available in the Objects
palette, as shown in Figure 37.29:

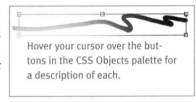

Hover your cursor over the buttons in the CSS Objects palette for
a description of each.

Figure 37.29
The CSS Objects palette.

1. Double-click a CSS Objects button to add it to your web page at the insertion point, or drag and drop the CSS Object, as shown in Figure 37.30.

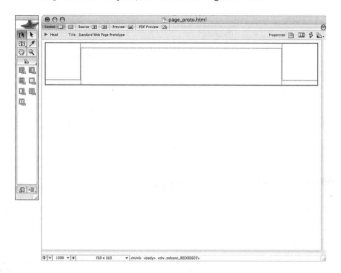

Figure 37.30
Insert a CSS Object on your page.

2. Insert content into the preformatted object space, as shown in Figure 37.31.

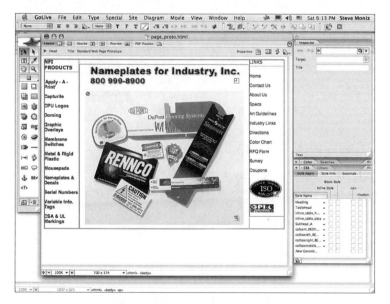

Figure 37.31
Insert content into the CSS Layout Object.

3. The content is formatted using the DIV tag and all the CSS styles appear in the CSS palette, as shown in Figure 37.32. Open the CSS Editor and edit the styles to customize the content for your site, as shown in Figure 37.33.

37

Figure 37.32
Styles from the CSS Objects
appear in the CSS palette.

Figure 37.33
Use the CSS Editor to edit the CSS
styles for the CSS Objects.

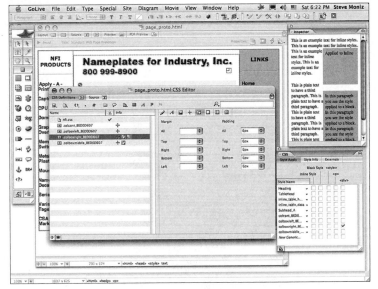

Cascading Style Sheets are an integral part of most websites these days because they enable you to exercise the most control over the format and appearance of your web content. GoLive's tools for CSS enable you to implement Cascading Style Sheets easily without the need to learn the entire set of code for CSS.

WORKING WITH SOURCE CODE IN GOLIVE

Although the need to work in source code becomes less and less with every new version of GoLive, there are occasions when it is necessary to work in the source code to achieve a particular effect or to format content a particular way. This is especially true of new technologies that are introduced and implemented after a software release of GoLive, where GoLive does not yet know about the new code required. You might also find it useful to work with the source code if you've been doing this a while and are more comfortable working in code. Then, of course, there are some things that still have to be inserted into the source code by hand, such as CSS ID selectors and certain attributes such as the `clear` attribute for the <BR> tag. Whatever your reasons for editing the source code, you will find GoLive's Source Code Editor useful and user friendly.

USING THE GOLIVE SOURCE CODE EDITORS

GoLive provides access to the source code of your pages in a variety of convenient ways. You can edit source code using the Source tab of the Document window in either *full mode*, as seen in Figure 38.1, or in *split view mode* with the Layout tab in the top and the Source code in the bottom, as shown in Figure 38.2.

If you like to edit your source code in a floating palette, you can open the Source Code palette, shown in Figure 38.3.

The Source Code Editor can be set up to display the source code in pretty much any format you like; you just have to spend a little time setting it up using the Source Code toolbar, if you're not happy with one of the default settings. See "The Source Code Toolbar," later in this chapter, for details about formatting the source code. See "Setting Source Code Preferences," later in this chapter, for more information about setting up the Source Code Editor the way you like.

The Outline Editor is another way you can work with the HTML source code in your document using an outline format that can be expanded and contracted to make it easier to isolate and work on sections of code, as shown in Figure 38.4.

The JavaScript Editor is designed to aid you in building scripts and provides all the tools necessary to embed and test a JavaScript in your document, as shown in Figure 38.5. The JavaScript code you create in the JavaScript Editor can be inserted in the <HEAD> section of your HTML code or exported to be used as an external JavaScript.

The Source Code Toolbar

The Source Code toolbar is located at the top of the Source Code Editor within the Source tab. The Source Code toolbar contains tools that affect the way the source code is displayed and also provides tools for checking your code syntax and navigating through the code. GoLive comes with some predefined themes that determine how the source is displayed. You can select these themes in the Source Code toolbar, as shown in Figure 38.6:

- **Check Syntax:** Ensure that your code complies with predetermined formats. See "Checking Syntax," later in this chapter.

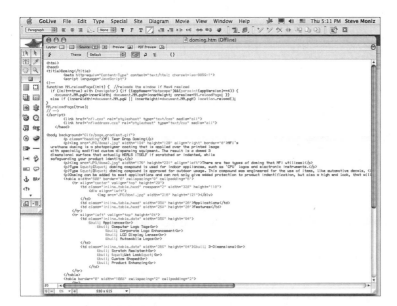

Figure 38.1
The Source tab of the Document window gives you full-screen access to your source code.

Figure 38.2
The split view mode of the Document window shows both the layout of your web page at the top and the source code at the bottom.

38

- **Select code formatting theme:** Choose a code formatting theme to make the code easier to read and follow. The available themes provide various methods of color coding the code as well as assigning different text sizes depending on how you'd like to look at source code.

- **Colorize Code:** Turn colorized text on and off.

- **Word Wrap:** Wrap the code to fit within the width of the window. All lines after the first are indented.

Figure 38.3
The Source Code palette gives you a floating window you can drag around the workspace as you edit your code and view a full-screen layout.

Figure 38.4
The Outline Editor in the Document window enables you to expand and condense the lines of source code, making it easier to locate and isolate specific areas of code.

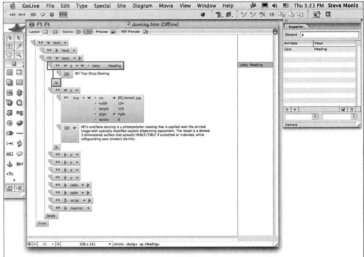

- **Display line numbers:** Turn on line numbers to make it easier to locate and remember places in the code. The line numbers also help when word wrap is turned on, since the line numbers refer to lines of code and assign a line number to only the first line of a wrapped line.

- **Navigate through code:** Set markers inside the code using the New Marker option in this button's menu and then easily jump to those markers using this same menu.

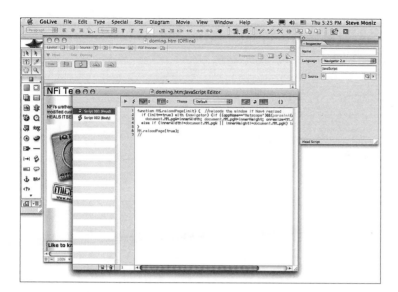

Figure 38.5
The JavaScript Editor helps you build scripts and provides the tools you need to embed and test a JavaScript in your document.

Check Syntax

Select code formatting theme

Word Wrap to window

Colorize Code toggle

Display Line Numbers

Navigate through code

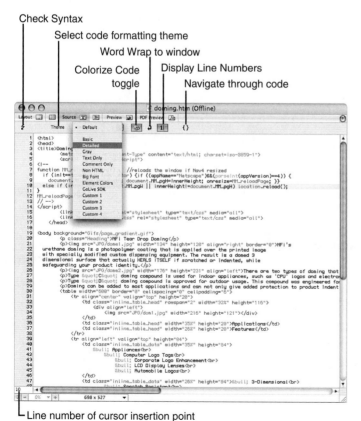

Line number of cursor insertion point

Figure 38.6
Select a theme that displays the source code in a variety of ways.

SETTING SOURCE CODE PREFERENCES

The Source Preferences window controls how the Source Code Editors and JavaScript Editor display their respective code. You can set theme preferences so you can easily switch to preferred methods of viewing source code and JavaScript based on settings you create:

1. Choose Edit, Preferences in Windows or GoLive, Preferences on the Mac to display the Preferences dialog.

2. Click on Source in the category column to display the source code preferences, as shown in Figure 38.7.

Figure 38.7
Set the general Source preferences in the Preferences dialog.

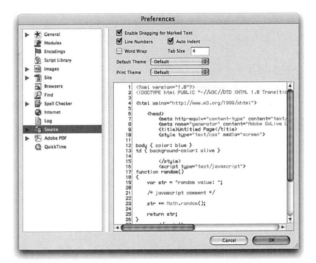

38

3. To control how the Source Code and JavaScript Editors work, set the following preferences:

- **Enable Dragging for Marked Text**: Select some text and drag it to another location or disable this feature.

- **Line Numbers:** Automatically display line numbers to the left of the source code or JavaScript code by default. You can toggle this feature on and off using the toolbar at the top of the Source Code Editor.

- **Auto Indent:** Automatically indent lines of text that wrap and cascade indents source code elements that are nested.

- **Word Wrap:** Wrap the source code to the window width in both the Source Code Editor and the JavaScript Editor by default. You can toggle this feature on and off using the toolbar at the top of the Source Code Editor.

- **Tab Size:** Set the size of the automatic indent and also control the number of spaces inserted when you type the Tab key.

- **Default Theme:** The default theme for displaying source code in the Source Code Editor and JavaScript Editor. You can override this setting using the toolbar at the top of the respective editors.

- **Print Theme:** Set the default code formatting for the Source Code Editor and JavaScript Editor when the code is printed to a printer. The Print Theme can be set different from the display theme so you can see your code one way and print it another.

4. To define your own themes or to modify the existing themes, click the triangle to the left of the Source category in the Preferences dialog box and click Themes, as shown in Figure 38.8.

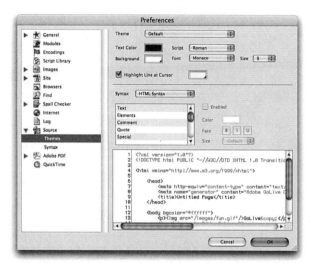

Figure 38.8
The Themes preferences enable you to customize the source code themes.

5. Select an existing theme from the Theme pop-up menu or choose one of the Custom theme options from the same menu. Set the other formatting options offered in the Themes preferences. All the settings in this dialog are purely for display purposes and do not affect the actual syntax of your code. You can customize the visual display of code by setting the color, size, and style of the text.

6. Click on Syntax in the category list to control the options for syntax checking, as shown in Figure 38.9:

- **Enable Code Completion:** Have GoLive intuitively complete your code for you when you begin typing.

- **Enable Immediate Completion:** Have GoLive insert end tags automatically. Be careful when this is turned on, because it automatically inserts them after the opening tag, so you could end up with extra tags when inserting code, like the <p> tag.

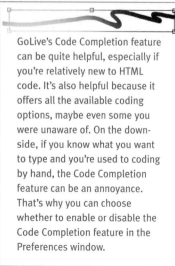

GoLive's Code Completion feature can be quite helpful, especially if you're relatively new to HTML code. It's also helpful because it offers all the available coding options, maybe even some you were unaware of. On the downside, if you know what you want to type and you're used to coding by hand, the Code Completion feature can be an annoyance. That's why you can choose whether to enable or disable the Code Completion feature in the Preferences window.

Figure 38.9
The Syntax preferences set basic rules about syntax and syntax checking.

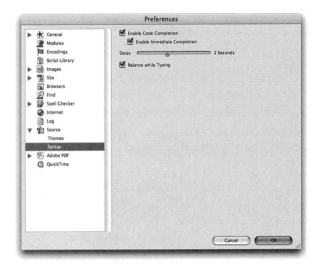

- **Delay slider:** Indicate a *delay speed* (the amount of delay before the code completion option kicks in). Set this value to a higher delay if you don't want it popping up every time you start typing code, especially if you know your code pretty well. If you're new to coding, you might want to decrease the delay time so the code completion feature kicks in sooner.

- **Balance while Typing:** Automatically jump to the next open bracket when you type a close bracket.

7. Click OK after you set all the Source Code Preferences.

> For advanced users, the Web Settings options in GoLive enable you to customize the way GoLive deals with code, markup, browser profiles, and file mapping. Be sure you understand what you're doing before changing any of these options. Choose Edit, Web Settings in Windows or choose GoLive, Web Settings on the Mac.

USING THE SPLIT SOURCE CODE VIEW AND SOURCE CODE PALETTE

You may find it easier to work with your source code when you can see the actual layout at the same time. You can achieve this in two ways with GoLive. Split the Layout Editor window to show the Source Code in half the space and the layout in the other half, or open the Source Code palette:

1. Click the Show/Hide split source button in the lower-left corner of the Document window to split the window, as shown in Figure 38.10.

   Alt-click (in Windows) or Option-click (on the Mac) on the Show/Hide split source button to change the orientation of your split window, as shown in Figure 38.11. Repeat to move the split window to different positions. This orientation will be the default orientation until you change it again.

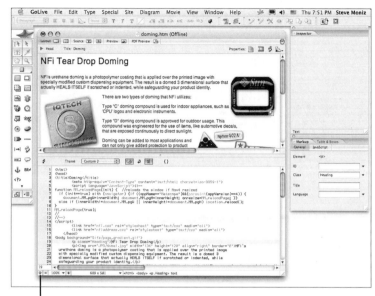

Figure 38.10
The split view mode.

Show/Hide split source

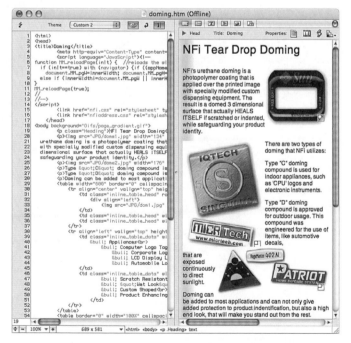

Figure 38.11
Alt-click (Windows users) or Option-click (Mac users) to choose an orientation for the split window.

2. To open the Source Code palette, choose Window, Source Code. The Source Code palette, shown in Figure 38.12, does not contain the Source Code toolbar and is formatted according to the settings in the Source tab of the Document window and any settings for source code in the Preferences window.

Figure 38.12
The Source Code palette.

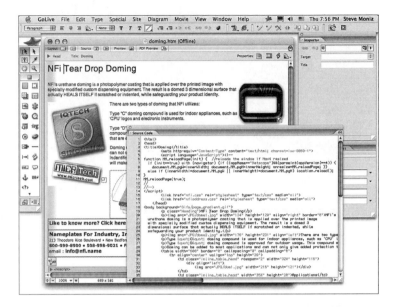

3. Click the palette menu in the upper-right corner of the Source Code palette to set the options for the palette, as shown in Figure 38.13. Choose the Dim When Inactive option if you want the code to be dimmed when you're not clicked inside the Source Code palette. If you choose the Local Mode option, the Source Code palette displays only the code for the currently selected elements, as shown in Figure 38.14.

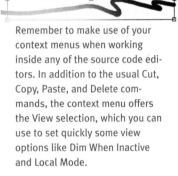

Remember to make use of your context menus when working inside any of the source code editors. In addition to the usual Cut, Copy, Paste, and Delete commands, the context menu offers the View selection, which you can use to set quickly some view options like Dim When Inactive and Local Mode.

Figure 38.13
The palette menu options for the Source Code palette.

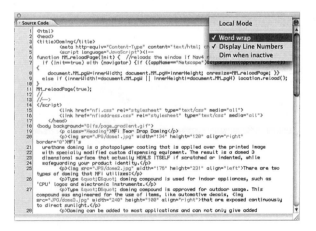

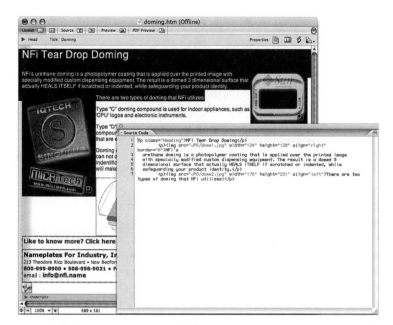

Figure 38.14
Selectively edit source code in Local Mode.

USING THE VISUAL TAG EDITOR

The Visual Tag Editor enables you to edit the source code of a single HTML element without using any of the Source Code editors and also enables you to insert new HTML code. The Visual Tag Editor can be quite handy when you want to insert a single code here or there:

1. Position your cursor within the Layout Editor where you want to insert new code or at a point after the code you want to edit.

2. Choose Special, Visual Tag Editor or press Ctrl+Shift+E in Windows or ⌘-Shift-E on the Mac to display the Visual Tag Editor, as shown in Figure 38.15.

Figure 38.15
The Visual Tag Editor.

3. Type code at the blinking insertion point or double-click any of the codes in the scrolling list on the left to insert the code at the location of the insertion point in the Layout window. When you type a space after the HTML code, the scrolling list displays the available attributes for the tag. Use a combination of double-clicking in the scrolling list and typing values to insert HTML code.

4. To edit existing code, click the code in the Markup string, as shown in Figure 38.16.

Figure 38.16
Use the markup string to edit source code selectively in the Visual Tag Editor.

5. Click OK to apply your changes.

USING THE OUTLINE EDITOR

Use the Outline Editor to manage and edit your HTML code in a hierarchical view that can be expanded and compressed to limit the amount of code you have to see at one time. Use the context menus within the Outline Editor to add HTML code and attributes, and use any of GoLive's drag-and-drop or point-and-shoot (Adobe sometimes refers to this as *pick-whip*) features to add elements through the Outline Editor:

1. Select the Outline Editor tab in the Document window to display your source code in outline format, as shown in Figure 38.17.

Figure 38.17
The Outline Editor enables you to view, add, and edit code in outline mode.

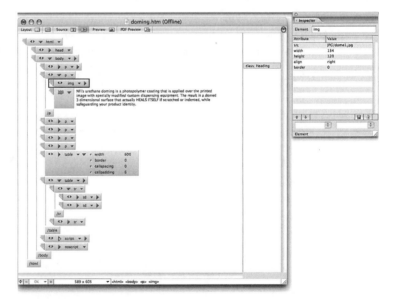

2. Click the triangles (on the Mac) or the plus/minus signs (in Windows) to expand and contract sections of code.

3. Click to select a tag, and either use the Inspector palette to edit the tag's attributes or click the attributes in the outline to edit them, as shown in Figure 38.18.

HTML Tag   Attributes

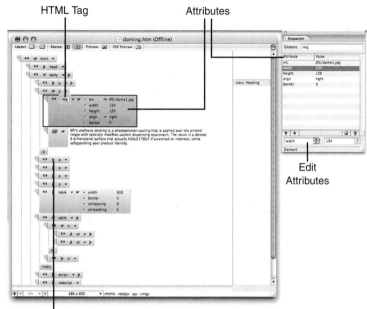

Expand/Contract Sections

Figure 38.18
Selectively edit HTML codes and attributes within the Outline Editor or by using the Inspector palette in concert with the Outline Editor.

Edit
Attributes

4. If you click the right-pointing arrow, called the *path pointer*, the Select File dialog appears so you can select an object like an image, as shown in Figure 38.19.

Path Pointer

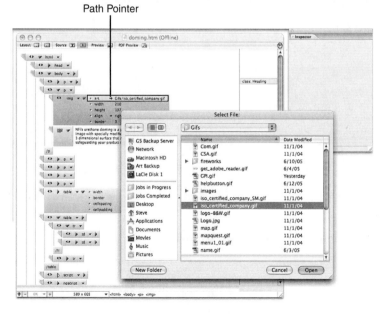

Figure 38.19
Click the path pointer to select a file.

38

5. Use the wedge-shaped icon at the beginning of each line of code to move the code by dragging and dropping. Click these same wedge-shaped icons to select sections, as shown in Figure 38.20.

Figure 38.20
Drag and drop the wedge icons to move sections of code in the Outline Editor.

6. Click the small arrows next to the attributes to display a list of available attributes for selection.

7. Use the tools in the Main toolbar to add new code, comments, and text, as shown in Figure 38.21:

- **Add new element button:** Insert a new HTML element after the current selected element. Type the code for the new HTML element.

- **Add new attribute button:** Add attributes by first selecting an HTML code, and then clicking this button in the Main toolbar.

- **Add new text button:** Insert plain text after the currently selected object.

- **Add new comment button:** Add an HTML comment to your code after the currently select object.

- **Add new generic item tool:** Add special codes such as ASP and SGML.

- **Unary and binary tags:** Toggle between these tags to control whether the closing tags are dimmed (unselectable) or not. This feature reduces the amount of code displayed to make it easier to look at all the source code. If you need to edit a closing tag, toggle binary back on and make changes.

Add new element
Add new attribute
Add new text
Add new comment
Add new generic item
Toggle between unary and binary tags

Figure 38.21
Add new elements using the tools
in the Main toolbar.

38

8. Use the arrow keys on your keyboard to navigate within the Outline Editor. Use the Tab key to jump from one text block to another. Press Shift+Tab to jump to the previous text block.

9. To view images within the Outline Editor, as shown in Figure 38.22, click the Images check box in the View palette. You can open the View palette by choosing Window, View. If you are using Low Source images with the `lowsrc` attribute of the <IMG> tag, click the Low Source check box in the View palette to display the low source images instead.

10. Drag elements directly from the Basic Objects palette onto the Outline Editor to add elements, as shown in Figure 38.23.

Figure 38.22
View images in the Outline Editor.

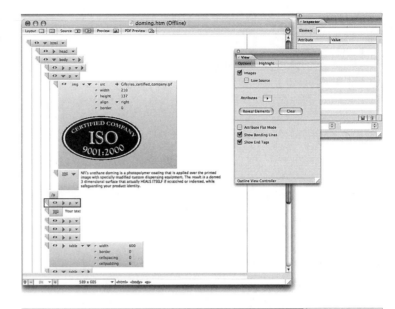

Figure 38.23
Drag and drop elements from the Objects palette into the Outline Editor.

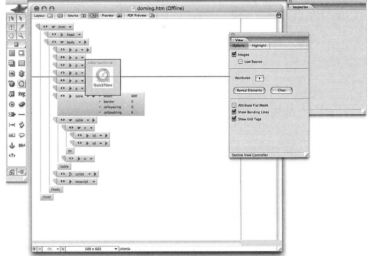

USING THE JAVASCRIPT EDITOR

The JavaScript Editor is a text editor that enables you to type in your JavaScript code and then check the syntax of the code. You must have some JavaScript in your document to open the JavaScript Editor. If you want to open the JavaScript Editor to create a script from scratch, start by choosing JavaScript from the Special menu; then select New Script Element to add a new JavaScript element to your document. You can then select Open JavaScript Editor from the JavaScript submenu under the Special menu. If you expand the <HEAD> section of your document at the top of the Layout Editor, you can double-click any JavaScript icon to open the editor.

You must have an understanding of JavaScript to create and edit scripts. GoLive creates JavaScript code for you when you use the Actions palette. Refer to Chapter 36, "Working with Images and Multimedia in GoLive," for specific information about the Actions palette and inserting JavaScript into your documents.

CHECKING SYNTAX

GoLive enables you to validate the source code on a single web page or the entire site to ensure that you have error-free, optimized source code on your site. The built-in syntax-checker checks your documents to see whether they're well formed and verifies whether your documents conform to a particular DTD (Document Type Description). Refer to Chapter 35, "Creating Web Page Layouts with GoLive," for information on specifying the DTD for your documents. You can check your documents against the DTD you have specified for the document or any other DTD of your choosing:

1. To check the syntax for a single document, open the document and click the Check Syntax button in either the Source Code Editor or the Highlight tab of the View palette, as shown in Figure 38.24. To check the syntax of the entire site, open the Site window and then select Edit, Check Syntax.

The Check Syntax button in the View palette's Highlight tab

The Check Syntax button in the Source Code Editor

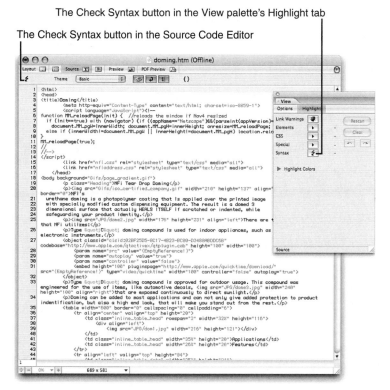

Figure 38.24
Click the Check Syntax button to check the syntax in the current, open document.

2. Select the DTDs to comply with in the list at the top of the Syntax Check dialog, as shown in Figure 38.25. You can select any number of DTDs, but keep in mind that some DTDs support formatting that others do not, so try to stick with the specific DTD with which you're trying to comply:

Figure 38.25
Choose the DTD with which you want your document's syntax to comply in the Syntax Check dialog.

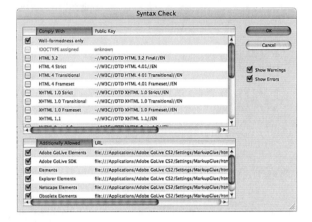

- Choose **Well-formedness Only** to ignore any DTD settings and check for the correct use of basic HTML rules.

- Choose **!DOCTYPE Assigned** to check the source code based on the DTD assigned to the document in the Head section of the HTML code.

- Scroll to the bottom of the list to select from the different browser types and versions, as well as options for mobile devices.

3. Click the check boxes for the Additionally Allowed elements that you want the syntax checker to check. Check them all just to be on the safe side, though keep in mind that you might be countering a DTD setting if you also select an option with looser compliance standards, such as Obsolete Elements.

4. Check the Show Warnings check box to display warnings about codes that might or might not be correct, such as a misspelled color name or invalid font size. Check the Show Errors check box to show syntax errors.

5. Click OK to display the result window, as shown in Figure 38.26.

6. Double-click the errors in the results window to highlight the corresponding code and make corrections. Recheck the syntax when you're done to be sure no additional errors remain.

> If you're not sure why GoLive is finding an error in your syntax, try removing the offending code if possible—it might not be needed. You might have to do some investigating on your own if you really want to know the whys and wherefores of a rejected code. A good place to start is at the World Wide Web Consortiums website, www.w3.org.

7. If you checked the syntax on your entire site, the results window displays all the pages that contain errors in expandable menus. Click the Save Collection button to save the collection in the Collections tab of the site window for later work, as shown in Figure 38.27.

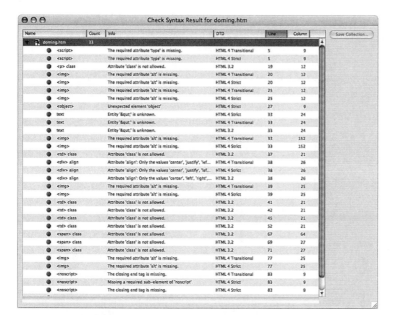

Figure 38.26
The results window of the Syntax Checker.

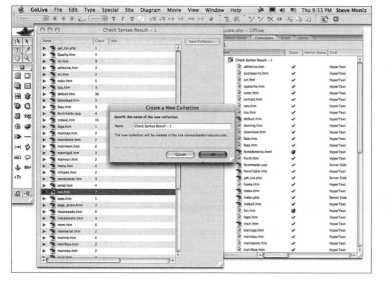

Figure 38.27
To work on them later, save the syntax check results in the Collections tab of the Site window.

FINDING AND CHANGING CODE ELEMENTS

You can use the Find Code Elements command to search for particular strings of code in a single document, a selection of documents, or every document in the entire site. Using the Change option you can search and replace code with ease in one dialog box. The Find Code Elements command can come in quite handy when you need to make a global change throughout your site, such as changing the background image for every page or changing the DTD for every page. In a single HTML document, search and replace outdated HTML codes like the `<font>` tag with cascading style sheet code like the `<div>` tag:

1. Regardless of whether you want to search a single file or the entire site (open a single Document window or open the Site window to start), choose Edit, Find, Find Code Elements.

2. Choose the element and any attributes you want to search for in the top section of the Find Code Elements dialog, as shown in Figure 38.28.

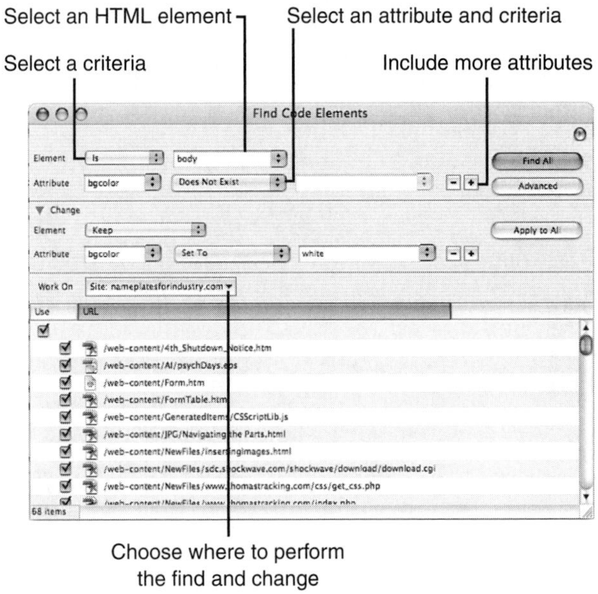

Figure 38.28
The Find Code Elements dialog.

Select an HTML element
Select a criteria
Select an attribute and criteria
Include more attributes

Choose where to perform
the find and change

3. In the Change section of the Find Code Elements dialog, choose Keep if you want to keep the element you're searching for and then set any new attributes you want to apply.

4. Select where you want to perform the find and change from the Work On pop-up menu in the bottom section of the Find Code Elements dialog.

5. Click Find All to find all occurrences and display them in the list at the bottom of the Find Code Elements dialog. Click Apply to All to make the change to every document selected in the bottom section.

You might find that you never have to edit source code in GoLive because GoLive does so much of the work for you in the background. However, if you *do* need to edit any of the source code on your website, GoLive has the tools to accomplish this. If your goal is to create web pages with the highest level of web compliance or if you're delving into the creation of mobile web content, the syntax-checking features of GoLive can be invaluable.

39

CREATING WEB FORMS IN GOLIVE

Web forms enable you to keep a line of communication open with visitors to your website at all times. Web forms provide a vehicle for receiving input from visitors to your site. Whether it's an involved survey or a simple search text field, web forms are an integral part of most every website. In GoLive, all the form elements are contained in the Form Objects palette, so creating forms is really a matter of dragging and dropping elements onto your page and then arranging them to look nice.

DESIGNING FORMS IN GOLIVE

Web forms can be presented on your web pages in a variety of ways. In GoLive, you can build your web form inside a table using the layout grid and layout text box. The basic function of forms is to gather information, but that doesn't mean you can't add a few graphics here and there to make the page look good.

Here are some suggestions for creating effective and appealing forms:

- Make forms visually appealing by including colors and graphics, just as you would for any other web page. This keeps the form connected to your site stylistically, and it also makes the exchange of information seem less intimidating.

- Keep instructions brief and to the point, and try to stay clear of confusing language and jargon.

- Group like information together. GoLive enables you to group form elements into sets, with visual cues such as bounding boxes to alert users that this information belongs together.

- Ensure that the tab order in the form enables easy and logical navigation through the form.

- Because some browsers display form elements much larger than intended, be sure to include extra space in your layout to compensate for any shifting that may occur. Be sure to test your forms often and thoroughly, on a variety of browsers and platforms, to make sure your layout remains intact.

- Keep your forms as short as possible. Collect only the information you really need. Make it quick and easy for your visitors.

- Don't make very many of the fields required—only those that you absolutely can't do without.

- Use fast selection tools such as radio buttons, check boxes, and pop-up menus, and prefill them with common selections.

CREATING A NEW FORM

The Form Objects palette, shown in Figure 39.1, contains all the elements you need to create a web form. Elements include buttons, labels, text and password fields, check boxes, radio buttons, pop-up menus, list boxes, hidden elements, a file browser, a key generator, and a fieldset creator. Each form element is actually an HTML element and serves as a means of transmitting information that is input by your users.

To create a web form, follow these steps:

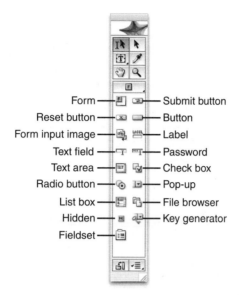

Figure 39.1
The Form Objects palette includes objects for all form elements.

1. Select the Form tab of the Objects palette to display the Form objects.

2. Select the Form object and drag it into place in your document window. The box that encloses this Form tag will house all the elements of your form, so it's essential that you place this icon first. Any elements not placed within this box will not function as part of the form.

3. Use the Form Inspector to name your form and provide essential information in the Action, Target, Encode, and Method fields. Use the Action field to indicate the URL of the script that will handle your form data when the Submit button is clicked. If the script that handles your form data returns a response web page, you can use the Target field to indicate what frame to display the content in when designing pages using HTML frames. The Encoding option indicates how the text is to be formatted when sent to the form-handling script. The Method field is usually set to POST for most forms and defines the method of delivery for the form data. Your web administrator or Internet Service Provider can give you all the specifics about what needs to be set in the Form Inspector.

4. Click the icon of any form element you want in the Objects palette and then drag it into place within the box enclosing the Form tag. You may also position your cursor within the Form tag box and simply double-click form element icons in the Objects palette to place them.

5. For each element, use the Form Inspector to provide any necessary details.

6. Continue to add form elements until your form is complete (see Figure 39.2).

7. Be sure to include a Submit button so users can send their information to you after they've completed the form online. You may also choose to include a Reset button so users can clear all the fields in the form.

8. Save your form and test it thoroughly in various browsers to ensure full functionality.

39

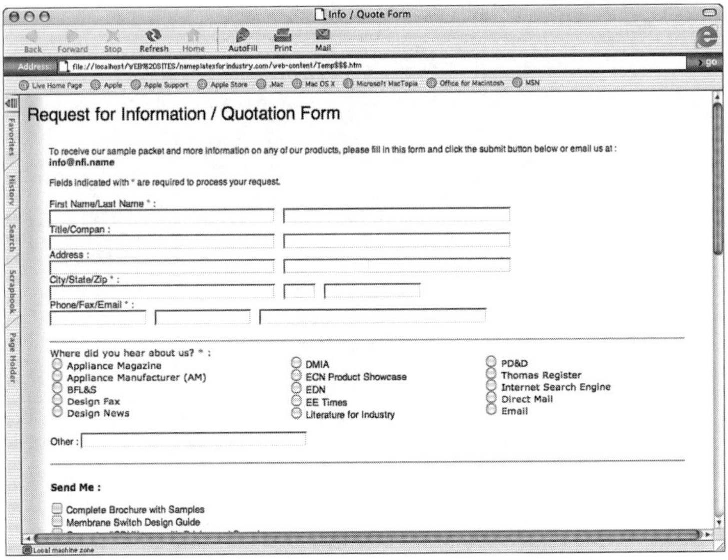

Figure 39.2
A completed form using a variety of form elements.

The Form Tag

The Form tag is the HTML tag that encloses all form elements. When a user clicks the Submit button, all of the variable data inside the <form> and </form> tags is submitted. The form tag also contains the information to process the form in its `action` attribute. The `action` attribute can contain a simple email address (not recommended) or a URL for a CGI script, PHP script, or ASP page for example.

Using the Form Inspector

Through the Form Inspector, shown in Figure 39.3, you provide the values that enable your form to communicate with the CGI scripts and transfer your data where it needs to go:

Figure 39.3
The Form Inspector provides a place to edit the characteristics of a form.

- **Name/ID:** This setting may be used for later reference. It is particularly important when you're using multiple forms simultaneously, but you can leave it blank if it is your only form.

- **Action:** This setting refers to the location of the script that will handle the data sent by the form. All forms need an action to tell the browser what to do when the user clicks the Submit button. Type the filename and directory of this script, or link to it using point and shoot or browsing. A form cannot function without calling a proper action, so be sure to talk to your Internet service provider or server administrator about what kinds of scripts are available for your use and where they are located on the server.

- **Target:** If you're using frames, use this field to specify a target where the page returned by the web server will appear.

- **Encode:** If you require special encoding, enter or choose the encoding type in the Encode field. Multipart/form-data is the most common, but this field can be left blank for most CGI scripts.

- **Method:** Use this menu to choose a form method. Although both are correct, the Get and Post methods function in slightly different manners. Use the Post method if you are unsure of which one you should use because the majority of form handling scripts rely on this method to store posted data. The Post method is most often used because it does not restrict the amount of data that can be transferred. The Get method stores the posted data in a variable within the script and greatly restricts the amount of data that can be handled. Ask your Internet service provider (ISP) or web administrator which method is best for your particular needs.

- **Inventory:** This button leads you to a dialog box that enables you to take a quick peek at what's included in your form so far (see Figure 39.4). This convenient feature helps you troubleshoot as you go, without sifting through lengthy lines of source code. In addition, you can export a list of the form elements you've used, or the action string as it stands, for use elsewhere. This comes in handy for duplicating forms, building databases, and troubleshooting your own form. The Action String section shows you just what will be sent to the receiving CGI script or form handler.

Figure 39.4
The Form Inventory dialog.

Creating Buttons

Three types of button icons exist within the Form tab of the Objects palette, each with its own unique function:

- **Submit:** This button sends the data entered in the form to the CGI script to be processed.

- **Reset:** This button clears the form and returns it to the original default values.

- **Button:** This button can be set up to behave exactly like a submit or reset button, or you can customize its appearance by adding an image, formatted text, or other content to make it more intuitive to the user (see Figure 39.5). These generic buttons can also be attached to HREFs or JavaScript actions using the onClick command in the Actions palette.

Figure 39.5
Examples of the Submit and Reset buttons, with an example of a customized button.

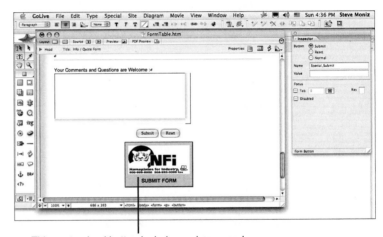

This customized button includes an image and
formatted text and acts as the Submit button

To create a button:

1. Select the Form tab of the Objects palette.

2. Click and drag the desired button icon into position within the Form tag box on your page.

3. Use the Button Inspector to specify the following details for your button:

   - **Select the button type:** Using the radio buttons in the Inspector, you can specify a button as Submit, Reset, or Normal. Custom buttons should always be set to Normal.

   - **Provide a name for each button:** This is strictly for your use when referring to the button and does not appear to the user on the form.

   - **Label the button:** This appears as text on the button itself. Submit buttons are by default labeled *Submit Query*, and reset buttons are labeled *Reset*, but you can change either label simply by checking the Label box and typing a new label into the field, as shown in Figure 39.6.

- **Custom button text:** Highlight the text on the button itself to change the label. You may adjust the font, size, and style of the text, just as you would in any regular text box, using GoLive's standard font tools.

- **Custom button images:** Drag the Image icon from the Basic tab of the Objects palette onto the top of the button to place an image there. Use the Inspector to select an image file and determine its dimensions, just as you would with any image element.

- **Custom button value:** Specify a value for your button (that is, an action or value to be passed to the CGI script, as suits the purpose of your form). For example, your custom button could say `Click this button if you like pizza` and the value to be sent to the CGI script would be `likes pizza`.

Figure 39.6 shows a Submit button set up in the Button Inspector.

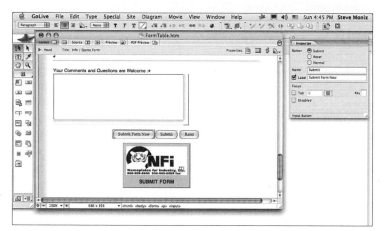

Figure 39.6
The Submit Button Inspector.

39

The Form Input Image

Another user-friendly option for sending information is the form input image. Like a custom button, an input image enables you to place a clickable image on your page:

1. Select the Form tab of the Objects palette.

2. Click and drag the Form Input Image icon into position within the Form tag box on your page.

3. In the Inspector, link to the desired graphic using the point-and-shoot lasso, browsing to the correct file, or typing the filename and path directly into the source field, as shown in Figure 39.7.

4. Specify details such as height and width, alignment, border size, and alternate text in the Inspector, as you would with any other image.

Figure 39.7
Images can also be used as buttons, shown here in the Form Input Image Inspector.

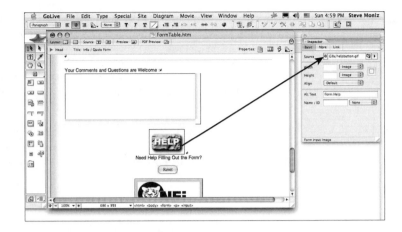

Labels and Text Fields

Although the Form tab features multiple text elements, each performs a slightly different role, as shown in Figure 39.8. Labels serve as titles or indicators for other elements, but they may also be used to activate or deactivate their associated elements. Text fields enable users to input single lines of text, such as individual words, numbers, or phrases. Password fields resemble text fields, except that the entered text string is not visible, providing protection to the user. Text areas provide additional space for multiline text entries, such as paragraphs.

Figure 39.8
Examples of a label, text field, password field, and text area.

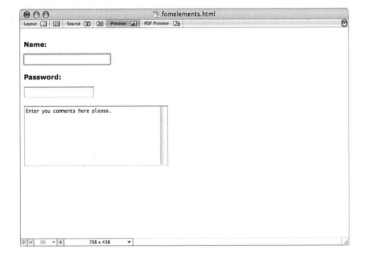

Labels

The Label icon inserts a small text box that enables you to define the purpose of another element (check box, radio button, and so on) for your users. Although the text of a label may be edited and formatted much like a standard text box, the label holds a distinct advantage over the text box in that it can also control the element it defines. By clicking the label, a user can activate or deactivate its associated object. Test this feature in your browsers, though, because it is not supported on some.

To create a label, follow these steps:

1. Select the Form tab of the Objects palette.

2. Click and drag the Label icon into position on your page, or simply double-click the icon in the Objects palette.

3. Place your cursor in the content area of the label and enter a name for it.

4. Select the name and format the text by adjusting the size, font, and/or style, as desired.

5. To link the label with an element, first select the label and then either point and shoot to the appropriate form element, or ⌘-click (on the Mac) or Alt-click (in Windows) the border of the label and drag it into the appropriate form element (see Figure 39.9).

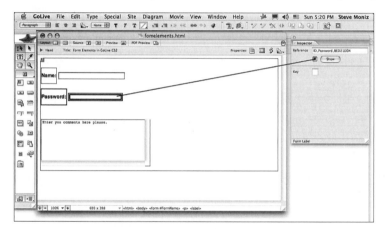

Figure 39.9
A label is selected in the Form Label Inspector.

Text Fields, Password Fields, and Text Areas

Although created with two separate objects, the text field and the password field are nearly identical, except for the privacy feature of the password field. Both fields are intended for short, single lines of text, although the line length can be adjusted to suit longer strings of data.

To create a text field, follow these steps:

1. Select the Form tab of the Objects palette.

2. Click and drag the text field or password field icon into position on your page, or simply double-click the proper icon in the Objects palette.

3. Select the field in your document.

4. In the Inspector, shown in Figure 39.10, enter a unique name to identify your field.

5. In the Value text field (in Windows) or the Content text field (on the Mac), insert any default text for users to see (or leave this text field empty).

6. In the Visible text field, enter the desired character length of your field. This setting refers to the number of characters that can be viewed in your new field.

7. Enter a character limit in the Max text field to set the maximum number of characters your field will accept. If you leave this text field empty, the limit is determined by the web browser used to view the form.

8. If your new field is a password field, enable the Is Password Field check box to indicate so. When this option is selected, the field displays bullets instead of displaying what's typed.

Figure 39.10
A standard text field shown in the Form Text Field Inspector.

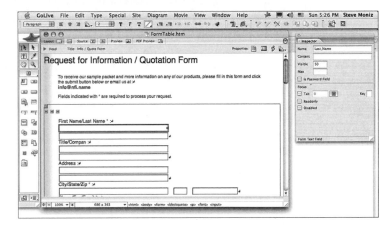

To create a text area, follow these steps:

1. Select the Form tab of the Objects palette.

2. Click and drag the Text Area icon into position on your page, or simply double-click its icon in the Objects palette.

3. Select the Text Area element in your document window.

4. In the Inspector, shown in Figure 39.11, enter a unique name to identify your text area.

5. In the Rows field, enter a number to determine the height for your text area. This setting determines the maximum number of rows visible in your text area.

6. In the Columns field, enter a number to set the width of the text area. This setting determines the maximum number of characters visible across your text area.

7. Choose a setting from the Wrap pop-up menu to control line breaks. Choose Default to use the default settings of the browser. Choose Off to keep text in a single line regardless of the Columns limit. Choose Virtual or Physical to wrap text within the Columns limit automatically. If you choose Physical, the text is submitted to the CGI script with returns where the lines break, whereas Virtual wraps the text on the web page but submits a single long string of text to the CGI script.

8. In the Content field, insert any default text for users to see, or leave this field empty.

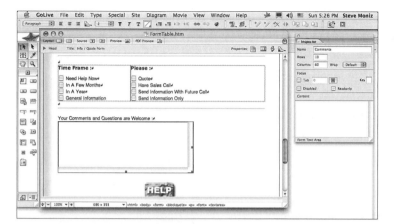

Figure 39.11
A text area is defined and described in the Form Text Area Inspector.

Check Boxes and Radio Buttons

When you're presenting multiple-choice questions, from a simple Yes or No to those with many possible answers, check boxes and radio buttons help you elicit quick, clear responses from your viewers. Figure 39.12 shows examples of radio buttons and check boxes along with the HTML source code generated by GoLive.

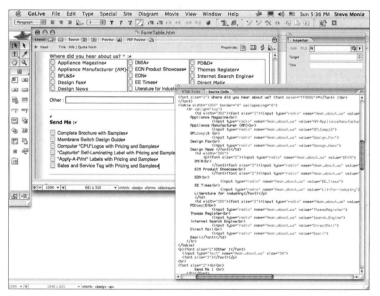

Figure 39.12
Examples of radio buttons and check boxes.

39

Check boxes and radio buttons enable you to maintain better control over the data submitted by the form. Unlike text fields, where user responses may vary widely, you actually predetermine the possible answers in a listed format. From here, you can sort the information into categories based on responses, set up scripts to flag certain criteria and perform designated functions according to the choices your users make, and calculate statistical data with greater accuracy. All these benefits make check boxes and radio buttons excellent choices for certain parts of forms.

Use the radio button any time answers are mutually exclusive, as in the Yes or No scenario or when you want to force users to choose the best answer.

Check boxes allow for multiple responses to a single question. Use these anytime more than one answer may be equally valid.

To create radio buttons, follow these steps:

1. Select the Form tab of the Objects palette.

2. Click and drag the Radio Button icon into position on your page, or simply double-click its icon in the Objects palette.

3. Select the Radio Button element in your document window by clicking it.

4. In the Inspector, type in the Group field the name of the group to which the selected radio button element belongs. The group name can be used, for example, to group all the buttons in response to a single question. In the likely event that several questions on your form make use of radio buttons, this ensures that only those from the same group are compared with one another. Choose a descriptive name for the group to which you want the selected button to belong and then type that name into the text field; alternatively, you can select an existing group name from the pop-up menu. After a group name has been entered, it becomes available as a choice in the pop-up menu.

5. Type a value in the Value field for the selected button. The value for the radio button is a unique response that serves to identify it within the group. This value may be any web-friendly alphanumeric character or a string of characters (without spaces). Values such as *A* (for lettered multiple-choice questions), *1* (for numbered lists or for questions involving mathematical calculations), *Yes* (for Yes or No questions), and *Always* (for questions of preference or frequency) are common examples. When a viewer submits the form, this value gets passed to the CGI script and then is sent back to you as usable data.

6. In the bottom section of the Inspector palette check the Selected box to indicate that this radio button should appear selected by default, as shown in Figure 39.13.

7. Repeat these steps for each button in the group.

Figure 39.13
A selected radio button shown in the Form Radio Button Inspector.

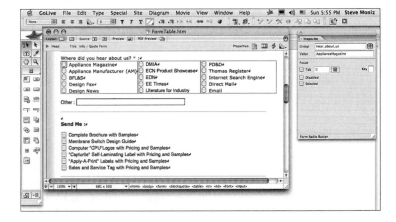

To create check boxes, follow these steps:

1. Select the Form tab of the Objects palette.

2. Click and drag the Check Box icon into position on your page, or simply double-click its icon in the Objects palette.

3. Select the check box by clicking it in your document window, and in the Inspector palette enter a unique name to identify the check box (see Figure 39.14).

4. Assign the check box a value in the Value field. This value may be any web-friendly alphanumeric character, or string of characters, without spaces. Values such as *A* (for lettered multiple-choice questions), *1* (for numbered lists or for questions involving mathematical calculations), *Yes* (for Yes or No questions), and *Always* (for questions of preference or frequency) are common examples. When a viewer submits the form, this value gets passed to the CGI script and is then sent back to you as usable data.

5. In the bottom section of the Inspector palette, enable the Selected box to indicate that this check box should appear selected by default.

6. Repeat these steps for each check box in the group.

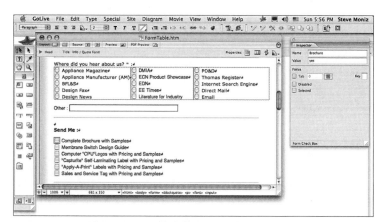

Figure 39.14
A selected check box is defined in the Form Check Box Inspector.

39

Pop-up Menus and List Boxes

Both the pop-up menu and list box accomplish the same task; each displays a list with multiple items from which the user may choose, as shown in Figure 39.15. The only real difference lies in the appearance of the lists. In a *pop-up menu*, only one item appears by default. Users must click the menu to view the full list, and the selected item becomes the one displayed. By contrast, the *list box* shows multiple items in a scrolling list. Users may use the scrollbars to view list items beyond the scope of the box, and any selections become highlighted. A list box enables the user to select multiple items from the list as well, by holding the Shift key while clicking.

Pop-up menu   List box

Figure 39.15
A pop-up menu and a list box are
shown here, with the source code.

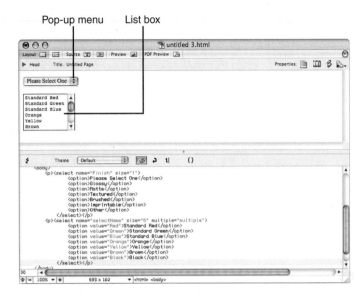

To create a pop-up menu or a list box, follow these steps:

1. Select the Form tab of the Objects palette.

2. Click and drag the Pop-up or List Box icon into position on your page, or simply double-click its
   icon in the Objects palette.

3. Select the Pop-up or List Box element in your document by clicking it, and in the Inspector, enter
   a unique name to identify the item (see Figure 39.16).

Create new item

Duplicate selected item

Figure 39.16
A list box shown in the Form List
Box Inspector.

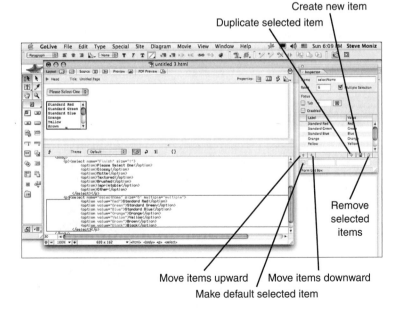

Remove
selected
items

Move items upward / Move items downward

Make default selected item

4. In the Rows field, enter a number to determine the number of rows you want to be visible. In a list box menu, viewers see this number of rows when scrolling through the menu.

5. Enable the Multiple Selection check box to allow your users to select more than one item, if desired. If you select only one row to display and disable the Multiple Selection check box, your element will be a pop-up menu. Any other settings revert it to a list box.

6. The Label/Value list box contains three entries by default, labeled First, Second, and Third with respective values of 1, 2, and 3. Select an item from the Label/Value list box and edit it to your specifications. Click Duplicate to make an additional copy of the currently selected item. Click New to add a new option.

Setting Up a File Browser

Insert a file browser form element when you want to provide a means for users to send you files, similar to the way you send attachments with email. The file browser element contains a field with a Browse button that enables the user to either type in the path name to the file they want to send or click on the browse button to navigate to the file's location on their hard drives. When the form is submitted by clicking the Submit button, the file that appears in the file browser field is uploaded as well. In the example shown in Figure 39.17, the user is prompted to send electronic artwork for a label to be ordered. In this example, the user is sending a JPEG file named `label.jpg`.

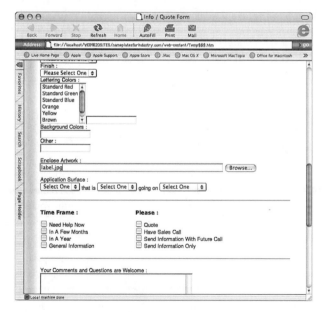

Figure 39.17
A file browser can be used to permit a user to upload a file to the web server. Here, a site visitor uses the form to submit electronic artwork.

39

To set up a file browser, follow these steps:

1. Select the Form tab of the Objects palette.

2. Click and drag the File Browser icon into position on your page, or simply double-click its icon in the Objects palette.

3. Select the File Browser element in your document window and, in the Inspector (shown in Figure 39.18), enter a unique name to identify the file browser.

4. In the Visible field, enter the number of characters that will be visible in the file browser text field, much like a text field.

Figure 39.18
Set the options for the file browser form element in the Inspector palette.

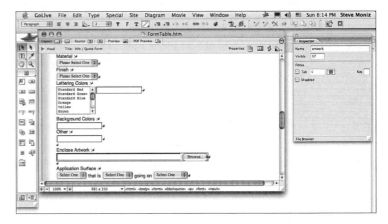

Creating Hidden and Disabled Form Elements

Sometimes you may want to keep elements of a form hidden from view entirely or activate them only when certain criteria are met. Hidden elements may include data or behind-the-scenes instructions not meant for the eyes of your users. An email address is often included in a hidden field to specify which address the form data is to be sent to if the CGI script has a variable for it, such as `recipient`, as shown in Figure 39.19.

Let's say you have a website that asks users to join your mailing list. In addition, let's say your site has three departments—appliances, furniture, and linens. In each of the departments you can provide an identical HTML form that enables users to join your mailing list, but each form has a unique hidden field indicating what department users were in when they filled out the form. In this example, the hidden field would be named `department`, and the value of the field would be `appliances`, `furniture`, or `linens` depending on which form users submit. In either case, the form would be submitted to the same script, which would gather the information in one place, with the `department` field indicating where users were on your website when they filled out the form. You could then use this information to customize marketing materials to suit users' interests. When a form is submitted, the hidden data is submitted as well, along with the users' input.

Disabled elements are regular elements that appear dimmed in the browser until a script activates them, based on a predesignated event or some condition being met. For instance, you could keep a Submit button dimmed until all required fields are filled. Legends, labels, text fields, password fields, text areas, submit buttons, reset buttons, check boxes, and radio buttons may be temporarily disabled in this way.

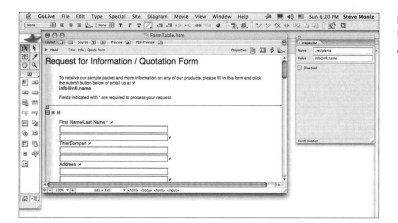

Figure 39.19
Hidden form elements appear as
a tiny H icon.

Follow these steps to create a hidden element:

1. Select the Form tab of the Objects palette.

2. Click and drag the Hidden icon into position on your page, or simply double-click its icon in the Objects palette.

3. Select the Hidden element in your document window and, in the Inspector (shown in Figure 39.20), enter a unique name to identify the Hidden element.

4. Assign a value to this hidden element. This will be carried by the CGI script.

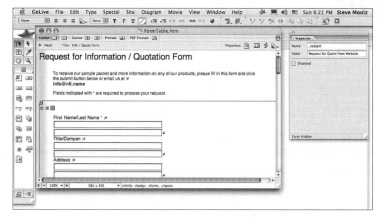

Figure 39.20
A hidden form element shown in
the Form Hidden Inspector.

To disable an element, follow these steps:

1. Select the element you want to deactivate in your document window.

2. Check the Disabled check box in the Inspector, as shown in Figure 39.21.

3. If you are familiar with writing scripts using scripting languages such as JavaScript or VBScript, you can write a script to enable the item based on logical conditions and attach the script to the page or to another button.

39

Figure 39.21
The Submit button set to Disabled in the Input Button Inspector.

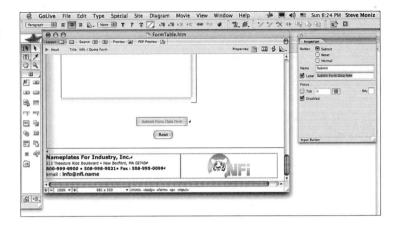

Creating Read-Only Form Elements

Any text form element may be set to read-only status. Simply select the element in your document window, and check the Read-Only box in the Inspector. These elements will not be transmitted when the form is sent, and they cannot be edited or otherwise manipulated by the user.

FACILITATING FORM NAVIGATION

To make your forms easier to navigate, you can assign a particular tabbing order and even assign keyboard shortcuts. These features enable users to select individual form elements by pressing Tab or a specific key combination. Not all browsers support form navigation control keys, but for those that do, it can be quite a time saver for your form users.

Tabbing Chains

You can define a tabbing chain for any set of form elements on the same page, as shown in Figure 39.22. The tabbing chain simply indicates in what order the form elements are selected when users press the Tab key repeatedly. Labels, text fields, password fields, text areas, submit buttons, reset buttons, check boxes, radio buttons, pop-up menus, and list boxes all support tab indexing.

Here's how to create a tabbing chain automatically:

1. Choose Special, Forms, Start Tabulator Indexing. Alternatively, select the first element of your tabbing chain and then click the Start/Stop Indexing button in the Focus section of the Inspector. (It looks like a number sign to the right of the Tab field.) A small yellow box appears on top of each index element on your form.

2. Click each element in the desired tabbing order, exactly in the order you want it to be tabbed. Each is assigned a number inside the yellow box on the element and in the tab index in the Inspector.

3. When you have finished creating the tabbing chain, choose Special, Stop Tabulator Indexing from the main menu or click the Start/Stop Indexing button in the Inspector.

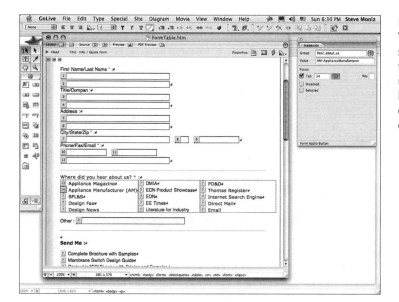

Figure 39.22
You can set a tabbing chain to specify the order in which your fields will be selected when the user presses the Tab key. A small boxed number appears to indicate each element's order in the chain.

To create a tabbing chain manually, select each of the form elements in the desired tabbing order and enter a number in the Tab text field of the Inspector for each element (see Figure 39.23).

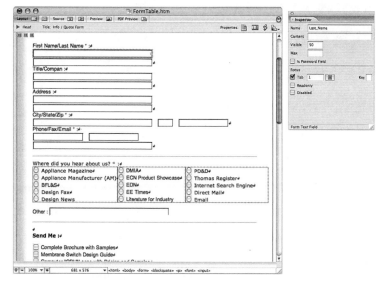

Figure 39.23
The First Name/Last Name field has been set to be the first in the tab order with a tab index value of 1.

39

To change an existing tabbing chain, follow these steps:

1. Select the element where you'd like to begin the tab order change.

2. From the main menu, choose Special, Start Tabulator Indexing, or click the Start/Stop Indexing button in the Inspector.

3. Click each element successively in the new tabbing order.

4. When you're finished, choose Special, Stop Tabulator Indexing from the main menu, or click the Start/Stop Indexing button in the Inspector.

Creating a Fieldset

The Fieldset icon creates a bounding box that visually groups form elements, making your forms more user friendly, as shown in Figure 39.24. A legend may be used to indicate a title for the group of elements or to give a reason why the elements are to be seen as a set.

Figure 39.24
Fieldsets help break up forms into logical groups of information.

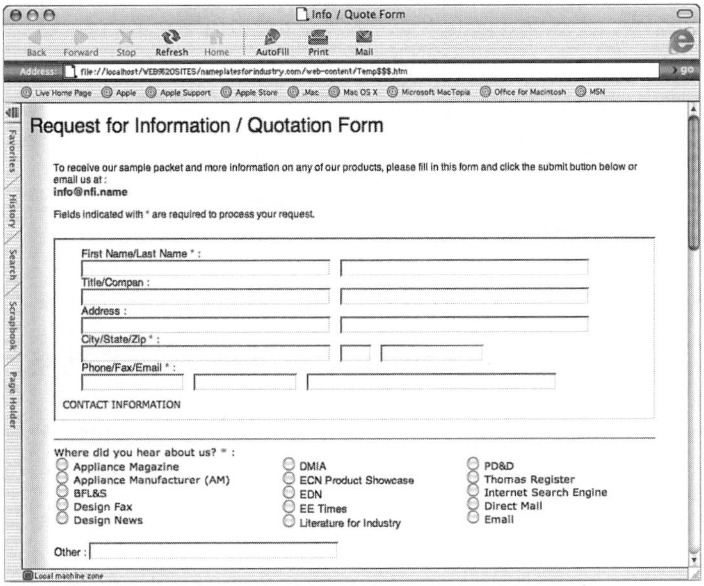

To create a fieldset, follow these steps:

1. Select the Form tab of the Objects palette.

2. Click and drag the Fieldset icon into position on your page, or simply double-click its icon in the Objects palette.

3. Select the Fieldset element in your document window by clicking it.

4. In the Inspector shown in Figure 39.25, select Use Legend if you want a legend to appear in the fieldset bounding box. In Figure 39.24, the legend depicted is *CONTACT INFORMATION*.

5. Use the Alignment pop-up menu to align the legend within your fieldset.

6. Highlight the legend in the fieldset in the document window and enter the text for the legend.

7. Drag an HTML element or other form elements inside the fieldset as desired.

Legend

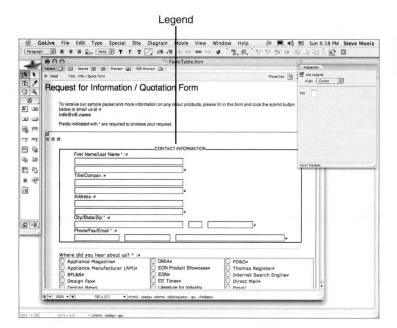

Figure 39.25
Options available in the Form
Fieldset Inspector.

ABOUT VALIDATING FORM DATA

To validate form data to determine whether all required fields have been entered, you need to perform a procedure known as *forms validation*. It can be done on the server side, where an application running on your web server checks the submitted data for validity and returns an error page if all is not well. However, it's often easier to run this procedure on the client side, using JavaScript forms validation.

When the Submit button is clicked, a JavaScript will first execute to check the contents of the form fields against criteria that you've specified for each field. If any required fields are empty, or any fields contain data not formatted correctly, a friendly error dialog appears, and the form is not submitted. This ensures that any form that *is* submitted is full and correct. Use GoLive's Action palette to create your own form validation:

1. Choose Window, Actions to display the Actions palette.

2. Click the F icon that represents the form tag in your document window to select the form.

3. In the Actions palette, scroll down in the Events list and select Form Submit, as shown in Figure 39.26.

4. Click the Create New Action button in the Actions palette to create a new action in the Actions column, as shown in Figure 39.27.

Figure 39.26
The Form Submit action enables you to create an action that is triggered when the Submit button is clicked.

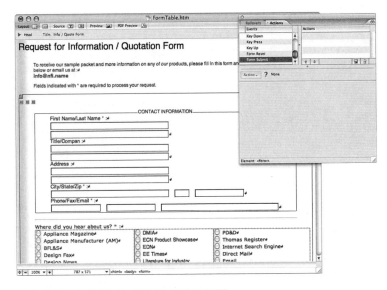

Figure 39.27
All of the available actions are found under the Action button, which becomes available after you select an event from the Actions palette.

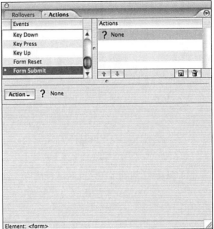

5. From the Action pop-up menu, select Getters, Field Validator, as shown in Figure 39.28.

6. In the Actions palette, select from the pop-up menus to specify your field validation, as shown in Figure 39.29.

7. Click the Create New Action button to add additional fields you want to validate and then test your form in a browser. A dialog box appears when the form validation is not met.

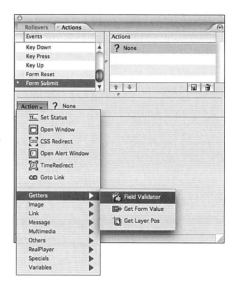

Figure 39.28
The Getters options pertain to forms specifically.

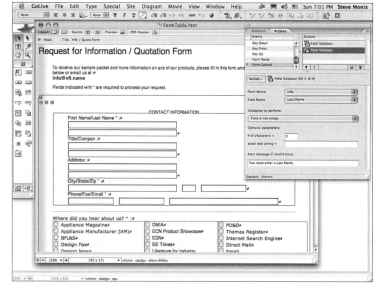

Figure 39.29
Add a Field Validator action for each field you want to validate.

39

SOURCES FOR FORM SCRIPTS

You can create your own customized scripts to handle the data submitted to your web server by the user. You need to learn how to program using a programming language such as C++, Java, or Perl. The most popular scripts are written using Perl. Scripts written for the purposes of handling form data are called *CGI scripts*. You can learn everything you ever want to know about CGI scripts at http://www.cgi101.com. You can even download predefined CGI scripts that you can use on your site with a few small modifications to the script.

Before you spend a ton of time learning to program in a programming language, explore the existing scripts available to you. Your server administrator or Internet service provider is an excellent resource for this kind of information. Chances are they already have a script that you can use or will be willing to write a script for you.

39

CREATING A WEBSITE
WITH GOLIVE

When it comes to creating a new site, this latest version of GoLive offers some exciting new features, such as the ability to create a new site based on a sample site provided with GoLive. You can, of course, still use the Site Creation wizard, which enables you to start from scratch or from an existing website. Larger and more complex websites, or corporate websites that require input from a large number of people for the content of a website, often use some method of version control, such as Adobe's very popular Version Cue. Regardless of how you want to create and build your site, all the initial site setup features are located in the New dialog, which opens when you choose File, New, as shown in Figure 40.1.

Figure 40.1
The Site options in the New dialog covers all the bases when it comes to creating a new site.

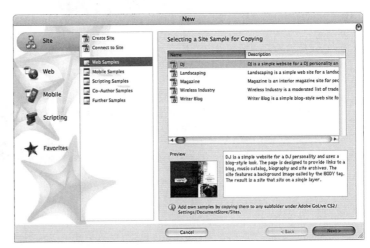

USING THE SITE CREATION WIZARD

The Site Creation Wizard is available when you select Create Site from the Site options, as shown in Figure 40.2. You can start by creating a blank site, which initially contains nothing but a home page, or select from the two other options for existing content. The Site From Existing Content option enables you to create a site in GoLive from an existing hierarchy of files, perhaps created by someone else, or with some other software package. The Site from a Site Locator file (.aglsi), enables you to open a previously created Site Locator file, which contains all the site information for a site. Site Locator files are created using GoLive's Export Site Locator feature under the File menu, where all the settings for the currently opened site are saved for future reference and use.

Creating a Blank Site

Creating a *blank site* means that you're creating a brand new root directory for your site. Whenever you create a site, GoLive assembles a complete package with all the things you need for that site. The site folder automatically contains a generic home page called Index.html and a default Cascading Style Sheet file called basic.css in the CSS folder of the Files tab in the Site window. The data folder contains empty subfolders for future elements of your site. The settings folder holds specifications for your site. And the site document itself—identified by the .site extension—opens to reveal the hierarchy of your site within a Site window.

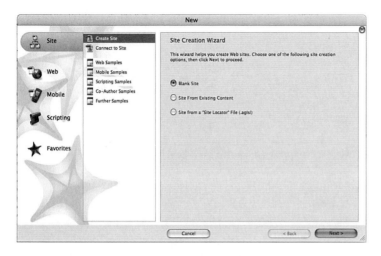

Figure 40.2
The Create Site option enables you to create a site with the Site Creation Wizard.

To create a new blank site, complete the following steps:

1. Choose Blank Site from the Site Creation Wizard options in the New dialog.

2. Click the Next button to specify a site name and location, as shown in Figure 40.3. You can assign any name you like. Click the Browse button to point to the directory where you want to create your new website.

3. Click the Next button and indicate whether you will be using a version control system—either Adobe's Version Cue or some other version control system. If you are using a version control system, click the Use Version Control radio button and select your version control system from the pop-up menu, as shown in Figure 40.4. See the section on Version Cue in Chapter 1, "Creative Suite 2 Basics," for information on Adobe's version control system.

4. The appropriate fields appear depending on which version control system you choose. See your system administrator or web administrator for information on what specs you need to put here. If you specify a version control system, you must also specify an actual server before you can continue by clicking the Next button.

5. Click the Next button to continue to the Publish Server Options. The *publish server* is the remote server that publishes your website on the World Wide Web. You have the option of specifying the server now or postponing it until later. Click Specify Server Now and enter the server information provided by your system or web administrator, as shown in Figure 40.5.

Click the Advanced button to set the Advanced URL Handling features. Use these settings to specify whether the references on your site will be case sensitive. If you're using a foreign language system or if your particular server requires some other method of URL encoding aside from the standard UTF8 encoding, you can also set this here. You might have noticed weird escape sequences like %20 in URLs that contain illegal characters, such as spaces. You can set the conditions that your site uses to determine when to apply escape characters. Unless you are creating a site that has specific settings conveyed to you by the System Administrator, *do not change* these Advanced settings.

40

Figure 40.3
Indicate the site name and location for your new website.

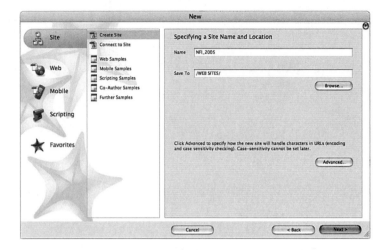

Figure 40.4
Select a Version Control system.

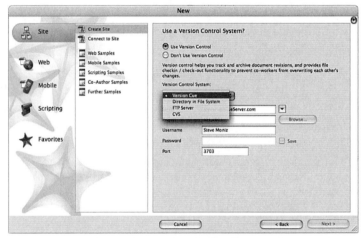

Figure 40.5
Specify your server information for the publish server.

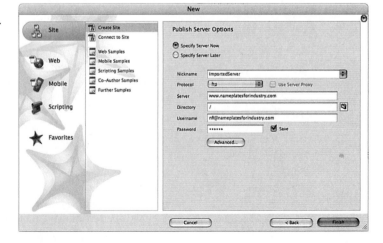

40

6. Click the Finish button and the Site window opens with your new site created in the Files tab, as shown in Figure 40.6.

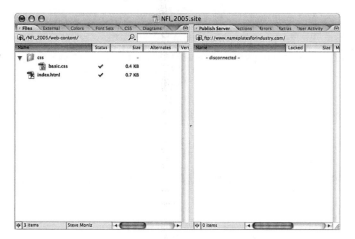

Figure 40.6
Your new blank site appears in the Files tab of the Site window.

Creating a New Site by Importing an Existing Site

If you want to work on an existing site, you can easily import the site for use in GoLive. The site can be located locally on your hard drive or remotely on an FTP or HTTP server. Either way, the process of importing creates a new site document and new site-related folders.

When working with a local site, the root folder is the folder that contains the imported site. When you import a site from a remote location, the site folder is downloaded to your hard drive. In either case, the site hierarchy is depicted in the Site window where you can open, organize, and manage your web content locally before uploading the site to a remote location.

To import a site from a local folder, complete the following steps:

1. Choose File, New to open the New dialog and click Site in the first column, Create Site in the second column and Site from Existing Content from the third column, as shown in Figure 40.7.

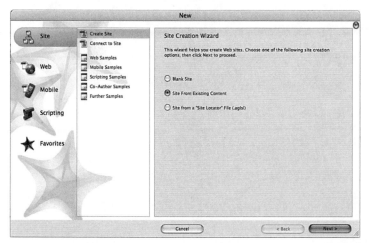

Figure 40.7
Create a new site by importing an existing site using the Site Creation Wizard.

40

2. Click the Next button and select where you want to import the existing content from, as shown in Figure 40.8.

- Choose **From a Local Folder of Existing Files** if the website files are located somewhere on your hard drives or on a server volume connected to your computer.

- Choose **By Downloading Files from a Remote Server** if your site files are located on another server such as an HTTP server or FTP server. You need all the connection info and passwords to access files this way.

- Choose **By Connecting to a Project on a Version Cue System** if you're using Adobe's Version Cue version control features. See the information on Version Cue in Chapter 1.

Figure 40.8
Select where the existing content is coming from.

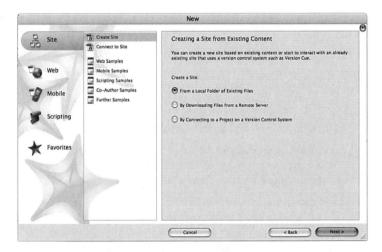

3. Click the Next button and specify the settings for how you want to import the site content. Follow the directions in the dialog for the specific method you select, as shown in Figure 40.9.

Figure 40.9
Indicate the location of the site you want to import.

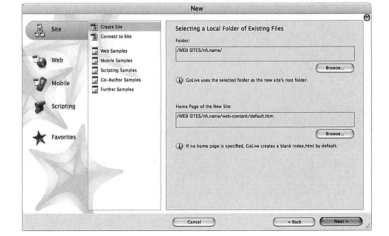

4. Click the Next button and specify a Site Name and Location if prompted to do so, as shown in Figure 40.10, and then click the Finish button to see the imported site in the Files tab of the Site window, as shown in Figure 40.11.

Figure 40.10
Indicate a site name of your choice and use the Browse button to indicate a location for the site files.

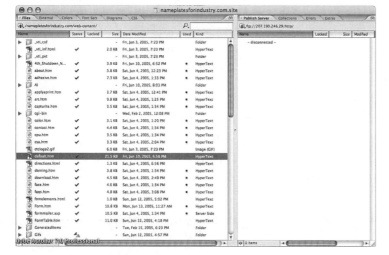

Figure 40.11
The Files tab in the Site window is populated by the files from the imported site.

USING VERSION CONTROL

Large workgroups often use some method of version control to ensure that only the latest revisions of their websites are published and that only a single user can work on a file from the website at one time. When you connect to a server that is set up with version control, you can check files in and out to work on them. If someone in your workgroup has a file checked out, you cannot also check out the file, and vice versa. GoLive supports Version Cue and CVS version control systems, and GoLive has some of its own built-in version controls you can use. See Chapter 1 for information about Version Cue, or visit www.versioncue.com to learn about Adobe's Version Cue CS2 system.

40

Concurrent Versions System (CVS) is free from GNU software and is in wide use around the world for a variety of software development projects and websites. Visit www.gnu.org for information on CVS and a host of additional free software offerings.

To use Version Control:

1. Choose File, New to display the New dialog.

2. Select Connect To Site and then choose Version Cue or CVS from the Version Control System menu, as shown in Figure 40.12.

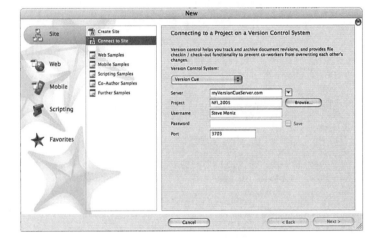

If you visit www.gnu.org and find some free software you'd like to use, consider donating to the Free Software Foundation (FSF) to keep sites like GNU operational.

Figure 40.12
Choose a Version Control System for an existing site.

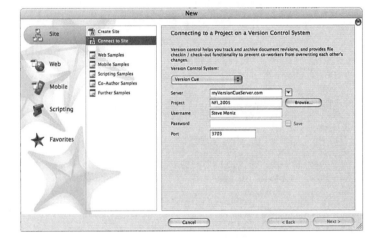

3. Enter the Server, Project, Username, Password, and Port information for your selection. If using CVS, choose an authoring type from the Authoring Type menu. Click Next.

4. Indicate a local mount location, as shown in Figure 40.13, and click Finish. Follow the onscreen instructions to complete the setup process.

Figure 40.13
Choose a local mount location where you want GoLive to keep the local versions of the files.

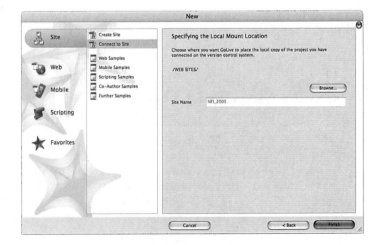

USING SITE SAMPLES AS TEMPLATES FOR NEW SITES

Use a site sample as a template to base your website on. GoLive comes with a number of samples for a variety of categories, as shown in Figure 40.14. You can also create your own sample sites (formerly called *site templates*) by saving files into any subfolder under Adobe GoLive CS2/Settings/DocumentStore/Sites. If nothing else, the site samples can help you to understand how to set up certain features used by popular websites.

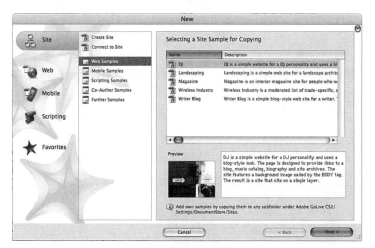

Figure 40.14
Select a site sample to base your new website on.

To create a site:

1. Choose File, New to display the New dialog, and then click Site in the first column and any samples choice in the second column.

2. After you select a site sample for copying, click the Next button and enter a site name for your new website, along with a path to where you want to save the files, as shown in Figure 40.15.

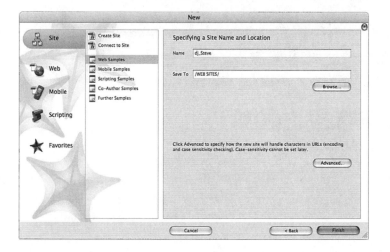

Figure 40.15
Give your new site a name and tell GoLive where to copy the site files to.

40

3. Click Finish and your new site based on a site sample appears in the Files tab of the Site window, as shown in Figure 40.16.

Figure 40.16
The Files tab contains the files from the site sample and any folder hierarchy.

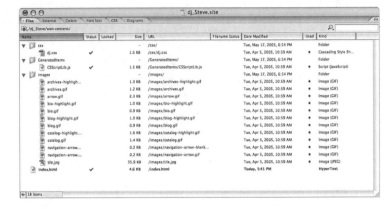

4. Double-click the home page (`index.html`) to open the home page so that you can modify it to your specifications, as shown in Figure 40.17.

Figure 40.17
Modify the file(s) included in the site sample to customize them to your requirements.

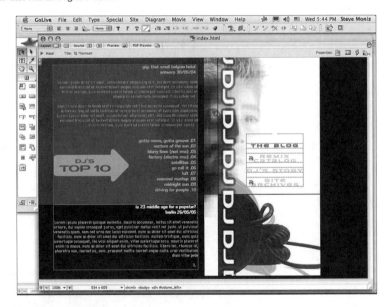

WORKING IN THE SITE WINDOW

Now that you've created a site, GoLive keeps track of every page you create and stores them all in one convenient place, together with all the other elements you need to keep your pages connected and functioning happily as a unit.

The Site window has a total of 10 tabs, split into two panes, with 6 tabs in the left pane and 4 tabs in the right. Each of these tabs also corresponds to an option in the Pane menu, a pop-up menu accessed by clicking on the small arrow in the upper-right corner of the Site window, as shown in Figure 40.18.

There are two additional tabs available in a floating secondary site window, making the total number of site tabs 12. Select Navigation or Links from the Pane menu to display the secondary site window, as shown in Figure 40.19.

For the most part, the Site window tabs behave like palettes. You can click and drag any tab just as you would a palette, to mix and match them in new windows, alone or in groups, in

> Explore some of the site samples, even if you don't intend to create your websites using them. You'll find that many of them contain interesting navigation features, icons, and images.

whatever arrangement works best for you. Your customized desktop of tabs and site windows returns the next time you open the site document. You can have more than one site document open at the same time. Although you can drag files between sites, dragging tabs from one site into the Site window of another site is not possible.

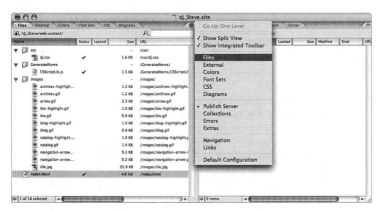

Figure 40.18
The site options and tabs are available in the Pane menu.

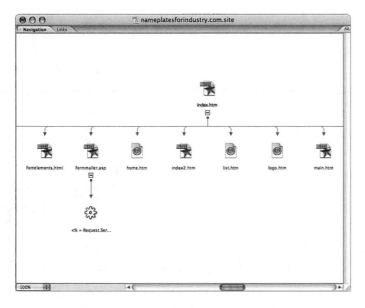

Figure 40.19
The Navigation and Links tabs appear in a secondary site window.

40

The Files Tab

The Files tab typically lists the content of your website root folder, although you can double-click folders to open them, or click the Up button located to the left of the path in the upper-left corner to go backwards. Click and hold on the Up button to display the path from your website folder to your current location and navigate to the directory of your choice, as shown in Figure 40.20.

Figure 40.20
Navigate backward using the Up button.

The Files tab operates exactly like a regular folder does elsewhere on your computer. You can open, close, or delete files; drag files to other folders; copy to the Clipboard; even spell-check any HTML files you have open. For each file, the Files tab lists particulars such as name, size, and date modified by column, just as you might see in a normal folder list view.

In addition, there are symbols specific to GoLive that indicate more details about the status of a file. These are located within the Errors tab:

- In the Status column, a check mark symbolizes that the file is free of errors and that all files referenced in it have been found.

- In the Filename Status column, an error symbol indicates that the name of the file violates some filename constraint.

- In the Locked column, a padlock indicates a locked file in Mac OS or a read-only file in Windows.

- A pencil icon in the Locked column indicates a locked workgroup file.

- In the Used column, a number indicates the number of links to the file from other files at the site. The links can be hyperlinks or references.

> When in doubt, try your context menu. Right-click (in Windows) or Ctrl-click (on the Mac) to display context menus in the Files tab of the Site window. With so many site options and their various icons, buttons, and pop-up menus, sometimes it's easier to check the main menus or context menus.

- In the Version Status column, the icons represent the state of files in the versioning system. Hover over the icons to read the status of the file. The absence of an icon means the page is in sync with the version server.

The External, Colors, and Font Sets Tabs

The External, Colors, and Font Sets tabs list items that are stored in the site file and assist in the storage of certain layout details:

- **External:** This tab lists URLs and e-mail addresses that are available to use as links on site pages, as shown in Figure 40.21. Simply point and click to insert one of the URLs or addresses on a page in a document window.

- **Colors:** This tab indicates which colors are in use on site pages and is a good place to set up your colors ahead of time to ensure color consistency on your site, as shown in Figure 40.22. To use a color, drag it from the tab onto selected text or a selected object on a page in a document

- **Font Sets:** This tab lists the fonts used on your site; you can create and edit font sets here, as shown in Figure 40.23. If you want to change a font set throughout your site, change it here and GoLive prompts you to update your site.

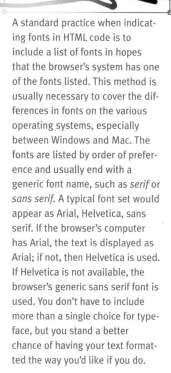

A standard practice when indicating fonts in HTML code is to include a list of fonts in hopes that the browser's system has one of the fonts listed. This method is usually necessary to cover the differences in fonts on the various operating systems, especially between Windows and Mac. The fonts are listed by order of preference and usually end with a generic font name, such as *serif* or *sans serif*. A typical font set would appear as Arial, Helvetica, sans serif. If the browser's computer has Arial, the text is displayed as Arial; if not, then Helvetica is used. If Helvetica is not available, the browser's generic sans serif font is used. You don't have to include more than a single choice for typeface, but you stand a better chance of having your text formatted the way you'd like if you do.

Create New Address Group
Create New Address
Create New URL Group
Create New URL
Delete Selected Item

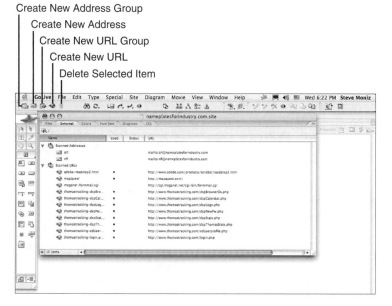

Figure 40.21
Manage external addresses here.

40

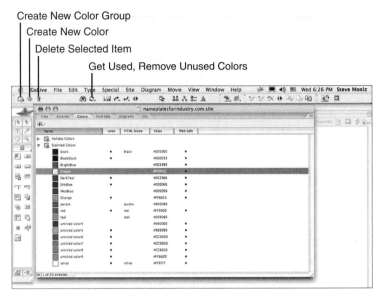

Figure 40.22
Manage your site colors in the Colors tab of the Site window.

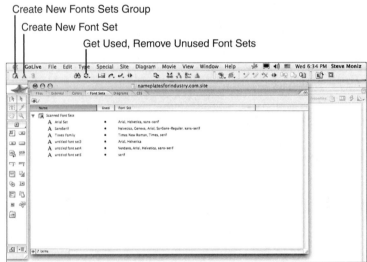

Figure 40.23
Manage the fonts on your site using the Font Sets tab of the Site window.

The Diagrams Tab

The diagram features of Adobe GoLive are useful for creating presentations and website flowcharts prior to creating a site, as shown in Figure 40.24. The hierarchy of the website can be clearly depicted, along with notes and links between pages, assets, and any other files. You can also include annotations, level indicators, custom objects, and boxes that hold text or images. Start by Choosing New Diagram from the Diagram menu; then double-click the diagram you create in the Diagrams Tab of the Site window. Use the tools in the Diagram Objects palette to create your diagram.

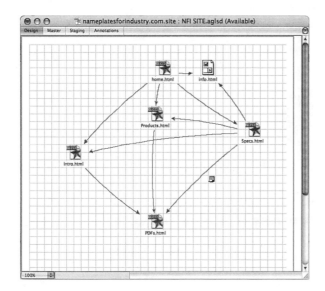

Figure 40.24
The diagram feature.

You can use any number of prototype diagrams to aid you in building and revising a site, enabling you to create and test designs as needed. The output options for diagrams enable you to print your diagrams or save them in Adobe PDF or SVG format. When you are ready to work with live pages, you submit a diagram using the Staging options under the Diagram menu, converting its pages to actual pages in the site. The details of creating and using diagrams is beyond the scope of this book, but you can use Adobe's Help files to learn how to diagram your site and then submit it for use in creating your site.

The CSS Tab

The CSS tab shown in Figure 40.25 enables you to control globally all the Cascading Style Sheets used on your website. If you use external CSS files, you can double-click and edit them from the CSS tab. You can likewise drag and drop the external styles onto your web pages or point and click to select them. Information on the Classes and Identifiers used on your site is available in the CSS tab, though you cannot make changes to these styles. The statistics in the #Times Defined and #Times Used columns can be of great help when managing large sites with lots of users inputting web pages.

The Publish Server Tab

The Publish Server tab shown in Figure 40.26 enables you to manage your remote files on the publish server and synchronize the local site with the remote site. Although there are a multitude of site management feats you can accomplish in the Site window, the most common events are the uploading and downloading of files between your local site (represented on the left side of Site window) and your remote site (represented on the right side of Site window). Use the site management features under the Site menu, the context menu, or the Main toolbar to move files between your local site and remote site.

40

Figure 40.25
The CSS tab helps you manage
your Cascading Style Sheets.

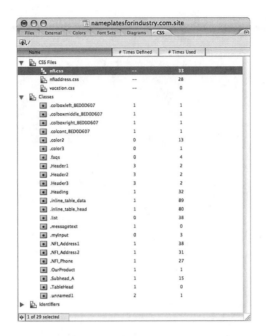

Connect to publish server/
Disconnect from publish server
Upload options
Download options
Synchronize local files with publish server

Figure 40.26
Put the files that are to appear on
your website in the publish server.

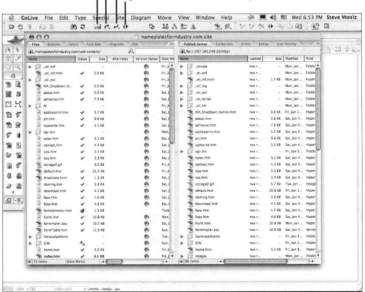

To set up the publish server, follow these steps:

1. Choose Site, Settings to display the Site Settings dialog, as shown in Figure 40.27.

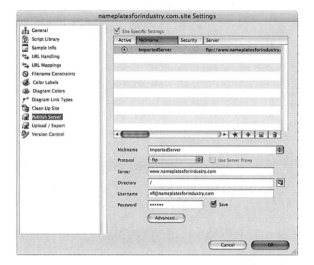

Figure 40.27
Control how everything on your site is handled in the Site Settings dialog.

2. Choose Publish Server in the category list and enter the appropriate connection information to connect to your publish server. Ask your system administrator or web administrator for assistance if you're not sure what to enter here.

3. Click OK to close the Site Settings dialog and click the Connect to Publish Server button in the Main toolbar to connect to your server.

4. Use the upload and download buttons in the main toolbar to send and receive files. Use the Synchronize button to synchronize your entire site. Whenever there's a difference between your local files and remote files, GoLive informs you in the Synchronize dialog, shown in Figure 40.28, so you can make decisions about what to do with the files.

5. Click OK to perform the desired actions on your files. Be sure to check the list carefully before clicking OK to avoid inadvertently uploading or downloading files.

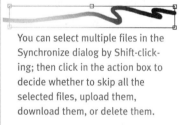

You can select multiple files in the Synchronize dialog by Shift-clicking; then click in the action box to decide whether to skip all the selected files, upload them, download them, or delete them.

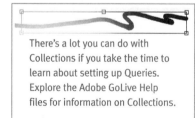

There's a lot you can do with Collections if you take the time to learn about setting up Queries. Explore the Adobe GoLive Help files for information on Collections.

40

The Collections Tab

The Collections tab displays custom sets of one or more files that you select manually or define as a result of a query, syntax check, or find operation. Create collections of your files to select groups of files quickly. Simply click the Create New Collection button in the main toolbar and then select a number of files in the Files tab and drag them over into the Collection folder. The files are not moved; only references to files are inserted in the Collection folders, as shown in Figure 40.29.

Show only downloads

Show only uploads

Show only deletions

Figure 40.28
The Synchronize dialog gives you complete control of which files get uploaded and downloaded.

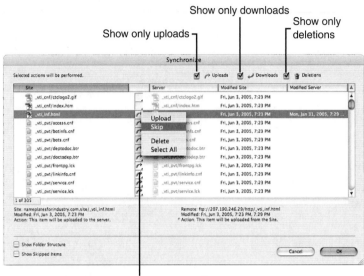

Click to choose how to handle file

Create New Collection   Collection folder

Figure 40.29
The Collections tab enables you to select collections of files quickly.

The Errors Tab

The Errors tab displays missing files, orphan files, Smart Object warnings, and files that have names that don't meet your filename constraints. An *orphaned file* is one that is referenced in a link but does not exist in the current site files. If you manage files in the site window, you can avoid creating orphan files. Double-click a file in the Errors tab to open the file and fix the error or use the Inspector palette to fix errors like missing links, as shown in Figure 40.30.

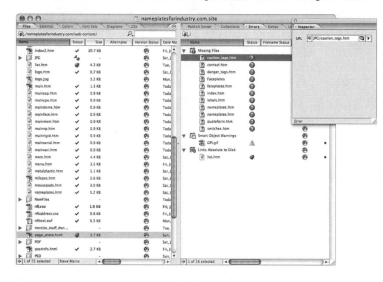

Figure 40.30
The Errors tab of the Site Window displays all site file errors in one place.

The Extras Tab

The Extras tab contains all the files and folders in the site's web-content folder and web-data folder. The web-data folder contains four types of reusable objects: components, stationery pages, snippets, and page templates. The Extras tab also contains diagrams, Smart Objects, web packages, queries, and files moved to the Site Trash, as shown in Figure 40.31.

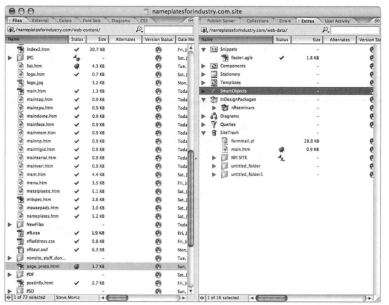

Figure 40.31
The Extras tab enables you to manage and manipulate the extra features available in GoLive quickly.

40

The site management features available in GoLive are quite extensive; you can learn a great deal about the available options and tools by exploring the Site menu. As you build your site, you should constantly think about what you can do to your site as a whole to standardize things, such as using consistent fonts, colors, and web assets. Finally, don't be intimidated by all the tabs in the Site window, you use the Files and Publish Server features most frequently, so concentrate on those at first.

40

V

ACROBAT, DISTILLER, AND DESIGNER

IN THIS PART

UNDERSTANDING THE ACROBAT WORKING ENVIRONMENT

IN THIS CHAPTER

It's difficult to imagine document transfers without PDF nowadays. Since its introduction by Adobe in 1992, the Portable Document Format (PDF) has become as essential to document distribution worldwide as computers themselves. This format has grown from a solution to cross-platform document portability (hence its name) to become the key piece that has made digital print workflow a reality. Together with PDF came Acrobat, Adobe's tool for creating and editing PDF documents.

The biggest difference between Acrobat and the rest of the Creative Suite 2 members is that, unlike Photoshop, Illustrator, InDesign, and Image Ready, the current incarnation of Acrobat is not just one program but three—or actually four. The fourth element is the Adobe PDF printer driver, a minisuite of sorts inside the Creative Suite. Add to that the Acrobat Reader and you have the full suite at your disposal. Each of these elements of Acrobat has its own defined function. Sometimes they overlap but not that often.

Sorting through these different parts of Acrobat may seem like a daunting task, but it's not. All you need to remember is what to use when. In this chapter, and the following ones, we demystify Acrobat for your benefit.

BEST PRACTICES (WHEN TO USE AND NOT USE ACROBAT)

How do you know whether you need Acrobat, and when? Perhaps the question should be when to use which part of Acrobat. It all depends on what line of business you are in and your needs. PDF is so versatile that it would be impossible to list all its uses, and if such a list existed there would be new items continuously getting added to it.

Adobe PDF Printer Driver

For most small tasks, The Adobe PDF driver (formerly known as PDF Writer) is enough. This is what we could call a "light" version of Acrobat, although there's a lot of power packed into it. If you are creating newsletters, brochures for online distribution, quick color proofs, or simple text documents with nonstandard fonts, the Adobe PDF printer driver shines. It quickly delivers no-nonsense PDF files from within any program, and the driver settings are good enough to keep most users happy. Adobe PDF installs as a printer. To use it you simply go to the Print dialog in the application you're using and select it from the list of available printers (see Figure 41.1). Hitting the Properties button gives you access to a variety of settings such as image compression, font embedding, color, security, compatibility, and more (see Figure 41.2).

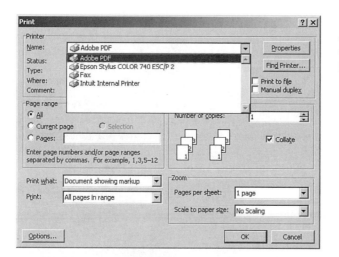

Figure 41.1
Although the Adobe PDF printer driver is good for lightweight presentation jobs...

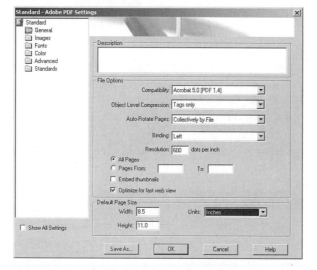

Figure 41.2
...it comes with a very detailed set of features.

Adobe Acrobat

If the features available in the Adobe PDF printer driver are not enough, you can open your PDF files in Acrobat for a boost (see Figure 41.3). With Acrobat you can now give your PDF the ability to take annotations in Adobe Reader for email collaboration.

Acrobat also enables you to spice up your PDF with video clips and audio tracks. Prepress professionals can use Acrobat to add or adjust trapping settings, bleeds, or crops; modify ICC color profiles; preview color separations; and much more. A very handy built-in Preflight tool helps you identify possible production conflicts before sending the file to press.

Figure 41.3
The main Adobe Acrobat program enables you to add annotation capabilities and other security features to the PDF document.

Adobe Acrobat Distiller

For high-volume publishing and PDF workflow the Acrobat Distiller is the tool to use (see Figure 41.4). Publishers and prepress professionals use the Distiller to batch process PostScript files into PDF format for press production of newspapers, magazines, catalogs, and anything that requires automation.

With Distiller you can save parameters for the file conversion and set a "watch folder." When a PostScript file is dropped in that folder, Distiller starts to process it using the parameters saved.

Figure 41.4
Use the Adobe Distiller when you want to batch-process PostScript files into PDF format.

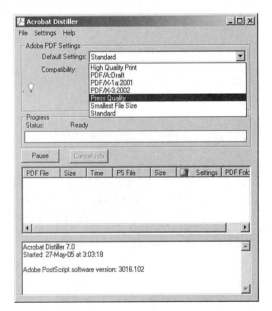

41

Adobe Designer (Windows Only)

If you have been looking for a better way to design PDF forms in your Windows environment, look no more. The Adobe Designer enables you to open DOC or PDF files and add text fields, radio buttons, and other form elements (see Figure 41.5). Or you can create your forms from scratch using one of its many premade templates and its simple yet comprehensive interface.

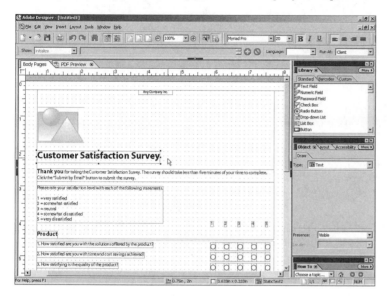

Figure 41.5
The Adobe Designer helps you create PDF forms.

PDF Engines

Many popular word processors and image editors come with built-in PDF engines these days, in case you need to create simple PDF files and don't have Acrobat. These PDF writers have varying degrees of complexity and for the most part serve the purpose of creating basic PDF files—something similar to what the Adobe PDF printer driver does. In Star Office, for example, you can choose File, Export as PDF or click on Export Directly as PDF icon in the Function bar. Either option opens a dialog box asking for a desired name for your PDF. After typing a name and clicking on the Export button, a new dialog box appears with a few options for your document. PDF files produced with these built-in engines generally have nothing to envy from files created with the Adobe PDF printer driver.

Other word procesors, like MS Word, do not come with a built-in PDF writer but instead recommend the use of third-party software. Adobe has addressed this. When you install the Creative Suite 2 with Acrobat, a Convert to Adobe PDF button is added to MS Word's toolbar.

Adobe Acrobat Reader

Although not part of the Creative Suite, the Reader is a vital member of the Acrobat family. Available as a free download from Adobe (http://www.adobe.com/products/acrobat/readstep2.html), the Reader installs as both a standalone viewer for PDF documents and a plug-in for most popular web

41

browsers. With the Reader your peers can view your PDF documents at different zoom levels and print them if required.

If you are distributing PDF forms (you'll learn more about them when we discuss Designer), the Reader enables users to fill them in and email them, submit them online, or print them. On PDF documents where this option has been enabled, the Reader also enables users to add several types of annotations.

NEW ACROBAT FEATURES

The new Acrobat shows that it has come of age by packing some nice surprises in the form of neat new features.

If you have used Acrobat before, the first thing you'll notice is that it's faster. A lot faster. Adobe engineers have done a great job at tuning up the Acrobat core to get rid of that tedious waiting time for Acrobat or the Reader to load (which was everyone's complaint).

Besides the speed, probably the most impressive new feature is Acrobat's novel ability to display 3D objects in addition to video and sound. To attract more clients, newsletter for a tour operator, for example, can contain a small video or a Flash movie instead of static pictures. Or how about embedding audio soundtracks or voiceovers in a PDF brochure? Similarly, engineers can use PDF now to showcase 3D CAD models saved in U3D format. And Acrobat now gives AutoCAD users the ability to save their files directly to PDF via a custom Convert to Adobe PDF button placed in the AutoCAD toolbar. This one-click PDF ability is also added to Microsoft Visio and Office programs such as Word and PowerPoint when you install Acrobat.

If you do a lot of document scanning for archival purposes you'll welcome Acrobat's revamped ability to scan images directly to PDF format; and if your scanner has an auto feeder, you'll be laughing. Acrobat can run the scanner and place each page into a page in your PDF document (see Figure 41.6). As an added bonus, The Create PDF from Scanner option also lists the contents of your digital camera if it uses a TWAIN driver. There is little that can be done with images placed this way, though; they can't be resized or edited. But if they are the right size (think preedited in Photoshop and stored back in your camera's memory), you can bring them into your document.

Adobe has listened to the many complaints that users needed to purchase the full version of Acrobat in order to be able to annotate files. That is no more. With Acrobat Pro you can set-up an email-based review system that enables your peers to receive your PDF files by email, annotate them using the free Acrobat Reader, and send them back to you. With Reader, your peers can enter comments in the form of text highlights; use comment boxes that act as sticky notes; use a replacement text tool to cross out text and type in revisions; customize stamps to display time, date, and even pictures; or even create pen drawings. Yes, it's official; with Reader, your peers can now doodle on your PDF (see Figure 41.7).

And then there is the Adobe Designer (also known by its official name, Adobe LiveCycle Designer). You'll explore this Windows-only program in a page or two, but for now think *forms*.

41

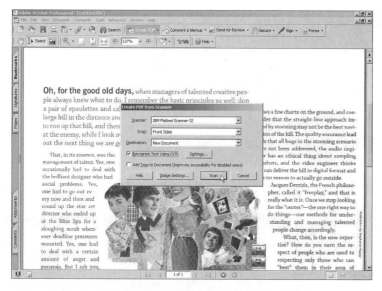

Figure 41.6
The Create PDF from Scanner option helps automate scanning and archival of long documents.

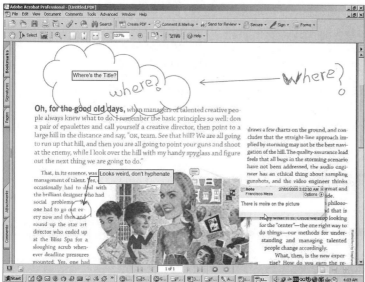

Figure 41.7
Adobe Pro enables you to send out PDFs to peers who can annotate the files using the free Reader; comments can be simple highlights, comment boxes, and even freehand doodles.

FILE FORMATS SUPPORTED

Acrobat doesn't come with an Import and Export feature as its Creative Suite siblings do, but that doesn't mean you can't bring files in other formats into your PDF documents. Here's a list of file types Acrobat enables you to bring in:

Category	Description
Graphics	Static graphics can't be directly imported into Acrobat; if you need to add graphics from your hard drive or a CD to an existing PDF, do it with Designer. Adobe Designer enables you to import image files in BMP, GIF, JPG, PNG, and TIF formats. You also can bring 3D CAD images in U3D format into Acrobat very easily.
Video	Many popular formats are supported, including AVI, MOV, MPG, RM, SWF, and WMV.
Audio	Audio tracks are supported in AIF, MP3, MP4, RA, WAV, and a few other less-popular formats.

Besides creating PDF files Acrobat gives you the ability to save your PDF to some useful formats that include

Category	Description
JPEG, TIFF, and PNG graphics	If you need to rasterize images, create thumbnails of your PDF files, and/or create rough pictures for quick proofing, these three formats fill the tab. The TIFF format allows for lossless compression and the PNG format has the added ability to retain transparency, in case your document needs it. Saving as JPEG can be useful when doing quick comps where image quality is not a big issue.
HTML and XML	In some cases you need to have a document as both PDF and HTML (or XML) in a website. Saving your PDF as HTML or XML saves you the trouble of having to re-create it in GoLive. When saving as HTML or XML, Acrobat creates an Images folder in which to place all the images included in the document. Images are saved as JPEG.
PS and EPS	Use these formats for prepress and print production purposes.
DOC, RTF, and TXT	Use these formats when you need a text version of a document for editing or archival.

THE DESIGNER ENVIRONMENT (WINDOWS ONLY)

If you're new to Adobe Designer you'll love it. You can open a Word document and use Designer to turn it into an electronic form. With Designer you can add interactive elements such as radio buttons, text fields, check boxes, and more—even bar codes in 32 different formats. All it takes is a simple drag-and-drop from the Library palette, and the Object palette offers a wide array of customization options. Adding colors, adjusting borders, rotating text fields—it's all done with just a few clicks and drags of the mouse. Viewers can use the Adobe Acrobat Reader to fill in the form and then submit it to a preset email address by hitting a simple button embedded in the form itself. Or they can print it for faxing or mailing. If you prefer, you can create new forms from scratch. Designer comes with more than 20 predesigned templates to choose. Or you can open an existing PDF and add form elements to it. You can also add pizzazz to your existing forms by importing images in a variety of popular formats.

Whichever way you want to use it, Designer is a delight to work with. After your form has been created, you can save it as a static or dynamic electronic PDF form file or as an XML file. And if you need to make continuous changes to the same form you can save it as a Designer template.

While you work on Designer, the Layout palette helps you position your objects precisely within the form, and the Hierarchy palette helps you keep track of all your objects. There is also a grid that can be turned on and off with one simple toolbar click.

Because Designer is a relatively new addition (it was previously available only as a standalone program) Adobe has included a very comprehensive How To palette that will have you zooming forms in no time (see Figure 41.8).

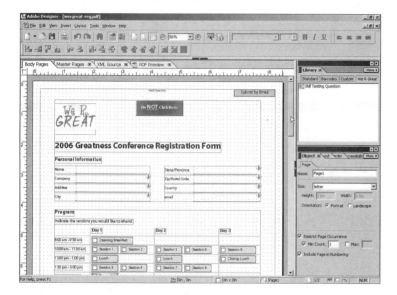

Figure 41.8
With Designer you can create forms from scratch using its comprehensive set of tools.

In the next few chapters you get your hands wet with Acrobat and PDF creation. If you're new to the Creative Suite you'll soon find that Acrobat gives you all the power you need to proof your work and to ensure that it is printed the way you intended it. If you are already familiar with Acrobat, you will appreciate all the new features and enhancements.

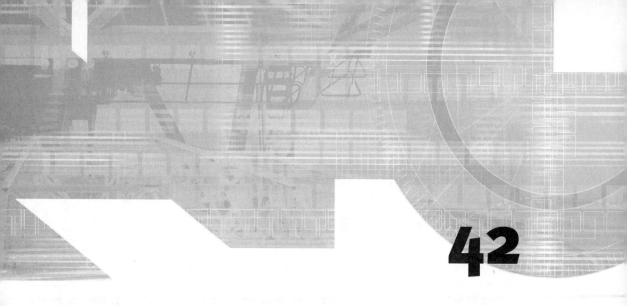

WORKING IN A PDF IN ACROBAT

IN THIS CHAPTER

The main reason Adobe created the PDF format was to offer a file format for documents that could be viewed across different platforms (Mac, PC, Unix) without users having to worry about fonts or format compatibility. Acrobat's mandate was to make the creation and display of PDF files not only possible, but to accomplish it in an easy and hassle-free way. Acrobat has grown since its introduction and many features have been added to it (and to the PDF format). The mandate of making the creation of PDF files easy remains. Let's see what you can do with your PDFs.

WORKING WITH FONTS

Font portability was a big issue before Acrobat came along. You could use any fancy font in your Mac to create an illustration, but if your client didn't have that font in his PC (or worse, if there was no PC version of that font), you had some rough choices. Limit your creative juices to the use of a common font like Arial or Times; or convert your text to outlines, rendering it uneditable. Or you could create the most amazing artwork in your PC and send it to print, only to get the final EPS file returned to you because the Mac-based printer didn't have the fonts used. And if you were working with long documents, good luck! Imagine converting to outlines all 120 pages in a magazine.

To overcome the font problem Adobe gave Acrobat the capability of embedding a copy of the font inside a PDF file and using it to display text the way it was originally created. Putting the technical jargon aside, what this means is that you don't have to worry about platform or font type anymore.

When creating a PDF with the Adobe PDF driver you're given the option to determine how fonts are handled through the Fonts panel in the PDF Settings dialog (see Figure 42.1). You can choose to embed entire sets of fonts used in a document, for example, or only a subset. The difference between these two approaches is that if you choose to embed a subset, Acrobat embeds only the characters used in the document. If you've used several fonts in a document and only a few characters of each, subsetting can help you make your resulting file smaller.

You can also specify a list of fonts to always embed (overrides the subset threshold) and another list of fonts to never embed (even if they're used in the document).

Figure 42.1
Some TrueType fonts can contain instructions to prevent embedding. In the Fonts panel of the PDF Settings dialog, these fonts show a padlock icon next to them.

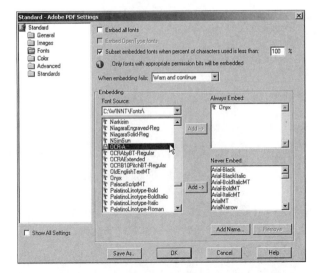

If you are working on a PDF created by someone else and/or in another computer, you can view a list of the fonts that are embedded in it by accessing the PDF Optimizer (choose Advanced, PDF Optimizer). From the PDF Optimizer dialog you can unembed a font that has been embedded in the document. This feature is helpful if you have deleted pages or parts of a document and some fonts are no longer required (see Figure 42.2).

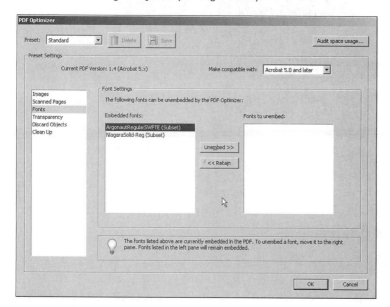

Figure 42.2
Fonts no longer needed can be unembedded from the PDF to make the file size smaller.

EDITING TEXT

Editing text is a limited option in Acrobat and the reason is simple. The PDF format was created with the objective of enabling a document to be viewed without the user's need to have the program that created it. If a document needs to be edited heavily, Adobe recommends that the editing be performed in the program that created it.

There are times, however, when a quick editing needs to be done and the originating program is not available—a misspelled word, for example, or a missing comma. For this purpose Acrobat comes with a very convenient TouchUp Text tool. And to prevent it from being overused Adobe has sort of hidden it inside the Tools, Advanced Editing menu. Sneaky, huh? Using it is simple: All you do is use it to select the text you need to edit and start typing. Or delete it. Or copy-and-paste. What you can't do is change font size. If you need to do something more advanced like changing font size or changing color you need to select the text to be edited, access the context menu, and select Properties to access the TouchUp Properties dialog (see Figure 42.3).

Keep in mind that if the font was embedded as a subset you can type in only characters that already exist in the document in that font. All other characters are not included in the subset.

Figure 42.3
Several formatting options are available in the TouchUp Properties dialog.

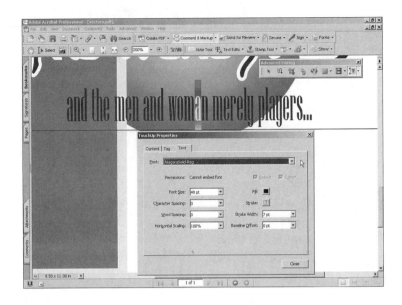

COMPRESSING IMAGES

Image downsampling and compression is another way to optimize your PDF file by reducing its final size.

Downsampling is a procedure through which a raster image resolution is reduced; and *compression* is when an algorithm (a mathematical formula) is applied to an image to compress it and reduce its size. Acrobat supports both.

The first time to use downsampling and compression in a PDF is when you create it, and the Images panel in the Adobe PDF Settings dialog is there to help you. Let's say you have a product sell sheet created for printing using InDesign, with some text and a few product photos at a resolution suitable for print. Now let's say you also want the sell sheet in a PDF file that you can easily email to some clients out of town. You can print the file to the Adobe PDF driver and use the Images panel to compress the images right there. The settings are very clear, offering you several compression methods (lossless ZIP or lossy JPEG) for different types of images and the ability to set downsampling parameters for each of these types of images (see Figure 42.4). For repeating jobs you can save those settings.

What if all you have is the PDF file and not the original document? You can apply the same downsampling and compression parameters from within Acrobat by opening the PDF Optimizer and navigating to the Images panel. After accepting your desired settings simply save your file.

42

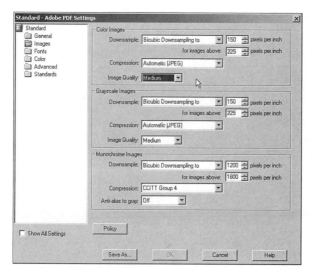

Figure 42.4
The Images panel in the Adobe PDF Settings dialog enables great customization.

REARRANGING PAGES

There are times when you need to move pages around in a document. Okay, this is not something you may need to do every day, but sometimes there's the need. Like when rearranging the pages of a portfolio, for example. Or a slideshow type of presentation. Acrobat enables you to do it without any effort.

All you need to do is open the Pages tab in your Acrobat window (choose View, Navigation Tabs) to see thumbnails of your pages. Click the thumbnail for the page you want to move and drag it to the position where you want it to be (see Figure 42.5). That's it. If you need to move more than one page you can use the Ctrl key (in Windows) or ⌘ key (on the Mac) to select more than one page. If you have automatic numbering set, you need to run the numbering routine again.

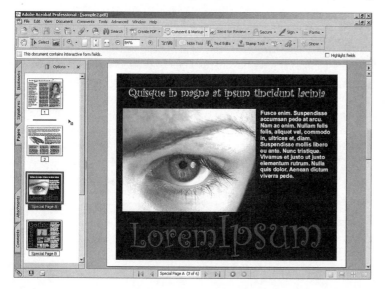

Figure 42.5
Page numbering is not affected when you move pages around but Auto-numbering is.

42

ADDING HEADERS AND FOOTERS

Headers and footers in Acrobat work the same way they do in any page layout or word processing program. When you open the Headers and Footers dialog (choose Document, Add Headers & Footers) you are presented with two tabs: one for headers and one for footers. Each tab has three fields to enter the contents for the left, center, and right sides of the page (see Figure 42.6).

If you want to add automatic page numbering to your document, use the Headers and Footers dialog. There are special codes to insert automatic numbering and dates in several types of formatting, options for font and font size, options for placement relative to the edges of the page, and a few more.

Figure 42.6
You can apply headers and footers to selected pages only or different types of headers and footers to selected parts of your document.

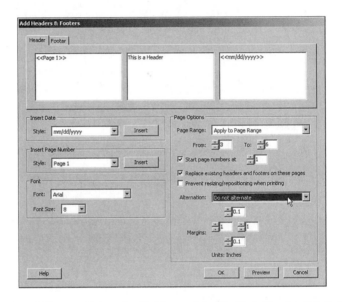

In addition to the Add Headers & Footers dialog, Acrobat has a separate Page Numbering dialog that doesn't affect the physical page order of the document but only the names that pages show in the Pages tab. The reason for these two numbering systems is that sometimes a document is prepared not only for print but for electronic distribution as well. Or both. Suppose you have a text document containing a collection of short stories. Your document has a cover page, a table of contents, and a preface. You set headers and footers to start numbering from 1 on the first actual contents page. Then you can open the Options menu at the top of the Pages tab and set individual numbering for each of the different sections and stories in your document. These numbers appear only under the page thumbnail in the Pages tab of the electronic version of your document and do not affect the numbers printed on the pages themselves (see Figure 42.7).

If your document already had page numbering before you convert it to PDF, these numbers are placed as regular text boxes in the PDF and lose their automatic flow capabilities. If you plan to merge several PDF documents into one or to move pages around, it would be better to avoid automatic page numbering in the originating program and do it in Acrobat after you establish the final page order.

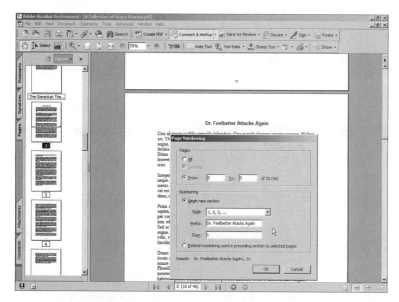

Figure 42.7
The Page Numbering dialog affects only the page names in the Pages tab.

ADDING WATERMARKS AND BACKGROUNDS

Watermarks and backgrounds are an easy and safe way to add a corporate identity to your document or to protect your copyrights.

The Add Watermark & Background dialog (choose Document, Add Watermark & Background to display the dialog) has all you need to create a custom text watermark or background. The only difference between these two elements is that a *watermark* shows on top of the page and a *background* shows behind it. You can select font, font size, font color, alignment, transparency level, and even a rotation angle. If you prefer to use an image—a corporate logo, for example—you can import it and scale it appropriately. Images can be BMPs, JPEGs, or PDF files. Transparency and rotation controls also apply to them (see Figure 42.8).

42

Figure 42.8
You can apply a watermark or background to only selected pages in your document.

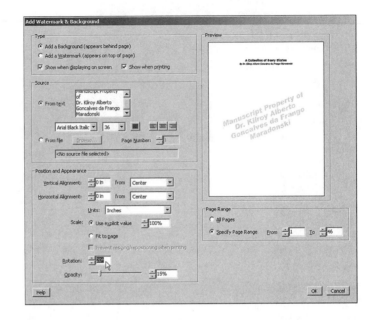

CREATING BOOKMARKS

In addition to page numbering, Acrobat provides you with a way to organize long documents by grouping sections or subsections and creating bookmarks at the start of each section (or assign bookmarks to any other individual pages, for that matter). This feature can be very valuable when working with technical manuals or any other kind of documents that requires a very organized multilevel structure.

To add a bookmark to a document, navigate to the page you want to bookmark. Use the Zoom and Hand tools to position your view of the page the way you want it to appear when the bookmark is clicked. When you are satisfied with the positioning of the page, access the Options menu at the top of the Bookmarks tab and select New Bookmark. The new bookmark shows in the Bookmarks tab. Highlighting a Bookmark enables you to change its name any time you want (see Figure 42.9).

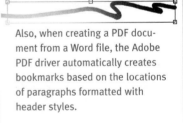

Also, when creating a PDF document from a Word file, the Adobe PDF driver automatically creates bookmarks based on the locations of paragraphs formatted with header styles.

42

Figure 42.9
Bookmarks help you keep your
document organized.

WORKING WITH DESTINATIONS

There are times when you need to work with several documents and establish links between them. Acrobat calls these links *destinations*. Destinations work in the same fashion as hyperlinks in a web page with an added bonus: You can choose the magnification level in the linked page (the destination).

Creating a destination is simple, all you need to do is think backwards. Be sure to have both documents available, the one where the link will be and the one where the link will lead to. Here we go:

1. In the destination document, navigate to the page you want linked and adjust the magnification and position of the page in the window. For example, if the link is to focus on a picture in a page, you can use the Zoom tool to magnify the page so that the picture takes the whole work area.

2. After you've set the view, choose View, Navigation Tabs, Destinations. You see the Destinations tab pop up on the page (you can drag it and dock it to the Tabs pane if you wish). If there are any destinations already created, they will be listed in it; otherwise, the tab will be empty.

3. In the Destinations tab, open the Options menu at the top of the tab and select New Destination. A new untitled destination will appear listed in the tab; click on it and give it a unique name (see Figure 42.10).

4. Now open the document where the actual link will be. Unlike web page links where you select a string of text or an image, Acrobat links are areas defined with the Link tool. Navigate to the part of the document where you want the link to be placed.

Figure 42.10
New links appear in the
Destinations tab.

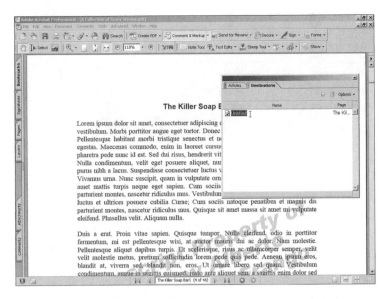

5. Pick the Link tool (choose Tools, Advanced Editing, Link Tool) and use it to draw a rectangle where the link will be. The Create Link dialog opens; use it to set the visual characteristics of this link. You can even make the link invisible if you want.

6. With the Create Link dialog still open, click on the Custom Link radio button under Link Action and click the Next button.

7. The next dialog to appear after clicking on Next is the Link Properties dialog. Click the Actions tab, select Go To a Page View from the pop-up menu, and click the Add button. You will see a new Create Go To View dialog appear. Don't touch it yet.

8. Use the Window menu to make your destination file and page visible again and only then click on the Set Link button.

9. The Link Properties dialog will appear again showing the location of the linked page. Select the newly recorded action and click on the Edit button. A new dialog titled Go To a Page in Another Document will appear.

Invisible links don't sound like a very bright idea, do they? However, there are cases when invisible links can come in handy. Imagine a presentation type of document where you have a photograph covering the first page. You could have invisible links placed over key features in the photograph, linked to pages that contain text explaining those features. Making these links invisible means that no boxes are visible over the photo that would detract from its visual integrity. Invisible links can be your creative ally.

10. Click on the radio button labeled Use Named Destination and then click on Browse.

11. Select your destination from the list shown and click OK (see Figure 42.11).

12. Click OK again and then the Close button to finish the operation.

If you want to make changes later you can always use the Link tool to right-click (in Windows) or Control-click (on the Mac) on any link to access its properties and edit them.

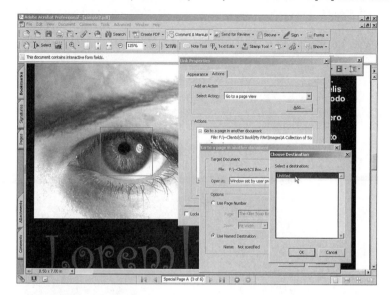

Figure 42.11
Any rectangular area can be a link.

COMMENTS

To enable collaboration without compromising the integrity of a document and maintaining portability at the same time, Acrobat includes a feature called comments. *Comments* are annotations that you or your peers can make to a PDF file without altering it. Think of them as electronic sticky notes that you or your peers can add anywhere on a page as part of a document revision process. You can resize them, make them invisible, have your printer ignore them or print them, add replies to them, and export their contents to a separate text file for review.

Comments go way beyond the sticky note model, however. Besides Notes Acrobat also gives you the ability to insert file and audio attachments to meet your different needs.

The greatest advantage of using comments, as opposed to doing reviews on a JPEG file, is that Acrobat uses a special separate layer for the comments; the pages themselves are not altered. You can hide all the comments and the page looks like it did before you added them.

Commenting tools are available from the Comments, Commenting Tools menu or through the Commenting toolbar. To activate the Commenting toolbar choose View, Toolbars, Commenting.

Notes

The basic sticky note is the most common type of comment. To create a Note select the Note tool from the Commenting toolbar or select the Comments, Commenting Tools, Add a Note option. With the Tool selected, click anywhere in the document where you want your Note to appear. You will see a small "call box" icon where you clicked and the Note beside it. Click inside the Note and type away.

You can use Notes to type a quick message, give instructions, ask questions—you name it. Because these notes can get quite large, they minimize when not focused on, leaving the small icon in their place. Click on that icon to open the note again. You can select what icon you want from a list in the Note Properties dialog, as well as adjust color, transparency, and more (see Figure 42.12). To access the Note Properties dialog, click the Options button and select Properties from the pop-up menu.

Figure 42.12
The basic Note comment.

Audio Annotations

There are times when the written word or the most ambitious doodling aren't enough. Acrobat gives you the option to add voice annotations to your document with the Record Audio Comment tool. To use it, choose Comments, Commenting Tools, Record Audio Comment or click the Record Audio Comment button in the Commenting toolbar. With the Record Audio Comment tool selected, click anywhere in the page, click the red Record button in the Recorder dialog, and start talking. Of course, a microphone is required (see Figure 42.13). You can also use an existing audio track in WAV or AIFF formats.

After you finish recording or inserting your audio file, Acrobat displays a small speaker-shaped icon on the page.

File Attachments

Although file attachments are not really comments, Acrobat considers them so. Files attached to a PDF work in the same way as files attached to an email message. Attached files can be of any format.

To attach a file to a PDF, use the Attach a File as a Comment button in the Commenting toolbar or select the option from the Comments, Commenting Tools menu. When attaching a file, Acrobat *makes a copy of the file* and embeds it within the PDF file. Mind you, this is not the same as placing an image in a PDF. Acrobat doesn't display the attached files.

42

Figure 42.13
Access the context menu and select Play File to listen to audio messages.

When creating the attachment, you are given an option to select between different types of icons (a paper clip, a thumbtack, a tag, or a chart) to display on the page. Your peers can click the icon to extract the attachment (see Figure 42.14).

Figure 42.14
Attached files can be extracted and saved from the context menu.

USING MARKUP TOOLS

In addition to Commenting tools, Acrobat also provides you with an assortment of Markup tools. If you're familiar with editorial work, you see that these tools, available from the Comments, Drawing Markup Tools menu, work in a manner similar to editorial markups.

Callouts

Callouts are similar to notes but they are a bit simpler. No cute icons and no minimizing. They are meant to be visible and accomplish that goal by remaining open on the page (see Figure 42.15). To add a callout select the Callout tool from the Drawing Markups toolbar or from the Comments, Drawing Markup Tools menu and then click the page. A yellow callout box appears, ready for you to type in. After you finish typing, use your mouse to click anywhere outside the box. Now you can click the box to drag it, resize it, or move its pointing arrow around. Right-clicking the box gives you access to its Properties dialog, where you can change its color and outline color.

Figure 42.15
Callouts are meant to be visible.

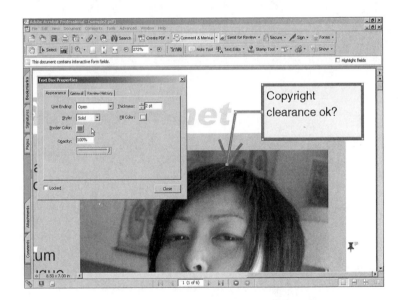

Clouds

Clouds are markup items to help you draw attention to page items when required. To draw a cloud, select the Cloud tool from the Drawing Markups Toolbar or from the Comments, Drawing Markup Tools menu and click on the page to place points forming an irregular polygon around the item you want the cloud to surround. After you close the line the cloud appears. You can customize its looks by right-clicking on it and selecting its Properties dialog (see Figure 42.16).

42

Figure 42.16
Use clouds to draw attention to an area of a page.

Text Box Tool

Text boxes are similar to callouts but have no arrows attached to them. To place a text box, select the Text Box tool from the Drawing Markups Toolbar or choose Comments, Drawing Markup Tools, Text Box and click your page. As you can with callouts, right-clicking a text box gives you access to its Properties dialog from which you can change its fill color, and border color, thickness, and style.

Dimensioning

Use the Dimensioning tool when you need to add dimensions or measurements markups to an image or an area of a document. This tool is available from the Drawing Markups toolbar or from the Comments, Drawing Markup Tools menu. After selecting it, use it to drag a line where you want your dimension marks to show. After releasing the mouse button, you are prompted to type whatever text you want displayed along the line. When you finish typing, click anywhere on the page. Right-clicking the line gives you access to its Properties dialog, from which you can change the line color, thickness, style, arrowheads style, opacity, and more (see Figure 42.17).

Figure 42.17
You can add text to your dimension markups.

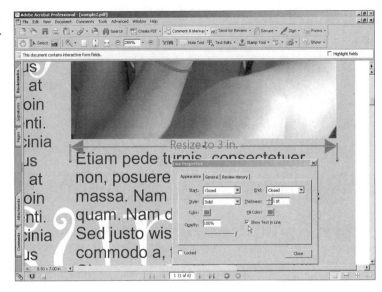

Geometric Drawing Tools

In addition to the previous markup tools, Acrobat also has some more freehand-style drawing tools for markup. Arrows, rectangles, ovals, lines, and open and closed polygons are available to meet your markup needs (see Figure 42.18). These tools are all grouped under the Comments, Drawing Markup Tools, Drawing menu and also under the third button in the Drawing Markups toolbar. To use them, select the tool you want to use and drag with the mouse over the page. Right-clicking enables you to access the drawing's Properties dialog, from which you can change color, line thickness, style, and more.

Figure 42.18
Acrobat gives you a wide assortment of geometric markup tools.

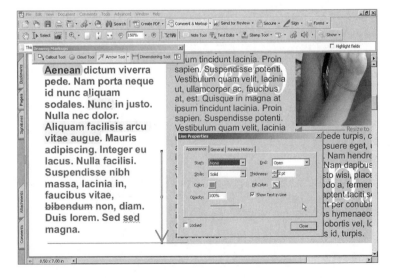

Pencil and Eraser Tools

If all the previous markup tools are still not enough to satisfy your creative doodling needs, Acrobat also has the Pencil and Eraser tools. You can find these tools under the same third button in the Drawing Markups toolbar or in the Comments, Drawing Markup Tools, Drawing menu. Use the Pencil tool just as you use a colored pencil; access its Properties dialog by right-clicking the line you've drawn to change color, thickness, and more. If you realize that you've gone a bit too far, you can always use the Eraser tool to remove the evidence (see Figure 42.19).

Text Edits and Highlighter

Text edits are a very easy way for you or your peers to edit the contents of text in a document without changing the original text. The easiest way to use text edits is by selecting the text to be edited with the Select tool. Access the context menu by right-clicking (in Windows) or Control-clicking (on the Mac) and select from it the kind of editing you want to do. Selecting Replace Text strikes out the selected word(s) and adds a typographic replacement symbol with a note attached where you can type the replacement word(s) to be used instead. Selecting Add Note to Text adds a small comment similar to a callout but with a smaller icon where you can type a note. The other options are self-explanatory: Highlight Text, Underline Text, and Cross Out Text. Right-clicking on the edited area gives you access to the Properties dialog where you can change color and transparency (see Figure 42.20). These options work only on text that is part of the PDF page and not on text that is typed inside other comment or markup elements.

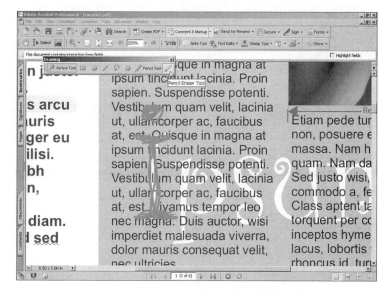

Figure 42.19
The Pencil and Eraser are the ultimate doodling tools.

Figure 42.20
Text edits enable you to add editorial markings to a PDF without altering the actual content.

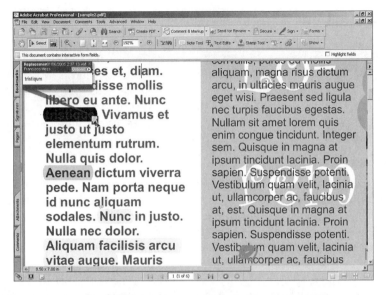

INITIATING REVIEWS AND COMMENTS IN ADOBE READER

One of the best ways to take advantage of comments is by initiating reviews. A *review* is a procedure through which you allow a designated group of peers to add comments to a PDF document or to add replies to existing comments. This is important when you're drafting documents or sending a copy of a design to a client for proofing. You can initiate an email-based review or a browser-based review, depending on your situation.

To initiate an email-based review choose File, Send For Review, Send By Email For Review. The first time you do this you are prompted to enter your name and email address. After that a wizard guides you through three easy steps that involve: confirming the name of the file to be sent; entering the email addresses of the persons authorized to add comments; and customizing an invitation message to be sent to your reviewers. The default message contains detailed instructions for your peers on how to submit their reviews back to you. After you're done, click on Send Invitation to prompt Acrobat to send emails to all the addresses you provided. The reviewers receive an email with the PDF file as an attachment (see Figure 42.21).

A browser-based review works in the same general way, except you need access to a web server to upload the PDF file to. When they are invited, your reviewers receive an email containing a link to the web address for the PDF file and all the appropriate instructions.

You can also manually send a comments-enabled PDF as an email attachment to a peer using your email client. To enable a PDF for commenting in Reader simply choose Comments, Enable for Commenting in Adobe Reader. If you use email- or browser-based reviews, the enabling is done automatically.

Keep in mind that if you don't enable the file and send it as an email attachment, users can add comments only if they have the full version of Acrobat. Enabling a file is equivalent to giving the Adobe Reader permission to add comments to it.

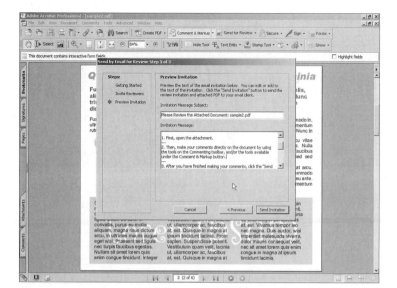

Figure 42.21
The Send By Email For Review wizard guides you through the steps of setting up an email-based review of a PDF.

WORKING WITH THE COMMENTS TAB

The Comments tab is a visual aid to help you manage comments and their status. Let's say you're doing changes to an InDesign document based on the feedback you received from reviewers. As you work in InDesign you can keep your PDF document open for reference and place checkmarks on those comments or edits you've already done. Or you can right-click (in Windows) or Control-click (on the Mac) on a comment to change its status to Completed, Accepted, or Rejected. You can also choose to clean up some clutter by deleting some obsolete comments. Or you can change their properties. You can also use the Comments tab to find comments—quite useful when working with large documents. Click on a comment in the Comments tab and you're sent to its location in the main work area.

The Comments tab also has a few useful buttons on its toolbar. You can display comments by only certain reviewers or sort them by status or alphabetical order. You also can add replies to comments right from the tab. Attached files and Audio Comments are also displayed in the Comments tab (see Figure 42.22).

Figure 42.22
The Comments tab helps you
keep your comments organized.

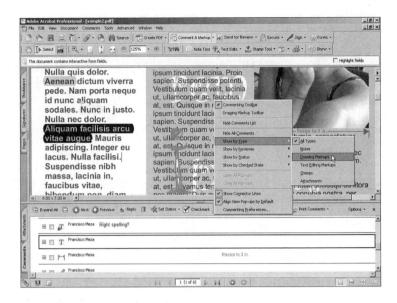

EXTRACTING DATA FROM COMMENTS

When you need to keep records of a review process Acrobat gives you the option to export and save comments made to a PDF. Comments can be exported in different ways.

Click on the Comments tab Options pop-up menu and select Export Comments. You have three options:

- **To File:** Create a FDF file containing the comments. This file can be opened with Acrobat or imported into another PDF using Acrobat.

- **To Word:** Open MS Word, choose a Word file, and import the comments into that file. This option is useful if you create your PDF off a Word file and use the PDF for the reviewing process. Importing the comments into the Word file makes it easier to edit it.

- **To AutoCAD:** Similar to the To Word option—if the PDF is generated off an AutoCAD file, you can use the To AutoCAD option to open AutoCAD and import the comments into the original AutoCAD file.

You can also create a new PDF document that displays the comments in separate pages (see Figure 42.23). This option uses the settings found in the Print with Comments Summary dialog (choose File, Print with Comments Summary to display this dialog).

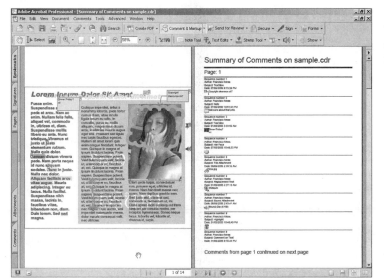

Figure 42.23
You can generate a new PDF that displays the comments listed side by side with the page they belong to.

USING THE TRACKER

The Comments tab helps you keep track of comments in one document. However, sometimes you have more than one document in a project. Enter the Tracker. This little utility shows you a list of all reviews you have initiated or all reviews you are participating in. The Tracker can be opened from the Comments menu or from the Options button on the Comments tab.

You don't need to add your review files to the Tracker; whenever you initiate a review or are invited to participate in one, the Tracker adds the files to one of two virtual folders in its left panel: My Reviews or Participant Reviews. A third folder, Offline Reviews, lists PDF files from browser-based reviews that you have saved to your hard drive. By selecting any of these folders and clicking the New Folder button in the Tracker's taskbar, you can add subfolders if you are participating in several projects and need to keep your reviews organized.

You can also use the Tracker to invite more peers to a review that you have already initiated. To do this, open the My Reviews folder in the Tracker, access the context menu for the file you are interested in, and select Invite More Reviewers. A dialog prompts you to enter the email addresses to which Acrobat must send the file.

Selecting a file in the Tracker's list displays some information about the file in Tracker's right pane, including the type of review, the date the review was initiated, and a list of the email addresses to which it was sent. Again, you don't need to enter any of this information manually; the Tracker does it automatically. If you want to work on a file listed in the Tracker, double-click it to open in Acrobat. If you need to send your users a reminder (in case some of them haven't sent their reviews yet), select the appropriate file in the Tracker's list, right-click the file, and select Send Review Reminder from the context menu. Tracker uses your default email client to create and display a new email message. You can customize the contents and the addresses in the To field before clicking the Send button.

UNDERSTANDING SECURITY AND DIGITAL IDS

Acrobat provides you with a way to verify that a peer has indeed read a document and approved it. This is especially important when confidentiality is an issue.

Using Passwords

To add security to a PDF file, Acrobat enables you to add two types of passwords so that only authorized persons can view and/or edit its contents. Passwords are stored inside the PDF itself and encoded with 128-bit encryption. Files protected with a Open Password prompt a dialog asking for the password to be typed. If the correct password is not entered, the document is not opened. Documents protected with a Permissions password can't be edited or printed unless the password is entered. There are several levels of Permissions password protection. You may choose to lock the entire document or to allow unauthorized users to view it but not to save attached files. You can make a document unprintable. Or you can make a document viewable but unchangeable, meaning no editing is allowed, including comments. You decide the level of protection you want in your file.

To apply a password to your PDF choose Document, Security, Secure This Document. The Select a Policy to Apply dialog shows you two default security policies that you can apply to your document, but you can also create your own. To do that, click on the New button in that dialog and a wizard guides you through the security-creation process. Select Use Passwords and click on Next. Select the options you want, enter the password(s), and click Next again (see Figure 42.24). After verifying the passwords, you're presented with a Summary of the security policy. Clicking on Finish ends the session and your document is protected. Remember to have a written-down copy of your password in a safe place for reference; if you forget the password you won't be able to open your own document.

Figure 42.24
The New Security Policy dialog guides you through the required steps to set up password-based security in your document.

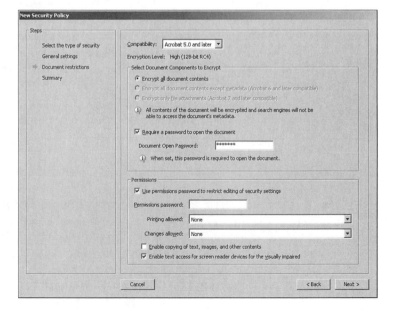

42

If you want to remove a password from a secured document choose Document, Security, Show Security for This Document to display the Security tab of the Document Properties dialog. Click the Change button. You'll need to enter the current password to make changes to security policies.

Certifying Options

There are situations where many users are opening a PDF file, as in the case of electronic forms, for example. You may need to have a form available for download with users being able to fill in data but not able to change the contents of the form itself. In a situation like that, posting a password defeats the purpose of securing the document.

Acrobat includes a Certification feature for this purpose. When you certify a document you add a signature to it locking those parts you don't want edited. If the document is modified in any way other than what you have allowed, the certification gets voided.

In addition to passwords, Acrobat has also implemented a verification method by means of ID signatures. The purpose of this security implementation is not only to restrict access to a document but to certify that a document has been reviewed or approved by an authorized person.

Digital signatures are electronic certificates stored in your computer that verify your identity. You can use your digital ID as a verification in a document or to secure it so that only you and persons authorized by you can view it.

To certify a PDF file in Acrobat you need to make sure that you have the final version of it, all revisions and editing done, and the file saved. Choose Edit, Preferences and select the Security panel in the Preferences dialog to select or create a new certification option. Then choose File, Save As Certified Document. You are prompted to obtain a Digital ID from a third-party vendor. If you already have a Digital ID click on OK. In the next dialog you're prompted to select the level of security you want to add (see Figure 42.25). In the next dialog you may get a warning if you have backgrounds, markups, or comments in the document. Next, if you want the certification to be visible in the document (it shows as a stamp) select that option. If you choose to make it invisible, that choice does not affect the certification itself. Next select the signature you want to use from those available and hit OK. You can also change the appearance of your signature and enter a reason for signing the document. When you're done, click on Sign and Save As to give the document a new name. This prevents the original unsaved version from being overwritten in case you need to do changes to it in the future.

To verify that a digital signature in a document actually belongs to an authorized person, you can request that person to send you a copy of his or her signature. Acrobat stores this signature file in a repository called Trusted Identities. To request a peer to send you a digital signature for this purpose, use the Advanced, Trusted Identities menu option. This command opens the Manage Trusted Identities dialog, which is a sort of address book for trusted people. Clicking the Request Contact button opens the Email a Request dialog. Enter your name, email address, and contact information (such as a phone number that people can use to contact you and verify that the email they got was from you). In this same dialog, enable the Include My Certificates check box if you want to send your certificate along with the request. You can also select whether you want to send the request as an email or to save it as a file to be sent later.

42

After clicking Next, a new Select Digital IDs to Export dialog opens (if you chose to send your certificate along with the request). Select a certificate from the list and click OK. This step is skipped if you don't choose to send a digital signature with the request. After clicking OK, a new Compose Email dialog opens. This dialog displays a standard request message that is sent to your peer. You can edit it at will. Enter your peer's email address in the To field and click the Email button to send the request. If you choose to save the request as a file, when you click Next in the Manage Trusted Identities dialog, a new Export Data As dialog appears, prompting you for a name and location to save the request, which is saved in FDF format. After saving it, you can send it to your peer as a regular email attachment.

Figure 42.25
You can choose the level of access allowed to your certified document.

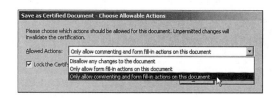

VI

WEB CHAPTERS

IN THIS PART

INDEX

Note: Page numbers preceded by "PDF:" can be found in PDF documents on the Que Publishing website. For more information about this book or another Que title, visit our website at www.quepublishing.com. Type the ISBN (excluding hyphens) or the title of a book in the Search field to find the page you're looking for.

NUMBERS

A

How can we make this index more useful? Email us at indexes@quepublishing.com

Filter, 363
Help, 364
Object, 362
palette menus, 360
Select, 363
Type, 362
View, 363
Window, 364
InDesign, 562
Edit, 564-565
File, 562-563
Help, 572-573
Layout, 565-566
Object, 567-569
Table, 569-570
Type, 566-567
View, 570-572
Window, 572
Photoshop
Edit, 64-67
File, 60-64
Filter, 71-73
Help, 75
highlighting options, 37
Image, 67-68
Layer, 69-70
Select, 70-71
View, 73-74
Window, 74
Merge effect (Illustrator), 479
merging layers, 70
mesh patches, 400
mesh points, 400
Mesh tool (Illustrator), 334, 401-402
Metadata panel (Bridge), 16-17
metric kerning (InDesign documents), 623
Mezzotint filter (Photoshop), 474
Microsoft Word
PDF writers, 913
importing documents
into Designer,
PDF:1036-PDF:1037
into InDesign, 643-644
midpoints, Photoshop gradients, 119
Migrate Comments command (Acrobat), PDF:974, PDF:986
millimeters, 41
Minus Back effect (Illustrator), 479

mixed inks (InDesign), 672-674
mobile devices, author web content with GoLive. *See also* **GoLive**
features overview, 732-733
file formats, 736
video editing tools, 732
Modify command (Photoshop), 157-158
monochrome colors, specifying in Illustrator, PDF:1000
monochrome images, PDF:1000
monotones, 107
Mosaic filter (Photoshop), 222
Motion Blur filter (Photoshop), 218
Move tool (Photoshop), 38, 46
Movie menu (GoLive), 756
Movie tool (Acrobat), PDF:978
moving
anchor points (Illustrator), 382
guides
Illustrator, 322
InDesign, 590
Photoshop, 38
moving tools (Illustrator), 342
MPEG-4 compression algorithm, 732
Multi-Page PDF to PSD command (Photoshop), 257
Multichannel color mode (Photoshop), 110-111
Multiply blending mode
Illustrator, 403
Photoshop, 131

N

Navigate through code theme (GoLive), 846
Navigation pane (Acrobat), PDF:946-PDF:949
Navigation tab (GoLive Site window), 897
navigation tabs (Acrobat), PDF:961-PDF:963
Navigation Tabs command (Acrobat), 923
Navigation toolbar (Acrobat), PDF:964

navigation tools
GoLive, 880-882
Photoshop, 54-55
Navigator palette
Illustrator, 360
InDesign, 556
Photoshop, 84
Neon Effects style library (Illustrator), 358
nested styles (InDesign text), 631
nesting layers (GoLive), 790-791
neutral density, PDF:1003
New Art Has Basic Appearance button (Illustrator), 357
New Art Maintains Appearance button (Illustrator), 357
New command (GoLive), 888
New dialog (GoLive), 770-772
New Document dialog (InDesign), 588-589
New Form Assistant (Designer), PDF:1028-PDF:1029
New Form command (Designer), PDF:1036
New From Template command (File menu, Illustrator), 361
New Graphic style button (Graphic Styles palette, Illustrator), 359
New View command (Illustrator), 364
New Window command (Illustrator), 364
newspaper images, resolution guidelines, 41
noise filters (Photoshop), 221
None swatch (Illustrator), 393
nonglobal colors, 675
Normal blending mode
Illustrator, 403
Photoshop, 131
Note tool (Acrobat), PDF:970
notes (PDF documents), 929-930
Notes tool (Photoshop), 54
NTSC Colors filter (Photoshop), 475
NTSC filter (Photoshop), 226
Number Pages command (Acrobat), PDF:986